Taste and Power

STUDIES ON THE HISTORY OF SOCIETY AND CULTURE

Victoria E. Bonnell and Lynn Hunt, Editors

Taste and Power
Furnishing Modern France

LEORA AUSLANDER

University of California Press

BERKELEY   LOS ANGELES   LONDON

University of California Press
Berkeley and Los Angeles, California

University of California Press, Ltd.
London, England

An earlier version of part of chapter 6 of this book appeared in
"Perceptions of Beauty and the Problem of Consciousness:
Parisian Furniture Makers," in *Rethinking Labor History:
Essays on Discourse and Class Analysis*, ed. Lenard Berlanstein
(Urbana and Chicago: University of Illinois Press, 1993).
Part of chapter 7 appeared in "After the Revolution: Recycling
Ancien Régime Style in the Nineteenth Century," in
Re-creating Authority in Revolutionary France, ed. Bryant T.
Ragan and Elizabeth Williams (New Brunswick, N.J.: Rutgers
University Press, 1992).

Library of Congress Cataloging-in-Publication Data

Auslander, Leora.
    Taste and power : furnishing modern France / Leora
Auslander.
        p.   cm.—(Studies on the history of society and
culture ; 24)
    Includes bibliographical references and index.
    ISBN 0-520-08894-8
    1. France—Civilization.   2. Furniture—France—Styles—
Social aspects.   3. Social change—France.   4. Politics and
culture—France.   5. France—Politics and government—
1789– . I. Title. II. Series.
DC33.A87   1996
944—dc20   95-715
                                           CIP

Printed in the United States of America
9 8 7 6 5 4 3 2

To my mother, Bernice Liberman Auslander,
and to the memory of my father, Maurice Auslander

This publication has been supported by a grant
from the National Endowment for the Humanities, an
independent federal agency.

Contents

Illustrations

Acknowledgments

Friends in Paris and the United States have sustained me and this work over the years it has traveled with me. I am delighted to be able to give them the finished product at last. Françoise Basch has been an example of intellectual accomplishment and chutzpah, political commitment, and great generosity in friendship. Marie-Noëlle Bourguet's warmth, welcome, and gifts as a historian have meant a great deal to me. Jacqueline Feldman has watched the unfolding of this book in Paris, in Normandy, and finally in Auvergne where a crucial draft was finished. Our conversations about feminism, science, and relativism have much enriched this work. I talked through many of the manuscript's initial stages with Maurizio Gribaudi and learned much from his intellectual curiosity and rigor. Cathy Kudlick's integrity, intelligence, and humor have been a great pleasure. While she has not read much of this book, our many conversations about the doing of history have made it different. Margaret Nickels and Moishe Postone have been great friends and intellectual comrades. Besides the good times, they were both very much "there" at a critical and difficult moment; without their friendship the book might not have seen the light of day. Tip Ragan has been a steady friend and colleague; his comments on the section dealing with the Old Regime and on an article that became part of part 3 were invaluable. Emily Stone has known me since before this book ever started. She has been enthusiastic about a project whose point must have often seemed rather mysterious. Annette Wilson has also known me forever and often wondered what I was doing—she will be glad to know that it's done. Marty Ward has been a good colleague, critic, swimming companion, and friend over the last few years. Her criticisms on the manuscript were most helpful. With Michelle Zancarini-Fournel and Jean-Claude Zancarini I have shared many evenings of riotous laughter, intense political and intellectual discussion, and encounters with goats. Their thoughts on the meaning of nations and nationalism in France have changed this book.

To my friends, colleagues, and students at the University of Chicago I owe a debt of gratitude. George Chauncey, Kathy Conzen, Norma Field, Michael Geyer, Jan Goldstein, James Grossman, Harry Harootunian, Linda Kerber, Peter Novick, and Bill Sewell, especially have provided consistent support and encouragement, even when this project caused me to disappear from circulation. Colin Lucas kindly read the first part and helped save me from egregious error.

The men with whom I worked at F. W. Dixon in Woburn, Massachusetts, and my grandmothers, Rose and Ida, provided the original impulse for this book. If they were to read it, I hope they all would find it interesting.

Lenard Berlanstein, Geoffrey Crossick, Victoria de Grazia, Gerhard Haupt, Yves Lequin, Philip Nord, and Michelle Perrot all gave crucial help and support at various moments, in various ways, to this project. I thank them all.

Karl Bahm, Robert Beachy, Louis Beilin, Paul Betts, Kate Chavigny, Allan Christy, Alex Dracobly, Jim Miller, Lisa Moses, Wendy Norris, Hannah Rosen, Carol Scherer, and Stephanie Whitlock all contributed invaluable research assistance to this book. Katie Crawford and Elisa Camiscioli did a heroic job of tracing down photographs in Paris.

I would like also to express my heartfelt thanks to Lynn Hunt, Tom Laqueur, Patricia Mainardi, William Reddy, Donald Reid, and to the three other (anonymous) readers of this manuscript. I was blessed with eight helpful critical reads of this book. It is much better for them. Thanks also to Sheila Levine at the University of California Press who believed in this book before it existed. Also at the press, Tony Hicks has helpfully shepherded the book through the production process and Edith Gladstone has done much to lighten and streamline my prose.

A School of Social Sciences' fellowship, supported by the National Endowment for the Humanities, allowed me a crucial year of extraordinary calm at the Institute for Advanced Study in Princeton. I am deeply grateful for the gift of that time.

Jacques Revel made possible a month-long stay at the Ecole des hautes études en sciences sociales in Paris where I tested very early versions of some of the ideas that ended up in this book. My thanks.

The Council for European Studies, Fulbright Foundation, Franco-American Foundation, Bourse Chateaubriand, Social Science Research Council, and the Tocqueville Foundation all provided funding for the initial research for this project. Without that generous support this book would not exist. The Social Sciences Division of the University of Chicago has also provided crucial funding for some of the research in this book.

The Maison Rinck was generous enough to allow me to forage through its records. The Schmit company let me take away a small portion of its extraordinary business records that it was in the process of jettisoning. The documentation of this book is much richer for their generosity.

The staffs of the Archives nationales, Bibliothèque nationale, Bibliothèque historique de la ville de Paris, the Bibliothèque Forney, the Archives de la Seine, and the Archives de la préfecture de police were all most helpful.

Special thanks are owed to Joan Wallach Scott, my former thesis advisor, current friend, and colleague. I can only say again how much her own work, her faith in this project, encouragement, and rigorous and helpful criticisms have meant to me.

My thanks to Chris Wilson without whom I would almost certainly never have become a furniture maker and for whose love, insights, and critical advice through the researching and writing of the dissertation that provided the basis for this book I will always be grateful. He has not seen the finished product; I hope it will please him.

Tom Holt, who normally does not spend his time thinking about either France or furniture, has cheerfully endured midnight queries and interruptions to his own work to see this one go forward. Our conversations about this book have kept me interested. His insights on the endless drafts he read have made it "mo' better." His intellectual and political work have inspired me. His love has sustained me and made me happy through the finishing of this book.

My family has always been there to give sustenance and support. My brother Philip has been ready with encouragement, intellectual debate, and inquiries as to when it will be done. I thank my parents Bernice Liberman Auslander and Maurice Auslander, to whom the book is dedicated, for providing models of what lives engaged in committed labor could look like as well as consistent encouragement to follow my nose and do what seemed right. This book can be but a partial repayment for that gift.

INTRODUCTION

Representation, Style, and Taste
The Politics of Everyday Life

 This book describes and explains the changing meaning of furniture in Parisians' lives from the mid-seventeenth to the early twentieth century. I will argue that the meaning borne by such objects was different to their makers, sellers, buyers, and arbiters; that production, distribution, and consumption were nonetheless interdependent systems, none necessarily having primacy over the others; and, that each of these systems and their interactions were as profoundly shaped by the form and logic of political regimes as by conjunctures in cultural and economic history.[1] Finally, I will argue that taste and style were the crystallizations of this complex dynamic. The goal of this book is thus less to explain the aesthetic forms of particular styles and tastes, than it is to explain the place of style and taste in the making of the political and social order, as well as of people's self-understandings.

Indeed, the analysis of both taste and style is crucial to grasp the interactions of these histories.[2] *Taste* has been, for at least the last two hundred years, a term laden with contradictions. It has been understood to be innate and emotional yet capable of improvement through education; individual and idiosyncratic yet absolute; transcendent of time and space yet socially constituted. *Style,* in contrast, has been understood to be historical and specific, resulting from either collective effort or individual genius. Almost always identified retrospectively, a style had characteristics,

---

1. Useful texts on the social and political history of objects are Arjun Appadurai, ed., *The Social Life of Things* (Cambridge, 1986); William M. Reddy, *The Rise of Market Culture* (Cambridge, 1984); Annie Phizacklea, *Unpacking the Fashion Industry* (London, 1990); Adrian Forty, *Objects of Desire* (New York, 1986).
2. Helpful on taste have been Terry Eagleton, *The Ideology of the Aesthetic* (Oxford, 1990); Luc Ferry, *Homo aestheticus* (Paris, 1990); and Pierre Bourdieu, *La distinction: critique social du jugement* (Paris, 1977).

1

could be named and dated, and was understood to be pervasive within a given moment. Thus, the two terms have been in perpetual tension and contradiction. Through a historically grounded analysis I hope to illuminate the relation between style and taste and the correlative relation between two different problems of representation: first, the ways in which political regimes—absolute monarchies, empires, restoration monarchies, second-generation empires, fragile and solid republics—attempted to use style and taste to represent and construct their power. Second, the process by which objects—in this case furniture—served to represent and perhaps even generate subjectivity and identity for their makers and consumers through shared taste.

French governments from at least the reign of Louis XIV were actively engaged in patronage and debate on French style and French taste. The quality of both were viewed as matters of national import, although in radically different ways and with very different implications under the various forms of polity. This book attempts to sort out how and why the appearance of domestic goods was a matter of state.

In the domain of taste, this book takes as its premise that judgments of aesthetic value emerge from a complex interaction of desires for emulation, distinction, and solidarity. This is not to say that people simply "choose" to find certain things beautiful or ugly depending on what contemporaries and ancestors have judged. Rather people come to find certain aesthetic forms desirable for very good reasons. They are not necessarily aware of those reasons, nor do they find their judgments changeable at will.

The study of these two kinds of representation—the political (state-based) and the civil—through analysis of style and taste, bring the "grand" narratives of political and economic history together with the "everyday" history of the organization, discussion, and experience of relations of production, distribution, and consumption. There is some degree of consensus among scholars on the object and the importance of political and economic history; the everyday is far more elusive and controversial. The everyday is, for certain authors, what people do in the interstices of time and space—walking down the street, riding the subway, daydreaming—when not occupied at labor or leisure.[3] Others use the everyday as a way

---

3. For examples, see Walter Benjamin's arcades project and Susan Buck-Morss's read of it in *The Dialectics of Seeing* (Cambridge, Mass., 1989); Michel de Certeau's approach in *The Practice of Everyday Life*, trans. Steven F. Rendall (Berkeley, 1984); that of Allan Pred, *Lost Words and Lost Worlds* (Cambridge, 1990). I emphasize that neither these authors nor I understand the everyday to be a space beyond politics.

to think about long-term structural transformation, including changes in geography, weather, reproduction, and death.[4] Still others employ the everyday almost mystically, characterizing it as the residuum of life, that which escapes from relations of production and from political institutions.[5] Some scholars invoking this definition of the everyday see it as perhaps the only space of freedom in a capitalist world and search within its boundaries for evidence of resistance, for signs that even when inhabiting seemingly totalizing systems, people nonetheless fought back in small but crucial ways.[6] More pessimistically, authors define the everyday as the private sphere, where false consciousness reigns.[7] Last, it serves to justify and to conceptualize the histories of people who left behind only fragmentary relics and sparse documentation of their lives.[8] The most interesting and important observation to emerge from this literature is that it is in the everyday world that politics and the polity, economics and the economy, aesthetics and beauty, are concretized, experienced, and perhaps transformed—in short, lived.[9] The everyday is historical and contextual, its boundaries shifting with the changing landscape. The everyday is sensual, bodily, emotional, and intellectual. There is no escape from the everyday, no position outside of it, for either the subjects of history or its writers.

It is perhaps important to emphasize here that I am not advocating a form of history that dreams of recuperating ordinary people's unmediated experience. All experiences must pass through some kind of classificatory, meaning-generating process in order to lodge in memory. Such processes are not necessarily linguistic—the "languages" of the ears, eyes, tongue, and skin, including music, painting, sculpture, food, and fabric are neither the same as nor reducible to natural language.[10] And there may be experiences that are not *expressible* through any communicative medium, but even these ineffable experiences are registered within memory—they are

4. Many of the French *annalistes* fall in this tradition; see, for example, Fernand Braudel, *The Structures of Everyday Life*, trans. Sian Reynolds (London, 1981).

5. Henri Lefebvre, *Everyday Life in the Modern World*, trans. Sacha Rabinovitch (New Brunswick, 1990).

6. See especially Detlev J. K. Peukert, *Inside Nazi Germany: Conformity, Opposition, and Racism in Everyday Life*, trans. Richard Deveson (New Haven, 1987).

7. Jean Baudrillard, *La société de consommation* (Paris, 1970), esp. 33.

8. That of the documentary includes much of the work from England's history workshop movement.

9. This usage is close to that of Alice Kaplan and Kristin Ross in their introduction to *Everyday Life*, a special issue of *Yale French Studies* 73 (1988).

10. Paul Gilroy, *The Black Atlantic: Modernity and Double Consciousness* (Cambridge, Mass., 1993), chap. 3 is especially eloquent on this point.

not unmediated, "immediate," or raw experience. Furthermore people are not in control of how an experience will be remembered.[11] Selves—neither unitary nor fully self-knowing—are thus made by complexly constituted, often mutually contradictory, experiences, some of which are known and expressed linguistically, some musically, some visually, and some in no known discursive framework. The multiplicities of experiences, of their inscription in memory, of their interpretation, and of their expression mean that neither experiences nor selves can be contained within such categories as class, gender, race, nation, or sexuality. Yet people who inhabit like locations within and among these categories often have similar experiences as well as similar memories and expressions of those experiences. The challenge, therefore, is to grasp the manifestations of the very large and abstract structures and transformations of the world within the small details of life; to recapture people's expressions—in all media—of their experiences of those abstractions, while also attempting to understand the forces shaping the multiple grids that mediate those expressions; and to analyze how concrete and mundane actions in the everyday may themselves transform the abstract structures of polity and economy.

This challenge is worthwhile because it is a means of thinking differently about the immensely influential feminist premise of the 1970s—the personal is political—to which parts of the current controversy over "political correctness" may be traced. That premise articulated the rage of the women of the New Left against their male allies' resistance to equality at home and in the movements for social change. It came out of a suspicion of a politics that seemed to do too little to transform the power relations of the everyday. It has proved to be a very rich, complex, and difficult precept by which part of a generation has tried to live. At its worst, it legitimates a kind of pettiness, of policing of the everyday, and, even more seriously, an assumption of rectifying through individual behavior injustices that operate on a structural level; it dissolves into a kind of moralism, into a liberal individualism. And yet, there is something of value in the slogan. Social

11. Denise Riley, Joan Wallach Scott, Dorothy Smith, and Konrad Jarausch have stimulated my thinking about this problem, although my own approach differs from each in specific ways. See Denise Riley, *"Am I That Name?" Feminism and the Category of "Women"* (Minneapolis, 1988); Joan Wallach Scott, "The Evidence of Experience," *Critical Inquiry* 17 (summer 1991): 773–97; Dorothy E. Smith, *The Everyday World as Problematic* (Boston, 1987); Konrad Jarausch, "Towards a Social History of Experience: Postmodern Predicaments in Theory and Interdisciplinarity," *Central European History* 22 (1989): 427–43. See also my "Erfahrung, Reflexion, Geschichtsarbeit. Oder: Was es heißen könnte, gebrauchsfähige Geschichte zu schreiben," *Historische Anthropologie* 3/2 (1995): 222–41.

relations whose causes may be traced to structural transformations *do* play out at the personal, individual level. Inquiries into power's capillary action and self-reflexiveness *do* have the potential for some kind of transformative politics; and politics devoid of them have been demonstrated to be highly problematic. A consequence of denying that the personal is political is unwittingly to change and stifle political transformation. And it is not only for the power*ful* that *power* works through the everyday.

Indeed, this very book emerged out of my preoccupation with the politics of the everyday and out of my own everyday life—produced from readings of fashion magazines, novels, newspapers, conversations, cities, music, furniture, buildings, advertisements, paintings, classrooms, meetings, conferences, and scholarly books. I am conscious of some of the multiplicity of experiences that produced this book, but I am no doubt ignorant of still others that may be relevant.[12] But since the point here is not self-revelation, nor even honesty, but rather the increased intelligibility of this project, the impossibility of complete transparency does not matter. Just as scholars critically select certain texts to cite, amid the many they read, so I have chosen to recount three lived experiences here (and cite others later), one from the world of production, one from the world of consumption, and one less classifiable within those categories.

When I began working as a cabinetmaker in a factory near Boston in the early 1980s, I assumed that my co-workers would be contesting hours, wages, and working conditions through union organizing.[13] I soon discovered, however, that although they would have appreciated improved material circumstances, they were far more distraught about the *aesthetic* failure of their labor. They found the objects we made ugly, devoid of creativity, artistry, or imagination, and useless, contributing nothing of value to the world. The workers' response to this form of alienation of labor was not to organize collectively but to stay in the factory after hours, using

12. In this genre two books of importance to me are Paul Rabinow, *Reflections on Fieldwork in Morocco* (Berkeley, 1977); and Patricia J. Williams, *The Alchemy of Race and Rights* (Cambridge, Mass., 1991).

13. I worked at F. W. Dixon in Woburn, a company that included a cabinet shop, an architectural model shop, an experimental machine shop, a display shop, a pattern-making shop; at Brouwer Woodworks, a custom woodworking shop in Cambridge that specialized in spiral staircases with a small production shop in Boston, where we made good quality hardwood furniture of Japanese inspiration; and at the Emily Street Cooperative, a workshop where there were fifteen or so independent woodworkers, who collectively owned the big machines and purchased wood.

the machines and stealing wood to make things they considered beautiful and useful. Two colleagues built guitars—one acoustic and the other electric—while another crafted a maple sled with runners carved from bubinga (an African wood). A fourth even redid the interior of his '72 Ford in mahogany veneer.[14] It was these objects that established respect among the workers in the factory, that gave them satisfaction, these objects that allowed them to talk with pride about their mastery. Here were artisans in full possession of their craft, but they were not being paid for its expert deployment on the job. Somewhat surprisingly, although deeply troubled by this loss, they did not perceive union organizing as a solution. The only response that made sense to them was to reclaim their trade for themselves, by making things they found to be beautiful and useful. Besides being impressed by their skill and perplexed by their lack of interest in collective action, I was intrigued and distressed by two of my co-workers' other reactions to their work. The first was their passivity in the face of an open labor market; these artisans could easily have found better (i.e., more interesting, better paid) work in the area, but they neither knew it nor, when told, really believed it. They appeared to have internalized or constructed a sense of the products of their paid labor as ugly and worthless and (perhaps consequently) their skills as valueless on the market. And yet they identified fully with their trade; they were proud to be cabinetmakers and outraged if mistakenly labeled carpenters. The second was the fierceness and rigidity of their definition of their work as masculine and their hostility to working beside a woman.[15]

Pained by these seemingly trapped lives, frustrated with my inability to intervene, and angered by their animosity toward women in the trade, I began to formulate the first questions that would ultimately produce this book: how had artisanal labor come to be devalued to the point that highly skilled and innovative artisans believed that they were doomed to making ugly and useless things? Could a kind of "aesthetic resistance" be an effective response to alienated labor, or were they simply trying to find

14. A well-known phenomenon analyzed most eloquently by de Certeau in *The Practice of Everyday Life*. Pred applies de Certeau's categories to late nineteenth-century Stockholm (*Lost Words and Lost Worlds*, 70–83). The contributions to John Calagione et al., eds., *Workers' Expressions: Beyond Accomodation and Resistance* (Albany, 1992) further this discussion.

15. I was the only woman on the shopfloor in a factory of sixty employees. The company, having recently won a contract for a partially federally-funded project, was subject to affirmative action. I happened to call looking for work the day the requirement became known and was, although completely untrained, precipitously hired.

apolitical solutions to what were ultimately political problems? How did the perception that they were being paid to make things of no value and that they could make worthwhile objects only on "their own time" influence their sense of self? Why did they cling so fiercely to the identity of cabinetmaker when it brought them so little in terms of pay or on-the-job satisfaction? Why did they so resent, even fear, the idea of sharing tools, machines, and the shop floor with women, even when they knew that women's labor posed no economic threat? The answers to these questions did not seem to be available on the shop floor, or accessible through discussion and thought confined exclusively to the present or even to the context of everyday experience and knowledge.

The historiography of industrialization, labor, and the working class, however fascinating and insightful, could not fully answer my questions either. Whereas my personal work experience had taught me that some late twentieth-century Boston woodworkers were most outraged by having to make objects lacking in beauty and utility, little hint of any such preoccupation appeared in the histories of artisans in late nineteenth-century Europe.[16] Did this mean that late nineteenth-century European artisans were concerned only with hours, wages, control of the labor process, and working conditions—as the literature implies—or had labor historians, trapped by their own vision of what workers "should" want, neglected to look at the full range of artisanal desires?[17]

Although labor historians have been very sensitive to issues of deskilling and workplace control, they have been less engaged in questions of workers' job-satisfaction through the creation of objects they find aesthetically pleasing. Control over the labor process and control over the appearance of the finished object are related but are not the same. Having

16. I am referring here to the classics of the old "new" labor history of France published in the 1970s and early 1980s. I was especially influenced by Michael Hanagan, *The Logic of Solidarity: Artisans and Industrial Workers in Three French Towns, 1871–1914* (Urbana, 1980); Yves Lequin, *Les ouvriers de la région lyonnaise (1848–1914)* (Lyons, 1977); Michelle Perrot, *Les ouvriers en grève, France 1871–1890* (Paris, 1974); Joan Wallach Scott, *The Glassworkers of Carmaux* (Cambridge, Mass., 1974).

17. There are by now many critiques of labor literature aimed at uncovering "true consciousness" or denouncing the false. An eloquent plea for another approach is Michelle Perrot, "On the Formation of the French Working Class," in *Working-Class Formation: Nineteenth-Century Patterns in Western Europe and the United States*, ed. Ira Katznelson and Aristide R. Zolberg (Princeton, 1986), esp. 71. A more general, theoretical critique of the concept is Stuart Hall, "The Problem of Ideology—Marxism without Guarantees," *Marx 100 Years On*, ed. Betty Matthews (Atlantic Highlands, N.J., 1983), 70.

accepted that by the nineteenth century workers were selling their labor rather than the product of their labor, labor historians largely ignored the relation between those alienated commodities and the people who made them. And after analyzing organized labor's systematic hostility to women's labor, historians are slowly turning to study the impact that the construction of labor as masculine had on the men who practiced those trades.[18]

Unlike most labor histories, this book assumes that workers may have been as concerned with the objects they made as with labor processes, wages, and working conditions. And, unlike most labor histories, the goal is not only to reexamine workers' relations to class-based politics but also to explore the broader range of questions concerning workers' relations to their labor and to the objects they produced. Why were particular pieces of furniture built, and how did their makers' think, feel, and speak about them? Did artisans simply make what they thought would sell or were they hindered by limitations in technique, skill, or materials? How did those possibilities and constraints change over time and how did artisans create and respond to those transformations? How did the persistent definition of the trade as masculine shape the expression of desire by its artisans as the terms of gender were transformed? Did the attitudes of the male producers change when furniture became something women consumed? No answers to these questions were in the extant labor histories because these are not the questions addressed by the classic productivist, labor, or working-class culture approaches.

This last silence was especially disappointing since studies of working-class culture had seemed initially closer to my preoccupations. Some studies of working-class culture take as their unit of analysis a "working-class community"; others focus on informal or organized leisure-time practices. They all cast their net beyond the workplace and union hall, to include the homes, churches, bars, streets, stores, and playing fields frequented by workers. But, by their choice of unit of analysis, studies of working-class culture tend to assume divisions between high and low culture, as well as to isolate the working class from the "general" culture.[19]

18. For further discussion of this point and historiographic references see chapter 6.

19. Michael Sonenscher effectively critiques the concept in the preface and conclusion to *The Hatters of Eighteenth-Century France* (Berkeley, 1987), as does Roger Chartier in the preface to *The Cultural Uses of Print in Early Modern France*, trans. Lydia G. Cochrane (Princeton, 1987). For an interesting and insightful genealogy of the concepts of high and low culture see Peter Stallybrass and Allon

And, while it is clear that workers were denied access to certain aspects of elite culture—and in fact this book is in part the story of that exclusion—defining a study as falling solely within the boundaries of working-class culture, or a working-class community, posits a too completely isolated working class. Yet studies of social mobility, usages of urban space, urban-rural ties, the importance of kin, and neighborhood social structures all demonstrate the manifold sites and interactions among members of the working class and other classes.[20]

So, just as I could find only partial answers to my questions on the shop floor or in the labor literature, answers were not forthcoming from the working-class culture literature either. Indeed, the constraints on, and possibilities for, my coworkers' lives at labor seemed to have been determined as much by the ultimate destiny of the goods they produced—or at least factory management's understanding of it—as by the culture of the shop floor and community. Some of what we made was being sold to other workers but most of it was not. Perceptions of the needs and desires of various consumers, as well as the organization of distribution, played fundamental roles in decision making about what objects would be produced. Thus to place the boundaries of the project either at the literal worksite walls or at some invisible fence marking the edges of the working-class community was clearly inappropriate. The constraints that management's perception of the market imposed on the choice of products to be crafted by my Woburn colleagues showed me that any attempt to analyze the labor process without analyzing consumer practices was doomed. I had to examine demand, both the structural and experiential aspects of consumerism. The structural aspects are how consumers' cumulative actions—what they bought at what price—affected the workplace. The experiential ones are why people bought what they did and what they said about it. Although I have distinguished between the structural and the experiential,

---

White, *The Politics and Poetics of Transgression* (London, 1986). For impressive *use* of the concept, see Les révoltes logiques, ed., *Esthétiques du peuple* (Paris, 1985).

20. An analysis demonstrating the complexity and importance of social mobility for conceptions of class and culture is Maurizio Gribaudi, *Mondo operaio e. mito operaio* (Turin, 1987). Using very different kinds of—contemporary rather than historical—evidence, the sociolinguist William Labov makes a similiar argument. See his *Sociolinguistic Patterns* (Philadelphia, 1972). For another kind of discussion again see the High Culture/Low Culture catalogue from the exhibit at MOMA 1991 and the example of Jelly Roll Morton's jazz, which combined a classical piano training and knowledge of "popular" black music to create a new form of music that was then deemed "black."

I know that they are interconnected. I know that in part because as I brooded about these things I started thinking about my grandmothers, their houses, and their conflicts over taste.

One of the things that bothered me as a child was why my two grand-mothers did not get along, and why they used judgments of taste to express their disagreements. My paternal grandmother, Ida, often accused my maternal grandmother, Rose, of buying things that were ugly and common. Rose, in contrast, accused Ida of expressing her snobbishness, arrogance, and competitiveness through her acquisitions. I was even more confused about the conflict and the form of expression of that conflict because my grandmothers seemed to me to come from like worlds.

Despite quite similar origins, however, by the time they were in their sixties, my maternal and paternal grandparents had radically different consumption habits and aesthetic languages. All of them were either Jewish immigrants from Eastern Europe or their children. They had all grown up in poverty but had fared better as adults. In both couples, the wife had the ultimate responsibility for the dwelling—its appearance, its cleanliness, and even who was invited into it. My father's father became a high-school English teacher in New York; and in the 1930s his wife, my grandmother, inherited the bankrupt plumbing supply business her father had founded in Philadelphia. Under her management the business eventually became profitable, sufficiently so that by the 1950s it employed both grandparents, enabling them to buy a small semidetached house. My maternal grandmother, after a stint doing piece-work at home for the garment industry, worked as a secretary for the Navy. Her husband, my grandfather, was a chemistry professor at the Columbia College of Pharmacy. Moving from the Lower East Side to Brooklyn, they always rented small apartments; they finally bought a modest condominium when they retired to Miami. According to contemporary sociological class definitions, my paternal grandparents were capitalists but, given the small scale of their business, hovered at the boundary of the petite bourgeoisie. My maternal grandparents, on the basis of my grandfather's position as a university professor, should have belonged to the bourgeoisie, although they occupied that problematic spot reserved for professional salaried workers, whose cultural capital outstrips their economic resources. But a man's relation to the means of production does not entirely determine the family's class position, and that of its members; even more pertinently, class location alone cannot contain or explain senses of self, and of solidarity. Understanding the likenesses and differences, as well as the conflicts between the two couples requires a much more complicated explanation, looking at other aspects of their lives besides their relation to the means of production.

One manifestation of the distance between the couples—and one that simultaneously provided a symbolic language for their differences and reified and concretized those differences—was their diverging definitions of the tasteful. My maternal grandparents maintained the taste of their youth throughout their lifetimes. Each apartment was furnished with a white "French Provincial" bedroom set, formica kitchen table and chairs, mahogany veneer living-room furniture in an "English" style, convertible sofa bed, a lazy-boy, and a TV. Despite the putative class status achieved through my grandfather's job as a professor, they continued to live with aesthetic norms that would probably be described by a sociologist as working-class.

Critical to their senses of self, and to the selves they created and represented through their furnishings, were their religious identities, their geographic stability, their interpretation of gender roles, and the constitution of their social world. Rose and Sam were orthodox Jews and did not leave the city of their youth until they retired to a microcosm of it in Florida. They participated in Jewish social organizations and lived essentially among other Jews who were from similar backgrounds. My grandfather talked little about domestic things; my grandmother had a more elaborated discourse about what she was buying and why. Dominating her conversation were references to what her friends and relations had bought and where. Rose bragged about getting "good value" on something and was ashamed of expensive purchases. To her, they were admissions of weakness. Discoveries of bargains she shared with her friends, and possessing exactly the same thing as her neighbor was more than acceptable—it was a pleasure. Thus Rose used furniture, clothing, and food to anchor herself and her family firmly in the social context into which she and many of her generation had moved in her young adulthood during the 1920s. They had escaped from poverty and their children would, to their parents' pride, establish themselves firmly in the middle class. My maternal grandparents themselves, however, were committed to the maintenance of the community of their youth, a community that had started as working-class and now cut across class differences. They used goods far more in the hopes of resembling their neighbors than in the hopes of differentiating themselves from them. Consumer solidarity was highly prized, and competition through goods frowned upon.

My paternal grandparents, in contrast, broke with the aesthetic of their youth and created a new definition of the tasteful. Their dwellings could not have looked less like those of my mother's family. Ida and Charles moved to Philadelphia and established a "modern" household. By the 1950s, they had acquired a house combining Danish modern with American "contemporary" furniture and even included a few custom pieces. The dining room was furnished with a matching contemporary pearwood set—table, chairs, sideboard, breakfront—in a moderately ornate design. The living room had carefully unmatched upholstered furniture with solid wood legs and arms, a glass and metal coffee table, and custom veneer cubes and display cabinets for some of their favorite crystal sculptures. Their bedroom was in Danish satinwood veneer, and the guestroom had also been purchased at Scandinavian Design. Furthermore, the basement housed a small dancing studio, with a hardwood floor and a very sophisticated sound system.

Any adequate explanation for my paternal grandparents' taste would have to include my grandmother's unusual role in taking over her father's business (and debts), the subsequent move from New York, their relative financial ease, their secularism, my grandfather's intellectual ambitions, and their love of dancing. On first glance, it would appear that they were trying to assimilate. They stopped practicing their religion, they bought international-style furniture, they had non-Jewish friends. But that is too simple; they did not want to be absorbed into WASP culture. Rather, they wanted to distinguish themselves from others for whom they might be mistaken (like my maternal grandparents). My grandmother appropriated from the dominant (i.e., middle-class WASP) culture its words of aesthetic praise—simplicity, elegance, quality, purity of line, originality—but gave different meanings to those words.[21] Anything "simple" was beautiful, anything "gaudy" was ugly. (She deemed most of what Rose bought gaudy.) Judgments with which most members of the dominant classes would be in agreement, until they saw the objects in question. Ida took immense pride in her house and garden and was quick to point out the uniqueness, cost, and specialness of her acquisitions and interior design. Like Rose, Ida sought to use goods to create and consolidate social ties. But, unlike Rose, she chose to weave those ties by differentiating herself from the others, highlighting her individuality.

21. See the contributions to Stuart Hall and Tony Jefferson, eds., *Resistance through Rituals: Youth Subcultures in Post-war Britain* (London, 1976).

Both couples, then, used their material goods as a means of self-representation.[22] Beyond the family, the primary audience for their domestic interiors was other Jews, often of similar geographic and class backgrounds. Despite one couple's secularism and the other's piety, both couples wanted their children to marry Jews and both wanted to be buried in Jewish cemeteries. Both had explicitly Jewish objects displayed prominently in their homes. My maternal grandmother bought and used things to create solidarity with others with whom she identified and to protect and reinforce those relationships in the face of material difference. My paternal grandmother created an interior that distanced her from those she feared she resembled and sought to flee through an insistence on the values of individuality, originality, modernity, and internationalism. But it was as much a process of differentiation from, as emulation of, the dominant culture, and both processes involved a complex use of objects and of the words to describe those objects. My grandmothers' consumer practices did not simply reflect their place in the world; they also defined that world and made that place.

Those consumer practices were not limited to the acquisition or arrangement of the goods themselves; the uses to which they were discursively put were equally critical. My maternal grandmother was terrified of standing out, of being different, of breaking rank with the friends and relations of her youth. She not only bought the same things they bought, but she talked about them in the same language and criticized those who deviated from the norm. My paternal grandmother either did not want to, or did not believe she could, be contained within the community in which she had come of age; she found other objects and other words with which to talk about them. Yet both used the language of taste as a language of social judgment, of inclusion and of exclusion. When they grew irritable with each other, their critiques were often in terms of taste.

My grandmothers, then, were anything but passive consumers, quietly buying what clever advertisers suggested to them. They were also doing something more complicated than dissolving unobtrusively into the American melting pot.[23] The identities they constructed and expressed

22. For a parallel discussion, but in contemporary Sweden, see Jonas Frykman and Orvar Löfgren, *Culture Builders: A Historical Anthropology of Middle-Class Life*, trans. Alan Crozier (New Brunswick, 1987), 148–50.

23. Stuart Ewen's discussion of immigrants' uses of goods in *All Consuming Images: The Politics of Style in Contemporary Culture* (New York, 1988), 76–77, is thus too simple, in its emphasis on assimilation and "passing," because it reduces immigrants to passive recipients of an ill-defined mainstream American culture. For

through the deployment of furniture in their homes were complex, fractured, and therefore by no means bounded by class, religion, or social or geographic origins. Even as my paternal grandparents described their taste in terms an American bourgeois of longer standing would recognize, they invented a personal and particular aesthetic. My maternal grandparents, seemingly less innovative in their consumer practices, likewise made a choice: not to produce an aesthetic representation of themselves that might distance them from the people they held dear. They chose to opt out of part of the American dream. Equally important—although by now a truism perhaps—is that this social labor was the responsibility of the women.

What relevance do observations about my grandparents have to the furniture makers in Woburn or in nineteenth-century Paris? My grandparents deployed their furnishings not simply as a source of sensual pleasure, but as a means of social differentiation and as the media to communicate those differences. Generalizing these observations, I began to ask myself if women had always had the final say on aesthetic matters, and whether furnishings had always been put to such uses. Had people in the eighteenth and nineteenth centuries used consumer goods to construct themselves—if they had, which consumer goods, which people, and what does it mean to "construct oneself"? What was to be made of the relation between what people bought and used and how they and other people talked and wrote about it, between the making and selling of goods and their use after purchase? With these questions in mind I turned again to the experience of scholarship, but this time to texts on the theory and history of consumerism and on identity formation.

There is, by now, a rather massive—economic, anthropological, psychological, sociological, and historical—literature on consumption and consumer practices. Theoretical studies, when they try to find the commonalities in people's use of objects across time and space, I have found of limited use. This work is often much more contextually and historically specific than its authors seem to realize: being a relatively young literature (in its modern form), it tends to start from consumption under late capitalism and unconsciously assumes either the uniqueness or the univer-

---

a very different example than my grandmothers' of consumers' creative use of objects, see Melanie Wallendorf and Michael D. Reilly, "Ethnic Migration, Assimilation, and Consumption," *Journal of Consumer Research* 10 (December 1983): 292–302.

sality of that formation.[24] Yet some of this work has been extremely useful in calling attention to the communicative capacity of objects, in their exchange and in their use.[25] Attempts to analyze consumer practices within a given time and space at a high level of abstraction have been more helpful in framing the analysis here.[26] This work is, however, most developed for the contemporary European and American world and is significantly less successful for distant times and places.[27] Furthermore, both the theoretical and empirical work on consumerism tend to come from either a liberal or neoliberal position, assuming the naturalness of demand, the autonomy of the consumer, and the justice of the market, or from a Marxist or neo-Marxist position that is often too critical of modern consumerism without a careful enough analysis of its particular historical manifestations.[28] I find neither approach fully adequate to the questions that troubled me.

More concretely, the historical debate over consumerism has concentrated on three issues: dating the onset of modern consumer practices; the relevance of demand as a causal agent for the first and second industrial revolutions; and the centrality of consumption to the class formation of the bourgeoisie. This literature is very rich but, in the case of work done on England, flawed for my purposes by the underlying agenda of making an argument for "home demand" as a catalyst for the first industrial

24. Economists and psychologists, in otherwise subtle analyses are most prone to these assumptions: see J. F. Bernard-Bécharies, *Le choix de consommation: rationalité et réalité du comportement du consommateur* (Paris, 1970); and Mihaly Csikszentmihalyi and Eugene Rochberg-Halton, *The Meaning of Things: Domestic Symbols and the Self* (Cambridge, 1981).

25. Most salient here is Mary Douglas and Baron Isherwood, *The World of Goods* (New York, 1979).

26. Jean Baudrillard, *Le système des objets* (Tournail, 1975); *Le miroir de la production* (Paris, 1968); and *La société de consommation;* also Daniel Miller, *Material Culture and Mass Consumption* (Oxford, 1987).

27. An important exception is Nicholas Thomas, *Entangled Objects: Exchange, Material Culture, and Colonialism in the Pacific* (Cambridge, Mass., 1991).

28. Striking examples of the liberal approach are Timothy Breen, "'Baubles of Britain': The American and Consumer Revolutions of the Eighteenth Century," *Past and Present* 119 (1988): 73–104; Neil McKendrick, "Home Demand and Economic Growth: A New View of the Role of Women and Children in the Industrial Revolution," in *Historical Perspectives*, ed. Neil McKendrick (London, 1975), 152–210; of the Marxist genre see Ewen, *All Consuming Images;* Rosalind Williams, *Dream Worlds: Mass Consumption in Late Nineteenth-Century France* (Berkeley, 1982); Wolfgang Fritz Haug, *Critique of Commodity Aesthetics: Appearance, Sexuality, and Advertising in Capitalist Society*, trans. Robert Bock (Minneapolis, 1986).

revolution.[29] Scholars, caught up in the standard-of-living debate, are eager to demonstrate that the industrial revolution was sparked by demand as much as by transformations in production, and that that demand was in England rather than abroad. These arguments become circular: they assume that all people are inherently prone to consume when they can, that ultimately wage levels determine consumer practices and economic take-off.[30] Because of its divorce of the economic from the political, and its naturalization of demand, this work has little relevance to the social and political meaning of consumption.[31] Efforts to think about both production and consumption in relation to the forms of political regime—a crucial linkage to an understanding of either—are few.

All of this work, the theoretical and the historical, set in Britain, the United States, and on the continent, did not satisfy my desire to understand what my grandmothers were doing in their homes. So I turned to the last of the scholarly literatures concerned with consumerism, in literary, film, and cultural studies, for analysis not just of what people bought but of what those acquisitions meant. This work, much of it feminist, much of it Gramscian or Lacanian in inspiration, some of it derived from the Frankfurt school cultural theorists, focuses on questions of subjectivity, identity, spectatorship, consumer-use, and resistance.[32]

29. On the uses of consumption in class formation, Leonore Davidoff and Catherine Hall, *Family Fortunes: Men and Women of the English Middle Class, 1780–1850* (Chicago, 1987); Marion Kaplan, *The Making of the Jewish Middle Class: Women, Family, and Identity in Imperial Germany* (New York, 1991); Bonnie G. Smith, *Ladies of the Leisure Class: The Bourgeoises of Northern France in the Nineteenth Century* (Princeton, 1981) are especially impressive examples.

30. On the standard of living see Lorna Weatherill, *Consumer Behavior and Material Culture in Britain, 1660–1760* (New York, 1988); D. E. C. Everseley, "The Home Market and Economic Growth in England, 1750–1780," in *Land, Labor, and Population in the Industrial Revolution*, ed. E. L. Jones, and G. E. Mingay (New York, 1967).

31. Important exceptions to this general trend are the work of historian Jean-Christophe Agnew, *Worlds Apart: The Market and the Theater in Anglo-American Thought, 1550–1750* (Cambridge, 1986); Peter Borsay in "The English Urban Renaissance: The Development of Provincial Urban Culture, c. 1680–1760," *Social History* 5 (1977); and, in a very different register, the work of Simon Schama, *The Embarrassment of Riches* (Berkeley, 1988).

32. Most notably Rachel Bowlby, *Just Looking: Consumer Culture in Dreiser, Gissing, and Zola* (New York, 1985); Jane Gaines and Charlotte Herzog, eds., *Fabrications: Costume and the Female Body* (London, 1990); Mary Ann Doane, *The Desire to Desire: The Woman's Film of the 1940s* (Bloomington, 1987); and Mica Nava, *Changing Cultures: Feminism, Youth, and Consumerism* (London, 1992).

It is a literature I find to be very useful, but with one caveat: in some cases, the commitment to a construction of consumers as either active agents (with the assumption that that agency has direct implications for resistance) or passive victims blurs investigation of the nature of the relationship between resistance and identity production (which mirrors the liberal/Marxist split described above).[33] Consumers may make choices and objects may become critical for the formation of self, and even for the formation of group solidarities, without necessarily engaging in any kind of resistance. Some of the difficulties of this literature seem to stem from confusion about what identity is, might be, and has been; so I turned to the literature more specifically concerned with those issues.

The literature on the process of identity construction is immense and diverse. It ranges from psychoanalytic discussions of the making of subjectivity, to feminist inquiries into the formation of gendered selves, to recent work on sexuality as a category of identity, to Marxist and post-Marxist discussions of class identity, to the archaeology of race and racial difference, to theoretical, empirical and historical investigations into the concepts of "other" and of "stranger," and even to the deconstruction of the very desire for, and idea of, identity.[34] Given the lack of consensus among or even within these diverse but interrelated discussions, and given the immense scope and complexity of these debates, I will not attempt even a brief critique or summary here. Suffice it to say, however, the issues they raise have been central to the formulation of my work.[35] This book worries a great deal about identity; about what the concept means, and about how both the making and buying of goods were at certain conjunctures important means of inventing a sense of self and at other moments one or the other, or both, of those activities were quite irrelevant to the process of

33. The most helpful historical work using this approach is Kathy Peiss's *Cheap Amusements* (Philadelphia, 1986), especially her introduction with its elegant discussion of the pitfalls of models of both liberation and victimization. Dick Hebdige, *Subculture: The Meaning of Style* (London, 1979) tends to emphasize the "resistive" capacity.

34. For a recent reevaluation of the "gender discussions" see Judith Butler and Joan Wallach Scott, eds., *Feminists Theorize the Political* (London, 1992). Judith Butler's *Gender Trouble* (New York, 1990) does an archaeology of the category. Zygmunt Bauman, "Strangers: Social Construction of Universality and Particularity," *Telos* 78 (winter 1988–89): 7–42 is helpful on the concept of the stranger. W. E. B. Du Bois, *Souls of Black Folk* (Chicago, 1903) is still one of the most compelling texts on raced identities.

35. See my critique and discussion of three texts within the feminist literature ("Feminist Theory and Social History: Explorations in the Politics of Identity," *Radical History Review* 54 [fall 1992]: 158–76).

self-creation. I also attempt to make some sense of the many identities in which producers and consumers found themselves—individual, familial, regional, gendered, classed, and national. Again, goods in general, and furniture in particular were not necessarily or inevitably used in the making of any or all of these potential identities.

It is important to emphasize here that I seek to not reproduce, in the domain of objects, the debate that reigns in the domain of discourse. I argue that objects cannot be understood to simply "re-present" an always-already-existing identity of the producer or the consumer, to the world. First of all there clearly has never been only *one* identity to represent. Second, the category of identity does not "cover" the problem of subjectivity, for it has misleading connotations, even when used in the plural, of the possibility of self-transparency, self-coherence, and the absence of internal contradiction. Within identity theory, contradictions tend to be understood as *externally* produced in adult social actors. But rather than explain the dissonance as the inability of others to let one simultaneously inhabit several identities, or let one choose an identity, I argue that contradictory desires and identifications are both internally and externally made and lived, that there are also contradictions *between* the internal and the external, and that one cannot always be conscious of these desires. Those desires are made in and through discourse, which I understand to mean language (and other symbolic systems) in use. Discourse does not merely reflect or represent realities or persons—it also constitutes them. Discourses have histories, sites of production, and levels of connotation. People use them with particular hopes, intents, and purposes in mind, but they do not always say what they mean, mean what they say, or even know what it is they mean.

In certain conjunctures, objects are likewise *both* constitutive and representative. They represent people's conscious identities and unconscious desires and fears; they also constitute them, because objects carry multiple potential meanings to different users and to the same user. When I go into a store to buy a chair, I carry Rose and Ida (as well as the rest of my family and digested and undigested childhood experiences) with me, both consciously and unconsciously. I also carry my—complicatedly generated—interpretive grid of what certain styles signify, in terms of social and political position. This baggage produces a judgment, or taste. I choose a chair. I take that chair home. Over the next months and years guests respond to me and to my chair, some seeing in it one thing, some another. They cannot see in it what I hoped for them to see because what I hoped was itself necessarily contradictory and occluded. They respond with their interpretations of my chair and me; I respond and am changed by their responses. I have been made by that chair and I have made the chair. The chair was full of meanings over which I had no control, and of which I had only partial knowledge when I acquired it. In my home it acquired new meanings. My guests have a certain understanding of me when they arrive in my home; as a result of viewing my chair they have somewhat different understandings. In their eyes I become different—perhaps also in my own.

This process is neither universal nor natural. It is a phenomenon of modernity, a creation of the bourgeois stylistic regime and its successor— the mass stylistic regime—and rests on the alienation of the producers from the product of their labor. When my co-workers' ancestors-in-trade had been paid to invent themselves (in all the infinitely complex meanings of that concept) through the making of things, "consumption" meant something very different than it does today. Likewise, when the political system was founded upon the concept of the embodiment of the nation in the king—when the king, the king's things, and the nation were one—objects meant something very different than they did under the republican system of the late nineteenth and twentieth centuries. The changing meaning of these objects became clear to me early in the project when I read late nineteenth-century discussions of contemporary and ancien régime taste and style. The dominant furniture style of the late nineteenth century was a pastiche of Old Regime styles. The debaters engaged in questions of taste in the late nineteenth century kept asking, Why can't we be as innovative as our prerevolutionary ancestors? I became curious about the meaning of these pastiches and this debate. To understand it, without grasping what seemed to have been going on in the Old Regime, was impossible.

In order to grasp the historicity of the meaning of objects in political and social life, therefore, the time frame of this book reaches across nearly two centuries. Its span, which is admittedly both audacious and uneven, was necessitated by the problem I address. Although the intellectual and personal experiences of my present—a "mass" society and mass stylistic regime—stimulated the problem, I knew that I could not begin to address it without a much better understanding of what preceded my present—the bourgeois stylistic regime of the late nineteenth and early twentieth centuries. To understand that regime, therefore, is the primary object of this study. In the course of my investigations, I came to see that the key to explain this aspect of French bourgeois society lay in the era before the Revolution. To extend an originally late nineteenth-century project back into the ancien régime risks not only the conventional errors that a nonspecialist is prone to but a teleological fallacy as well: to raid the ancien régime solely to illuminate the modernity that followed. I decided to chance these risks because the contrast between the ancien and bourgeois regimes underscored so clearly the intricate interrelations between production, distribution, and consumption, between public and private spheres, and between the political and the social necessary to understanding the deployment and constitution of power in the everyday of absolutist and bourgeois political orders.

Consequently, the periodization of this story is determined by the approximate moments at which furniture came to occupy a different place in social and political negotiation than it had before. The story of shifts in the uses of furniture is divided into three periods: the Old Regime, the transition to the bourgeois stylistic regime, and the bourgeois regime. During the first period, domestic objects were constitutive of political power and the state served as a direct patron and determiner of style; the period from Revolution to 1871 was a transitional one, marked politically by two imperial regimes, two monarchies, war, civil war, two revolutions, the birth and death of the Second Republic, and the establishment of the Third. The state tried and failed to sustain its role as patron, but it was unable as yet to assume another role. Furnishings appear to have served both political and social ends, although neither very clearly. This transitional moment continued through the Second Empire and into the first decade of the Third Republic, marked by a strong renewed state involvement in matters of taste and rapid transformations in the organization of production and distribution. The period 1880 to 1930 may be characterized as a mature bourgeois stylistic regime, in which domestic goods became essentially irrelevant for the constitution of political power but crucial for the making of social power. The state was now largely absent as patron, although very present in the training of producers; meanwhile new market mechanisms trained consumers in taste. The story ends with the beginnings of a mass stylistic regime in the twentieth century.

I will argue that consumption as a set of actions constitutive of the social fabric was especially a phenomenon of the nineteenth century. During the Old Regime, and to a diminished extent until 1848, durable, symbolically rich objects were used primarily to represent royal and aristocratic political power; after mid-century they were used by the bourgeoisie as part of the process of class formation and to consolidate their power, excluding thereby both the aristocracy and the working class. In the twentieth century, the working class in its turn gained access to this system of class, identity, and subjectivity formation through consumption.

Furthermore, when consumption as an occupation constitutive of society came into being, it was defined as feminine or effeminate. From the Old Regime onward, acquiring subsistence for the family was a task that fell to women. But the nineteenth-century gendering of non-subsistence consumption was not simply an extension of women's traditional role in providing for their families. Rather, the nineteenth-century invention of the female consumer was closely linked to the transformation of the place of everyday objects in the making of social and political life. At the moment that domestic objects ceased to be important as means of representation of political power and became means of production and consolidation of the newly invented world of the "social," women were defined as consumers and men as producers. The redefinition was a matter of importance not only to the consumers, but also to the producers, for the possibility of being paid for making beauty diminished when beauty came to be defined as a feminine preserve. This re-gendering of the aesthetic was implicated in a shift in the mechanisms of power from the seventeenth to the nineteenth centuries and from an absolutist to a republican state.

The theme of my story is that domestic objects worked very differently in the constitution of social place, individual identity, and state power from the seventeenth century to the early twentieth. The nature of that difference was a product of the change in form of politics, including not only the move toward representative forms of government but also the changing nature of state intervention. In the Old Regime the crown regulated all relations of production and distribution and chose at moments to allow those regulations to be broken. But part of that process of regulation was granting great autonomy—for the internal policing of their trades and the training of successor generations—to the producers and distributors of goods. And, in this structure the appearance of goods was non-arbitrary; they had not yet become completely commodified. After the end of the guild structure, and the development of industrial capitalism, first the bourgeoisie and then the state became increasingly involved in direct control over the processes of training and production and less involved in patronage. Artisanal men came to be less able to produce themselves through creative work, as their labor became more fractured and divided. Bourgeois women came to be able, and obliged, to fashion themselves and their families through commodities. In a bourgeois stylistic regime, bourgeois men were to represent the family through the vote and women were to represent the family on and in their bodies and homes. After the First World War, with the move into mass consumption and mass politics, the dynamic of commodities, and the gendering of production and consumption would change yet again.

For parallel reasons, this book uses both a synchronic and a diachronic organization. Each part represents a moment I have found to be crucial in tracing the trajectory of the meaning of domestic objects in the constitution of political and social life. The ancien régime, from the apogee of absolutism to its crisis in the eighteenth century; a transitional moment from the Revolution through the Second Empire; and the bourgeois stylistic regime of the late nineteenth and early twentieth centuries. The chapters within each part examine a particular aspect of its historical moment; their relation to each other is temporally concurrent rather than sequential. Each discusses a different aspect of the making of meaning through objects within that moment.

The broad sweep of this book and the nature of the questions it attempts to address require a wide variety of sources ranging from the objects themselves (and images of them); to archival documentation on production, distribution, and consumption; to primary printed texts (including government reports, memoirs, political theory, novels, magazine articles, and aesthetic treatises); to the work of other historians (writing in both the nineteenth and the twentieth centuries); and to texts by theorists writing about production, consumption, and citizenship in abstract terms. Some chapters rely more on one kind of inspiration and evidence than another. To forestall readers' concern about such disparities, I point to the necessarily collective nature of scholarly production. That I should redo the labor of others merely to have the authority of an archival citation seems arrogant and foolish. That I should limit my interpretive work to those areas in which I have done "primary" work would be a fetishization of the archive and of the primary source. I choose instead to take advantage of all the tools available to me to address the problems posed by this project.

In parallel to the wide range of sources upon which this book is based, I also have recourse to diverse modes of argumentation. There are moments of abstract, theoretical arguments and moments of empirical, concrete narration. The movement between these two forms is deliberate and reflects the movement between the theoretical and empirical that marked the evolution of the research and writing of this book. The historical sources alone could not and did not tell the story, and the story I found in those historical sources was not merely an illustration or a case of an abstract or general argument. There are moments when I rely on a cited abstract argument concerning, for example, the power of the family metaphor in the structuring of social relations, to support an argument. The empirical evidence is presented within that framework, and is intended to demonstrate the argument, just as the theory is intended to make the empirical evidence meaningful. Neither the empirical evidence nor the theoretical discussion alone is intended to prove the argument.

This movement between the abstract and the concrete is, therefore, partially a result of the sources used but is equally a reflection of the dialogues in which I have been and hope to continue to be engaged. This book is the result of an engagement with historians, anthropologists, art historians, and political, feminist, and critical theorists. I hope that the book will make a contribution to debates in that broad interdisciplinary arena. Despite this age of interdisciplinarity, however, all who have participated in interdisciplinary forums know how durable disciplinary conventions remain. There are, therefore, moments in this book that I fear will be read as painfully anecdotal to the theorists, and others as absurdly abstract to some historians, art historians, and anthropologists.

More specifically this introduction, the introductions to each of the three parts, and the epilogue all provide the conceptual architecture of the book. They both explain in broad strokes the historical unity of each part and offer the theoretical context of the discussion within the debates on representation, commodification, and nation building. They are, therefore, intentionally abstract. It is my hope that readers unfamiliar with French history, but engaged in similar questions in some other context, will find this material helpful in making this book speak to their own preoccupations.

This work emerges from the melding and contradictions of a complex array of experiences both within and outside the academy. Beginning as an effort to understand what artisans might have thought they were doing in the practice of their trade and what shaped those thoughts, the project came to focus instead on the biography through time of a particular object. This book uses an analysis of that one object to explore the general history of the place of things in the constitution of social and political life. The object is furniture, the place is Paris, and the time is from the seventeenth century to the early decades of the twentieth. In order to answer the questions that bothered me, I found it necessary to break the traditional chronological and substantive divisions into Old Regime or new, into design or production or distribution or consumption of furniture. The book could not be about only the working class, or only the bourgeoisie, nor just about women nor just about men. It could not analyze society while leaving the state and the economy as residual categories, nor vice versa.

Thus this book, which started from a small and not terribly significant object, turned out to be about a rather vast number of institutions and social

transformations. The choice of the time frame and the decision to reconstruct the cycle of design, production, distribution, and consumption I have
already explained. But the questions remain, why France and why furniture? To start to explain both why I chose to explore these questions in
modern France, and what this optic helps us understand about France, I will
tell my last personal story.

My family changed countries and continents a number of times when
I was a young child at an age to be taught to write. I learned, in the end,
how to write three times in three different countries—the United States,
Uruguay, and France—for no pedagogic culture could accept the handwriting learned in another. All agreed that there was *one* way for handwriting to look, and all tried to instill a unified style. The experience of
mastering one hand only to be defined as in need of urgent instruction the
next year made me realize that the judgment of small things, like how one
shaped one's p's, was both arbitrary and a matter of great import. Its
importance was made clearest in France, for despite competing efforts my
handwriting became (and remains) far more French than American or
Uruguayan. While acculturation of children into the nation was to be
accomplished in all three countries in part through the disciplining of the
body that handwriting norms represented, the French were at once the
most insistent and the most successful at inscribing their nation on my
hand. Both the determination and the skill with which French schools
succeeded in remaking my style of writing—reflecting the capacity of
French culture to remake individuals from other cultures in its own image—appeared to me to be unique. Consequently, while the story told in
this book is at moments comparative and always has implications beyond
France, it is specifically French. It is the emphatic French commitment to
French modes of living the everyday and the role of the state in creating
those modes that this book hopes to explain.

By the 1960s, when I was a child in France, the French state had a history
of efforts to homogenize the speech, clothing, and habits of its inhabitants
that reached back nearly two centuries to the Revolution. France became
one of the most consistent and determined advocates and practitioners of
nation making through culture as well as one of the most highly centralized
states, in both political and bureaucratic terms, in Western Europe or in
comparison with North America. Unlike in the United States or Germany
or even, to a lesser extent, in England, notions of regional interests and
regional differences were little tolerated by the French state. The country
was divided into political districts because of the pragmatic exigencies of
elections, not because it was understood that each region was entitled to

its own representative in the capital. Likewise, education was under national control from very early on with an explicit agenda to build a more unified nation through homogenized schooling. The French state attempted to eradicate regionalisms and to assimilate foreigners both out of a belief in the possibility of transformation through culture and in the interests of national cohesion and solidarity. The history of this intense centralization and homogenization has been told before but will be told again and differently here (see chapters 9–10). Whereas previous studies have analyzed the institutions through which the state clearly had a mandate to shape the nation—schools, universities, the army—this study tackles the problem more obliquely, tracing when and how the state was involved in matters of taste and when and how processes of nation building through taste occurred without direct state intervention. This book also demonstrates the ways and moments in which national identities competed with others and how those competitions were resolved or not.

Furniture is an especially apt object by which to tackle this set of problems in France for three reasons. First of all, furniture, unlike steel, bottles, or wheat is an object of style and requires taste for its production and consumption. Taste has been uniquely salient to both national identity and to export production in France. As early as the seventeenth century the French understood themselves as possessing, as a nation, more refined taste than other European nations. In the nineteenth and twentieth centuries, while England and later the United States and Germany could export goods made more cheaply and more efficiently, France competed economically through taste. Furthermore, French commentators were more likely than others to declare "crises in national taste" and to argue that such crises were indicative of more profound upheavals in French society.

French conceptions of taste in the nineteenth and twentieth centuries, however, contained a necessary paradox. Unified French taste was understood to be essential to the well-being of the nation and yet that nation was internally divided by class and gender and different tastes were thought appropriate to each class and gender. An investigation of the language in which these crises in taste in furniture were enunciated, the responses to these perceptions of crisis, and the styles and tastes which were in fact produced and used, all elucidate the ways in which the dynamics of representation and identity were constructed in France.

Second, because furniture is a good essential to both the domestic space of the home and the public space of the government, its analysis enables, indeed forces, a rethinking of the divisions between state and society, public and private, and ultimately masculine and feminine. After the Revolution, in the era of laissez-faire, the state should no longer have had anything to do with the production or consumption of style. Both the workshop and the home were defined as private and beyond the purview of the state. And yet the state was deeply concerned with what people made and bought because it was understood that those who did not live in properly French homes were not properly French and that artisans' inability to produce distinctively French furniture endangered the French economy. Thus an examination of the complex and changing role of the state in the design, production, distribution, and consumption of furniture enables one to seize the limits and paradoxes of nineteenth-century republican liberalism as well as of nation and class in modern France.

Third, for the entire time period of this study furniture was an expensive and durable consumer item. Its acquisition was therefore a weightier act than for many other, more transient, consumer goods. Its making required elaborate expertise, both technical and aesthetic, and was therefore particularly vulnerable to transformations in the organization of production, including systems of training. And since furniture makers were notorious for their subversive and revolutionary tendencies, crises in the industry were perceived to have particularly worrisome political implications. Such tendencies, together with furniture's important place in the export economy, gave furniture a special interest for the state. Thus changes in furniture style reflected and produced changes in social relations in a more tangible way than did the stories of other objects.[36]

At all moments of its life cycle, from its conception through its design, production, advertisement, display, sale, purchase or acquisition, use, gift, loan, legacy, and abandonment or destruction, furniture had the potential to crystallize social and political possibilities and tensions in French society.[37] It did not, of course, always do so in the same way. At some moments

36. In all these ways furniture differed from clothing, another obvious object of style by which one might address the set of questions I have outlined. Furniture had, because of its durability, its cost, its relative immobility and immutability particular capacities for expressing and representing political power and authority at certain moments. A parallel study of clothing would be fascinating but would reveal different things. On clothing see Philippe Perrot, *Les dessus et les dessous de la bourgeoisie* (Paris, 1981); Elizabeth Wilson, *Adorned in Dreams* (Berkeley, 1987). See also Rosalind Coward, *Female Desires* (New York, 1985); Hebdige, *Subculture*; and, Alison Lurie, *The Language of Clothes* (New York, 1981).

37. Others have, of course, noted the importance of interiors for the construction of bourgeois identities. For work on France see Adeline Daumard, *Les bourgeois et la bourgeoisie en France depuis 1815* (Paris, 1987), 56, 109–11, 115–17; Debora L. Silverman, *Art Nouveau in Fin-de-Siècle France* (Berkeley, 1989); Whitney Walton, *France at the Crystal Palace* (Berkeley, 1992).

furniture was important in constituting political power and legitimating regimes, and at others it was irrelevant in that domain but still crucial in producing and reproducing the social order. At some moments it was critical in constituting the symbolic repertoire of the nation, at others interior decoration served as a means of class consolidation, at still others as a means of making manifest intraclass schisms. At times it did many things at once. In some periods, but not all, furniture styles were used to differentiate gender and generational roles. The actors in this story—the producers, distributors, "taste professionals" both private and public, and consumers—engaged in an endless process of negotiation over who would control style, how they would learn to make aesthetic judgments, and what those styles would mean. Those battles occurred in the context of a changing kaleidoscope of institutions and terrains through which furniture passed or was discussed. These included the guilds, journeymen's organizations, apprenticeship, royal workshops, antique dealers, specialized furniture stores, custom furniture stores, advertisements, schools, museums, universal exhibitions, department stores, trade unions, auction houses, etiquette books, and decorating magazines.

This book poses, then, from a different angle, the very classic problem of the relation of state, culture, and economy. For in talking about representation through goods and through politics, we are ultimately talking about capitalism and democracy. So while this book cannot hope, through the close study of only one commodity, to resolve the very long-standing debate on feudalism and absolutism, or on the nature of a capitalist state, I hope that by radically shifting the perspective from the very abstract and general, to the very concrete and specific, to shed some light on these crucial questions—questions all the more urgent in these times when the connection of mass consumption and democracy is too often assumed without any question at all.

PART 1

THE PARADOX OF ABSOLUTISM
The Power of the Monarch's Limits

Objects, especially domestic objects, played a distinctive role in the representation and maintenance of power under absolutism; the crown displayed its strength both through its possessions and through its control of those who made, sold, and bought them. An absolute monarchy would in principle have only one style in domestic objects, and the state would determine it. That style, like military uniforms under any state form, would have variations to represent the different positions in the political hierarchy. The appearance of even the most domestic possessions of its enfranchised subjects would concern an absolute monarchy, because given the powerful familial metaphor grounding the power of the father-king, the dwelling was a constitutive part of the polity. Such a style-system never existed, for no French monarchy was ever in fact absolute. Even Louis XIV, the epitome of absolute monarchs, had far from absolute power. There was, thus, slippage in the system.

The absolute king could never survive in pristine detachment above the actual exercise of power; he could authenticate its majesty only by engaging in testing its limits. Sustaining an absolutist regime required an endlessly careful, sometimes paradoxical, manipulation of power: the crown's power had to be used to prove its existence, but some uses diminished while others augmented it; sometimes select exceptions to absolute control helped secure the illusion of total control. Thus were the discursive representations of power inextricably bound up with the material bases of that power. Under the Old Regime, monarchical power articulated with complex relations of production, distribution, and consumption. Seeming contradictions within relations of production and of distribution, and of consumption were actually reflections of royal uses of objects to consolidate and reproduce its power, within a cultural and political order that the crown dominated but could not completely control.

Qualifying the king's capacity to determine aesthetic form was the fact that neither the king nor his court could *make* anything. The crown was dependent on artisans, architects, and artists to create visual and mechanical forms. Whereas the symbolic meaning of, and access to, objects and style belonged to the crown and the court, the form of the objects and the dynamic of stylistic transformation did not. Style emerged from diverse sites and processes: out of the interaction among the patronage of the crown and court, initiatives of the distributors, and the "culture of production" that transmitted artisans' skill, knowledge, and craft sense; out of archaeological finds, discoveries of new raw materials, the expansion of commerce to the Americas, Africa and Asia; and out of diplomatic needs and economic cycles.[1] All these provided the seedbed for the invention of forms.

The complexities of the organization of production allowed the king to use his capacity to grant and undermine monopolies and to adjudicate among the competing needs and demands of the crown, the city of Paris, and the Catholic Church. The institution through which the king was supposed to regulate the production of all objects (including furniture) was the guild (also called corporations and communities)—an instrument of city government as well as of economic regulation—but in the case of furniture the crown undermined its own mandate of monopoly power by giving competing privileges to certain artisans working under the authority of the crown itself or of the church. As we shall see, however, such actions were simultaneously concessions to real weakness and demonstrations of symbolic power. The demonstration of strength lay in the rights of patronage: the king gave and the king took away. Even when a privilege had been paid for it could be legitimately undermined by an ostensibly omnipotent crown.

The crown acquired furniture from all available sources—court artisans, royal manufactories, guild producers, guild merchants, and "free workers" (who were not members of a guild) under church patronage—fostering competition among them. That process created another contradiction: although the crown sought to sustain the guilds so as to protect the rights

---

1. By "culture of production" I refer to a relatively autonomous artisanal system of passing down the knowledge, skill, and craft sense needed for the creative practice of the trade but do not therefore treat the seventeenth and eighteenth centures as a "golden age of labor." Sonenscher (*Hatters*, 169–72) and Andreas Grießinger (*Das symbolische Kapital der Ehre* [Frankfurt, 1981], 426–29) describe a similar phenomenon, although they do not use the term.

of producers and consumers alike, in the case of goods of high symbolic valence, like furniture, it also perceived a national interest in producing the highest quality goods possible. Thus, France competed in the strategic world economy and polity through its aesthetic prowess. By creating a competitive world in the decorative arts, by encouraging the immigration of foreign artisans, by establishing workshops within its palaces, the crown hoped to push French furniture to new heights so as to reinforce its power abroad as well as at home. Consequently, the organization of production was far more complicated, and formed far more by the construction of power under absolutism, than reading guild statutes would lead us to believe.

Complicating matters further was the effect of the dominant metaphor of king-as-father on relations of distribution, because a critically important task of the father-king was to assure the availability of goods (especially bread) at a just price. But while the culture of production lay largely within this paternalist metaphor, distribution sprawled across it into other conceptual grids, making contemporary perceptions and practices correspondingly contradictory and tortuously complex. On the one hand, within the moral and philosophical context of the seventeenth and eighteenth centuries, those who only sold and did not make were considered parasites on society, entitled to less respect even than those who tilled the fields. On the other hand, the merchant guilds—which had the right to sell but not to make—were often the most prestigious and the most powerful, while those who made the products they sold were disdained far more than they were honored.

It was not through the institutions of production and distribution alone that the king's power was made manifest, but through the structures devised to assure the creation and transmission of knowledge, skill, and craft sense—the ensemble that enabled artisans to create new forms. Just as under an absolute monarchy the king was to be the father of his people, and the father within the household was to be as the king was to his subjects, so in the Old Regime model of labor the master was to be the fictive father of the apprentice. A corollary of the importance of the family to the state and the mirroring of the state in the family was the centrality of fathers and fictive male kin to the running of both the household and the larger family and kin system.

The workshop was a masculine family in which the father, brothers, and sons had central roles, while the women, although vital to the success of the household, were left to hover on the periphery. In this masculine structure of production—with its close relation between production and distribution and a relatively weak gendering of consumption—men's interest in the beautiful and competition among themselves over the creation of the beautiful were considered appropriate. The masculine gendering of the making of domestic objects of beauty may have also been an effect of the fluidity of the boundaries between the public and the private and of the importance of these particular goods in constituting political power. The transmission of the trade was thus male- and craft-controlled through a system of fictive kinship analogous to the ideal relation between a king and his people postulated within the system of absolute monarchy. An identity as a furniture maker did not follow inevitably from the practice of a trade; it was a conscious construction. Institutions mirroring those of the political order of the ancien régime provided the framework for that construction and for the elaboration of a culture that gave meaning to that construction. Thus investigation of the complex relations between the organizations of production and the crown is crucial to better understanding the nature of political power under absolutism and of the ways in which artisans and merchants responded to the exercise of that power.

In the consumption of goods of style, the king had a delicate line to tread between preserving the uniqueness of his self-representation through objects and his need to demonstrate power by allowing certain privileged people to have things that resembled his own. Just as the crown reinforced its power through granting and undermining monopolies, and just as it acknowledged the limitations of its power posed by the church, the corporations, and the nobility through granting special favors to each, so the crown could not completely monopolize style either but rather judiciously allowed and even encouraged emulation. The systems of production, distribution, and consumption of goods of style in the ancien régime thus illustrate the complexity of the everyday workings of absolutism as well as the ways in which its apparent weaknesses could become its strengths, and its strengths its weaknesses.

This political system was complicated and challenged by the development of capitalism during this period. Much debate surrounds the timing and nature of French economic development, but by the eighteenth century the economy was expanding and escaping the bounds of state regulation. This development of industrial capitalism contributed to the vulnerability of France's monarchical regimes in this period. By the second half of the eighteenth century, the political system was subject to acute challenge from an increasingly wealthy group of non-nobles. Furthermore, wealthy individuals could buy objects that closely resembled courtly objects and unsettle not only the social but the political order as well.

Such possession of objects of royal style by the Third Estate could be understood as a political claim (and threat) because of the tradition of political power embedded in, and represented by, all royal objects. In contrast, the possessions of *the people,* that is, the vast majority of the French population, including peasants, artisans, servants, and laborers, were of little interest to the state. The poor had furnishings that no doubt were replete with aesthetic, symbolic, and social meanings, but they were devoid of political meaning.[2] Before the Revolution, even if a poor person could have gained access to royal style, it would have been a containable gesture, like that of the charivari, a ritualized reversal of power—potentially threatening perhaps—but largely understood as reinforcing the established order.

Part 1 traces the story of the production of political meaning through furniture from the reign of Louis XIV until the eve of the Revolution. Chapter 1 is concerned with explaining the forms of style under each successive monarch, from the point of view of each king's efforts to sustain and reproduce his political power. Chapter 2 traces the complex organization of production and distribution that were devised under absolutism, that both created the conditions of possibility for stylistic change and ultimately undermined royal monopoly on style. Chapter 3 narrates the implications for the organization of the transmission of the skill, knowledge, and craft sense of a society organized within a patriarchal or paternal model. On one level, then, part 1 narrates the workings of style during the apogee of absolutism and its subsequent decline. On a different level, however, it is intended to reframe some familiar elements of the conventional stories of production, consumption, and absolute power so as to enable our better understanding of the role that the objects of everyday life—specifically furniture—held in the power relations of the ancien régime.

In order to analyze the changing construction of power under absolutism, we must sustain a dialectic between analysis of stylistic change, on the one hand, and of political and economic changes, on the other. The specific use of materials, the historical repertoire of forms, and the products of

2. I rely on two exhaustive archival studies of popular consumption in this period: Annik Pardailhé-Galabrun, *La naissance de l'intime: 3,000 foyers parisiens XVIIe–XVIIIe siècles* (Paris, 1988); and Daniel Roche, *Le peuple de Paris: essai sur la culture populaire au XVIIIe siècle* (Paris, 1981).

distant cultures emerged out of a set of perpetual dialogues between the culture of production, the system of distribution, and the culture of the court. The relations of power characteristic of absolutism—including especially the legitimization of the king's authority, and the specific ways in which an absolutist king represented his people—shaped both these cultures and the system of distribution that mediated among them.

1

The Courtly Stylistic Regime
Representation and Power
under Absolutism

 When servants and courtiers at Versailles came and went about the royal bedroom they bowed before the royal *nef*, a gold shiplike vessel containing the king's knife, fork, and napkin. This was done whether the king was present or not. [Like t]he genuflections of the faithful before altars in churches at all times . . . [1]

As the image conjured by Orest Ranum renders vividly, a particular form of fetishism characterized the apogee of absolutism. The very mundane objects used to assist the king in the satisfaction of his bodily needs were encased in gold and granted the same gestures of respect as the king's body itself. The king's objects *were* the king, and consequently the style of those objects belonged to the king. Royal acquisition and display of possessions luxurious and rare beyond the imagination of even the nobility helped establish and reinforce the theoretically boundless power of the king.[2] An essential purpose of royal goods was to demonstrate the creative and economic strength of the monarch and the loyalty of his court against both domestic and foreign challenges. Or as it was put in a complaint to Jean-Baptiste Colbert (1619–83), contrôleur général des finances, concerning bourgeois emulation of the court, "the court of sovereign princes is the principal place where is manifested the magnificence from the splendor or obscurity of which foreign princes or their ambassadors make inferences about the strength or weakness of the kingdom."[3]

1. Orest Ranum, "Courtesy, Absolutism, and the Rise of the French State, 1630–1660," *Journal of Modern History* 52 (September 1980): 433.
2. For elegant discussions of the negotiations over power engaged in through symbolic and discursive means see Sarah Hanley, *The Lit de Justice of the Kings of France* (Princeton, 1983); and Ralph E. Giesey, "Models of Rulership in French Ceremonial," in *Rites of Power*, ed. Sean Wilentz (Philadelphia, 1985), 41–64.
3. "Plaintes des dames de la cour contre les marchandes ou bourgeoises de Paris," quoted in Carolyn Lougee, *Le Paradis des femmes: Women, Salons, and Social Stratification in Seventeenth-Century France* (Princeton, 1976), 96.

Figure 1.   *Marie-Antoinette, Josephine, Jeanne
d'Autriche, reine de France et de Navarre* (1769).
Cabinet des estampes, Bibliothèque nationale.

The meaning borne by royal objects is shown even more dramatically
in the print of Marie-Antoinette (Figure 1). Marie-Antoinette stands in
front of a very elaborate Louis XV–style chair with her hand on a very small
crown that rests on the edge of an extraordinary table leg. A grotesque bird
of prey intently eying the sardonic face that graces the leg joint makes the
print maker's opinion of Marie-Antoinette more than clear: she depicts
royalty run amok. The table in the print could never have existed, for both
the bird and the face would have been impossible to carve. The artist counted
on the furniture to convey a critique that he chose not to inscribe directly
on the body of the queen (in contrast to the many pornographic depictions
of Marie-Antoinette in the last years of the eighteenth century). The artist
expected royal character and royal being to be read through royal things.

Thus both the court at home and embassies and ambassadorial residences abroad stood in for the king, and the king's power, just as the king stood in for the nation as a whole. Keith Baker argues that the absolute monarch in the ancien régime "exercised a representative function" in that "the realm is re-presented, or made visible to the people as a whole, in his very person" and that "the king is representative . . . in the strong sense that a multiplicity can indeed be made one only in the unity of his person. . . . [T]he king represents the whole, not in the sense that he is authorized by the body of the nation to act on its behalf, but *precisely because the nation exists as a body only in the individual person of the monarch.*"[4] In this form of representation there was no separation between the king, the nation, the state, and the people. The people as a whole, the nation, could be united only in the person of the king, because the people were divided by orders and estates. This was a corporatist world in which people shared interests (and perhaps identity) with those of the same order and no other; only the king transcended corporatist specificity to both *be* and *be above* the nation as a whole. He stood in for the nation, and his things stood in for him.

Following a similar line of argument, Joan Landes claims that the court was not the home of the monarch but represented the state to its subjects.[5] I argue further that just as the king was the nation, the court—as the residence of the monarch—*was* the monarch. If the buildings were not of sufficient splendor, the power of the king was diminished. There was no room in this symbolic system for an experiential or spatial split between the king as (public) monarch and the king as (private) human being. The king's mortal human body, which might need or want a home, was entirely secondary to the king's immortal body, which must have a palace.[6] The lack of separation between public and private space within Versailles—the palatial exemplar of French absolutism—unlike in the British royal palaces, demonstrates the point.[7] Furthermore, royal ceremony generally occurred

4. Keith Michael Baker, *Inventing the French Revolution* (New York, 1990), 225–26; emphasis added.

5. Joan B. Landes, *Women and the Public Sphere in the Age of the French Revolution* (Ithaca, 1988), 20.

6. This discussion emerged from a reading of ibid.; Giesey, "Models of Rulership in French Ceremonial," 46–51, 57–58. See also Roland E. Mousnier, *The Institutions of France under the Absolute Monarchy 1598–1789*, trans. Brian Pearce (Chicago, 1979), 1:646–56; Alain Boureau, *Le simple corps du roi: l'impossible sacralité des souverains français XVe–XVIIIe siècle* (Paris, 1988), 5–23.

7. Guy Walton, *Louis XIV's Versailles* (Chicago, 1986), 39. See also Peter Burke, *The Fabrication of Louis XIV* (New Haven, 1992).

inside, and the solemn and magnificent setting of those ceremonies was essential to their effectiveness and performative power. The interior decoration of the residence of the crown was therefore at least as critical to the making of absolute power as the external appearance of the buildings, or the construction of monuments.[8] These objects constitutive of the king's power—buildings, furniture, clothing, jewelry, paintings—were objects of style.

The crown could not quite control or monopolize style. The slippage between the dates of reigns and the dates of the styles named for those reigns demonstrates vividly that despite the king's use of style under absolutism, he could not make style. Styles in the Old Regime were named for kings, yet the dates of the reigns and the dates of the styles are not concurrent. Louis XIV was on the throne from 1643 to 1715, Louis XIV style was dominant from 1670 to 1700. The Regency lasted from 1715 to 1723; Regency-style furniture was made between the beginning of the century until about 1735. Louis XV came into his majority in 1723 and died in 1774; the style named after him dates from approximately 1735 to 1755. Louis XVI arrived on the throne in 1774 and was removed in 1792, but the provenance of the style that bears his name preceded his ascension to the throne by nearly twenty years.

These styles, like most others, were named retrospectively, in the second half of the nineteenth century, and defined at that time. Yet furniture from the late seventeenth and late eighteenth centuries does indeed fall into styles, in a way different from furniture following the Revolution. Elegant Old Regime Parisian furniture is placeable and datable by its distinctive forms and materials. This was, in part at least, an effect of the construction of political power through things. Objects of style then, had a *political* meaning; they placed their possessor in a certain relation to the state.

With this elaboration of royal style, discussions of taste and luxury multiplied. At first glance such simultaneity would appear paradoxical. What place is there for training in taste, when style is set largely by the court and is therefore not a matter of taste? In the pure logic of absolutism's relation to objects, there ought to have been no need for discussion of taste. Codifications of the appropriate goods for particular ranks—as in sumptuary legislation—should have sufficed. But there was too much necessary

8. I refer to royal patronage, not collecting. On the distinction see Antoine Schnapper, "The King of France as Collector in the Seventeenth Century," in *Art and History: Images and Their Meaning,* ed. Robert I. Rotberg and Theodore K. Rabb (Cambridge, 1988), 185–202.

slippage in the system for that to be the case. Seventeenth- and early eighteenth-century discussions on taste emerged in the context of the anxiety and confusion resulting from the sale of noble office.

Furniture of style in the Old Regime was ideally to be unique and univocal; there was to be one style at a time—the crown's. And yet there were to be many variations on that style, appropriate to the proximity to the crown of members of the royal family and of the successive positions within the noble ranks with whom the absolute monarch shared power. Aesthetic objects had political as much as social meaning; furnishings were bought as noble status could be bought—to produce place. Any noble or ennobled family necessarily possessed the manners and the household— the style—symbolic of that nobility. The style of each period was to create a harmonious and unified visual world. There is a logic, therefore, to the appearance of the furniture that has come to be known as Louis XIV, Louis XV and Louis XVI, respectively; a logic whose dynamic can be found in the interaction of the different monarchies' needs and strategies of legitimation and the constraints and possibilities offered by the organization of production and distribution.

Marking furniture of style, from Louis XIV to the Revolution, was the influence of the classical world, the importation and domestication of the "exotic," a refusal of historicism, a valorization of the novel, and virtuoso display of artisanal skill. In its emphasis on novelty and transcendence rather than historical borrowing, furniture design of the late Renaissance, seventeenth and early eighteenth centuries simultaneously reacted to and emulated the styles most immediately preceding but involved few adoptions from the accumulated cultural heritage. Revivals and pastiche, which would become the norm of design in the nineteenth century, were exceptions in this world of courtly style. Thus, even the neoclassical revival in the mid-eighteenth century—following the discoveries of Herculaneum and Pompeii in 1748, which would appear to be a clear moment of temporal and spatial pirating—was understood in other terms by contemporaries. Eighteenth-century neoclassicism was defined as a reappropriation of abstract principles of aesthetics simply codified or discovered (and not invented) by the ancient Greeks. It was not perceived as an instance of borrowing but rather as an enlightened appropriation of transhistorical, universal, aesthetic principles.[9] Likewise borrowings from distant cultures,

9. Svend Eriksen, *Early Neo-Classicism in France*, trans. Peter Thornton (London, 1974). On Greek aesthetics from within the trades see André-Jacob

such as the incorporation of actual elements of Chinese furniture into French pieces, were considered to be complete appropriation rather than a sign of succumbing to the influence of another culture.[10]

A corollary of this lack of interest in historicism was, until late in the eighteenth century, the lack of interest in antique furniture. The old had no intrinsic cultural value; secondhand objects were essentially worthless unless they could be remounted to look like something new.[11] Decorative details were painted, gilded, or otherwise altered and combined with new elements to make new objects. While the previous generation's and even previous decade's acquisitions were left to molder in country houses, the court spent fortunes on elaborate, and often renewed, ensembles of furniture.[12]

The central tropes of ancien régime style, then, were the symbolic relation between the crown and its subjects, of the new and the novel, and—ultimately—the place of history and the historical. All of these figure into the stylistic changes in furniture from the late seventeenth to late eighteenth century and—given that style was constitutive of monarchical power—bear witness in turn to the changing nature of representation under the late ancien régime.

TRUE ABSOLUTISM AND ITS STYLE: LOUIS XIV (1643–1715) AND LOUIS XIV STYLE (1670–1720)

Louis XIV came of age shortly after the crisis of the Fronde, and his reign was marked by the consolidation of absolutism. A key problem for this absolutist regime was not only the constitution and fortification of the monarch's power, but also the historical legitimation and legacy of the reign. Thus representation was—in both senses—crucial to consolidating

---

Roubo, *L'art du menuisier*, 2 vols. (Paris, 1769–70); and from the nineteenth century Agricol Perdiguier, *Le livre du compagnonnage*, 2 vols. (Paris, 1841).

10. On the thoroughness with which Chinese forms and materials were de-exoticized see Hugh Honour, *Chinoiserie* (London, 1961), chaps. 3–4.

11. Gerald Reitlinger, *The Rise and Fall of Objet d'Art Prices since 1750* (London, 1963), 21.

12. Ibid., 19; Maurice Rheims in *The Strange Life of Objects*, trans. David Pryce-Jones (New York, 1961) even suggests that people kept storerooms of furniture to permit redoing their drawing room on a moment's notice. See also Yvonne Brunhammer and Monique Ricour, "Les ébénistes parisiens du XVIIIe siècle," *Jardin des arts* 14 (December 1955): 75.

and perhaps even establishing the absolutism of the monarchy. Louis XIV was as concerned with safeguarding his memory and the power of future French kings as with justifying his own use of power by the judicious use of historical precedent.

Louis XIV's reign inherited a complex legacy of historical writing, including medieval epics and narratives recapitulating what the Greeks and Romans had said about themselves; but the seventeenth century was most profoundly marked by the quarrel between the Ancients and the Moderns. In the quarrel, those who held that the study of history ought to be limited to the classical world faced off against those who argued for the primacy of national history, a position premised on the idea of progressive history. This debate was itself shaped by the needs of the crown; its two sides were reproduced in the placement of his person and his reign within the history the king chose to patronize. Over time his reign moved among national, classical, and transcendent narratives.

The style that came to be known as Louis XIV mirrored and reinforced (and perhaps even produced) the changing depiction of the monarch's place in history. Before the creation of the Académie des inscriptions in 1663 under Colbert, Louis XIV patronized artists and authors who placed him in either the classical or French national tradition. In 1652, just after his majority, the king reoccupied the ancestral home of French kings, the Louvre; although he abandoned it by 1667, in the interval he undertook important redecorating work that, while carefully reconnecting Louis XIV to a glorious (French) past, had also already started to insist on his transcending that past.[13]

Corresponding to these moves, the earliest of royal furniture commissions combined French Renaissance forms with new techniques, new materials, some new objects, and new modes of ornamentation, thereby taking from the French traditions and improving on them—making them more luxurious, more elaborate, and more elegant. Marquetry using precious woods was introduced; veneers, including ivory and dyed horn appeared for the first time; *marqueteurs* fashioned elaborate inlays using gemstones and trompe l'oeil. These were novel developments, for earlier French furniture, even royal and courtly furniture, had been made of domestic wood—decorated with sculpture, bas relief, and turned columns rather than marquetry—and chairs had been, when upholstered, covered in leather rather

---

13. Alain Merot, "Décors pour le Louvre de Louis XIV (1653–1660)," in *La Monarchie absolutiste et l'histoire en France* (Paris, 1986), 113–37.

Figure 2.   French buffet, first half of sixteenth century. Sculpted and turned indigenous wood (oak). 1.41 × 1.02 × 0.56 m. Musée des arts décoratifs. Photo: L. Sully-Jaulmes.

than in embroidered fabric or tapestry (see Figure 2).[14] With the expansion of overseas exploration, the elaboration of trading with other parts of Europe, especially the Italian peninsula, and the transformation of courtly society, the furniture of the crown came to incorporate these newer, richer, and more exotic elements.

The early work of *ébéniste* Pierre Gole (died 1684), who worked extensively for the crown, was characteristic of this initial period. He was first commissioned by the crown in the 1650s to make furniture for the redecorated Louvre and he continued working for the crown after the move

14. See Catherine de Médicis's furniture inventory in Edmond Bonnaffé, *Inventaire des meubles de Catherine de Médicis en 1589* (Paris, 1874); Guillaume Janneau, *Les ateliers parisiens d'ébénistes et de menuisiers aux XVIIe et XVIIIe siècles* (Paris, 1975), 25.

to Versailles. While the form of Gole's early pieces was reminiscent of Renaissance furniture, the materials and the technique were not. He specialized in ivory marquetry and chinoiserie as well as precious metal. His marquetry work was extremely elaborate and beautifully executed—and novel in the second half of the seventeenth century—while chinoiserie was essentially unheard of.[15] Gole's work, begun in a period when Louis XIV's connection with previous French monarchs was strongest, combined historicist referents with fantastically luxurious and only newly available materials.[16]

By the late 1660s, courtly society moved toward the position that no past ruler—either Greek, Roman or French—could provide an adequate model for Louis.[17] His predecessors on the French throne became the occupants of earlier stages on a progressive march toward perfection, rather than models and legitimators of his reign.[18] After 1670, poets and historians took to saying not only that Louis XIV was unique but that he was superior to all who came before. Such uniqueness required novelty in design. Thus the Italian *ébéniste* and bronze caster Dominique Cucci (d. 1705), employed at the royal Gobelins works, and the Dutch Alexandre-Jean Oppendordt (d. 1715), *ébéniste ordinaire du roi,* elaborated and extended the pattern of new materials and techniques started under Gole.[19]

After the death of Colbert and the passing from favor of the modernists' faction, the attitude toward history changed yet again, stressing its irrelevance to the now transcendent king. Furniture styles and historical writing both reflected Louis XIV's vision of himself in relation to the past and future, yet they were not in lockstep. Even well before Colbert's death, and the conceptualization that Louis XIV marked the beginning of a new historical era, Louis XIV's unique place in history was to be established for all time through the building and furnishing of Versailles. Versailles was

---

15. His prices were often commensurate: a desk for Versailles in 1672, for example, cost 1,800 livres.

16. Alexandre Pradère, *French Furniture Makers,* trans. Perran Wood (London, 1989), 45–51.

17. Here I follow Christian Michel's finer-grained chronology ("Les enjeux historiographiques de la querelle des Anciens et des Modernes," in *La Monarchie absolutiste et l'histoire en France* [Paris, 1986], 139–54). Edouard Pommier dates the change to 1670 ("Versailles, l'image du souverain," in *La nation,* ed. Pierre Nora [Paris, 1986], 451–95). For a contrasting interpretation see Anne-Marie Lecoq ("La symbolique de l'état," in *La nation,* 145–92, esp. 147).

18. François Furet, *In the Workshop of History,* trans. Jonathan Mandelbaum (Chicago, 1982), 80–81.

19. For a discussion of the Gobelins, see chapter 2.

Figure 3.   The king's bedroom in the Grand Trianon at Versailles. Photo:
La Goélette.

to demonstrate the absolute monarch's mastery over the animal world,
over the seasons, over the plant world, and over the oceans, as well as his
superiority among kings on earth. Versailles became a showplace for the
best that France could produce. The move from the Louvre in Paris to
Versailles brought with it different modes of court life, greater emphasis
on wealth and splendor, and new styles in decoration, later known as "Louis
XIV." The architecture and furniture served to represent and display
Louis's place in history past and future. Thus, Louis XIV was very involved—through the architects and designers he employed—in the aesthetic decisions for the remodeling of the Louvre and the building of
Versailles.[20] The richness of the setting and of the furnishings is visible in
Figure 3.

From the 1680s, furniture came to be marked by proportions artisans
learned from a study of classical architecture—in the profiles, proportions,
curves, and angles of the structures. But the classical influence went no
further than proportions and geometry; the decorative motifs were all
newly conceived. This style came, therefore, as close as a style could to
matching a transcendent king. It was impossible to create a style ex nihilo,
but this very creative borrowing of the abstract principles and forms of both
French and classical aesthetics effectively created a new form.

20. G. Walton, *Louis XIV's Versailles*, 35, 38.

The furniture of André-Charles Boulle (d. 1732) marked the epitome of this phase of Louis XIV style, initiating a definitive break with Renaissance form with his own techniques, forms, and materials. Characteristic of Boulle's furniture, and the feature that rendered it thoroughly original— although he too was influenced by his immediate predecessors—was the integration of metal, sculpture, marquetry, and the more traditional elements of *menuiserie*. The bronzes were not simply ornaments or necessary hardware or decorative protective elements, added after the fact. Rather, they were an integral part of the work and merged without pause into the marquetry elements; the marquetry itself now combined materials that were very precious, exotic, and difficult to work, for example in the virtuoso cabinet on a stand attributed to Boulle (Figure 4). Here Boulle constructed a veneered image from ebony, tortoiseshell, pewter, brass, ivory, horn, boxwood, pear, thuya, stained and natural sycamore, satinwood, beech, amaranth, cedar, walnut, mahogany, and ash. By his use of the two large sculpted figures shown supporting the cabinet, Boulle at once played with the massiveness of the form, marked his piece as unique, and underscored his status as an *artiste*.

The transformation in materials, including the nascent use of tropical wood, marble, gilding, marquetry, tortoiseshell, elaborate upholstery tapestry, and bronzes, broke with all that had come earlier. And, in addition to fresh techniques and materials, Boulle also participated in the creation of forms of furniture: the *commode, bas d'armoire,* and *bureau plat.*

Boulle worked most intensively for the crown between 1680 and 1710, that is, during the heyday of the making of Versailles and of Louis XIV's vision of transcending history. But while the changing imagined relation of Louis's reign to history was critical in shaping these forms, equally salient were the relations of production and distribution to be discussed in the next chapter, themselves created or reinforced under Louis XIV; they allowed and encouraged immigration of foreign artisans, freedom from guild restrictions, and encouraged the transmission of the culture of production from one artisan to another. Indeed, the fact that Cucci was Italian trained and Oppendordt, Dutch, was surely important in enabling the earlier moves to a new style as well.

Louis XIV's transcendence went beyond his relation to history and predecessors. Not only did Louis XIV set out to build an incomparable, inimitable, palace to represent his power, he attempted to control access—by legal and economic means—to furnishings resembling his own. For example, Louis XIV commissioned and purchased furniture whose materials and crafting made it uniquely royal, including, of course, Boulle's

Figure 4.   Cabinet on stand, Paris, ca. 1675–80. Attributed
to André-Charles Boulle; medallions after Jean Varin. Oak
veneered with ebony, tortoiseshell, pewter, brass, ivory, horn,
boxwood, pear, thuya, stained and natural sycamore, satinwood,
beech, amaranth, cedar, walnut, mahogany, ash; with drawers
of lignum vitae; painted and gilded wood; bronze mounts.
7′6 1/2″×4′ 11 1/2″×2′ 2 1/4″. J. Paul Getty Museum,
Malibu, California.

tortoiseshell inlay. Tortoiseshell was both extraordinarily expensive and difficult to work; it was also distinctive, unique. Even more dramatically, following the full exploitation of South American mines, Louis XIV had made for his use furniture cast of solid silver. Contemporaneous sumptuary legislation prohibited the use of silver and gold gilding on furniture or silver and gold thread in fabric—laws from which the crown was exempt.[21]

Louis XIV was willing to pay a high price for the uniqueness of his household possessions. In 1689, at a moment of fiscal crisis, Louis XIV had his solid silver furniture melted down rather than sell it either domestically or abroad for the far greater price it would have brought as furniture than as molten metal. While such a move might have been motivated by simple expediency—selling the metal was faster and easier—it was consistent with his self-positioning to argue that the great price the furnishings would have brought indeed made them "priceless" to the crown; they would have been worth a fortune, in part because of the labor, but more because they were identifiable as Louis XIV's furnishings. In selling his furniture, Louis XIV would be selling symbolically a measure of his own power.

Yet noble dwellings were patterned on royal habits; for example, seventeenth- and early eighteenth-century aristocrats, like the king, held audiences in bed.[22] The move of the court from Paris to Versailles (in 1682) brought a contingent of the nobility out of the city to live in the new palace and to rent or occasionally build private homes near it.[23] The importance of Versailles, the practice of renting, and the very high cost of interior decoration helped limit the nobility's architectural and decorative presence in Paris during the reign of Louis XIV. The contrast in domestic architecture in this period between Paris and Florence is striking. By the fifteenth century the Florentine bourgeoisie were building elaborate palaces to uphold their civic responsibility and establish their dynasties, while their

21. Louis XIV's reign revived laws regulating clothing and other consumer items. Two of the most relevant were "Déclaration contre le luxe des habits, carrosses et ornemens," Paris 27 novembre 1660 (reprinted in François-André Isambert, *Recueil général des anciennes lois françaises* [Paris, 1829], 17:382–85) and "Ordonnance faisant de nouveaux défenses de porter des passemens d'or et d'argent, vrais ou faux" (ibid., 18:26).

22. On noble emulation of royal style see Peter Thornton, *Seventeenth-Century Interior Decoration in England, France, and Holland* (New Haven, 1978), 6.

23. See Jacques Wilhelm, *La vie quotidienne des parisiens au temps du Roi-Soleil, 1660–1715* (Paris, 1977), 15–21, 225–54; Jacques Wilhelm, *La vie quotidienne au Marais au XVIIe siècle* (Paris, 1966). Of those sampled in the Marais, 77 percent rented rather than purchased their dwellings.

French counterparts, and even the nobility, did nothing of the kind until much later.[24] In France monumental building was largely left to the state.

Inside their homes, the noble and ennobled, along with the princes of the blood and the other members of the royal family, did their best to emulate courtly style. For this elite clientele the workshop of André-Charles Boulle supplied objects ranging from the sumptuously luxurious for the royal family, the elegant and rich, to the rather simple. Thus the new style could be firmly identified with the king and carefully allowed to permeate only the upper reaches of the court society.[25] Boulle's role as supplier to the nobility, the ministers, and financiers, church officials, and foreign princes as well as the royal family and the king himself, is illustrative of the ways in which the organization of production and distribution articulated under the absolute monarchy served the stylistic needs of that monarchy.

The furniture made by Boulle and other court-patronized artisans to furnish these dwellings was, predictably, extremely expensive. The 1684 inventory of Pierre Gole gives prices of 10 livres for a very modest desk in walnut or cedar, 80 for a walnut desk. Marquetry desks sold for 200 livres and individual items could cost as much as 1,000 livres.[26] Imported woods, stone, and mirrors would add even more to these costs. Thus, the high cost of furnishings assured only limited emulation by those not working on a courtly budget.[27]

Art historians have claimed that Louis XIV's furniture was all so stately and magnificent as to be intrinsically unadaptable to nonpalatial interiors. This is something of an overstatement. Both the market for genuine antique Louis XIV furniture and contemporary reproductions, as well as the pastiche style based on it in the last third of the nineteenth century, demonstrate that there was nothing intrinsic to the style that made it unusable in domestic interiors.[28] It is the case, however, that the furniture was intended to be impossible to imitate though possible, if difficult, to emulate. Moreover, the emulations were, by their scale and materials, always identifiable as such. There was no risk, in this style, of someone

24. See Richard Goldthwaite, *The Building of Renaissance Florence* (Baltimore, 1980).

25. Pradère, *French Furniture Makers*, 70.

26. Ibid., 26.

27. Albert Babeau, *Les bourgeois d'autrefois* (Paris, 1886), 35.

28. For patterns in antique furniture sales see Janine Capronnier, *Le prix des meubles d'époque, 1860–1956* (Paris, 1966).

confusing a noble's copy of a Louis XIV chair for one that would be found in Versailles.

Paradoxically the same king who attempted to restrict access to his symbolic power was willing to sell noble office, an act that potentially diluted the political power of the nobility on which the monarch's hegemony rested. Historians have long debated the impact of those sales on the positions of the nobility and their implications for the relation between the nobility and the crown, as well as with the non-noble elite, the ennobled, and the noble.[29] The crown's reluctance to sell its furnishings and its willingness to sell noble office might suggest that, whatever the real effect of the expansion of venal office, Louis XIV did indeed intend to weaken the power of the nobility. Making nobility available through purchase necessarily lessened its value to those born noble, while increasing the king's power through patronage. Rather than allow either French nobles or other European monarchs to possess *his* furniture and dilute his power, so the king sold noble office and diminished the value of nobility: by limiting emulation of the crown he protected its uniqueness.

There were limits to such a strategy, however, because the sale of offices would ultimately diminish their value and thus the value of the king's patronage and control. And yet Louis XIV's successors discovered that there were limits to the reverse strategy as well: restricting the sale of office while relaxing control of emulation undermined both income and royal prestige. The coincidence of the crown's later increasing *limitation* of venal office (despite the greater number of plausible candidates for such office) and its diminishing protectiveness of its own symbolic power as constituted in objects is telling.[30] When the crown was strong and relatively unchallenged, it allowed the nobility to expand and protected its symbolic representation—though planting the seeds of future dissension. When the crown was weak, it limited mobility into the ranks of the nobility and allowed closer emulation of its symbolic power—which ultimately weakened it further.

29. William Doyle ("Was There an Aristocratic Reaction in Pre-Revolutionary France?" *Past and Present* 57 [November 1972]: 5–6) suggests that the nobility's position was strengthened by the expansion of venal office. Ruth Kleinman suggests that despite venality of office, the crown continued to favor the nobility of the sword over other elite groups ("Social Dynamics at the French Court," *French Historical Studies* 16 [spring 1990]: 517–35).

30. There seems to be general agreement that venal offices did become scarcer over the eighteenth century. See Colin Lucas, "Nobles, Bourgeois, and the Origins of the French Revolution," *Past and Present* 60 (August 1973): 114.

The sale of office, in a world in which the performance and display of power constituted power, was ultimately more corrosive to royal power than Louis XIV realized. The newly ennobled needed to learn to behave nobly and the institution founded to school them in nobility—the salon— became a seedbed of antimonarchical thought in the next century. Before late in the seventeenth century, "[f]estivities and functions, formal dinners, formal suppers, lavish hospitality and receptions extending beyond an intimate set are the exclusive province apparently of the Court and of princely houses."[31] By the middle of Louis XIV's reign a parallel social world to Versailles developed in Paris. At that time, Carolyn Lougee argues, salons provided a crucial means of integration of the recently ennobled into the ranks of the nobility. The ideology of the salons rested on substitution of behavior for birth: "The cultural development of the seventeenth century was, in this context, the process by which behavior superseded birth as the criterion of status. The *honnête homme* was the man of whatever social origin who appropriated to himself noble *civilité*." Those who defended the salons, for they were highly controversial, argued that one who behaved like a noble should be considered noble. Indeed, the women who ran the salons may have been invested in this process because many of their own had only recently secured noble status.[32]

The salons were controversial because they allowed newcomers to "pass" as noble and also because they were run by women. According to Lougee, "Ladies made gentlemen, then, in an existential sense. This was the social mission of women in seventeenth-century France." Antifeminists objected to women in public roles, "the *monde* was evil because the women who led it were using the tools of leisure, luxury, venality and illicit love to upset the social hierarchy." Women undermined the association between particular goods, especially clothes, and certain ranks. Some contemporaries argued that this salon culture was a cause of noble impoverishment—the old nobility had to continuously increase its rate of expenditure in order to keep ahead of the newly ennobled. According to the antifeminists, "[l]uxury was a tool for the reinforcement of authority. A person occupying a position of dignity used luxury ornamentation legitimately, and this purposeful splendor was not a result of sinful pride or vanity. *But the spread of luxury necessarily undermined its effectiveness as a tool of authority*

31. Edmond and Jules de Goncourt, *The Woman of the Eighteenth Century: Her Life, from Birth to Death, Her Love and Her Philosophy in the Worlds of Salon, Shop, and Street*, trans. Jacques Le Clercq and Ralph Roeder (Westport, Conn., 1988), 41.
32. Lougee, *Paradis des femmes*, 52, 41–48.

and therefore could not be tolerated. So ornamentation without rank was made a sin; although ornamenting position was legitimate, ornamenting one's person was pride."[33] Undermining the careful edifice of inimitable splendor created by Louis XIV was an institution (the salon) whose need was created by the sales of office that helped provide the money to build the glories of Versailles. The king could to some extent protect his style but the aristocracy could not protect theirs, and even though no autonomous noble style was born—and certainly no autonomous ennobled style—the salons did create the site for cultural, political, and intellectual developments beyond the direct control of the world of the court. This movement, started under Louis XIV, would gain strength in the next reign.

The reign of Louis XIV, long considered the apogee of the absolutist form of rule, was characterized by monarchical power created and reinforced through a hegemonic control of the extravagant display of luxury in all spheres of aestheticized consumption. Little distinction was made between inside and outside or domestic and public. Access to the king's things was limited because the things—not only the wealth invested in those things—*were* the king and his power. But this system of absolute power, which could never be totalizing, necessarily had internal contradictions. The expanded sale of venal office and the multiplication in number and importance of the salons accompanying that sale was one critical site for the future troubling of absolutism. The construction of Louis XIV as a monarch who transcended history, who was unique in time and space, Louis the incomparable, was also—by definition—a problematic legacy for his heirs. In order for the complex construction of power that was absolutism to be viable, its head had to be embedded within his nation and its history. The absolute power of an absolute king was not like the absolute power of God, and the legacy undercut that power when the fantasy played out. Louis XIV's relation to history, to the nobility, and to the future were concretized in the *style Louis XIV*. The heirs of *le Roi-Soleil* would inherit the style, the glory of the reign, and the tensions and contradictions that gave it dynamism.

THE DECLINE OF ABSOLUTISM: THE REGENCY TO THE REVOLUTION

During Louis XV's minority the Regency marked an important stylistic watershed and a departure with respect to how absolute kings used their

---

33. Ibid., 54, 70, 72–73, 95 (emphasis added).

furnishings. Over the course of the Regency (1715–23) and the reigns of Louis XV (1715–74) and XVI (1774–93), increasing boundaries were drawn between the public and the private, the courtly and the urbane, the masculine and the feminine. New styles—Regency (ca. 1710–35); Louis XV (ca. 1736–55); and Louis XVI (ca. 1755–Revolution)—came into being. A philosophical, political, social, and literary world exterior to the court rapidly developed and challenges to absolutism emerged from that world. Sumptuary laws were allowed to fall into abeyance and, while innovations in style still systematically originated with the court, far more emulation was permitted and even encouraged by the crown.[34] Many of these developments were nascent during Louis XV's reign; it was only in the second half of the century that the public sphere came into its own, but the conditions of possibility for that noncourtly world were established during this reign.

After Louis XIV's death the regent Philippe, duc d'Orléans, moved the court from Versailles to the Palais-Royal in Paris. Many of the nobles who had been housed at Versailles moved back to private homes in Paris. The crown engaged in major redecoration of the Louvre and the Tuileries and the nobles of their *hôtels*. From the Regency onward, despite the reopening of Versailles in 1722, the focus of court life returned to Paris and private salons gained in importance.[35] The move back to Paris and the reoccupation of the old royal palaces marked a distancing from the reign of Louis XIV and the need to create a new place (even if it were a new-old place) for the new reign, and a new style to go with it. But the change in style also resulted from imagining a distinct place for history and history writing in the making and legitimating of reigns.

With the fading of the Sun King the location of the kings of France in history became once again uncertain, although history remained essential to the construction of power in the eighteenth century. Under Louis XIV all parties to the debate over history supported the concept of absolutism and an absolute monarchy; they were merely arguing over its best rep-

---

34. Charles Bauthian, *Droit romain . . . droit français* (Paris, 1891). Some furniture authorities argue that the nobility and bourgeoisie dictated taste in the eighteenth century (Jacqueline Viaux, *Le meuble en France au XVIIIe siècle* [Paris, 1962], 84), and others that the taste of the non-noble elite triumphed only after the Revolution (Pierre Verlet and Claude Frégnac, eds., *Les ébénistes du XVIIIe siècle français* [Paris, 1963], 18–19). Michel Vovelle suggests that the prerevolutionary non-noble elite lived a noble life-style rather than making one of their own (*The Fall of the French Monarchy, 1787–1792*, trans. Susan Burke [Cambridge, 1984], 9). I think that the nobility and the bourgeoisie became important customers and copied the court but did not create style.

35. Jean Meyer, *La vie quotidienne en France au temps de la régence* (Paris, 1979), 104; Verlet and Frégnac, eds., *Ebénistes du XVIIIe siècle*, 23–25.

resentation. In the eighteenth century, by contrast, François Furet argues, the history of civilization (that is, the classical world) came to be associated with a defense of absolutism, and that of the nation (that is, France) with its critique.[36] History served equally to justify absolutism and to argue for the importance of a contract between the people and the king. Some invoked it to argue for an unbroken transmission of civilization's transcendent truths from the classical world to the present, others to argue for the specificity of French culture, for the notion of progress, for the idea of a nation. Furthermore, Roger Chartier asserts that the nobility may have used history to "provide them all with a base for their particular culture, rooting their aristocratic ambitions in the past and justifying them."[37] Thus, what history was to mean, which history was to be remembered, and how it was to be written and transmitted came to be part of the contest for power in a new way in the eighteenth century. With this new fight over history, the development of the world of the salons, and expansion of other sites of a noncourtly public sphere, royal furniture styles divorced themselves further from history and a pattern of greater emulation and even imitation of royal furniture by the noble and non-noble elites ensued.

Whereas the Sun King had his shining silver furnishings destroyed rather than fall into the hands of others, Louis XV auctioned off much of what was left of Louis XIV's furniture in order to raise money to support his own style. Three sales were held during the reign of Louis XV (in 1741, 1751, and 1752) in which much of the contents of the Tuileries and Louvre was sold. Rather than a matter of simple financial necessity, the selling off of the embodiments of Louis XIV's reign and the subsequent commissioning of works in a style marked as his own was part of Louis XV's means of claiming power in his own right. In voiding his court of Louis XIV's things (or at least many of them), Louis XV turned his back on one possible route of legitimation for his own reign. He chose not to reinforce his place as Louis XIV's heir but rather to mimic Louis XIV's efforts at transcendence by sponsoring and supporting a new style, even if it was, necessarily, a style less magnificent and less luxurious than that of his predecessor. Not only was the style less magnificent: Louis XV delegated responsibility for its patronage to his wife and consorts, thereby diminishing the centrality of furnishings for the making of royal power.

In selling Louis XIV's things, moreover, he not only distanced and differentiated himself from the preceding king but demonstrated a new

---

36. Furet, *In the Workshop of History*, 125–26.
37. Chartier, *Cultural Uses of Print*, 194–95.

understanding of the ways in which power was manifest in objects. Louis
XV was not afraid of letting others have what once had been his, for he
knew that he could commission a new unique and distinctive object. Louis
XIV's silver furniture had been his power; Louis XV's furniture was not
his power, even though the wealth invested in it was critical to the representation of that power. Wealth and power could as easily be reinvested
in another object, leaving the original object divested of its royal meaning.
In other words, the objects had become more commodified since the reign
of Louis XIV. It was a complex trajectory and not one that neatly followed
the path Marx would lay out. Commodification and fetishization did not
go hand in hand; under Louis XIV objects of style were more thoroughly
fetishized and less commodified than they were to be later in the eighteenth
century. Louis XIV's power was inseparable from his things—his things
were the fetishes of his power; Louis XV and Louis XVI were separable from
their things, but their power was inseparable from the capital invested in
those things. Like their predecessors, Louis XV and Louis XVI could not
afford to be without objects of an unsurpassed magnificence, but objects
once faded could unproblematically pass into someone else's possession as
new royal objects took their place.

The critical importance of furnishings to the constitution of Louis XIV's
power—and their fetishization—had resulted in part from the greater
conflation of the public and the private, the domestic and the political in
seventeenth and early eighteenth-century France.[38] With Louis XV, this
system started to change. While the family analogy for absolutism and the
power of the king continued, the development of sites of conversation,
aesthetic invention, and political discourse outside the purview of the court
challenged the theoretical omnipresence of the king on which absolutism
relied. The transformation in the understanding of objects was embedded
in challenges to royal power in the eighteenth century, the development
of a noncourtly public sphere, changing meanings and uses of history, and
the expansion of commercial culture.

The aesthetic outcome of these transformations in French polity and
society in the early eighteenth century was the Regency style, which
Charles Cressent's work exemplified. Charles Cressent (d. 1768), a master
sculptor originally, used his training in wood sculpting to design relatively
simple, geometric marquetry, overlaid with elaborate bronzes. Rather rap-

38. The king's household was considered less rather than more familiar in the
earlier period, a point reinforced by Simon Schama's discussion of royal family
portraiture ("The Domestication of Majesty," in *Art and History*, ed. Robert I.
Rotberg and Theodore K. Rabb [Cambridge, 1988], 155–83).

Figure 5. Writing and toilet table, Paris, ca. 1750–55. Jean-François Oeben, *ébéniste du roi*. Oak veneered with burl ash, holly, tulipwood, and other stained and exotic woods; leather, gilt-bronze mounts. 2′ 4″ × 2′ 7 1/2″ × 1′ 4 7/8″. J. Paul Getty Museum, Malibu, California.

idly, Regency style yielded to the rococo of Louis XV. Louis XV style was, in fact, hegemonic for only some thirty years, 1720 to 1750, starting during the Regency and ending well before the end of that reign. This furniture favored curves over straight lines, fragile forms, lightness, elaborated marquetry, complex veneer work, and highly decorative bronzes, as can be seen in a writing and toilet table by Jean-François Oeben (Figure 5).

The case of Oeben (d. 1763) underlines the centrality of the court in the patronage of innovative artisans under Louis XV. Oeben was one of the most innovative of eighteenth-century cabinetmakers, inventing techniques, forms, and objects. As a young man Oeben had worked as an independent artisan in the shop of Charles-Joseph Boulle, and in 1754 he

Figure 6.   Commode, Paris. Pierre II Migeon. French lacquer and imitation Chinese lacquer. Musée des arts décoratifs. Photo: L. Sully-Jaulmes.

was granted the title of *ébéniste du roi,* setting up shop first in the Gobelins and then in the Arsenal. Oeben worked almost exclusively for the court and the high nobility, and while his work is quite homogeneous in style, each piece was clearly unique and built to order. Falling somewhere between rococo (associated with Louis XV) and neoclassicism (associated with Louis XVI), his very fine and detailed wood marquetry combined complex geometric patterns (like vanishing cubes) with still lifes, pastoral scenes, or other virtuoso realistic images. Bronzes were still present but as detail and emphasis rather than as an integral part of the design, and the work usually featured legs of rococo inspiration and bodies of neoclassical linearity. Besides his expertise in marquetry, Oeben's other passion and talent was for mechanical furniture; included in his production was Louis XVI's rolltop desk.

Another theme of Louis XV style—orientalism—may be seen in the commode made by Pierre II Migeon (Figure 6). The commode illustrated here demonstrates both the new shapes, and popularity of lacquer and oriental motifs in Louis XV–style furniture. The forms of the furniture are fully French, and fully within the norms of Louis XV style. Pierre II

Figure 7.   Center table. Support, Paris, ca. 1745; top, Rome, ca. 1600. Gessoed and gilded wood; *piètre dure* and marble mosaic top. 2′ 10 1/2″ × 6′ 5 5/8″ × 3′ 9 4/8″. J. Paul Getty Museum, Malibu, California.

Migeon attempted to imitate Chinese lacquer, and the bronzes repeat the orientalized motif. He appropriated and assimilated Chinese lacquer techniques more to create a variation on the Louis XV theme than to evoke China. Migeon was a dealer as well as an *ébéniste* and clearly not only commissioned work but provided drawings for that work. Over five years he delivered several hundred *secrétaires* that had a critical role in diffusing this style among the elite class.[39]

Louis XV style was every bit as "rich" as that of Louis XIV, but in a different form. The luxurious material of Louis XV style—precious woods, gold-gilded cast and chiseled bronze feet, railings, locks and drawer pulls, ornate tapestry, and beautiful marble—were not of much easier access, but with money were possible. Furthermore, as the pair of tables (Figures 7–8) indicate, the style could be produced in less luxurious materials. In the 1745 table of Figure 7, the wood is gessoed and gilded, and the top is made of imported Italian marble. In Figure 8, the table from approximately the same date, the table is painted, rather than gilded, and the marble is imitation. Here the form of Louis XV style remains, but the materials are much less rich.

As these tables demonstrate, after mid-century the crown came to allow, and perhaps even encourage, the production and distribution of versions

39. Pradère, *French Furniture Makers*, 163.

Figure 8.   Table, probably Paris, ca. 1700–30. Louis XV style. Sculpted and painted wood, fake marble. Musée Carnavalet, MB 237.

of its furniture—not exact copies, but scaled down, less luxurious versions. Many art historians go so far as to talk about Louis XV– and Louis XVI–style furniture as bourgeois styles.[40] I would describe them rather as royal styles that some elite non-nobles were able to emulate. Limited emulation of the court was apparently understood to be helpful to the court's prestige: the court retained its monopoly on the creation of new style but permitted certain forms of copying. Everyone in court society came to participate in this system, with the less powerful reproducing a version of a courtly interior appropriate to their station. In the seventeenth century elaborate interior decoration had remained the province of the nobility, but by the eighteenth century even the wealthier non-nobles were investing heavily in interior decoration.[41]

Expenditures for a noble life-style were very high.[42] Despite their wealth, the court nobles—whose incomes of a hundred thousand or a

40. For Janneau (*Ateliers parisiens*, 30), 1750 marks a break point.
41. Pardailhé-Galabrun, *Naissance de l'intime*, 144–45. Neither political power nor history went uncontested during the ancien régime, but such struggles over memory and the past did not play themselves out in decoration (Baker, *Inventing the French Revolution*).
42. Michael Stürmer, "An Economy of Delight: Court Artisans of the Eighteenth Century," *Business History Review* 53 (winter 1979): 500.

hundred fifty thousand livres and assets of two or three million livres made them the wealthiest group in eighteenth-century Paris—lived deeply in debt, resulting from their efforts to emulate the wealth of the royal household. Consequently, until the mid-eighteenth century there was a considerable economic divide between the nobility and the bourgeoisie, with very few non-nobles able to afford a noble life-style; after 1750, however, the gap narrowed.[43] But even then, with a strengthened economic position, and the development of a lively, relatively autonomous cultural sphere, other elite groups, ennobled and not, strove to emulate a noble life-style rather than create a style of their own.

It must be acknowledged, nonetheless, that the story of furniture consumption and of the symbolic valence of objects in the Old Regime is greatly complicated by the convoluted history of the relation among non-noble, noble, and ennobled elites and the unresolved historiographic debate over the "bourgeois revolution." One set of questions turns around the relations between the noble and the ennobled, between the nobility of the sword and of the robe. Some historians see conflict and tension within the nobility, while others see the formation of a coherent elite, capable of concerted action against both the king and the commoners.[44] It does seem clear that the relatively widespread sale of office under Louis XIV slowed after his death, as did the opportunities for social mobility through the professions, both having the effect of creating a disjuncture between wealth and social and political place.[45] So, in addition to the questions on the effects of venal office on the nobility, a second set concerns the existence of a distinctly bourgeois class in France during the eighteenth century—with wealth but little political power—that perhaps sparked the Revolution to right the balance.[46] Some hold that there was a capitalist bourgeoisie clearly differentiated from the noncapitalist nobility; others claim that while the

43. Mousnier, *Institutions of France*; Adeline Daumard and François Furet, *Structures et relations sociales à Paris au milieu du XVIIIe siècle* (Paris, 1961), 38; Pardailhé-Galabrun, *Naissance de l'intime*, 149.

44. Jonathan Dewald argues for a unified aristocracy in *The Formation of a Provincial Nobility* (Princeton, 1980); Roland Mousnier emphasizes conflict between the robe and the sword, at least in the sixteenth and early seventeenth centuries, while conceding that the new larger aristocracy united at times against the crown (*La vénalité des offices sous Henri IV et Louis XIII*, 2d ed. [Paris, 1971]). For a concise summary of current positions see the forum on the revolution in *French Historical Studies* 16 (fall 1989).

45. Lucas, "Nobles, Bourgeois," 112, 114.

46. Michel Vovelle and Daniel Roche, "Bourgeois, Rentiers, and Property Owners," in *New Perspectives on the French Revolution*, ed. Jeffry Kaplow (New York, 1965), 34.

nobility and the non-noble elites both earned income by capitalist and noncapitalist means, the legal distinction between the nobility and commoner was still of fundamental importance.[47] The "bourgeois revolution" position, hegemonic for many years, is fiercely contested by others who see no meaningful way to distinguish a unified bourgeois class in the ancien régime. Given that there was no distinctly bourgeois class in its relation to the means of production, they assert that there could not have been a bourgeoisie conscious of itself as distinct from the aristocracy—that is, a bourgeoisie that existed as a class-for-itself.[48]

Jürgen Habermas helped turn unresolved debate on the bourgeoisie as a politically conscious class and on different groups' relation to the means of production toward inquiry into the public sphere: the political climate, political debates, and the sites for and participants in those discussions in the eighteenth century.[49] This work established the existence of a noncourtly, sometimes oppositional, culture—salons, newspapers, cafés, theaters, and restaurants inhabited by the elite, noble and bourgeois alike—flourishing in the capital.[50] These studies indicate that not only was this public sphere distinct from the court, but that there was a strong non-noble presence in political and intellectual debate, and, more significantly, that those non-nobles made significant and distinctive contributions to those debates.

So, given that elite groups in contemporary Holland, England, and America developed relatively autonomous aesthetic styles, why did no distinctive style in interior decoration emerge out of this new public sphere in eighteenth-century Paris? Why, given the noncourtly public sphere, and a group outside the court with the financial means to invest in style, did no separate style emerge—particularly in a political context in which

47. James B. Wood, *The Nobility of the Election of Bayeux, 1463–1666* (Princeton, 1980), 12.

48. The classic argument is G. V. Taylor, "Non-Capitalist Wealth and the Origins of the French Revolution," *American Historical Review* 72 (1967): 469–96. James Wood sees a crucial distinction between the nobility and the commoners, though a legal and not economic one (Wood, *Nobility of the Election of Bayeux*, 12).

49. Jürgen Habermas, *The Structural Transformation of the Public Sphere*, trans. Thomas Burger and Frederick Lawrence (Cambridge, Mass., 1989).

50. See Daniel Gordon, "'Public Opinion' and the Civilizing Process in France," *Eighteenth-Century Studies* 20 (spring 1989): 302–28; Bernadette Fort, "Voice of the Public," *Eighteenth-Century Studies* 22 (fall 1989): 368–94; Keith Michael Baker, "Politics and Public Opinion under the Old Regime," in *Press and Politics in Pre-Revolutionary France*, ed. Jack R. Censer and Jeremy D. Popkin (Berkeley, 1987), 204–46.

objects were of immense importance? Those who inhabited the public sphere had the economic means to buy furniture comparable to the nobility if not to the crown, and the structure of furniture production and distribution might have allowed it access to whatever furniture it chose to negotiate with the makers and dealer. It is not, then, that the noncourtly elite lacked the economic means to make a style, rather that economic reasons did not determine the matter.

We must approach the particular form of style in eighteenth-century France through analysis of the relation between political representation and the use of things to represent their owners, because the uses to which objects could be put in the constitution of social and political life were shaped by the form of political power. But in order to grasp the nature of that relation we must first clarify the definition of political representation itself and the relation between the governed and the governors.

It is crucial to understand the use of objects and of display in the ancien régime as a political as much as a social usage. As I argue in greater detail below, objects, in nineteenth-century France, became crucial for the constitution and the representation of self, and they may have served that purpose in eighteenth-century England and America and even seventeenth-century Holland; but in prerevolutionary France what was at stake was political power at least as much as social place.[51]

This distinction between the prerevolutionary use of objects to occupy position and their postrevolutionary use to invent the individual and the social group can be discerned in the move from courtesy books to etiquette books. One of the classics of the courtesy book genre was Antoine de Courtin's *Nouveau traité de la civilité qui se pratique en France parmi les honnêtes gens*, which went through fifteen editions between 1671 and 1730. Such books were models of the *politesse mondaine* designed to organize life at court. The emphasis was on knowing what to say to whom, and how to act according to the position one occupied.[52] These courtesy books were distinct from the etiquette books that would replace them as a genre in the nineteenth century. Courtesy books were written by aristocrats and addressed to aristocrats. Etiquette books were written by the bourgeoisie and addressed to the bourgeoisie. Courtesy books were addressed to men; etiquette books to women. Courtesy books melded morals

51. R. Williams (*Dream Worlds*, 20–30) correctly emphasizes the importance of expenditure on luxurious goods within the French court, but her reading of it as conspicuous consumption is anachronistic.
52. Chartier, *Cultural Uses of Print*, 71–109.

with manners; etiquette books were preoccupied with the detail of social ritual.[53] As long as things and rituals were constitutive of political power and that political power was justified theologically, then the proper enacting of those things and rituals were also matters of morality. When things and rituals became constitutive of social place, and that social place was justified through the possession of those things and rituals, then the proper use and deployment of goods and social actions became simply a matter of propriety, place, and ambition.

By the late eighteenth century some hybrid forms were appearing. The treatment of the appropriate forms for different ranks in the 1780 sensationalist architectural treatise by Nicholas Le Camus de Mézières is telling. He argued that "the building which a grand Seigneur has built, a Bishop's palace, a magistrate's hotel, the house of military officer, and that of a rich individual, are objects which should be treated differently." The fundamental distinctions here were still among the three estates, although that was not the language he used. Le Camus de Mézières went on to specify the "fixed and invariable rules which form taste"; they were not to be altered. The appropriate stylistic differentiation by *état* was to be marked by symbols in order to provoke the right emotions in the viewer. The military officer's room was to be redolent of Mars, the officer's of Themis. Furthermore specific orders of architecture were deemed appropriate for particular rooms: boudoirs were to be Corinthian, libraries Doric, dining rooms Ionic, and kitchens Tuscan.[54] Men's rooms and women's rooms were to be differently appointed as were those of children and adults. Le Camus de Mézières's text is a hybrid. Categories of individuals were to be represented by various styles that were all Greek orders of architecture. Despite the very detailed discussion and Le Camus's known interest in furniture, there was no discussion of how these rooms were to be furnished.

In Holland and England the move from the predominantly political to the social use of domestic objects happened earlier: in seventeenth-century Holland and eighteenth-century England. Here the absence or abolition of absolute monarchy meant that the history of the polity's and society's relation to objects was very different. In England the development of a

53. Here I elaborate Michael Curtin's argument in "A Question of Manners," *Journal of Modern History* 57, no. 3 (September 1985): 395–423. Roger Chartier argues that French courtesy books in the eighteenth century had little to do anymore with morality (*Cultural Uses of Print*, 71–109); I think Curtin has a more accurate sense.

54. Nicholas Le Camus de Mézières, *Le génie de l'architecture, ou l'analogue de cet art avec nos sensations* (Paris, 1780), 8–9, 14, 150, 116, 164, 180, 191.

bourgeois consumer society followed the Civil War and revolution and the resulting abolition of absolute monarchy. After 1688 the crown depended on parliament (more directly than did the French crown on the Estates General—given that they were not called for over 170 years), and during the reign of Anne the electorate was the largest and most frequently consulted in Europe; extraparliamentary politics were also critically important. There were both growing numbers and influence of the "middling sort"; in 1730 about 60,000 adult men out of 1.4 million exercised a profession. By 1800 there were 500,000 well-educated men with money to spare, although they could not vote until suffrage was expanded in the reform of 1832. This is not, of course to argue that aristocracy did not matter. It revived after 1649 and remained very important until 1880, but its power had been broken in a decisive way.[55]

Whereas England did not, in any sense, have an open democratic regime following the upheavals of the seventeenth century, the power and centrality of the crown were permanently diminished, leaving in place an aristocracy larger and more powerful than that of the French as well as a bourgeoisie, still politically disenfranchised but free of a society of orders headed by an absolute monarch that constrained their counterparts in France. So, while it is clearly an overstatement to argue, as does Neil McKendrick, that England in the eighteenth century was a mass consumption society, it did appear to be a nascent bourgeois consumer society— one whose equivalent would appear in France only well after the Revolution.

The Dutch case is, in some senses, more striking, for Holland by the seventeenth century had an even better developed noncourtly (in this case burgher) stylistic regime.[56] Simon Schama depicts in rich detail the central importance of the home and its contents as well as the development of a distinctively burgher style. The home in Holland was the bedrock of the political order, not because every father was the king writ small, but because the government was composed of independent cities, and each city was understood to be made up of the households it contained. The government

---

55. A. McInnes, "When Was the English Revolution?" *History* 67, no. 221 (1982): 377–92; J. H. Plumb, *The Origins of Political Stability in England, 1625–1725* (Boston, 1967); John Brewer, *Party Ideology and Popular Politics at the Accession of George III* (London, 1976); John Brewer, "Commercialization and Politics," in *The Birth of a Consumer Society: the Commercialization of Eighteenth Century England*, ed. Neil McKendrick, John Brewer, and J. H. Plumb (London, 1982); Lawrence Stone and Jeanne C. Fawtier Stone, *An Open Elite? England 1540–1880* (Oxford, 1984).

56. See Schama, *The Embarrassment of Riches.*

existed to protect the cities and their inhabitants, not the other way around. Calvinism and its ambivalence toward worldly wealth shaped Dutch burghers, whose homes were understood to provide protection against the corruption of the material world (although rooms were also beautifully decorated with material things). But the crucial point here is the obvious one—Holland could not develop a courtly stylistic regime because it had no court. The combination of nascent but flourishing capitalism, Calvinism, and republicanism created a particular aesthetic and style in interior decoration unique in Europe and the Americas at the time. And, yet, given the English and especially Dutch examples, the question of why the domestic in Paris, especially the domestic in the form of the salons did not foster a new aesthetic, and the corollary question of the role of women in interior decoration emerges even more strongly.

The absence of a style of noncourtly initiative in France, then, must be explained by the development and transformation of salon culture in the eighteenth century, by the place of courtly women in the making of that style, by the still hegemonic role of the crown in regulating the production and distribution of goods, and by the way the crown continued to use the invention of style and access to courtly style to consolidate its position. The efforts of the crown to regulate the production and distribution of goods will be sketched in the next chapter, but the relation between absolutism, women, and objects may be elucidated here. That relation raises a series of questions in turn. What was the place of women in making courtly and salon culture? Were they important patrons and did they shape taste? How and when were associations between certain ancien régime styles and femininity or masculinity developed?

By mid-century, one of the crucial challenges to the authority of the king came in the addition of a nonroyal, nondomestic political public sphere to the salon culture already established under Louis XIV. The salons continued their role of training noble initiates in the manners crucial for social mobility; but this was no longer their dominant role.[57] Dena Goodman asserts that during the eighteenth century salons came to be a means of entry into the republic of letters, rather than into aristo-

---

57. Landes argues the dominant position that the salons were crucial to both women and the society they created through them (*Women and the Public Sphere,* 19, 25). Cissie Fairchilds, in contrast, sees a rampant new domesticity as women turned from the salons and the court to marriages newly filled with love (Cissie Fairchilds, "Women and Family," in *French Women and the Age of Enlightenment,* ed. Samia I. Spencer [Bloomington, 1984], 97–110).

cratic society.[58] Consequently, salons became a critical base for the Enlightenment and a site of contestation of the monarchy and of the nobility. Whereas seventeenth-century salons had questioned nobility on the basis of birth, many eighteenth-century salons came to question nobility per se.

This form of salon appears to be unique to France.[59] It is possible that the particular form of the salon in France resulted from the simultaneous development of an elite group of considerable economic power that needed access to a group different from itself in order to gain political power. The newly noble in France required an apprenticeship in noble manners, unlike their counterparts in England, where nobility was not for sale. In France, the courtly structure of political power, despite the development of a noncourtly public sphere, remained hegemonic.

These salons were not completely divorced from court life. Some salons were open only to women who had been presented at court, and some participated in both worlds. Despite some overlap, the court and the salon inhabited two different social, political, and cultural spaces. In the salons women became the midwives of republican thought and of new literary forms.[60] In the world of the court women became the midwives of new aesthetic forms in the decorative arts.[61] This split was far from accidental. Eighteenth-century salons occupied a complicated space between their origins as parallel but compatible structures to the court that prepared the newly ennobled for court life and their newer, more thoroughly contestatory role as sites for discussion of Enlightenment philosophy, avantgarde literature, and political theory—especially republicanism.

58. Dena Goodman, "Enlightenment Salons," *Eighteenth-Century Studies* 22 (spring 1989): 329–50.

59. In Spencer, ed., *French Women and the Age of Enlightenment*, see Katherine M. Rogers, "The View from England," 357–68; Charlotte C. Prather, "The View from Germany," 369–79; Carolyn Hope Wilberger, "The View from Russia," 380–94. Also Deborah Hertz, "Salonnières and Literary Women in Late Eighteenth-Century Berlin," *New German Critique* 14 (spring 1978): 97–108.

60. Generally, women provided the site for men to produce work and they trained younger women in the arts of conversation, literature, and music; Dena Goodman sees "the self-determined educational needs" of the founders as primary. But women's place in salons was always liminal, and by the 1780s the public sphere had become an exclusively masculine space (Dena Goodman, "Filial Rebellion in the Salon," *French Historical Studies* 16 [spring 1989]: 28–47; Goodman, "Enlightenment Salons," 333; Sarah Maza, "The Diamond Necklace Affair Revisited (1785–1786)," in *Eroticism and the Body Politic*, ed. Lynn Hunt [Baltimore, 1991], 68–69).

61. For women's influence in literature and the fine arts see Roseann Runte, "Women as Muse," in *French Women and the Age of Enlightenment*, ed. Spencer, 143–54, esp. 144.

Much has been written and debated in recent years concerning the ways in which contract theory, liberalism, and republicanism necessarily excluded women from full participation in the body politic.[62] Part of the reason that participants in the salons, and other sites of the new public sphere, did not invent a new or specific aesthetic in the decorative arts derives from the association of luxury, of beauty, of the interior with the absolutism of Louis XIV on the one hand and, on the other, with the wives and mistresses (and implicitly the corruption) of the reigns of Louis XV and Louis XVI. The salons were not far enough from their origins as a means of access to the court, to do the obvious—invent an oppositional, ascetic aesthetic in dress, furniture and interior decor, as was to happen during the Revolution. Instead the patronage of new aesthetic forms was left to the crown and especially to the women closely associated with that crown; consequently, those participating in salon culture inhabited watered-down versions of court styles.

Just as the salons were at the edge of the domestic and the public, of the noble and the bourgeois, of the feminine and the masculine, rococo style lodged precariously on those same boundaries. It was a style that originated with the court but predated the ruler most strongly associated with it and was far more deeply shaped by city life than Louis XIV style had been. It was influenced by women but deemed masculine; it was to epitomize French taste but was made largely by foreigners.

Furthermore, as the next chapter relates, the particular organization of production in the ancien régime made limited emulation of the crown possible. At the very moment that the royal institutions of style production—the guilds and the royal workshops—were weakening, permitting a greater diffusion of royal style, women came to have a different role in the making of that style and in the furnishing of royal dwellings. Whereas Louis XIV, despite the importance of Mme Rambouillet, had kept a tight control over the aesthetic direction of his reign, Louis XV and Louis XVI appear to have allowed, or even encouraged, their mistresses and wives to have considerable authority over the definition of the beautiful in royal interiors.[63] This feminization coincided with the elaboration of mediated

62. Carole Pateman, *The Sexual Contract* (Stanford, 1988); Landes, *Women and the Public Sphere*; Lynn Hunt, *The Family Romance of the French Revolution* (Berkeley, 1992).

63. Wendy Gibson suggests that noble and royal women were important patrons during this period (*Women in Seventeenth-Century France* [Basingstoke, 1989], 168–71).

relations between consumers and collectors by the distributors and experts; it foreshadowed—although it was still radically different from—nineteenth-century domesticity.

Mme de Pompadour (Louis XV's mistress) took a central role after mid-century in making style.[64] The account books of the merchant Lazare Duvaux, as well as the diary of the *ébéniste* Pierre II Migeon, reveal that the marquise de Pompadour was interested in, knowledgeable about, and spent vast quantities of the crown's money on furniture.[65] She had at least three châteaux to furnish and did not let her status as mistress rather than wife deter her from furnishing those châteaux in kingly splendor.

After Mme de Pompadour's death in 1764, Louis XV took Jeanne Bécu, comtesse du Barry, as his mistress in 1769, installing her promptly at Versailles and a bit later at Louveciennes and Fontainebleau. For all her residences Barry ordered a vast amount of furniture from the *menuisier* Louis Delanois, to be sculpted by Joseph-Nicolas Guichard and gilded by Jean-Baptiste Cagny. She also used the services of the merchant Poirier. Unlike Pompadour, she frequented only the artisans used by the crown and seems to have had little initiative in these matters.[66]

Adding weight to the argument for women's influence in the making of Louis XV style are the inventions of the dressing table, the bedside table, women's writing desks, the chiffonier, and many other specifically "feminine" pieces of furniture.[67] To the architectural furniture that constituted the only furnishings of the sixteenth and seventeenth centuries and rarely moved, eighteenth-century households added new mobile, "comfortable and agreeable furniture."Rooms often held a mixture of "movable" and immovable furniture: the duc de Nevers's salon, for example, had five canapés and ten fauteuils that were immovable as well as twelve fauteuils that were moved to suit the social occasion.[68] *Ebénistes* arranged clever drawer mechanisms so that a woman would be spared the necessity of pulling a drawer toward her, a gesture deemed ungainly and inelegant.

64. Janneau, *Ateliers parisiens*, 43.
65. Louis Courajod, ed., *Livre-journal de Lazare Duvaux, marchand-bijoutier ordinaire du roy 1748–1758* (Paris, 1873).
66. Charles Baulez, "Le mobilier et les objets d'art de madame du Barry," in *Madame du Barry: de Versailles à Louveciennes*, ed. Marie-Amynthe Denis, et al. (Paris, 1992), 26, 40–41, 54–55; Jean-Paul Samoyault, "L'appartement de madame du Barry à Fontainebleau," in ibid., 87–100.
67. Guillaume Janneau, *Les styles du meuble français* (Paris, 1972), 29.
68. Pierre Verlet, *French Furniture in the Eighteenth Century*, trans. Penelope Hunter-Stiebel (Charlottesville, 1991), 113, 58.

Roger Chartier documents the development of chairs designed for private reading, most often occupied by women, including "the *bergère*, with its armrests and cushions, the *chaise-longue* or *duchesse*, and the two-piece *duchesse brisée*, with its upholstered stool."[69] No longer relegated to sitting on backless stools as in the seventeenth century and early years of the eighteenth, women at court or in noble salons of the 1760s could sit on one of the innumerable chairs specially designed to accommodate their dresses. The comfort or ease of women (or of men) was not the goal of Louis XIV–style furniture; the appropriately magnificent display of the king's power was. With the relegation of decorative schemes to courtly women, the forms of furniture did indeed change.

Yet with the "feminized" style known as Louis XVI came the most marked break between a monarch and the style named for him, the *style Louis XVI* having been born approximately twenty years before Louis XVI assumed the throne.[70] The initiative behind the new aesthetic lay elsewhere than in Louis XVI's sense of how he should be represented, or in his relation to the past, or to the future. The dissociation between the king Louis XVI and the style Louis XVI is all the more striking as the latter was even more of a departure from Louis XV style than Louis XV had been from Louis XIV. Whereas Louis XV style had been rococo, characterized by extravagant curves, organicism, and asymmetry, Louis XVI style was neoclassical in inspiration, characterized by right angles, straight lines, architectural proportions, fluting, and decorative elements borrowed from Greece and Rome.

This dissociation between the initiation of a style and the monarch whose name it bears is indicative of the complexity of the relation between monarchy and style under absolutism. Louis XIV style went through changes and permutations in a close correspondence to the king's self-presentation to the world, and his furniture was French-derived—when he defined himself as the true heir of the French monarchs. But as he borrowed legitimacy from the classical world, the forms turned Greco-Roman; and when he strove for uniqueness, the style became more differentiated from either aesthetic tradition. Yet Louis XVI style was, in fact, born under the patronage of Louis XV. The early masters of the style worked directly for the crown, as well as for other clients, and the style shift reflected the recent classical discoveries and the corresponding taste of the marquise de Pom-

69. Chartier, *Cultural Uses of Print*, 221.
70. Francis J. B. Watson, *Le meuble Louis XVI*, trans. Robert de Micheaux (Paris, 1963).

Figure 9. Commode, Paris, 1769. Gilles Joubert, royal cabinetmaker, 1763–75. Oak veneered with kingwood, tulipwood, holly or boxwood, and ebony; gilt-bronze mounts; sarrancolin marble top. Has inventory number from the Garde-Meuble royal. 3′ 5/8″ × 5′ 11 1/4″ × 2′ 2 1/2″. J. Paul Getty Museum, Malibu, California.

padour. The shift from a naturalistic, organicist style in the 1760s may have largely to do with the monarchy's effort to restate a claim to legitimacy consistent with its partisans in the intellectual debate who argued for the legitimacy of absolutism on the basis of an unbroken continuity with the ancient world.

The case of Gilles Joubert (d. 1775), who was a *marchand-ébéniste* and the principal supplier of the Garde-Meuble royal between 1751 and 1775 (thus largely during the reign of Louis XV), illustrates the complexities of aesthetic changes. Between 1748 and 1774 Joubert delivered to the crown nearly four thousand pieces of furniture, some of which he made, many of which he either had made in his own shop or subcontracted out to other producers.[71] To some extent his style also varied according to the type of piece; his tables and commodes tended to be in a rococo style, while his *secrétaires* and some *encoignures* were definitively neoclassical. The commode in Figure 9 in fact displays an intriguing mixture of the two styles. This commode was made for Versailles in 1769 for the youngest daughter

71. Pradère, *French Furniture Makers*, 209.

of Louis XV. The design of the legs and feet and most of the bronze work are distinctly neoclassical, while the curves of the front and top make reference back to rococo style. But while Joubert's story demonstrates the certainty of the support of Louis XV's court for the neoclassical style that would become known as Louis XVI, it cannot account for the stylistic shift in the middle of a reign, nor why neoclassicism later acquired the label Louis XVI. The latter question is a problem for a later chapter, but the former is of immediate concern here.

The dynamic of this stylistic shift reflected the strengths, quasi-autonomy, and creative possibilities of the organization of production and distribution under absolutism. The policies put into place by Louis XIV to encourage diversity of production, immigration of foreign talent, and collaboration across disciplinary boundaries produced an extraordinary culture of production with enormous generative capacities. Consequently, there was relative autonomy—from the direct exigencies of representing the crown—in the development of style within the furniture trades as well as in the other arts. The crown established structures in its own interest that then took on a life of their own. Styles remained court-based, in the sense that the court still set the style emulated by the royal family and the nobility, but the court was itself following the court artisans. Thus the paradoxes of absolute power evident in royal consumption were replicated within the domain of production.

It is significant that even more than under the previous two reigns, the core of courtly artisans under Louis XVI was dominated by foreigners, in this case Germans. Two of the three artisans often identified as the initiators of neoclassicism—Joseph Baumhauer, Pierre Garnier (d. 1800) and Jean-François Oeben—were German in origin, and all three passed a significant moment of their professional lives in the faubourg Saint-Antoine—an area independent of the guilds. All three worked extensively for the courts of Louis XV and Louis XVI, as well as for others of princely and noble wealth and position. Part of the explanation for the aesthetic transformation of the middle years of the eighteenth century lies in the dynamism of the trades when freed from the monopoly of the guilds and the continued royal and elite support for what those trades could produce.

Although the creative energy of a trade itself might explain why stylistic change happened, it does not explain why the change was in the direction of neoclassicism. Neoclassical style in furniture moved away from the curves and organicism of the rococo toward an emphasis on

Figure 10. Watteau de Lille, *Le départ du volontaire*. Musée Carnavalet, P 1272.

geometric marquetry, involving trompe l'oeil, beautifully cut veneers of precious imported wood, delicate bronzes. It was still virtuoso, luxurious furniture, although often the materials were less rich than for either Louis XIV– or Louis XV–style furniture. Some observers assert that architects and furniture makers moved toward the classical under pressure from their customers, themselves influenced by a passion for things classical sparked by recent archaeological finds. But Mme de Pompadour appears to have initiated the fad for the style.[72] Others argue (perhaps overstating the case) that the bourgeoisie originated styles in this pe-

72. Janneau, *Ateliers parisiens*, 42.

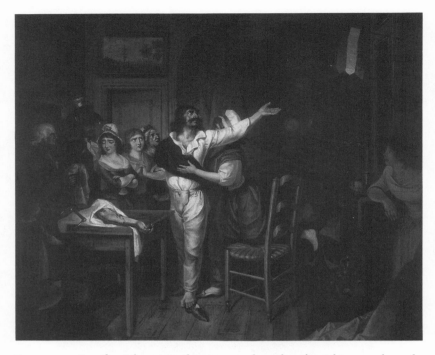

Figure 11.   *Sacrifice à la patrie,* showing popular urban furnishings at the end of the eighteenth century. Musée Carnavalet. Photo: Andreani.

riod, which did mark the beginnings of a transition away from the dynamic characteristic of the absolutist consumption regime toward that of the bourgeois order of the next century. From the mid-1760s until the Revolution, more French furniture appeared in more modest forms, and artisans were more influenced by aesthetic developments elsewhere in Europe. The relatively modest but still very distinctively Louis XVI–style furniture in Figures 10–12 reinforces this argument. These pieces resemble those in use at court, but the materials were less elegant, the decoration less elaborate, and the work somewhat less finely done. There is little evidence for a bourgeois style at the eve of the Revolution, but conceptual transformations well outside the boundaries of the court—like the general rebirth of interest in the rationality of the classical world during the Enlightenment—may have had a new impact on furniture design in this period.

Two other trends—the making of copies of old furniture, especially Boulle's, and the refurbishing of old pieces—signify a similar socially and

Figure 12. Small writing table, Paris, late eighteenth century. Possibly by M. G. Cramer. Henry E. Huntington Library and Art Gallery, San Marino, California.

politically marked transition that prefigures the end of the Old Regime's relation to style. These trends were especially striking since both Louis XV and Louis XVI had, at other moments, held sales to liberate themselves from Louis XIV–style furniture. Exemplifying the trends is the cabinet in Figure 13. Philippe-Claude Montigny mounted seventeenth-century marquetry panels, by Boulle or in the style of Boulle, onto a thoroughly Louis XVI–style cabinet. The greatest master of this pastiche form was Guillaume Benneman, whose story may well reflect the significance as well as the poignancy of the moment. Benneman came from Germany to live and work as a free artisan in the faubourg St-Antoine, although he was hastily granted guild status in 1785, a year after receiving his first royal commission. Amidst the building crises of the last years of the monarchy, he turned out copies of previous *ébénistes'* work and refurbished worn pieces.

Figure 13.   Cabinet, ca. 1785–90, with marquetry panels and some gilt-bronze mounts of the late seventeenth century. Attributed to Philippe-Claude Montigny. Oak veneered with ebony, brass, pewter, tortoiseshell, and amaranth; gilt-bronze mounts; *blanco e nero antico* marble top. 3′5 1/4″ × 5′4 5/8″ × 1′10 1/2″. J. Paul Getty Museum, Malibu, California.

Thus a system of rule dependent on the display of objects to mark its place in history and its relations to the ruled found itself, metaphorically if not literally, rummaging through the closets of its more glorious past. As an interesting and poignant comment on the Old Regime, we observe it in a final populist moment—with a humble German artisan of the Faubourg making-over pieces to maintain the polish of the monarchy that has become rather tarnished.

2

Negotiating Absolute Power
City, Crown, and Church

 The crown's need of objects to represent it and its dependency on others to design and make those objects shaped the complex organization of the furniture industries in Old Regime Paris. Another determinant of that organization was the monarchies' need to balance concessions to, and demands from, the church and the municipalities, as well as from the consumers of furniture. From the reign of Louis XIV onward, the crown supported three institutional and legal structures of furniture production: the guilds, the royal workshops, and certain privileged areas of the city. The normative institution—the guilds—never accepted the existence of the other two and there was intense rivalry among all three. The crown upheld them all despite the competition and conflict thus engendered because an absolute monopoly of any one institution did not fit its complex interests. The objects themselves represented the monarchy's power, but so too did the way those objects were produced and distributed.

The organization of the production and distribution of furniture was not simply, or even largely, an economic problem; it was also political and symbolic. The crown needed to ensure its possession of unique goods; it needed to encourage a high level of furniture production to safeguard the economic health of France; it needed to allow a degree of emulation of its things to keep political peace. To achieve these goals it needed to negotiate with the municipalities in which the guilds played a central role and keep a stable relation with the large number of urban religious communities. The complex and apparently contradictory organization of production—insofar as the crown granted monopolies that it then undermined—may stem from the need to assure all these different purposes at once.[1]

---

1. This diversity in the organization of production was by no means unique to the furniture trades. See William M. Reddy, "The Structure of a Cultural Crisis,"

This chapter tells the story of the possibilities and limits for the making of furniture contained in the tripartite division among guilds, the royal workshops, and the faubourg Saint-Antoine. It is not simply a political story of the crown's negotiations among the church, the guilds, and its own representational needs but involves the exigencies of the trades themselves resulting from the raw materials used, the composition of the workforce, and the knowledge, skill, and craft sense needed to create successful furniture. Through control of style the crown exhibited its absolute power; but control of style rested on production and distribution, processes it had to negotiate. In that negotiation process lay possibilities for both enhancing and undermining royal power.

This chapter also sketches the parameters of the organization of production and distribution in the furniture industry, established in the Old Regime but enduring after the legal world in which they were embedded evaporated after the Revolution. The taxonomy of the trades persisted throughout the nineteenth century, as did the centrality of the faubourg St-Antoine to furniture production. The royal workshops formed a precedent for a particular structure of state patronage in the decorative arts, a precedent that would be frequently cited in later years.

The story of the organization of production and distribution in the Old Regime explores how taste and style worked under absolutism in its relatively pure form and in its decline and sets the stage for the place of furniture in the postrevolutionary world.[2]

THE TAXONOMY OF THE TRADES

The division of labor in the furniture-making trades was determined by the interaction of three factors: the trades' technical skills; the presence of artisans trained within other aesthetic and technical traditions; and the guilds' juridical boundaries. Because the boundaries of the guilds were not identical with the boundaries of the trades, it is important to differentiate between the two in order to grasp the structure of production and the conditions of design innovation.

---

in *The Social Life of Things*, ed. Arjun Appadurai (Cambridge, 1986), 261–84; and Reddy, *Market Culture*; Cissie Fairchilds, "Forum: Three Views on the Guilds," *French Historical Studies* 15, no. 4 (fall 1988): 688–92; Gail Bossenga, "Protecting Merchants," *French Historical Studies* 15 (fall 1988): 693–703; Michael Sonenscher, *Work and Wages* (Cambridge, 1989), 146; Sonenscher, *Hatters*, 47–49.

2. References in this chapter are drawn from both Old Regime and nineteenth-century sources in instances where I wish to demonstrate continuity.

The basic divisions within the wood trades were carpentry, *menuiserie en bâtiment, menuiserie en meubles, ébénisterie,* marquetry, turning, sculpting, and millwork.[3] Though the trades all involved working wood, distinctions among them were not simply protectionist and arbitrary.[4] The system of specialization in the furniture trades was shaped by a complex composite of a relation to the materials used; the techniques and knowledge needed to create certain forms; the social histories of the different sub-trades; and the structuring of the guilds.

For example, *ébénisterie* and *menuiserie* were separate trades within one corporation. *Menuisiers* and *ébénistes* perceived the skills, tastes, and especially the talents necessary to practicing each trade as very different. *Ebénistes* were understood to need a taste for precision, an eye for color and for surface design.[5] *Menuisiers* were thought to need a firmer mastery of architectural drawing because their task was to design and build weight-bearing structures; to visualize and define a chair required a certain imag-ination, separate and distinctive, and perhaps incompatible with that of designing a sideboard. The design problems involved in making weight-bearing structures, such as chairs, stools, and sofas, were different from those in making either surface-producing structures—such as tables—or space-producing structures—such as chests and cabinets. Likewise the knowledge and skill needed to make successful sculptures—that is design in three dimensions—were different from those needed to produce

3. I keep French terms for the various trades since most have no exact analogue in English. Two indispensable treatises on eighteenth-century furnishings trades are Roubo, *L'art du menuisier;* and Denis Diderot and Jean Le Rond d'Alem-bert, *Encyclopédie, ou dictionnaire raisonné des sciences, des arts et des métiers,* 30 vols. (1751; reprint, New York, 1975). The most useful standard secondary works on the trades are Paule Garenc, *L'industrie du meuble en France* (Paris, 1957); two works by Pierre Verlet: *L'art du meuble à Paris au XVIIIe siècle* (Paris, 1958); and *Les meubles français du XVIIIe siècle* (Paris, 1956); Janneau, *Ateliers parisiens;* Bernard Deloche, *L'art du meuble: introduction à l'esthétique des arts mineurs* (Lyons, 1980); Pradère, *French Furniture Makers;* Steven L. Kaplan, "The Luxury Guilds in Paris in the Eighteenth Century," *Francia: Forschungen zur westeuro-päischen Geschichte* 9 (1981): 257–98; and two works by Michael Stürmer: *Herbst des Alten Handwerks: Quellen zur Sozialgeschichte des 18. Jahrhunderts* (Munich, 1979); and "Economy of Delight."
4. Michael Sonenscher, Jacques Rancière, and Simona Cerutti all make such arguments (Sonenscher, *Work and Wages; Hatters;* Jacques Rancière, *La nuit des prolétaires* [Paris, 1981]; Simona Cerutti, "Group Strategies and Trade Strategies," in *Domestic Strategies: Work and Family in France and Italy, 1600–1800,* ed. Stuart Woolf [Cambridge, 1991], 102–47).
5. "Planche 6: portes de placard Louis XIII," *Journal de menuiserie* 1 (1863): 21; Roubo, *L'art du menuisier-ébéniste* (Paris, 1774), 811, 995. See also Diderot and d'Alembert, *Encyclopédie,* 10:346.

two-dimensional "paintings in wood." Some artisans did master the knowledge, skill, and craft sense needed to practice within more than one discipline, but they were exceptionally gifted, much as would be a contemporary who is equally creative within the domains of mathematics and physics.

The invention of a woodworking trade specializing in movable objects dates from the split in 1290 of *huchiers* (or chest makers) from carpenters.[6] In the early Middle Ages the skills and techniques needed to build dwellings and furnishings were barely distinguishable. Most people had little furniture and made what they had. The very high geographic mobility of monarchical and princely courts and the lack of security in empty dwellings meant that furniture was either built-in (like benches along the walls), roughly hewn (like tables), or portable (like chests). Even churches had few furnishings. By the end of the thirteenth century, with the elaboration of church and royal furnishings, furniture making was becoming a distinct discipline, requiring training and different everyday practices. The creation of separate guilds both reinforced and transformed an already existing practical distinction. The *huchiers* themselves quickly subdivided into the two trades considered fundamental to the modern furnishings industry—*ébénisterie* and *menuiserie*.

Ebénistes specialized in surface-producing and space-containing furniture such as tables, desks, sideboards, and wardrobes, especially those with large inlaid or veneered surfaces. Their discipline consisted of designing, working the surfaces of furniture, and coordinating the construction of a piece or set of furniture. They often did not build the structural elements of a piece but subcontracted that work out to a *menuisier*, although they were not required to do so.[7] *Menuisiers* tended to work exclusively in solid wood, within a subtrade: either making chairs or constructing the carcasses of furniture that would later be upholstered, carved, veneered, or inlaid. There were also *menuisiers en bâtiment*, or finish carpenters, who made built-in cabinetry, staircases, doors, and moldings. The division between the *ébénistes* and the *menuisiers* also often reflected a difference in what their clientele could afford. According to a contemporary observer, Jacques Savary des Bruslons, the most critical distinction was one of the luxuriousness of the goods produced: *ébénistes* made veneered furniture "most often decorated with gilded bronzes, which serve to adorn the richest rooms

6. "Ancien statuts des maîtres huchiers de Paris, donnez par le prévost de Paris" [December 1290] (Bibliothèque nationale [hereafter, BN] mss fr. 21679).
7. Roubo, *L'art du menuisier-ébéniste*, 891.

of palaces and beautiful homes."[8] In any case, the skills and aesthetic traditions of the two crafts were distinct.

Marqueteurs practiced a subtrade of *ébénisterie;* they were the ones who carried out the most elaborate inlay work, who possessed the skills necessary to dye woods all colors of the rainbow and to "paint" realistic scenes on the surfaces of furniture using a palette consisting of dyed and natural wood, tortoiseshell, ivory, stone, gems and precious metals. "[T]here is nothing that this art is not capable of imitating," wrote a contemporary enthusiast. "It can, like painting, represent not only animals, fruits, flowers, and grotesques but also human figures" (see Figures 14 and 15).[9] To be a successful *marqueteur* required not only a good sense of chemistry and materials but also elaborate drawing and imaginative skills. Marquetry was a technique most highly elaborated in the German lands. Part of the logic of the defense of the faubourg and the development of the royal workshops, as will be seen below, was to allow and even encourage the immigration of German artisans who could contribute these skills to the French pool.

The analogues of the *marqueteurs,* for the three-dimensional aspect of the work, were the sculptors and turners. The sculptors were entrusted with the carved ornamentation of the panels of sideboards, and the arms and legs of chairs. Sculptors worked with hand tools—chisels, gouges, and files—while turners worked on a lathe.[10] The turners produced regular decorative patterns; turning consisted of taking off layers of wood from a rotating piece with differently shaped chisels and cutting tools. They most often made chair legs, columns, and banisters. Their work was much more limited than that of the sculptors but was still crucial to the construction of many pieces of furniture. The turners were something of a special case within the furniture trades as their trade was a result of very precocious mechanization. The foot-powered lathe dated from 1561 and came into common usage in the seventeenth century. Turners took over work that *menuisiers* and sculptors had previously done and sometimes entered into conflicts with them.[11]

8. Jacques Savary des Bruslons, *Dictionnaire universel de commerce* (Paris, 1761), 224–25.

9. Ibid., 792–93.

10. Archives nationales (hereafter, AN) AD XI 25. The turners' guild dated from 1691 and lasted until 1776 when combined with that of the *menuisiers* and *ébénistes.* See the *Statuts et ordonnances de la communauté des maîtres tourneurs de la ville, fauxbourgs et banlieue de Paris* (Paris, 1742).

11. Perhaps eighteenth- and early nineteenth-century technical literature on turning is richer than for *menuisierie* and *ébénisterie* because its newer technology

Figure 14. "Paysage et figure en bois de rapport avec leurs développements." André-Jacob Roubo, *L'art du menuisier-ébéniste* (Paris, 1774), pl. 307.

Figure 15. Writing table (detail), Paris, late eighteenth century. Bernard Molitor. Henry E. Huntington Library and Art Gallery, San Marino, California.

All the artisans within the wood trades were dependent on the *scieurs de long* (sawyers) or mill-shop workers who prepared the wood for other artisans. The standard means of moving wood, from domestic forests or from its port of entry into France, was to form "herds" of logs that would be floated down river. Once the logs arrived at the port of Paris they would be landed, taken to the mill, and sawn into either planks or veneers. The wood was taken to the Isle Louvier and processed there. The wood then had to dry. Early drying was handled at the lumber yard, while the later stages were surveyed either by the mill shops or the furniture makers themselves.[12] The drying process varied in length from at least twenty years for

encouraged practitioners to have recourse to new print media rather than shop culture alone. See for example Hulot, père, *L'art du tourneur mécanicien* (Paris, 1775); and Charles Plumier, *L'art de tourner, ou de faire en perfection toutes sortes d'ouvrages* (Lyons, 1701). On conflicts see "Arrest de nos seigneurs de Parlement rendu entre la communauté des Tourneurs de la ville et fauxbourgs de Paris et les maîtres menuisiers de la dite ville et autre" [1 September 1698] (BN mss fr. 21679).

12. The constancy over time of such advice is suggested by its appearance in Roubo (*L'art du menuisier*, 1:32) in 1769 and—ninety years later—in A. Mangeant ("Façon et empilage du bois," *Journal de menuiserie* 2 [1864]: 92–96). Both the value of wood and the weight of the taxes can be seen through attempts by the crown to control tax evasion and theft. See for example "Arrest du Conseil d'Etat du Roy. Portant confiscation et condamnation d'amende contre François Villot, Marchand de Bois" (AN AD XI 2).

wood destined to become a fine violin or guitar, to a few years for a soft wood used for the carcass of a mediocre dresser. The drying process was a long, tedious, risky process (the danger of fire being great), but to speed it up meant considerable sacrifice to the quality of the wood. There were attempts to dry wood in ovens, helped along by chemical injections, but wood dried artificially was often unstable in color, unevenly dried and therefore warped—overall it was generally less than satisfactory.[13] For furniture makers, to age lumber themselves both improved the chances that if they needed a particular piece of wood it would be on hand and permitted them to design with a special piece of wood in mind. After an artisan lived with an especially dramatic piece of mahogany burl for ten years, an inspiration might strike as to what that wood was destined to become.

Next the wood was milled. Workers cut the logs into handleable lengths, sawed them into rough planks, and sometimes planed and jointed them— that is, rendering the edges of the plank parallel to each other and per-pendicular to the faces, and making all of the surfaces absolutely smooth. At least the sawing stage of this work had been specialized since the Middle Ages, done by the sawyers in separate workshops more closely related to wood merchants than to *ébénistes* or *menuisiers*. Sawyers also cut veneers, a task that according to André-Jacob Roubo "demands much attention and practice on the part of the worker" and his illustration of how to cut veneer so as to create different effects, brought the message home (see Figure 16).[14] Veneers were sheets of wood, cut as thinly as possible, to be glued onto other, thicker planks. Artisans used veneers rather than solid wood either when the desired visible wood was expensive and solid pieces would be prohibitively costly, or to create certain decorative patterns. To make two doors of a sideboard with the grain of the wood in mirror image—known as bookmatching—for example, was possible only with veneers,by cutting the faces of the two doors from the same piece of wood as closely together as possible (since the grain changes through the plank). The appearance of the wood varied greatly depending on how it was cut. If a log was peeled,

13. See, for example, Nosban, *Manuel du menuisier en meubles et en bâti-ments suivi de l'art de l'ébénisterie contenant tous les détails utiles sur la nature des bois indigènes et exotiques . . . la description des outils les plus modernes* (Paris, 1827), 14.

14. Roubo, quoted in Hans-Ulrich Thamer, "*L'Art du Menuisier:* Work Prac-tices of French Joiners and Cabinet-Makers in the Eighteenth Century," European University Institute, working paper no. 85/171; Roubo, *L'art du menuisier-ébé-niste*, 820.

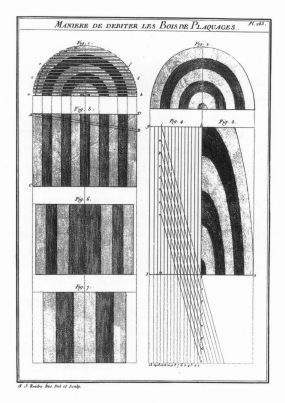

Figure 16. "Manière de débiter les bois de plaquages." André-Jacob Roubo, *L'art du menuisier-ébéniste* (Paris, 1774), pl. 283.

that is, transformed into one long continuous sheet (as one unrolls tinfoil), then the grain had a certain appearance. If it was first cut into quarters (the long way) and then sliced, the grain would look completely different. Veneers could also be cut into simple sheets to be bought by *marqueteurs* who created designs or images out of small pieces of wood.

The wood itself, therefore, played a unique role in the economic (and cultural) structuring of the industry. The critical importance of the constraints on an industry based on a living, fragile, and unpredictable raw material should not be underestimated.[15] Those constraints strongly in-

15. By the end of the eighteenth century there were 240 wood merchants listed in the La Tynna Paris directory (compared with 51 *ébénistes*, 120 sculptors, and 42 *tabletiers*). Their specialities in different kinds of wood are often listed (J. de La Tynna, *Almanach du commerce de Paris, pour an VIII de la république française*

fluenced the geographic location and the organization of production of the trade, as well as the appearance of the objects. The very name, *ébénisterie*, came from ebony, the wood—too heavy to use alone easily—originally most common in inlay work. The availability and cost of different kinds of wood had a large part in determining what furniture would be made. Before the extensive importation of wood from West Africa, the West Indies, and the Americas, starting with mahogany in the late seventeenth century, French furniture makers were largely limited to the timbers of Europe, often decorated with precious metals, stones, fabrics, and leather. Trees grown in temperate climates have many beauties and qualities, but they lack two important ones: dramatic range of color, and closeness of grain. The native trees of Europe all fall within a relatively narrow color range, from the slightly red of cherry through the pale browns of walnut and oak to the very palest of maple and birch. Tropical woods, in contrast, grow in a much wider range of color, from the brightest of yellows and reds to the true black of ebony. The hues of tropical woods provided an extraordinary resource on which one tradition in French furniture-making was based. Even before the widespread importation of wood, artisans were dyeing domestic wood, and some colors always had to be dyed; for example, there is no natural occurrence of blue, green, orange, or gray wood, and to produce them caused woodworkers no end of sleepless nights.[16] And almost as soon as the exotic woods became available they were understood to be scarce and terribly expensive. Savary des Bruslons writing in the early eighteenth century was already commenting on the rarity of true ebony and its replacement by fraud.[17] So availability was not all-determining. Artisanal skill, together with global exploration and international trade circuits, was a critical factor, modifying the intrinsic qualities of the natural materials. Consequently, the commercial expansion of the eighteenth century amplified a tradition already present in French furniture-making.

But wood was not the only necessary material; indeed, from the late seventeenth century on furniture was not made exclusively of wood. It also

---

[Paris, 1799]). For eighteenth-century discussions of wood and its beauty and difficulties, see Nicholas Le Camus de Mézières, *Traité de la force des bois* (Paris, 1782); Henri Louis Duhamel du Monceau, *Du transport, de la conservation et de la force des bois* (Paris, 1767).

16. Charles Paul Landon, *Annales du musée et de l'école moderne des beaux-arts* (Paris, 1800); see also Pierre Chabat, "Coloration des bois," *Journal de menuiserie* 14 (1877): 29–31; Roubo, *L'art du menuisier-ébéniste*, 787–88.

17. Savary des Bruslons, *Dictionnaire de commerce*, 223–24.

often included fabric, tortoiseshell, brass, silver, gold, marble, gems, leather, and mirrors. Elegant "shoes" were cast of bronze to protect the feet of furniture, as were railings that bordered shelves and bands protecting edges.[18] The bronzes were generally cast, chiseled, filed, and polished by the bronze maker and then mounted by an *ébéniste*, and last, gilded in gold leaf by a gilder. Marble, for table tops, had to be cut, polished, and mounted. Mirrors had to be produced and carefully placed. Tortoiseshell, gems, porcelain, and precious metals used in inlay work required special tools and techniques.[19] Those who specialized in fabrics, the *tapissiers*, while not dealing with the most precious materials, had the greatest influence (after the *ébénistes* and *menuisiers*) over the ultimate appearance of the object and of the room. *Tapissiers* upholstered armchairs, poufs, and sofas.[20] They also provided the textiles necessary for the decoration of a room: drapes for the windows, curtains for the bed, carpet for the floor, and fabric for the walls. The *tapissiers* do not, of course, bring the list of the trades involved in the production of furniture in the eighteenth century to a close—there were also *tabletiers*, workers who specialized in mother-of-pearl inlay and other detailed crafts—but the taxonomy sketched here does lay out the critical divisions among the trades as they were understood by those working within them.

The reality of differences among the wood trades is made manifest by the durability of their separation in the two areas beyond guild regulations, the royal workshops and the faubourg St-Antoine. Free to do as they pleased, artisans working outside the guilds were more likely to transgress the boundaries between specialities based on materials than on technique. Thus *menuisiers* who did upholstery were not uncommon, nor were *ébénistes* who designed and cast bronzes. *Ebénistes* who made chairs were, however, quite rare. The taxonomy of the trades did not exactly match the groupings of trades within the guilds, for the corporate divisions reflected politics as much as they did the exigencies of wood, fabric, and metal. The coexistence of these taxonomies of practice and of the juridical order helps reinforce the argument that guilds were political structures and that the history of the trades can be limited neither to the taxonomies of practice

18. The bronze workers were included in the guild of "doreurs, argenteurs, démasquineurs, ciseleurs, et enjoliveurs sur fer, fonte, cuivre, et laton."

19. *Dictionnaire portatif des arts et métiers* (Paris, 1766).

20. The *arrêt* of 18 April 1598 gave the *marchands tapissiers* the right to sell furniture if they bought it from a *maître menuisier* and stamped it with their mark (AN AD XI 27).

nor to those of the guilds; all bear on the resources available to the crown and the limitations on its power.

THE TRIPARTITE ORGANIZATION OF PRODUCTION
The Guilds

The normative organization of production and distribution in the furniture trades, as in all others during the ancien régime, was the guild.[21] The medieval corporate system—which as a legal structure died in 1791 with the Le Chapelier law—was based on principles of exclusiveness, intense specialization, and protection of a trade's members and customers through heavy self-regulation. The guilds were to exercise monopolistic control over craft production. Each guild, therefore, carefully defined the labor processes and objects that fell under its domain, to limit its members to those practices and to exclude all others from engaging in them.

In theory, each guild had a monopoly on the production of a given object within a particular municipality. For the privilege of this monopoly, each guild paid a yearly tax to the crown, raised through dues, and especially through admission fees charged each new master. Besides being used to pay taxes, the guild's income provided aid to sick or disabled guild members, money for funerals and celebrations, and sometimes funds for the religious confraternity often associated with a guild. The guilds attempted to work as monopolies that controlled prices, quality, and working conditions, as well as moral and religious communities. Each guild had its own statutes (granted by the crown), imposed its own entry fees and rules concerning apprentices, journeymen, and masters, and governed the rights of widows. Guilds were to provide training for the young, and regulations governing the conditions of production and distribution.

The boundaries of these corporations did not define the furniture-making trades. The *menuisiers* and *ébénistes* practiced genuinely different branches of the woodworking trades, tended to be of different national origin, and lived in different neighborhoods in the city, but were still systematically grouped in one guild.[22] In 1751, as part of the general reform of the guilds, the distinction in practice between *ébénisterie* and *menuiserie* was officially acknowledged, although they continued to belong to the same

21. One of the best recent analyses of the guilds is Sonenscher, *Work and Wages*. For the guilds' political place see Mousnier, *Institutions of France*, vol. 2 chap. 10.

22. Raymonde Monnier, *Le faubourg Saint-Antoine, 1789–1815* (Paris, 1981).

guild.[23] In 1776 the guild reforms of Anne-Robert Turgot, Louis XV's contrôleur général des finances, following the failed effort to abolish the corporate system, redrew many of the boundaries among trades. The new combinations did not necessarily reflect, although they did in some cases produce, changes in the organization of production and distribution. The *ébénistes* and *menuisiers* were combined by the crown with the turners and *layetiers* to become the thirty-second community in Paris.[24] The painters, gilders, varnishers, sculptors, and marble workers formed a single guild. The guild of *marchands merciers* became the guild of the *drapiers-merciers*. The *tapissiers* were grouped with the *fripiers en meubles* and the *miroitiers* and were therefore entitled to make and sell a wider range of goods than previously. Other combinations would have been equally, if not more, rational from the point of view of the practice of the trades at the time, but that was not the dominant consideration.[25]

The guild structure imposed an intense specialization by material and process. *Tapissiers* were not supposed to work wood, for example, nor *menuisiers* fabric, bronze, or leather; and turners were not to sculpt nor sculptors to turn. The border between *tapissiers* and *menuisiers* was often more permeable than the guilds would like; *menuisiers* would have an upholsterer working in their shop, and *tapissiers* would sometimes have their own woodshops that employed *menuisiers*. Yet the guild ethos discouraged specialization in many microprocesses. No one, for example, was only to sand or glue. Finally, there was supposed to be no division of labor by object—no *ébéniste* within the guild was supposed to make only bed-side tables, for example. Each *ébéniste* had to be capable of making, and to make, a variety of objects—tables, desks, dressers, sideboards, and similar items.

Not all the trade distinctions made sense in terms of the labor processes, however; some were largely protectionist or anachronistic. Artisans chafed at the limits these regulations imposed on them, with conflicts tending to arise over issues of materials and design. Many artisans did not want to be

23. "Statuts et privilèges ordonnances et réglements de la communauté des maîtres menuisiers et ébénistes de la ville fauxbourgs et banlieue de Paris" [20 August 1751] (AN AD XI 11), 1–3.

24. The tendency of the artisans grouped under the new guild to keep their trade identities can be confirmed by their identifications in the *Tableaux de la communauté des maîtres menuisiers, ébénistes, tourneurs et layetiers de la ville, fauxbourgs et banlieue de Paris*, 3 vols. (Paris, 1782, 1787, 1789).

25. "Recueil de Réglements pour les corps et communautés d'arts et métiers commençant au mois de février 1776" [1779] (AN AD XI 11), 58.

limited to the materials of their guild, and while the design of a piece was often delegated to the *ébéniste* or sometimes to the *menuisier* in charge, in fact the problem was much more complex. To design for materials one had not worked was very difficult, and furniture necessarily involved many specialities. There were, from at least the early eighteenth century, *ébénistes, menuisiers,* decorators, designers, architects, *ornemanistes, tapissiers,* and furniture merchants (and often one individual would wear two hats, being both an *ébéniste* and a designer, or a *menuisier* and a decorator) who were involved in design through the creation of pattern books, sketches, three-dimensional models, and the simple making of innovative pieces that would be seen and then copied.[26]

If we follow the idealized trajectory of a sideboard, as imagined by an *ébéniste* who was master in his guild, it would look something like this: the sideboard would be designed by the *ébéniste* inspired perhaps by the drawings of an *ornemaniste,* or by a piece recently acquired at court, or by items shown in the combined fashion–home decorating magazines of the period. The process of design would also include consulting clients (whose orders launched the entire process) about their wishes, looking at drawings of earlier objects of similar style and function, and discussing the design with other members of the furniture trades. After a first impressionistic drawing, the *ébéniste* would produce working drawings. From these more precise drawings he would make a wax or wood model, sometimes with several variations of the decorative details and sculptural motifs, and show them to the purchaser for final decision and approval. The last stage of the design process was the drawing of life-size plans as templates for rough cutting the wood. The work would then begin. First the carcass, or frame, would be subcontracted out to a *menuisier en meubles* (who would have the wood rough-cut by a *scieur de long*). The *menuisier* would more or less follow the *ébéniste*'s drawings but add his own curves here and there. While the *menuisier* made the body, a bronze maker would cast the bronzes for the handles and feet; a marble worker would cut the marble, a turner would make the legs, and a *marqueteur* would do the most complicated of the inlaid work. Finally the *ébéniste* would assemble all the pieces, doing all the flatwork not done by the *marqueteur,* and arrange to have the piece sanded

26. For detail on the *tapissiers'* role as decorators, see J. F. Bimont, *Principes de l'art du tapissier: ouvrage utile aux gens de la profession et à ceux qui les emploient* (Paris, 1770). For the architects' designs for furniture see Jean-François de Neufforge, *Recueil élémentaire d'architecture* (Paris, 1757–68); Jean-Charles Delafosse, *Oeuvre,* vol. 3 (Paris, 1772).

and varnished. So between the *ébéniste*'s original design and delivery of the finished piece to the client, many hands were involved, and the finished piece might or might not look like what the *ébéniste* had in mind. If innovative, the design was always in some sense a collective achievement.[27]

Yet new designs were rare because the weight of tradition in the guilds was also heavy; it was difficult to break out and do something completely new with the years of passed-on work routines and styles behind one. Working in the faubourg St-Antoine or in a royal workshop freed artisans from these constraints at the same time that their status made them vulnerable to attack by the guilds. The guild divisions reflected commercial and political interests and conflicts, on the one hand, and the specific training in the building of beautiful and technically sound furnishings, on the other.

The Royal Artisans

As well as granting statutes to the guilds and privileges to artisans living on church territory and in other privileged enclaves, the crown created its own organizations of production.[28] There were four structures within which royal artisans worked: the royal workshops, workshops with royal patents, individually named royal artisans, and another structure through which furniture was commissioned, the Garde-Meuble royal. The royal workshops—the Louvre (1608), the Gobelins (1667), and the Arsenal— like the academy of architecture, were under the control first of the Surintendant des Bâtiments du roi, then the Direction générale des Bâtiments du roi. Their founding and expansion coincided with the founding of the other academies: the Académie française (1635); the Académie royale de peinture et sculpture (1648), the Académie royale de musique (1669), Académie royale d'architecture (1672), which systematized the teaching, evaluation, and hierarchization of art and artisanal work. Artisans working under these institutions worked for the crown—either by direct commission or for the Garde-Meuble royal. They also had the right to work

27. Bernard Deloche has a detailed investigation of this process in *L'art du meuble*.

28. This discussion has been shaped by Emilia Frances Strong Dilke, *Art in the Modern State* (London, 1888); and Thomas Crow, *Painters and Public Life in Eighteenth-Century Paris* (New Haven, 1985), chap. 1; Stürmer, "An Economy of Delight." Also helpful are Sonenscher, *Work and Wages*, esp. 216 on the *manufactures royales* and the *artisans du roi*; and Charles Coulston Gillispie, *Science and Polity in France at the End of the Old Regime* (Princeton, 1980), chap. 6; Verlet and Frégnac, eds., *Ebénistes du XVIIIe siècle* (Paris, 1963).

for all others who could afford their very high prices; it has been estimated that they supplied between 20 and 25 percent of the elite furniture
market.[29]

Consequently the royal workshops of the Louvre, the Gobelins, and the
Arsenal, though they employed only a few artisans, had a central role in
France's furniture production. The heyday of these royal workshops was
under Louis XIV, their budget being seriously reduced under Louis XV.[30]
This blow followed the general decline in amounts spent by the Direction
des Bâtiments on large public commissions during the last few years of the
reign of Louis XIV. Many of the most distinguished furniture makers of
the seventeenth and eighteenth centuries worked in one of the royal
workshops supplying the crown through the Garde-Meuble royal, or
through direct commissions. Along with all other state institutions the
Garde-Meuble suffered under the financial crises of the end of the ancien
régime. In a gesture toward economy, it started subcontracting out parts
of works commissioned to various artisans rather than giving a contract to
an *ébéniste* to fulfill as he saw fit.

Artisans were sometimes granted residency in a royal workshop as a
reward for their accomplishment. The *mécanicien* Loriot, for example, was
given a berth at the Louvre, following his invention of an ingenious
mechanical table; regulations limited the number of artisans who would be
so privileged.[31] The court artisans all had high prestige and could engage
in artistic and technological innovation but were also rather vulnerable to
disaster. It is striking how many of them died bankrupt, perhaps because
of the costs of living like *valets de chambre.*[32]

The Galeries du Louvre were founded by Henri IV in 1608 with the
explicit intention of improving the quality of artisanal production through
increased competition. He also began the practice of bringing in workers
from elsewhere in Europe, to take advantage of other artisanal traditions.[33]
In 1671 they were reorganized to include, among others, two *tapissiers*, one
embroiderer, six painters, three *ébénistes* and *marqueteurs*, twenty-three
sculptors, five goldsmiths, and two *émailleurs*. André-Charles Boulle, one

29. Stürmer, "Economy of Delight," 514–15.
30. Alfred de Champeaux, *Le meuble* (Paris, 1885), 2:110.
31. Paul Mantz, "Les meubles du XVIIIe siècle," *Revue des arts décoratifs* 4
(1883–84): 379. "Recueil de Réglements" (AN AD XI 11), 92–102.
32. On the housing and living habits of the royal artisans, see Pardailhé-
Galabrun, *Naissance de l'intime*, 205.
33. For the creation of the Galeries du Louvre see "Lettres Patentes du Roi,
Portant Privilèges accordées aux Ouvriers qui demeurent dans la Gallerie du
Louvre" [22 December 1608] (AN AD XI 10).

of the most celebrated artisans of his time (see chapter 1), appears to have become a master *menuisier* before 1672, after which he moved to the Galeries du Louvre where he became the *ébéniste, ciseleur, doreur, et sculpteur du roi* of Louis XIV. In so doing he broke the guild separation of metal- from wood-working. He was also considered competent to practice architecture, painting, mosaics, engraving, chiseling, marquetry, and arithmetic.[34]

The Manufacture de la couronne aux Gobelins was created by Colbert in 1667. The workshop at the Gobelins was under the direction of Charles Le Brun who had the notion of creating a total world, "to unify all the arts and to establish an ensemble of formulas in which the rules of Absolute Beauty would be fixed forever." The artisans working and housed there were categorized with scientists, artists, architects, and writers and given the status of *valets de chambre* of the king. They were also allowed to train apprentices who would be permitted to join the guilds.[35] This was in part to compensate them for the nonhereditary nature of their position—they, unlike the guilds artisans, could not found dynasties—and to differentiate them from the artisans of the faubourg St-Antoine, who were not allowed to train apprentices (and whom I discuss below). Savary des Bruslons noted that the most innovative work was being done at the Gobelins.[36]

Some of those who worked for the Garde-Meuble were members of the guild and some were the bearers of individual privilege. Jean-Baptiste I Tilliard (d. 1766), for example, came from a long line of *menuisiers* and was a long-standing member of the guild when he started working for the royal house as *menuisier ordinaire du garde-meuble* in 1730. He won a number of important commissions, including the furnishings for the queen's apartment, and the *chambre* and the *cabinet* of the king at Versailles, as well as furnishings for the prince de Soubise.

These royal artisans were free of any guild restriction and worked under the direct patronage of the crown, the royal household, and the princes.

34. The discussion here is based on Champeaux, *Le meuble*, 2:68–71; Emile Molinier, *Le mobilier royal français aux XVIIe et XVIIIe siècles* (Paris, 1902), 53–80; Henry Havard, *Les Boulle* (Paris, 1898).

35. Le Brun quoted in Christine Bertrand, *Le meuble et l'homme: essai sur une philosophie du meuble* (Verviers, 1946), 33. For the creation of the Gobelins see "Edict du Roy pour l'établissement d'une manufacture des meubles de la Couronne aux Gobelins, registré en Parlement le 21 décembre 1667" (AN AD XI 45). See also the very helpful discussion in Stürmer, "An Economy of Delight."

36. Savary des Bruslons, *Dictionnaire universel de commerce*, 224–25.

Many were foreign and all broke the divisions between trades held sacred by the guilds.[37] Perhaps as a consequence of their freedom, they built pieces displaying extraordinary richness of material and craft and constituted a key site for stylistic innovation in royal furniture. They were hated by the guilds but immune to harassment because, unlike the artisans of the faubourg St-Antoine, they were directly under the crown's protection.

The royal workshops established the French crown as a direct patron of the decorative arts, able to set style through the support of the artisans whose work matched its image of itself. By maintaining an exclusive right to the production of the royal workshops, and by acquiring its furnishings only from the royal artisans, the crown could in theory acquire unique goods. That the crown did not do so, that it allowed all who could pay the price to buy from the royal artisans and that it bought furnishings from the guilds and the faubourg, is indicative of its need to allow emulation and to patronize the city- and church-based modes of production and distribution.

The Faubourg Saint-Antoine

Most furniture makers who worked outside the guilds were located in the faubourg St-Antoine, which had been under the control of the Cistercian convent of St-Antoine-des-Champs since 1471.[38] Artisans here were free to work as they pleased, although they were not to have journeymen or apprentices. The faubourg St-Antoine was, in the medieval and early modern period, an ideal location for the furniture trades; it was still rural, so land was available to store wood, and it was at a convenient point in the river to unload logs. Georges Rudé estimates that in 1791 there were 8,000 workers in the furniture trades, of whom 4,500 lived in the faubourg. Within the guild in 1790, by contrast, there were about 895 masters, of whom about 200 were *ébénistes* and 100 chair makers.[39] Competition between the guild and the faubourg was serious: the privileged furni-

37. Sonenscher, *Work and Wages,* 137.
38. On the special status of the faubourg St-Antoine see AN Y17291. A significant recent article on the faubourg is Steven L. Kaplan, "Les corporations, les 'faux ouvriers' et le faubourg Saint-Antoine au XVIIIe siècle," *Annales: Economies, sociétés, civilisations* 43 (1988): 353–78.
39. Georges Rudé, *La population ouvrière parisienne de 1789 à 1791* (Paris, 1967), 28. There were 59 workshops on the rue de Charenton, 24 on rue de Charonne and 114 in the faubourg St-Antoine (Janneau, *Ateliers parisiens,* 9). On the guild, François de Salverte, *Les ébénistes du XVIIIe siècle, leurs oeuvres et leurs marques* (Paris, 1927), xii.

ture makers were free from taxes and could therefore sell their work cheaper than their colleagues in the guild; they could organize their production and distribution as they chose; and, foreigners were not excluded from the faubourg as they were from the guilds.[40] The products of the faubourg thus offered consumers a wider variety of goods, often at a lower price.

The organization of production—that is, the division of labor and the specialization of manufacturing—in the faubourg St-Antoine was complex and more varied than that within the guilds. The unit of manufacturing varied from the individual *chambrellan* working alone in his room, or with his family, to workshops of sixty employees. As a measure of manufacturing even the unit of production could be deceptive, since the size and number of employees did not correlate with the production of simple pieces or only parts. A workshop specializing in turning chair legs was one extreme and an atelier, which included a mill shop, marquetry shop, finishing room and upholstery shop, was the other. This distinction between the division of labor and the specialization of production—between what an individual worker did and what a shop produced—is an important one because a workshop employing fifty people in specialized tasks could seem from the outside very Taylorized and factorylike; yet the work that went on inside could be very individualized and creative. At first glance, nothing seems more artisanal than the furniture maker alone in his or her shop or his or her room, working with hand tools. And yet that artisanal, skilled surface might hide someone whose skill consisted of making one kind of chair, and who was infinitely more "proletarianized" than colleagues in the large shop. Consequently, to evaluate the degree of division of labor and specialization of manufacturing during the Old Regime is difficult, because the sources are sketchy; it appears, however, that there were already artisans whose labor was sharply divided both by task and by object even in this early period. The larger manufacturers often employed a variety of skilled artisans, gathered under one roof. The artisans owned their own tools but did not own or provide the wood. Moreover, not only was the work done differently in the faubourg than in the guilds, but the resulting work often was of a different style.

40. "Ordonnance de Police de la Prevôté de l'hôtel du roi, et grande Prevôté de France, Portant Réglement pour les Marchands et Artisans et Privilegiés établis à Paris" [30 July 1766] (AN AD XI 10), on guild masters' regulation of the employment of journeymen and privileged workers but clearly more anxious about laxness among the privileged.

The production trajectory of a sideboard, if it had been made in the faubourg rather than by a guild master, could be identical or very different indeed. One possibility was that one artisan made the entire piece or nearly the entire piece, himself, on speculation. The artisan would sketch the design, draw the blueprints, build the carcass, do the veneer work, turning, and marquetry himself. He might even design and cast his own bronzes and cut his own marble. The sideboard would really be the work of one individual. The artisan might take the finished piece around to furniture merchants and try to sell it, or he might have made it on commission for a client. Another possibility was that the piece was made in a large, diversified workshop that employed artisans in each of the traditional trades. The process of production would be very similar to that of the guilds, but the artisans would be united under one roof, able to work more or less collaboratively. And a piece made in the faubourg might be designed and drawn by one artisan who contracted out much of the work to *chambrellans*, individual artisans working in their homes.

The faubourg St-Antoine was largely peopled by foreigners and migrants from other parts of France, trained in other aesthetic traditions, as well as by the children of those who themselves had settled in the faubourg.[41] For example, the eighteenth-century fashion for veneered furniture had a dialogic relation to the strong German presence in the Parisian furniture trades. Veneer work had long existed in Germany and emigrating workers brought with them to Paris both the talent and the capacity to produce a taste for the new technique.[42] Given the guilds' restrictive policies, settling in the faubourg was sometimes the only way such immigrants could work in their trade in Paris. But even if the artisans who lived and worked in the faubourg did so because of guild restriction, they took full advantage of the aesthetic freedoms there. Contemporaries considered them more innovative than the guild artisans, and more creative in their practices.[43]

Joseph Baumhauer (d. 1772), discussed in the previous chapter, one of the initiators of neoclassical style in furniture, was trained in Germany and settled in Paris sometime before 1745, where he married into a family of *menuisiers* and became *ébéniste privilégié du roi* around 1749. His marquetry work was pictorial, geometric and floral. He never joined the guild

41. Monnier, *Le faubourg Saint-Antoine*, 27–28.
42. De Salverte, *Ebénistes du XVIIIe siècle*, xiii.
43. Jacques Hillairet, *Evocation du vieux Paris* (Paris, 1952–54), 686.

and was never invited into a royal workshop; like Joubert he was skilled in both rococo and neoclassical styles and worked almost entirely through the merchants Duvaux, Poirier, and Léger Bertin, and several others.[44] Baumhauer's work was purchased by the crown, the royal family and the nobility.

Some of the most famous and celebrated furniture makers of the eighteenth century had their origins in the faubourg, and many continued to work there even after joining the guild, and sometimes even after rising to positions of responsibility within it. The Bernard Van Risen Burgh dynasty was faithful to the faubourg. Bernard I Van Risen Burgh (d. 1738) arrived in Paris from Holland and settled in the faubourg at the end of the seventeenth century, although he did become a master of the guild sometime before 1722. His son Bernard II Van Risen Burgh (d. ca. 1765) continued the workshop in the faubourg and became a master sometime before 1730. He seems to have worked primarily for the *marchands merciers* (and through them, for the crown). His son, Bernard III Van Risen Burgh (d. 1800), took advantage of the suppleness of the organization of labor in the faubourg to change careers from *ébéniste* to sculptor. Roger Vandercruse (d. 1799), the son of a privileged Flemish artisan of the faubourg (François Vandercruse), took over his father's workshop on the rue du faubourg St-Antoine in 1755. He worked regularly for the Garde-Meuble royal (as did his son Pierre-Roger), and received commissions from the duc d'Orléans and Mme du Barry, as well as working for the *marchands merciers.* He held rank in the guilds rising from *juré* of the guild from 1768 to 1770; to *adjoint aux syndics* in 1781; and to *syndic* in 1782.

Unsurprisingly, the faubourg became the topic of debate, in the eighteenth and nineteenth centuries, between the advocates of free trade and those in favor of maintenance of regulation. Jean-Baptiste Say, on the one hand, used the faubourg as an example of the benefits of free trade.[45] Louis-Sébastien Mercier, on the other hand, in his *Tableau de Paris* was caustic on the subject of the quality of production there:

> All the *menuisiers* who make readymades work through the *tapissiers.*
> Be suspicious of those who live in the faubourg St-Antoine. One will sell
> you a drop-front desk that will unglue itself within three weeks. You

44. Pradère, *French Furniture Makers*, 231–42.
45. Jean-Baptiste Say, *Traité d'économie politique*, 6th ed. (Paris, 1841), 195.

have a wardrobe, wait until the end of the month and it will let drop its panels. There is furniture that leaves their shops that is a mere ghost—at the end of twenty days, it will list and become worm-eaten.[46]

He further complained that the *tapissiers* exorbitantly marked up—at 60 percent—the furniture they sold. Mercier asserted that they could get away with this because their customers were largely either prostitutes or men furnishing the apartments of their mistresses, who had money to spare and who were concerned above all with discretion and ease of purchase![47] Thus, according to Mercier, only those outside society, the immoral and depraved, would go buy their furniture beyond the law in the faubourg St-Antoine.

In fact, the tensions between the guilds and the faubourg St-Antoine point to the inherent strains of absolutism, corporatism, and the development of the market. While negative publicity like Mercier's presumably did the furniture makers of the faubourg St-Antoine little good, they were also subject to even more serious harassment by the guilds. The guilds systematically attacked the workers of the faubourg St-Antoine and tried verbally and legally to rid themselves of this thorn. Many of these conflicts produced *arrêts royaux*.[48] The most common ground for attack was that the artisans of the faubourg were producing low-quality furniture and that the state was not, therefore, fulfilling its obligation to protect the consumer. Clearly, these accusations often masked simple protectionist efforts. For example, the guild attempted to retain its traditional rights to send its *jurés* (the elected officers of the guild) into the faubourg four times a year to confiscate furniture that was not deemed to be of sufficiently high quality. This right was sometimes recognized and sometimes not. In any case, however, in 1751 the guild required its members to stamp (or brand) their furniture with a distinctive, nontransferable mark, in order to be able to distinguish it, in the boutiques of the *tapissiers* and the *marchands merciers*, from the faubourg's production.[49] This rule clarifies the issue of the relative quality of intra- and extraguild production. If, as the guild claimed, the artisans of the faubourg were producing furniture of poor quality and ruining the reputation of the furniture makers of Paris, then it would be unnecessary to specifically identify, with a brand, the guild-made objects;

46. Louis-Sébastien Mercier, *Le tableau de Paris* (Amsterdam, 1782–88), 245.
47. Ibid., 240–46.
48. For an interesting case of conflict between the guilds, the *marchands merciers*, and the faubourg, see AD XI 22 and S. Kaplan, "Luxury Guilds," 259–61.
49. Janneau, *Ateliers parisiens*, 9.

they would be identifiable by their quality alone. Indeed, the fact that guild and nonguild production were often indistinguishable was one of the grounds given for the abolition of the guilds in 1776.

The guilds and the faubourg divided the victories in court. The faubourg's *lettres patentes* were consistently renewed, although sometimes with crippling limitations. In 1675, for example, the masters in the faubourg were ordered either to join the guild or not to set foot outside the faubourg; they were also prohibited from making "masterpieces." These conflicts involved all the furniture guilds, including the *tapissiers,* the *ébéniste-menuisiers,* and the gilders.[50] And yet, while the guilds generally won the right to send in inspectors, the artisans of the faubourg often won the right to have those visits prearranged. After the guild made an appointment to inspect, artisans could hide furniture that they were afraid would be confiscated.

A conflict in 1710 between the guild and five *menuisiers* of the faubourg in which their goods were seized caused the abbess of the convent of St-Antoine-des-Champs to petition the king.[51] At the end of the eighteenth century the guild finally relaxed its prohibitions against foreigners in an effort to get people living in the faubourg to join the guild—an attempt to shore up its finances. In 1776, the crown made further concessions to the artisans of the faubourg in order to entice them into membership, if not full, then at least adjunct of the guilds. By 1785, one-third of the guild masters were foreign-born.[52]

None of these strategies achieved the ultimate goal of eradicating furniture production in the faubourg St-Antoine. The fact that the abbess of the convent was still taking her responsibilities for the workers of the faubourg seriously enough to petition the king on their behalf in the early eighteenth century indicates the continued connection of the Catholic Church and the faubourg. Attacks on the privileges of the faubourg were

50. For some of the multitude of conflicts between the guild and the faubourg see AN AD XI 10. There were *arrêts royaux* in 1557, 1558, 1559 and 1581 against extraguild production in general on the grounds that the consumers were not being adequately protected from bad merchandise. *Arrêts* against the faubourg continued into the next century; see also those of 31 July 1659, 17 April 1662, and 27 June 1662 (AN AD XI 22); and "Arrest de la cour des monoyes rendu en faveur des Maîtres doreurs, argenteurs, démasquineurs, ciseleurs, et enjoliveurs sur fer, fonte, cuivre, et laton de cette ville de Paris" [29 August 1711] (AN AD XI 18).

51. "Arrest du Conseil d'Etat du Roy Concernant les Privileges du Fauxbourg Saint Antoine et autres lieux Privilegiez" [15 August 1710] (AN AD XI 10).

52. "Déclaration du Roi portant réglement en faveur des Ouvriers et Artisans du Fauxbourg Saint-Antoine de Paris" [30 December 1776] (AN AD XI 11), 109–13. On foreign-born masters see de Salverte, *Ebénistes du XVIIIe siècle,* xiii.

read as impinging on the prerogatives of the church—a move the crown did not want to make more often than necessary. Thus, its refusal to do so reflects a complex story involving negotiation of relations of production and consumption that it commanded but could not absolutely control—or, in short, that it had to finesse. Nonguild production and emulation were crucial parts of that story, further complicated by the fact that after its manufacture furniture had to be sold; and distribution posed yet another set of conceptual conundrums under absolutism, one at the very core of the relation between the king and his subjects.

Distribution: The Tension between Protection and Competition

All thoughts on distribution took shape within the template provided by the overriding distribution problem of the Old Regime—that of food, and especially, bread. The king, as father, was to guarantee the supply of food—and by analogy all other goods—of acceptable quality and at a just price.[53] He was not, perhaps because he was the father rather than the mother of the nation, to provide the food; rather he was to see that the food was provided.[54] This provisioning was to be assured through the close policing and regulating of the distribution of flour and of bread. Thus the central role of the crown in assuring the well-being of the consumer through the strict control and regulation of goods is the background against which the story of the distribution of furniture played out, because this concern with fraud and malfeasance in the distribution of bread influenced the perception of other goods.

William Reddy holds that until the development of free trade, and the kinds of knowledge specific to it, people were haunted by the fear of the fraud and deceit that they felt would inevitably follow deregulation.[55] In 1761 it was found necessary to create a police ordinance that prohibited "any merchant to run after another to sell his or her goods, or to use any artifice to deceive the buyers, or to manipulate the purchasers so as to inhibit the freedom of exchange. Nonetheless certain merchants of this city have distributed leaflets with their name to announce the sale of fabrics and other goods at a price they claim to be lower than custom has

53. I follow Steven L. Kaplan, *Bread, Politics, and Political Economy in the Reign of Louis XV* (The Hague, 1976), 1:5–10 and passim.

54. For the absolute monarch's obligations as father, see Jeffrey Merrick, "Patriarchalism and Constitutionalism in Eighteenth-Century Parlementary Discourse," *Studies in Eighteenth-Century Culture* 20 (1990): 317–30.

55. Reddy, "Structure of a Cultural Crisis," 274–75.

established for the sale of those goods by other merchants."[56] The ordinance claimed that low prices inevitably meant that the merchandise was of low quality. Although there were advocates of deregulation by the 1760s, the view that competition was inimical to the consumer's interest was still widely held.

The solution was further complicated by the fact that eighteenth-century views of merchants were highly ambivalent. On the one hand, those who made money off other people's labor and other people's needs — merchants — were sometimes considered little better than usurers.[57] And for nobles, investing in wholesale trade was an acceptable activity whereas participation in either retail trade or manual labor was cause for derogation of their status. The shame attached to manual labor was great enough for the king to transform his court artisans into court *artistes;* and, as noted above, many of them went deeply into debt trying to live up to their putative status. Moreover, the guilds with the right only to sell, and not to make, goods had the highest prestige and the greatest power. They occupied an important place in official ceremonies, royal and princely entrances into the city, and marriages, births, and funerals of those of high birth.[58] Their prestige may relate to their place within a world system, because the distributing guilds engaged more in international negotiation and travel than the producer-distributors, thereby gaining access to scarce information and resources valuable to a king as well as to a merchant.[59]

Further complicating the situation was the contradictory relation of the crown to the distribution of durable goods. As noted in chapter one, the

56. "Ordonnance de Police, qui fait itératives et très-expresses défenses à tous Marchands en gros et en détail, de cette Ville et Fauxbourgs de Paris, de courir les uns sur les autres pour le débit de leurs Marchandises; et leur défend notamment de répandre ni autrement distributer aucuns Billet, pour en annoncer la vente, et ce sous quelque prétexte que ce soit . . . " [10 April 1761] (AN AD XI 10).

57. See for example Diderot's encyclopedia entry, quoted in Pierre Verlet, "Le commerce des objets d'art et les marchands merciers," *Annales: Economies, sociétés, civilisations* 13 (1958): 11.

58. See for example the hierarchy in *Liste générale et roolles de tous les arts et métiers qui s'exercent tant en la ville et fauxbourgs de Paris* (Paris, 1656). A *mercier grossier* (wholesaler) fits in the first rank along with apothecaries, jewelers, drapers, and a few other largely distributing trades. *Bahutier, cofretier, maletier, charpentier,* and *menuisier* are in the third, or *médiocre* rank, while *doreur, miroitier, bibelotier,* and *tabletier* are in the fourth between the *médiocres* and the *petits,* while a *tapissier* is relegated to the fifth. The ranking parallels the lines of production and distribution. The other critical factor for the distributors was the scale of operation. See also Pardailhé-Galabrun, *Naissance de l'intime,* 72.

59. On the distribution of the products of the Parisian luxury trades through Europe, see Sonenscher, *Work and Wages,* 214.

crown needed both inimitable and imitable possessions—the inimitable to represent its absolute, unique, and inviolable power to rule; the imitable to represent its willingness to share some of that power and to grant symbolic standing to some of the ruled. The systems of production and distribution worked in tandem to ensure this outcome.

Thus, despite the monopoly that each guild was to have over the production of particular items within a given geographic region, competition was built into the system along with mistrust of it. A number of guilds consisted exclusively of merchants, most notably, the guild of *marchands merciers*. The *marchands merciers* sold, among many other items, readymade furniture that was to be made only within the guilds, to be antique, or to come from abroad. They tended to sell high-quality, expensive furniture and were a central source of furniture for the king.[60] The *huissiers-commissaires-priseurs* (who did not formally constitute a guild) also sold but did not make furniture and dealt only in furniture seized for nonpayment of debt and after bankruptcy; they were sometimes in conflict with the *merciers* over who had the right to sell what and where. But the *ébénistes* sometimes sold furniture whose production they had entirely subcontracted, *menuisiers* sometimes sold upholstered chairs, and the *tapissiers*, unupholstered ones.[61] Some furniture was sold at auction. Until the mid-eighteenth century old furniture was not especially prized, but at the end of the century Boulle's furniture was selling well and auction houses became an important means of distribution of antiques. The existence of these multiple structures created great anxiety over quality and price.

The problem of price was a complex one. Few goods were sold on the basis of a fixed price and many were sold on credit. Price was a matter of negotiation and discussion, either privately through bargaining, or publicly at auction. Goods were to be sold at a "just price" and that just price was

60. AN AD XI 22; Pradère, *French Furniture Makers*, 30, 38–39; Verlet, "Le commerce des objets d'art," 14, citing Savary des Bruslons's dictionary. On the importance and power of the *merciers*, see Bossenga, "Protecting Merchants," 700–703.

61. "Arrest de la cour de Parlement portant Réglement entre les Six Corps des Marchands de la Ville de Paris et les Huissiers-Commissaires-Priseurs au Châtelet de Paris. Au Sujet des Ventes de Fonds de Boutiques, Marchandises et Meubles Neuf" [17 June 1777] (AN AD XI 10). By 1800 there were 260 *huissiers* (compared with 51 *ébénistes*), and 240 *tapissiers* and *marchands de meubles* listed in La Tynna, *Almanach du commerce*. On subcontracting see Sonenscher, *Work and Wages*, 31–38, esp. 31–32; 133.

to be a matter of negotiation between buyer and seller rather than a one-sided decision by the seller individually or even by all the *corps* of merchants. Charles Smith notes that "auctions . . . are not exclusively or even primarily exchange processes. They are rather processes for managing the ambiguity and uncertainty of value by establishing social meanings and consensus."[62] While this observation is almost certainly truer in a world in which most exchanges are fixed-price and negotiating and bargaining are the exceptions, the fact that the dominant form of determining price in the Old Regime was negotiation, and an important secondary one the auction, indicates the degree to which the determination of a just price was a social process.

The task of protecting consumers of furniture created an intricate system of distribution that matched the complexity of the organization of production. Furniture was sold by various producer-guilds, by diverse distributor-guilds, by both producer-distributors and distributors in the faubourg St-Antoine, by *huissiers* at auction, and in open-air markets. Or it was delivered directly by the court artisans to their royal and noble patrons. From early in the eighteenth century until its end, there was intense conflict among these different distributors, each of whom claimed the exclusive right to sell a given good at a given place; yet another complication grew from moves toward a market economy, which culminated in the attempt to abolish the guilds.

Some effort was made to force distributors to specialize in categories of goods because success at selling was held to derive from expertise in particular goods, rather than from the art of selling itself.[63] Even the *marchands merciers*, who had the right to sell anything, tended to specialize in certain goods. Most goods were still made to order and sold by the merchant who commissioned them. The making of goods on speculation to be sold by the art or wiles of the salesclerk, rather than by the reputation of the maker, seller, or the guild was to wait until the nineteenth century.

Even if the art of sales as a distinct craft was not a thoroughly acceptable notion in the Old Regime, eighteenth-century distributors were not unwilling to adapt to their consumers' needs and habits. Although Old Regime Paris tended to segregate its classes vertically (in buildings) rather

---

62. Charles W. Smith, *Auctions: The Social Construction of Value* (New York, 1989), 163.
63. William Reddy goes so far as to argue that there were no clear entrepreneurs in the eighteenth century (*Market Culture*, 46).

than horizontally (in neighborhoods), neighborhoods were wealthy or poor, aristocratic or laboring. Most of the well-established nobility would shop by having the artisan or distributor come to them, but by the second half of the eighteenth century shopping was beginning to be an acceptable pastime for the fashionable, in certain neighborhoods only.[64] Merchants with aspirations to the elite market tended to group together on the rue St-Honoré and adjacent streets, at a distance from the faubourg St-Antoine, or on the rue de Cléry where much of the production was located; those customers who were willing to go to a shop rather than have the goods come to them—noble women, for example, reluctant to engage in public shopping—would enter a shop on the rue St-Honoré but would never set foot in the faubourg.[65]

Sellers' reputations came from their links to the court. The merchant-suppliers of crown and court were patronized by others who could afford their prices. The major forms of advertising before the late eighteenth century were the *almanachs,* which provided information about what was being shown at court and the addresses of the fashionable suppliers.[66] The 1691 edition of *Le livre commode,* for example, gave the reader several addresses of establishments from which to buy furniture, along with the court calendar, snippets of royal etiquette, and a description of royal ceremonies.[67] By the end of the eighteenth century, there was also a directory of "persons of quality," which probably helped distributors locate likely consumers.[68]

Even in the domain of women's fashion, often considered the earliest commodified domain, the first magazine to discuss fashion, the *Mercure Galant* (founded 1672), was dominated by descriptions of what was being worn at court. The late eighteenth century saw the apparition of *annuaires*

64. For a description of elite shopping habits in the eighteenth century see Pardailhé-Galabrun (*Naissance de l'intime,* 71).

65. Pradère, *French Furniture Makers,* 31.

66. These included the *Almanach parisien en faveur des étrangers et des personnes curieuses* (Paris, 1765–93); the *Almanach des corps des marchands et des communautés des arts et métiers de la ville et fauxbourgs de Paris* (Paris, 1758, 1769); and *L'esprit du commerce pour 1754* (Paris, 1754), which had addresses and current prices on goods throughout France.

67. Abraham du Pradel, *Le livre commode,* cited in Emile Mermet, *La publicité en France: guide pratique* (Paris, 1878), 216. The *Almanach royal* first came out in 1679, eliminating the competition.

68. *Almanach de Paris contenant la demeure, les noms et qualité des personnes de condition dans la ville et fauxbourgs de Paris* (Paris, 1772–81).

providing addresses as well as information on the goods being sold.[69] Nearly a century passed before *Le courrier de la mode* (founded 1768) offered the first signs of a style in clothing detached from that of the court. The burgeoning of fashion magazines—*Le courrier* was quickly followed by four others—indicates the advance of this sector. That a style distinct from the courts emerged in the domain of clothing, and women's clothing, rather than in furnishings more directly associated with the king's household may be more than a coincidence. Even here, although all included addresses of fashionable suppliers, no magazines carried explicit advertisements.

So the world of eighteenth-century distribution was not one in which shops wooed customers through savvy advertising and skillful salesclerks or sold products at any price the market would bear. Reputations were made through court patronage, and the notion reigned that a just price—the price at which an item of good quality, made by artisans paid at the standard rate, could be sold—should be determined and goods should be sold at that price. Distributors worked hard to avoid accusations that they were out to defraud their clients by selling shoddy goods, at inflated prices, and by dubious means.

The list of important *marchands merciers* in the eighteenth century runs to a dozen, all closely tied to the court.[70] They included Gersaint (d. 1750) who sold pictures, clocks, mirrors, and marquetry, as well as objects imported from Japan (and even some "items of natural history"). More prominent was Thomas-Joachim Hébert (d. 1773), the *marchand privilégié du palais*. He had shops both in the château at Versailles and on the rue St-Honoré in Paris. He specialized in lacquer work and may in fact have inaugurated the practice of reusing panels taken from Japanese objects. He was a major supplier of the crown—the exclusive supplier in lacquer—and commissioned work from Parisian artisans as well. Hébert was succeeded by Lazare Duvaux (d. 1758), originally a jeweler, who had a massive business supplying the court and nobility. Simon-Philippe Poirier (d. 1785), himself the son of a *marchand mercier*, became one of the most successful merchants in eighteenth-century Paris, supplying the prince de Soubise, the prince de Condé, the Garde-Meuble royal, among others. He

69. Le Vent, ed., *Almanach général des marchands, négocians, armateurs et fabricans de la France et de l'Europe et autres parties du monde* (Paris, 1778); *Almanach du commerce de Paris* (1797).

70. This paragraph draws on Pradère, *French Furniture Makers*, 32–40. I disagree, however, that merchants were the imaginative force behind stylistic innovation while *ébénistes* provided the labor (40).

commissioned work from creative and skilled artisans and began the fashion for porcelain inlay on furniture. Poirier's business was taken over by Dominique Daguerre (d. 1796) who was the most famous dealer in Paris in the 1780s and became the major supplier of the king and queen. He also imported furniture from Britain. The Julliot family were powerful merchants for three generations; in the 1770s Claude-François Julliot commissioned one of the very few pieces in historicist pastiche as well as sponsoring fashions for old furniture, particularly by Boulle. His passion for Boulle old and new was shared by Pierre Lebrun (d. 1791), who bought quantities of it at auction between 1776 and 1788. Claude Delaroue was a *marchand ordinaire* who regularly supplied the mid-century court with *ébénisterie* and *meubles de toilette*.

The role of merchants in creating and selectively diffusing royal styles can be seen also in the case of the Bernard Van Risen Burgh family. Bernard II (d. 1765/6) has become known as one of the most innovative and graceful *ébénistes* working during the reign of Louis XV. Under commission from a succession of merchants, first Hébert, next Duvaux, and then Poirier, he supplied large quantities of furniture to the crown, reviving and transforming floral marquetry, which had been dead in France since 1700, then making furniture incorporating lacquer panels dismantled from Japanese objects, and finally crafting furniture either entirely covered in porcelain or with elaborate porcelain decorations. He spent his entire life in the faubourg and was a master in the guild but avoided most direct dealings with clients, preferring or perhaps being obliged to work through merchants. In both instances flexibility and diversity in the systems of production and distribution enabled the court to encourage innovative work.

The question of who had the right to make and to sell what was never satisfactorily resolved, as a multitude of lawsuits attest. In a court sentence from 25 June 1669, a *menuisier* was condemned and forced to pay a fine because he had sold four *chaises garnies*, which he had no right to do: selling upholstered chairs fell within the monopoly of the guild of *tapissiers*. The *tapissiers* and the *menuisiers* came into conflict, as did the *tapissiers-menuisiers* (now unified) and the *merciers*. An *arrêt* of Parlement in 1724 prohibited masters and merchants of the guild of *tapissiers* to "live with the *merciers*, to lend them their name, to do business or socialize with them, and forbade the apprentices and journeymen of the trade from working with them, for the month, the year, or the day."[71]

71. Husson, *Artisans français*, 172, 222.

The desirability of becoming a merchant rather than a mere artisan can be demonstrated by the frequency with which *ébénistes,* when successful, transformed themselves into distributors.[72] Léonard Boudin (d. ca. 1804) started his career very modestly in the faubourg St-Antoine until he came to the notice and then patronage of the celebrated and successful *ébéniste* Pierre III Migeon.[73] Despite being a Protestant and working in the faubourg, Migeon was a guild master, the son of a favorite of Mme de Pompadour, and a supplier of the Garde-Meuble. Migeon commissioned furniture for the nobility from Boudin. In 1761 Boudin joined the guild and enlarged his workshop but stayed within the faubourg. In the 1770s he opened two stores, one on the rue Fromenteau and another on the cloître St-Germain-l'Auxerrois. After the Revolution he gave up furniture production and worked exclusively as a decorator.[74]

Some very successful *ébénistes* like René DuBois (d. 1799), who was listed in the *Tablettes royales de renommée,* had commissions from the prince de Soubise and the court and in 1779 was named *ébéniste de la reine,* may have used their reputations established building furniture to guarantee their future as merchants.[75] DuBois gave up building furniture the same year he was named the queen's *ébéniste* and set up a business on the rue Montmartre. But it was not just artisans who started their professional lives outside the guilds who became merchants later in life. Pierre Michel Roussel, son and grandson of master *menuisiers* and himself accepted into the guild in 1766, opened a store in the rue St-Honoré specializing in luxury goods.

This multiplicity of distributors existed in a symbiotic relation with the multiplicity of producers. The existence of distribution guilds, for example, helped undermine the monopoly of the producer guilds over production. For despite the illegality and risks of the practice, members of the guild of *marchands merciers* regularly bought goods from shops in the faubourg St-Antoine. They did not, therefore, ally with the producer guilds in an effort to get the privileges of the faubourg revoked but rather strongly

72. This pattern is confirmed by Monnier, *Le faubourg Saint-Antoine,* 214.

73. Saint-Sere, "Deux ébénistes favoris de la favorite," *Plaisir de France* 6 (December 1956): 73–77; André Boutemy, "Pierre II Migeon," *Connaissance des arts* 83 (January 1959): 66–73.

74. Little has been written on Léonard Boudin; Paul Guth, "Le roman d'un estampilleur, L. Boudin," *Connaissance des arts* 54 (August 1956): 26–31.

75. The *Tablettes royales de renommée, ou almanach général d'indications des négociants, artistes, célèbres fabricants des six corps, arts et métiers de Paris* (Paris, 1773) was a listing of well-known artisans in Paris, all working for the crown. See Sonenscher, *Work and Wages,* 216.

supported the artisans in the faubourg while seeking to undermine the court artisans, whose direct negotiations with the court posed a far greater threat to the merchants' livelihood.[76]

Royal tolerance and even encouragement of competition in distribution increased toward the end of the eighteenth century. The revised statutes of 1776 allowed *drapiers-merciers* (formerly, *marchands merciers*) to "hold and sell wholesale and retail all kinds of merchandise in competition with all of the manufacturers and artisans of Paris, even those included within the six *corps* [of the guilds], but he may not produce, nor have worked any merchandise, even under the pretext of embellishing it."[77] These regulations are very explicit in their acknowledgement of competition among the guilds and the *corps*, as well as of their refusal to allow the competition to expand by letting merchants modify the goods they sold. The revised guild statutes of 1776 also encouraged competition between the producer guilds and the distributor *corps:* they gave the guilds of manufacturers and artisans the right to sell what they had made and also to sell what they had the right to make regardless of where it had in fact been made, thereby implicitly acknowledging the separation of production and distribution.

The forty-first community—the *tapissiers, fripiers en meubles et us-tensiles,* and *miroitiers*—could also sell furniture. The guild of *tapissiers, fripiers en meubles et ustensiles, et miroitiers* had the right to make new chairs, if they were entirely covered with upholstery; otherwise they had only the right to embellish and sell already existing objects.[78] As members of this new corporation they pursued what had been earlier a sideline; the *tapissiers* became interior decorators and started to deal largely with ready-made goods. By 1788 the six *corps* (the distributor guilds) of Paris petitioned the king to have a place at the Estates General, arguing that whereas in the past commerce had not been important to the well-being of the nation, because of its primitive state, now "it has become, so to speak, suddenly one of the largest bases of the political power of states."[79] Coming on the eve of the Revolution, their polemical and instrumental argument illustrates the kind of claims that could be made in the name of commerce.

76. Gail Bossenga's claim ("Protecting Merchants," 703) of generally positive relations between production and distribution guilds, to assure reliable goods on the market, may need modification.
77. "Recueil de Réglements" (AN AD XI 11), 58.
78. Husson, *Les tapissiers,* 25, 226.
79. *Mémoire présenté au roi par les six corps de la ville de Paris* (Paris, 1788), 4.

The notion of the natural rights of both producers and consumers had been deeply eroded.

One plot line of this story leads to the nineteenth century and the increasing importance and autonomy of commerce and of distributors. That story also necessarily involved a transformation in the nature of knowledge, which would culminate in the 1880s with the advent of sales and advertising theory. That development was still a century away, but the growing differentiation of production and distribution, with greater expertise associated with distribution rather than production during the eighteenth century, established the conditions of possibility for the maturation of the art of sales and of the discipline of art history, as well as the expansion of experts I dub the "taste professionals" in the second half of the nineteenth century.

The other plot line, however, is of the eighteenth century and reflects the multiple tensions and contradictions involved in exercising and sustaining monarchical power. The paradoxes absolutism confronted in managing production and distribution were strikingly parallel to and interdependent with those of consumption. In granting autonomy to the artisans under monastic communities' protection, for example, the crown not only reinforced its own power—by displaying its prerogative to make exceptions to its own rules—it also sustained its commitments to another powerful institution—the Catholic church and the monastic system. The largest privileged area of the city in which furniture was made, the faubourg St-Antoine, was under the control (however nominal) of a Cistercian convent. The privileges of the woodworkers were a concession granted by the absolute monarch to the church.

Second, through the creation and support of the royal workshops, the crown could guarantee the uniqueness of the objects in its own possession and thus of representations of itself, because the crown exercised more direct control over the artisans within the crown workshops and could therefore require unique commissions. Through the royal workshops and the naming of royal artisans, the crown could invite foreign artisans (whom the guilds would exclude) to contribute their knowledge, skill, and craft sense to the Parisian trades. The general level of French production improved, as well as the crown's own decoration.[80]

---

80. In *Herbst des Alten Handwerks* (Munich, 1979), 13–14, Michael Stürmer argues that the court artisans were the avant-garde of capitalist manufacturing.

Third, and central to the political organization and autonomy of cities in ancien régime France were the guilds—legal persons or corporations similar to universities, juridical bodies, and academies.[81] In the Middle Ages seigneurial cities, like Paris, were composed of the corporations they contained, which divided the administration and policing of the city among themselves and could at times contest royal power.[82] Until the seventeenth century cities had little unitary identity, rather they existed as a consolidation of corporate bodies. After the upheavals of the Fronde, Louis XIV's policy was to restrict the autonomy of the municipalities and therefore of the guilds, but the guilds continued to be structuring units of urban life, as much political as economic organizations in this period. The crown needed their support and their revenues; it also needed to limit their power.[83] But guilds as economic institutions put too much emphasis on stability, and the crown needed the production of luxury goods to ensure its dominance in the international competition over representation.[84] Guilds were necessary but not sufficient to the productive and political needs of the crown.

Once this tripartite system was in place it could not be closed down. It created a complex division of labor and specialization characterized by an unwieldy mix of the marginally skilled poverty-stricken furniture makers who worked at home alone or with their families, alongside traditional workshops of a master, a journeyman, and a couple of apprentices, and much larger workshops. This complex system could not have been reconstrained within the borders of the guilds without great political and social cost.

Consequently, the royal creation of competition for the very organizations to which it had granted monopolies initially appears perverse but makes more sense on closer inspection. Both the organization of production and the exercise of monarchical power under the Old Regime produced certain structural antinomies. The absolute monarchy needed to demonstrate its power through the creation of exceptions to its own rules; that it could *undermine* monopolies as well as *grant* them was a clear illustration

81. This argument is drawn from Mousnier, *Institutions of France*, 1:429–31; and Sonenscher, *Hatters*, 7 and passim.

82. Here I follow Orest Ranum, *Paris in the Age of Absolutism* (New York, 1968), chaps. 2, 4, 9, 12.

83. On efforts of the crown to limit autonomy of craft guilds, see Emile Coornaert, *Les corporations en France avant 1789* (Paris, 1941).

84. Richard Gascon, "La France du mouvement," in *L'état et la ville*, ed. Fernand Braudel and Ernest Labrousse (Paris, 1977), 231–479.

that the king's prerogative was superior to his own rules. From the furniture trades' close ties to the structural and representational needs of the absolute monarchy, and delicate negotiation among these differing demands, came conditions for innovative production, for seventeenth- and eighteenth-century French furniture often considered unsurpassed in its originality, beauty, and craftsmanship.

3

Fathers, Masters, and Kings
Mirroring Monarchical Power

 The analogy legitimating kingship was that the king was to his people as a father to his children. Masters in their turn were to be as kings and fathers in their workshops. Consequently, although the crown did not intervene as directly in the reproduction of the trades as it did in their regulation, the forms of masculine kinship used to structure relations within the trades and the transmission of knowledge, skill, and craft sense to the next generation were modeled on those of kingship. And, like the tripartite division into guild, royal workshop, and faubourg St-Antoine, the organization of training in the trades had some unanticipated consequences.

Just as the needs and desires of absolute monarchy shaped the structural organization of the trades, they formed the trades' social relations as well. As we have seen, the king needed stylistic innovation in order to respond to the changing and complex requirements for representing and projecting his power, and the conditions for an expanding repertoire of forms were rooted in complex modes of production and reproduction. Actual creativity and innovation, however, could come only from the craftsmen themselves and no conceivable system of monarchical hegemony could guarantee such initiatives. It was in some sense then, still another example of absolutism's limits; and yet absolutism supplied the organizing principle—the paternal model—for the craftsmen's relation to each other and thus to their craft.

THE CULTURE OF PRODUCTION: CREATING AND TRANSMITTING KNOWLEDGE, SKILL, AND CRAFT SENSE

> [A] good *menuisier-ébéniste* should not only be in the state [*être en état*] to do ordinary woodworking well, but he also needs to know how to glue and polish all of the different kinds of wood, both French and foreign. He should also know how to dye the woods and darken them, and to work diverse kinds of materials, like ivory, tortoiseshell, mother-of-pearl,

pewter, copper, silver, and even gold and precious stones. He cannot do this without perfectly knowing all of these materials, which are all used and worked differently. Wood-dying also requires some idea of chemistry to formulate the dyes. To this theoretical-technical knowledge, *menuisiers-ébénistes* must add that of taste which is to be acquired through drawing of all kinds, including architecture and perspective, ornament, landscape, and even the figure, in order to be able to represent all kinds of subjects with all of the precision of which their art is capable.[1]

As André-Jacob Roubo, in his 1772 treatise on woodworking, described the craft of furniture maker, it involved the mastery of diverse materials, chemistry, manual technique, various kinds of drawing, architecture, proportion, and art history.[2] Unmentioned by Roubo, but equally crucial to mastering the craft, were arithmetic and geometry. Until the mid-nineteenth century those who had knowledge, skill, and craft sense had learned it from other artisans in the trades, supplemented perhaps by an occasional evening course.[3] Training took place in two stages: apprenticeship and journeymanship. The artisan then either became the master of his own shop or continued life as a waged worker.

Possessing basic skill—the ability to plane a board so the two faces were true, to saw in a straight line, or to cut the male and female parts of joints so that they would perfectly meet—brought the capacity to produce parts of given dimensions. But manual skill alone did not enable an artisan even to copy an object in wood.[4] To do anything but the most routine tasks, a furniture maker needed to be able to read a drawing, which involved visualizing and making a three-dimensional object from a two-dimensional one. This second level of skill in eye-hand coordination added a level of abstraction: the artisan needed to be able to look at a flat drawing and see a projected object. There was an implied act of translation if not of creation.

1. André-Jacob Roubo, quoted in Thamer, "Work Practices of French Joiners."
2. Commissioned by the Académie royale des sciences, André-Jacob Roubo's treatise consisted of *L'art du menuisier*, 2 vols. (Paris, 1769–70); *L'art du menuisier-carrossier* (Paris, 1771); *L'art du menuisier en meubles* (Paris, 1772); *L'art du menuisier-ébéniste* (Paris, 1774); and *L'art du layetier* (Paris, 1782), which was not part of the commission. There were many reeditions in the nineteenth century.
3. Free evening courses for artisans were available from the late eighteenth century at the Ecole spéciale de dessin and at the Ecole polytechnique; for the offerings see AN F^{21}1422 and F^{17}12530.
4. This discussion draws on the approximately 150 technical manuals dating from 1760 to 1920 available at the Bibliothèque Forney, the Bibliothèque des arts décoratifs, and the Bibliothèque nationale, as well as my own practice of the trade.

More complicated and enabling than the ability to read a drawing was the ability to make one. Drawing pushed the abstracting capacity from the relatively passive act of reading a drawing and translating that act of absorption into a chair, to the more active accomplishment of drawing a plan and then making the chair. The first and simplest level of drawing was technical drawing, by means of which the artisan formalized an object or a sketch into a working drawing.[5] Technical drawing, however, entailed only imitation and copying, not innovation. Beyond technical drawing lay the *trait*, or study—through drawing—of perspective, proportion, and basic geometry.[6] The *trait* was based on the five classical orders of architecture, Tuscan, Doric, Ionic, Corinthian and composed. Or, as Le Camus de Mézières defined them, "By the word Order is understood a regular and proportioned arrangement of volumes, moldings, and ornaments which in a facade or another element of architectural decoration, compose a beautiful whole. . . . Each order is made up of three essential parts: a pedestal, a column, and a capital." Since furniture was considered architecture in miniature, and all architecture was deemed to be based on the classical Greek, knowledge of these orders was important.[7] Most technical manuals for *ébénistes* included a short course on architectural proportion, including the drawing from *Le livre du compagnonnage* in Figure 17.

Technical drawing, the most elaborate kind of transitional ability, provided the foundations for innovative and creative design, but was not sufficient. Technical drawing was crucial because without having drawn the geometrical and architectural forms, an artisan could not really know or understand them. Yet it enabled artisans to assimilate geometry and the orders of architecture without necessarily enabling them to create new forms.[8] Mastery of technical drawing sufficed for detailed drawings from an existing object or sketch, but the creation of a new form required another

5. For the importance of drawing to the eighteenth-century *ébéniste*, see Roubo, *Art du menuisier-ébéniste*, 763. See also J., "Concours de l'art décoratif," *L'art décoratif* 7 (April 1899): 94.

6. A. O. Paulin-Desormeaux, *Art du menuisier en bâtiment et en meubles, suivi de l'art de l'ébéniste, ouvrage contenant des éléments de géométrie descriptive appliquée à l'art du menuisier*, 3d ed. (Paris, 1829), 1:43. This was the first new study of the *trait* intended for woodworkers since Roubo and the *Encyclopédie*.

7. Le Camus de Mézières, *Le génie de l'architecture*, 23. For example, the architect Jacques-François Blondel's *Discours sur la nécessité de l'étude de l'architecture* (1754; reprint, Geneva, 1973) argues for the importance of a training in architecture for artisans.

8. Perdiguier, *Livre du compagnonnage*; see also Jean Gentry, *Le petit menuisier* (Paris, 1892–96).

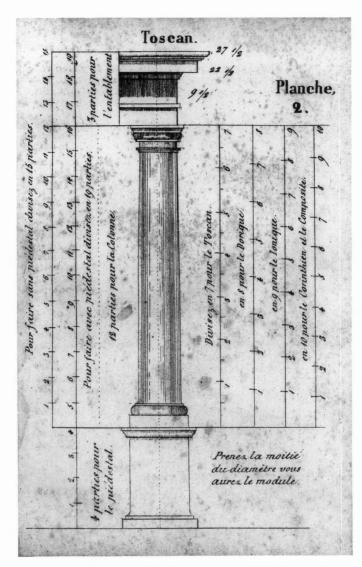

Figure 17.   The orders of architecture. Agricol Perdiguier, *Le livre du compagnonnage*, vol. 1 (Paris, 1841), pl. 2.

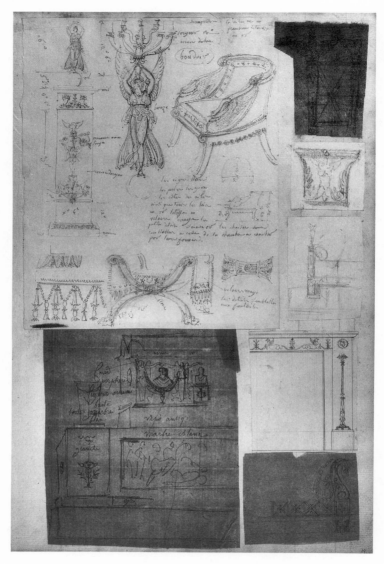

Figure 18. Charles Percier (d. 1838), sketches of furniture. Scrapbook
of sketches in pencil and pen and ink, mounted in a parchment-covered
album from the stationer Renault, folio 19. Elisha Whittelsey
Collection, Metropolitan Museum of Art, 63.535.

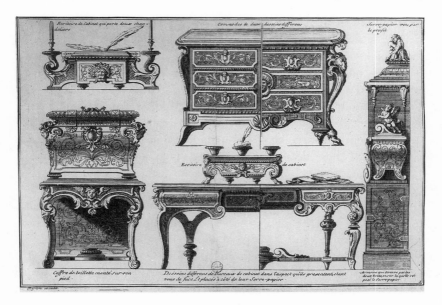

Figure 19. André-Charles Boulle, engravings of furniture. Cabinet des estampes, Bibliothèque nationale.

capacity. The second level of drawing involved the rendering of figures as well as flora and fauna. This drawing was done freehand from nature or the model and trained the eye to more sophisticated perception, the hand to greater sureness, than technical drawing done with the aid of compass and ruler. The next step was the depiction on paper of images born in the imagination.[9] Charles Percier's sketchbook (Figure 18) demonstrates the kind of "thinking with a pencil" (and training in freehand drawing) necessary to conjure new forms, while the engraving of the much more formalized drawings of André-Charles Boulle in Figure 19 demonstrates the process of working out the variations on a given form that advanced training in both drafting and drawing allowed.

Knowledge allowed the artisan to conceptualize a new piece of furniture: without knowledge one could only repeat what had been done before; without an image of the beautiful in one's head, a dream of what the world could look like, even the desire to do anything but repeat would be lacking.

9. Gustave Geoffroy, "Causerie sur le style, la tradition et la nature," *Revue des arts décoratifs* 18 (1899): 181. For a contemporary argument emphasizing the crucial importance of drawing to furniture making, see Deloche, *L'art du meuble*, 165.

While skill consisted of learning a number of strategies for arriving at a defined goal, knowledge gave the artisan the possibility of defining that goal. Skill was specific and limited in application, knowledge was general. The cause and effect in learning a skill was clear: one learned to make a mortise and tenon joint, perfected that skill, and then could make the joint until the end of one's days. In the domain of knowledge cause and effect were less clear; one might spend months looking at the architectural detail of seventeenth-century châteaux without immediately miniaturizing a composite of those details into a canapé, but the time was not wasted. Someday, one element of one château closely studied would provide the critical idea for a successful dining room set.

Acquiring knowledge meant learning the histories of art, architecture, and furniture, and through that study obtaining an agility of mind and the means of grasping the full range of possibilities and functions for visual forms.[10] Besides a semiotic repertoire, an understanding of the dynamic of aesthetic change, and a stock of forms and images, furniture makers needed geometry to improvise, reuse, and create furniture aesthetics. Artisans had to understand how two-dimensional shapes and three-dimensional volumes were constructed and could be joined. Geometry was necessary as the basis of a simple kind of structural mechanics. As Roubo's illustration of the projection of a curve of a chair indicates, a knowledge of geometry was the necessary scaffolding behind drawing and design (Figure 20). To make chairs that would withstand the weight of a well-fed customer, bookcases that would not list, and spiral staircases that would not collapse, it was helpful to know that a triangle is a much stronger form than a rectangle and that one could easily turn one weak rectangle into two much stronger triangles. Furthermore, geometry was needed for the mastery of perspective, itself essential for much marquetry work, including the popular "vanishing-cube" design. It was also necessary for calculating quantities of wood.[11] A knowledge of geometry (and arithmetic) provided the technical and theoretical knowledge necessary to create the imagined designs, as well as ideas of what was, in fact, possible.

10. Emile Molinier, "La décoration dans l'ameublement," *Revue des arts décoratifs* 18 (1898): 48; Georges Duplessis, "Le département des estampes à la Bibliothèque nationale," *Revue des arts décoratifs* 6 (1885–86): 334–41.

11. Perdiguier, *Livre du compagnonnage,* 34; A. Mangeant, "Des ouvrages de menuiserie," *Journal de menuiserie* 3 (1865).

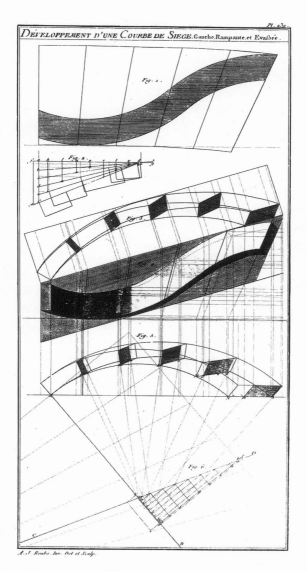

Figure 20. "Eléments de perspective, nécessaires aux ébénistes." André-Jacob Roubo, *L'art du menuisier-ébéniste* (Paris, 1774), pl. 297.

For the creation and transmission of knowledge books were essential. The technical treatise that was later to become such an important means of teaching the trades was already an established genre in the eighteenth century, even if cost rendered diffusion limited.[12] Few artisans owned books—although ownership seems to have been increasing in the eighteenth century—but most were literate and many had access to books owned by others.[13] Producing a series of elevations had been an acceptable masterpiece within the German guild tradition from the sixteenth century, and artisans continued to study and reproduce them in their efforts to learn architecture, geometry, and perspective. The two great eighteenth-century treatises, Roubo's and Denis Diderot's, were written to many purposes beyond that of instructing artisans in their trades, yet book knowledge was an important part of the culture of production. Charles Gillispie's argument that by the time Roubo and Diderot wrote they were describing dead trades is misleading. Although few artisans would have had Roubo's experience of training under an architect of the status of Jacques-François Blondel, the range of technical treatises was wide, they were used, and the trades they served were far from dead in the late eighteenth century.[14]

The last element of the trilogy of skill, knowledge, and craft sense is perhaps the hardest to define. It was of the same epistemological order as good sense (in Gramsci's usage); it consisted of informal, practical knowledge vital to the practice of a trade that passed from one person in a community to another and from one generation to the next. Possessing craft sense meant being able to judge what a log would look like on the inside, where its faults would be, and what it was destined to make; sensing

12. Pierre Quef, *Histoire de l'apprentissage: aspects de la formation technique et commerciale* (Paris, 1964), 94. For eighteenth-century examples, see Alexandre Jean-Baptiste Leblond, *Desseins de développement d'assemblages de differens ouvrages de menuiserie* (Paris, 1711); Plumier, *L'art de tourner; Secrets concernant les arts et métiers,* 2 vols. (Paris, 1716); Filippo Buonanni, *Traité des vernis, où l'on donne la manière d'en composer un qui ressemble parfaitement à celui de la Chine* (Paris, 1723); Bimont, *Principes de l'art du tapissier;* de Lormois, *Le Vernisseur parfait, ou manuel du vernisseur* (Paris, 1771); Jean-Félix Watin, *L'art de faire ou d'employer le vernis, ou l'art du vernisseur auquel on a joint ceux du peintre et du doreur* (Paris, 1772).

13. Philippe Ariès, introduction to *Passions of the Renaissance,* ed. Roger Chartier, trans. Arthur Goldhammer (Cambridge, Mass., 1989), 4. According to Roger Chartier, about 75 percent of artisans in eighteenth-century Lyons could sign their names. In mid-eighteenth-century Paris 12 percent of master craftsmen owned books, and in 1780 35 percent of wage earners owned them (*Cultural Uses of Print,* 188–89).

14. Gillispie, *Science and Polity,* 340–50, esp. 348–49.

when glue was the appropriate consistency to match the weather and the woodgrain; and knowing how a flaw in the wood would react to the bite of a plane's knife. Craft sense was not a mystical phenomenon; it was taught but not in the same way that skill and knowledge were taught, because it contained a large component of experience, time, and habit as well as notions of tastefulness and innovation. As they passed down old tricks, artisans encouraged one another to invent forms and techniques.

Amid all the discussions of the furniture-making trades in the Old Regime, none took up the problem of selling the goods produced. This intriguing and significant omission suggests that contemporaries thought that if one knew how to conceptualize, design, draw, and build, one could sell what one had made. In whatever structure an artisan worked, the guilds, the faubourg St-Antoine, or the royal workshops, the emphasis was on *making* beautiful things; publicity and sales would automatically follow. Even practices we normally associate with sales, like the display and the delivery of goods, had, in this world, more to do with the culture of production than with a consumer culture.

Artisans normally left furniture in the workshop for a few days after finishing it so workers from the neighborhood could drop in, study it, and learn from the work of their colleagues.[15] And great pomp and circumstance surrounded the delivery of goods—in procession—not as would become the case with nineteenth-century department store deliveries to impress the neighbors, but as a display of the artisans' prowess and pride in their creation of beauty. The importance of such processions was part of why the furnishing guild chose to attack the free artisans of the faubourg by winning the right to confiscate their products between the shop and the customer's home. They thereby forced the artisans of the faubourg to deliver their work secretly, in shame, under the cover of darkness, rather than in proud procession. The culture of production thus involved the trades as a whole. Without knowledge, skill, and craft sense artisans were doomed to repetitive, uncreative work, and to a vulnerability to changes in the organization of production resulting from the pressures of external competition.[16]

15. Pardailhé-Galabrun, *Naissance de l'intime,* 94.
16. Stoerckel and Prévost, "Tourneurs sur bois," in *Exposition universelle de 1867, à Paris,* ed. M. F. Devinck (Paris, 1868), 3:11 (each article in this useful work begins with a new page 1. For all subsequent note citations of the Devinck edition I list only author, subject, and vol. + pp.); Emile Gallé, "Le mobilier contemporain orné d'après la nature," *Revue des arts décoratifs* 20 (1900): 334.

The culture of production provided artisans with a mastery of their trade analogous to linguistic mastery. Creating a piece of furniture was not unlike creating a sentence for a native speaker of a language. In both cases the makers of furniture or of speech had a repertoire, which consisted of the rules of the trade, or the grammar and vocabulary of a language; a sense of audience, which constrained what could be made or said and how, if one wanted to be understood; and individual creativity, which enabled one to construct unique objects or utterances that were both correct and comprehensible.[17]

Artisans working within the variegated structures of production of the Old Regime and trained within the culture of production invented an ever-expanding repertoire of form. Studying style, in the genealogical sense—looking for the chain of individual master-pupil relationships—or in the hermeneutic sense—looking for the form which represents the Truth—is not the way to understand what furniture looked like or why. For any style, there were few true innovators, in the sense of creating a form or object.[18] Changes in style might alter the form of an existing piece of furniture, such as curving what was once a straight line, adding inlay, using a new kind of varnish; they might create entirely new pieces of furniture. Either case involved a first time, an inventor; all who followed, whether they lived in the same block at the same time or practiced the same trade a century later, were mere imitators.[19] Yet unless a worker made a perfect reproduction, it was never a case of pure imitation, any more than an individual can imitate another's speech. The end result, the appearance of a chair, was a product of a process of which artisanal innovations, marketing inspiration, influence from abroad, and consumer needs were critical elements.

Any change in the existing form, material, or technique of furniture was an innovation. It did not have to be dramatic. Even the most minor shift in the degree of curvature of a leg, or of the form of a dresser could fundamentally alter its appearance and was innovative, as was a small technical one—an alteration in the glue formula or a new joint. The

17. Bernard Deloche has constructed a related but different linguistic model for furniture production (*L'art du meuble*, 128–36). For a similar, non-linguistically based argument see Bertrand, *Le meuble et l'homme*, 83–84.

18. On a parallel track, see Carla Hesse on the revolutionary invention of the male author in "Reading Signatures," *Eighteenth-Century Studies* 22 (spring 1989): 469–87.

19. André Boutemy, *Analyses stylistiques et essais d'attribution de meubles français anonymes du XVIIIe siècle* (Brussels, 1973), 11–12.

creation of a new object, however banal, was innovative. Examples of successful eighteenth-century changes were rolltop desks; needlework tables; movable chairs; love seats; a kind of lacquer called *verni Martin;* a new gilding process; the vanishing-cube style of marquetry; the use of mother-of-pearl in inlay work; new leg curves on tables and chairs; and the generalized lightening (both visually and materially) of furniture. The use of a new material or of an old material in a new way was innovative. Thus, innovations with dramatic stylistic consequences could be subtle, individual, and technical.

Changes in style were in part the result of the accumulation of innovation. To study changes in style is therefore to study the end of a long process that had its origins not only in previous works of masters but of hours spent in workshops on a piece's smallest detail. One artisan would discover a way to make a joint a little stronger; he would tell another. That artisan, after testing the joint, would adopt it. Two years later another artisan, unknown to the first, would realize that the strength of this new, and by then common, joint allowed him to make another chair shape, one he had been imagining for years. If his dreamed-of new chair sold, and if the form could be adopted to other pieces besides chairs, a new style was conceived. If it did not sell, the innovative joint would be put to other uses. The innovation had, nonetheless, happened.

Understanding the process of innovation within the culture of production is crucial to understanding shifts in style; but understanding the culture of production requires examining the complex of material and symbolic relations among the practitioners of the furniture-making trades and their transmission. During the ancien régime the reproduction of those relations was still predominantly internal to the trades. Two institutions that would later channel the transmission of knowledge, skill, and craft sense—schools and museums—had already made their appearance by the late eighteenth century, but their role in reproducing the trades was still very limited.The beginnings of French technical education were in the seventeenth century, but the Ecole spéciale de dessin (founded in 1766) sought to provide all workers in the "mechanical" arts with training in classical as well as technical subjects.[20] The Ecole nationale des arts décoratifs—intended for the children of workers—was created in 1763 on the initiative of Bachelier and sustained by private donations before it became the Ecole royale gratuite de dessin in 1767 with lettres patentes of Louis XV by request of the guilds of the city of Paris; it continued into the

20. Quef, *Histoire de l'apprentissage,* 77; AN F^{12}1422.

nineteenth century, changing name from time to time. The Ecole nationale d'arts et métiers was founded around 1780 by the duc de la Rochefoucauld-Liancourt for the children of soldiers. In the nineteenth century it became an engineering school, the Ecole des arts et métiers at Châlons-sur-Marne, but in the eighteenth century it remained primarily a military school.[21] The Convention (1792–94) created the Conservatoire des arts et métiers (1794), and under the Empire the Rapport d'Acquier (1799) determined the rules of technical instruction.[22]

These schools, however important as models for the later transformation of the trades in the second half of the nineteenth century, trained very few furniture makers in the eighteenth. Museums, where artisans could learn from what others had done, were even scarcer and more inaccessible.[23] Most artisans in the Old Regime, if they were to have the knowledge, skill, and craft sense necessary for true mastery of their trade, including the processes of innovation, started their professional life as apprentices, followed either by a *tour de France* as a *compagnon* within the *compagnonnage*, or journeymanship, in the town in which they had been apprenticed.

The "Sons": Apprenticeship

> It means a trained body, which lives on its nerves; and the training, the restructuring of the body is what apprenticeship is all about. So it may be said that while bakers make the bread, the bread also makes the bakers; if the population needs bread to live, the artisanal form needs the bakers' bodies in order to survive. The relations of production produce the people who will reproduce them.[24]

Apprenticeship was the norm of artisanal training in the furniture trades, whether they were being practiced in the guilds, royal workshops, or in the faubourg St-Antoine. To get started in a trade, a child would be sent out in early adolescence to live, work, and learn in the house and work-

21. Edouard Thomas Charton, ed., *Dictionnaire des professions, ou guide pour le choix d'un état*, 3d ed. (Paris, 1880), 55–56, 62–63.

22. Gaston Valran, *Préjugés d'autrefois et carrières d'aujourd'hui* (Toulouse, 1908), 276.

23. Ibid., 267.

24. Daniel Bertaux and Isabelle Bertaux-Wiame, "Artisanal Bakery in France," in *The Petite Bourgeoisie*, ed. Frank Bechhofer and Brian Elliott (New York, 1981), 175.

shop of a master.[25] The parents would sign a contract with the master specifying the terms of the apprenticeship, including whether the apprenticeship was to be fee-paying or free of charge.[26] Payment of a fee spared apprentices from domestic labor in the master's household but presumably made their status within the household somewhat less filial.[27] The master would teach apprentices the basics of the trade so they could emerge five, six, or seven years later as competent journeymen. The length of the apprenticeship was set as much by the perceived labor needs of the trades as by the length of time demanded for mastery of the craft. An accepted, if tacit, feature of the system was that apprentices took on a certain amount of errand running, cleaning, and preparatory rough work—tasks not central to their education but necessary to the shop's existence. The role of the master and spouse as substitute parents was, in contrast, an explicit element in the arrangement. They were responsible for the moral as well as trade education of the apprentice. Apprenticeship thus served multiple functions: it provided cheap labor for some of the industry's dullest, heaviest, and least skilled tasks; it was a period of hazing, of teaching boys to be men; and it was the time to begin acquiring the elements necessary for the trade. In a heavily familial trade, where sons often followed their fathers, it separated parents and children at the moment when the strains of adolescence may have been especially fierce, rendering the training of children by parents difficult.[28]

25. On apprenticeship and journeymanship as important means of socialization and hazing, see S. Kaplan, "Luxury Guilds," 288–92. For eighteenth-century apprenticeship within the guild see "Statuts et privilèges ordonnances et règlements" (AN AD XI 11); and Verlet, *L'art du meuble*, 22.

26. For the apprenticeship contract and the paternal/filial relation between master and apprentice, see Hippolyte Blanc, *Les corporations de métiers* (Paris, 1898), 133–37.

27. This argument is made by Quef (*Histoire de l'apprentissage*, 79), whereas Kaplan ("Luxury Guilds," 283) argues that apprentices in the luxury trades tended to pay for their training while those in the more common trades did not.

28. For the paternal role of the master, the contractual nature of the relationship, and the obligations of the apprentice, see H. Blanc, *Les corporations de métiers*, 133–37. For an analysis of the importance of apprenticeship in teaching masculinity, see Ava Baron, "Questions of Gender," *Gender and History* 1 (summer 1989): 178–99; and Keith McClelland, "Masculinity and the 'Representative Artisan' in Britain, 1850–1880," *Gender and History* 1 (summer 1989): 164–77. For the need to separate parents and children in training in the trades, see Jacques-Louis Ménétra, *Journal of My Life*, trans. Arthur Goldhammer (New York, 1986), xi; Carole Shammas, "The Domestic Environment in Early Modern England and America," *Journal of Social History* 14 (fall 1980): 3–24. Dena Goodman notes an

Sons tended to follow fathers in all of the woodworking trades. There were famous examples like the Foliot, Delorme, and Cresson families, as well as many less celebrated families. Guild *menuisier* Nicolas Foliot (d. 1749) ran a distinguished workshop—which counted the crown and court among its clientele—within the community of guild *menuisiers* in the rue de Cléry. He had three sons, one of whom became a *marchand mercier*, the other two, Nicolas Quinbert (d. 1776) and François (d. 1761) became *menuisiers*. François married, had two sons—François II and Toussaint— and in his turn took over his father's workshop. François II became a *menuisier* and Toussaint became one of the king's sculptors. In 1761, François II took over his dead father's workshop under his mother's di- rection. François II became even more distinguished than his father and grandfather had been and not only worked for the Garde-Meuble but made Louis XVI's Versailles bed. Nicolas Quinbert Foliot left his father's work- shop to establish his own in the colony of the rue de Cléry. He came to play an important role in the guild as well as to build furniture for Versailles, Trianon, Compiègne, and Fontainebleau. He counted among his patrons Marie-Antoinette, the comtesse de Provence, the comte d'Artois, and Mme du Barry. Whereas the Foliot family was unusual in its continuity and productivity across generations, their story is far from unique.

It may appear paradoxical that relations of pseudo-kinship should be so important in trades in which sons tended to follow fathers and daughters of *ébénistes* and *menuisiers* tended to marry other woodworkers, but the character of pseudo-kinship is crucial. Apprentices in the Old Regime were not taken on in the case of "missing" sons; apprentices were to be "like" sons but were not sons.[29] Simona Cerutti's work on Italian guilds em- phasizes the same point in a different way. Her research makes clear that apprentices were not taken on because there were no sons—sons of the appropriate age were sent elsewhere to be replaced by apprentices from outside the family. Thus the trade bonds of pseudo-kinship were reinforced even at the cost of the literal bonds of fathers and sons.[30]

interesting parallel here: *salonnières* often "took apprentices," who were rarely their own daughters ("Filial Rebellion in the Salon," 28–47, esp. 37).

29. On the intimacy of the relations among furniture makers see Janneau, *Les ateliers parisiens*, 10, chap. 4; Raymonde Monnier, *Le faubourg Saint-Antoine, 1780–1815* (Paris, 1980), 209. As Sonenscher argues, "The act of apprenticeship was analogous to the primordial alienation of natural liberty. It implied entry into the rule-bound social existence of civil society, embodied in this instance by the statutes of particular corporations" (*Work and Wages*, 75).

30. Cerutti, "Group Strategies," 115–18.

Michael Sonenscher emphasizes the nontechnical needs fulfilled by apprenticeship: "The elaborate prescriptions of eighteenth-century apprenticeship regulations conceal imperatives that owed as much to formal definitions of adulthood, family strategies, and local economic circumstances as to the techniques of the trades." I am not sure that they "conceal" imperatives as much as reveal that definitions of adulthood, family strategies, and local economic circumstances were not separable from teaching the techniques of a trade.[31] All this is not to say that the system was without problems in the eighteenth century; there were certainly abuses. Many apprentices did not fill out their time, and masters sometimes used them simply as cheap labor.[32] Under the familial-cum-political order of the ancien régime, such abuses did not threaten the system as such. By contrast, when the *Cahiers de doléance* demanded the continuation of apprenticeship contracts, though voluntary, they indicated their acceptance of apprenticeship as a viable system, one best regulated by law.[33] After the Revolution, after the death of the father-king and the development of a new system of state- and family-based paternal authority, the fictive paternity that underlay apprenticeship became more and more difficult to sustain.

The "Fathers": Mastership and the Masterpiece

The paternal figures in this system of pseudo-kin were the masters. They bore responsibility for their "child-son" apprentices and for their "adult [rival?]–son" journeymen. The master furniture maker was to work in his own shop with his own journeyman and two apprentices. The workshop was to be integrated into the home and family of the master, to ensure the paternal relation between apprentice and master. Very large workshops and isolated artisans as well violated this guild ethos. Just as the guilds were imagined as fundamental organizing units within the corporatist society,

---

31. Sonenscher, *Hatters,* 35. On the importance of the family analogy for apprenticeship and its socialization function see Grießinger, *Das symbolische Kapital der Ehre,* 57ff.

32. For a classic text of complaints about apprenticeship in the book trade see *Les misères de ce monde, ou complaintes facétieuses sur les apprentissages de differens arts et métiers* (London, 1783), 111–44; royal ordinances also indicated conflict between masters and their apprentices and journeymen, as for example, "Ordonnance du roi, qui défen aux Garçons et Compagnons de quelque Profession, Art et Métier . . . de s'attrouper, cabaler contre les Maîtres" [19 March 1786] (AN AD XI 11); and John Rule, "The Property of Skill," in *The Historical Meanings of Work,* ed. Patrick Joyce (Cambridge, 1987), 105–6.

33. Quef, *Histoire de l'apprentissage,* 110.

so the families and workshops of the masters were organizing units within the guilds.

Whereas the apprenticeship system emphasized the importance of the fictiveness of the kinship relation, guild regulations concerning mastership emphasized biological kinship. Sons of masters had to pay little or nothing to join the guilds and were exempt from the masterpiece requirement, those defined as "foreign" had higher fees to pay as well as a masterpiece to produce. There was a finely calibrated scale of foreignness: an artisan who was not the child of a master but who had been apprenticed in the same town paid more than a biological son, but less than a stranger to the town, and was usually required to prepare a masterpiece.[34] Thus the corporate system, in its encouragement of exogamous apprenticeships, helped to extend the family-in-trade beyond the immediate biological family while, in the rules governing access to mastership, it reasserted the idea of genetic inheritance. A fictive father was not a biological father.

No doubt both the relative openness of apprenticeship and closure of the ranks of masters assured an adequate supply of apprentices even when a shortage of sons minimized competition by limiting access to the mastership. But there was another logic as well. Guild masters were not only the fathers of their apprentices, and the father-rivals of the journeymen, but were also municipal fathers. In becoming a master of the guild, an artisan became an incorporated member of the city, a full-fledged citizen with civic and religious responsibilities. The high financial cost of mastership for "foreigners" to the city reflected the difficulties they faced in terms of social place as well.[35]

This is not to say that all masters were equal, for that was far from the case; there was a hierarchy of *syndics* and *jurés*, of "maîtres modernes et jeunes." Guilds were elaborate hierarchical structures, which organized municipal relations to the crown and kept social and religious order in the cities as they dealt with the economic relations of the trades.[36] In theory,

34. Verlet, *L'art du meuble*, 20. Before the reform of 1776, the fees varied from 121 livres for the son of a *maître juré* or an *ancien maître juré* to 536 livres (and another 100 livres to replace six years of compagnonnage) for someone foreign to the community. The reforms of 1776 leveled this variation at 500 livres.

35. For detailed information on mastership within the guild of *menuisiers ébénistes*, see *Statuts, Privilèges, Ordonnances et Reglemens de la Communauté des Maîtres Menuisiers et Ebénistes de la Ville, Fauxbourgs et banlieue de Paris* (Paris, 1751); AN AD XI 18, 22, and 27; and Verlet, *L'art du meuble*, 12–23. On recruitment within the furniture trades see Kaplan, "Luxury Guilds," 281.

36. For a persuasive discussion of the political role of the guilds see Cerutti, "Group Strategies," 102–47.

Figure 21. *Secrétaire en armoire*, France, transition period. Rosewood, dyed pearwood, *bois de violette, mahogany, buis, ivory, amarante.* 39 × 31 × 14.5 cm. *Chef d'oeuvre de maîtrise* (masterpiece for admission to the guild). Collection Vendeuvre, Louvre des antiquaires.

every master was to produce a masterpiece to prove his worth as an artisan, as a fictive father, and as a man. This masterpiece was defined in aesthetic as well as technical terms, as the chef d'oeuvre shown in Figure 21 indicates. This was an eighteenth-century *secrétaire* done in miniature scale to render the task more demanding and more delicate. Men had to demonstrate their ability to produce beauty in order to be deemed truly adult men within the trade. This demonstration, rather than a show of strength, of entrepre- neurial success, or of wealth, justified their roles as fathers. The emphasis on manhood through aesthetic and technical prowess continued a tradition masters had learned as journeymen.

The Fraternity of Compagnons: A Contentious Symbiosis

> [T]he innkeeper is the father of the compagnons, his wife is their mother; the children of the hotelier and the servants are their brothers and sisters.[37]

The intermediate stage in becoming a fully fledged artisan was that of journeymanship. In principle, one then moved into full adulthood as a master, but by the eighteenth century many journeymen were unable to become guild masters.[38] In the structuring of pseudo-masculine kinship discussed here, the journeymen occupied a complicated place. They, like the apprentices, were within the familial metaphor, being in a certain sense their masters' sons, and the apprentices' older brothers. But they could also be independent and therefore rivals of the father-masters. Indeed, it was a frequent practice for the widow of a master to marry her dead husband's journeyman. The two most celebrated instances were the marriage of Jean François Oeben's widow with Jean Henri Riesener and of Joseph Poitou's widow with Charles Cressent. Cressent (d. 1768) went to work in the workshop of the *ébéniste* Joseph Poitou in 1714.[39] In 1719 he took over the workshop and the store on the fashionable place des Victoires as well as the title of *ébéniste du duc d'Orléans* (the regent), when he married Poitou's widow. He continued to do well, working for the nobility and royalty of Europe—including Jean V of Portugal and the elector Charles-Albert of Bavaria—although he died deeply in debt. The story of Jean François Oeben (d. 1763) was similar. He trained in the workshop of Charles-Joseph Boulle (the son of André-Charles Boulle) and at his death in 1754 took over his title of *ébéniste du roi aux Gobelins*, with its accompanying workshop and

---

37. *Almanach des métiers pour 1852* (Paris, 1852), 62.

38. Alfred Franklin, in *Comment on devenait patron* (Paris, 1889), 90–91, associates the sixteenth-century development of journeymanship with an effort by the masters to limit access to, and the practice of, the trade; earlier artisans had passed directly from apprentice- to mastership. On becoming guild masters see Merry E. Wiesner, "Guilds, Male Bonding, and Women's Work in Early Modern Germany," *Gender and History* 1 (summer 1989): 125–38; Sonenscher, *Hatters,* 139–40.

39. Marie-Juliette Ballot, "Charles Cressent, ébéniste du régent," *Revue d'art ancien et moderne* (1919): 237–53; André Boutemy, "L'avènement du style Louis XV," *Connaissance des arts* 70 (December 1957): 132–37.

apartment. In 1756 he moved his workshop to the Arsenal where he started his labor on Louis XV's desk of state.[40] In 1763, three years after starting the desk, he died and his wife declared bankruptcy, although she continued to operate the business with the help of two of her dead husband's compagnons: Jean Henri Riesener and J. M. Leleu. Riesener and Leleu entered into an all-or-nothing contest—for control of the business, the right to finish the king's desk, and for the master's widow. In 1767 Riesener won, although both went on to have spectacular careers.[41]

Journeymen were, in a certain sense, then, their masters' adult sons and rivals—rivals for expertise in the trade, rivals sexually, and perhaps rivals for the younger sons'—the apprentices'—admiration and respect. To complicate the story yet further, journeymanship refers both to the status intermediate between apprentice and master and to the organization of those in that status—the compagnonnage. Journeymen's associations were very specifically male organizations. Merry Wiesner documents how German journeymen often did not marry even after all chances of achieving mastership had passed but continued to live in all-male housing.[42]

Compagnonnage was the unofficial, and illegal, organization of male workers who had finished their apprenticeships and were embarking on their *tour de France* as journeymen. The tour lasted from three to seven years and was intended to give young workers the opportunity to finish their training and to learn a variety of techniques in their trade. It was also designed to create an identity based on work and on an allegiance to a trade. Woodworkers were to learn to be artisans and compagnons first, with other identifications weakened. The compagnonnage was a central element in the construction of the culture of production, at least from the Old Regime through the early part of the nineteenth century.[43]

40. Janneau, *Les ateliers parisiens*, 159ff.; Alfred Darcel, "Oeben, Riesener, et Maugie aux Gobelins," *Nouvelles archives d'art français* 3d s., 1 (1885): 166; Nadine Gauchat, "A Royal Desk by Oeben and Riesener," *International Studio* 98 (February 1931): 47–48; Jules-Joseph Guiffrey, "Oeben, Riesener: le bureau du roi au Louvre," *Forum artistique* (March 1887): 39–45.

41. Charles Séné, "Contrat de mariage de Riesener avec la veuve d'Oeben," *Nouvelles archives d'art français* (1878): 319–38; Pierre Kjellberg, "Leleu, le plus grand ébéniste français sous Louis XVI," *Connaissance des arts* 123 (May 1962): 58–65.

42. Wiesner, "Guilds, Male Bonding, and Women's Work," 129.

43. On illegality, see "Arrest de la Cour du Parlement" of 12 November 1778, in AN AD XI 11. On socialization of journeymen and the unity of identity, status, and group memberships see Grießinger, *Das symbolische Kapital der Ehre;* Cynthia M. Truant, "*Compagnonnage:* Symbolic Action and the Defense of Workers' Rights in France, 1700–1848" (Ph.D. diss., University of Chicago, 1978); and Mary

Compagnonnage was an elaborate and complex network of institutions modeled on both the corporations and the confraternities of the Old Regime.[44] It provided a structure for every aspect of the compagnon's life from the time of initiation through death, although active participation usually ceased when the compagnon completed the tour. Rituals played a crucial role in the lives of the compagnons. The chain of ritual started with the initiation, which Cynthia Truant argues took the form of a classical rite of passage. After initiation, the compagnon was to belong exclusively to his brothers. The compagnonnage did, however, retain the values the initiate had learned in his old world: obedience, loyalty, honesty, and brotherhood. This retention of old values served a functional purpose for the compagnonnage: "*Compagnonnage*, by informing its own association with the same types of values and norms found in these legally recognized institutions of French society, sought to legitimate itself in the eyes of its members and to appropriate for itself the powers inherent in such institutions."[45] In the last stage of initiation, the initiate was given a new name in a secular baptism.

Mary Ann Clawson further develops this argument, stating that compagnonnage provided an alternative family for late adolescents who were waiting to take their place in society.[46] Compagnonnage created a fictive kin system for young men, giving them a community and an affirmation of their distinct place in society as men. Each town within the system had a lodging house for the compagnons, called the *mère*, which was staffed by a mature couple known as the *père* and the *mère*. It is interesting

---

Ann Clawson, "Early Modern Fraternalism and the Patriarchal Family," *Feminist Studies* 6 (summer 1980): 368–91. For the place of the compagnonnage in the training of furniture-makers, see Ministère du travail, *Associations professionnelles ouvrières* (Paris, 1894–1904), 2:674–75; Rémi Gossez, *Les ouvriers de Paris* (Paris, 1968), 143; Alphonse Baude and A. Loizel, "Ebénistes," in *Exposition universelle de 1867, à Paris*, ed. Devinck, 1:5; Pierre du Maroussem, *La question ouvrière: les ébénistes du faubourg Saint-Antoine* (Paris, 1892), 68, argues that *ébénistes* were only very rarely compagnons, but he is a rather lone voice.

44. The position I have taken here is closer to that of Sewell than of Sonenscher in their debate on the meaning of compagnonnage (Sonenscher, *Hatters*, 144; and "Mythical Work: Workshop Production and the *Compagnonnages* of Eighteenth-Century France," in *The Historical Meanings of Work*, ed. Patrick Joyce [Cambridge, 1987], 31–63; William H. Sewell, Jr., *Work and Revolution in France* [Cambridge, 1980]).

45. For the rituals see Cynthia M. Truant, "Solidarity and Symbolism among Journeymen Artisans: The Case of the *Compagnonnage*," *Comparative Studies in Society and History* 21 (April 1979): 214–25; and her "*Compagnonnage*," 121.

46. Clawson, "Early Modern Fraternalism and the Patriarchal Family."

to note that while the *père* was only a person, the *mère* was both a person and a place—nurturer and nurturing environment. The *mère* served as a convivial gathering point for the compagnons in the town; the individuals *père* and *mère* may have been available for advice to the young compagnons. I agree that the compagnonnage created a structure modeled on the family yet emphasize that these symbolic ties were fundamentally *masculine* kinship ties. The only female elements in these networks of fictive kin were the *mères*. There were no sisters, aunts, or female cousins. Nor were there wives; compagnons could be full-fledged, active members only if they remained unmarried. The consistent exclusion of women from all the formal systems of training in the wood trades reinforces their general exclusion from the domain of production.

Notwithstanding the governing familial metaphor, women had very little place in this organization of economic and municipal space. Women did work in the furnishings trades, as varnishers, sanders, gilders, and upholsterers. Both varnishing and gilding were finishing processes involving a high level of meticulousness but little possibility for creativity.[47] All these auxiliary trades altered little from the late eighteenth century to the 1920s. They were not mechanizable and had always been highly specialized. The wood trades themselves employed essentially no women since the taboo against women handling sharp tools and working wood was very strong. Clearly, masters' wives were often heavily involved in the businesses, but since they could have no role in the polity, their role within the guild structure was very limited as well. Women did take a critical role in the running of the trade as widows. Within the guild, widows of masters usually had the right to continue their dead husband's business if they were employing qualified journeymen, or if they had sons who could continue in the trade. They could run the businesses alone in an exceptional instance—by virtue of their relation to a man.

The rarity of women carpenters, *menuisiers*, and *ébénistes* is underlined by a postcard of a woman carpenter, proudly displayed at the Maison de l'outil et de la pensée ouvrière in Troyes and noted as the only such in the region. The other exception was the practice in the late nineteenth century of woodworking as a hobby for leisured women.[48] Furniture making was a masculine trade, in which men proved their manliness through the

---

47. For a concise technical description of gilding see *L'art et l'industrie* 1 (1877): text before pl. 17.

48. Antony Valabrègue, "Les arts de la femme," *Revue des arts décoratifs* 18 (1898): 174.

creation of beauty. In both the eighteenth and nineteenth centuries women would, although in very different ways, take on significant roles as the consumers of this furniture, but that is a story for later chapters.

Breaking ties with real kin and fostering a social network of brothers were essential ingredients in a culture of production that transmitted artisanal knowledge, skill, and craft sense within the political economy of an absolutist regime. Even though many young men did follow family tradition in becoming woodworkers, it was nonetheless crucial, if the trade was to grow, that the younger generation of artisans learn from workers other than their parents, and be tied by other than literal familial ties to the trade. Beyond craft skill, creating a culture of production meant creating a community, based in the work process, and extending far beyond it. The compagnonnage linked artisans within a social world and a work world, with rules of sociability along with craft technique. The next generation of artisans needed the skill to carry out their trade, the knowledge to design, and the sense of community and loyalty to protect their trade from encroachments.

Following his initiation, the compagnon began his tour. He would be met in each new town by a *rôleur*, whose job was to greet the brother, make sure of his authenticity, and provide the welcoming ritual. The *rôleur* would place the newcomer in a job in town; if no work was available, the compagnons of that town would give him enough money to get to the next. The compagnon's leave-taking was also accompanied by great ceremony. Once a man was accepted into the compagnonnage he was assured of work, if there was any to be had. He was also assured of a decent wage; in each town the compagnons negotiated wages with the masters and boycotted any master who tried to pay less. In case of illness or accident a compagnon was also guaranteed financial assistance, and a proper funeral at the time of his death. In exchange for these privileges and services, the compagnon was pledged to secrecy, reciprocity, and to defense of the rite. These trade-union-like activities presumed not simply that each compagnon was a wage earner but that he was a fellow artisan, sharing knowledge, skill, and taste with his brothers.

A side effect of the modeling of the compagnonnage on the corporate system of the Old Regime was its disunity. There were different, and rival, corporations within what could have been defined as one trade—the division between the corporations of the *menuisiers* and *ébénistes* being one example—as well as a lack of solidarity among guilds controlling the same trades in different cities, or different guilds within the same city. Similarly two rival groups, or rites, within the seventeenth-century compagnonnage spawned a third in the late eighteenth century. Each rite accused the others of inauthenticity. When two journeymen met on the road, they would inquire as to the affiliation of the other. If they belonged to different rites, or if one of the journeymen claimed to be a compagnon while practicing an "unworthy" trade, they fought, sometimes to the death. The source of conflict was not just allegiance to a sect; workers in the traditional construction trades contested the legitimacy of the trades that had come more recently to the compagnonnage: the shoemakers, upholsterers, bakers, weavers, carriage makers, and others. The discrimination was based on knowledge.[49] Besides provoking these bloody confrontations, the rites also served to regulate the flow of labor. Each trade within a town was "owned" by one rite, and all intruders from other sects were summarily evicted (exceptions were large cities like Paris where the rites might divide the city instead).

The splits and the conflicts they engendered did not undercut the most important aspect of the compagnonnage, which was augmenting and transmitting the repertoire of knowledge within each trade.[50] Unity within each trade and across the different rites was unnecessary for knowledge and skill to be effectively passed on. The conflicts between rites may even have helped foster adolescent fidelity to a rite and to a trade. Thus, the compagnonnage was not an early trade union and was not based either on notions of class consciousness, nor even on "trade consciousness," in the nineteenth-century definitions of the terms. Notions of art and of aesthetic capability were deeply embedded in the very identity of a compagnon.

The importance of the chef d'oeuvre—the piece to demonstrate mastery—within the compagnonnage clearly demonstrates the difference between this organization and the trade unions that were to follow in the 1860s.[51] At the end of his period of compagnonnage, each individual was to make a masterpiece. Works of fantastic complexity, taking years to complete, they were intended to demonstrate mastery of all the techniques of the trade and to show a capacity for innovation. As the compagnons generally crafted their chefs d'oeuvre during the years spent on the road as journeymen, those who worked in trades where one normally produced

49. Perdiguier, *Livre du compagnonnage*, 2:207.
50. Ulrich-Christian Pallach, "Fonctions de la mobilité artisanale et ouvrière," *Francia: Forschungen zur Westeuropäischen Geschichte* 11 (1983): 365–406.
51. Fine examples of the masterpieces of the compagnons may be seen at the Musée du compagnonnage in Tours, and at the Musée des arts et traditions populaires in Paris (hereafter, ATP).

Figure 22. "Arbre à sabots." François-Louis Touzet (d. 1940).
Compagnon's masterpiece. Musée des arts et traditions populaires.

large objects—the wrought-iron workers, *menuisiers*, carriage makers—
made miniatures. Those who worked in smaller scale objects, the *sabotiers*
(wooden-shoe makers), for example, sometimes made gigantic wooden
shoes. The works produced were often humorous: they included, by a
compagnon-sabotier, a carved tree, approximately three feet tall, well
adorned with leaves, and, in the guise of fruit, miniature wooden shoes
(Figure 22). Another wooden-shoe maker made a pair of gigantic sabots,
carved out of one piece of wood, each about two feet long and linked
together at the toes by an unbroken wooden chain (in the Musée du
compagnonnage in Tours). The list could go on. There were wooden shoes
whose surface was worked to look like lizard, or patent leather, inlaid
wooden shoes, giant and miniature wooden shoes. The blacksmiths, too,

created a range of astonishing objects, all made out of either full-, exaggerated-, or reduced-scale products of their trade: horseshoes, nails, and other shoeing equipment. A *marqueteur* who specialized in mother-of-pearl made a miniature of a mother-of-pearl-polishing lathe, itself in mother-of-pearl, decorated with a greyhound and a rabbit.[52]

The *compagnons-menuisiers'* chefs d'oeuvre were, in some sense, more limited than those of the wooden-shoe makers or blacksmiths; the *menuisiers* did not have the same possibilities of playing with scale. They could, and did, reduce the scale, but they could not increase it. Another distinction was that the *compagnons-menuisiers* did not suffer from the banality of *sabotiers* and locksmiths. Even a perfect reduction of a well-conceived chair was an object of beauty and intrigue; the miniaturization itself forced a use of particularly developed skills. But a horseshoe, a nail or a wooden shoe, whether large or small, unless one transformed it, was of a crushing familiarity. But in any case we see considerable fantasy, imagination, and skill in Agricol Perdiguier's spiral staircase, or other otherwise complicated staircases built by a variety of compagnons.[53] The compagnons often conceived their masterpieces as objects that could, technically, have been built full scale, but that never would be because while structurally and technically sound they were functionally useless or prohibitively complex. The *compagnons-menuisiers, compagnons-tourneurs* (turners), and *compagnons-tapissiers* (upholsterers) presented numerous miniaturized pieces of furniture as chefs d'oeuvre. Like the staircases, in these masterpieces the inventiveness sometimes showed itself through the extraordinarily virtuoso nature of the design rather than through a more obvious humorous quality. Demonstrating the virtuosity of the turner in the masterpiece shown in Figure 23—and giving it the tremulous quality of a "trembleur"—was the combination of the exceedingly narrow central shaft and the rings ornamenting it. Innovativeness, ingenuity, and audacity, as well as humor, were part of the definition of a successful chef d'oeuvre.

Chefs d'oeuvre were also used to resolve conflicts between rival sects.[54] In the case of a dispute over the "ownership" of a town, the best workers

52. These objects are in the Collection Vendeuvre and were shown in an exhibit, "Mobilier miniature: objets de maîtrise XVI–XXè siècles," at the Louvre des Antiquaires, 7 November 1986–1 March 1987.

53. See the drawings in Perdiguier, *Livre du compagnonnage*, opposite 1:204, 205.

54. As Sonenscher notes ("Mythical Work," 53), men competed through the demonstration of skill.

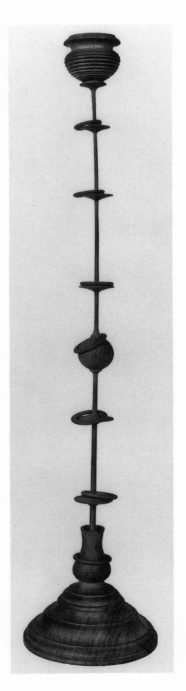

Figure 23. "Trembleur."
Compagnon Maurice
Puisais, dit Tourangeau.
Buis. Compagnon's
masterpiece. Musée du
compagnonnage, Tours.

of the two sects would be enclosed for a set time, during which period they were to produce a collective masterpiece. The two works were judged—by "a number of conscientious men who are expert in architecture and the *trait.*"[55] Whichever sect won would have undisputed exclusive rights to work in that town. In the end, the right to work was to be determined not on the basis of brute force, longevity, necessity, or an ideal of a universal "right to work," but on the basis of skill and knowledge. The chefs d'oeuvre were the products and symbols of that knowledge.

In the eighteenth century the compagnonnage was a national organization, uniting unattached young male workers into one of three rites that gave them fictive kin, support in times of trouble, training, and work. It wove a lively ritual life, spiced with secrecy and mystery, along with an elaborate series of myths describing the origins of the organizations. Individual compagnons were in perpetual motion, their ties to their families and their native regions weakened, their whole lives structured by the compagnonnage. And, while the compagnonnage was fundamentally in an adversarial position toward society at large, it was based on it and shared many of its values. Likewise intended to defend compagnons from masters, the organization was patterned after the masters' own, and ties with ex-compagnons who became masters were maintained. Attempts were made during the Old Regime to abolish the compagnonnage, but they were halfhearted, because just as the compagnonnage appropriated parts of the dominant culture, it was, in some ways, useful to that society.

This ambiguous position of interiority and exteriority, imitation and opposition, was a consistent theme of artisans' organizations, and of artisans' aesthetic from the Old Regime until the First World War. Neither organizational models nor aesthetic forms could emerge exclusively from within an artisanal culture of production; yet innovation in both areas required possession of knowledge as well as a certain position in the social organization of production.

This particular paternalist system for bringing the young up in a trade suffered a severe shock with the Revolution. With the Revolution came a shift in the familial metaphor from the king and queen as father and mother to a fraternal image of the nation.[56] The beheading of the father-king, combined with the ideology of the free worker selling his labor for the best price on the market, fatally undermined the culture of production. Compagnonnage continued in a weakened form for another forty years,

55. Perdiguier, *Livre du compagnonnage*, 1:72.
56. Ibid., 49.

and versions of it and apprenticeship remain to the present day, but the state was to come to play a different role in the transmission of knowledge, skill, and craft sense. With the Revolution came increasing encroachment of the public into the private in a very direct, rather than solely meta-phorical way.[57]

Under the absolute monarchies of the Old Regime, not only was the king's hegemony productive of social forms but, paradoxically, the limits to the monarch's power also contributed to richness of the stylistic repertoire constitutive and representative of political power. The crown could not have an absolute monopoly on style but rather needed to allow emulation; yet, that emulation enhanced rather than diminished the crown's centrality in matters of style. The crown could not limit production to its royal work-shops, nor could it protect the guilds from the competition of the faubourg. Yet this complex system of production and distribution enabled foreigners to settle and work in France, bringing their contribution to its aesthetic heritage. The crown even set the model for how the trades were to be reproduced: the paternalism of the state was mirrored in the paternalism of the trades. Governing relations of production, distribution, consumption and style were the exigencies produced by both the strengths and weak-nesses of the monarch.

Any system of rule necessarily implies some way of thinking the relations between the politics and the everyday and such a system must be pursued through relations of production, consumption, and distribution. Despite the Enlightenment, the elaboration of a noncourtly public sphere, and other challenges to absolute monarchy, long before 1789, the Revo-lution marked a watershed. The place of style and taste in the making of political power and order could no longer be the same once the principle of the centrality of the individual rather than of the corporate body was raised, and once the language of social groups within the nation became that of class rather than of order. With the end of absolute monarchy came the end, in France, of the possibility of the constitution and representation of the power of the state through a single style, for that form of power is characteristic of authoritarian rather than representative regimes. The state continued to be deeply preoccupied with the everyday, with the social relations of production, distribution, and consumption and with the taste

57. Lynn Hunt, "Révolution française et vie privée," in *De la révolution à la grande guerre*, ed. Michelle Perrot (Paris, 1987), 22.

of the people. But what the state was to be and how it was to achieve legitimacy and hegemony was highly uncertain for a long time. The making of bourgeois society and polity was not instantaneous; it was only late in the nineteenth century that new conceptions of individual, class, and nation took firm hold.

PART 2

FROM STYLE TO TASTE

Transitions to the Bourgeois Stylistic Regime

> The laws of taste have this fortunate quality—they accommodate themselves perfectly to the diverse *états* and they are applicable to all degrees of fortune.[1]
>
> The duration of a national taste is that of a phase of a civilization.[2]
>
> In the history of art, each century or each reign has its style.[3]

These three citations summarize the complicated relation between style and taste that arose following the Revolution. Taste came to be understood simultaneously as defined by class and wealth, and as linked to the nation as a whole, at least as long as its whole mode of life held. Style was regime-bound (in a monarchical system) or time-bound (in a republican system). The complex and varied positions on taste and style resulted from the rich and productive chaos nineteenth-century France inherited from the Revolution concerning the fundamental concepts of representation, nation, and state. With the destruction of absolute monarchy came the end of a system of social representation and economic organization as well as a political order. The nation and the state were no longer to be embodied in the king; the ruler, the state, and the nation could no longer be represented by the king's things. After 1789 people would no longer bow to the king's knife and fork but would come instead to pay homage to the flag, a much more abstract symbol of the nation and the state. And, as the abbé Sièyes

---

1. Charles Blanc, "Etude sur les arts décoratifs: les meubles," *Journal de menuiserie* 12 (1875): 22.
2. César Daly, *Architecture privée de Paris et des environs sous Napoléon III* (Paris, 1864), 1:13.
3. "Planche 6: boudoir Louis XVI," *Journal de menuiserie* 3 (1865): 34.

put it at the beginning of the century, "in the social state [*l'état social*] all is representation. It is to be found everywhere" rather than concentrated in the person of the king.[4]

Determining what it meant to be represented politically and socially and what nurtured the welfare of the nation, given the overthrow of the old system, became dominant problems of the century. The king as father had held the responsibility for the provisioning of his nation-children, but in the year III or 1794, Sieyès argued, "representation is the mother of manufacture and commerce as it is of economic and political progress [*progrès libéraux*]."[5] What was that to mean concretely? The problem of representation might also be understood as a problem of mediation—what or who was to mediate between the individual, the state, and the society? The mode of mediation that rapidly came to replace corporations and orders as the vehicle for the social (and sometimes political and juridical) representation of the individual was *class*. Classes were defined not only, and perhaps not even largely, by relation to the means of production, but also by knowledge and taste. With the shift from a society of orders to a society of classes, from an absolute monarchy to a constitutional monarch, came a shift from style as constitutive of political power to taste as constitutive of social place, leaving unresolved the relation of style, taste, and the nation.

In the first half of the nineteenth century, styles continued to be made by the interaction between the court and networks of production and distribution no longer tied to the court. The creation of a putatively free market in goods and in labor, the political weakness of the crown, the development of the bourgeoisie as a political and social force, and transformations in training meant that the system of production no longer produced a hegemony of one style. It was the very multiplicity of styles that created the possibility of *taste* as a means of constructing social meaning. It now appeared possible for all classes to be represented by their taste, rather than having their place in a society of orders and their relation to the king revealed by their *style*.

Thus, the French Revolution, while not eradicating monarchical regimes in France for all time, eliminated the possibility of absolute monarchy and broke the dynamic of the absolutist stylistic regime. With the destruction of the corporate system, the closing of the royal workshops, and the

4. Abbé Sieyès's opinion on constitutional matters, quoted in Pierre Rosanvallon, *Le sacre du citoyen: histoire du suffrage universel en France* (Paris, 1992), 66–67.

5. Ibid, 67, n. 1.

elaboration of the mythic goal of a "free" market in labor and goods, the state's relation to objects, to style, and to the aesthetic was necessarily transformed. Imbricated within this aesthetic transformation—if not caused by it—were new dynamics of how social and political power were constituted and deployed.

Successive imperial and monarchical governments tried, of course, with varying degrees of success to sustain a relation to style like that of the absolutist monarchies of the Old Regime. Napoleon was able to patronize a distinctively First Empire style along the lines of the courtly stylistic regime, but his was also the last regime to do so. The styles associated with the subsequent restoration monarchies did not dominate the market but competed with other styles. After the First Empire, styles were plural rather than singular, and the end of unitary style was itself indicative of the distance of nineteenth-century monarchies and empires from the abso-lutism of the Old Regime. Postrevolutionary monarchies and empires could not use style to signify their own power as had been possible before 1789; the styles they patronized were simulacra of a more regal era. For these were anachronistic monarchies coexisting with a society and polity dom-inated by the bourgeoisie (rather than by the court and aristocracy), challenged periodically by revolutions, and interspersed among republican regimes. Thus, the period from the First to the Third Republic, a transi-tional one between absolutism and republicanism, was characterized by the waning importance of the direct political usages of furniture and design and the onset of their social use.

Transforming the social as well as the ideological basis for political hegemony, the Revolution brought to political and social prominence for the duration of the century the elite group most commonly called the bourgeoisie. Its members did not work with their hands, work for hourly or piece wages, or have particles before their names. The bourgeoisie had no single political, religious, and philosophical outlook, yet within the bourgeoisie from the 1830s onward were identifiable, if conflicting, bour-geois positions on the newly framed "social question," by which members distinguished themselves first from the aristocracy and later in the century from the working class.

The "social question" emerged from the visible hardships, glaring in-equities, and urban growth accompanying industrial capitalism, in tandem with the breakdown of earlier understandings of responsibility for the poor. The bourgeoisie's search for a solution to the "social" problem entailed the elaboration of three—at times incompatible—theories: social economy with its rationalist vision of the household; moral economy with its hope of creating social peace through the universal imposition of bourgeois norms of family behavior; and political economy with its philosophy of noninterventionism.[6] Out of these competing philosophies emerged a complicated and contradictory web of discourses.

These discourses were not born ex nihilo; indeed, the seeds of all may be found in texts dating from the ancien régime. Yet they were distinctively postrevolutionary. The intellectual roots of political, social, and moral economy were deep; the dynamic of their development into social and political movements, policies, and practices came in the revolutionary rupture and transformations of the first thirty years of the nineteenth century. And throughout the century these discourses were critical in framing interventions by philanthropists and the state, on the one hand, and, on the other, artisanal and working-class interventions into the domain of the aesthetic and the everyday.

The notions of social utility and of a social domain were also results of the Revolution, which ended absolutism's paternalist metaphor (although not, of course, paternalism itself) for social and political relations. The regicide in 1793—which was also a parricide—forced a reconceptualization of the metaphorical apparatus of the state. The culture of production based on a metaphor of masculine kinship could not survive the beheading of the father, and much of the century was marked by the quest to replace that system with some other. The task required new means of training both artisans and consumers, a task complicated by a liberal state that frowned on state intervention. Recourse to the conception of "the social" marked off a space from the political—neither public nor private—to assure the reproduction and stability of the state and allow it to intervene, although only in carefully mediated ways.

The innovators in the construction of the social were private philanthropists, intellectuals, and individuals I call the "taste professionals." They worked through universal expositions, schools, and libraries in their attempts to "make" the working class. New institutions were to replace the culture of production, creating a specifically working-class repertoire that differentiated the producers according to the technical skills they possessed. Limitations on working-class knowledge and the invention and the imposition of an ostensibly working-class style were to make the class itself.

---

6. I use "political economy" in two senses: to describe the system of relation of polity and economy, as in the political economy of the ancien régime; and to refer to the liberal economic theory its practitioners call "political economy."

The bourgeois making of the working class had, however, some unexpected outcomes, including stimulating a sense of shared working-class interests in opposition to the bourgeoisie. Artisans used the universal expositions of the Second Empire to express their desire to create beauty and their right to creative labor as well as authorship. In so doing, they kept the culture of production briefly alive. The other major (and more enduring) site of artisanal expression was trade union activity, where through the languages of their mobilization, working-class men participated in the destruction of the culture of production and in a definition of working-class manhood that excluded fine aesthetic training and creative labor. Paradoxically, perhaps, in the context of unions working-class men set the stage for their social participation and representation as consumers rather than producers. That is, their focus on increased wages and shorter hours and the abdication of creativity and knowledge left them dependent on leisure and consumption for self-expression and satisfaction.

Meanwhile, the ideological move toward a free market in goods and services would eventually transform relations of production and distribution fundamentally. Both the division of labor and the specialization of manufacturing gradually increased early in the century, and the expansion of production and distribution already appeared to promise democratized access to goods. The ending of sumptuary legislation together with the prospect of an abundance of goods appeared both exciting and threatening to contemporaries. Capitalist organization of production and distribution meant that the bourgeoisie could envision representing themselves, claiming a collective identity, through goods. And indeed, by the 1820s, bourgeois women were already being cast in the role of domestic decorators whose interiors were to be carefully differentiated from the classes above and those below.

Embedded in all these changes—and contradictions—were the seeds of the bourgeois stylistic regime that would develop in the last decades of the century. That development had to wait on the consolidation of the economic and political power of the bourgeoisie, the definitive establishment of a republican regime, the development of marketing and the expansion of production. There was nonetheless—even in this earlier period—a perception of danger in this possibility of an increased availability of "things." Just as "inappropriate" knowledge could cause working-class producers to have "inappropriate" aspirations, the logic ran, so the possession of the wrong things could cause working-class consumers to step out of their place. The taste professionals conjured a working-class style to compensate for the working class's "lack of taste" in consumption, just as they imagined a working-class curriculum to compensate for the artisans' "lack of taste" in production. By the last twenty years of the century, the simultaneous paradoxes of, on the one hand, universal manhood suffrage and the need to educate the working class to responsible citizenship and, on the other, expanding productive capacity and the need to create an adequate domestic market would pose problems for this system. But for this, transitional, moment the focus was on keeping people in their places through knowledge and taste.

4
Revolutionary Transformation
*The Demise of the Culture of Production
and of the Courtly Stylistic Regime*

 The furniture trades, like many others, were thrown into disarray by the Revolution. The old tripartite organization of production and distribution was no more, in its place an ostensibly free market in labor and goods. The trades were not being taught very well, contemporaries observed. What would become of the industries and their workers, unless they had new means of training? But first, some consensus on the nature of responsibility for social welfare and education was needed, and that was slow to take shape. More commercialized relations of production and distribution further threatened old systems of training. And, despite the imperial and monarchical courts extant in the first seventy years of the century, the courtly stylistic regime also ended with the Revolution. This era witnessed the end of the old system of regulation and the struggle to redefine the nature of state intervention into the newly defined "private" and "social" domains, all shaping the meanings of style.

This chapter takes up the shifting relation between the state and style, from the Revolution through the Second Empire—the first stage in the transition to the bourgeois stylistic regime—and discusses state intervention in production, distribution, and consumption. It looks at discourses on style during these regimes, the decay of the culture of production, the early commercialization of conditions of production, and legislative initiatives. Chapter five will examine more activist forms of intervention into production and consumption.

REVOLUTIONARY FURNITURE

The years during and immediately after the Revolution were catastrophic for the Parisian furniture trades. The first terrible crisis came in 1795, the year IV, when nearly everybody in the faubourg St-Antoine received some kind of government aid and the people worst hit were the "lumberyard

147

workers, *ébénistes*, and carpenters."[1] The economic situation remained perilous through the year IX, 1800–1801 and beyond. The crisis can be explained by the bankruptcy of the crown, by the disruption of the market provided by courtly and elite clientele dispersed in the 1790s, by the irregularities in supplies created by the war, by the emigration of significant numbers of highly skilled artisans, and by the reluctance of most people to buy large, expensive, objects in such unsettled times. Colin B. Bailey argues with respect to painting that by 1794 the "diverse Parisian elite whose patronage had developed, in emulation of State practice, to support the latest trends in French contemporary art" had disappeared.[2] With the end of the guilds and the closing of the royal workshops, the organization of the trades was fundamentally disrupted. Furthermore, the artisans of the faubourg were active in the taking of the Bastille, turning to politics rather than furniture design during the revolutionary years. Because of the revolutionary emphasis on the restructuring of all aspects of everyday life, however, these were not completely infertile years for the furniture trades, despite these economic difficulties.

The period of the Revolution, Directory, and First Republic saw the sponsoring of a new aesthetics of everyday life and artistic production. An important element in the effort to create a new society and a new aesthetic was the pedagogical restructuring of drawing and of the fine and decorative arts during the Revolution—an attempt to replace the guild-based organization of training. Some of these institutions, like the Conservatoire des arts et métiers, built on Old Regime initiatives such as the Ecole spéciale de dessin. Others, like the first free public museum, the Museum central des arts, which opened in the Louvre in August 1793, had a more novel design.[3] These new institutions were to replace training structures abolished by the Revolution and to provide the context for the invention of distinctively revolutionary art including furniture.

Despite these institutional innovations, the rapidity of political change and the gap between political and cultural transformation during the 1790s did not allow redesign of the fundamental structures of furniture but did

1. Monnier, *Le faubourg Saint-Antoine*, 83 and chap. 5.
2. Colin B. Bailey, "'*Quel dommage qu'une telle dispersion*': Collectors of French Painting and the French Revolution," in *1789: French Art during the Revolution*, ed. Alan Wintermute (New York, 1989), 11–26.
3. AN F²¹1422. For an incisive discussion of the Louvre's political significance see Carol Duncan, "Art Museums and the Ritual of Citizenship," in *Exhibiting Cultures*, ed. Ivan Karp and Steven D. Lavine (Washington, D.C., 1991), 88–103. More extensive is Andrew McClellan, *Inventing the Louvre* (Cambridge, 1994).

Figure 24. Armoire (detail), probably Paris, end of eighteenth century. Mahogany, *orme* burl, walnut crotch, oak, and *buis gomme-lacque*; gilded bronzes. Musée Carnavalet, MB 200. Photo: Berthier.

encourage changes in existing furniture styles, to make them more appropriate to the moment. The furniture and objets d'art produced in the early years of the Revolution of 1789 employed self-consciously republican iconography—scenes of the taking of the Bastille, clasped hands (to show fraternity), triangles with an eye in the middle (to embody reason), Phrygian hats.[4] Ancien régime structures (skeletons) were reused but given a republican skin. The piece shown in Figure 24 demonstrates the explicit politicization of this furniture. Besides revolutionary symbols, *marqueteurs*

4. See introduction to Paul Avril, *L'ameublement parisien avant, pendant, et après la révolution* (Paris, 1929).

Figure 25.   Commode, probably Paris, during the Revolution. Light mahogany and marquetry, *brèche d'Alep* marble. Drawer pulls with pictures of the taking of the Bastille. Musée Carnavalet, MB 196. Photo: Joffre.

inscribed patriotic and revolutionary phrases on the surfaces of the furniture and bronze makers turned their talents to decorative pikes. As in Figure 25, the fundamental forms of the furniture remain those of Louis XVI style, albeit hastily made with the cheaper indigenous wood available in wartime. Despite the continuity, this furniture reflects the sense that in order for the Revolution to be successful, the objects of the everyday must convey the revolutionary sentiment. It was not enough to remove royal symbolism, nor to produce simpler, more popular, furniture (although that was also done). *Ebénistes* and customers of the revolutionary years knew that revolutionary change required the changing of patterns of thought through reminders in the world of the everyday.

The next few years of the Revolution—encompassing the style known as Directory—continued this trend, as well as the exact reproduction of motifs and objects from the Greek and Roman republics and Etruscan-inspired motifs.[5] Rather than use the Greek orders of architecture and principles of geometry as the theoretical framework for the creation of new forms, revolutionary artisans turned to the archaeological finds of Pompeii and Herculaneum and copied objects directly. This was an early and quite literal version of historicism, apparently motivated by a desire to recreate the life-style of the republics. It was carried to considerable lengths as is made clear by the production during the Revolution of an entire (700-piece!) ensemble of accurate, historically specific, Greek furniture.[6]

Art historians often denigrate the impact of the Revolution on style, arguing that the Directory style was simply a continuation of Louis XVI style, and that Empire style was merely a sequel to Directory. For example, Jacqueline Viaux claims that much of the apparent innovation merely changed names; one fashionable magazine, the *Journal des dames et des modes*, renamed pieces: a "petite commode" became a "chiffonière," an "athénienne" became a "vide-poche," and a "bonheur-du-jour," a "gradin."[7] The above illustrations, however, belie this argument. Moreover, her interpretation seriously underestimates the difficulty of imagining and carrying out a "new" style under the wartime conditions of the Revolution and First Republic and, consequently, the significance of the stylistic transformations that did occur. Developments in interior decoration during the revolutionary moment both resembled and differed from contemporary transformations of other elements of the symbolic order. New festivals, calendars, and clothing regulations all served to split from the past and to set novel temporal and ritual cycles.[8] In their borrowings from the past as in their simultaneous breaks from it, revolutionary rituals paralleled the innovations in decoration.

One of the most enduring consequences of the Revolution on the furniture trades was the damage to the traditions of training embodied in apprenticeship and compagnonnage.[9] Within the ideological scaffolding

5. Jean-François Barrielle, *Le style empire* (Paris, 1982), 15–16.

6. Avril, *Ameublement*, 8–10; Spire Blondel, *L'art pendant la révolution, beaux-arts, arts décoratifs* (Paris, 1887), 302–3. See also Barry George Bergdoll, "Historical Reasoning and Architectural Politics" (Ph.D. diss., Columbia University, 1986), 28–29.

7. Viaux, *Le meuble en France*, 124.

8. See Mona Ozouf, *La fête révolutionnaire, 1789–1799* (Paris, 1976).

9. Ministère du Travail, *L'apprentissage industriel: rapport sur l'apprentissage dans les industries d'ameublement* (Paris, 1905). For a nuanced analysis of the status of apprenticeship in the Parisian furniture trades see Lee Shai Weissbach, "Entrepreneurial Traditionalism in Nineteenth-Century France," *Business History Review* 57 (winter 1983): 548–65. Yves Lequin claims that apprenticeships

provided by the patriarchalism of absolutism, training in the furniture crafts was largely controlled by the trades themselves. More experienced artisans taught the younger the knowledge, skill, and craft sense needed for effective practice of the trade and also brought them into the community of the craft. The two basic stages of artisanal training under the Old Regime—apprenticeship and journeymanship—were enmeshed in familial discourse and relationships; they reproduced not only the knowledge of the trades but the solidarity of its practitioners as well. Combined with the particular organization of production under the Old Regime and linked by patronage to the court, the system was a fertile environment for innovative design. In the course of the nineteenth century the reconfiguration of training, the steady deterioration of the apprentice-journeyman structures, the commercialization of relations of production and distribution, the changing nature of the market, and the altered relations between the state and style eroded that environment.

The effect of the ideological break in the paternal metaphor was not immediate, but rapid efforts were made to buttress the relations of pseudo-kin in the apprenticeship system through legislation passed during the Revolution. The law of 19 July 1791, art. 19, for example, held that an apprentice's crime against his master or his master's family would be more severely punished than one against any one else.[10] The law of 22 Germinal year X (1801; titre III, règlement sur l'apprentissage et sur les ateliers) governed the delegation of paternal authority to the master. If the apprentice stole something from his master or from his master's shop, it was to be considered domestic theft and punished by *réclusion et peine infamante* (code pénal, art. 386). Likewise, the master was as responsible for damages caused by his apprentice as he was for his children (code civil, art. 1384). The existence of this legislation indicates both a commitment to the familial metaphor and the increasing fragility of these relations.

The next step of training—the compagnonnage, or journeymen's organizations—had similar difficulties within the revised social relations of the evolving world of industrial capitalism. This trade structure worked

---

continued in factories in the late nineteenth century but agrees that the general situation was deteriorating ("Apprenticeship in Nineteenth-Century France," in *Work in France*, ed. Steven L. Kaplan and Cynthia J. Koepp [Ithaca, 1986], 456–74). An equally bleak assessment is found in Lenard Berlanstein, "Growing Up as Workers in Nineteenth-Century Paris," *French Historical Studies* 11 (1980): 551–76.

10. Cited in 12 January 1842 report on apprenticeship contracts in AN F^{12}4830, p. 556.

effectively only as long as the compagnonnage mirrored the structure of the larger society; thus its integrity and cultural logic were fractured by the ending of the corporate system of the Old Regime. The decline of apprenticeship and compagnonnage in the nineteenth century had both as cause and as effect the changing configuration of the culture of production in the furniture trades. (Chapter 3 offers more detail.)

One contemporary paean to the virtues of home work and deregulation reinforces the shift in training. A spokesman from the recently founded Chamber of Commerce of Paris argued, in the year V (1796–97), that deregulation and outwork produced an ideally flexible work force. Workers were no longer limited to one trade but could move into neighboring ones when their own was no longer viable.[11] Thus rather than artisans knowledgeable in a specific trade, they were becoming alienated labor, subject to deployment wherever the economy needed them.

Despite this drama of deregulated production and distribution, some scholars assert that the impact of the Revolution on furniture production and distribution was inconsequential, because a great deal of furniture was built and sold outside the corporate structure, the organization of production in the furniture trades was already complex, and the division of labor and specialization of manufacturing already widespread under the Old Regime.[12] It is true that the scale of production changed very slowly—for much of the nineteenth century the faubourg was dominated by small shops with few employees—and there was relatively little capital investment in machines until much later in the century.[13] But the existence of a complex organization of production and distribution—including shop work, home work, the combination of production and distribution and their separation—had meant something very different when guilds were the normative structure and these other organizations of production existed outside that structure. Once guilds were abolished, the meaning of the faubourg and of the royal workshops changed as did the direction of growth in the furniture trades. Just as pressing was the need to restructure a market once the motive force of the court had diminished. The freedom of the market unsettled the organization of distribution, which in turn reinforced and created certain tendencies in the dynamic of the organization of production. All these changes brought contemporaries to understand that the

11. AN F¹²1569.
12. For example, Roger Price quoted in William Doyle, *Origins of the French Revolution* (Oxford, 1980), 20–21.
13. Monnier, *Le faubourg Saint-Antoine*, 191, 207.

relation of artisans in the furniture trades to their labor had been permanently transformed.

RESURRECTION OF ANCIEN RÉGIME STYLE: THE CONSULATE (1799–1804) AND EMPIRE (1804–1815)

Napoleon shared with the Old Regime monarchs and with some revolutionary leaders a belief in the importance of the symbolic in the everyday. Napoleon's regime needed to differentiate itself symbolically from the Revolution but could not simply return to the ancien régime for legitimacy. Like many authoritarian rulers and regimes, therefore, he attempted to foster a new style, fitting his own person and his vision of the nation, harking back to the ancien régime but at the same time unique.

Empire style was in a new relation to the styles of the ancien régime. Designers borrowed freely from ancien régime styles but neither recaptured old objects, as in the later years of the Revolution, nor inscribed explicit political messages onto their surfaces.[14] The styles of the Directory and Empire were most strongly characterized by a mixture of neoclassicism and exoticism; sphinxes and other Egyptian motifs glorified and commemorated Napoleon's campaigns in Egypt as early as 1798.[15] In addition, the desire to memorialize (and perhaps legitimize) the military accomplishments of Napoleon led to an emphasis on martial themes in the early years of the Empire. The forms were hybrids based on the one hand on classical forms borrowed from Louis XVI and the Directory and, on the other, laden with exoticism.[16] The chest shown in Figure 26 is typical of this moment in Empire style.

Perhaps unsurprisingly, given the reliance on state patronage, First Empire was a highly centralized style. It was, furthermore, the first architect-created style in France, with official architect-decorators Charles Percier and Pierre Léonard Fontaine having a controlling influence over the construction of forms.[17] Their intent was to create both a style and a representation of history appropriate to the imperial project. Their work

---

14. Emile Bayard, *Le style empire* (Paris, [1914?]), 56–57.

15. Baude and Loizel, "Ebénistes," 1:13.

16. Viaux, *Le meuble en France*, 129.

17. Charles Percier and Pierre Léonard Fontaine designed the interior of the Louvre, the Cabinet of the Emperor at the Tuileries, as well as other Napoleonic interiors. Their *Recueil de décorations intérieures comprenant tout ce qui a rapport à l'ameublement* (Paris, 1801, 1812) rapidly became a classic text of interior decoration, more influential than works by Vivant-Denon, Prudhon, and even David.

Figure 26.   Commode, Paris, First Empire. Musée des arts décoratifs, D 11188. Photo: L. Sully-Jaulmes.

was seconded by Prudhon, the official decorator of the city of Paris—a post created in this period.[18] Architects in the ancien régime had designed furniture and had influenced the development of styles, but no prerevolutionary styles had found their sole or dominant source in an architect's sketchbooks.

Throughout the First Empire, there was always one dominant style and one popular wood; others would also be used, but in a secondary market or as the secondary effect of technical exigencies. Cabinetmakers recast neoclassical ancien régime forms in new woods, especially mahogany in the early period, to create imperial interior decoration. Figure 27 of a chest of drawers produced around 1800 is typical of a modest version of this style. The chest is mostly veneered in mahogany with ebony accents, while the columns, the ormolu mounts, and the porcelain plaques show a clear neoclassical heritage. Even very modest furniture of this period, like the small tier table made about 1800 reproduced in Figure 28 was crafted from

18. M. Jullian, *L'art en France sous la révolution et l'empire* (Paris, n.d.), 80–81.

Figure 27.   Chest of drawers, ca. 1800. Veneered with mahogany
and ebony; decorated with ormolu mounts and blue and white
porcelain plaques; mottled white marble top, also marble panels
supporting and behind the columns. Henry E. Huntington
Library and Art Gallery, San Marino, California.

mahogany. This taste in wood changed abruptly with the blockade of 1807,
however. After the onset of the blockade, there was a shift to a very limited
range of domestic wood.[19] The difficulty in persuading both artisans and
consumers of the desirability of these woods is indicated by the fact that
the emperor created a special prize for furniture displayed at exhibitions
using French timbers.[20] The needs of the administration and the course of
international politics determined aesthetic forms of the hegemonic, official
style, as they had under the ancien régime, yet there was enough autonomy
of production and of consumption to require the Empire to exert persuasive
pressure.

Moreover, the disrupted conditions of production of the Revolution put
severe constraints on Napoleon's ability to emulate the Old Regime's

19. "L'histoire prouvée par les modes," *Journal des dames et des modes* 36
(September 1811): 252.
20. Denise Ledoux-Lebard, *Les ébénistes parisiens du XIXe siècle* (Paris, 1965),
xviii.

Figure 28.   Small tier table, Paris, ca. 1800. Jean-
Baptiste Gamichon. Mahogany. Henry E. Huntington
Library and Art Gallery, San Marino, California.

stylistic hegemony. The early days of the Empire saw little improvement
in the economic health of the furniture industries. It has been estimated
that there were only six thousand artisans making their living largely
through the production of furniture in 1810.[21] There were severe crises in
1805 and 1806; things looked up in 1807–10, but then in 1811 *tabletterie*
and *ébénisterie* suffered nearly 80 percent unemployment. The bankruptcy
rates in 1810–11 and 1813–14 were very high.[22]

The catastrophe resulted from the permanent loss of the courtly structure of the Old Regime, an absence further exacerbated by the temporary
loss of the export market. Napoleon did commission large quantities of

21. For the sources of these figures and their difficulties see Leora Auslander,
"The Social Life of Furniture in Paris, 1860–1914" (Ph.D. diss., Brown University,
1988).

22. Monnier, *Le faubourg Saint-Antoine*, 219–22.

furniture, but Parisian artisans had heretofore depended ultimately not only on the crown itself but on the courtly world surrounding it; those relations were not reproduced under the empires and monarchies of the nineteenth century. Indeed, a proposal designed to reinforce a centralized style by reviving the ancien régime Manufacture royale des Gobelins was rejected as inappropriate to the new era.[23] And yet the inadequacy of the free market is attested to by the resurrection of the Garde-Meuble, and by the large loans made by the imperial government to the industry in 1807 and 1811. The Garde-Meuble was a workshop that produced furniture for official use within the Empire and a warehouse of furniture commissioned directly from woodworkers rather than from merchants.[24] Had elite society been consuming furniture the way it had in the Old Regime, or had the free market been effective, recourse to state patronage in the form of the Garde-Meuble might not have been necessary.

The new national schools for arts and crafts—really low-level engineering schools—at Châlons-sur-Marne (1806), and Angers (1811) were created under the Empire, according to the same principles as that of Liancourt founded by La Rochefoucauld.[25] They were to admit the children of artisans and turn them into skilled workers and foremen; the children who attended them, however, were not the children of artisans but rather of low-level civil servants and soldiers, whose households could subsist without the waged labor of children. Rather than learn a trade, the students stayed in school long enough to become literate and then left for a commercial job. An attempt was made to resolve this defection by requiring an apprenticeship as a prerequisite for admission, but significant numbers of artisans were never trained in these schools.

Through extensive commissions to its architects and artisans the First Empire did succeed in creating an identifiable style. Art historians debate at much length the merits and faults of this style, some declaring it dry, ponderous, and lifeless, others finding it somber, dignified, and masculine. Whatever the style's aesthetic virtues or faults, it came from workshops employing a relatively limited number of artisans who worked to architects' drawings. Tellingly, the major supplier of imperial furniture, Georges Jacob (d. 1814), employed 332 workers, but only 9 apprentices, divided among fifteen workshops including *ébénisterie, menuiserie en meubles,*

23. Edmond Bonnaffé, *Etudes sur l'art et la curiosité* (Paris, 1902), 221.
24. Monnier, *Le faubourg Saint-Antoine,* 226–27, 213.
25. C. R. Day, "The Making of Mechanical Engineers in France," *French Historical Studies* 10 (spring 1978): 439–60.

menuiserie en bâtiments, two for sculpture, one for painting and gilding, with others for forging, chiseling, mounting, marquetry and inlay, metal gilding, polishing, turning, sawing, and locksmithing.[26] In contrast with the Old Regime, where royal-style furniture was produced by a multitude of workshops employing relatively few artisans, much of First Empire–style furniture was produced in a factory.

The consular and imperial years thus brought the return of an industry that superficially resembled its prerevolutionary self but was in fact fundamentally unlike it. The Garde-Meuble was restored, Napoleon had much furniture commissioned, and a distinctively imperial style emerged. What remained was but a simulacrum of the trades as they had existed during the ancien régime: the industry suffered severe unemployment; elite society did not follow Napoleon in supporting innovative design; the system of reproducing the trades was in shambles. This was also a period of reconfiguration of the relations between the state and the family, between men and women, between workers and employers, between the public and the private, a reconfiguration crystallized in the Napoleonic Code. The Empire instituted a paradox: the official ideology of the regime (and of those that followed) was liberalism—that is nonintervention into the private sphere—yet the civil code regulated the most private of relations within the family. Thus economic liberalism functioned in the context of an authoritarian political regime, where production, distribution, and consumption were not as free from state interference as the ideology of laissez-faire would have it. While trying to recreate the courtly stylistic regime, Napoleon also sought to implement a laissez-faire economic regime—and ultimately the two were not compatible.

RESTORATION MONARCHIES (1815–1830)

Ironically, Napoleon carried out aspects of the monarchical-style production system—such as court artisans and patronage—more ably than the kings who followed him. Napoleon's was France's first empire, and the monarchies that followed—Louis XVIII, Charles X, and Louis-Philippe— were all restoration regimes, hoping to reconstruct monarchical rule in a postrevolutionary moment. The difficulty and ambiguity of this task were reflected in the styles patronized, and in the relation of all three monarchs to the production and distribution of the decorative arts.

26. AN F¹²2410.

We see Louis XVIII's desire to recapture the objects of Old Regime monarchies and his weakness in comparison to those monarchs in the possibly apocryphal story told on him by Germain Bapst in 1888 about Louis's attempts in 1814 to have two chests moved from Versailles to the Tuileries, thwarted repeatedly by government bureaucracy.[27]

All three restoration monarchies were marked by striking stylistic continuities with earlier regimes, which in turn reflect the continuities in royal administrations and commissions.[28] When Louis XVIII was still the comte de Provence he had, over the five years between 1781 and 1786, commissioned 140,000 livres' worth of furniture from Georges Jacob.[29] After the Revolution the Jacob shop, now known as Jacob frères and run by François H. G. Jacob Desmalter (d. 1841), continued an active business in the nineteenth century, first playing a central role in the elaboration of First Empire style and then supplying the restoration monarchs. This continuity may be seen in the cabinet featured in Figure 29 in which Louis XVI and First Empire forms are melded. Similar continuity from the Empire to the Restoration may be seen in the work of Charles-Joseph and Louis-Edouard Lemarchand. Charles-Joseph Lemarchand trained under the Old Regime (he became a master in 1789); after he died in 1818, his shop was continued by his son, Louis-Edouard Lemarchand. And the individual who took over the king's household, Thierry de Ville d'Avray, was the son of the *commissaire* of the Garde-Meuble under the Old Regime.[30] Even more striking was the appointment of Jean-Démosthène Dugoure, who had been the dessinateur du Mobilier de la couronne in 1784, to become the new dessinateur du Garde-Meuble et des Manufactures in 1816. Continuing the Old Regime tradition, Louis XVIII commissioned a great deal of furniture from the shop of Alexandre-Louis and Pierre-Antoine Bellangé. Born in 1760, Pierre-Antoine Bellangé had become a guild master under the Old Regime but enjoyed great success in the nineteenth century, becoming licensed by the Garde-Meuble in 1817, its director under Charles X, and his son became

27. Germain Bapst, "Exposition Louis XIV et Louis XV de l'Hôtel Chimay, à Paris," *La Nature* 1 (1888): 404.

28. In further parallel to the reigns of Louis XV and XVI, a woman, the duchesse de Berry, was a patron of stylistic innovation and ordered quantities of furniture from Pierre-Antoine Bellangé.

29. Jacques Robiquet, *L'art et le goût sous la Restauration, 1814–1830* (Paris, 1928), 49.

30. Colombe Samoyault-Verlet, "L'ameublement des châteaux royaux à l'époque de la Restauration," in *Un âge d'or des arts décoratifs 1814–1848* (Paris, 1991), 42.

Figure 29. Cabinet (*commode à vantaux*), with sliding shelves enclosed by folding doors, three drawers above, Restoration. Jacob-Desmalter's shop. Oak, thuya wood veneer; gilt bronze ornaments including griffin monopodia at corners and center medallion with bust of Minerva framed in a laurel wreath; white marble top. Metropolitan Museum of Art, 19.182.5.

ébéniste du roi under Louis-Philippe.[31] As Figure 30 demonstrates, Alexandre-Louis Bellangé's style was more reminiscent of Louis XVI than of the Empire. He returned to the use of exotic wood veneer and porcelain plaques rather than the plainer mahogany or indigenous veneer or solid wood that characterized the Empire. The *secrétaire,* in fact, shows the first hint of a revival style.

The nineteenth-century monarchies' uncertain relation to style reflected their own ambivalent relation to history, which was in turn a possible consequence of their uncertain place in the ongoing historical transformation. Unsurprisingly, therefore, all three restoration styles were historicist in a way different from any ancien régime style. Louis XVIII largely continued First Empire style, and Charles X in his turn made little effort to devise a style for his reign. The table made for Charles X by Louis François Puteaux shown in Figure 31 was characterized by a ponderous dignity, elegant work, and extensive use of native wood. The furniture was

31. For additional discussion of this phenomenon see Robiquet, *L'art et le goût sous la Restauration,* 7–18, 104.

Figure 30. *Secrétaire*, Paris, ca. 1824. Attributed to Alexandre-Louis Bellangé. Oak veneered with amaranth, thuya wood, ebony, and pewter; set with twelve hard-paste porcelain plaques; mirrored and painted glass; gilt-bronze mounts; *rouge griotte* marble top. 5 ′ 3/8 ″ × 2 ′ 10 5/16 ″ × 1 ′ 4 3/4 ″. J. Paul Getty Museum, Malibu, California.

Figure 31. Table, Paris, 1830, made for Charles X. Louis François Puteaux. *Loupe de frêne et d'orme-sycomore et amarante.* Musée Carnavalet, MB 235. Photo: Habouzit.

massive without having the drama and power of Louis XIV's equally substantial pieces. The plainness of the materials was in an uneasy relation to the scale, perhaps an accurate reflection of the position of Charles X in French politics and society. Of all the restoration monarchs, Louis-Philippe was the most engaged in matters of the decorative arts, but he focused on furnishing the restored châteaux of the ancien régime in their original styles, or in styles deemed appropriate to the different functions of the rooms.

The Restoration crowns largely kept Empire style and resurrected somewhat modernized versions of Louis XVI style. There appears to have been little direct royal influence on these styles, and even more important, the Restoration did not bring a revival of the widespread and very luxurious courtly life of the Old Regime.[32] The society of notables of the early nineteenth century was a highly fashion-conscious one, but it did not

32. Ibid., 47.

necessarily follow the lead of the crown. Furthermore, many of the old nobility were impoverished, spending what moneys they put into furnishings for renovation rather than new purchases. For example, records from the château de Rosny show very few purchases for the decade of the 1820s. Its total furniture expenditures consisted of one major furniture restoration project in 1821, followed by an order of seven buffets in 1827–28.[33] There were of course still major purchases. The duc de Berry spent 5,000 francs with the *tapissier* Grand Jean, 1,500 with the *tapissier* Bonnemain, and 4,000 with the furniture maker Jacob during the month of September 1821 alone.

The furniture makers of the Restoration did not go back in time only to find inspiration and motifs, nor to locate the models for exact copies, nor to make pastiches of the old. Their concern for authenticity (linked to the legitimation of the new Bourbon regime) led them to reuse the ancient objects themselves, combining them into new forms appropriate to the representation of the new king. Under the Bourbon Restoration artisans found remains of real medieval and Renaissance furniture and combined them into new pieces in a kind of precocious Dadaist gesture, thus producing a mode of representation perhaps appropriate to this period with its weak "legitimate" monarchy.[34] By returning to the relics of the deepest ancien régime—the era of masculine, strong, kings—they apparently found the best way of reinforcing the Bourbon legacy and transcending their contemporaries' image of the weak, effeminate kings of the eighteenth century.

Not surprisingly, during the Restoration of Louis XVIII and under Charles X, new royal styles competed with relics from the past and revivals of Old Regime styles, which came in and out of fashion sequentially according to the needs for symbolic representation of the current political regime. Louis XVIII in fact expressed appreciation for Empire style and kept much of Napoleon's furniture with small changes of decorative elements; the new objects sustained the same basic forms. Louis XVIII had little personal interest in creating a style for his reign or in supporting institutions that could have done it for him. He depended rather on the stylistic innovations of his predecessors.

Even more dramatically than Napoleon, the restoration monarchs lacked two key ingredients of the older stylistic regimes: a court perceived to be

33. AN 371AP11, archives du château de Rosny.
34. Lesieur, Lagoutte, and J. Durand, "Menuisiers en meuble antique," in *Exposition universelle de 1867*, ed. Devinck, 2:1; Robiquet, *L'art et le goût sous la Restauration*, 20.

hegemonic in the production and distribution of political power, and a sense that emulation of the crown's possessions would produce political place as well as social position.

THE JULY MONARCHY (1830–1848) AND THE SECOND REPUBLIC (1848–1851)

The bourgeois age in France began with the July Monarchy of Louis-Philippe. The 1830s and 1840s witnessed the expansion of a new class of notables enriched by capitalist development, the growing prominence of the liberal professions, and the increasing political representation of the propertied classes. Adeline Daumard notes that the bourgeoisie during this period came to represent 15 to 20 percent of the population.[35] Accompanying this economic and social growth was a building boom, itself provoking debate among architects about the appropriate representation of the French nation and the French people. Much as during the age of Louis XIV, historians and histories became important to the construction of a sense of Frenchness. Unlike their predecessors, these historians were not patronized directly by the crown and some understood themselves to be creating competing narratives of France's past in the interests of the people, rather than the government. Thus the bourgeois monarchy was as much bourgeois as it was a monarchy, a fact that would deeply influence its relation to style, as well as to the people who made and bought furnishings.

Louis-Philippe continued and elaborated the stylistic patterns established under the Restoration monarchies.[36] When he assumed the throne in 1830, he had already spent, as the duc d'Orléans, fifteen years restoring and furnishing the Palais-Royal in Paris, the château de Neuilly, and a country château at Eu. Now Louis-Philippe set about restoring the Tuileries, Fontainebleau, Compiègne, Trianon, Pau and the other royal dwellings. But framing all his decorating effort was the fact that he was "restoring" ancien régime royal dwellings as the successor to the Restoration crown. He did not, however, get rid of First Empire or Restoration furniture; rather he added both reproductions and pastiches to the furnishings of his predecessors. These styles were also available on the market, as an advertisement from 1833 indicates, appealing to potential customers in the epistolary form typical of ads of the period: "We saw a chair in an elegant salon that looked exactly like one of those pretty armchairs of the period

35. Daumard, *Les bourgeois et la bourgeoisie,* 22–26, 85.
36. I follow the argument of Samoyault-Verlet, "Louis-Philippe de 1830 à 1840," in *Un âge d'or des arts décoratifs,* 230–34.

Figure 32.   Gothic style chairs, Paris, 1830s. Musée des arts
décoratifs, W 22 660 and D 32 601. Photo: L. Sully-Jaulmes.

of Louis XIII, over which collectors fight for the decrepit remains. . . . This
piece of furniture was made in the workshop of M. H. Chenavard."[37]

Louis-Philippe's efforts focused on historicism, on finding or making
furnishings and decorations appropriate to each of these château, suited to
the stylistic period of each. For one, he had new objects made in old styles:
a billiard table such as André-Charles Boulle would have made—had he
made billiard tables. The Gothic-style chairs shown in Figure 32 are a
beautiful example of this form. But even this effort at "authentic" historicism competed with Louis-Philippe's son's eclecticism. The duc d'Orléans would combine anything he found beautiful in one room without
anxiety about matching historical styles. Both legacies would be important
later in the century. The period from 1835 to 1845 was characterized by
free copies of earlier styles, while after 1845 there was a greater emphasis

37. See the furniture series at the Bibliothèque historique de la ville de Paris
(BHVP), which contains advertising materials from approximately 220 Parisian
stores: BHVP 120, ameub. C, Chenavard, 1833.

on exact reproduction. Therefore, Louis-Philippe's reign saw increased precision in dating and characterizing styles.

The historicism and eclecticism at court were resonant with debates over history, philosophy, and design. Historiography under the July Monarchy was dominated by a liberal, progressive, narrative, although it competed with others. Already in 1827 influential translations of the historical philosophies of Vico by Jules Michelet (1798–1874) and of Herder by Michelet's friend Edgar Quinet (1803–75) enlarged the conception of the doing of history far beyond the classical world. Liberal historians came to see their task as reconstructing past societies rather than retelling the tales of the ancient world. Augustin Thierry (1798–1856) and François Guizot (1787–1874) in particular, as well as other liberal historians, turned their attention to transitional moments in the past, rather than golden moments, hoping to learn rather than to copy.[38]

Changes in architectural thought, being more closely linked to design, provide an even sharper delineation of the issues at stake. In the 1830s, the leading young architects of the day—Félix Duban (1796–1871), Henri Labrouste (1801–75), Louis Duc (1802–79), and Léon Vaudoyer (1803–72)—sought "to find principles so basic that they could embrace the entire history of architecture and remain valid for the nineteenth century as well. They wished to understand the whole of the world's architectural speech and discourse in a universal language."[39] But that universalist position was not uncontested. Or, as one contemporary rather plaintively wrote in 1839, "the Revolution and the Empire imposed Greek and Roman style on us . . . the Restoration saw our clocks, our armchairs, and our commodes crowned with arches and imitating cathedrals; today we're becoming Florentine and Byzantine. When are we going to be French?"[40]

During the first half of the nineteenth century architects debated at length whether buildings ought to represent the society for which they were made or should strive rather for transcendent beauty. The 1820s through the 1840s saw the development of a revival of Gothic style, as well as efforts to invent a truly new style appropriate for the century. Conflict over the form of historicism ended at last in agreement that simple emulation of the Greeks based on the assumption of their transcendent aesthetic accomplishments was no longer tenable. This position was supported by the contemporaneous romantic, and later realist, movements in all

38. Bergdoll, "Historical Reasoning and Architectural Politics," 127, 88–89.
39. David Van Zanten, *Designing Paris* (Cambridge, Mass., 1987), xv.
40. *Exposition des produits d'industrie française en 1839* (Paris, 1839), 175.

aesthetic genres, which argued for the crucial importance of style being linked to the time and place that it was to serve.[41]

The architectural debates found echoes in the furniture trades, which also benefited from the expansion of the 1830s and 1840s, at least in terms of the numbers employed in the trades. Significant innovations appeared: a few new, specialized furnishings stores began to merchandise their own goods or sell those made by others, and the earliest *magasins de nouveautés* opened. The Deux Magots, the Coin de Rue, the Ville de Paris (1841), Ville d'Amiens (1830), and the Petit Saint-Thomas specialized in fabrics and notions, with the goods divided into departments with fixed prices, easy return policies, and no obligation to buy. As far as furnishings were concerned, the importance of the *magasins de nouveautés* was largely conceptual; they demonstrated the possibility of a new kind of merchandising (although one specialized store—Vervelle—advertised as early as 1831 in *La mode* that it sold furniture at fixed prices).[42] Department stores started to appear in Paris in the 1850s but little furniture was sold through them until the 1890s (and even then fabric and clothing made up a much more important part of their sales).[43] The only exception was the Colonnes d'Hercule, later becoming the Colosse de Rhodes in 1861, which specialized in bedding and furniture.[44]

The increased use of advertisements also marked the period. The commercial directory, the *Almanach du commerce de Paris*, heir to the ancien régime guides to shops and consumers in Paris, expanded both in breadth and scope, starting in 1820 to carry advertisements as well as listings, and in 1827—in response to competition from new publications—establishing a policy of free advertising. Even by the 1830s, newspapers still did not carry advertisements, because their owners thought that they were responsible to their readership for the quality of the merchandise advertised.[45] The 1820s and 1830s marked a transitional moment in such merchandising, therefore; advertisements were no longer purely informational, but they still often attempted to be personal; and by the 1840s, they had become far more ubiquitous in urban space. By 1830 the *almanachs de commerce* listed

41. Linda Nochlin, *Realism* (Harmondsworth, 1971), epilogue.
42. BHVP 120, ameub. V, Vervelle, *La Mode* 1831, 327–28.
43. The Bon Marché was founded in 1852, the Grands Magasins du Louvre in 1855, Au Printemps in 1865, the Bazar de l'Hôtel de Ville in 1860, and La Samaritaine in 1869 (Philip G. Nord, *Paris Shopkeepers and the Politics of Resentment* [Princeton, 1987], 60–61).
44. Georges Renoy, *Grands magasins* (Zartbommel, NL, 1978), 48–71; see also Paul Jarry, *Les magasins de nouveautés* (Paris, 1948).
45. Mermet, *La publicité en France*, 223–26.

seven poster hangers, and one company advertised that it provided posters attached to carriages. In 1844 an umbrella store was using a wallet-sized calendar as advertising, a practice that was becoming quite common. By 1845 the *Almanach* included an entry for the distributors of printed materials and cards, which included newspapers and advertisements. Finally in the 1850s came long advertisements in the form of newspaper articles for furniture.[46]

Paralleling and supporting the commercialization of distribution was growth in the industry—its periods of crisis and underemployment, not surprisingly, often synchronous with periods of political transformation (i.e., 1831–32 and 1847–48). In 1810 only about six thousand artisans made their living largely through the production of furniture but by 1850 that figure rose to around thirty-two thousand. We should not take this growth to mean that the industry had returned to its prerevolutionary health. The expansion of the trades reflected the general growth of Paris; even more important, the increase was concentrated in certain branches of production. Furthermore, this development was marked by deteriorating conditions of labor: hours lengthened and the regularity of work decreased. This period also saw the beginning of the steady shift from day rates to piece rates, and wages appear to have fallen.[47]

Not only did working conditions generally deteriorate but the division of labor, the specialization of manufacturing, and subcontracting intensified. Before the Revolution, the conditions of labor in the Parisian furniture industry had been very poor for most workers, and little had changed during the early years of the nineteenth century. For a substantial minority of the elite of the trades, however, conditions of production and especially of training did deteriorate in this period. More workers now knew how to do fewer things, specializing their labor either by task or by object. While there had always been an elaborate division of labor in the trades, specializing in marquetry was not the same as specializing in sanding. Working exclusively in marquetry could lead to greater expertise, artistry, and

46. Sebastien Bottin, *Almanach du commerce de Paris, des départements de la France, et des principales villes du monde* (Paris, 1830), 2; Archives du département de la Seine (hereafter, ADS) 6AZ 1814; Bottin, *Almanach du commerce de Paris* (Paris, 1845), distributions d'imprimés, cartes; on 1850s, see article by Jules Ladimir, in the *Gazette de Paris*, 18 April 1858 (BHVP 120, ameub. V, Vieuge).

47. For the loans made by the government following the Revolution of 1830, see ADS DQ^{10}1667 dossier 351; on numbers of artisans see Bonnaffé, *Etudes sur l'art*, 221. And on rates see the discussion in L. Descamps and Beaujean, "Tourneurs en chaises," in *Exposition universelle de 1867, à Paris*, ed. Devinck, 3:1–2.

creativity than a more general practice of the trade; spending an entire working life at sanding could lead only to boredom and frustration.

Specialization by object—between *menuisiers en sièges* and *ébénistes*, for example—had long existed. Yet that specialization had a different logic and different consequences than did the postrevolutionary version of specialization. In the Old Regime the specialization was based in part, at least, on the different knowledges needed to build weight-bearing and surface-producing structures, and between assembling structures and decorating the surfaces. It was a specialization, in other words, in a general category of object determined by the exigencies of its successful production. In the nineteenth century the dominant form of specialization came to be based on a superficial knowledge of a wider array of skills. One speciality was in bedside tables. Artisans in this speciality would often not know how to design a table; they simply made essentially the same objects over and over on the basis of drawings and jigs. And they often worked at home rather than in a workshop, with less access to other artisans' knowledge, with a much more limited supply of wood and of tools. The goal became the quickest production with the minimum tools of a very narrow range of goods.

Not only had the definition of the *métiers* tended toward increased specialization by object or task, but the same trend could be seen in the workshops themselves. By 1830, for example, there were twenty-five billiard-table makers and eight specialists in the sale of billiard cues; eight manufacturers of iron beds; and, in 1845, there were eight listings of stores specializing in *fauteuils mécaniques*.[48] As early as 1799, and emphatically by 1830, the *almanachs de commerce de Paris* listed producers so specialized that their listings could only have been of interest to fellow woodworkers (gilders, nail makers, casters, and sculptors), indicative of the elaboration of the specialization of production. Thus, three organizations of production existed simultaneously. There were workshops that specialized either in an object, like chairs, or in a process, like turning. There were workshops that diversified by uniting different processes and trades involved in the production of one object under one roof. And there was the subcontracting system in which much of the work was done by home workers or in specialized workshops and merely assembled by its ostensible

48. J. de La Tynna, *Almanach du commerce de Paris, des départements de la France et des principales villes du monde* (Paris, 1815); Bottin, *Almanach du commerce de Paris; Annuaire des notables commerçants de la ville de Paris* (Paris, 1861).

maker. Although no simple correlation can be made between the degree of specialization of manufacture and the quality of the work produced or the conditions of labor, the general trend over the century was toward outwork and more intense specialization of labor.

This period was further marked by the development of pattern books, including the *Nouveau recueil en divers genres d'ornements* published by Charles Normand in 1803, the *Recueil de décoration intérieure*, published by Brance in 1828, the *Vademecum du tapissier*, published by Charles Muidebled in 1835, and the *Meubles et objets de goût*, by Pierre de la Mésagère (1802–1835). The use of pattern books initiated by Percier and Fontaine under Napoleon had had the effect of centralizing style. But their multiplication in this period meant *at once* a new multiplicity of designs and less shop-based innovation.

The transformations of the period crystallize in the person of the *trôleur* (derived from the verb *trôler*, to carry a load on one's back). Most *trôleurs* worked at home, alone or with their family, bought their own wood, and made objects on speculation. Once they had finished a piece they carried it from market to market and from store to store until they succeeded in selling it (hence their name).[49] *Trôleurs* owned the minimum of tools and stock. They were sometimes very highly skilled and produced elegant furniture, sometimes their mastery of their craft was minimal.[50] They made complete objects but may have specialized in only one object.

These effects were understood by contemporaries and feared for the impact they would have on the quality of the goods produced and on the training of the workers. For example, on 15 March 1848 the citizen Moricet—the president of the Comité des orphelins of the third arrondissement—outlined the crisis in the furniture and other trades, identifying *trôleurs* (here called "ouvriers en chambre") as the main victims and retailers as the main enemies. The *trôleurs* paid an inflated price for their raw materials, Moricet argued, and were terribly vulnerable to the vagaries of the market: "[i]t is reasonable, it is fair, it is necessary that the great principle—to each according to his ability, to each according to his work—finally be enacted. A worker must be recompensed for his labor, his name must be attached to his works."[51] For Moricet, *ouvriers en chambre* sold not their labor but the product of their labor. Some were making useful

---

49. See for example an exposition catalog from the Musée Carnavalet, *Du faubourg Saint-Antoine au bois de Vincennes* (Paris, 1983), 44.

50. AN F^{12}2441.

51. Ibid.

objects, some masterpieces, but all were entitled to appropriate payment and had the right to a signature. Moricet was not alone in his perception of the problems in the industry, nor was he the first.

Furniture makers joined forces in the 1830s to protest what they perceived to be a deterioration in the conditions of their labor. The first documented militant action of the nineteenth century came in 1831 with an attempt by furniture makers in the faubourg St-Antoine to destroy new milling machines.[52] In November and December 1833 the *ébénistes* and turners of the faubourg went on strike to obtain an increase in wages.[53] In 1838 the woodworkers of the faubourg fought with foreign workers who they felt were undercutting the French workers' attempts to control hours and wages. In 1840 the *ébénistes* of Paris (at least twenty-two thousand of them) joined in the general strike that had been started by the carpenters and *menuisiers en bâtiment*, they too concerned with issues of control over the quality and price of work.[54] In 1846 and 1847 the workers of the Maison Krieger, one of the largest shops in the faubourg and also one of the earliest to mechanize, struck. The 1846 strike was won, but the 1847 strike for workers' control of production ended in the arrest of many of the participants and with no gains.[55] Thus, whereas historians discuss the complex and nondeterminate implications of some changes during these years, to piece rates rather than hourly rates, for example, furniture makers at the time appeared almost unanimously opposed to these developments.

The expansion of new forms of distribution, the elaboration of advertising, and increasing proletarianization of labor were indicative of the growing distance between consumer and producer and, more saliently, the expansion of capitalist relations of production and distribution. Under these conditions the possibility of court or state control of style became increasingly difficult; in the long run, it would be inconceivable.

In the short term, however, the Second Republic did choose to maintain state support of the decorative arts by putting the manufactures of Sèvres, Gobelins, and Beauvais under the control of the minister of agriculture and commerce and by holding a special exhibition of the products of the national manufactures in 1850. Indeed, the budget of the manufactures was sus-

52. Ministère du Travail, *Associations,* 2:675.
53. Jean-Pierre Aguet, *Les grèves sous la monarchie de juillet* (Geneva, 1954), 100.
54. Ibid., 215; Ministère du Travail, *Associations,* 2:675.
55. Aguet, *Les grèves sous la monarchie de juillet,* 292.

tained under the Second Republic despite fiscal difficulties.[56] The motivation for the maintenance of the state manufactures was not the creation of a state style but the support of workers—a rationale distinctly different from that of earlier regimes. The discussion in the women's magazine *Le conseiller des dames* suggests an even more profound sense of difference—making a state style was no longer considered an appropriate state or republican project.

The founders of *Le conseiller des dames [et des demoiselles]: journal d'économie domestique et des travaux d'aiguille* intended it to be an "intelligent" women's magazine, different from mere fashion magazines. Nearly every issue contained household advice; menus; poetry; historical anecdotes; obituaries; discussions of literature, theater, and fashion; embroidery and needlepoint designs to copy. It took women and their domestic lives profoundly seriously, making comparisons between domestic economy and the state budget and emphasizing that the magazine was carrying on the tradition of the prerevolutionary salons.[57]

The editorial in the April 1848 issue of *Le conseiller des dames* opened with words of praise for the Revolution and the provisional government, then continued with a discussion of women's place in this new regime. As "the voice of women, the newspaper of the home, the echo of the elegant world, the guide to domestic economy," its editors felt that the journal had no obligation to "occupy [itself] with political affairs." It was not that the editors were indifferent to the transformations of their world for, "like our subscribers, we wish for the progress of civilization, the gentling of mores, the relief of the needy classes, the extinction of resentments, and the union of all parties, for these principles are those of the first legislator of the world, our Lord Jesus Christ." But they identified women's interests and concerns as charitable and religious rather than political; women were to seek social peace rather than social justice. It was men who were to worry about politics: "Whether women are the wives of republicans or the wives of royal subjects, their mission remains the same . . . to preserve France's old reputation of distinction, by their taste and their spirit, to encourage the beautiful in arts and letters, to teach their families love of country and fear of God." Thus women were to be the wives and mothers of political men,

56. For the organization of the manufactures under the Second Republic see Edouard Gerspach, "Chronique de l'enseignement des arts appliqués à l'industrie," *Revue des arts décoratifs* 3 (1882–83): 152–55; 219–22.

57. *Le conseiller des dames*, February 1848.

but they themselves had no political positions and could be neither republican nor royalist. Furthermore, the task of encouraging the production
of beautiful things was deemed equivalent to teaching children patriotism
and Christianity.

In any case, according to the editors, society had changed little after the
first excitement of the Revolution. Salons had reopened, and it was, in fact,
people's obligation to continue to throw large parties: "The government
itself, in the interests of the laboring population . . . wants parties, . . . precious source of work for all industries. To continue one's habits of yes-
terday, therefore, is to serve more seriously than one would have thought,
to come to the effective aid of national commerce. The elegant woman, who
tastefully and intelligently composes her attire, the mistress of a house who
ordonne avec théorie les honneurs d'un dîner, is using her fortune nobly."[58] At home, woman was to assure the continuity of society.

The divisions, and the connections, made in this editorial, between the
domestic and political worlds, between the feminine and the masculine, the
religious and the secular, are telling. At one moment the implication was
that the world could turn upside down and backward and nothing was to
change in everyday practice—women must continue to educate their children, give dinner parties, donate to charity, worship God, and patronize
beauty. At such a moment it appears that the personal was conceived as
very distant from the political. But at other moments in the text the
personal took on profoundly political meaning: for that very reason it had
to remain unaltered.[59] Elite women were obliged to consume luxuriously
because through that consumption, they provided women workers with
labor, they encouraged beauty, they served God, and they brought up the
next generation. The editorial was conscious enough of the Republic of
Labor to insist on the contribution consumption made to the welfare of the
laboring classes but stated equally clearly that matters of taste and style
belonged in the feminized home, away from politics.

The implication of all this was that the state must assure the conditions
of possibility for the cultivation of good taste in domestic objects—appropriate domestic style—but need no longer make a style. Style was no longer
an affair of state as during the Old Regime, rather taste was now an affair

58. Z. Bourkey, *Le conseiller des dames,* April 1848, 161–62.
59. Hinting at a more activist position, the editors planned to use their new
freedom from censorship to discuss "the increase in work and of wages of women
workers; the protection for nurseries and orphanages to be demanded from the
government, changes in the rules of admission for women teachers." This more
activist position was, however, muffled under the "business as usual" stance.

of elite women. Here is an early statement of a conceptualization that would come to maturity under the Third Republic, when state-supported creation of style turned into state-fostered good taste; when matters of everyday aesthetics moved from the state to the nation. But the end of the Second Republic in 1851 brought a temporary halt to that trajectory. Only desultory efforts went on, under the authoritarian Second Empire to create a new style of state. The task proved an impossible and anachronistic one.

THE LAST STATE STYLE: SECOND EMPIRE

These patterns continued under the Second Empire in a complex combination of authoritarianism and liberalism under the regime of Napoleon III. Unlike some of his royal predecessors, Napoleon III was personally uninterested in the decorative arts and, until the 1860s, commissioned little work, and even then only to boost employment in the luxury trades.[60] Also unlike nineteenth-century monarchs, Napoleon III, insofar as he was engaged in matters of style, did not encourage borrowing from eighteenth-century styles but rather favored a return to the Renaissance, safely distant from monarchist claims.[61] In contrast, the Empress Eugénie was very engaged in interior decor. The styles favored by the empress mixed real eighteenth-century furniture, especially Louis XVI, with contemporary pastiches of it; the old furniture was often reupholstered in colors uncharacteristic of the eighteenth century. Compare, for example, the two Louis XV armchairs in Figures 33 and 34. The chair shown in Figure 33 was made in the 1860s, that in Figure 34, in the 1730s. The radical differences in proportions, geometry, and curve-tracings are obvious. The chair in Figure 34 was a pastiche in that it played on the forms of the Louis XV but made no effort to reproduce them. Finally, the Second Empire did see some novel forms like that of the chair shown in Figure 35 and the *meuble d'appui* in Figure 36. The chair mixed Louis XV and orientalist forms, including mother-of-pearl and lacquer in its decorative elements. The *meuble d'appui* was vaguely reminiscent of other times and places yet very much identifiable as a piece of the 1860s. Its surface was decorated with painting, mother-of-pearl, and papier-mâché rather than inlay and bronzes; the effect was not really that of trompe l'oeil, but rather the

60. Jean-Marie Moulin, "The Second Empire: Art and Society," in *The Second Empire, 1852–1870*, ed. George H. Marcus and Janet M. Iandola (Philadelphia, 1978), 12. On its laissez-faire stance in the fine arts see Patricia Mainardi, *The End of the Salon* (Cambridge, 1993), 39.
61. Reitlinger, *Objet d'Art Prices*, 130–31.

Figure 33. *Chauffeuse*, 1850s or 1860s. Louis XV style. Musée des arts décoratifs, 22566. Photo: L. Sully-Jaulmes.

Figure 34. Armchair, Paris, ca. 1735–40. Gessoed and gilded beech. 3′ 7 1/2″ × 2′ 6 1/8″ × 2′ 8 7/8″. J. Paul Getty Museum, Malibu, California.

Figure 35. *Fauteuil à gondole,* 1850s or 1860s. Wood covered with black lacquer, *carton bouilli,* mother-of-pearl inlay. Musée des arts décoratifs, 48965. Photo: L. Sully-Jaulmes.

adaptation of old forms to new techniques. Napoleon III style was, thus, identifiable but competed with many other styles and was never hegemonic, even within the court.

Thus the direction given to style in interior decor by the ruling couple, insofar as there was one, was contradictory. To quote David Van Zanten's analysis of architectural style under Napoleon III, "the Empress Eugénie was a partisan of Viollet-le-Duc's Gothic (which was secretly Republican); the Minister Fortoul helped conceive Vaudoyer's authoritarian Byzantine; the monument most widely accepted today as embodying the style Napoleon III was Garnier's parvenu Baroque Opera. And the structure awarded the Grand Prix de l'empereur in 1869 . . . was Duc's Palais de Justice, the style of which seemed so obscure that many contemporaries judged it mad."[62] The court and the state were both important patrons, yet

62. In Van Zanten, *Designing Paris,* 177.

Figure 36.   *Meuble d'appui*, 1850s or 1860s. Papier mâché,
painted wood, and mother-of-pearl inlay. Musée des arts
décoratifs, 48964. Photo: L. Sully-Jaulmes.

neither the emperor's nor the empress's taste was critical because styles
were set not by them but by bourgeois consumers.[63]

Notwithstanding the chaos and relative unimportance of imperial stylistic leadership the state became much more heavily engaged in institutional attempts to influence matters of style than earlier in the nineteenth
century.[64] The struggle to determine the appropriate form of state intervention by an authoritarian regime, in a capitalist economy, and under a
pervasive ideology of laissez-faire produced Laborde's confused vision of
a process for renewing the industrial arts.

In 1856 Laborde suggested the creation of a new version of the Gobelins
(now to be called the *grande manufacture modèle*) that would produce only

63. Moulin, "The Second Empire: Art and Society," 13. For bourgeois taste
in the creation of taste in the fine arts see Patricia Mainardi, *Art and Politics of the
Second Empire* (New Haven, 1987), 3, 33, 47, and passim.

64. Kathryn B. Hiesinger and Joseph Rishel, "Art and Its Critics: A Crisis of
Principle," in *The Second Empire, 1852–1870,* 29.

for the imperial residences and museums, although his project gathered little more support than a similar one by Talma had under the Consulate.[65] Laborde's suggestion that the goods not be sold but be displayed in palaces and museums was indicative of contemporary reluctance to expand state intervention in the economy. Colbert's manufacture des Gobelins had produced objects of style for the crown and, to some extent, the court. Talma had wanted simply to sell the goods to all who could buy, combining the logics of free markets and of state involvement in the economy. Laborde understood that displaying goods and style in the imperial dwellings was no longer sufficient—that "the public" had to have direct access to them if these objects were to change the process of style production. Furthermore Laborde emphasized training. The new *grande manufacture modèle* would not intervene directly in the market through the distribution of goods made under state patronage; it would train artisans and then send them out to work in the trades. His suggestion failed, however, partially because it would have required a far more extensive degree of state intervention than would have been palatable at the time. By the 1850s and 1860s, it was understood that imperial patronage was no longer enough, that the training of both artisans and the taste of the consumers needed to be transformed if style was to change, but no consensus on a solution could be obtained.

Furniture of the Second Empire thus came to be characterized, to the despair of Laborde and others, by fully upholstered, tufted, comfortable chairs, cabinets of vaguely Louis XVI dimensions, and a continued Gothic revival.[66] Aside from these, there was no Napoleon III style marked by distinctive geometry, form, or decoration. The explanation for this failure must be sought in ideological changes as well as materialist ones.

I argue that that "failure" of style was in part the result of a reconceptualization of the universal and the particular or national, of the transcendent and the historical, of the public and the private, and of order and liberty under the Second Empire, a reconceptualization that can be vividly seen in the work of Eugène Viollet-le-Duc (1814–79) and César Daly (1811–94). Viollet-le-Duc tried to find a means of combining historicism and rationalism, but he occupied an uncomfortable position between the universalist and the historicist. On the one hand, he argued that architecture was not the simple expression of culture, and on the other he was deeply regionalist and nationalist, urging the discovery of a uniquely French style

65. Bonnaffé, *Etudes sur l'art*, 222–23.
66. Colombe Samoyault-Verlet, "Furnishings," in *The Second Empire, 1852–1870*, 74.

rooted in a uniquely French genius.[67] Viollet-le-Duc's monumental *Dictionnaire raisonné du mobilier français*, first published in the early 1860s, was an alphabetically organized guide to furnishings. The first section gave a history of the changing forms and usages of all the major pieces of furniture, followed by a historical analysis up through the Renaissance in the second half of the volume. He argued that there was continuity from this much earlier period, "because they are part of the very nature of our national character." For Viollet-le-Duc, the "true" French were those who lived before the age of absolutism. The period of royal furniture, of the seventeenth and eighteenth centuries, was to be avoided. "To want to imitate the habits of luxury, the ideas, and even the prejudices of a period separated from us by the chasm of 1792 is, at the very least, a failing." He claimed that "as citizens of a country we are worth more, it seems to me, than in the Middle Ages, but as private men, we are far from equaling the definite, energetic, and individual characters that one encountered at every step until the century of Louis XIV." Viollet-le-Duc argued for Gothic furniture on the grounds of "its taste and the rationality of its adoption of forms . . . its true use of the material according to its quality." Gothic furniture was honest and true, and good taste consisted of "appearing what one is and not what one would like to be."[68] For example in *The Story of a House* he argued that "the dwelling ought to be, for a man or his family, a garment made to his measure; and that when a dwelling is in perfect accordance with the manners and habits of those who are sheltered beneath its roof, it is excellent."[69] His work created a series of tensions between the notion of the furniture and taste accurately and truly reflecting the individual, and accurately and truly reflecting the true French character.

Viollet-le-Duc's contemporary César Daly, founder of France's first major architectural magazine, *Revue générale de l'architecture et des travaux publics*, had similar concerns, but his work was marked by an important difference. Viollet-le-Duc was a revivalist who believed that the Gothic aesthetic best exemplified not only "Frenchness" but republicanism.[70] Daly advocated and helped introduce the concept of "eclecticism," the reappropriation of the entire French historical repertoire of style and form, rather than the privileging of one form in particular. Neither ar-

67. Paul Rabinow, *French Modern* (Cambridge, Mass., 1989), 65ff.

68. Eugène Viollet-le-Duc, *Dictionnaire raisonné du mobilier français de l'époque carlovingienne à la renaissance* (Paris, 1868) [2d ed.], 295, 428, 364, 431.

69. Eugène Viollet-le-Duc, *The Story of a House*, trans. George M. Towle (Boston, 1874), 33.

70. Van Zanten, *Designing Paris*, 156.

chitectural nor aesthetic theorist, however, advocated the making of new forms from old styles, which was the style that would, in fact, come to dominate French interior decor in the last half of the century.

César Daly made complicated and sometimes contradictory arguments for universal laws of beauty and individual taste. These are worth discussing in some detail, for Daly was immensely influential during the Second Empire and well into the Third Republic. In the introduction to his *Architecture privée de Paris et des environs sous Napoléon III* (1864), Daly articulated the problem of contemporary design as one of relating public and private interests or of balancing freedom and order, problems that he understood to be two sides of the same coin. "To respect the laws of the beautiful, the rules of art, the taste of the public, that is to make *order*. To respect the rights, even the fantasies of the client, that is to recognize one of the forms of *individual liberty*." It was clear, however, that reconciling these requirements would not be easy because of the tension, even "positive hostility" between order and liberty.[71] To resolve this hostile relation he suggested different rules of design for public and private dwellings: universal laws of beauty for public buildings, the vagaries of individual taste for private dwellings.

Thus Daly tried to establish two parallel rules of taste and style, the public and private; the first, the domain of constraint, the second that of freedom. This meant that architecture and design intended for private use could be left up to the market, while that intended for the public should be subject to the rules of order. In many ways this stylistic system mirrored that of the Old Regime, when it had not mattered what "the people" possessed since their possessions had no bearing on the national interests. But the situation was more complicated now, because the "nation" and the "public" could no longer, in the 1860s, be defined as simply the emperor and his court (although Daly tried to do so when he defined the palaces and dwellings of men of state as public buildings). The "people" were now part of the nation; they were citizens as well as subjects.

Daly also equated the taste of the public with a transcendent, universal set of laws of the beautiful. This traditional foundation of aesthetics sat uneasily with Daly's historicization of taste and beauty, for he went on to state a definition of public taste that made it specific to the French nation and the French race: "The beauty of a public monument should be a radiant and direct emanation of the living genius of all, a profession of the aesthetic faith of the race. Thus, the architect is . . . only the sonorous trumpet

71. Daly, *Architecture privée de Paris et des environs*, 1:5, 12.

through which passes the powerful breath of the nation; it resonates with the immense vibrations that emerge from the lungs of an entire people."[72]

The nation was understood in this argument to consist not in king or court or some universal ungrounded general will, but in the inhabitants of France, the French race. Daly was well aware of the difficulty such a conception posed. It disrupted his carefully constructed barrier between the public and the private, carrying with it the distinction between private, idiosyncratic taste, and public, transcendent style. By historicizing and nationalizing the Beautiful, he also threatened to popularize and temporize it. "One should not accuse me of pleading the cause of *vulgarity* in art," he hastened to add in a footnote. "That which is *common* is not necessarily *vulgar* and *base*. To love one's mother, one's father, one's *patrie*, is at the same time common and noble. A *national sentiment of art* is tied to a patriotic sentiment, and from this point of view, imperiously commands respect. Which is not to say that all national tastes are of equal worth."[73] The sentimentalism of this last gesture did little to resolve the fundamental contradictions involved in trying to foster a state role for the sponsorship of style in a postrevolutionary, laissez-faire, ethos, in which all inhabitants of the nation were to be citizens, and in which the economic sphere— including what people made, sold, and bought—was to be free of state intervention. Indeed, the last sentence of this note is ambiguous: it may mean that the national taste of different nations varies in quality, or, that the private taste of citizens within a single nation varies in quality. This ambiguity was part of an even larger conceptual tangle.

At different moments in this text Daly argued that Beauty was transcendent and universal; that there was a particularly French form of Beauty; that that French Beauty was an emanation of a single will of a people; and, that French taste was an aesthetic composed of a multiplicity of private, individual tastes. Attempts to work among these incompatible positions would continue to plague French efforts to define a new national style well into the Third Republic. The fact that it was voiced under an authoritarian imperial regime is itself a measure of the distance between Napoleon III's form of authoritarianism and that of Louis XIV. There were two linked issues here to resolve. One concerned the relation between capital and the nation, between the private and the public. Under a laissez-faire economic regime in which people were free to make and buy what they chose, how could one have a unified national style? Second, if the French race shared

72. Ibid., 1:11–12.
73. Ibid., 1:12 n.

a genius and a definition of the beautiful, how could one account for the fact that the French did not all spontaneously identify the same forms as beautiful? The presence of private tastes that were not simply fragments of the public taste mirrored the more general issue of representation. As Pierre Rosanvallon eloquently argues, since the time of the Revolution the French polity (unlike the English or the American) had been understood to be a whole, not a composite of individual, or local interests. The French were one. And yet they were tangibly divided by class, gender, region, religion, age, race, and language. Coping with that paradox became a dominant preoccupation of the Third Republic.

Characteristic of all the styles from the Revolution through the Second Empire was a reuse and recombination of old forms. Greater degrees of innovation marked some periods—like the First Empire—and a greater fascination with the antique marked others—like the Second Empire—but no styles were comparable to those of the Old Regime. The place of style in the making of French political power and of state power in the making of style had been irrevocably weakened with the Revolution. The monarchical and imperial regimes of the nineteenth century became less and less able to even emulate or imitate the courtly life of the Old Regime. Unitary, innovative style disappeared with the organization of production, distribution, and consumption of absolutism as did the capacity of style to embody the power of the state. When absolutism died, absolute style died.

But why exactly, given the renewed monarchies of the nineteenth century and the efforts of successive imperial and monarchical governments to sustain a relation to style like that of the absolutist monarchies of the Old Regime, did the place of objects in the constitution of power change definitively with the Revolution? Most fundamentally because the constitution and deployment of political legitimacy could no longer be the same after a revolutionary moment in which the king was beheaded and a republic established on the basis of liberty, equality, and fraternity. But we cannot understand the force of that revolutionary rupture apart from the complex changes in the state's role in production and consumption.

The period from 1789 to the middle of the nineteenth century saw the decay of the culture of production and the dismantling of the court system of patronage of the decorative arts. Thus nineteenth-century monarchies did not, could not, provide their subjects with one royal style or hierarchy of stylistic modifications according to rank. None attempted to restore feudal social relations or a courtly political and social world. Not surprisingly, therefore, these anachronistic monarchies sponsored anachronistic styles. Despite this anachronism, there was no competition to the courtly definition of style. There was no one courtly style to be followed, but there was still no competition from outside the courtly world to the furnishing habits of the crown and the royal family.

Whatever its choices of style, the crown could no longer regulate and control style as it had in the Old Regime, because it no longer controlled the organization of production and distribution. The apparently contradictory, but in fact finely tuned, tripartite structure of production and distribution of the Old Regime—guilds, royal workshops, faubourg St-Antoine—that encouraged creativity and innovation was no more; the combination of laissez-faire and remnants of old royalist institutions was an inadequate replacement.

From the early years of the First Republic through the 1840s, French governments did try in new and different ways to influence style—systematically sponsoring industrial exhibitions to inspire industrialists to extend their efforts—but could not replace the uniformity of the courtly stylistic system of the ancien régime. The organization of production and distribution in the Old Regime had been ideal for the production of royal stylistic hegemony (underscored by limited access to emulation), but the nineteenth-century royal courts had a role more comparable to that of an extremely wealthy patron.

To recreate a courtly stylistic regime in this period would require the bourgeoisie to exist in a relation to the court analogous to that of the notables of the Old Regime: it could not be. The Restoration did not in any sense restore feudal relations; venal offices were no longer bought and sold. The sites and sources of political power were no longer unitary but rather fragmented. The court was not the absolute center of political and social power; the institutions of the potentially oppositional public sphere—salons, cafés, theaters, newspapers, and boulevards—flourished, despite rigid censorship. Style could no longer be made at court, or as one nineteenth-century critic devastatingly put it: "The Restoration, that anachronism, was a lacuna, or at best a halt in time in furniture. . . . It is thus very true to say that the renaissance of French furniture is due to romanticism and Victor Hugo."[74]

Relations between social and economic elites and the monarchs of the first half of the nineteenth century were tension-ridden, and those tensions could no longer be soothed by the king's granting gracious permission for a limited degree of emulation on the part of his subjects. Deregulation of

74. Auguste Luchet, *L'art industriel à l'exposition universelle de 1867* (Paris, 1868), 93.

distribution meant that all could have what they wanted as long as they could pay for it. Distributors were also beginning to learn how to generate that desire through advertising, although the thorough commercialization of relations of distribution would happen only in the last years of century. Even so, stores were offering more goods to more consumers, which enabled many elite consumers to seek other satisfaction beyond echoing court and king. Such consumers were not yet numerous enough to create their own designing class and foster a properly bourgeois style.

The development of outwork and mechanization, the commercialization of relations of production and distribution brought with them not only an increased availability of luxury goods but also very visible urban poverty, social unrest, and enormous anxiety concerning the appropriate role of the state in the regulation of everyday life in the workplace, on the street, and at home. With these changes and the expansion of commercial culture came a new way of conceptualizing the space that both separated and linked the state and the people—a space heretofore framed by the paternal metaphor; that new spatial concept was "the social." Eventually it would help reframe how objects could represent power.

5

The New Politics of the Everyday
Making Class through Taste and Knowledge

 The 1830s through the 1860s were unsettling years for French commentators on style and taste in furniture. The traditional culture of production was understood to be no longer capable of producing skilled and inventive furniture makers, they remarked, and new distribution methods seemed to contain the seeds of a democratized market in goods; the taste professionals found bourgeois consumers to need advice. The central trope to emerge out of the cacophony of discourse concerning style and taste in these midyears of the century was a mélange of anxieties about class. How could artisans be provided with enough knowledge to make innovative furniture but not enough to make revolutions? How could working-class consumers be persuaded to buy furniture appropriate to their station, rather than cheap imitations of royal furniture? How could the bourgeoisie be guided in their consuming activities, to represent their increasingly important political and social positions? All these questions, moreover, implied a transformed and transforming conception of the relations between style and social and political power.

Many sharply contested views emerged on these matters because nothing less than social and political peace and stability were understood to be at stake. And, because the discourses were inherently paradoxical, no clear consensus was possible. Crucial to the elaboration of those discourses was the early nineteenth-century transformation of the paternal metaphor for state and society, and the consequent construction of an imaginary space called the social, in which a new group of investigators could intervene. In particular, a subgroup of actors appeared in that social space—the taste professionals—to shape the taste of bourgeois consumers and working-class producers and consumers in the period from the 1820s through the 1860s.

THE CRISIS OF PATERNAL-MASTERLY LEGITIMACY

The Revolution precipitated not only breakdowns in the social organization of production and distribution but a new conceptualization of the location of responsibility for the well-being of members of society. After the revolutionary upheaval it was no longer possible to imagine that the successive nineteenth-century kings were the father of all, given that their paternal responsibilities could no longer be enacted through corporations, courts, and other regulatory structures. Commerce in goods was now, in theory, liberated from restriction, and labor was now something freely sold on the market.[1] In fact, although the transition to a market economy was never complete, workers were left with little protection against the vagaries of the economy and the greed of their employers.

The expansion of large shops and in the numbers of the *ouvriers en chambre* in the furniture trades and elsewhere in French industry hastened the decay of apprenticeship already visible during the Revolution and Empire periods. As we have seen, revolutionary and Napoleonic legislation attempted to reinforce and support the paternal relation between master and apprentice. Masters were still to be substitute fathers for their apprentices. The state was not to intervene in relations between fathers and sons, or masters and apprentices, except to reinforce in law the identity between authority of father-master and obligation of son-apprentice. By the late 1830s, however, it was understood that the state might need to intervene in a new way in relations between masters and apprentices, between employers and employees because employers might not be taking appropriate responsibility for their child employees—who were in fact now often not apprentices but child laborers.

In this period officialdom assumed that many if not most working-class parents could not afford, or were not willing, to do without the wages their children could earn in factories. For example, as a M. Corne insisted in

1. For a terrific discussion of the complexity of the history of the market see Reddy, *Market Culture*. For artisans' refusal to accept that they were selling their labor rather than the product of their labor until well into the nineteenth century, see his "Skeins, Scales, Discounts, Steam, and Other Objects of Crowd Justice in Early French Textile Mills," *Comparative Studies in Society and History* 21 (April 1979): 204–13.

December 1840, speaking in defense of child labor legislation: "Oh, doubt-less the father's authority is a respectable and sacred thing, but [only] when the father understands and respects his mission. . . . Only then is he re-alizing the fullness of his right because he fulfills all the sanctity of his duty. But if he is brutalized by ignorance or poverty . . . if in order to satisfy real or artificial needs he hastens to traffic in his child . . . if he coldly cashes in on the future of this unhappy creature—oh, then he has stripped himself of the power that was given him toward a whole other end. And society has the right to say to him: 'This child no longer has a father. It is I who shall protect him.'"[2] M. Corne depicted working-class men, themselves brutalized, as too often taking advantage of their children and their capacity to labor. A father's authority was defined as sacred but only insofar as a father was deemed responsible. If he was not, it was society's obligation to deprive him of his paternal rights. The state stepped in, however, not as father, but as the public.

In 1841, after much debate concerning the infringement of paternal rights over children, a law regulating child labor was passed in France, the first, according to Lee Shai Weissbach, "to break with the rather consistent policy of noninterventionism." Justified in part by the need for interven-tion in large factories, where the owner's paternal presence was necessarily diluted, it dealt the assumption of paternal beneficence and the father's capacity to protect his children a severe blow.[3]

Subsequently, in a report by the Conseil général du commerce in 1842, the authors argued for state regulation of apprenticeship in small work-shops and domestic labor (not covered under the law of 1841) in the following terms. "There is [in apprenticeship] a kind of delegation of paternal authority [*puissance paternelle*] . . . to which the public authority [*puissance publique*] cannot remain either indifferent or ignorant."[4] In their minds the fact that the father had delegated his authority to a substitute father meant that the state should be concerned. The master was not the real father and did not have the same rights and obligations as a real father. Furthermore, since the law of 1841 regulated child labor in factories, small workshops too must be subject to state regulation. The

2. M. Corne quoted in Katherine A. Lynch, *Family, Class, and Ideology in Early Industrial France* (Madison, 1988), 196–97.

3. Lee Shai Weissbach, *Child Labor Reform in Nineteenth-Century France* (Baton Rouge, 1989), 86; Lynch, *Family, Class, and Ideology*, 194.

4. Minutes of the Conseil général du commerce, 12 January 1842 session (AN $F^{12}4830$, p. 556).

crucial matter now was not scale, but the fact that the child's real father was no longer taking direct responsibility for his child.

Even more salient, perhaps, was an ideological change in the understanding of the place of the father and the role of the state in the metaphorical and everyday relations in the workshop. Whereas in the Old Regime and even into the early years of the nineteenth century, the master was really like a father—and the state held the relations between masters and apprentices to be inviolable—by the 1830s, the master was only a substitute father, and therefore a father whose claim over his adoptive son was limited and conditional. The strong metaphor of the Old Regime had been grounded in the complex nexus of paternal and political identities under absolutism: the king was not as a father to his people, the king *was* at once father to his people and the embodiment of the people. The Revolution closed off the possibility of such an identity. Consequently, the kings of the nineteenth century were only in a very weak metaphorical paternal relation to their subjects, and the state's relation to the people was in flux.

The parallelism between *puissance paternelle* and *puissance publique* is telling. In the common phrase for paternal authority, *puissance* also meant potency. By the 1840s, sending one's child to be trained in another's workshop had become comparable not only to delegating one's paternal authority, but also to losing one's potency (one's paternal and reproductive potential and capacity). Implicit in this conceptualization was that a properly potent father would be able to support his children.

The logic behind the legislation of 1841 involved a simultaneous essentializing of the paternal relation and an implicit argument that once a father's power had been delegated, it could be again. The legislators appeared highly ambivalent as to whether to expect from working-class fathers a proper expression of paternal authority and paternal potency, for both working-class fathers and working-class pseudo-fathers were now fundamentally mistrusted. The public's children needed protection both from greedy fathers who sold them into apprenticeship before the age at which they should have been working, and from abusive masters.

The most benign solution was in some sense the *livret*—a kind of worker's passport that each employer was to sign when a worker moved on—designed to enforce a familial relation between apprentices and masters.[5] But the *livret* was not understood to be sufficient, and by 1845 specific proposals for state regulation of apprenticeship were once again being

5. Rapport, délibérations et vote (ibid.).

made—some of them quite radical changes. César Fichet, a teacher and the founder of a school of *arts et métiers*, proposed in 1847 that apprenticeship be replaced by an apprenticeship school, claiming that the conditions of apprenticeship were abominable—bad food, terrible hygiene, little instruction in the trades—and that artisans could be better trained in school.[6] His advice was ignored; only in the 1880s did widespread public technical schools emerge in France.

The erosion of the apprenticeship system of training was a result of both political and economic change. The commercial expansion of the 1830s and 1840s brought with it increasing possibilities for child labor and made the choice to apprentice a child appear a greater sacrifice than ever for the parents. Social investigations and reports increasingly labeled working-class fathers incompetent parents and by implication incompetent masters. At the same time, the state was undermining both working-class fathers' authority and employer-masters' authority, following the end of the Old Regime's version of paternalist social and political power, the king-father.

FROM THE PATERNAL TO THE SOCIAL:
BIRTH OF THE TASTE PROFESSIONALS

One logic of bourgeois response to the breakdown of the culture of production and the awareness of abusive conditions of labor was to promote and work for ameliorative protective legislation. But many of those opposed to the child labor law of 1841 argued that such legislation was unacceptable because it impinged on the laissez-faire principles of political economy. Workers were entitled to freely contract their labor. The child labor law was finally passed on the basis of an argument that children were not in full possession of themselves and therefore could not freely contract their labor; that their parents (usually really their fathers) were incapable of acting responsibly for them.

The political fights over protective legislation were only one sphere of a more general debate over the definition of new and appropriate relationships between the government, businesses large and small, families, the working class, and women and children of all classes. There was, on the one hand, the ideal of a laissez-faire system in which factory and shop owners were free of government regulations, workers were free to sell their labor to whom and at whatever price they could, and fathers were free to raise

6. César Fichet, *Mémoire sur l'apprentissage et sur l'éducation industrielle* (Faubourg de Paris, 1847) (ibid.).

their children as they saw fit. On the other hand there were the harsh realities of an industrializing economy: since men's wages were not enough to support a family, the contribution of women and children to the household was necessary, under working and living conditions that were often abominable. Elite groups seeking to produce a reliable working force feared potential working-class responses—militancy and revolution—to such blatant inequities. Rather than the abolition of inequalities, the solution was seen to lie in the improvement of working-class morality. If working-class children could be taught in school instead of in the supposedly insalubrious, dangerous world of the shop, then they would, according to some bourgeois observers, avoid exposure to the culture of production and to dangerous knowledge—either or both might give them inappropriate hopes and expectations.

Not all discourses of bourgeois origins focused on defense of the bourgeoisie and the containment of the working class. Some authors found the society in which they lived not only destructive of artisans and workers but of the materially better-off. Nonetheless, a crucial shared characteristic of early nineteenth-century discourses of reform and transformation—by the defenders of bourgeois privilege and by the reformers—was their insistence on a transformation in relations of production, consumption, and reproduction, that is, of the organization of labor and of life. It was not enough to change the workplaces; homes and their furnishings also needed to be remade.

Equal to the shop in its significance as a site for bourgeois intervention into working-class life was the home. The debates about the appropriateness of state intervention into the workplace and into relations between employer and employee and between master and apprentice coincided with the practice of social investigation into the living conditions of the working classes. If young workers lived, ate, played, and drank according to standards deemed appropriate for their class, that, it was thought, would also forestall revolution. Thus did habits of consumption as well as production enter the state's discourse about its role in a new way in the 1830s and 1840s.

Two of the earliest and most influential French social investigators were Louis Villermé and Frédéric Le Play, who studied the conditions of working-class life. In the 1830s the Academy of Moral and Political Sciences charged Villermé to make detailed inspections of workers' dwellings including commentary on their furnishings. He concentrated on textile workers and concluded that they suffered from moral degradation because of their environment. He argued that if their physical circumstances could be improved, including their domestic surroundings, then their morality would likewise be rectified. In each of his examples, he moved within the same paragraph from a description of the dwelling and its furnishings to the inhabitants' sexual habits. In his analysis of Lille, for example, after describing the armoire, planks, stove, table, two or three bad chairs that composed the furnishings of the dwelling, he went on: "I do not want to add anything to the detail of these hideous things that reveal, at the first glance, the depths of the poverty of the unhappy inhabitants, but I have to say that in many of the beds I just described I saw lying together individuals of the two sexes of very different ages, for the most part without nightshirts and revoltingly filthy."[7] Villermé implied that had the inhabitants of these dwellings had better furnishings, they would also have had more acceptable social practices.

A very different and equally important intervention into private lives came from the utopian socialists. Despite their great differences, all three strands of utopian socialism born in the 1830s and dying by 1848—Saint-Simonianism, Fourierism, and Icarianism—envisaged a transformation of the everyday.[8] The movements occupied the boundaries of working-class and bourgeois worlds and planned new societies where, in addition to the more familiar demands to reorganize labor and property, people's love lives, relationships with their children and with their friends, schemes to change how and what they ate, what they wore, and where they lived and what those dwellings looked like would unfold. All held a complex mixture of faith in science, in progress, in individual genius; even more saliently, all envisaged new, planned communities, rather than piecemeal changes in the existing social fabric. Their holistic vision did not divide public from private, productive from reproductive, masculine from feminine, or political from social. All aspects of life were to be simultaneously and willfully transformed.

None of the utopian socialist movements succeeded in creating durable communities able to challenge industrial capitalism, but all did establish communities, all did attract significant numbers of followers, and all did

7. Louis Villermé, *Tableau de l'état physique et moral des ouvriers employés dans les manufactures de coton, de laine et de soie* (Paris, 1840), 83. See also Sewell, *Work and Revolution in France,* 224–32.

8. For this argument see Christopher H. Johnson, *Utopian Communism in France* (Ithaca, 1974); Frank Manuel, *The Prophets of Paris* (Cambridge, Mass., 1962); Frank Manuel, *The New World of Henri Saint-Simon* (Cambridge, Mass., 1956).

influence more mainstream political and social thought. They are significant to this story, therefore, both in the fact of their existence and in the influence they had on others. Although nothing that happened in the French utopian socialist communities directly affected the style of furniture made (unlike the Shakers in America) or the working conditions in the furniture industries, many of those responsible for major changes in aesthetic thought, conceptualizations of urban planning (e.g., César Daly), and the development of social policy were deeply influenced by utopian socialist, and especially by Saint-Simonian thought.

The sociologist Frédéric Le Play, a Saint-Simonian and general commissioner of the 1867 universal exposition, followed and expanded on the work of Villermé by doing detailed investigations of the living conditions of families. Supervising the gathering of family *monographies* between 1829 and 1855, Le Play, like many other social investigators of the period, believed that the social fabric depended on individuals behaving morally in all domains of life.[9] Social investigation was to reveal moral turpitude and the job of private philanthropists and the state was to provide the means for individuals to "better themselves." The whole technique assumed a close connection between having goods appropriate to one's class and morality. The monograph of Bernard D., used as an example of a "manual laborer with a large family," illustrates this point.[10]

According to Le Play's research associates, MM. Courteille and J. Gautier, Bernard D. lived with his eleven dependents in a three-room apartment in the faubourg St-Martin. The family was much praised for its piety, cleanliness, sobriety and for the fact that their furniture "expressed order and cleanliness and demonstrated a particular inclination toward bourgeois habits." The investigators stated that nearly all this admirable furniture (along with some equally "appropriate" clothing) had been bought with a prize of 3,000 francs won unexpectedly by Bernard. A few pages later, however, Bernard was condemned for the foolishness of his expenditures. Bernard made these purchases because he wanted to return to the petite bourgeoisie in which he had been raised but was unable to do this because of "certain intellectual deficiencies." Not understanding that the reality of his impoverished situation required a rigorous savings plan for success, he instead "used his resources to give himself, in his clothing and furniture,

9. Rabinow, *French Modern*, 86.

10. Frédéric Le Play, "Manoeuvre à famille nombreuse," in *Oeuvres complètes de Frédéric Le Play*, 2d ed. (Tours, 1878), 6:327–86.

some of the *attributes* of the bourgeoisie. . . . That is how he unproductively wasted 3,000 francs."[11]

Completely unconsciously as far as the text reveals, Le Play put Bernard in an impossible double bind. If he had not bought furniture and clothing with his windfall, he would have been condemned for not providing his family with the basis of a moral existence. As it was, he was both praised and condemned for his bourgeois aspirations. According to Le Play, rather than looking bourgeois, he should have behaved like a bourgeois—by saving his money. But Bernard may have realized (just as Le Play must have known) that money in the bank, if one was housed in a hovel and dressed in rags, did not make one bourgeois. Ultimately, of course, one needed a bourgeois income, bourgeois things, and bourgeois habits to be bourgeois.

Diverse groups contributed to the making of the powerful new conceptual space—the social. Elaborated in a number of domains as a buffer space between the public and the private, the concept opened out the private sphere and served to justify and legitimate state and philanthropic intervention.[12] Furthermore, the concept was also central in justifying, and transforming, private intervention. With the definition of the social as an arena legitimately accessible to the gaze of outsiders, intervention was no longer limited to benevolent gestures but now included the inquiries of social scientists and social workers.

The right of the state and of private investigators to enter the private sphere to enquire into the conditions of labor and life had been long established by the mid-nineteenth century, but the nature of the obligations and responsibilities of the state and the privileged classes toward others was still highly contested. Private philanthropists in the social sphere were understood to be acting benevolently, altruistically, and therefore voluntarily in the interests of others. Until the 1880s, the state was understood to be justified in social intervention only when the private sector failed to act. In the middle decades of the nineteenth century, the concept of the social allowed both private and public intervention into the private lives of those deemed potentially dangerous to the stability of society and state—the working class. The 1830s, 1840s, and 1850s witnessed both the deterioration of the culture of production and of state-based style, as well as expanded

11. Ibid., 342, 348; emphasis added.

12. Catholic organizations were also involved in these moralizing projects as well as creating trade schools. See for example an 1842 dossier on the Ecole chrétienne in AN F^{12}2334. On the category of the social see Sewell, *Work and Revolution in France,* chap. 10. A general discussion of it as a gendered category, is Riley, *"Am I That Name?"*

industrial production and the commercialization of distribution. All these phenomena sparked debate and inspired reform projects aimed at intervening in the relations and practices of the social sphere.

The projects varied greatly in content, form, and intended audience, but all had one thing in common—they saw tastefulness as class-specific. Etiquette or decorating books addressed to well-off housewives, sociological reports on the state of the working classes, or proposals for exhibits at the universal expositions, all agreed that furnishings of certain styles and not others represented one's social position and in fact constituted it. They went even further, linking tastefulness, morality, and forms of knowledge. Just as certain classes were to have goods of a certain appearance, certain classes were to have certain kinds of knowledge. Thus the projects to replace the culture of production fit these class-based conceptions of taste and knowledge. I call the individuals involved in these projects taste professionals—the growing number of men and women (but mostly men) engaged in commenting on matters of taste and style.[13]

The taste professionals in the decorative arts had previously dealt only with the most expensive furniture; they now found greatly expanded roles and redefined authority as arbiters of public taste, given the failing hegemony of courtly style. They did not form a coherent group or think alike. In fact, their independent appearance in different discursive and institutional sites attests to the new anxiety and interest in matters of taste. These taste professionals worked with a pen and paper or pencil and sketch pad, not with their hands. They included architects interested in interior decor; owners of the largest and most prestigious furniture companies, who typically had built furniture in their youth; successful interior decorators and designers; members of the Académie de l'industrie and other such organizations; writers concerned with taste and beauty; and, legislators preoccupied with aesthetics and working-class dwellings. In general they earned their living through their role as expert commentators on questions of taste, not through the sale of particular objects, as various individuals in these professions and expert amateurs had done since the eighteenth century.

During the 1830s taste professionals grew more numerous and more prominent, filling the vacuum left by the expiring culture of production,

13. I obviously do not mean "professional" in a corporatist sense. I coined the term but many scholars have worked on the groups and individuals within the category. See Silverman, *Art Nouveau in Fin-de-Siècle France*, part 3; Nancy J. Troy, *Modernism and the Decorative Arts in France* (New Haven, 1991); W. Walton, *France at the Crystal Palace*. The classic on the American case is Russell Lynes, *The Tastemakers* (New York, 1949).

helping mediate the new more distanced relations between producers and consumers, and giving advice to the socially uncertain. Until being recruited into the service of the state during the organization of the Paris exposition of 1855, the taste professionals worked largely through private organizations. They wrote etiquette books, technical and decorating guides, marriage manuals, and the early decorating magazines. They created private philanthropic organizations. They wrote reports on the universal expositions.

The taste professionals worked through the Académie de l'industrie, the Association des inventeurs et artistes industriels, and the Société du progrès de l'art industriel. The Académie de l'industrie, claiming 2,553 members in 1840, saw its goal as defending French taste and industry against competition from abroad. It sponsored juried exhibitions and encouraged manufacturers to link "good taste . . . with the comfortable and a reasonable price."[14] The Comité de l'Association des inventeurs et artistes industriels was a similar organization and defined its goal in an 1863 letter to the minister of public works, agriculture, and commerce: "[U]niting art with work, that the art of the rich should become the art of the poor as well; in order to do that we would like that art be applied as much to pine as to ebony." Not wanting simply to encourage art for art's sake, its founders hoped that "by adorning the home with forms that are agreeable to the eye, [we] will encourage and invite the artisan to accept the sweetness of the domestic home, instead of pushing him to flee it by the enormity of the contrast that strikes him everywhere." In a letter signed by forty-one artisans, businessmen, and professionals, the Société du progrès de l'art industriel requested that an exhibit of industrial art be joined to the agricultural exhibit of 1860, arguing that since the creation of the royal workshops of the Gobelins and Sèvres, industrial artists had not received the recognition due them and that therefore the traditional prestige of French crafts was suffering.[15]

The list of organizations created by the taste professionals from the 1830s through the 1860s could go on for many pages, but it is their ubiquity, rather than their individuality, that makes them crucial to our story. From the 1830s to the end of the nineteenth century, an extraordinary and extraordinarily large number of people in France set out to write, speak, and act on matters of taste and style. Intense debate and anxiety surrounded the determination of the appropriate style and taste for each class in society.

14. *Exposition IVe des produits des membres de l'Académie de l'industrie à l'Orangerie des Tuileries, en 1840* (Paris, 1840), 44; AN F^{12}2334.

15. Letter to the Ministre de l'Agriculture, du Commerce et des Travaux publics, 24 January 1860 (AN F^{12}2334).

Some taste professionals came to specialize in providing advice to the bourgeoisie, while others were far more concerned with the taste of the working class. They were intimately and directly linked to the better known social reformers such as Villermé and can be considered part of a broadly linked project.

We observe their centrality by the 1860s, and contemporary preoccupation with matters of taste, during a crisis in the teaching of drawing in schools, which was acute enough for the city of Paris to set up a commission to investigate the problem in 1863. An improved level in the teaching of drawing was deemed necessary for France to preserve its dominance of the luxury trades. The commission decided that the solution lay in creating examinations for potential instructors, dividing the field into "art" and "geometry," improving facilities for drawing, and setting up annual contests among the students. The division of drawing into geometric and artistic, or technical and free drawing, reveals the persistent desire to create a differentiated artisanal class. Artisans destined to become designers learned free as well as technical drawing; those destined to produce simple variations on set themes usually learned only technical drawing. The commission did have some egalitarian intentions: drawing was to become compulsory for both genders and all classes. This project had a strong moralizing component and well-defined limits on what knowledge artisans needed to have. Or as Brongniart concisely put it in 1867: "The art of drawing is useful in all social positions . . . the study of drawing raises the general level of taste."[16]

A crucial context for the taste professionals' intervention into the conditions of training and of production was the revolutionary history of the faubourg. Furniture makers participated in the revolutions of 1789, 1830 and 1848 in disproportionate numbers. Of those involved in the taking of the Bastille nearly three-fourths were from the faubourg, approximately one-third working in furniture. Most were poor artisans, working alone or doing piecework with their families.[17] The revolutionary tradition continued into the nineteenth century. The revolutionary crowd of 1830 much resembled that of 1789; once again it was the skilled artisans and the workers from the faubourg who occupied a central role. David Pinkney estimates that carpenters, joiners and cabinetmakers were present in one-

16. Edouard Brongniart, "De l'enseignement du dessin en 1867," in *Exposition universelle de 1867, à Paris: rapports du jury international,* ed. Michel Chevalier (Paris, 1868), 13:402–11; citation on 403.

17. Monnier, *Le faubourg Saint-Antoine,* 122–25; de Salverte, *Ebénistes du XVIIIe siècle,* 15; Verlet, *L'art du meuble,* 64–65.

third greater numbers than might be expected. Sporadic violence in the faubourg St-Antoine in September 1846 presaged the Revolution of 1848. In June, crowds of between eight and ten thousand there protested the abolition of the National Workshops. Whether most of the revolutionaries in June came from within the old industries or the new is still debated, but it is agreed that the *ébénistes* and *menuisiers* were present in disproportionate numbers.[18]

Contemporaries acknowledged the faubourg's reputation as the seat of sedition, and of furniture workers as being ever ready to revolt; that reputation influenced policy, including educational policy, throughout the nineteenth century. In 1834 the city councillor Bonneville declared the faubourg to be "the home of revolt, the terror of the capital," carrying "in its breast the germ of the revolutions that exploded in Paris, and appeared to be the lever of popular fury."[19] The faubourg was understood to be especially explosive because of its poverty and the vulnerability of its inhabitants to economic vagaries, rendering it a "theater of unrelenting and murderous battles, one of the most formidable ramparts" of the uprisings of 1848 and 1852 when "giant barricades made it like a fort . . . [where] armed socialism made a supreme effort."[20] The examples could be multiplied.

Thus, the faubourg came to be the symbol of working-class misery, of poverty, of the striking contrast between the objects produced by these workers for a luxury trade and their own living conditions. The taste professionals saw one of their fundamental tasks to be the improvement of conditions of production in the faubourg, and of living conditions in working-class neighborhoods throughout Paris, ultimately in the interest

18. David Pinkney, "The Crowd in the French Revolution of 1830," *American Historical Review* 70 (October 1964): 3–5. On the crowd's elements see Georges Duveau, *1848: The Making of a Revolution*, trans. Anne Carter (New York, 1967); as support for Duveau's argument that most of those who revolted belonged to traditional trades, see Lynn Lees and Charles Tilly, "The People of June 1848" (working paper no. 70, Center for Research on Social Organization, 1972), although they intend to show something quite different. Out of 4,022 people arrested after the June days, 319 were *ébénistes* and 495 were *menuisiers*, a combined figure of 814 or just about 20 percent. Of these, 3,376 were deported to Algeria for participating in the revolution; 328 were *menuisiers* and *ébénistes*. Since only 773 came from the department of the Seine, and most of the woodworkers were probably from Paris, the proportion of woodworkers involved was high.

19. A. S. Bonneville, *Le faubourg Saint-Antoine* (Paris, 1834), 7–8.

20. Auguste Van Doren, *L'ébénisterie à Bruxelles et à Paris* (Brussels, 1860), 51. This point of view was repeated in the very widely read article, Thomas Funck-Brentano, "La ville du meuble," *La nouvelle revue* 76 (1892): 272.

of social and political peace. Not a simple task, it was complicated by contemporaries' very mixed stances toward both popular education and state intervention. On the one hand, better education for the furniture makers was perceived as necessary so that the economic health of the industry and of the faubourg could be improved and guaranteed. On the other hand, knowledge was perceived to be potentially dangerous when put in the hands of the working class. Furthermore, throughout this period most commentators agreed that the state should not meddle in the private relations between parents and children, between employers and employees. Accordingly during the 1840s, initiatives were largely limited to protective legislation for children and private efforts to create evening courses and libraries for artisans. But by the 1850s and especially the 1860s the state was becoming engaged through a change in the format of the universal exhibitions.

Trying simultaneously to improve the taste (and thereby the morality) of working-class consumers, expanding on the work of the social investigators of the 1830s and 1840s, the expositions' organizers argued that workers who lived in salubrious, tasteful, comfortable, clean dwellings would be happier, more productive, and better behaved. But here too the stance was paradoxical. If on the one hand workers lived more like bourgeois then they would behave more like them, reformers thought. But on the other hand, having goods like theirs, they would expect a bourgeois quality of life. Thus the question of state intervention into private homes grew more fraught.

THE TASTE PROFESSIONALS AND THE
CULTURE OF PRODUCTION

> There are two equally important although distinct principles that are necessary to the production of all perfect pieces of work: the conception and the execution. The precious qualities that we should strive for in all our work—beauty, simplicity, and solidity—rest on the union of these two principles, that is to say in thought served by skilled hands.[21]

> The *artiste* who designs and the *exécutant* who is in charge of realizing [the vision] always know how to respond to all the problems that daily come their way.[22]

These two quotations from anonymous articles in the *Journal de menuiserie* date from 1863 and 1865. Despite their proximity in time, they mark

21. "Planche 10: panneau de porte Louis XIV," *Journal de menuiserie* 1 (1863): 39.
22. "Planches 3 et 4: magasin," *Journal de menuiserie* 3 (1865): 9–10.

two opposing positions on the role of knowledge in furniture making. The first advocates the marriage of the imagination and the hand in the same artisan, insisting that only through that union would one arrive at beauty, simplicity and solidity. It articulated the traditional notion of craft, still held by many artisans in the trades. The 1865 quote notes a division between the operative who produced, using all technical possibilities, and the artist who designed; the two—one possessing skill and technique, the other knowledge and creativity—combined to produce an objet d'art. This divergence became both possible and necessary in this period because of the breakdown of the culture of production and the commercialization of relations of production and distribution. Both discourses could coexist in the 1860s, but by the turn of the century the split between the artist and the operative would be definitive.

At midcentury, the divergence reflected the larger problematic implicated in interventions designed to replace the educational functions of the culture of production. These interventions involved technical journals and books as well as night courses and universal expositions. The earliest institutions were publicly funded and privately run evening courses organized by the Conservatoire des arts et métiers and the Association polytechnique, followed in the 1860s by the Collège des beaux-arts appliqués à l'industrie (a middle school), the Bibliothèque des arts décoratifs and by the pioneering journals, the *Journal de menuiserie* (1863–81) and *Art pour tous: encyclopédie de l'art industriel et décoratif* (1861–1905). The goal of the *Journal de menuiserie* was to guide the craft of *menuiserie* into the nineteenth century, in part by serially reprinting Roubo's famous (but out of print) 1782 treatise.[23] *Art pour tous* was somewhat less technical in its orientation, emphasizing precise lithographs of masterpieces in French furniture production.

The two most visible institutions in Paris from the 1830s through 1850s that provided educational possibilities to artisans were the Association polytechnique and the Conservatoire des arts et métiers. The Association polytechnique offered free evening courses to the workers of Paris, expanding and organizing hierarchically the curriculum of the old Ecole spéciale (which it had absorbed), based on positivist principles.[24] Arithmetic, geometry, drawing of figure and ornament were its basic courses,

23. "Aux abonnés," *Journal de menuiserie* 1 (1863): 65. See mention of Roubo's work in chapters 2 and 3.

24. AN F²¹1422. On the Conservatoire des arts et métiers see the director's report of 2 February 1858 (AN F¹²4861). The association did have informal support from the state in this period (AN F¹⁷12529, p. 4).

followed by descriptive geometry, stone cutting, the building of wooden structures, mechanics, machine design, physics and chemistry; last came the optional or accessory courses of grammar, accounting, and hygiene. The curriculum held only materials directly applicable to the trades and those understood to be morally beneficial and excluded dangerous subjects such as history, architecture, art history and philosophy—the subjects necessary for innovation, creativity.

Continuing its explicit goal of "exercising a moral influence on the workers by giving them good habits," the association had between four hundred and five hundred members by the early 1830s and a broad network of classes for workers. It started a branch in the faubourg St-Antoine and actively recruited students, gathering by the 1840s an estimated eighty to one hundred *menuisiers, ébénistes, mécaniciens,* and employees in architecture offices. Despite complaints about low attendance, the employers' trade groups (*syndicats patronaux*) adopted the association's methods in the 1860s and urged cooperation within the corporation, trying through their efforts in education to persuade workers that employees and employers in their industry had like interests.[25]

The *polytechniciens* never reached large numbers of artisans and—a more serious defect—never offered the range of knowledge, skill, and craft sense that the culture of production had made accessible to some artisans. Courses were in lecture format, scheduled in the evening after a long workday. The materials covered may also not have been those of greatest interest to the artisans of the faubourg. Neither the association's nor the employer unions' schools' teachers were especially concerned about enabling artisans to do creative, innovative work—to make beauty. The association restricted its mission to giving workers "solid and elementary knowledge that will allow them to improve their position and perfect themselves in their *état,* and not advanced knowledge that most of them are too old to completely assimilate and that will alienate them from their trades without giving them the means of successfully moving into another."[26] Such training and its "moral" corollary might enable workers to perform specified tasks and might bias workers against unions but would not help them write poetry or think or act politically.

25. Rapport présenté par le comité d'enseignement, 1837 (AN F^{17}12529, p. 11); association polytechnique; documents pour servir à l'histoire de cette association, 1830–55 (ibid., pp. 4, 23). See also in F^{17}12330; the Patronage des apprentis tapissiers founded a school in the faubourg in 1882.
26. AN F^{17}12529, compte rendu, 1856.

Matching the efforts of the *polytechniciens*, the Conservatoire des arts et métiers, the public engineering school founded during the Revolution, expanded its evening courses, library and display rooms, claiming in 1856–57 an average audience of 270 people at each of its 550 lessons, nearly 10,000 readers in its library, and nearly 3,500 viewers in the Galerie du portefeuille industriel. The Conservatoire concentrated its evening curriculum on technical matters, including applied geometry, mechanics, chemistry, agriculture, industrial legislation and civil construction.[27]

The class logic of these projects is made especially clear in another proposal suggested by César Fichet. Education should be organized by social class, he argued in 1847, because the materials introduced into popular education—astronomy, cosmography, geology, ancient history, natural history, rhetoric "and other ornaments of the salon spirit"—were too abstract. He proposed a three-tier hierarchy of schools: "*collèges artistiques* for engineers and future heads of businesses, *écoles d'arts et métiers* for second-ranking managers, and *écoles communales d'apprentissage* for the vast majority."[28]

The Union centrale des beaux-arts appliqués à l'industrie took up Fichet's program, but without being completely straightforward as to the class location of its intended student body. Located at the edge of the faubourg, (in theory so that it would be accessible to workers), this middle school sought to combine "for the first time, a serious classical and literary education" with "the broadest study of art," educating the mind and the hand of children "destined to a career in the industries directly concerned with art."[29]

Their curriculum was indeed very broad, being much more inclusive than that of the Association polytechnique or of the *écoles patronales;* but the school was not really intended to train artisans. There were no scholarships and the cheapest tuition rate was 800 francs per year. Most working-class families in this period could not survive without their children's wages; paying out 800 francs a year was clearly impossible. A small footnote in the school's prospectus qualifies the rhetoric about its broad potential public: "We ask you to note, moreover, that the Collège des beaux-arts appliqués à l'industrie has been founded above all to train the leaders of the industrial arts." The founders of the school loudly proclaimed that they were going

27. Report of the directory of the Conservatoire to the minister, 2 February 1858 (AN F^{12}4861).

28. Fichet, *Mémoire sur l'apprentissage*, 33.

29. AN F^{12}2334, pièce 9.

to emulate the example of England, Germany, Austria and Russia and teach "the entire youth" but then quietly acknowledged that the school was really intended for future employers. As a consequence, the proposed curriculum of this elite middle school was the most abstract, and the most preoccupied with knowledge, of any school claiming interest in the industrial arts. As one descended the social ladder, the range of knowledge considered of relevance to the students became narrower and narrower.[30]

Such private institutions helped define the working class by a process of exclusion; access to knowledge observed class lines. The library of the Union centrale followed the same pattern. The library opened in 1866 in the place des Vosges, in the middle of an artisanal neighborhood. At its founding the library was private, supported by donations to the Union centrale; it served large numbers of both *travailleurs* and *visiteurs*. In 1867 the collection included books on art and industry, engravings, figures and ornaments, drawings and manuscripts, framed pictures and drawings, and fabric samples, together with a vast assortment of costumes, wallpaper samples, objets d'art, ceramics, plaster busts, and assorted objects.[31] But the library had no technical treatises, geometry books, or works on wood dyeing. Its collection blurred the distinction between the fine and the decorative arts—by including objects falling into both categories—but it did not include materials that would enable artisans to learn how to *make* the new forms that the collection enabled them to *imagine*.[32]

In sum, through the 1860s efforts to construct alternatives for artisans to the old culture of production—evening courses, schools, and libraries—were ineffectual. The new institutions intended for working-class audiences may have foundered because they hoped to blend moral and pedagogic functions. The Collège des beaux-arts was successful but did not train artisans or students of working-class origins. The impact of new trade journals and books is difficult to assess.

One institution did find an important place in artisans' lives: the universal exposition, a state-administered form of involvement in the training of artisans. Even before the Third Republic, industrial expositions came to

30. Ibid., note 4; also preface to the 1880 exposition review issue of *Revue des arts décoratifs* (3 [1882–83]); Victor Champier, "Le pavillon de la commission française organisé par l'Union centrale à l'exposition d'Amsterdam," *Revue des arts décoratifs* 4 (1883–84): 75.

31. AN F^{12}2334, pièce 2.

32. Cornélia Serrurier, *Bibliothèques de France* (The Hague, 1946), 238; Eugène Morel, *Bibliothèque: essai sur le développement des bibliothèques publiques et de la librairie dans les deux mondes* (Paris, 1909), 1:91.

seem ubiquitous and occurred as often as twice a decade. International trade fairs had existed since ancient times, and the first half of the century saw a series of national expositions, but expositions like the London Crystal Palace Exhibition of 1851 and its successors were novel in their cosmopolitanism, their efforts at comprehensiveness, as well as in their founders' hopes of effecting social change through the expositions. Paris hosted universal exhibitions in 1855, 1867, 1878, 1889, 1900, and finally the big decorative arts exposition in 1925. The expositions grew enormously in size from midcentury to its end: seeing vast increases in exhibitors, attendance, and space.[33]

When the 1867 universal exposition was hosted in Paris, exhibitions had become a linchpin in the system of institutions that were designed to replace the culture of production and were the main locus of state-sponsored activities and influences in that effort. They were far more complex than a hegemonic imposition of new productive relations; in fact, they involved two separate but interrelated functions. First, expositions became a context in which artisans were to increase their knowledge of their trade, a place where their taste was formed—a function that draws our attention to the structure of the exhibitions, what was exposed there, who went, and what they retained of what they saw. Second, the expositions were a critically important location for the taste professionals' efforts to differentiate the styles and aspirations of working-class and bourgeois consumers.

The organizers of the imperial expositions put considerable effort into assuring a working-class presence—displaying items by workers as producers and items for them as consumers.[34] They were equally careful to "mark" the working-class visitors and the exhibits intended for their benefit. The 1855 exposition charged admission for the first time, but tickets cost more on some days than others, to encourage workers to come to the exposition but not to mingle with the wealthier classes; exhibitors were encouraged to display goods the working class could afford—within general exhibits on domestic economy—but carefully labeled them "working-class." For the exhibition of 1867 artisans were invited by Napoleon III to participate as "worker delegates."[35]

---

33. Pascal Ory, *Les expositions universelles de Paris* (Paris, 1982), 26.

34. Madeleine Rébérioux, "Approches de l'histoire des expositions universelles à Paris du second empire à 1900," *Bulletin du centre d'histoire économique et sociale de la région lyonnaise* 1 (1979): 198.

35. See *Rapports des délégués des ouvriers parisiens à l'exposition de Londres* (Paris, 1862); and Eugène Tartaret, ed., *Exposition universelle de 1867: commission ouvrière*, 2 vols. (Paris, 1868–69).

These exhibitions of the Second Empire were serving many diverse—and sometimes contradictory—interests: they provided a showcase for technological, craft, and artistic innovation; they served as advertisements for exhibitors; they gave artisans from many parts of the world a place to meet; they stimulated world competition in productivity. They were festive events, offering a break in the routines of everyday life; they displayed, through the colonial exhibits, a representation of European domination; and, they were educational events.[36] The universal expositions were caught in an interstitial position between the culture of production and "modern" relations of production, between the "moral" concerns of the taste professionals and the commercial interests of the producer-distributors, between a world dominated by producers and one dominated by consumers.

For example, one traditional means by which artisans learned from each other had been the display of pieces produced in a workshop and left there for a few days so that other artisans could come to admire them and educate themselves. The goods would then be carried, in procession, to their ultimate owners. Incompatible with increasingly rationalized labor practices and consumption patterns, the practice declined over the nineteenth century, a development *ébéniste*-delegates to the 1867 exposition strongly regretted.[37] In its stead, museum and fair exhibitions formalized the competition of manufacturers—both in the world market and against their neighbors. Not only did a medal won at a universal exposition bring recognition by one's peers, it also increased sales. With the creation of exhibitions, moreover, an additional level of expertise was installed between the makers and the buyers—the taste professionals now accepted the products to be displayed at an exposition and later judged which items to immortalize in a museum. Both the status and education of artisans suffered as a result.

These universal exposition exhibits may be understood in one sense as a transformed version of the chefs d'oeuvre of the masters of the Old Regime as well as of the compagnons (discussed in chapter 3). The chefs d'oeuvre of the masters were strictly individual projects designed to demonstrate the worthiness of a journeyman to become an entrepreneur and a teacher in his trade, as well as its representative to the city. Those of the compagnons were also usually individual and always self-generated, made

36. Charles Rearick, *Pleasures of the Belle Epoque* (New Haven, 1985), 119. For a rather different interpretation, see Werner Plum, *Les expositions universelles au 19e siècle*, trans. Pierre Gallissaires (Bonn, 1977), 63; Richard D. Mandell, *Paris 1900: The Great World's Fair* (Toronto, 1967), 4.

37. Baude and Loizel, "Ebénistes," 1:13.

Figure 37.   Chair in precious wood,
ca. 1820. Toulousain le Tranquille.
Compagnon's masterpiece. René
Edeline Collection.

to be seen and judged by one's peers. As Figure 37 indicates—in the maker's
name painstakingly carved into the front of the chair, as legible decoration—authorship was often, although certainly not always, central to the
chef d'oeuvre of the compagnons. By contrast, Figure 38 shows the exhibit
of chairs entered by the maison Rébeyrotte in the 1889 Exposition universelle. The chairs are displayed with other furniture (probably produced
by other shops) in a domestic setting rather than as discrete items, which
would have emphasized that they had been produced by chair makers. They
bear no signs of their labor and are identified only as having been produced
by the maison Rébeyrotte.

Figure 38. "Exposition universelle—Paris, 1889. Sièges et meubles exposés par la maison Rébeyrotte (à Paris)." *Le Garde meuble: collection de sièges*, pl. 1791. Louis XV style.

In contrast to all these forms of chefs d'oeuvre, the exposition exhibits were typically the products of an entire workshop and represented the congealed, fragmented, and anonymous labor of a large number of artisans. Worker delegates to the 1867 exposition expressed great irritation over employers' refusal to give credit to the workers involved in producing a piece. For example, admiring a masterpiece of French cabinetwork, they asked for the names of the workers who created it, only to be frustrated by the exhibitor's insistence that only the employer be credited since he drew the design. When pressed to credit at least the sculptors' work (the most "artistic" element), he insisted that since more than sixty workers had a hand in sculpting the piece they were effectively anonymous. In response, the cabinetmakers refused to give the names of either the employers or the workers.[38] The cabinetmakers clearly did not accept the argument that employers could legitimately take sole credit for the pieces emerging from their workshops. Confronted with a representative's obstructionism, they were willing to accept the anonymity of the cabinetmakers and other workers, but when it became clear that no worker (and they used the word *worker*, not *artisan*) was to be named, they strongly objected. These

38. Ibid, 1:22–23.

workers did not accept that they were *simply* selling their labor; they had indeed sold their labor, but they wanted recognition for their talent and knowledge nonetheless.

The limitation of the expositions as a means to perpetuate the culture of production was not only that authorship went unacknowledged. Although the expositions did partially replicate a central role of traditional production, the communication of innovations among artisans, their display was but a pale reflection of earlier practices. Various forms of direct contact within an artisanal culture—apprenticeship, compagnonnage and visiting—had helped workers learn from one another. Now, innovation and production of creative new pieces was encouraged by awarding prizes. But encouraging the submission of prize-winning pieces would not serve anything like the same function. The expositions were supposed to provide a place where artisans could exhibit their work and view the work of others, but as the makers of "antique" furniture complained, the cost of exhibiting a piece was prohibitively high.[39] This expense was not a result of display charges but an effect of the role of the universal expositions as sites of international competition. Individual producers could rarely afford to submit pieces to the exhibitions, and the prizes awarded were always given to the owner of the shop responsible, never to the individual creators. Last, although artisans might still learn from the objects on display, they could rarely talk to those responsible for its innovations.

Artisans, or rather the entrepreneurs who controlled the workshops, devoted enormous resources to exhibition pieces in the hopes of winning prizes of considerable commercial value. Unlike the pieces earlier displayed in the workshops, which had been partially paid for before any work was invested, exhibition pieces were made on speculation and were often never sold. Few artisans could afford the luxury of making a masterpiece of this order. Moreover, in the profusion of luxury goods, not only was there competition between individual producers, but between nations; each country was trying to show itself at its best.[40] Exhibit pieces were chosen to compete in a capitalist world market, not to establish an individual's place in a community, nor to regulate relations among communities. Knowledge, skill, and craft sense were now to be used much more directly in the interests of the state and in the interests of capital. The alienation of

---

39. Lesieur, Lagoutte, and Durand, "Menuisiers en meuble antique," 2:1.
40. *Exposition universelle de 1855: rapports du jury mixte international* (Paris, 1856), 1114.

workers from the works displayed at the expositions may find its echo in a union discussion in 1889 over when to strike: *ébénistes* of the faubourg decided that "this was the appropriate moment because the bosses had a hundred displays to do for the exposition."[41]

Successful competitors influenced production because their rivals in France and abroad imitated or adapted their designs, both to garner retail sales and to compete at the next exhibition. The exhibitions did allow individual manufacturers to have great impact. For example, Henri Fourdinois, who won gold medals in 1851, had enormous influence and Fourdinois imitations were numerous in the years following.[42] Individual decorators—Liénard, Reiber, Rambert, Brunet, Langfeld—also gained influence. The exhibitions were also heavily reviewed in the specialized and general press, with articles on individual accomplishments, new machines, and technical and aesthetic innovations. Undoubtedly people within the trades read the articles and studied the results, deciding for themselves what they could learn or use.

The expositions were bourgeois in origin, the result of an alliance between the state, moral reformers, and taste professionals. They were part of the state's effort to respond to the perceived crisis in taste provoked by the fading of the culture of production. Moreover, expositions in the 1850s and 1860s had the goal of promoting French "art industries" and French products in general and of maintaining class peace.

The two worlds of the culture of production and of the taste professionals came together—and at times collided—in these expositions. The taste professionals determined the structure of the expositions, the definitions of the categories of exhibits, the number of prizes to be allocated, the price of admission and other administrative matters. They named the judges. But the artisans themselves submitted work, sat in judgment on the work in their trades, and, as we shall see in chapter 6, used the expositions and the reports published after the expositions as an alternate forum to organized labor. The expositions were a hybrid, combining the last vestiges of the culture of production of the Old Regime with the scientifically, bureaucratically, rationally organized knowledge and skill of the late nineteenth century; suspended between the exigencies and interests of production and

41. Archives de la préfecture de police (hereafter, APP) Ba 1422 [2000.44.51], report of a meeting on 17 February 1889.

42. *Exposition universelle de 1855: rapports du jury mixte international,* 1402–3; and J. Fresson, *Enseignement professionnel: conférences sur le meuble* (Paris, 1887), 65–66.

consumption; and located at an ambiguous juncture between organizations of bourgeois and artisanal initiative.

Although advocates of this separation of knowledge, skill, and craft sense can be found in writings from as early as the Old Regime, the idea came into prominence only in the mid-nineteenth century. The debate spawned the concepts and institutional structures of the almost synonymous "industrial arts," "decorative arts," "applied arts," and "design." These new domains were cordoned off both from the fine arts—painting, sculpture, and drawing—and from industry. The institutions of unified craft died, to be replaced by disarticulated art, design, and industry.[43] By the end of the century it was thought that an elite of school-trained *artistes* and a substratum of unskilled workers could replace the artisan.

TASTE PROFESSIONALS' INTERVENTION
INTO WORKING-CLASS CONSUMPTION

Part of the work of taste professionals—especially those concerned with the state of working class life—was closely allied and in fact overlapped with the work of the social investigators Louis Villermé and Frédéric Le Play. By the 1850s government officials as well as private interests were worried that the working classes were buying furnishings inappropriate for their station in life. Rather than furnishing their homes with utilitarian, practical, durable goods, they were buying—at least in the imaginations of the commentators—monarchical-style furniture that appeared luxurious but was really shoddy, thus representing false and foolish aspirations.

From the 1830s, therefore, how and if class difference was to be marked by furniture style became an issue in a new way. In the eighteenth and early nineteenth centuries, the cost of furniture that resembled that of the wealthy made it clearly and obviously inaccessible to the laboring classes, so the only possible style slippage across class lines occurred between nobles and very wealthy commoners. Few nineteenth-century consumers yearned for the old era when the crown set style and regulated consumption, yet most found the idea of an open market in goods little easier to accept. But the midcentury had brought changes in marketing and retailing practices—department stores, chain stores, rationalized consumer-credit procedures, elaborated advertising and display techniques—developments that caused

43. This move was not greeted uncritically by contemporaries. See, for example, Bonnaffé's scathing critique (*Etudes sur l'art*, 212–15).

considerable anxiety. M. Delamarre, for example, in a book published in 1851, provides one example of many texts that waxed eloquent against the evils of distributors.[44] Delamarre's focus was on the dangers of fraud, but behind many of the tirades against commercial techniques was fear of what this solicitation of consumers and the availability of goods might produce in social disruption.

Few of these developments directly concerned the furniture trades until later in the century, yet by the 1850s the possibility that the poor could acquire furniture in the style of kings appeared imminent enough to worry critics. Theirs would not be high-quality royal furniture, but its forms might echo those of the courtly society of the ancien régime and, equally important, might equal the pieces acquired by their contemporary wealthy neighbors.[45] The king might well allow and judiciously limit emulation of his things, but many bourgeois at midcentury panicked at the prospect that the working class might aspire to be like them. Critics understood these changes to bear the seeds of a mass-consumer society (although they would not, of course, have called it that). They envisioned this new world as one in which social differences would be invisible and, far more seriously, one in which the working class would refuse to stay in its place, would attempt to move, through knowledge and taste, into the bourgeoisie.

The bourgeoisie were far from unified in this class project, however. Given the internal division among social Catholics, social investigators, state officials, pedagogues, social scientists, and other members of the elite, their perceptions and prescriptions for the working class varied. Yet nearly everyone involved in the discussion agreed that knowledge and style were the stuff of which class was made and that the differentiation of the working class from the bourgeoisie was critically important. The possibility of a class blurring of interior furnishings, at the same time that divisions between

44. Théodore-Casimir Delamarre, *Economie pratique: la vie à bon marché, économie pratique, reformes utiles* (Paris, 1851). On the cost of furniture during the ancien régime and the difficulties the poor had in acquiring it, see Roche, *Le peuple de Paris;* Pardailhé-Galabrun, *Naissance de l'intime,* chap. 6; David Garrioch, *Neighbourhood and Community in Paris, 1740–90* (Cambridge, 1986). On the development of department stores see chapter 8.

45. The BHVP 120, ameub. series supports this claim: C, Au confortable moderne, 1902, 57 bis avenue de la Motte-Picquet; and V, Ville d'Aboukir, 1880s, 143 rue d'Aboukir. Part 3's introduction discusses laborers' buying abilities. As Jeanne Gaillard notes, department stores had few working-class customers (*Paris, la ville, 1852–1870* [Paris, 1976], 541).

classes were deepening in other ways, raised the question of where social boundaries were to fall and how they were to be marked.

Commentators on consumption found themselves in a double bind parallel to that encountered by the commentators on production. Social and moral reformers had, for years, been urging the "bourgeoisification" of working-class homes. The extensive commercialization of society seemed to promise exactly that: the erasure of the commodity markings of class. But these reformers had not been advocating a classless society. If anyone could buy a Henri II–style dining room, how was the social peace that depended on acceptance of class stratification to be maintained? An apparent solution to the problem, typified by Le Play's analysis of the case of Bernard D., was the creation of different styles for different classes, a parallel to the forms of knowledge and skill appropriate to various classes. Individuals of the working class were not to be excluded from the new world of commodities, they were simply to be given a precise location within it. This idea was in some sense an extension of the work of Daly and Viollet-le-Duc, who argued that for each culture there was an appropriate style. If classes were defined as cultures, then it made sense that each should have its own form of dwelling, furnishing, and clothing. And in fact, the fruit of the social investigations and architectural innovations of the 1830s and 1840s was, in the 1860s, the creation by bourgeois designers, of a specifically working-class style.

This style was not widely purchased and was therefore never widely produced. It is not, however, in the rather predictable commercial failure of bourgeois-imagined working-class style that the significance and irony of this story lies. In the creation of working-class style, the taste professionals and the state prescribed the creation of the working class itself, a class with a sense of its interests and identity distinct from those of the bourgeoisie. That they could envision such a relation between style and class making suggests the new relations among taste, style, and social power emerging in the nineteenth century. Their discussions, moreover, were less a response to actual transformations in working-class consumption habits than they were expressive of both the perceived possibility of mass consumption and the effects of the recategorization of the working-class home into a social space open to the eyes and commentary of concerned state officials and private philanthropists. They emerged from the same assumption about the general aesthetic limits of workers as compared to the bourgeoisie. And in these discussions we glimpse the hope that, if the working class could come to live not like the bourgeoisie, but in a manner the bourgeoisie deemed appropriate, then the social conflict threatened by industrialization could be held at bay.[46]

The universal expositions were the central site of bourgeois attempts to "make" the working class through appropriate life-styles, furniture style, and domestic taste. An ideal medium because they attracted very large numbers of working-class visitors, the expositions were state-controlled and ostensibly disinterested. Exhibits like the Galerie de l'économie domestique seemed value-neutral but, like other attempts at class making in this period, were riddled with contradiction and confusions. At moments, for example, the crucial lines of social demarcation as marked by furnishings seemed to fall between consumers and producers; at others between the moral and the immoral, or workers and bourgeois. Though to some extent chronological moments, these were also simultaneous, cross-cutting categorizations of the aesthetic and the functional.

The Galerie de l'économie domestique at the 1855 exposition had two basic objectives: to push industry to create new kinds of furniture and to provide information to consumers of limited resources.[47] The furniture displayed there was to include only affordable products, characterized by "good quality, good conditions of solidity and durability; practicality and easy maintenance; low price."[48] On the consumption side, the purpose of the *galerie* was to inform consumers of the sound furniture and other domestic items available. The organizers shifted the emphasis of the exposition from a locus for the producers to show off their art and skill through a presentation of masterpieces in the ancien régime tradition— with the retail cost of prize-winning furniture equivalent to several times a well-paid bourgeois's yearly salary—to an effort to improve consumer taste and provide a bridge between producers and consumers.

Following the model of the Société d'économie charitable de Paris and the London-based Society of Arts, the organizers divided consumers into a four-tier hierarchy, originally to be in separate divisions (not carried out). At the bottom they put the poorest, who had little choice and were limited to necessities, followed by those who could afford to be more selective but who were still limited by economic and practical considerations, and finally

46. I would therefore modify Katherine Lynch's argument that there came to be *one* familial norm (*Family, Class, and Ideology,* 13).
47. Rébérioux, "Approches de l'histoire," 203–4.
48. *Exposition universelle (de 1855): galerie de l'économie domestique* (Paris, 1855), 8–9.

those who could "add to the useful, the practical, and the agreeable."[49] Not included, and not intended to attend this exhibit, were the wealthy, for whom money was no object. Consumers of different wealth were to have different furniture, but the exposition addressed them all as consumers similarly in search of self-representation and good taste.

The organizers planned a catalogue to give consumers useful information such as the name of the manufacturer, price, and sales location. They urged that not only the prices of goods be displayed, but the cost breakdown of labor, materials, distribution, and profit. With such frankness they hoped to improve relations between distributors and consumers (much tarnished at that point).[50] Predictably, manufacturers resisted the idea and the organizers were unable to enforce it. Clearly, the organizers hoped to mediate between distributors and consumers, urging the latter to adopt "realistic" and "appropriate" tastes.

The idea that different classes were to have different things was made very explicit: "Therefore instead of that furniture known under the name of *'camelote'* that apes luxury by elaborate forms and fraudulent appearance and offers only illusory good value, woodworkers who would really like to work with intelligence and success for the middling and laboring classes, should present furniture in domestic woods, solid, practical, and elegant in its simplicity, and above all perfectly adapted to the service that it will provide."[51] The passage was one of many implying that should laborers buy this "fraudulent" furniture, they would not only be pretending to be something they were not but would receive "only illusory" quality and be cheated.[52] The exhibit was to include "a successive progression of specimens of the domestic home at each step of the social scale, from poverty to affluence." The working class was now to live in specially designed working-class dwellings, with working-class furniture, and its own aesthetic of practicality.[53]

49. Ibid., 13.
50. Ibid., 7, 12.
51. Ibid., 44.
52. Adrienne Cambry, *Fiançailles et fiancés* (Paris, 1913); M. A. Cochin, "Classe 91: meubles, vêtements et aliments de toute origine, distingués par les qualités utiles, unies au bon marché," in *Exposition universelle de 1867, à Paris: rapports du jury international*, ed. Michel Chevalier (Paris, 1868), 13:775–76. See also *Exposition universelle de 1855: rapports du jury mixte international*, 1402–3.
53. *Exposition universelle (de 1855)*, 13. On working-class housing see Lion Murard and Patrick Zylberberg, *Disciplines à domicile* (Paris, 1977) and *L'Haleine des faubourgs* (Fontenay-sous-bois, 1978). For another perspective on working-

Such aesthetic guidelines were heavily burdened by the idea of appropriateness: to make an everyday object luxurious was in poor taste; for everyday people (workers) to own luxurious objects, or luxurious-seeming objects, was—implicitly—inappropriate. The dangerous quality of appropriateness was its fluidity: who was to judge what was appropriate for what purpose and for whom? According to these taste professionals, clearly, neither producers nor consumers were capable of such judgment.

Even though working-class people were not to ape their superiors, they were not to be deprived of all ornamentation in their houses either. The *galerie* was divided into *meubles de service* and *meubles d'agrément.* In the former were the necessary goods (tables, armoires, beds, chairs); in the latter, the decorative objects (clocks, vases, sculptures). "Even those that constitute but pure decoration should not be excluded from the category of domestic economy, if one reflects on all that contributes to making a *chez soi* agreeable, in attaching a master of the family to his home and to his interior, to bring him home with pleasure. These decorative items exercise an incontestable influence on the happiness of the home and of the family."[54] The subtext of this class of economical furnishings, here made explicit, was to keep working-class men at home, off the street, and out of the bars.

Despite the impressive rhetoric, the exhibit of goods in classe XXXI— produits de l'économie domestique: ameublement—was not, in 1855, a great success. A very limited exhibit, with only Parisian exhibitors and few even of them, its only complete line of furnishings was produced by M. Fourdinois. In fact, Fourdinois designed a special collection for the exposition; furniture in this price range was not part of his regular line. His work was praised for being "perfectly designed, and in the conditions of genuine economy . . . solidly made, and with excellent materials," demonstrating "a healthy appreciation for the comfort appropriate to each level of income."[55] With his success attributed in part to the fact that he had once been a worker himself and therefore knew the "tastes and needs" of the working class, the unstated argument was almost genetic; that those who came from the working class, regardless of their current social location would always somewhere possess the (limited) taste of their class and no

---

class housing see Anne Louise Shapiro, "Paris," in *Housing the Workers, 1850–1914,* ed. M. J. Daunton (London, 1990), 33–66.

54. *Exposition universelle (de 1855),* 44.

55. *Exposition universelle de 1855: rapports du jury mixte international,* 1402–3.

working-class person when making or buying something could be truly possessed of "good taste."[56] From the manufacturers' point of view, then, success in this humble category was a mixed blessing. To succeed was to be linked with the working class. In Fourdinois's case it was a reminder of his social origins; for any manufacturer it invited a reputation as exclusive producers of working-class furniture. The compliment made to Fourdinois was also perhaps an attempt to remind him that he was, despite his consistently prize-winning, highly luxurious furniture, only a worker after all.

The discourses concerning appropriate representation of the working class combined in complicated ways paternalist concern for working-class welfare and a preoccupation with the construction of class boundaries. The ancien régime–style furniture offered to workers was itself judged not only inappropriate but also deceptive because inexpensive versions of luxury furniture required cutting costs—usually in materials and workmanship— and, it was alleged, making the furniture unsound.[57] Tellingly, the standard criticism of bourgeois consumers when they too bought "fake" Old Regime–style furniture—that the work was imitative and therefore not original—was not made of working-class consumers. Working-class consumers were understood to have no need for original furniture.

By 1867, the 1855 classification Galerie de l'économie domestique had been transformed, possibly exemplifying a continuing ambivalence toward production and producers. It was now "six categories . . . containing not only inexpensive objects, but also a broad array of exhibits: methods and materials used in elementary schooling; folk costumes; work techniques and products of master artisans; housing blueprints and models. In brief . . . it [now] concerned all of the objects specially displayed with a view to improving the physical and moral condition of populations."[58] Working-class consumers had been shunted with working-class producers to their own autonomous world; they became an anthropological object analogous to the colonial villages imported for later exhibitions.

In this new version of the gallery of domestic economy, moreover, the world had come to be divided into wealthy consumers and a population in need of betterment. Even the conditions for work presented here were

56. *Exposition universelle (de 1855)*, 44.
57. On this aspect of the problem see Arnould Desvernay, ed., *Rapports des délégations ouvrières contenant l'origine et l'histoire des diverses professions* (Paris, 1867), 5:67–68.
58. Cochin, "Classe 91," 13:775–76. See also *Exposition universelle de 1867: enquête ouverte par la réunion des bureaux du 10e groupe* (Paris, 1867), 2.

marked. Exhibitors were obliged to give prices for their goods in this exhibit category but not in others. The organizers still hoped that this category would encourage the production of affordable goods and thereby improve the standard of living of the working class, albeit not because a minimum quality of life was an inalienable human right but because people living under too great a strain of deprivation were judged inevitably doomed to become vicious, since "only exceptionally can morality develop or last in the grip of absolute destitution, and a bit of happiness is necessary to a bit of virtue."[59]

In the discourse of the taste professionals, the working class was saturated with its class position. The bourgeoisie perceived themselves as highly differentiated and stratified, but they understood the working class as a basically unified entity, segmented only by bourgeois images of what it ought to be. Within and between households, inhabitants of a bourgeois home were to be carefully distinguished by their precise status, location, gender, age, and religion; the interior of working-class space was to be undifferentiated. True, the cramped space of working-class housing did limit the possibilities of elaborate subdivisions but did not dictate furniture marked simply by class. The fundamental purposes of working-class furniture were to keep the man of the house at home rather than out on the street and to reproduce the social order. The bourgeoisie drew only one line of demarcation within the working class—between the domesticated and the undomesticated—these being the grandchildren of the laboring and dangerous classes earlier in the century. But all were without the aesthetic sensibility to make or buy tasteful furniture.[60]

For the working class, cleanliness, practicality, and solidity were to take priority over aesthetic pleasure, and all its members were to have interiors in which all the spaces looked identical. While the guides to furnishing bourgeois dwellings emphasized the specificity of each room and what style would be appropriate to it, laborers had simpler lives in which such specialization was unnecessary. Furthermore, in this schema, the working class was to have no opportunity to construct its continuity with a national past through appropriating objects with "history"; the project of establishing a familial past or an individual past through objects had no relevance. The furniture recommended to the working class was to be practical for the

59. Cochin, "Classe 91," 13:776–77.
60. *Exposition universelle (de 1855)*, 44; Louis Chevalier, *Laboring Classes and Dangerous Classes in Paris during the First Half of the Nineteenth Century*, trans. Frank Jellinek (New York, 1973).

everyday; it was not the stuff from which dreams, or history, or individuality were made.

Far from reaching a consensus on what furnishings to represent or on how to categorize those who owned them, even the organizers and commentators at the 1867 exposition could still confound social class boundaries, the old distinction between the laboring and dangerous classes with that between virtue and immorality.

> Here is . . . the horoscope of Parisian furniture. For the worker, the artist, the lawyer, the doctor, the scientist, the man of letters, oak—the strong, robust wood—and solid walnut, or their analogues. For wealthy households, sculpted furniture in the dining room, the living room, and study; veneered furniture from Boutung or Godin [stores that sold expensive, fashionable furniture] in the bedroom. For châteaux and palaces, elaborate furniture: mantelpieces, canopy beds, bookcases, filing cabinets, wardrobes. . . . For the dubious professions, for shady opulence, for boudoirs that are really salesrooms, junk. Birds of a feather should flock together.[61]

Here the most crucial divide was between legitimate or illegitimate labor, rather than working-class or bourgeois social location. Workers, doctors, scientists, and lawyers all did honest work and were therefore entitled to solid, strong, robust wood. Those who were wealthy (and the author implies that they were wealthy by birth rather than by labor) were best represented by highly ornamented pieces; those who existed by dishonest labor were to possess fraudulent furniture. The furniture thus stood in for, represented, a man's moral standing; it matched his mode of being in the world.

This was an unusual position by the late 1860s. Most commentators would agree that the furnishings were to match the man of the household's place in life but argued that the fit concerned his class rather than his moral position (and most would argue that class and moral position were necessarily identical). The grouping of both consumers and producers from the laboring poor into one category, separate from that of the middling classes, was more typical of the moment, but it is significant that moral differentiations could still confound clear class divisions.

In fact, the efforts at the expositions of 1855, 1867, and 1889 appear to have failed; few producers were willing to display their goods in the designated categories, and working-class as well as bourgeois consumers

---

61. Luchet, *L'art industriel à l'exposition universelle de 1867*, 134.

were fondest of pastiche ancien régime furniture.[62] The evidence from working-class furniture retailers—through sociological investigations or novelistic and photographic evidence—reinforces this image.[63] Working-class stores sold largely cheap pastiches of ancien régime style (although the style was often even less determinate than that from more expensive stores), and there is evidence that the furniture sold in open air markets was also generally historicist.[64]

The possibility that furniture in the style of the ancien régime could be available at a price the working class could afford caused deep distrust and chagrin in conservative and socialist commentators alike, as the debate ranged far beyond the universal expositions and taste professionals. The conservatives argued that the working class should have furniture appropriate to its station, such as would encourage good and moral behavior; the socialists hoped for furniture that would assist in building class solidarity.[65] For conservatives, surroundings of courtly style led (laborers) to unreasonable expectations and a dangerous sense of social entitlement; for socialists, they contributed to (all workers') false consciousness. The following quotation from an etiquette book published just before the First World War captures and perpetuates a conservative point of view common thirty years earlier: "Today, the display of false and imitation [furniture] has given to modest households the ambition of elegance and the vanity of appearances. This failing would be moving, if it did not damage the most serious of interests, for on the one hand it exaggerates coquetry and on the other leads to extravagant spending."[66]

62. *Exposition universelle de 1855: rapports du jury mixte international,* 1402–3; Cochin, "Classe 91," 13:777; Alfred Picard, ed., *Exposition universelle internationale de 1889, à Paris* (Paris, 1891–92), 3:6–7.

63. See Lenard R. Berlanstein, *The Working People of Paris, 1871–1914* (Baltimore, 1984); on Eugène Atget's work as a historical source see the introduction to the Atget catalogue (Margaret Nesbit, "Atget's *Intérieurs parisiens,* the point of difference," in *Eugène Atget, 1857–1927: intérieurs parisiens, photographies* [Paris, 1982], 25–28).

64. The BHVP advertisements include detailed flyers from twenty stores serving popular consumers; some of the furniture was given an ancien régime attribution.

65. Gaston-Louis Marchal, *Jean Jaurès et les arts plastiques* (Castres, 1984); and Benoît Malon, *Des réformes possibles et des moyens pratiques* (Paris, 1890–91). For conservative sociological views on style and the working class see Frédéric Le Play (*Les ouvriers des deux mondes,* 5 vols. [Paris, 1857–85]) and Octave Du Mesnil (*L'hygiène à Paris: l'habitation du pauvre* [Paris, 1890]).

66. Cambry, *Fiançailles et fiancés,* 122.

Other critics thought that members of the bourgeoisie too should not live in prerevolutionary interiors, but the logic of their complaint was different. Bourgeois individuals who acquired courtly furniture were judged unfaithful to their age and class and lacking in courage; the working class was simply deceitful.[67] Indeed, no commentators thought that ancien régime style of *any* description was appropriate for the working class.

This process of class making through style was slow and complex. The class boundaries in these discussions solidified only gradually in the second half of the nineteenth century, being further complicated by the expansion of the rather nebulous class of the petite bourgeoisie. But a discourse grouping individuals of diverse social classes into the same stylistic categories—and thus defining other criteria, such as character, religion, region, as more relevant—would become much rarer as the century neared its end. So although the route to class boundaries marked by style was long and somewhat tortuous, by the end of the century such distinctions were firmly in place (at least in the minds of bourgeois commentators). Even if all had had the means to live in the style of kings, it was not to be; distinctions on the basis of consumer goods were as sharply drawn as during the ancien régime.

THE TASTE PROFESSIONALS AND THE ADVENT OF BOURGEOIS DOMESTICITY

Another sphere of class formation through taste in which the taste professionals intervened was the bourgeois household. Research into death inventories allows Adeline Daumard to document both the homogeneity of bourgeois furnishings and the fact that by this period bourgeois couples did not live with their parents' furniture, but rather bought furnishings of their own.[68] The task of acquiring this furniture and decorating the home fell to women.

By the third decade of the nineteenth century, wives and daughters of Parisian large manufacturers, professionals, and civil servants had largely been excluded from paid labor. Part of the very definition of a bourgeois householder was that his wife and daughters not work for wages but have

67. For the critique of bourgeois taste, see Henri Fourdinois, "Quelques réflexions sur le mobilier à propos de l'Union centrale," *Revue des arts décoratifs* 3 (1882–83): 164–65.
68. Daumard, *Les bourgeois et la bourgeoisie*, 22–27, 73–74. The timing of this intervention seems to have been similar in the United States (Lynes, *The Tastemakers*, chaps. 1–2).

at least one servant to give them managerial status within the home.[69] The bourgeois "home" (a word the French borrowed from the English in 1816) was invented along with the housewife. Among the manufacturing bourgeoisie, the sites of production and domesticity were distinct and set the manufacturer apart from the petit-bourgeois artisan, whose home was still over the shop, and whose wife still worked in the business.[70] Individuals in the expanding class of civil servants also took umbrella in hand and left home every morning. The separation of workplace from home was not absolute; professionals—doctors, lawyers, notaries, and architects—often still worked out of an office at home. But even when the dwelling was physically segregated from the workplace, the location, cost, and appearance of the home was far from irrelevant to the professional success of the husband-father and to the economic well-being of the family.

Bourgeois women, as consumers, had a doubled task; they were to adorn themselves and they were to constitute and represent the family's social identity through goods. Bourgeois daughters, when on the marriage market, were encouraged to increase their value through the cultivation of beauty and the acquisition of clothing, jewelry, and culture. That obligation did not end with marriage, for in the bodies of wives, and in the homes they created, inhered the position of the family. Brides often brought furnishings for the use of the couple into the household, while grooms often brought goods for their personal use.[71] Hence bourgeois wives did not produce only

69. Louise Tilly and Joan Wallach Scott, *Women, Work and Family* (New York, 1978), 77 and 149–51; B. Smith, *Ladies of the Leisure Class;* Adeline Daumard, *Les bourgeois de Paris au XIXe siècle* (Paris, 1970), chap. 5; Anne Martin-Fugier, *La bourgeoise* (Paris, 1983), 10–14.

70. Frank Bechhofer and Brian Elliott, eds., *The Petite Bourgeoisie* (New York, 1981), 182–200, esp. 194; Daumard, *Les bourgeois de Paris au XIXe siècle,* 191–92.

71. For example, the marriage contract between M. Arson and Mlle Hackenberger on 11 October 1841 shows that M. Arson brought diverse objects for his personal use (including furniture) while Mlle Hackenberger brought "various pieces of furniture and a trousseau for the use of her husband" (ADS DE¹, fonds Lestringuez). Some arguments sketched here appear in greater detail and with different emphases in Leora Auslander, "After the Revolution: Recycling Ancien Régime Style in the Nineteenth Century," in *Re-creating Authority in Revolutionary France,* ed. Bryant T. Ragan and Elizabeth Williams (New Brunswick, N.J., 1992), 144–74. Other key texts include the classic work on bourgeois women in France, B. Smith's *Ladies of the Leisure Class;* a path-breaking study on consumerism, R. Williams, *Dream Worlds;* and an insightful economic study of bourgeois women, W. Walton, *France at the Crystal Palace.* See also Anne Martin-Fugier, *La vie élégante, ou la formation du Tout-Paris, 1815–1848* (Paris, 1990), chaps. 3–4; and Daumard, *Les bourgeois de Paris au XIXe siècle.* On women's critical role in

themselves as cultural objects, they were responsible also for the purchase, arrangement, and use of those goods—especially furnishings—to represent and constitute the family's social position.

Consequently, although the home was characterized as a "feminine sphere," a haven from the outside world, that home and the women contained within it were fully part of the world outside. Recent studies take up the degree to which such homes were private familial spaces and suggest that bourgeois women were not protected from the fierce world of capitalism and exchange. Bourgeois women's normative homemaking activities—hiring and supervising servants, keeping a budget, visiting and being visited, mothering children, shopping and decorating, visiting museums and doing charitable or other improving cultural activities—involved them in the world and opened the home to that world. Wives and daughters ventured out to others' homes and to shops, museums, concert halls, churches, restaurants, theaters, public parks, tearooms, and libraries.[72] They received their extended families, a wide social circle, and their husbands' business acquaintances. Social and business networks overlapped; the workday, therefore, did not necessarily end when the man of the household crossed his threshold but rather when the last guest departed. Likewise, wives' "afternoons" were not merely for pleasure and friendship, but also to consolidate relationships that had economic implications. Bourgeois women needed sophisticated social skills and a level of literary, musical, and artistic culture in order to be successful wives.

In the early years of the nineteenth century, bourgeois women were to enhance themselves and acquire goods to represent their families and their class. Although the seeds of a discourse of nationalist consumption were planted in the 1830s and 1840s, they were only to come to maturity later. The prescriptive literature of this period included few exhortations for *self*-expression through dress and interior decor or condemnations of those who consumed the same goods as others of their class. The complex and paradoxical task of individuation through "appropriate" goods, "appropriately" deployed was not yet an element of the bourgeois wife's obligations.

British bourgeois projects see Davidoff and Hall, *Family Fortunes*. For Germany see M. Kaplan, *The Making of the Jewish Middle Class*.

72. Geneviève Fraisse, "L'éducation ménagère et le métier de femme au début du XIXe siècle," *Pénélope* 2 (1980); Leonore Davidoff, *The Best Circles: Women and Society in Victorian Britain* (Totowa, N.J., 1973). And see the contributions to Perrot, ed., *De la révolution à la grande guerre*.

By the 1820s, this model of domesticity, with the woman-wife as consumer, was already quite apparent in the developing genres of women's magazines, etiquette books, marriage manuals, and furnishings guides— genres largely, although not entirely, controlled by men.[73] This literature was dominated by discussions of fashion, style, society news, and women's responsibilities. While not all the publications were very expensive, they all addressed an elite audience with considerable disposable income. They, along with novels, plays, and salon culture, elaborated a feminine public sphere. Unlike the salon culture of the Old Regime, this feminine public sphere was no longer a primary site for the discussion of politics and philosophy; rather salons, etiquette books, and women's magazines were building blocks of the feminine and the social, the world of style policing (but not stylistic invention), of consumption, and of "good" works.

For example, in her *Manuel de la maîtresse de maison, ou lettres sur l'économie domestique*, published in multiple editions in the 1820s, Mme Pariset used the epistolary form to sketch the obligations and responsibilities of a wife. She outlined how, first of all, it was crucial to keep careful and exact accounts of household expenditures so as to be able to show them, on a moment's notice, to one's husband. Through her condemnation of boudoirs and her advocacy of account books, Mme Pariset located her audience in the wealthy bourgeoisie rather than the aristocracy. Decorative style was to be motivated by *confort* (the code word in this period to distinguish bourgeois from aristocratic taste—the objects in question were often not actually comfortable): "real good taste involves buying useful, practical, durable goods that should, above all, go together. I think that this harmony is the essential aspect of what the English express in the word *comfortable* [in English in the text]."[74] Mme Pariset's suggestion of the English as models would become much more problematic later, as the web among style, taste, and "the national" was spun. In this text, however, she offered readers entry into a Bourgeois International; the salient category was class, rather than nation or self.

Beyond generally advocating furnishings that conveyed comfort, durability, and utility, Mme Pariset gave precise instructions—in fact a formula—as to how to furnish the various rooms of the house, down to the color of paint, number and kind of furnishings, and placement of pictures. Despite her own exact advice, she urged her reader not to even

73. I follow Evelyne Sullerot, *La presse féminine* (Paris, 1966).
74. Mme Pariset, *Manuel de la maîtresse de maison, ou lettres sur l'économie domestique*, 3d ed. (Paris, 1825), 8–9, 22.

attempt to choose her furniture herself but rather to consult a reputable decorator and let him take care of the purchasing. Indeed, her advice on furnishing was embedded within a broader discourse urging women to be comfortable in their confinement at home and not strive for individuation and accomplishment in the world beyond, as men did.[75] Women were to exist only as representatives of their families; the boundaries of the self and of the family were coterminous. This focus on familial representation, the importance of tasteful consumption, and the encouragement of self-abnegation through consumption did not end with etiquette books. It was at once very durable (lasting through the century) and widely diffused in women's magazines and in novels.

The early fashion magazines of the Old Regime grew rapidly during the midcentury, when there were many women's magazines, most weekly and some with very large distributions, such as *La mode illustrée* with forty thousand subscribers in 1866. The classic, *Journal des dames et des modes,* indulged itself in 1811 with a backhanded assertion of its own importance. An article, "Sur la tyrannie de la mode," commented ironically on the nature of fashion while emphasizing the cost of disobeying it. And to arbitrate fashion for its readers, the article noted, "the prettiest women and the nicest young men are its Prime Ministers; the most expensive stores are its Finance offices. Its legislation . . . lasts only a day, but it is obeyed."[76] Thus fashion became the new force of power.

Another issue of the same magazine argued that the government should send taste professionals along with the army and scientists to "civilize barbarous peoples." "How, in fact, can one civilize a nation without giving it the taste for adornment. . . . There is no need for cannons, or bombs, or guns, or generals, or supplies, or armies . . . fashion has always been the queen of the world and nothing resists its empire."[77] While these articles took a mock-serious attitude, they mark the conceptual distance traveled since the Old Regime. It was no longer the state that made style, but fashion that made the state. Social power, with its links to political power was to be made in the everyday, through knowledge, taste, and style appropriate to each rank in society.

75. Ibid., 33–34, 52, conclusion.

76. "Sur la tyrannie de la mode," *Journal des dames et des modes* 23 (August 1811): 226–30. The theme recurs in the issues for November 1811; the magazine began in year VI (1797) and cost 30 livres per year.

77. *Journal des dames et des modes* 6 (floréal, an VI [April 1798]), 1–3.

6

The Separation of Aesthetics and Productive Labor

 A by-product of bourgeois interventions in the culture of production was the making of a self-conscious working-class identity among male furniture makers. Male artisans had observed and participated in the disintegration of the institutions for transmitting knowledge, skill, and craft sense—apprenticeship, compagnonnage—and witnessed efforts to replace them in the 1850s and 1860s with universal expositions. They had experienced the dislocations of their livelihoods and working conditions that accompanied the new patterns of distribution, the novel vagaries of consumer demand, and new relations of production. In response they founded mutual aid societies and trade unions, to organize their trades and demand their place in society as consumers as much as producers.

Both sets of interventions—those by workers as well as those by the bourgeois taste professionals had the effect of redefining what it meant to be an artisan and a worker. There was no simple replacement for the culture of production, no single site. Its successor institutions had to redefine who was to have what forms of knowledge, skill, and craft sense, and new relations to aesthetic concerns. Some workers, in some sites, responded by conceding the aesthetic domain entirely, while militantly asserting their claims to better productive relations, leaving the universal expositions as the only sites for artisanal claims to a concern for craftsmanship and beauty.

As a consequence, the transformation of the culture of production was accompanied by changes in the very definition of working-class masculinity and its traditional links to the making of beauty. Thus, from the 1860s to the end of the century furniture makers' expressions of their hopes and expectations for their lives at labor were framed by new definitions of what it meant to be "a man," what it meant to be a "worker," and what it meant to be a working-class man. By the end of the century the relations of artisans to the making of style had been thoroughly changed and with them the conditions of possibility for the creation and consumption of style in a bourgeois social order.

From the 1830s through the 1870s male furniture makers had access to and operated within four discursive contexts: the remnants of the old culture of production, especially the compagnonnages; republican political organizations and, after 1848, the National Assembly; universal expositions; and labor associations and unions. Furniture makers spoke in each of these discourse communities in their identity as producers. In the context of the culture of production they claimed solidarity with other men who worked in trades with a relation to knowledge similar to their own. In republican political contexts they spoke as men who had the right to citizenship because of their contribution to the state as producers. In universal expositions they spoke as worker delegates—as men who had particular expertise because of their role in the making of objects. Within labor associations and unions, furniture makers claimed their likeness to others who shared their relation to the means of production as wage laborers. The terms varied, but in all four contexts it was as producers, not as consumers or individuals, that they spoke. As producers, and as men.

Women did work in furniture trades but they were marginalized within them. They worked in the finishing processes of caning, gilding, polishing, varnishing, and upholstering, tasks that demanded skill but not the knowledge needed for the initial stages of sketching, drawing, calculating, cutting, and assembling that men monopolized for themselves. The fact of women's exclusion from many of these trades does not mean that they were irrelevant to our story, but their relevance is not as real competition, nor as workers, but rather as consumers. Therefore, this chapter discusses artisans' hopes for their trade in the contexts of efforts to modernize the failing compagnonnage, producers' voices in republican discourse of midcentury, worker delegates' efforts in the Paris universal exposition of 1867, and wage laborers' votes in the trade unions of the 1880s. In each of these contexts the individuals are men.

Conceptions of masculinity were shaped in part in the workshop, but not only there. I will argue that the expanding role of the elite male taste professional, discussed in the last chapter, fundamentally altered what being a man could mean to artisans. Despite the construction of diverse discursive identities as producers, even in their working lives furniture makers were not confined to the workshop. Changes in modes of distribution and consumption structured their senses of self. Further challenges to traditional artisanal links between knowledge, beauty, and manliness were the simultaneous expansion of the feminization of consumption and the multiplication of elite male taste professionals, who as a result of their close links to dandyism were not perceived by many male artisans to be fully masculine, and because of their aristocratic or bourgeois class locations, were viewed as potential class enemies.

THE CULTURE OF PRODUCTION, COMPAGNONNAGE, AND REPUBLICAN POLITICS AT MIDCENTURY: AGRICOL PERDIGUIER

Although journeymen's organizations had increasing difficulties recruiting members and sustaining their practices in the 1830s and 1840s, given the dissolution of the guilds and paucity of unions (made illegal by the Le Chapelier law of 1791), the compagnonnage remained an important associational form throughout that period. Some artisans had hopes of modernizing the organization and making it adequate to the labor conditions of the mid-nineteenth century. The best known of these reformers was Agricol Perdiguier (1805–75), himself a *menuisier* and a former compagnon, and his story illustrates the transitions in the culture of production observed through the changing political practices of one worker. Perdiguier's trajectory—from his origins as a provincial *menuisier*, through his *tour de France,* his later work in the faubourg, his beginnings as a writer and reformer in the 1840s to his decision to turn to politics during the Revolution of 1848 and the Second Republic—is at once unique and quite extraordinary and yet exemplifies the complex place of knowledge, skill, and craft sense in the forging of masculine working-class identities at midcentury.

Born in 1805 in a small town outside Marseilles, Agricol Perdiguier pursued his father's trade of *menuiserie.* Following an apprenticeship in his home town, Perdiguier took the requisite *tour de France* as a compagnon. After finishing his tour in 1829, he settled in the faubourg St-Antoine where he worked as an employee in several shops before an accident disabled him in 1835. No longer able to work in his trade, Perdiguier organized a school in 1836 to teach design to the woodworkers of the faubourg. In 1838 he married. Up to this point, his life does not appear unusual for a woodworker of this period, except for the fact that after he had worked his daily ten hours in the shop, he read widely, wrote poetry, and composed songs. But, as Jacques Rancière eloquently shows, "worker-poets," while not the norm, were also not rare.[1]

Perdiguier's life can be divided into three periods: his youth spent as a woodworker, with a traditional apprenticeship and period as a compagnon; a middle period spent as a defender and reformer of compagnonnage; and a last period committed to republican politics. These three eras in his life were also marked by different social worlds and influences. As a child and as a young man, he was immersed in the artisanal world. By the end of his life, his closest allies were bourgeois radicals.

The first step in Perdiguier's reform project was an 1834 book of uplifting, unifying songs for the compagnons. He argued that their traditional bloodthirsty tunes incited battles between compagnons, so he wanted to substitute peaceful ones.[2] After a second book of songs, Perdiguier published the work that was to become the first edition of the *Livre du compagnonnage* (in 1839), which first appeared serially in the worker newspaper, *l'Atelier*. This first edition of the *Livre* attracted the attention of a number of bourgeois intellectuals and reformers, most notably George Sand, who gave Perdiguier the means to set off on a new tour of France, to gather material for a second edition of his book (published in 1841) and to make progress toward his goal of the reform of the institution.

The *Livre du compagnonnage* inspired hundreds of laudatory letters and the assistance of five hundred compagnons in underwriting the second edition. Its argument followed three threads. Perdiguier insisted first that "it was necessary to form a durable and intimate alliance among all of the *corps d'état*." He urged an end to the warfare among the rival groups of compagnons and the creation of a union, based not on their relation to the means of production, but on whether they were producers or consumers, since all employers and employees shared the same interests and should work together for their mutual benefit. Workers would profit from this new unity not only or even largely through improved material conditions—hours, wages, and working conditions—but because they would have the time and the energy to study and read more. Once artisans had made peace and worked in conjunction with their employers for the betterment of all, they would be able to return to their "natural state" in which they would

1. Perdiguier, *Livre du compagnonnage*, 2:65; Rancière, *Nuit des prolétaires*. On Perdiguier's life I use the standard biography by Jean Briquet (*Agricol Perdiguier: compagnon du tour de France et représentant du peuple, 1805–1875* [Paris, 1955]).

2. Perdiguier, *Livre du compagnonnage*, 1:2.

"once again devote themselves to the peaceful study of arts and sciences, the study that has such a strong attraction and so many charms for us."[3]

The design of the *Livre du compagnonnage* was structured by the exigencies of this argument and the need to make the book accessible and desirable to an artisanal audience. Divided into seven kinds of materials, it appeared at first glance very heterogeneous, including dialogues (usually between reactionary and enlightened compagnons), cautionary tales (on the dangers of ritual fighting), model songs (encouraging union), the history of the compagnonnage, letters praising the book, and treatises on architecture, geometry, drawing, and a complete bibliography for *menuisiers* and *ébénistes*. The four hundred fifty pages of the *Livre du compagnonnage* skillfully used a range of forms and rhetorical devices to give the illusion of variety, and to enable each reader to find what he was looking for in the book.

Perdiguier thought that once aware of the dangers of isolation and of conflict within their ranks, compagnons would come to rely on one another, on knowledge, and on the love of their trade (and moral behavior) to make their lives meaningful and to cause their exploitation to cease.[4] Strikes, or a permanent state of conflict between the owners of capital and the dispossessed, were not to be seen in the *Livre du compagnonnage*. Perdiguier was not advocating the transformation of the compagnonnages into mutual aid societies or trade unions, based on the shared interest of labor under capitalism. Indeed, he spent the next seven years (until the Revolution of 1848) pursuing a defense of the knowledge, taste, and skill needed for mastery of the trades and still believed that both workers and employers shared an interest in that project.

William Sewell asserts that Perdiguier was misguided in these attempts to reform compagnonnage because he did not realize that its divisions were intrinsic to the organization, having evolved out of the corporate structure of the Old Regime.[5] The compagnonnage, he insists, became fundamentally anachronistic in the postrevolutionary, postcorporate era. While I agree with Sewell that the corporate history is crucial, I argue that Perdiguier's reform efforts could not succeed for another, equally relevant, reason. The compagnonnages had been a part of an entire culture of production in which knowledge, skill, and craft sense were fundamental to individual male artisans' identity and sense of self (which was not coterminous with a

3. Ibid., 2:207; 1:110–11, 91.
4. Ibid., 1:91.
5. Sewell, *Work and Revolution in France*, 54.

corporate identity). Possessing the craft, possessing the ability to create beauty and to innovate had been part of the fundamental definition of manliness. Trying to hold on to the past fusion of art and work—the old culture of production—Perdiguier was not fighting for better material conditions, he was fighting for artisans' right to be the masters of their crafts. He blamed unruly workers for losing that culture and urged them to reform themselves. He had recognized, therefore, that a split was occurring between art and work and tried to mend it through the old institutions. Perdiguier himself was well aware of some of the paradoxes of his project. He knew, for example, that fundamental and intense pride in their specialized knowledge and skill had been as responsible as bloodthirsty songs for the compagnons' battles. "At this word of 'alliance,' the members of many *sociétés* will protest. They will say that they do not want to unite with *corps d'état* in which one does not need profound knowledge of architecture and geometry."[6] But Perdiguier himself could not abdicate his commitment to the conception of a community based on shared knowledge.

He was perhaps then, as Sewell argues, a man of the nineteenth century, but he was a man of a particular vision of the nineteenth century. Indeed, Perdiguier belonged to the first half of that century, with strong links to the Old Regime. He believed in the power of knowledge and craft, and the dominant thread of working-class discourse in the second half of the nineteenth century took up the worker's relation to the means of production, not the specialized knowledge, skill, and craft sense of a particular trade. This distinction would not clearly emerge until the 1880s. Through the 1860s Perdiguier may have been on the losing side of history, but he was not the only one.

Nonetheless, a fundamental contradiction underlay Perdiguier's project in the years of the July Monarchy. He wanted to unite all workers and he wanted to preserve the central place of knowledge in artisanal life. But knowledge in the trades was not only inherently divisive, its role in the evolving social relations of production and consumption had diminished. In the dominant bourgeois vision of these relations, artisans were to be given the minimum education needed to be able to carry out their tasks. There was little discussion yet of the possibilities for social mobility through education. A new form of teaching was to replace the relatively autonomous culture of production: schools would replace apprenticeship, museums would replace the culture of production, along with notions of a bourgeois-sponsored "style for the people."

6. Perdiguier, *Livre du compagnonnage,* 2:207.

During and after the Revolution of 1848 Perdiguier abandoned his efforts to reform compagnonnage and turned his attention to electoral politics. Announcing his candidacy for a seat in the Chamber of Deputies in *l'Atelier* on 12 March 1848, Perdiguier ran as a moderate republican, won the elections from Vaucluse and Paris, and chose to sit for the capital. This move may seem surprising, given Perdiguier's mordant comments on politicians in the *Livre du compagnonnage,* where he accused them of encouraging the compagnons in their fighting so that they would not have time to look around and realize how exploited they were.[7] But many artisans in the furniture and wood trades turned from the compagnonnages and mutual aid societies toward politics. Part of what had changed was the context of politics—becoming a representative during the republic of labor had a radically different meaning than under the authoritarian regime of the July Monarchy (Perdiguier paid for his political activity with imprisonment followed by exile from 1851 to 1855). The Second Republic represented a brief moment of citizenship and hope for direct political transformation that would not recur until the Commune and the subsequent Third Republic. During the interim, workers had to find other sites in which to articulate their aspirations and visions of change.

ARTISANS AT THE EXPOSITIONS: BETWEEN THE CULTURE OF
PRODUCTION AND CAPITALIST RELATIONS OF PRODUCTION

During the 1860s universal expositions offered an important site for workers to express their hopes and desires for their trades as well as transmit knowledge, skill, and craft sense. By the end of the century, decades of economic crises rendered demand a matter of increased concern, and it was the consumer, rather than the producer—and certainly rather than the worker—who became the honored guest at the fairs. But for a brief moment in the 1860s artisans used the fairs to express their intense concern for the objects of their labor, as distinguished from the conditions under which they labored. In that moment, male artisans still voiced their concern with beauty for its own sake and for their own satisfaction. The process of feminizing taste and beauty, the increasing stratification of the furnishings trades, and the new centrality of consumption had not yet driven these voices underground, as they would by the 1880s.

In fact, the general commissioner of the 1867 exposition, the sociologist Frédéric Le Play, arranged the most extensive worker participation of any

7. Ibid, 1:10.

exposition in history. He established a commission for the encouragement of workers' studies, composed of sixty members—manufacturers, economists, bankers, and engineers. Assisted by local mutual aid societies, the commission formed committees in each *département* to see to the election of worker-delegates by universal manhood suffrage.[8] The elections were widely publicized; all those working in the trades were eligible, including foreigners; voting was encouraged by the allocation of a free admission ticket to each voter; and significant numbers did in fact turn out to vote. The end result was the selection of 314 worker delegates. They became the Commission ouvrière centrale, with a Proudhonian *ébéniste*, Eugène Tartaret, as secretary. To ensure their presence in Paris for the exposition, the commission arranged for the trips to be paid and provided lodging, food, health care, and compensation for missed wages. Thus 67,000 workers attended the 1867 exhibition in Paris, among them 40,000 foreign workers who were also given free lodging by the French government.[9]

The official delegates were to go to the exhibitions, study both domestic and foreign exhibits, assess the problems and merits of French production techniques, products, and prices against those of competing displays, and compile all this into the written report that Tartaret would edit.[10] The

8. Rébérioux, "Approches de l'histoire," 198–99, for this paragraph. See also AN F^{12}3103 on the composition of the regional committees. The groups argued, the Conseil de prud'hommes (labor arbitration board) of the *ébénistes* insisting that it alone could rightfully represent the workers (letter from the Conseil de prud'hommes, Paris, 20 March 1867, to M. le président Devinck, AN F^{12}3106). Eighteen *dessinateurs en ameublement* voted, 173 wood gilders, 793 *ébénistes* (nearly 200 of them were foreign); the gilders elected 2 delegates out of 8 candidates, the *ébénistes*, 3 out of 11 (AN F^{12}3106).

9. The very free distribution of admission tickets may have boosted the attendance; the *ébénistes* of the faubourg obtained an extra thousand, for example, and asked for more! (letter of 18 October 1867 from Roy, the *délégué ébéniste* to M. Devinck, président, AN F^{12}3106). On the numbers attending see Mandell, *Paris 1900*, 13.

10. Mandell says that the artisans were completely uncensored in their reports (*Paris 1900*, 13). For the format of the report's questionnaires see Victor Dillais's introduction to *Exposition universelle de 1867, à Paris*, ed. Devinck. The upholsterers complained about its "narrowness" ("Tapissiers," in ibid., 3:15). Most of my examples of artisanal opinion expressed at the fairs—and all the rest I cite in this chapter by volume only—come from Devinck's edition, which has fuller texts than those in Tartaret, ed., *Exposition universelle de 1867: commission ouvrière*.

The crucial issue here is neither whether the discourse reveals class consciousness, nor whether it can be taken to be the "authentic voice" of the artisans. The questions used limited the content of discussion, but it is also clear that there was no censoring, since the organizers needed the artisans to appear uncensored. The voices of the artisans in the unions may appear more "authentic," but they were

reports of the worker delegates followed the same general format, starting with a brief survey of the history of the trade, from ancient times to the present. They listed and evaluated the works displayed in their trade, reported on the contemporary state of the trade, and ended with expressions of their desires and needs. All the worker delegates agreed, notwithstanding their complaints about domestic conditions, that France was clearly superior to the other nations represented. Those from the furnishings trades repeated certain topics and complaints, which emerge clearly and consistently, under five themes: aesthetic control; organization of production; collective organization; wages; and management of the exposition.

The fact that these reports were solicited by those at the center of power tends to make historians skeptical of the authenticity of these expressions, yet worker-delegates were not hesitant to express their grievances about the organization of the exhibitions themselves or the deteriorating conditions of labor. They used the expositions, as well as the reports published after the expositions, as an alternate forum to that provided by organized labor.[11]

Artisans consistently complained about competition from work done in jail and in the provinces. Wages, they said, were simply too low, and all wages ought to be set high enough so that a worker could support his wife and family. Related to complaints about wages were those concerning the high cost of living and demands for fixed wages. The *trôle* (domestic labor on speculation or contract) was another topic of endless complaints, for reasons very similar to those later given by organized furniture workers. The solution to such ills was seen to be cooperative production because that would do away with competition between producers and the ills of piece rates.[12] A different kind of demand was for the suppression of the *livret*

also limited and biased by other sorts of constraints. The discursive contexts in fact organized what stood for workers' perceptions and experiences in either case, so the whole idea of "authenticity" makes little sense.

11. See, for example, the debate between Kaplow and Rancière (Jeffry Kaplow, "Parisian Workers at the Universal Exhibitions of 1862 and 1867" [paper presented at the conference on Work and Representations, Cornell University, 1984]; Jacques Rancière and Patrice Vauday, "En allant à l'expo: l'ouvrier, sa femme et les machines," *Les révoltes logiques* 1 [1975]: 5–22).

12. Descamps and Beaujean, "Tourneurs en chaises," 3:6–8; Lesieur, Lagoutte, and Durand, "Menuisiers en meuble antique," 2:1–2; Stoerckel and Prévost, "Tourneurs sur bois," 3:17; "Tabletterie et fantaisie de Paris," 3:20; Poirier, Gobert, and Levallois, "Découpeurs marqueteurs," 1:20. For the problem with competition between producers, the lowering of quality and people buying work from abroad, see Destrès and Spoetler, "Menuisiers en siège," 2:16.

d'ouvrier, the worker's identity card, that every worker had to get stamped by the employer on taking or leaving a job. It was felt to be demeaning; the argument went that if workers had to have these identity cards then so should all French citizens, otherwise it was invidious discrimination. If the workday could only have a fixed length, the wood gilders thought, then the conditions of labor would improve. There was concern for the safety of tools and hope and interest in the possibility that workers might influence the kind of tools used as well as their form.[13]

A last complaint concerning wages had to do with women's work. In these artisans' eyes work and production were clearly masculine activities. They made a sharp distinction between the domains of production and consumption, leaving little room for women in production. But no common line of argument united the trades. The gilders were simply opposed to women's work (as were all other groups within organized labor), though the upholsterers were in favor of equal pay for equal work.[14]

In addition to these issues of wages and collective organization, artisan-delegates went on at greatest length about artistic training, aesthetic control, the quality of the pieces produced, and recognition for their creative labor: "A large part of the successes earned by the exhibitors are ours by right and the active part we've taken is not less obvious for the fact that it's not officially recognized and consecrated." The upholsterers who made this statement thought they brought to their work not only *connaissances* (in this context, a concrete, multiple, and plural form of knowledge), but also *savoir* (here more abstract, unitary, atemporal, and singular) and *soins,* or care. *Soins* had a double meaning: attention and diligence. In making those distinctions, the workers were refusing to accept the fragmentation of their craft and the loss of creative possibilities at work.[15]

---

13. Descamps and Beaujean, "Tourneurs en chaises," 3:8; Crisey and Lorémy, "Doreurs sur bois," 1:8; Michel, Jules, Waaser, and Lejeune, "Découpeurs à la mécanique," 1:7.

14. Crisey and Lorémy, "Doreurs sur bois," 1:7; "Tapissiers," 3:15.

15. "Tapissiers," 3:15. For this use of *connaissances,* see Ludovic Simon's piece on the Bibliothèque Forney that praises it for providing the workers with *connaissances* and says nothing about *savoir* ("Une grande oeuvre," *Ville de Paris,* 4 July 1884, in ADS VR216). Other artisans as well as upholsterers made similar objections: Poirier, Gobert, and Levallois, "Découpeurs marqueteurs," 1:19; C. Niviller, "Dessinateurs d'ameublement," 1:22; Michel, Jules, Waaser, and Lejeune, "Découpeurs à la mécanique," 1:7; Destrès and Spoetler, "Menuisiers en sièges," 2:16. Skill has no commonly used equivalent in French—*habileté* or *qualification* or *compétence* are about as close as one comes.

The jigsaw operators emphasized the importance of abstract knowledge in a different way, one reminiscent of concepts from the eighteenth century, insisting that a craftsman could achieve "varied, beautiful [and] artistic" results only by combining the skills of *découpage* with those of a draftsman, an architect and a historian of the craft.[16] Emphasizing the finished product, these artisans wanted greater knowledge so they could produce more successful, innovative products. They insisted that the successful practice of their trade depended on architecture, the most abstract form of knowledge they listed.

Their position contrasts sharply with another group that was concerned about apprenticeship but not in general in favor of trade schools—the trade union movement. There was in fact, considerable debate as to what position the furniture workers' unions should take on schools. The *ébéniste* worker delegates made a specific proposal for a free school to train furniture workers; there were to be evening classes a couple of nights a week, and the curriculum was to include both theoretical and practical lessons. The students were to come in with a solid elementary education; knowing how to read and write, to do arithmetic and basic drawing and ornamentation. Theoretical education was to be strictly limited to what was of immediate use to workers in their trade: "In the theoretical classes we shouldn't lose sight of the trade, and sacrifice it to art and to science, because in that case it becomes a waste of time for the mass of workers who have very little time to devote to their instruction."[17]

In this instance, the artisans came down on the same side of the debate over practical and abstract knowledge as the taste professionals discussed in the last chapter. There are, however, two important differences. First of all, a glance at the proposed curriculum makes the modesty of the preamble less credible. The deemphasized theoretical training nonetheless included "chemistry, physics, accounting (industrial accounting, prices of raw materials, calculating estimates, etc.), laws on workers' organizations, apprenticeship contracts, comparative statistics, worker hygiene, geometry, architecture and ornament, study of styles, metrage and cubage, mechanics, machines, inventions, native and exotic woods, colors and varnishes."[18]

16. Michel, Jules, Waaser, and Lejeune, "Découpeurs à la mécanique," 1:8.
17. The unions' position on schools was very ambiguous; there was major debate in 1875 (Ministère du travail, *Associations*, 2:687); "Extrait du rapport des délégués ébénistes à l'exposition universelle de 1867," in *Exposition universelle de 1867: commission ouvrière*, ed. Tartaret, 1:107–108.
18. "Extrait du rapport des délégués ébénistes," 1:107.

This was a much more inclusive curriculum than that actually offered in the majority of the trade schools created in the period. Second, in contrast to the taste professionals, the artisans' misgivings about schools with too abstract a focus concerned limits on training time; workers simply did not have time to learn subjects too distant from their trade. The taste professionals were more worried about workers' rebellion and unseemly expectations.

Abstract training (or the conveying of knowledge) was to be matched by practical education (or the transmission of skill). Practical education was to include the more elaborate technical aspects of the trades. The potential pitfalls of the practical courses were perceived to be opposite those of the theoretical lessons; in manual training one had to be careful not to repeat what workers already knew. The practical as well as the theoretical curriculum placed a heavy emphasis on instructing workers in all the details of the construction of a piece, from its conception to its installation. The artisans also felt that workers should become familiar with machine tools; they were not looking to return to the past but rather to form the best skilled and most knowledgeable workers possible in a modern world.

Worker delegates focused on two other issues of central importance to artisans: specialization within the trades and the presence of middlemen. The *découpeurs marqueteurs* (marquetry workers) wanted greater specialization by trade within the exhibitions so that they would be able to work independently from the cabinetmakers.[19] But since the *marqueteurs* did marquetry only on the surface of a piece, and whole pieces of furniture had to be displayed rather than just elements of a piece, they had to cooperate with the cabinetmakers. Although some artisans involved in the union movement and Left politics often insisted on the importance of eliminating all barriers among people united by their relation to the means of production, in this context many expressed deep reluctance at abdicating the historical definitions of particular trades in the interest of working-class solidarity. The workers in gilding were not, for example, at all pleased that manufacturers specializing in other things were beginning to do gilding as well: "We ask those in the gilding business to sell their products themselves. . . . We ask the decorator, upholsterer, the antique and old furniture dealers to stay out of a trade they don't understand."[20]

Even when there was not outright hostility to the competition posed by the encroachments of other trades, the traditional specialization of man-

19. Fresson, *Enseignement professionnel,* 66.
20. Crisey and Lorémy, "Doreurs sur bois," 1:8.

ufacture by corporation was touted by some workers as a good thing, improving the quality of the work. "We don't think foreign manufacturers will be able to compete for long with us in the antique furniture business. Aside from taste, the main obstacle blocking them—given that most of them aren't specialists—is that they don't know all the resources of art and therefore can't execute bold projects."[21]

Others were also certain that economic pressures were much greater than they ever had been, and that the result was a loss of taste and skill. "These days the commercial and industrial side of our profession is greatly expanded and leaves little leisure for the artistic side, which is regrettable from the point of view of taste, of skill, and of the art of good work." They went on to lament the declining responsibility of the master who now had only to deliver a piece meeting the manufacturer's specifications. "He deals with the workers, he pays them by the hour or by the piece . . . in order to earn a living wage, the worker is forced to work like a dog, to turn out thoroughly defective work, and little by little our beautiful industry is falling into decay. . . . [I]t's getting harder and harder to find serious and able workers in the trade."[22] These artisans assumed that "art, taste, skill, and *l'art de bien faire*" were constitutive elements of the trades, elements that had depended on a limited division of labor, a reasonable work pace, and some autonomy in the interpretation of a piece. If all workers were to do was produce an exact version of a precise working drawing in a very reduced amount of time, the trades would die. And that, they argued, was exactly what was happening. Most of the increase in the furniture maker population cited in chapter four was composed of workers whose labor was increasingly specialized and increasingly under time pressure (as a result of the domination of piece rates). The *tourneurs en chaises* (chair turners) were clearly dismayed about what they felt to be a rampant division of labor, that was completely deskilling their trade. "This division of labor by specialities started in 1839 in our trade . . . the worker in this specialized labor rarely does anything other than his task, which will mean that soon workers will not be able to make a chair by themselves and that a man *sans état* will be able to work in our trade easily with the help of [only] a laborer."[23]

By the 1860s many artisans in the trades, as well as outside observers, added their voices to the chorus: too many artisans no longer had access

21. Destrès and Spoetler, "Menuisiers en sièges," 2:16.
22. Cited in Ministère du travail, *Apprentissage industriel,* xxii.
23. Descamps and Beaujean, "Tourneurs en chaises," 3:2.

to the knowledge, skill, and craft sense they needed for innovative design. The fundamental question was whether this erosion in the furniture makers' ability to practice their craft was the inevitable by-product of the anonymous forces of industrial capitalism and its necessary accomplice, proletarianization. If this was the case, then the most artisans could do was improve the material conditions of their unsatisfying labor as best as they could. If matters were otherwise, then artisans could defend their trade and their possibilities for creative labor. In the 1860s there was no consensus on this question, nor could there have been. The situation was still fluid and no one could foresee the future of the trades. In the context of the universal expositions, however, furniture makers acted as if the right to creative labor was still a defendable goal.

Ideas on how to reconstruct the furniture trades came from all the delegates. The jigsaw operators suggested the founding of a school specializing in *découpage* because those in existence were limited, teaching only what was already being done, not what was possible. The chair turners and furniture designers further specified that they thought the public schools should teach drawing. Many worker delegates asserted that there was need for both a revived and improved apprenticeship system and training in school. Other artisans thought that the aesthetic crisis could be resolved through the creation of specialized libraries or museums, paid study time, or the elimination of consumer influence.[24]

The worker delegates also did not lack ideas on how to improve the organization of production. Many objected to mechanization but stated firmly that the problem was not the machines, but rather how they were used.[25] Others even insisted that mechanization was a good thing, that improved tools improved the condition of work because "in tiring work, machines take over the heaviest of the labor [and] workers need only their intelligence." Mechanical inventions could transform the *ébéniste* from artisan to artist: "Drawing a sketch, designing a project, adjusting and polishing—that's the work of *ébénisterie*. His intelligence, hitherto neglected, will demand its legitimate supremacy. Subjected and disciplined raw materials will obey his commandments, and man will take the place God intended him to when he made him the king of creation."[26]

24. Descamps and Beaujean, "Tourneurs en chaises," 3:2, 8; Niviller, "Dessinateurs d'ameublements," 1:22; Crisey and Lorémy, "Doreurs sur bois," 1:7; Baude and Loizel, "Ebénistes," 1:13.
25. Destrès and Spoetler, "Menuisiers en sièges," 2:17.
26. Baude and Loizel, "Ebénistes," 1:16.

This 1867 quotation offers a utopian vision of the machines' potential, rather than an accurate image of their role in the furniture industry during the 1860s. Its interest lies precisely in its inaccuracy. The statement implies that machines were widespread in the industry in the 1860s—which was not the case—and that their effect was entirely positive. It asserts that the real work of the *ébéniste* was sketching an idea, drawing designs, fine assembly and final polishing. The *ébéniste* delegates to the exposition hoped that machines could transform man—that is the artisan—into the creative, intelligent being he could be rather than the workhorse he actually was. No longer struggling with the exigencies of his raw materials, the woodworker could bend wood to his will. The *ébénistes* appear completely uninterested in the potential of increased profitability and productivity through mechanization, as well as reduction of their hours of labor. They simply wanted to use machines so that they could do the artistic work to which they aspired.

Delegates defended the culture of production through their vigorous protests, on aesthetic grounds, against piece rates. The makers of "antique" furniture complained that piece rates meant not only that artisans were not making enough to be able to eat, but also that the quality of the work had deteriorated: "The worker obliged to obtain a certain wage to feed his family, pay his rent, supply all those needs that are so expensive today, works without *taste*, putting aside all his pride as an intelligent, skilled, worker, he sets his sights on one thing only—to produce, because one has to eat." And when workers were paid by the day, they did creative work, "because, whatever one says, the worker is proud of earned praise."[27]

We could add more detail to this varied list of suggestions for improving artisans' knowledge of the disciplines that make up a fine aesthetic sensibility. The crucial point here is the amount of attention artisans, in the context of the expositions, and in contrast to that of organized labor, were paying to this problem in particular. Furthermore, they were making these demands not in terms of defending either wages or the traditional labor process but rather in the interest of producing beautiful objects. This point is even more striking because these delegates were selected with the assistance of the mutual aid societies and were therefore likely to have been participants in organized labor.

Directly and forcefully, furniture makers at the expositions during the 1860s and 1870s expressed their desire to make beautiful objects, but in union meetings they were silent on the same matter. Each of these contexts

27. Ibid.; emphasis added.

had its historical logic; deciphering that logic leads to a deeper understanding of the social meaning of labor and of workers' experience. The
discourse of the universal expositions and that of the unions coexisted,
although by the end of the century that of the unions had become pre-
ponderant. The gilders, for example, objecting to the chauvinistic nature
of the competition in the universal expositions, argued that "the industrial battle started in Paris should avoid all prejudice of nationality."
The *ébénistes*, in contrast, had few qualms about the expositions' implications for internationalism: "One does not exhibit to earn money but to
support the honor of our national industry."[28] Neither the internationalism nor the militancy of the gilders was present in most of the artisans'
discussions.

Indeed, issues of organization and militancy were—in this period—far
more controversial than the desire for the right and possibility of making
beautiful objects. Although the details of artisans' ideal solutions to aesthetic problems might differ, they rarely raised tempers. Conflicts and
contradictions over problems of organized labor seemed inevitable: some
trades expressed a strong desire to abolish all strikes, while others talked
equally forcefully about the necessity for diverse forms of organization.
Thus while other artisans argued more straightforwardly for the importance of creating unions, credit unions, retirement funds, and the right to
hold meetings, the representatives of other trades expressed opposition to
strikes, arguing that they had become redundant and unimportant in their
contemporary world.[29]

But even some of the most determined expressions of concern about
organization tended to be couched in elliptical terms. "We will finish with
some general considerations on work, which is the saving law of humanity;
it makes us grow, it develops our faculties, it enhances our intelligence and
prepares us for the era of fraternity to which the world aspires. Glorify
work, because it frees us from poverty. . . . Through work we can hope, not
only to respectably raise our families, but to insure our last years against
need, and to preserve our dignity by being dependent on no one. We will
then be able to taste in peace the sweetness of rest among our children who
will follow us on the route of honor. . . . But in order for work to produce

28. Poirier, Gobert, and Levallois, "Découpeurs marqueteurs," 1:19; Baude
and Loizel, "Ebénistes," 1:23.
29. Crisey and Lorémy, "Doreurs sur bois," 1:8; Lesieur, Lagoutte, and Durand, "Menuisiers en meuble antique," 2:2–3; Descamps and Beaujean, "Tourneurs en chaises," 3:8; Poirier, Gobert, and Levallois, "Découpeurs marqueteurs,"
1:20.

this modest outcome for us, we need more freedom. We must be given the right to assemble."[30]

The language of this text is extraordinary. The quotation starts with the statement that work was the saving law of humankind; it developed capabilities, improved intelligence, and prepared all for the era of fraternity to which the world aspired. In this context work existed prior to man and shaped his existence. Here is impressive hopefulness about the liberating possibilities of work and no desire to be liberated from work. But the rest of the paragraph takes another tack, becoming distinctly more pragmatic and materialist. What work really allowed, according to the bulk of this text, was the possibility of not living in misery, of being self-supporting. Work was the way of obligation (or service) and honor in life, but this was so largely because the authors perceived starvation as dishonorable. The quotation started in the dominant corporatist discourse of the eighteenth century—when work, in theory at least, provided one with one's place in life—and ended in the nineteenth-century discourse of political economy, the dominant language of capitalism—where liberty had become the crucial human quality, and labor something one sold.

Indeed, the equivocal, or multivocal, artisanal discourse of the midcentury threads through these workers' reports. A number of different trades argued for the importance of *prud'hommes* (arbitrators) for each trade, insisting that their needs were so specific that generalized *prud'hommes* services could not suffice. In their emphasis on the uniqueness of each trade and on the importance of the knowledge, skill, and craft sense that each trade entailed, these worker delegates were much closer to Agricol Perdiguier than to their colleagues in the unions. Similarly, echoes of the protests against the end of shop displays and remnants of Old Regime corporatism can be heard in their protest against distributors, the worker delegates making the argument that middlemen drove wages down because they took a cut in the finished object. The workers could not accept that these distributors added necessary value and performed a useful service for which they should be paid. The central issue was an alliance between the producers of all classes—both employers and workers—against the nonproducers or parasites—the middlemen and consumers.[31] Artisans also

30. Poirier, Gobert, and Levallois, "Découpeurs marqueteurs," 1:19–20.
31. Descamps and Beaujean, "Tourneurs en chaises," 3:6, 8; Crisey and Lorémy, "Doreurs sur bois," 1:8; Lesieur, Lagoutte, and Durand, "Menuisiers en meuble antique," 2:1, 3; Stoerckel and Prévost, "Tourneurs sur bois," 3:17; "Tabletterie et fantaisie de Paris," 3:20; Destrès and Spoetler, "Menuisiers en sièges," 2:17.

understood that the new occupations of distributor, advertiser, and salesclerk transformed their relation with the consumer and undermined their
aesthetic authority—or at least competed with them for it.

ORGANIZING LABOR, FORGETTING CRAFT

From their tentative beginnings in the 1830s and 1840s to their heyday
during the depression of the 1880s, the role of the furniture unions in the
formation of a trade definition of the beautiful and innovative was largely
a negative one. Indeed, the question is not what the unions had to say about
taste and beauty but rather why they said nothing at all. A thorough
reading of the expressed concerns of furniture workers participating in
mutual aid societies and strikes in this period makes clear that the issues
at stake, or at least the demands explicitly stated, were identical to those
of all the other artisanal trades of France: hours, wages, and working
conditions.[32] Under the rubric of working conditions there were occasional
efforts to maintain traditional work habits, but the dominant efforts of
organized furniture workers aimed mostly at improving the material conditions of work. Little attention went to defending the level of skill, knowledge, or craft sense that had defined workers as artisans and permitted
individuals to innovate. This lacuna reflects the ambivalent relation between the new unions and the traditional culture of production, between
the requirements of labor mobilization and the other needs of workers, and
perhaps reflects artisans' acceptance, during the depressions of the 1880s,
of the inevitability of the transformation of their trades.

According to nineteenth-century French working-class historiography,
the history of mobilization in the Parisian furniture trades emerges as a
classic case of a relatively militant artisanal trade. The chronology of
organizational patterns is also typical. The *ébénistes* and *menuisiers,* in the
associations created following the February 1848 revolution, paralleled
other trades in the making of two new kinds of organizations, producer
cooperatives and mutual aid societies. Mutual aid societies concentrated on
workers' pensions and benefits in case of illness or unemployment, taking
over two old functions of the compagnonnage—material aid and a trade

---

32. For the very slow involvement of craft unions in the creation of museums
see Arthur Fontaine, "Musées et expositions," in *Notes sur Paris,* ed. Société de
statistique de Paris (Nancy, 1909), 194. More detailed discussion and documentation of union activities may be found in my "Perceptions of Beauty and the
Problem of Consciousness," in *Rethinking Labor History,* ed. Lenard R. Berlanstein
(Urbana, 1993), 149–81.

community—but leaving behind the effort to transmit knowledge, skill, and craft sense. Efforts to control production took the form of producer cooperatives.[33]

The militant tone of the written expressions of collective action intensified under the Second Empire, and the period from 1849 to 1870 was one of extensive labor organization for the woodworkers of Paris. Nonetheless, such organizations, especially the producer cooperatives created after February 1848, faced numerous difficulties. The 1860s to the 1880s also saw the organization of unions (*chambres syndicales*) in many of the trades in the furniture industry and engaged in numerous strikes over issues of wages, hours, and control. The organizing efforts included an attempt, in 1868, to form a general union of all the trades involved in furniture production and the successful founding of a union for all *ébénistes* that was affiliated with the Chambre fédérale des sociétés ouvrières de Paris. This union, like many others, foundered in the period following the Commune.

During the depression of the 1880s and 1890s the industry went through a period of very heavy unemployment followed by intensive organization and strike actions, largely over issues of wages, hours, and worker control. New worker cooperatives continued to be founded, to last a few years, and then to founder. All the organizations—mutual aid societies, unions, and cooperatives—were plagued both by financial instability and ideological conflict. The issues raised during the strikes of the 1880s were provoked by the economic situation: wages, the employment of foreign workers and women, the *trôle*, responsibility for worker welfare, and unification across trades.[34]

The following statements from two strikes, one in 1882 and the other in 1886, show the distance—at least the discursive distance—between 1848 and the 1880s, between the early days of the Second Republic and the second decade of the Third. In 1848 artisans had argued the desirability of unity and of discussion between workers and employers. In a statement from 1882, the *ébéniste* Jeannin claimed that unions were needed to resolve problems that the politicians were too cowardly to address. The *chambres syndicales* had become units of negotiation with responsibilities and ambitions far beyond the improvement of working conditions in a specific

33. Ministère du travail, *Associations*, 2:186–87; Gossez, *Les ouvriers de Paris*, 141–43.
34. Ministère du travail, *Associations*, 2:691–700. See for example APP Ba 168, January 1882; APP Ba 168, 26 November 1881.

trade. In 1886 other *ébénistes* took the argument a step further, arguing that the state and capitalist employers had an explicit alliance and that the workers should take over the state. The 1848 discussion was still internal to the trade; by the 1880s the goal was to force the intervention of the state. The furniture makers had abandoned the strike discourse of direct discussion with the employers and now talked about their political as well as their economic goals. The *ébénistes* still had faith in the idea of the republic but none at all in the politicians currently in office. The language of strikes had expanded beyond the improvement of working conditions to the takeover of the political system.[35]

Efforts to get artisans to join the union often employed three tactics: the first was to argue that working conditions had badly deteriorated and that artisans were no longer respected; the second, that the bosses were leading the industry to wrack and ruin through mismanagement; and the third, that wages were perpetually dropping and the only solution was organized refusal to accept pay cuts. "The workshops are being turned into slave galleys, where the worker is constructed as an irrational and defective production machine, this will very soon bring the loss of our universal reputation and the dispersion of our industry. Add that to the steady drop in our wages, matched only by the steady rise in taxes."[36]

Besides attempts to get workers to join the union, there were also endless calls for unity among furniture workers. In 1886 the Syndicat du meuble sculpté merged with that of cabinetry. In the propaganda for this union the proponents claimed that unification was a good idea "because of the collective interests of the two corporations, which do the same kind of work."[37] This claim illustrates the continued rhetorical importance of identity based on work processes, even though the idea never entirely fit the case. Certainly in the 1880s the work of the *ébénistes* and that of the *menuisiers* were not the same. But this history of labor conflict—internal and external to the trades—is only part of the explanation for the limitations of labor discourse.

Mutual aid societies, trade unions, and strikes functioned as speech communities; they created a relatively unified discourse that transcended the differences between crafts and constructed alliances in the increasingly fragmented and adversarial Left of the late nineteenth century. These

35. APP Ba 182, 20 November 1882; and APP Ba 1422, 23 April 1886.
36. APP Ba 1422, notes from 5 January 1894.
37. APP Ba 1422, notice entitled "Manifeste de la Caisse de Change de l'Ebénisterie du meuble sculpté," 24 December 1886.

speech communities could be either longstanding and reified into institutions, as in the case of mutual aid societies and unions, or transient, as in the case of strikes. In each case, coherence within the group, as well as the agreement needed for action, was created by limiting the range of topics for discussion. Legitimate topics for conversation within organized labor were defined to create at least temporary consensus. Many matters of interest to even a majority of members of the organization may have disappeared into silence, to be discussed elsewhere or lost forever. For example, furniture unions, like others, often explicitly deemed politics to be beyond discussion. Beauty and craft knowledge were never formally banned from debate, but one suspects the topics seemed so inappropriate that there was no need to suppress them.[38]

Discourses used within speech communities must accomplish at least two things: they must be intelligible to their interlocutors; and they must not fragment the group. Labor historians state that the primary audience for much labor action was the state, and feminist scholars explain that much of organized labor (except in trades where women formed a clear majority of the work force) was fundamentally masculine in identity.[39] Both of these

38. APP Ba 1422, union meeting of 27 February 1890, where it was stated that there was to be no talk about politics. See also APP Ba 1422, 15 April 1889, which contains the new statutes of the trade union that split from the local for political reasons and (perhaps to heal the schism) forbade political discussion. For a theoretical discussion of speech communities see Joshua A. Fishman, *Sociolinguistics: A Brief Introduction* (Rowley, Mass., 1970); Dell Hymes, *Foundations in Sociolinguistics: An Ethnographic Approach* (Philadelphia, 1974); John Gumperz, *Discourse Strategies* (Cambridge, 1982). On consensus and silence see Erving Goffman, *Forms of Talk* (Philadelphia, 1981), 68–69. In talking about strikes, mutual aid societies, and unions in one breath I ignore distinctions that are valid in other contexts: for example, Michelle Perrot points out that strikes developed in response to economic liberalism independently from unions and that in 1890 heavily organized unions ended the heyday of strikes, which began in 1864 (Perrot, *Les ouvriers en grève*).

39. The argument for the state as interlocutor occurs in the labor histories cited above. The masculinity of organized labor, veering toward misogynistic images of women workers as evil competition, is well documented in the classic text, Marie-Hélène Zylberberg-Hocquard, *Femmes et féminisme dans le mouvement ouvrier français* (Paris, 1981). Two important analyses of the British case are Sonya O. Rose, "Gender Antagonism and Class Conflict," *Social History* 13 (May 1988): 191–208; and Barbara Taylor, *Eve and the New Jerusalem* (New York, 1983). On the gendering of labor within political economy to which organized labor was responding, see Joan Wallach Scott, "L'ouvrière! Mot impie, sordide," in *Gender and the Politics of History* (New York, 1988), 139–63, and her chapter on French workers' discourse on women, "Work Identities for Men and Women," 93–112; also Michelle Perrot, "L'éloge de la ménagère dans le discours des ouvriers français au XIXe siècle," *Romantisme* 13–14 (1976): 105–21.

attributes of the discourse of organized labor shaped what could and could not be said.

Because the unions' dominant interlocutor was the state (and secondarily the employers), it made sense to speak not only the language of political economy but also a familiar (however inverted) language of class. The work of social investigators (like Louis Villermé) in the 1830s insisted that the laboring—and dangerous—classes had special needs. This work marked the founding of a conservative concept of class that was clearly distinct from the socialist heritage. Thus, just as the compagnonnage mimicked and inverted relations with the masters, the unions and socialists accepted and inverted the terms of conservative class definition.

The apparent necessity of basing demands on the commodification of labor and on membership in a class formed by relation to the means of production limited the available language. Once artisans accepted that they were entering these negotiations as vendors of their labor power— as political economy dictated—they were limited to material demands. In a crude sense, what they had to sell was their bodies and the ability of those bodies to do the tasks demanded of them. They could claim better terms for the sale, but they could not offer another object. Had they struck over the right to define the knowledge needed to practice a trade, to control the transmission of that knowledge, and to make objects they found beautiful, it is unlikely that they would have won anything at all—or that they would even have been understood. There was no clear way to put a price on knowledge, skill, craft sense, or innovation.

Further reinforcing the material orientation of the claims of organized labor was the logic of class as the basis for worker solidarity. An emphasis on material grievances would help foster unity among the trades, diverse in their skills and knowledges but common in their experiences of wage cuts, long hours, and increasingly limited control over the labor process. An emphasis on knowledge and taste, by contrast, had already proved to be divisive—to the point of pitched battle—in the compagnonnages.

Finally, discussions of the beauty or even the usefulness of the objects workers made, within a discursive space defined as masculine, became increasingly problematic as the century reached its end. Although the notion of speech community may help explain the limited range of demands made by organized labor, it does not explain the exclusion of aesthetic issues from workers' demands. As we noted, in the context of unions artisans did not talk about beauty and creativity. We might argue that this silence was simply a result of acceptance of the deterioration of working conditions since the 1867 universal exposition, yet a more adequate explanation lies in the gendering of the aesthetic in the nineteenth century as well as in the language of political economy.

GENDERING BEAUTY, ALIENATED WORK

The union world was a homosocial one defending itself against perceived blurring of gender boundaries. Male artisans were preoccupied with protecting themselves against female artisans, who they perceived to be encroaching on their territory. Questions of beauty and knowledge had played a different role in the equally, but differently, masculine culture of production, when competition over who could produce the most beautiful object decided rivalries between men. The culture of production had very fixed gender positions; women did certain things within the shop and did not do others; and as consumers, they were dependent on the authority, knowledge, and good taste of the producer. In that culture, there was no need to define masculinity by absolute opposition to femininity. In contrast, organized labor responded to the threat from women workers who undersold them by fiercely defending a version of masculinity taken from the political economists.

Organized male workers unwittingly sabotaged themselves by participating in this gender system. Organized labor's acceptance of the logic of political economy in which men produced and women consumed further undermined unions' capacity to defend workers' right to make beautiful objects; consumers judged their beauty and utility, assisted not by producers but by distributors and taste professionals. An interest and expertise in matters of aesthetics came to be defined as both feminine and effeminate, for in fact it was the taste professionals, at least as much as the consumers, who became authoritative in matters of taste, playing the newly crucial role of mediating between the now alienated producers and consumers. With the multiplication of the taste professionals from the 1870s onward, the category of beauty and aesthetic pleasure may have become increasingly suspect in the aggressively masculine context of organized labor. The taste professionals were both male and female and occupied a space not clearly masculine or feminine; neither producers nor consumers, they worked on the interior but did so from the outside and were often paid for it. The solidarity of unions was fundamentally a masculine solidarity, defending labor in terms sometimes reminiscent of

Gracchus Babeuf. It was an alliance of manly men who wielded tools and could bear arms.[40]

Most of the taste professionals were men, although a significant minority were women. That gender is not as simple as biology is illustrated by the appearance of dandies in the third decade of the nineteenth century, men who passed their lives worrying and writing about matters of beauty and who were not perceived as entirely men anymore—suggesting part of the reason "real" working-class men could not claim the creation of beauty as a desire of their own.[41]

Dandies appeared in England at the end of the eighteenth century with Beau Brummel and had crossed the Channel by the 1820s; they remained a significant presence in French society until the end of the century. All were men for whom living elegantly was essential. They dressed carefully, expensively, and distinctively. They furnished their apartments with like extravagance and attention. They cultivated their bodies, disciplining their gestures, their gaits, and their stances. Some were heterosexual, some homosexual, and most did not marry. Many had to work to support their style; all acted as if they were men of leisure.[42] A very few were dandies for a lifetime; far more were dandies for a while.

Dandies were men who refused to play the male role assigned to them of living economically productive, or even artistically creative, lives. Rather, dandies made the aesthetic pursuits of life their object. Dressing appropriately, finding the right furnishings for their homes, the right posture and the right tilt of hand, the right horses and carriages consumed practically all their time and money. Dandies turned their bodies and their

40. For an insightful discussion of this phenomenon in America see Elizabeth Faue, "'The Dynamo of Change': Gender and Solidarity in the American Labour Movement of the 1930s," *Gender and History* 1, no. 2 (summer 1989): 138–58.

41. I am endebted to George Chauncey and Carla Hesse for bringing this point to my attention. On dandies and the masculinity of men interested in aesthetics see Marylène Delbourg-Delphis, *Masculin singulier: le dandysme et son histoire* (Paris, 1985); and Michel Lemaire, *Le dandysme de Baudelaire à Mallarmé* (Montreal, 1978).

42. This discussion has emerged from readings of Jules Barbey d'Aurevilly, *Du dandysme et de George Brummel* (1845; Paris, 1989); Patrick Favardin and Laurent Bouëxière, *Le dandysme* (Paris, 1988); Martin-Fugier, *La vie élégante*; Arnould de Liedekerke, *Talon Rouge: Barbey d'Aurevilly, le dandy absolu* (Paris, 1986); Ellen Moers, *The Dandy: Brummell to Beerbohm* (Lincoln, 1960); Thomas Spence Smith, "Aestheticism and Social Structure," *American Sociological Review* 39 (1974): 725–43; R. Williams, *Dream Worlds*. It was very expensive to maintain a dandy's life-style: *L'Entracte* of 10 January 1839 estimated the annual budget of a dandy at 94,500 francs (Martin-Fugier, *La vie élégante*, 355).

surroundings into art for art's sake. They made a morality of the aesthetic, of the everyday.

Dandies do appear to have been terrifying to their contemporaries; they attracted much abuse. "In making himself into a dandy," wrote Balzac in 1830, "a man becomes a fixture in a boudoir, an extremely ingenious mechanical doll [*mannequin*] that one can set on a horse or on a sofa, who gracefully nibbles or sucks the head of a cane; but a thinking being . . . never."[43] Here Balzac typified the derogatory commentary of contemporaries. Such accusations derided the dandies' intelligence, utility to society, masculinity, and sexuality.

Some taste professionals were dandies but certainly not all, and not all dandies were taste professionals in the sense in which I use the term. Dandies qua dandies were not interested in developing a bourgeois aesthetic nor inventing an aesthetic for the working class. They put themselves outside and above the social fray and set an important nineteenth-century—that is, modern—precedent for masculine involvement in the decorative arts. They also created a link between masculine engagement in matters of beauty and a rejection of bourgeois society and of reproductive responsibility. In nineteenth-century discourse they were seen as men who by turning their lives into art abdicated their class, their gender, and normative heterosexuality. By contrast, when men made art—fine art, not decorative art or industrial art—they remained men, for that was a matter of genius. The fine arts came to be understood as transcending the everyday, the domestic. The great sin of the dandies, therefore, was not their interest in art, which was a perfectly acceptable interest for a man. The great sin of the dandies was their interest in their own adornment and the adornment of their domestic space.

The male taste professionals inherited the legacy of the dandies and thereby came to constitute part of a "third sex." Once the dandies had made aesthetic sensibility suspect as masculine virtue, taste itself came to be defined as falling within the feminine domain.[44] Yet good taste was one of France's major claims to international prestige and to a place in the new

---

43. Balzac, *Traité de la vie élégante* (1830), quoted in Martin-Fugier, *La vie élégante*, 351. For contemporary comment see Stendhal, *De l'amour* (Paris, 1876); Eugène Ronteix, *Manuel du fashionable, ou guide de l'élégant* (Paris, 1829); Jules Janin, *Journal des débats* (1843), quoted in Martin-Fugier, *La vie élégante*.

44. On the "feminine" nature of taste, among many other texts, see Valabrègue, "Les arts de la femme"; and Armand Audiganne, *La lutte industrielle des peuples* (Paris, 1868), 184–89. Two famous taste professionals of the late nineteenth century whose sexuality was the subject of some speculation were the brothers Goncourt.

industrial world. The dissonance and anxiety created by France's reliance for distinction and solvency on expertise defined as feminine or effeminate is strikingly evident in the many efforts by taste professionals and others, including political economists, to find a way to partially remasculinize taste.

In an 1868 text Armand Audiganne, a social investigator associated with the Académie des sciences morales et politiques (one of the institutional homes of political economy), commented on this issue. He attempted to assert France's coexistent masculine prowess and tastefulness by tracing the origins of French aesthetic superiority to the tournaments of the Middle Ages, where manly men jousted for women's approval. This rhetorical move is rather baffling, until one arrives at the phrase claiming that the universal expositions were contemporary jousts. In the expositions, men were competing to produce beauty, not because they cared about the beautiful but because women did. Men competed through beauty for women. Even if men produced beautiful objects for the home, it was women who ultimately judged and consumed them.[45]

The tortuous recourse to medieval jousting underscores the anachronism of the image, however. By the 1860s the traditional masculinity of the woodworking trades could not be comfortably reconciled with the recently feminized connotations of aesthetic judgment. Furniture makers without taste were nothing, yet furniture makers with taste were no longer fully men. This had not always been the case; there had been a time when manly men could think about beauty. In the second half of the nineteenth century, the universal expositions kept that moment briefly alive, while trade unions left it behind.

Artisans in the second half of the nineteenth century faced a series of dilemmas. Their old means of transmitting knowledge, skill, and craft sense were no longer viable. They themselves could no longer persuade their younger colleagues to complete apprenticeships, and few could afford to take them on. The state was increasingly intervening in education and the workplace. Moreover, they were part of a society that distinguished among men who labored to produce exchange value, women who consumed aesthetic value, and men—neither fully men nor members of the artisanal class—who assessed aesthetic forms. Artisans who wanted to defend their possibilities of acquiring and deploying their knowledge, skill, and craft sense to make beautiful objects at work risked both their gender and their class—and that was a terrible price to pay. The artisans sustained a defense

45. Audiganne, *La lutte industrielle des peuples,* 184–89.

for a brief moment in the already anachronistic institutions of the production-centered universal expositions, but the more thoroughly "modern"—and therefore ultimately hegemonic—trade unions abandoned the field.

Organized labor became the loudest voice of the artisans by the century's end, but its voice did not even whisper the desire for beauty. The aesthetic experts were now bourgeois women and bourgeois and petit-bourgeois men perceived to be of dubious masculinity, none of whom knew much about the production process. Meanwhile, the making of furniture was carried out by workers, whose resolutely masculine demeanor ruled out public discussions of aesthetics and beauty.

The delegates' reports of 1867 make clear that artisans were indeed concerned with taste, education, and knowledge. They used that forum to express their desire to maintain their culture of production. The workers were hired as experts to assess the state of their craft and suggest ways to make French crafts more competitive on the market. Their emphasis on the products of their labor and their desire to innovate and create beauty were precisely what was expected of them. When they spoke in both unions and exhibitions, artisans necessarily attempted to be effective by speaking in a discourse recognizable, even acceptable, to their interlocutors, bending and shaping it to reflect their hopes and desires as best they could. The agency of the workers was, in both instances, created contextually.[46]

Even if we understand why, in this venue, artisans were able to talk about beauty—and perhaps even felt obliged to talk about it—the context does not explain what happened to their gender anxieties. As was made clear above, to talk about aesthetics threatened the collective masculinity of the artisans in unions, so why did it not threaten worker delegates? The answer is that it was not demasculinizing for artisans to talk about beauty; indeed, they had been doing so for a long time in the context of the culture of production. In the gendered construction peculiar to organized labor they could not. The universal expositions of the 1850s and 1860s, by bridging the old culture of production and a new world, retaining qualities of each, provided a space in which to voice aesthetic concerns.

While organized labor spoke the modern language of political economy, the language of the universal expositions of the 1860s and 1870s was a

46. As is made even clearer by the unions' detailed response in 1902 to government questions about training and apprenticeship (AN F^{12}7621, enquête d'apprentissage, syndicat des sculpteurs-décorateurs, Paris). My point is that constraint on members of unions concerned not their opinions but where they could express them.

creole, structured by a collision between the language of the culture of production born of the Old Regime and the language of mid-nineteenth-century political economy. The universal expositions of the 1880s left the producers of goods aside altogether—left them indeed speechless—as the expositions moved into the service of a mature bourgeois consumption regime.

As the century neared its end it became more and more difficult to persuade workers to participate in mixed-class events, and artisans became increasingly committed to separatist organizations.[47] The unions eventually came to dominate even within the context of the universal expositions. There were fewer written worker reports; the last ones were from Vienna in 1873 and Philadelphia in 1876. After 1867 the worker-delegates were chosen by unions and not by a "universal" vote in the département, assisted by the mutual aid societies.

The expositions themselves were changing. Their shift of emphasis from production to consumption also reflected a move from didacticism to pleasure. They were no longer places where the most qualified artisans displayed their competence. As a result, the universal expositions no longer fit neatly into the space between the artisanal culture of production and the taste professionals' vision of artistic renovation. That positioning had depended on the possibility of cross-class alliances and the didactic function of the expositions. Both possibilities had in turn depended on a society dominated by relations of production and on a world view in which production played a central role. By the end of the century, consumers were beginning to replace producers on center stage, and institutions of distribution were starting to rival institutions of production.[48] The universal expositions were providing spectacles for the amusement of consumers.

The exhibitions of the Third Republic were plagued by far more controversies than the early ones had been. The exhibition of 1889 was in large part a fête to commemorate the centenary of the Revolution, and as such faced bitter opposition from the Right. The exhibition of 1900 also faced serious, organized opposition. Features of the exhibitions that had passed without controversy under the empire suddenly became problematic. The paid visits of provincial worker-delegates stirred few emotions when the host had been the emperor; those same paid trips when the host was the socialist Alexandre Millerand raised enormous problems for the Right.[49]

47. Réberioux, "Approches de l'histoire des expositions," 199.
48. Ibid., 201.
49. Mandell, *Paris 1900*, 91.

Besides the indignation from monarchists and conservatives, the workers themselves were far less interested or compliant than they had been. The split between working-class events and organizations and bourgeois events was deepening.

By the first exhibitions of the Third Republic the universal expositions had come much more to resemble our contemporary expos than the early models of peace, progress and harmony that had been influenced by the utopian socialists. As such, the exhibitions of the Third Republic had a very different purpose than those of the Second Empire. Their emphasis was on distracting people from the problems of the Republic and the difficulties of everyday life. Without jettisoning the old didactic and competitive intents, the organizers sought "a new kind of quasi-educational amusement that served the purposes of industrialists, artists, scholars, entertainers, and politicians alike."[50] But the emphasis had definitively shifted away from cross-class alliances, from artistic and industrial prowess. It was now a matter of entertainment and fun.

The logic of political economy, the exigencies of creating a sentiment of cohesion among workers from different trades with varying histories and powerful rivalries, and working-class men's sense of what it meant to be a man in the context of the union hall all framed the discourse of organized labor. Unions helped create the working class as much as they represented it. There was no single discourse common to all artisans but rather a field of competing discourses.[51] If this perspective is valid, it counters labor historians' tendency to privilege union discourse above other expressions of working-class desires in an effort to find the one "true" voice speaking for the class of artisans. Historians typically examine when and how workers decided to organize unions, to strike, or to revolt and for what

50. Rearick, *Pleasures of the Belle Epoque,* 138; Ory, *Expositions universelles de Paris,* 123; Mandell, *Paris 1900,* 16. For a contemporary critique of the lack of support given the "exposition ouvrière" at the fair see Paul Bluysen, *Paris en 1889: souvenirs et croquis de l'exposition* (Paris, 1890), 174–78.

51. On the creation of class by representation see Pierre Bourdieu, "What Makes a Social Class?" *Berkeley Journal of Sociology* 32 (1987): 1–16. For a cogent analysis of the multiplicity of speech communities (and identities) that members of the working class may inhabit and possess, see Hall, "The Problem of Ideology," 57–85, esp. 77. Even Hall, however, assumes here too much fixity of identity; individuals interact in the world in different roles at different moments—as workers or parents or consumers—and do not always speak in the same voice or in the same way or say the same thing. This multivocal and multilocational approach has been most thoroughly elaborated by feminist theorists. See Riley, *"Am I That Name?"* chap. 1. For another perspective see Henri Lefebvre, *Critique de la vie quotidienne* (Paris, 1958), 1:22 and passim.

goals. What often emerges from their efforts is a falsely unified image of a working class concerned above all with hours, wages, working conditions, and narrowly defined revolutionary politics. Although these issues were indeed crucial, they were not—as we have seen—the only issues of intense concern to late nineteenth-century Parisian furniture makers. They were also interested in maintaining the aesthetic traditions and creative possibilities of the trades.

Knowledge and aesthetics did not exist beyond, above, or outside power relations but were embedded within them and in the context of institutions besides those of organized labor, notably the universal expositions, trade schools, museums, and libraries. Some artisans continued to exchange ideas and argued and learned in shop libraries, workshops, and cafés. These sites—because of their informality—were relatively immune to the commercialization of the late nineteenth century. Neither the anonymous forces of industrial capitalism nor the efforts of the taste professionals could still the culture of production, and the seeming hegemony of the logic of political economy could not silence artisans altogether; it only constrained what they said and where.

PART 3

THE BOURGEOIS STYLISTIC REGIME

Representation, Nation, State, and the Everyday

> Yes, things animated by an artistic spark are gifted with a personal exis-
> tence. . . . They live . . . but they . . . also imprint us with their spirit.
> They are ours, but we are also theirs. . . . A desk understood in that way
> is more than a comrade, a companion of every day; it is a real friend,
> and perhaps even a literary friend, a collaborator.[1]

This animist spirit expressed by Rioux de Maillou in the 1880s marked part
of the new place of objects in the constitution of the world in the late
nineteenth century. If they contained "an artistic spark," domestic objects
were alive, shaping how their *owners* (rather than their *makers*) lived.
Furniture could now be one's friend, represent one's position in the social
world, keep one's family safe, assure one's heritage, and help constitute the
nation itself. Much was being asked of "things." Yet this was still not a
world of mass consumption, in part because it is doubtful that the masses,
in France at least, had the means with which to constitute meaning through
the acquisition and deployment of things. Equally salient was the role still
attributed to labor—"the artistic spark" we saw above. In a world of mass
consumption, the labor that produced such an object would become invisible, and the object's meaning would be divorced from that of labor. That
world would not arrive in France until at least the interwar years, if not
the 1950s.

I mark the period from the 1880s until at least the First World War as
the bourgeois stylistic regime to differentiate it from earlier courtly and

1. Rioux de Maillou, "Causeries sur le mobilier: le bureau," *Revue des arts
décoratifs* 6 (1885–86): 139.

transitional eras and the world of mass consumption that followed. The period was one of representative government elected by universal manhood suffrage, and the dominant social group behind and within the regime was the bourgeoisie. Individuals of noble lineage were still of social and political import, but they functioned within a laissez-faire republic of industrial capitalism. Individuals who worked with their hands could participate in this system and at times move it to their will, albeit as an opposition force.

As we noted in part 2, fear that the lower classes could acquire furniture too much like that of the bourgeoisie had been prevalent since the 1850s. But in the early and middle years of the nineteenth century, the vast majority of Parisians did not have enough disposable income to justify that fear. The taste professionals were responding less to a reality of emulation than to its awful possibility. Had that situation changed in the late nineteenth century? Was the late nineteenth to early twentieth century period in France one of mass consumption? I would argue, insofar as mass consumption involves not just the acquisition of goods but their frequent replacement, as well as shopping as a leisure-time identity and group-forming activity, that—at least as far as expensive items like furniture were concerned—the turn of the century was not a period of mass, but of bourgeois, consumption.

The ideological investments, intellectual difficulties, and resulting irresolution of the standard-of-living debate keep us from determining whether capitalism and industrialization improved the material means of the majority of the population. Even the more modest task of assessing the popular classes' ability to buy furniture is daunting, but some parameters may be established. It is difficult to estimate the real incomes of working-class people and determine how consumers spent their money. On the one hand, a pair of studies published in 1898 and 1910 by Lucien March stated that the standard of living had indeed improved and that more people had more disposable income with which to enjoy the fruits of the expanding economy.[2] On the other hand, an investigation in 1907 demonstrated that families headed by unskilled and service workers spent more than 80 percent of their yearly income on food and rent, and that artisans in the same period spent about 65 percent of their income on perishable necessities. Another study from the same year gave an even bleaker image of

2. Lucien March, "Influence des variations des prix sur le mouvement des dépenses ménagères à Paris," *Journal de la Société de statistique de Paris* (April 1910): 135–65; and Lucien March, "Les salaires et la durée du travail dans l'industrie française," pt. 1, *Journal de la Société de statistique de Paris* (October 1898): 347.

the disposable income of a Parisian *menuisier-ébéniste's* family: they were in debt at the end of the year without buying any durables at all. Adeline Daumard confirms this pessimistic image of Parisians' poverty with an example: "the room of the silk salesman in the rue Montmartre was furnished with only the indispensable pieces of furniture, lacking even an armchair. The retired shopkeeper, if he had a little margin, would add to his armoire, bed, and chest of drawers—the basic furnishings—armchairs, *secrétaire,* and sometimes a 'room set,' that is to say a sofa with matching armchairs and chairs, that allowed him to receive intimate friends."[3]

Working-class families did invest once in a lifetime in furnishings—at the moment of marriage—or again perhaps, if their fortunes considerably improved. The last decade of the century saw the opening of a significant number of stores catering to a working-class public.[4] Whatever their dreams, few laborers could afford the frequent refurbishing that characterized bourgeois households. Lenard Berlanstein agrees and notes that those wage earners buying durable goods were more inclined to spend their money on clothing and on food and drink in bars and cafés than on furniture and other decorations for the home.[5] This perception mirrors bourgeois conceptions of the period, but its validity remains uncertain.

Further complicating our view of economic possibility and aspiration is the fact that average household incomes among the petite bourgeoisie in this period were no higher than among those in artisanal occupations, yet petit-bourgeois households spent their money very differently. Unlike couples in the working class, Berlanstein states, they augmented their relative disposable income by marrying later and having fewer children. They did not invest heavily in their children's futures and spent most of what they earned on rent, furnishings, clothing, and leisure.[6] The petit

3. First 1907 study quoted in Berlanstein, *Working People of Paris,* 46; Gaston Cadoux, "Contribution à l'étude des salaires réels et du coût de la vie des ouvriers des grandes villes," *Journal de la Société de statistique de Paris* (December 1907): 414; Daumard, *Les bourgeois de Paris au XIXe siècle,* 70.
    4. For a detailed discussion of stores see chapter 8.
    5. Berlanstein, *Working People of Paris,* 51.
    6. Ibid., 148–50. In the 1880s petit-bourgeois households had annual incomes in the range of 2,500 to 3,500 francs per year; in 1876 annual working-class wages (for men's labor) were around 1,500 francs and in 1911 2,400 francs—thus if working-class households included at least two workers, their incomes were not necessarily much lower (Jacques Rougerie, "Remarques sur l'histoire des salaires à Paris au XIXe siècle," *Le mouvement social* 63 [1968]: 103). Michael Miller notes that in the 1880s the Bon Marché's male clerks earned approximately 1,500 francs a year, and many could increase that sum with commissions (Michael Miller, *The Bon Marché: Bourgeois Culture and the Department Store* [Princeton, 1981], 92).

bourgeois were interlopers in the bourgeois world of representation. Thus one of the strengths of this bourgeois regime was persuading those who aspired to its ranks to consume in a bourgeois fashion, while excluding those who did not do so.

Introducing a moment of bourgeois hegemony, the 1880s led to the consolidation of the French nation, French state, and French empire; the establishment of the Third Republic in 1871 and the strengthening of French republicanism during the next decade marked a new step in this story. The 1880s saw the development of a new logic of consumption and its relation to social and political representation. To talk about a "logic" of consumption is not, however, to imply a functionalist explanation.[7] Consumption's simultaneous location in economic, political, and social worlds necessarily produced historically specific contradictions and paradoxes— within as well as between each of these domains. In the world of the economy the capitalist ideal sometimes required maximum consumer expenditure so as to stimulate production, and sometimes limited consumer spending so as to liberate capital for investment or taxation. In the political world the stability of the state depended on both a universalized Frenchness and strong class differentiation through goods. In the social world, women's and men's different forms of simultaneous dependence and independence produced conflicting goals for, and patterns of, consumption. Bourgeois women were to consume appropriately for their family, class, and nation yet, by the end of the century, were to do so through the expression of their individuality. Bourgeois men were supposed to marry and have children, to reach immortality through their name and their lineage. Yet that was not enough; they were also supposed to be innovative and creative, to achieve immortality through the work they did. They were to represent their families in the outside world and yet inhabit a domestic space that they paid for but did not directly manage. These tensions, contradictions, and paradoxes grew from efforts to negotiate the complex relations of state, nation, and capitalism under a democratic republican regime.

Paradoxically, the furniture that embodied the dominant style of this republican period was historicist pastiche—that is, new versions of ancien

---

A woman retiring in the 1880s from a petit-bourgeois job might have less than 2,000 francs per year (Susan Bachrach, *Dames Employées: The Feminization of Postal Work in Nineteenth-Century France* [New York, 1984], 26, 27, 35).

7. I use the language of a "logic" of consumerism in part to avoid emancipatory and false-consciousness narratives of modern consumerism: I consider them equally problematic.

régime–style furniture. While historicist pastiche was also popular in England, Germany, and the United States, styles of past epochs did not constitute a repertoire out of which the bourgeoisie could effect subtle distinctions within their class or from other classes, or make bourgeois history as they did in late nineteenth-century France.[8] Industrial capitalism evoked in French, English, and German consumers a similar fascination with the styles of a pre-industrial age, yet the French experience of the Revolution was unique. The dramatic end of the ancien régime in France, combined with the particular course of history in the first seventy years of the century, made the French manifestation of the general stylistic phenomenon of historicist pastiche distinctive.

Analysis of this phenomenon—the dominance of historicist pastiche as bourgeois style in France—offers a privileged point of access to the restructuring of relations between nation and state, the social and the political, the bourgeoisie and the other classes, and men and women during the Third Republic. The popularity of historicist pastiche cannot be explained by the incompetence or the cowardice of the consumers, as some contemporaries claimed.[9] Consumers, distributors, and many taste professionals held historicist pastiche to be the appropriate bourgeois style. That consensus resulted from the fact that this particular form of historicist furniture was a uniquely appropriate response to the dilemmas facing French bourgeois society as a result of the complex interaction of the process of legitimizing the Third Republic, the revolutionary legacy, the development of industrial capitalism, and the particular problem of bourgeois class formation in the last years of the nineteenth century.

8. I worked out this argument after reading and reflecting on Alastair Service, *Edwardian Interiors* (London, 1982); Bernard Denvir, *The Late Victorians* (London, 1986); Lyndel Saunders King, *The Industrialization of Taste* (Ann Arbor, 1985); Gertrud Benker, *Bürgerliches Wohnen* (Munich, 1984); Sonja Günther, *Das Deutsche Heim* (Berlin, 1984); Gert Selle, *Die Geschichte des Design in Deutschland von 1870 bis heute* (Cologne, 1978).

9. See an 1815 statement anticipating consumers' power to determine production, "Sur la tyrannie de la mode," 226–30; and a bitter comment by the furniture manufacturer Fourdinois on late nineteenth-century consumers' refusal to buy new designs ("Quelques réflexions," 162–65); for additional critiques of the conservatism of consumers see Picard, ed., *Exposition universelle internationale de 1889, à Paris*, 3:6–7; Victor Champier, "La maison modèle: études et types d'ameublement," *Revue des arts décoratifs* 3 (1884–85): 20; in the same issue see also "Le goût du vieux en art," 592–94.

7

The Bourgeoisie as Consumers
Social Representation and Power
in the Third Republic

 "Furniture is the clothing of life," Mazaroz, a great artist of the factory said to me one day. "One's furniture reveals one's taste and the quality of one's spirit. Furnishings are incorruptible witnesses, condemning or glorifying those who own them."[1]

If furniture revealed one's spirit, as Mazaroz claimed, then the French bourgeoisie from the last quarter of the nineteenth century were inhabiting the souls of their ancien régime ancestors, for contemporary versions of prerevolutionary styles had come to dominate urban homes. Despite the efforts of some furniture makers and critics to promote new developments, including bentwood furniture, *style moderne, art nouveau,* and later *art déco,* these were largely rejected by consumers in favor of Henri II–, Louis XIII–, Louis XIV–, Louis XV–, and Louis XVI–style furniture.[2]

Art historians tend to condemn these furnishings as bad copies of dead styles, but they were in fact inventions of a particular sort—historicist pastiche. Furniture makers borrowed historical forms and altered their curves, angles, and colors, thereby inventing furniture reminiscent of, although distinguishable from, the old.[3] These nineteenth-century versions

---

1. Luchet, *L'art industriel à l'exposition universelle de 1867,* 67.
2. See C. Blanc, "Etude sur les arts décoratifs," 22–48, which describes ancien régime styles available to the producer and consumer as opportunities to make precisely the appropriate object for the particular consumer. For the relative commercial failure of *art nouveau* and *style moderne* see Madeleine Deschamps, "Domestic Elegance: the French at Home," in *L'art de vivre: Decorative Arts and Design in France, 1789–1989,* ed. Catherine Armijon et al. (London, 1989), 125. For further detail on the commercial history of *art nouveau* and *style moderne* see chapter 8. On marketing bentwood furniture see Alexander von Vergesack, *L'industrie Thonet: de la création artisanale à la production en série—le mobilier en bois courbé* (Paris, 1986).
3. For contemporary woodworkers' remarks on using old techniques and forms in their work see "Planche 3: porte Louis XV," *Journal de menuiserie* 3

were based on ideal types rather than concrete embodiments of particular ancien régime styles combined with contemporary forms. Each historical style was understood to contain essential identifying characteristics— twisted columns, with sculpture and dark wood for Henri II, dramatically curved forms for Louis XV, and extreme delicacy for Louis XVI, to cite just a few. Indeed, all pastiches of those styles contained those elements, some- times combined or assembled in startling ways. Thus the furniture shown as Renaissance in the advertisement from the maison Krieger in the late nineteenth century (Figure 39) bears only a vague resemblance to the comparable piece from the early sixteenth century (see Figure 2, p. 42). Yet each piece was perfectly recognizable as Renaissance style in its use of dark wood and heavy carved and turned columns.

Sometimes the nineteenth-century artisan stayed a bit closer to the model. The *meuble d'appui* made by Beurdeley around 1880 was remi- niscent of the *meuble d'appui* made by Guillaume Benneman one hundred years earlier (Figures 40 and 41). Where Benneman used *piètre dure* plaques, lacquer, and ebony veneer, Beurdeley used oil painting, gilded bronzes, and satinwood veneer. Both were pieces of very high quality and Beurdeley was clearly inspired by a Louis XVI piece like Benneman's but the aesthetic of the 1880 piece is very different.

Another kind of copying may be seen in Figures 42 and 43. The desk in Figure 42 was made by Adam Weisweiler in the late eighteenth century, that in Figure 43 in the style of Weisweiler sometime in the second half of the nineteenth century. The pieces are not identical, but Weisweiler's characteristic ornate geometric base and delicate legs are used as an in- spiration and the bronzes have a similar feel.

Exact reproductions were rare and tended to be clearly identified as such. Making an exact copy might be easier than an imaginative pastiche, but often neither consumer nor producer wanted an exact copy. It was dull for

---

(1865): 28–29. After poring over original ancien régime furniture and drawings, comparing them with their nineteenth-century descendants, I concluded that the makers of the later pieces did not intend them to be copies: variations from the original were too systematic. In the French case a distinction between historicist pastiche and reproduction is more apt than "creative" and "historical" revivals, the terms Witold Rybczynski uses for pastiche (borrowing them from William Searle, quoted in Witold Rybczynski, *Home: A Short History of an Idea* [New York, 1986], 175). For (incompatible) theoretical discussions of the complexity of pastiche that influenced my analysis see Fredric Jameson, "Postmodernism and Consumer So- ciety," in *The Anti-Aesthetic: Essays on Postmodern Culture*, ed. Hal Foster (Port Townsend, Wash., 1983); and Butler, *Gender Trouble*, conclusion.

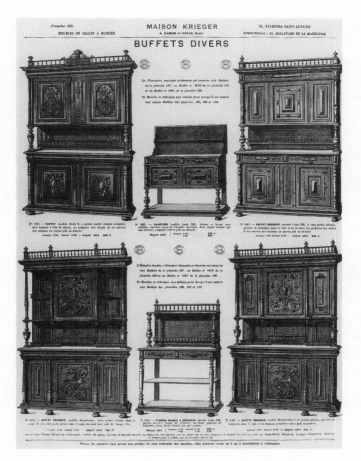

Figure 39. Advertisement depicting assorted *buffets* from maison Krieger, late nineteenth century. They are all in either Henri II or Louis XIII style, available only in waxed oak.

the maker, and late nineteenth-century bourgeois taste and eighteenth-century royal taste were not identical, nor were their means, though the pastiches were not necessarily made from cheaper materials. Late nineteenth-century furniture used a doubled visual vocabulary of old and new, historical and contemporary, but was labeled as simply historical. In short, this furniture "passed" as historically authentic discursively, but not visually.

The French bourgeoisie, in a manner unique in Europe, used the accumulated stylistic remains of previous epochs to consolidate their posi-

Figure 40. *Meuble d'appui*, Paris, ca. 1880. Beurdeley. *Palissandre* veneer, chiseled and gilded bronzes, varnished oil painting, *griotte* marble. Musée des arts décoratifs, 44514. Photo: L. Sully-Jaulmes.

tion—setting themselves off from other classes, marking internal diversity and individual family histories, and laying claim to their role as the new heirs of France's history and patrimony.[4] Rather than blindly emulate the crown and aristocracy of the Old Regime, the French bourgeoisie used the ancien régime as a source of raw material for both a new bourgeois social and political order and a new bourgeois history.

MAKING CLASS BOUNDARIES: BOURGEOIS REPRESENTATIONS OF WORKING-CLASS AND PETIT-BOURGEOIS TASTE

One can . . . divide the inhabitants of a town by [social] category, according to the number of rooms in their dwelling. A workspace without a home represents the deepest poverty; a room with a stove that serves as

4. It is not accidental that the elaboration of domesticity, as in other countries, was simultaneous with the increased employment outside the home of working-class and petit-bourgeois women. In 1866 some 40 percent of women worked while by 1906, the percentage had risen to about 60 (Zylberberg-Hocquard, *Femmes et féminisme*).

Figure 41. Cabinet, Paris, 1788, made for Louis XVI. Guillaume Benneman. Gilles-François Martin (modeler), Etienne-Jean Forestier (caster), Denis Bardin (caster), Pierre-Philippe Thomire (chaser), André Galle (gilder), and Pierre Auguste Forestier. Oak veneered with ebony, mahogany, and lacquer, set with *piètre dure* plaques of seventeenth- and eighteenth-century date; gilt-bronze mounts; *bleu turquin* marble top. Stamped "G. Beneman" twice on top of the carcass and stenciled with a partial mark, possibly for the château de St-Cloud, on the back. 3' 1/4" × 5' 5 1/8 " × 2' 1 1/4". J. Paul Getty Museum, Malibu, California.

> a bedroom and kitchen is the worker's dwelling; if the kitchen is separated from the room, then it's one step up. If one has a dining room, that's an indication of a higher situation; if one has a salon, then one has definitively emerged from the inferior classes.
>
> The dwelling is above all the exterior and permanent sign of the social situation.[5]

Just as in the eighteenth century the story of style was the story of the court, so in the late nineteenth century the story of style is the story of the bourgeoisie. The bourgeoisie used furnishings both to accomplish internal consolidation and to mark their class off from the classes above, and especially below, theirs. Regardless of the working class's and petite bourgeoisie's *real* buying capacity, how the bourgeoisie perceived the

5. Babeau, *Les bourgeois d'autrefois*, 8, 3.

Figure 42.   Desk. Adam
Weisweiler, late
eighteenth century.
Louvre, OA 5509.
Photo: R.M.N.

Figure 43.   Small writing
table, probably mid-
nineteenth century.
In the style of Adam
Weisweiler. Mahogany.
Henry E. Huntington
Library and Art Gallery,
San Marino, California.

consuming habits of the classes "beneath" them is central to their self-portrayal. A sampling of popular novels together with the photographs of Eugène Atget and several extant memoirs can help us grasp contemporary understandings of the meaning of furnishings in creating social place.

In fact, one of the most striking aspects of late nineteenth- and early twentieth-century novels was the assumption that certain goods would be understood by readers to carry certain meanings. Thus the classic narrative in Emile Zola's *L'assommoir* of a working-class couple's rise and subsequent fall from respectability was punctuated by the acquisition and loss of a particular array of furnishings. In *L'assommoir*, Gervaise and Copeau painstakingly saved the 350 francs they needed to furnish their home over seven and a half months of privation. It was worth waiting, because on "the day they bought their furniture at a used furniture store . . . they took a walk . . . their hearts bursting with joy. There was a bed, a night table, a chest of drawers, a wardrobe, a round table with its oilcloth, and six chairs. It was all made out of mahogany. . . . It was for them like a serious and definitive start in life, something that, by making them property owners gave them importance in the milieu of well-off people of their neighborhood." The detail of the description that included even the "almost new bedding, sheets, and kitchen utensils" was clearly understood to have a specific meaning—combining condescension, admiration, and empathy—for the readers. Only the cheapest of furniture was sold in complete sets and only the poorest bought from used furniture stores. The reader was clearly meant to understand the limits of the dreams possible in a working-class milieu and the ties of ownership and domesticity to respectability. This image was reinforced by Gervaise's relation to her furnishings: "She had a religion for these pieces of furniture, she wiped them with maternal care, heartbroken at the sight of the smallest scratch. She stopped, startled, as if she had been hit herself, when she knocked them while sweeping. The chest of drawers was especially dear to her; she found it beautiful, solid, and of a serious air."[6]

It is hardly surprising then, that Gervaise and Copeau's decline in the world was also recorded in the fate of their furniture. Three hundred pages after acquiring the furniture, Gervaise found herself first cramming her dresser into an apartment much too small for it, not having had the courage to sell it. In another ninety pages Gervaise was reduced to selling first the wool out of the mattress, then the fabric cover of the empty mattress, then the pillows and bolster, and finally the wooden frame of the bed itself piece

6. Zola, *L'assommoir*, (Paris, 1877), 123, 124, 125.

by piece.[7] Just as Zola had used the acquisition of furniture to mark their rise in the world, he used the gradual disappearance and then the actual destruction of the furniture to underscore Gervaise and Copeau's ill fortune. According to Zola, furniture provided status in the eyes of their neighbors and a sense of stability to the owners themselves. Their acquisition and loss traced the family's fortunes. Most important, Zola assumed that this fetishism was recognizable, even commonsensical to his readers.

We find a similar representation of social meanings through objects in a working-class interior included by the photographer Eugène Atget in his *Intérieurs parisiens*. Atget's photograph shows what appears to be a two-room apartment, sparsely furnished; what furniture it did have was of the vaguest style. A woman worker's interior was even more modest, containing a bed, a stove for cooking and heating, a chest of drawers, a night table and a stand on which she put her pitcher and bowl. Atget's goal in producing these photographs was not a documentary one; the meagerness of the furnishings and the clutter he chose to photograph as representative of working-class interiors was as much a commentary on working-class life in Paris and an exercise in the formal possibilities of photography as an act of documentation. The emptiness of these rooms seems to stand in for material and existential emptiness.[8]

Atget's depiction of "respectable" petit-bourgeois interiors was in sharp contrast with those inhabited by his working class. The first was the home of a *petite rentière* living near the southern periphery of the city on the boulevard de Port-Royal (Figure 44). A dining-room set composed of a massive Renaissance-style buffet and table, with a piano off in the corner, a very small bedroom with an iron bedstead, and a vaguely Louis XV–style bedside table—these marked the habitat of a petite bourgeoise. The apartment also had a salon furnished in nineteenth-century variations on Louis XV style. The apartment of a milliner followed a very similar pattern, except that her living room was devoted to a display of hats and a massive, mirrored, three-door wardrobe. The very definition of petit-bourgeois status was having bourgeois-style furnishings, arrayed in a bourgeois manner. But it was only "bourgeois style," because pianos did not belong in dining rooms, and iron bedsteads were appropriate only for servants. Like the apartment of the *petite rentière* and the milliner, Atget's depiction

7. Ibid., 371, 462.
8. *Eugène Atget, 1857–1927*, 10–13. For a very interesting article on Atget as a historical source see Nesbit's introduction to this catalogue ("Atget's *Intérieurs parisiens*," 25–28) and her book, *Atget's Seven Albums* (New Haven, 1992).

Figure 44. Eugène Atget, "Intérieur de Mme la petite rentière, boulevard du Port-Royal." BHVP divers, XXIII, no. 39.

of the living room of an employee at a large department store is equally crowded, even claustrophobic (Figure 45). All three are shown having the right things, but in contrast to the emptiness of the working-class dwellings and the spaciousness of the financier's apartment (Figure 46), the apartments of the petite bourgeoisie are overcrowded, stuffed. The novelist Ponson du Terrail likewise used a very precise description of an interior in his 1859 novel *Rocambole* to locate a character's place in the social world: "[T]he furnishings which were those of a salon of a petit-bourgeois household, whose income varied between two and three thousand francs: a mahogany-colored sofa in old Utrecht velvet, red damask drapes, a clock

Figure 45. Eugène Atget, "Intérieur d'un employé aux Magasins du Louvre." BHVP divers, XXIII, no. 51.

with columns, accompanied on the mantle by two vases of artificial flowers under glass, a table beneath a pier glass, and well-waxed tiles."[9]

Furniture was also used in late nineteenth-century literature to create atmosphere and convey information about the character and morals of its possessors. For example, the Goncourt brothers first established the social and moral place of a woman who appeared in their 1878 journal, Mme Descaves: she was "a young woman of twenty-six years, who was the ideal

9. Ponson du Terrail, *Rocambole*, ed. C. A. Ciccione (1859; Monaco, 1963–65), 78.

Figure 46.   Eugène Atget, "Intérieur de M. financier." BHVP
divers, XXIII, no. 11.

type of the good and honest wife of the petite bourgeoisie." They launched
immediately into a description of her neighborhood, Montrouge: a "mis-
erable neighborhood without character, with its melancholy silent factories, bounded by the city wall even sadder here than elsewhere." Mme
Descaves was nonetheless able, "in this pitiful ramshackle dwelling . . . [to]
introduce a bit of the elegance of the literary."[10]

10. Edmond and Jules de Goncourt, *Journal*, ed. A. Ricatte (1878; Paris, 1959),
4:902.

Huysmans's 1879 description of his protagonist in *Les soeurs Vatard* marked out the boundary line, to bourgeois eyes, of working-class conceptions of the commodity and life-style differences between themselves and the petite bourgeoisie.

> [S]he wanted a husband who did not have stains on his overalls, who washed his feet every week, who did not pocket part of his paycheck, and who would allow her finally to realize her dream: to have a room with flowered wallpaper, a bedroom set in walnut, white curtains at the windows, a knickknack made of shells, a cup with gilded initials on the dresser, and . . . to live quietly, to be able to devote 10 francs a year to keeping a dog and to have beyond her room a small bit of a bathroom, where behind a curtain of green serge she could put her water pitcher and her coke.[11]

The oppositions were clear. A working-class man would be engaged in manual labor that would dirty his overalls, would spend some of his money on himself (perhaps on drink), would not even bathe his feet once a week. His wife would have had painted rather than papered walls, no curtains, or dark ones to hide the dirt, and an unmatched array of bedroom furniture probably bought piece by piece over time and made out of pine rather than the much more expensive walnut. And the privacy of bathing that her green serge would provide was beyond the reach of a working family, as was the money to feed a dog. Huysmans depicted her as wanting little but made clear that this little was a great deal. The judgments of sociologists like Frédéric Le Play and Louis Villermé defined petit-bourgeois status in large part by reference to propriety, such as the separation of living and sleeping spaces and the prioritizing of representational, public rooms.

Many writers stigmatized petit-bourgeois status itself as a hybrid place. For example, the Goncourt brothers' attacked Michelet, republicanism and liberalism through a description of Michelet's wife and of his home. "They went so far as to decorate their apartment with little turned-wood sconces and artificial flowers under glass! It is extraordinary that the thought of Michelet should soar, rise, take flight, glide out of this milieu, out of this life that he shared with his wife, the wife of a petty employee. I had never seen such a contrast between a man and his home, between the nest and the egg." By 1878 only the greatest disingenuousness would venture to label Michelet a petit bourgeois. The Goncourt brothers used this rather vicious description to deride the political Left as provincial and narrow; to belittle a celebrated contemporary historian, whose politics the Goncourts

11. J.-K. Huysmans, *Les soeurs Vatard* (Paris, 1879), 56.

found reprehensible; to heap excessive praise on Michelet's work and cast doubt on his judgment by sneering at his wife, his company, his apartment, and her taste.[12]

The representation of class differentiation by domestic form and objects in the last years of the century was not limited to the work of novelists and photographers but continued within social science as well. In Chapter 5, we traced the work of Villermé and Le Play in establishing the social as a space between public and private in which the philanthropists and ultimately the state could intervene. The elaboration of the welfare state under the Third Republic only increased those tendencies. An anonymous reviewer of the next generation of family *monographies,* by Cheysson and Toqué, mirrored the novelists' conceptualizations of class constitution in other language. "All the acts of the life of a family culminate in bringing in or spending money. To reconstruct the budget of this family is, therefore, to dissect it even to the marrow, and to penetrate the secret of its material and even moral situation. . . . The budget is the key that opens all doors including the sanctuary of the family."[13]

Thus a study of how a family spent its money, how and what it consumed, was understood to act as guide to its innermost essence. These texts and images disclose the bourgeoisie's fears and fantasies of the permeability of class boundaries and the social meaning of goods far more than they display the actual consumption habits of either the working class or the petite bourgeoisie. What they make abundantly clear is that the nineteenth-century bourgeoisie used furniture to represent to themselves how others in society lived. The fascination with observing the inner dynamics of families through looking over their budgets and their possessions did not stop at lower classes. The bourgeoisie also turned anxious eyes on themselves.

MAKING CLASS SOLIDARITIES: BOURGEOIS FAMILIES
AND FAMILY HISTORIES

The bourgeoisie did not simply use taste, or descriptions of taste, to mark boundaries between themselves and other classes; objects figured into a

12. Goncourt, *Journal,* 2:18. This attribution has a certain irony as the petite bourgeoisie, both urban and rural, are famous for their reactionary rather than republican tendencies.

13. A. T., review of *Les budgets comparés de cent monographies de famille,* by E. Cheysson and A. Toqué, *Journal de la Société de statistique de Paris* (May 1891): 182.

process of self-constitution, recording the origins and legacies of the family. Bourgeois furnishings crystallized the present, the past, and the future, because assemblages of furniture constituted family histories. The place of furniture in the making of family histories was more marked than that of other commodities because it tended to be acquired at significant moments in the life cycle—marriage, birth of children, and death of parents.

The construction of family histories through furniture involved an ambiguous relationship between the nineteenth-century bourgeoisie and the past. Not only were bourgeois households filled with new "old" furniture, but the moment of marriage was marked by the creation of a new household filled with newly bought furniture. People usually did not want to be subjected to the past generation's taste or to live surrounded by the unmediated history of their own or their spouse's family. The horror of a young bourgeois woman, Valérie Feuillet, who described in her memoirs the house of her husband's parents to which they moved upon marriage, may be somewhat extreme, but it dramatically demonstrates the hideousness, to a young woman, of being tied to the past of things and to people dead and gone:

> On the ground floor was the dining room with a few chairs lined up along the walls, a large dining table dancing on three legs, a piano whose strings sang a melancholy melody during damp weather, and a desk on which were scattered newspapers received since 1830. Then there was M. Feuillet's study, which he had not used since he had taken to his bed. This room was inhabited by many books entombed under dust, scientific instruments, and a headless statue sitting in the middle of the mantle.
>
> On the first floor was the living room, furnished with the aridness and the stiffness of the First Empire. Everything there was faded, dusty, torn; it all reflected the depression and discouragement of the master of the house. The lamp shades disappeared under spiderwebs, the mirrors [having lost their silvering] no longer reflected [the viewer's gaze], only the clock, covered by its dome, was preserved from the ravages of time.
>
> An enormous room, which was supposed to be mine, came after the living room. This room had belonged to the mother of my husband. It had not been opened since her death. The wallpaper, succumbing to the cold dampness, was falling off the walls. The "swan's neck" mahogany furniture now listed. Only a painting by Boucher retained its charming freshness.[14]

This text deploys a depiction of the house and its furniture to evoke a sense of entombment and a loss of identity following the enclosure within the

14. Valérie Feuillet, *Quelques années de ma vie* (Paris, 1894), 138–39.

author's husband's family upon marriage. Not accidentally, the only objects described as having withstood the passage of time are also the only eighteenth-century objects—the domed clock and the canvas by Boucher.[15] The privileged exclusion of genuine eighteenth-century artifacts from the general horror of the more recent nineteenth-century past perhaps underlines the bourgeoisie's desire to create links with the prerevolutionary past. But even if the memoirist found the eighteenth-century relics less revolting than the others, she was disinclined to take over the ancestral home.

The idea of taking the place of her husband's mother in this animate house where the piano played mournful tunes without human assistance was not attractive. The quotation is full of illness, death, and decay. The description clearly implied, with its insistence on the details of the interior, that the house and its furnishings symbolized the marriage. In a house that was not one's own, furnished with the moldy goods of another generation, the crucial contract between two families did not happen, no new family was formed—history ended.

Certain objects, especially beds, carried a very direct symbolic connection with family lineage and history (as well as with sexuality) and were more likely to be maintained from one generation to the next. As Mme Octave Feuillet recounted her own birth, "I was placed, as soon as I had given my first cry, on the bed of cloth of gold where my mother rested. That bed had belonged to my aunt Beauffrement. It was a sacred object with which they had honored the birthing mother."[16]

The contemporary ideal, in fact, was to create a new household with earmarked money received from both sides of the family for the specific purpose of constructing a new-old story. Money for the purchase of furniture was often a nuptial gift. The account books of Jean Pariset show the contributions of various of his relatives, designated for specific purchases, on the occasion of his marriage in 1873. The largest contribution, 31,500 francs, was from his future wife's family. His father provided 3,000 francs for furniture, an uncle gave him 150 francs for knives, his grandmother provided 200 francs for decorative objects for the mantel over the fireplace. Several people identified only by name gave large sums: 2,000 francs for a bedroom, 550 francs for bronzes, 200 more for ornamenting the mantel. The account books in the following months record the purchases made with this money.[17]

15. I am endebted to Tom Mitchell for this point.
16. Feuillet, *Quelques années de ma vie*, 19.
17. Comptes de la famille Pariset, 1887–1914 (AN AB XIX 3503).

By giving money allocated for particular pieces of furniture, but not the furniture itself, relatives asserted the importance of the home and claimed their own place in that home (the new couple would remember who had paid for what) but at the same time allowed the new generation to establish itself. Not only would the couple remember and perhaps tell their children the source of their possessions; the account books recorded for posterity the continuity of capital, and of the family. So allocated, monetary gifts protected both the future of the family and the integrity of the new couple.[18]

Bourgeois families, through the purchasing of objects and the keeping of accounts, were also writing their own family histories, creating a legitimate bourgeois past, uniting on paper families joined through marriage.[19] Just as the cohabitation of objects from both sides of a new family testified to the separate past histories and joint future history of the family, so too the accounts recorded the details and history of that merger for all time. The account books reveal bourgeois acceptance of individual mortality and the assumption of familial immortality. Families would endure.

Bourgeois families often inherited furnishings from their parents or other relatives, but inheritance of furnishings was ideally (and in fact) for later in life. When couples took over their parents' or relatives' homes, for example, they generally acquired the contents. Heirs did not feel obliged to keep all their relatives' furniture and, given the absence of primogeniture, rarely inherited a complete household. At the death of a relative, the heirs or their lawyer would draw up a room-by-room inventory of the contents of the house, often with approximate values in the margins of the document. The heirs would then go through the house, each claiming goods of comparable worth.[20] The old was assessed in monetary terms, divided, dispersed, fragmented, and recombined. The ensemble was, in effect, a kind of literal pastiche. Thus, the bourgeois world of the late nineteenth century

18. See also the record of Victor and Clélie Dujardin, who brought into the marriage the precise sum of 35,484 francs and 55 centimes, which represented Clélie's dowry and their liquid assets but not furniture or personal goods; Victor had 1,500 francs' worth of personal goods, Clélie 3,000. They recorded all wedding presents received and their worth (AN AB XIX 3496 72G).

19. Marguerite Perrot uses the fact of keeping accounts as her definition of bourgeois (*La mode de vie des familles bourgeoises* [Paris, 1961], 3).

20. Camille Marbo [Marguerite Borel], *A travers deux siècles, souvenirs, rencontres, 1883–1967* (Paris, 1967), 364; Edmée Renaudin, *Edmée au bout de la table* (Paris, 1973), 115; and an example from Feuillet, *Quelques années de ma vie*, 39–40. The records of auction houses provide detailed evidence for the tendency of family members to sell off inherited furniture; in the collection of auction catalogues at the Bibliothèque Forney see for example, décès de Mme A. Allotte de la Fuye, 3 janvier 1898: partage, Georges et Maurice [her sons] (AN AB XIX 3498).

deeply understood the cultural and economic capital provided by the old. The use of historicist pastiche was therefore unsurprising—it provided a link to the past and a reconfiguration in the present.

MAKING THE SELF: THE FEMININE
IN A GENDERED CONSUMPTION REGIME

> It is in the arrangement of the *home* that the qualities of inventiveness and taste—so natural and so feminine—show themselves.[21]

> For the husband, public life and productive work; for the wife, private life and the management of the home.[22]

The contents of bourgeois households helped constitute solidarities across generations and families, but they were also used to create and reinforce conceptions of the self—especially the gendered identity of that self. In the historiography of nineteenth-century France, it has become a truism—and for good reason, as the above passages indicate—that bourgeois women were excluded from paid labor and ensconced within the home. The bourgeois home in the late nineteenth century was not the exclusively feminine, entirely private, space often described by both contemporaries and historians, however.[23] Rather the home, like much other space in the period, was composed of feminine and masculine, private and public, youthful and adult places.

It is claimed, further, that the social identity of "producer" became a critical constitutive element of masculinity, and that the social identity of "consumer" became a critical constitutive element of femininity. I will argue, in contrast, that the production-consumption dichotomy is misleading, that the bourgeoisie of both genders were cast as consumers, albeit consuming to different ends. All acts of consumption were also acts of production, but some modes of consumption were defined as almost exclusively feminine, while others were defined as largely masculine.[24] This gendering of forms of consumption was not stable across the century, however, nor were the boundaries between the masculine and the feminine impermeable at any given moment.

21. Henri de Noussane, *Le goût dans l'ameublement* (Paris, 1896), 144.
22. Louis Legrand, *Le mariage et les moeurs en France* (Paris, 1879), 58.
23. On the domestic sphere see chapter 5 notes 71–72. The strongest version of this argument is B. Smith, *Ladies of the Leisure Class.*
24. Bowlby, *Just Looking,* 29. De Certeau makes the argument that consumption is a form of production (*The Practice of Everyday Life*).

Women's tasks of acquisition and deployment of furniture to represent the bourgeois household established in the earlier years of the nineteenth century continued, but in a changed form. In the first part of the century the focus for women's consumption was the making of the family and the class; to these tasks, that of representing the nation through domestic consumption was added from about midcentury, that of representing the self from the 1880s onward. After the turn of the century single women—divorced or never married—started to use their interiors to create and represent themselves alone and to write about their creation of such interior spaces. The tasks were cumulative, not sequential. Women were to produce the social representation of the family and class throughout this period but had the projects of making the nation and the self added onto the earlier obligations and possibilities.

Contemporaneous with the development of the bourgeois housewife's consuming activities in the 1830s were the elaboration and expansion of two forms of consumption associated with men: collecting and dandyism. Consumption, like many other social activities, tended to be deemed appropriately masculine when it was productive of self and of a durable legacy beyond the self.[25] Collecting could, therefore, be characterized as appropriate masculine behavior, while dandyism was understood to be an activity of men but one threatening to their masculinity in the eyes of contemporaries.

Although consumption was not an exclusively feminized activity, it would appear at first glance to mirror and reproduce stereotypes of masculinity and femininity. But the story is more complicated: the "appropriate" always bears the seeds of its opposite.[26] Collectors could also be dandies, and dandies collectors. Women could create collections and could also construct a self and a legacy through their consumption. All was not always equally fluid, however. "Masculine" forms of consumption became more accessible to women at the end of the nineteenth century than they had been earlier, but men had been playing with "feminine" forms since the 1830s. The changing gendered meanings of the acquisition and use of

25. It is striking that when consumption became the basis for organized political action in the nineteenth century, it became as much a masculine as a feminine domain. Ellen Furlough, *Consumer Cooperation in France* (Ithaca, 1991).

26. See Emily Apter's analysis of "cabinet fiction" at the end of the nineteenth century, in which the dandy and the collector merge (*Feminizing the Fetish: Psychoanalysis and Narrative Obsession in Turn-of-the-Century France* [Ithaca, 1991], 39–64).

goods both reflected and produced multiple and changing meanings of femininity and masculinity.

The records of the furnishings that the unremarkable bourgeois couple Victor and Clélie Dujardin brought into their marriage in 1876 reflect the distribution of tasks and space according to gender: Victor brought his mahogany, glass-doored bookcase "garnie de livres," a leather-topped mahogany desk, and a caned mahogany desk chair. He also had a gilded Louis XV picture frame, assorted statues, a barometer, and a bust of Voltaire. He did not bring his, or any other, bed; indeed, it was carefully noted that his iron bed remained with his parents. Clélie, in contrast, brought a mahogany bed, complete with bedding (which cost 250 francs— exactly the same amount as Victor's bookcase and books), matching curtains for the bed and bedroom window, chairs, wardrobe, bidet, mirror, armchair, bedside table for the bedroom, sewing basket and table as well as a sewing machine. She also brought a piano, a music stand, and a few things that might have been intended for a living room, such as shelves and their accompanying *objets,* a bentwood chair, an inlaid bookcase. Victor's room, his space in the house, was clearly to be the study, which was furnished according to his taste, and with his furniture. Her space was the bedroom and the salon. He had his bookcase "accompanied" by books, she had her shelves "accompanied" by knickknacks.[27]

This gendering of space within the home was matched by the gendering of style. By the 1880s contemporaries had come to define ancien régime reigns as masculine or feminine depending on how far back in time the monarchies lay. The earliest were the most masculine; closer to the Revolution they became increasingly feminine. One exposition visitor went so far as to argue that under Louis XV, "the effeminate tastes of the king and his court were apparent everywhere."[28] Thus nineteenth-century furni-

27. Livres de compte de la famille Bernard (AN AB XIX 3496 72G).
28. As evidence of this temporal gendering see, among many others, Etincelle [Henriette Marie Adelaïde Double], *Carnet d'un mondain: gazette parisienne, anecdotique et curieuse* (Paris, 1881–82), 50–51; la comtesse Jean de Pange, *Comment j'ai vu 1900* (Paris, 1962), 247; Judith Gautier, *Le second rang du collier* (Paris, 1909), 35; Gustave Droz, *Monsieur, madame et bébé* (Paris, 1884), 135–36. In the private archives of the furniture manufacturer and distributor Maison Rinck (passage de la bonne Graine), account books of 1901 to 1905 and earlier photographic documentation of their production show earlier styles being used for public rooms and later styles being used for private rooms. For other contemporaries, O. E. Ris-Paquot, *L'art de batir, meubler et entretenir sa maison* (Paris, n.d.), 192–211; *Exposition de 1889,* 10. For confirmation by a leading historian of design see Forty, *Objects of Desire,* 65.

Figure 47.   Assorted chairs. Louis XIII–style. *Le carnet du vieux bois*, no. 3, pl. 17.

ture going under the name of Louis XIII and Henri II was unquestionably masculine, as was all more vaguely labeled medieval or Gothic or Renaissance furniture (Figure 47). Louis XIV and Louis XV were potentially androgynous, but intrinsically masculine, while Louis XVI exemplified femininity (Figure 48). Louis XVI style was "modest, alluring, indulgent, gracious, svelte, light, and varied." Liminal styles might change their gender. According to the taste professionals of the late nineteenth century, furniture made in Louis XIV, and especially Louis XV, style could be specially modified for women to make it feminine.[29]

The most "public" of rooms, the dining room, was almost always furnished if not in Henri II then in Louis XIII (Figure 49). Because Henri II and Louis XIII were explicitly defined as masculine, they were also often seen in a study (by definition masculine), but very rarely in a bedroom or boudoir (by definition feminine).[30] Thus the potentially feminine Louis

29. Vicomtesse Nacla [Mme Th. Alcan], *Le boudoir: conseils d'élégance* (Paris, 1896), 219–20. See the discussion of Mme Pompadour's desk in Maillou, "Causerie sur le mobilier," 138–42, 234–55.

30. See for example Edouard Bajot, *Du choix et de la disposition des ameublements de style* (Paris, 1898). The only dining rooms shown are Louis XI, Henri II, and Louis XIII. All of the Louis XIV and later furniture is for the more private spaces (salons, boudoirs and bedrooms, with the exception of a Louis XV library). See AN

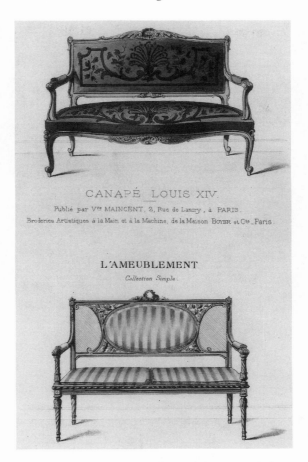

CANAPÉ LOUIS XIV.

Publié par Vᵉ MAINCENT, 2, Rue de Lancry, à PARIS.

Broderies Artistiques à la Main et à la Machine, de la Maison BOYER et Cⁱᵉ _Paris.

L'AMEUBLEMENT

Collection Simple.

Figure 48.   Louis XIV and Louis XVI *canapés*, late nineteenth century. *L'ameublement*, pls. 3605, 3606.

XIV, Louis XV, and always feminine Louis XVI were generally excluded from dining rooms. Bedrooms, especially women's bedrooms, were best furnished in Louis XVI style. It was therefore appropriate, in the dominant classification scheme, to furnish a living room (which was a liminal space) with the feminine version of Louis XV. Thus, a hermaphroditic style was created for a relatively androgynous space.

AB XIX 3496–503 series for evidence from decorating guides, advertising materials, company archives, and death inventories; two accounts traverse two generations.

Figure 49.   Henri II–style dining room. Paris, early twentieth century.

Illustrating the choice of styles, the 1887 marriage contract between the wealthier M. Lestringuez and Mme Arson had the newly married couple possessing a bedroom entirely in Louis XVI style. Likewise, the novelist Gustave Droz had his protagonists in *Monsieur, madame et bébé* sleep in a Louis XVI bedroom on their wedding night.[31] We observe the gendered division of styles for different rooms in the home of Mme Lhiabasters at 114 boulevard Malesherbes. At the time of her death in 1885, the public rooms of her home—the dining room, vestibule, and waiting room—were entirely furnished in antique, reproduction, or pastiche versions of sixteenth- and seventeenth-century style furniture. The petit salon and the cabinet de toilette were done in Louis XVI style. Her boudoir and bedroom were also very largely Louis XVI in style but with a few Louis XIV–style pieces mixed in. The most eclectic room was the very copiously and luxuriously decorated grand salon. It contained one sofa, eleven chairs of various kinds, two screens, one mirror, one footstool, two display cabinets, one desk, and two small tables. More copious even than the furniture of Mme Lhiabasters's grand salon was that of Mme Lucie Dekerm, which

31. ADS DE[1,] fonds Lestringuez; Droz, *Monsieur, madame et bébé,* 135–36.

Figure 50.   Grand salon of Lucie Dekerm, Bibliothèque
Forney, CV 27–30 April 1885.

contained four *meubles d'appui,* two desks, one harp, one clavecin, one
chaise longue, two tables, four screens, two sofas, one additional sofa with
a matching set of eight armchairs, and an additional twelve chairs, as well
as a *cartonnier* (filing cabinet). The dominant theme in the room was Louis
XV, but there was some representation of Louis XIV and XVI as well
(Figure 50). The same pattern was repeated in the very large array of
furniture to be found in the home of M. de Lafaulotte.[32] This frequent

32. Forney CV 2 March 1885, 6030 1035; 27–30 April 1885, 6030 1038; 5–13
April 1886, 6030 10338.

practice of gendering was also to be found in the prescriptive literature (see chapter 10).

The notion of certain styles being appropriate for certain rooms in the house, depending on how public or private, masculine or feminine they were, obtained in the prices paid for antiques in the nineteenth century. On the domestic antique market Louis XIV furniture, the oldest real furniture extant in any quantities and that used for public rooms, generally brought the highest prices before 1900 and remained strong until the 1930s, whereas Louis XVI—used largely for very private rooms—only started bringing very high prices after 1910. We might imagine that those prices merely reflect the relative scarcity of the older pieces, but the fact that the prices for Louis XIV furniture dropped dramatically in the 1930s makes such an interpretation more difficult. More plausible is that people chose to spend more money on furnishings for their public rooms. Likewise, Louis XV dining tables—to be used in salons—were systematically selling for prices considerably higher than Louis XVI dining tables (Louis XVI not being considered, between 1860 and 1920, an appropriate style for the dining room). In contrast Louis XV and Louis XVI commodes—often bedroom objects—despite the generally lower selling price for those styles, were sometimes outpricing Louis XIV.[33] Thus Victor and Clélie's spatial division of their apartment was commonplace.

The code of appropriate uses of different styles was complicated, however, and often contradictory. The advice in an 1895 etiquette book for a male customer trying to furnish his bedroom clearly shows the complexity and fluidity of this system. A taste professional counseled that "a bedroom for someone of princely wealth [should be] close to the style Louis XIV; . . . if you are a severe diplomat, a notary, or a magistrate, and sleep alone in [your room], you would certainly seek inspiration from the Renaissance or Louis XIII. On the other hand, the style Louis XVI would definitely be the thing if you were in the habit of sharing your room with your wife."[34] According to this author, therefore, Louis XIV was a style suited to someone who could live like a prince in a republican age; Louis XIII, a Renaissance style, was appropriate to those of high dignity and seriousness; while Louis XVI or feminine furniture represented a necessary compromise if you were to break the bourgeois custom of separate bedrooms.

33. Capronnier, *Le prix des meubles d'époque*, 37.
34. Nacla, *Le boudoir*, 201.

For men the critical issues were wealth, social position, and sexual habits, but female consumers were to consider their coloring and age as paramount when they furnished their apartments, and especially their bedrooms. Yet another commentator insisted that brunettes should buy Louis XV and Louis XVI, blondes Louis XIV, which suggests that other considerations could interfere with the rigid gender code: Louis XIV was identified at most other moments as masculine, while here it was attributed to women, if they had hair of a certain shade.[35] The novelist Paul Bourget described the color scheme designed "to harmonize with [his character's] colourless brunette complexion. . . . Its walls hung with yellow silk, in stripes alternately dull and lustrous, the dark mahogany of its furniture in the style of the Empire, and its delicate green carpet." But age was important too: "If at forty years of age, you need to seek refuge in majesty, you have the choice between François I, Henri II, Louis XIII and Louis XIV."[36] In this schema, in other words, the masculine, public styles became appropriate for a woman's room after she had passed the age of sexuality (at forty!).

This coding was, at moments, very explicit in its social lessons: "As to a young girl's room, Louis XVI style with its gracious curves. . . . A *chiffonnier-secrétaire*, where one scribbles [*chiffonne*] more than one writes. . . . A three-footed little table . . . holds all unfinished work. . . . A boy's room should look entirely different. It should be in *style moderne* made out of old varnished mahogany and have the appropriate somber air . . . a bookcase . . . permits the display of pottery, sculpture, engravings, weapons, or photographs that all boys have in quantity. The desk should be unpretentious and there should be a swivel chair. . . . This is a room in which work should play the largest role."[37]

The coding of the rooms, their appropriate uses, and the tasks to which it was understood that young men and young women would devote their time is quite striking. Young women needed rooms that were flattering to their looks, writing desks that doubled as diminutive work tables, where little writing was done, and where the only work referred to was unfinished. Furthermore, the young girl's room was to be in an eighteenth-century, aristocratic style (Figure 51). The young man was given a modern room,

35. Georges de Landemer, *Le carnet de fiançailles: livret de famille* (Paris, 1890), preface.

36. Paul Bourget, "Other People's Luxury" in *Domestic Dramas*, trans. William Marchant (New York, 1900), 154; Landemer, *Le carnet de fiançailles*, preface.

37. BHVP 120, ameub. S, Soubrier, 1904: 14 rue de Reuilly, 12th arrondissement (hereafter, arr.).

Figure 51.   Advertisement for a young girl's bedroom. BHVP 120, maison Roll.

devoted to work; there was no question of the room suiting his looks, and it was to be sober and heavy. Another variation was the homology between the pastoral and the feminine created in the following advertisement. "The models shown here were specifically designed to furnish the bedrooms in villas; they would be equally appropriate for the bedroom of a young girl. The structure of this furniture is entirely made from varnished solid pine, which makes an excellent frame for the panels of white bird's eye maple, enlivened by fine marquetry in colored wood." This gendering of woods as well as of styles was a commonplace by the 1880s. Besides maple's or pine's appropriateness for girls, oak was deemed distinctly masculine, walnut on the edge of androgyny, mahogany and rosewood unproblematically feminine.[38]

This gendering of ancien régime style—Renaissance as masculine, late eighteenth century as feminine—was entirely a construction of the late nineteenth century. Clearly, people living in the periods when the original versions of this furniture were made did not consider it gendered by style.

38. BHVP 120, ameub. N–R, Pérol frères, 1906: successeurs de Mons Chaillet, Barzin, Pérol Ainé, Pérol Mouflier, 4, 6, 8, 28 bis and 30 rue du faubourg St-Antoine, 12th arr.; Champier, "La maison modèle," 57.

Furniture was made in each style during its period for all rooms of the house and for the use of both sexes. There was nothing intrinsically masculine about early furniture, nor anything essentially feminine about late eighteenth-century furniture. Even within the gendering of aesthetics in the late nineteenth century, the rococo of Louis XV, full of curves, highly decorated and ornate, or indeed the elegance and exuberance of Louis XIV style could as easily have been dubbed feminine as masculine, or variable. The gendered attributions had nothing to do with absolute aesthetic associations between certain forms and the masculine or feminine, but everything to do with the gendering of the past and of history.[39]

In the eyes of the late nineteenth century, the Renaissance was the epoch of robust, manly monarchs and the late eighteenth century the period of corrupt, effeminate kings.[40] The conservatism in this discourse—in its negative evaluation of the Revolution—and the implicit causal explanation of the Revolution as an outcome of the corruption and effeminacy of Louis XV and especially Louis XVI is fascinating, especially as it appears to have been unreflectingly adopted by consumers and critics of all political persuasions. Figure 52 of Louis XVI style and a Renaissance-style bedroom from the maison Krieger makes the arbitrariness of the gendering of these styles even clearer—given that the two bedroom sets are almost indistinguishable.

This system was not divorced from the visual content of these styles, rather it was made possible by a coincidence between certain aspects of the styles and contemporary conceptions of femininity and masculinity. Decoration in the earlier styles was effected by carving the solid structural wood composing the object. Louis XV and Louis XVI, in contrast, were fundamentally veneer styles, where the structural elements of the piece were covered by thin sheets of carefully dyed and shaped wood, mother-of-pearl, or tortoiseshell. Veneer could be dubbed feminine because it was ornamented through overlay; a frame was disguised (clothed, made-up)

39. Few have been brave or foolhardy enough to try to correlate politics and furniture style in any direct way. An interesting discussion of the issue in the American context is Edward O. Laumann and James S. House, "Living Room Styles and Social Attributes," *Sociology and Social Research* 54 (April 1970): 321–42. The authors found that consistency of style correlated with consistency and extremity of political position, but not the same style with the same party (335).

40. Among the evidence for this claim are many etiquette books and decorating magazines discussing what one ought to put in each room, novels describing imagined rooms, and memoires providing other evidence. For example, see Mantz, "Les meubles du XVIIIe siècle," 359, 380.

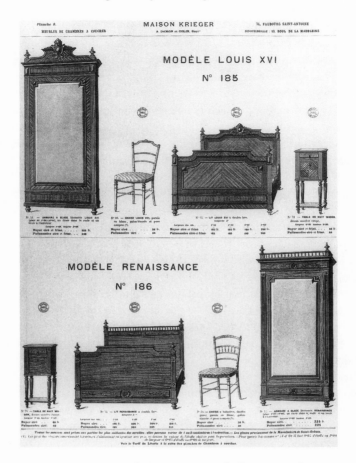

Figure 52.   Two pastiche ancien-régime bedroom sets from
maison Krieger, one Louis XVI and one Renaissance. Available for almost the same price in waxed walnut and waxed
"palissandre." Structurally very similar; details of veneer and
of decoration differ. Both quite expensive; cheaper Louis XVI
model cost 488 francs.

with decorative elements including trompe l'oeil and precious stones.[41]
Sculpture, in contrast, transformed the essence of the form and the wood
itself; it was done by penetrating the wood with a chisel. Sculpture was the
product of manly labor. According to the assessment of the eighteenth-

41. On the transhistorical association of femininity with decoration and especially makeup, see Jacqueline Lichtenstein, "Making Up Representation: The
Risks of Femininity," *Representations* 20 (fall 1987): 77–87.

century furniture industry by a worker delegate to the universal exposition of 1867, "furniture became precious . . . [in the eighteenth century], it put on makeup and jewels. It was gallant, nonchalant. . . . The pretty instead of the beautiful, the gracious instead of the heroic. The art of furniture from then on became more and more feminized and dainty."[42]

Discursively each person, each activity, each gesture, had a place and an appropriate piece of furniture. This image was mirrored in the bourgeoisie's dwelling practices. Bourgeois apartments generally contained a living room, a dining room, a boudoir with an attached bedroom for the mistress of the house, a study for the master and often a bedroom for him as well, together with rooms for the children, maids' rooms, and a kitchen. Besides these basic rooms, large bourgeois apartments or villas sometimes contained additional living rooms, music rooms, billiard rooms, libraries, antechambers, large front halls, multiple salons, and greenhouses, all of which had to be furnished appropriately.[43] As the scale of the apartment expanded, the number of rooms grew more dramatically than their size. The specializations of style and of space were products of the bourgeoisie's process of internal differentiation, which was effected in part to make the social code a puzzle to outsiders. As Edmée Renaudin put it, remembering the years before the First World War, "[The women] obeyed the complicated rules of *savoir-vivre.*" The apartment and its contents were to reveal the social position of the family as well as to contain its past and

42. Artisans in the trade understood (and understand) sculpting to be the most masculine of the woodtrades; an enduring belief is that having women working in a shop blunts the tools. Desvernay, ed., *Rapports des délégations ouvrières contenant l'origine et l'histoire des diverses professions,* 5:86–87. A similar quote identifies Louis XVI furniture as feminine: Mantz, "Les meubles du XVIIIe siècle," 381–83.

43. Bedrooms held a double bed, often a canopy bed with curtains, a wardrobe, a dressing table, a chaise longue, a couple of other comfortable chairs, a small writing table, and a dresser or two. The boudoir had a sewing table, a vanity, a chaise longue, a wardrobe, a few decorative small tables, some delicate shelves, and perhaps a couch. The public rooms of the house held even more pieces than the private. A medium-size living room had a couch or love seat, six armchairs, four chairs, a fire screen, a few tabourets, a firewood chest, a *table-guéridon,* and a piano. The assortment varied for larger or smaller rooms, but a piano was an absolute requirement whether or not anyone played. Dining rooms generally contained a table with leaves, six chairs, a sideboard, and sometimes, a *desserte* or a *panetière.* To these pieces of furniture add carpets, curtains, tablecloths, doilies, photographs, paintings, sculptures, clocks, small statues, vases, crucifixes, souvenirs, mirrors, ashtrays, silver tea services, decorative plates, dried flower arrangements, and assorted other objects. See for example Gautier, *Le second rang du collier,* 181–82; Pange, *Comment j'ai vu 1900,* 189; Renaudin, *Edmée au bout de la table,* 13.

future: "A young household that succeeded, moved its home with each step up." Or, as Viollet-le-Duc noted, after saying that people changed furniture six times in a lifetime, "Everything is connected . . . in the lives of men; it would be illogical to ask nineteenth-century families to sustain a perpetuity in their furniture that no longer exists in customs or morals [*moeurs*]."[44] But these furnishings also ensured that every member of the family and of the class learned their place within the class.

Bestowing connotations of gender, age, and profession (by style, wood, and color) on the very forms of furniture, so that it could suit both the individual within the household and the entire family, produced a rather complex and often contradictory set of semiotic codes that had to be mastered if one were to be a successful consumer. How much autonomy married women had in making expensive purchases like furniture has been much debated and will probably never be empirically resolved; but in a sense it may not greatly matter. Wives may have sought their husbands' approval before purchases of this scale, but the fundamental responsibility (and perhaps pleasure) of furnishing the home was theirs.[45]

As the following passage illustrates, wives were constructed novelistically to be part of, to manage, and even be acquired for the household's public presence as much as its private sustenance:

> Mme Rougon, in three months, had brought a sober atmosphere to the house in the rue Marbeuf, where a licentious mood had dominated before. . . . Rougon smiled when complimented on his home. He insisted on saying that he had married following the advice and the choice of his friends. His wife delighted him; he had wanted a bourgeois interior for a long time, an interior that would be a material proof of his honesty. That was all that was needed to separate him completely from his dubious past, to place him with respectable people.[46]

As this almost perverse passage from Emile Zola's *Son excellence Eugène Rougon* indicates, the construction of wives, in their persons and through their buying activities, to constitute their husbands' social presence and identity was expected to resonate with a late nineteenth-century reading public. Zola depicted Rougon as urgently needing a wife who was capable

44. Renaudin, *Edmée au bout de la table*, 190, 82; Viollet-le-Duc, *Dictionnaire raisonné du mobilier français*, 404.

45. Unlike their American contemporaries, French women did not get heavily involved in theorizing the transformation of the domestic sphere, redesigning homes and neighborhoods (Dolores Hayden, *The Grand Domestic Revolution* [Cambridge, Mass., 1981]).

46. Emile Zola, *Son excellence Eugène Rougon* (Paris, 1876), 151–52.

of creating the home required for bourgeois respectability. Zola was per-haps criticizing bourgeois society through his critique of the place of wives and of furniture in the constitution of social life, but he counted on the familiarity of the image to make his point. Had the idea of a wife being a social asset or making a home been absurd to contemporaries, his goal of character painting would have failed—in fact it was a very common trope by the 1880s.

The novelist René Boylesve in his extremely popular novel, *Madeleine jeune femme* (1912), likewise depicted the centrality of the aesthetic con-struction of the home to the role of the wife. Here he is conveying the ruminations of the female protagonist (facing an undesired marriage) as finding solace in her fantasy of her future domestic life: "The trousseau and then the representation of the apartment where we would live, those are the two things that consoled me. I saw a young woman coming and going . . . leaning against the mantel, sitting in a particular corner to judge the effect of a picture."[47] Again, the way the image is used implied that the novelist did not expect it to startle or shock his readers, who would take it rather as a commonplace.

Such novels were one element of a large discourse productive and representative of the uses to which the bourgeoisie put furniture and other goods, and the role of women in that deployment. They did not simply document an existing reality but assumed their readers' recognition of the social relations they portrayed. Even as these French novelists were often critical of, ironic about, or distanced from bourgeois domesticity, its cen-trality in their texts reflected and reproduced its centrality in life. Thus, novelistic renderings of bourgeois consumption and gender roles both reflected and produced social practices.

It was not accidental, or without meaning, therefore, that Zola chose to disclose the dubious past, instrumental nature, and social ambitions of his protagonist through his choice of wife for Rougon and of the interior the novelist had her make for him. Such literary examples could be multiplied a hundredfold. Most striking in them is the simultaneous presence and absence of the wife. These novelistic wives existed to yield information about the husband; they themselves were not of much interest to their inventors. Women were present through the interiors they created, through the sets they provided the family.

Bourgeois women, in their memoirs, generally written in old age, used elaborate descriptions of furniture and interiors to convey a sense of their

47. René Boylesve, *Madeleine jeune femme* (Paris, 1912), 10.

lives. For example, in her memoir, Judith Gautier described the interior of her childhood home with considerable humor (and perhaps some estrangement):

> The dining room no longer looks so small, now that curtains hang in the window, that the gilt of picture frames laughs on the walls, and that there is paint on the moldings. A very beautiful set . . . of antique silver shines in the mirror of the sideboard. On the stove is sitting a porcelain jug that fills the whole corner . . . the salon is made to appear larger by a mirror placed above a gilded sideboard on which rests a bronze bust of Lucius Verus . . . chairs lined up along the walls disappear under the large and small canvases . . . in a dark corner, near the window, an immense armchair in purple damask, which makes one think of a bathtub, reclines.

Gautier was not alone in producing memoirs and novels in which interiors played an important role.[48]

Women also seem to have acted on the instructions to "be themselves." Married women's construction of aesthetic palettes through commodities became less limited to their homes than they once had been. Whitney Walton finds that the proportions of expenditures on clothing and jewelry compared with linen and silver were markedly higher in the period 1869–70 than in 1828–30. This shift could be read to indicate increasing concern among bourgeois wives about their personal appearance and less about their family's image. By the 1890s bourgeois women's preoccupation with self-validation had spread from a diversion of the family's money to clothing instead of furnishings to demands for education and suffrage. As Debora Silverman asserts, the efforts to elevate the status of women within the home and persuade them of the importance of domestic activities and of the potential of those domestic activities for their self-realization, may have been a response to the threat posed by the "New Woman." By the early years of the twentieth century that threat was becoming more and more real. More women divorced or never married.[49] With the consumption of

48. Gautier, *Le second rang du collier*, 31–33. See also Feuillet, *Quelques années de ma vie*, 193.

49. W. Walton compared the expenditures of 16 bourgeois households from the Restoration (1828–30) with 16 from the Second Empire (1869–70), defining "bourgeois" as households with goods worth at least 3,000 francs (*France at the Crystal Palace*, 72–73, 101). For feminists' use of the liberal tradition of individualism, see Laurence Klejman and Florence Rochefort, *L'égalité en marche: le féminisme sous la Troisième République* (Paris, 1989); and Silverman, *Art Nouveau in Fin-de-Siècle France*, 198–206. Another source, the labor census, shows the shifting relation of the individual and the family. The 1872 census divided the labor statistics among individuals really engaged in the trade; relatives of all degree living

divorced and single women at the turn of the twentieth century, the complexity of consumption's gendering becomes clear, for in many ways these women more resembled collectors and dandies than they did their married sisters.

> —I'm having all of the divan cushions re-covered, you know. And then I'm pushing the divan itself right into the corner, and I'm going to have an electric lamp fixed above it.
> —Splendid! It'll look just like a brothel, says Brague gravely.
> —Silly ass! And besides that, oh well, I've heaps of things to do. It's such ages since I paid any attention to my home.
> —It certainly is! agrees Brague drily. And who are you doing all this for?
> —What d'you mean, who for? For myself, of course![50]

Thus did Colette, in this 1911 dialogue, have her protagonist in *La Vagabonde* express many of the complications of being an independent woman in the early twentieth century. Her protagonist enthusiastically describes creating an interior for herself that broke with bourgeois conventions, only to be faced with a double put-down: such a room must be for a prostitute, because a woman could not create an interior only for herself. The theme of the independent or divorced artist or writer creating her own home and replicating in her home the liminality of that independence recurred in the memoirs (published in 1967 but describing here events of the teens) of the writer Camille Marbo:

> These women opened their apartments . . . which usually had only two rooms, to their friends. For example, Mme Mantelin, the divorced wife of the musician Groviez, rue du Bac, welcomed her guests in a mauve tunic, her gray hair worn *à la garçonne* above an androgynous body. In each of the rooms, there was a large divan covered with black, yellow, and blue cushions. The furniture consisted of a Norman wardrobe, a round table, and straw chairs, and a piano reserved for the composer Florent Schmitt.[51]

The women writers Camille Marbo described were living modestly, surrounded by furniture whose color scheme, style, and quantity would have been deemed singularly inappropriate for their bourgeois households of

---

off their labor or fortune; domestic servants engaged in their personal service; and total number supported directly or indirectly by each of the trades (*Statistique de la France: résultats généraux du dénombrement de 1872* [Nancy, 1874], 125–28). After this census, the family as an economic unit disappeared, replaced by individual, seemingly solitary, workers.

50. Colette, *The Vagabond*, trans. Enid McLeod (New York, 1955), 69. I am grateful to Ellen Furlough for calling this text to my attention.

51. Marbo, *A travers deux siècles*, 197.

origin. Indeed, she used the description to mark the distance between these women and other women of their class. The only comfortable seating consisted of two large sofas, strewn with pillows in a combination of colors associated with prostitutes in the etiquette books of the period. The straw chairs and Norman wardrobe were also out of place in a Parisian apartment—those were country, not city furnishings. Last, the piano, the fixture of every bourgeois salon, here waited for a visiting composer, rather than dutifully responding to the efforts of a cultured daughter of the bourgeoisie. Even if this description was entirely a figment of the memoirist's imagination, it is significant that the representation of autonomous women, dressed androgynously, should include a radically different decor. According to Marbo's image, these women had bought what they wanted to create interiors that suited them. They were not chosen to adequately represent a husband nor to assure a social place within the bourgeoisie. By the early years of the twentieth century divorced women were expressing their right to have a home even though they were alone.

Furthermore, not only did independent women furnish their homes for themselves and choose to play on styles associated with prostitution, they also took up collecting in more significant numbers. The 1946 description by the actress Cécile Sorel demonstrates the distance traveled from the decorating advice of Mme Pariset in the 1820s:

> Our furnishings are our friends. Works of art are extensions of ourselves. Near them, I ennobled my personality . . . the perfect art of the Regency inspired in me an obsessive passion. I loved this style. . . . How many times have I gotten up during the night, to see, to touch a unique piece of furniture which I had just purchased? As I looked at it, my eyes filled with voluptuousness. I knelt before its perfect forms to caress it with devotion. . . . I went into my bedroom. There, on a platform, reigned the bed of the "Dubarry", in gilded wood, crowned with roses, with its four columns topped with incense burners. I slid into bed, as the favorite once had, finally liberated from her court dress, waiting for her royal lover. The room breathed, beat, like a heart. Was it not Louis XV who wandered amidst the scented smoke? And I pursued this vision which evaporated slowly in the dreams of the night.[52]

Like the Goncourts, discussed below, Sorel was nostalgic for an earlier, courtly world. She, however, dreamed of a world where fine artisans made beautiful objects for lovely women, a world in which she could have a royal

---

52. Cécile Sorel, *Les belles heures de ma vie*, quoted in Nesbit, "Atget's *Intérieurs parisiens*," 8–10. Sorel's memoirs were published in 1946, but Atget had already photographed these rooms by 1910.

lover. In the last paragraph, Sorel was transformed into Mme du Barry waiting for Louis XV to come into her bed. Yet this is the bed that she, Cécile Sorel, had bought and it is she who, at night, rather than passively waiting to be caressed, actively caressed the furniture she had acquired. She used her power to acquire these goods to allow herself fantasies of both dominance and submission. Sorel was "unwomanly" in acquiring and enjoying objects for herself, "unwomanly" in her fetishistic and active relation to her furniture, but "womanly" in imagining herself waiting for a male lover.

Colette, Marbo's writers, and the actress Cécile Sorel were perhaps exceptional in their autonomy and in their choice of careers. But their behavior as consumers, and as writers who used the tropes of consumerism, was also the logical outcome of the final addition to the panoply of obligations a bourgeois woman incurred as a consumer—that of expressing herself. By the interwar years and especially after the Second World War, when France moved into a society of mass consumption and one in which women had the vote, the gendering and meaning of consumer practices in the making of the nation and the state would change again. But that is another story.

For the women contained within bourgeois families throughout the nineteenth century, the appropriation of consumption repertoires was much harder and took different forms. Some married women turned the images and metaphors of the prescriptive literature that assailed them—the advertisements, magazine articles, decorating and etiquette books—into a repertoire of images they could use when writing their memoirs and sometimes novels. Housewives could use the language of consumption and domesticity to feed their literary imaginations, giving them the tools with which to represent themselves in prose rather than in goods. Whereas single women, like men, could sometimes tell their own stories and constitute their social beings through goods, some wives could tell their own stories and constitute their social beings only through narratives in which imagined, fictional furnishings and interiors carried crucial information. A description of a living room, rich with transformed imagery borrowed from advertisements and etiquette books, could effectively and economically convey volumes about a memoirist's emotions concerning her marriage, or her childhood.

It is possible that this form of individuation through commodities, and through narratives about commodities, provided the conditions of possibility for thinking about other forms of individuation—the right to education, and for the vote, for example. As Hubertine Auclert wrote in 1908,

"Woman, who is taxable, a producer *and a consumer,* should be an elector and eligible for office in the *commune.*"[53] The taste professionals and distributors could not turn women into puppets enacting their will, could not even turn them into vehicles for simply enacting their husbands' wills, both because of the contradictory instructions they themselves provided and because of the focus on individuality and individual expression in their own discourse. Yet formidable obstacles blocked women's efforts to turn domestic objects to satisfy or represent their own autonomous desires within a stylistic regime that had defined them, the objects, and their interrelations. Perhaps the power of that discursive regime is most striking in the form of consumption dominated by men—collecting. For it is in the case of male collectors that the process of individuation through consumption can most clearly be seen.

SELF-MAKING: MASCULINE CONSUMPTION
AND THE PROBLEM OF INDIVIDUATION

> [Collecting] is the hunt for the masterpieces! . . . one finds oneself face
> to face with adversaries who defend the quarry! it's trick against
> trick! . . . it's like in fairy tales, a princess guarded by sorcerers![54]

Balzac's classic description of collecting suggests how certain forms of consumption were characterized so as to make them male and compatible with definitions of masculine individuation and citizenship. Collecting for Balzac was a challenge, a proving ground, a hurdle separating the boys from men and men from women.[55] While bourgeois wives and mothers were to make families through their activities as consumers, bourgeois men were to make themselves into individuated men through theirs. We have no systematic study of the collecting practices of women and men in nineteenth-century France, but it does appear that the vast majority of collections were assembled by men, and certainly masculine models of collection dominated in literature, where most collectors were depicted as men and the activity of collecting was assimilated to the hunt and conquest.[56]

---

53. Hubertine Auclert, *Le vote des femmes* (Paris, 1908), 13; emphasis added.
54. Honoré de Balzac, *Le cousin Pons* (1846; Paris, 1973), 75.
55. Susan Stewart's work on the self and the collection (*On Longing* [Baltimore, 1984], 158–59) has been very helpful here, but she does not analyze the gendering of the processes. For similar descriptions of collectors see Léo Larguier, *Au vieux saint de bois* (Avignon, 1944), 18, 20, 55.
56. Steven Gelber ascribes different collection practices to nineteenth-century American women and men, the men's scientific and the women's aesthetic; as goods entered the commodity state—acquiring value on the market—they came to be

But the story was more complicated than this, for when collectors went too far and sought their individuation, emotional satisfaction, and immortality exclusively through their collections, they were calumnied by critics and incorporated into the category of dandy. In nineteenth-century France collecting was conceptualized as a properly masculine activity if it did not emotionally replace the family; if it could be conceptualized as investing— that is, if it could be understood as knowledge producing.

Collecting, in its modern form, was largely an invention of the 1830s, before which it had been oriented largely to scientific specimens or art and motivated and organized very differently than in the nineteenth century.[57] In the 1830s expertise came to play a new role in collecting. With the development of art history as an academic discipline came an increasing preoccupation with attribution and with creation of a canon. This new development led to an expanded role for the picture merchant and the art expert—who could assess attribution. Krzysztof Pomian argues that collectors, through the creation of categories and because of the collaboration of experts, came to control a domain of knowledge.[58] The creation of a respected collection may have allowed a recently wealthy consumer more prestige than investing the same amount of money in other commodities. A corollary of the utility of collecting for establishing social position was its status as a creative act, an act of taste.[59]

---

collected by men rather than women (Steven M. Gelber, "Free Market Metaphor," *Comparative Studies in Society and History* 34 [October 1992]: 748). Walter Benjamin also emphasizes the order-making aspect of collecting ("Unpacking My Library," in *Illuminations*, ed. Hannah Arendt, trans. Harry Zohn [New York, 1968], 60). Paula Findlen claims that late sixteenth-century men first used collections to masculinize domestic space ("The Museum," *Journal of the History of Collections* 1, no. 1 [1989]: 69–71). This, in some sense, continues the eighteenth-century scientific voyages to "collect" the world, classifying and displaying samples and thereby producing mastery and order (Daniel Defert, "The Collection of the World," *Dialectical Anthropology* 7, no. 1 [1982]: 11–20). James Clifford's work supports and extends these conclusions, esp. "On Collecting Art and Culture," in *The Predicament of Culture* (Cambridge, Mass., 1988).

57. Gerald Reitlinger argues that even in the 1860s the value of antiques had not yet been firmly established (*Objet d'Art Prices*, 13). Paul Eudel insisted that Victor Hugo convinced the French that antiques had value (*Le truquage: altérations, fraudes et contrefaçons dévoilées* [Paris, n.d. (1880s?)], 296–97).

58. See especially Krzysztof Pomian, "Marchands, connaisseurs, curieux à Paris au XVIIIe siècle," in *Collectionneurs, amateurs et curieux* (Paris, 1987), 185, 51–52.

59. Capronnier, *Le prix des meubles d'époque*, 15; Rheims, *The Strange Life of Objects*, 23, 25.

Appropriate consumption for bourgeois men was deemed to be highly individual, often authenticity-based, creative, self-producing, order-making activity—all best enacted in collecting. The sites at which collectors consumed offer insights into the differences between masculine and feminine consumption. In Balzac's and others' fantasies, rather than shopping in the banal department stores and specialty or custom shops frequented by female consumers, collectors were—with great ingenuity and intrepidness—to hunt down and uncover unexpected, unrecognized treasures at auctions, flea markets, and in antique stores. Finding and acquiring the object of one's desire in each of these places was understood to require different talents. Buying at auction required persistence, guile, quickness, and a willingness to take risks, as did sifting through flea markets, characterized as exotic and dangerous places, to uncover treasures amidst heaps of junk, stolen objects, and dubious characters. Buying furniture from antique dealers also required the pitting of wits, where the collector by bluff would try to persuade the dealer that an object was worth less than it was. Many of the innovations of the department and specialized stores, developed simultaneously with the elaboration of bourgeois women's roles as consumers, were absent here—there were no fixed prices, and advice represented as "expert" was often as much challenge as help.[60]

In auctions, the hunter did have some information before entering the contest—auctioneers published catalogues detailing, and whetting the appetite for, the goods for sale. But once in the auction room the collector would have to mobilize all his wiles to snatch his quarry. In bidding auctions the auctioneers took a percentage of the total sales, so the challenge was to win over the other bidders but also to force the auctioneer to accept a lower price. Collectors were competing against one another in auctions but also against antique dealers trying to acquire goods for their stores. Unlike other situations, the buyers competed for the right to buy what were often unique objects.

Perhaps paradoxically, just as the taste professionals were central to the place of consumption in bourgeois women's lives, so they were central to the elaboration of collection as a masculine activity. Modern collectors depended on authentication of their goods to establish the legitimacy and

60. André Warnod, *La brocante et les petits marchés de Paris* (Paris, 1914); Larguier, *Au vieux saint de bois*. The best discussion of the auction dynamic is C. Smith, *Auctions*. Three major auction houses in Paris—Drouot, Petit, and Charpentier—sold a wide range of goods, either as complete lots or as individual items. For detailed discussion of transformations in the organization of distribution see chapter 8; M. Miller, *The Bon Marché*; R. Williams, *Dream Worlds*.

value of their collections. Whereas the taste professionals and distributors attempted to dictate to female consumers what they should buy, the experts on whom the collectors relied were to confirm that an object was what it was claimed to be. Experts did not get to define what objects were appropriate material for a collection or what the categories should be. An expert could not say that a collection of Chinese porcelain was inappropriate for a collector occupying a particular social location; he could only state that a vase that claimed to be from seventeenth-century China really was one. It was then up to the collector to decide if he wanted it. Of course, since some collections were secret, they played a more complicated role in establishing social position; but their owners could promise special access to some, thus creating privileged relationships.

Understood to be the reflection and the creation of their possessors, collections represented the fantasy of immortality. The major function of the objects acquired for collections, as opposed to the function of the collection as a whole, was that they took their place in the collection, that they contributed to the collection's wholeness. A chair acquired for a collection of Louis XIII chairs did not serve the usual functions of providing seating, blending in harmoniously with the other furnishings of the salon or dining room, or even representing the personality of the purchaser and the status of the family to the outside world. Thus, for example, the furniture manufacturer and taste professional Henri Fourdinois had, in what appears to have been his personal collection at the time of his death, sixty-three chairs, including many that lacked their upholstery. The objects composing a collection did not even have to be beautifully displayed to function well. They had to suit the collection, filling some gap in the search for completeness and perfection.[61] By contrast, a Louis XIII chair purchased for use in a dining room, had to match the other chairs and furniture, be reasonably comfortable (or acceptably uncomfortable) to sit on, convey the tastes of the mistress of the house, and be an accurate indicator of the wealth and social position of the family.

Assembling a collection was understood to be an individualistic act, more akin to making a sculpture or painting than to decorating a living room. The Baron J. de Pinchon, in the foreword to the sale of the collection of his friend M. le comte de la Béraudière, insisted strongly on the individuality

61. Catalogue des meubles d'art anciens et modernes . . . le tout appartenant à M. Fourdinois (Forney 6030 1051 January 1887, 41–50). See Atget's photograph of "the collector"'s room: a row of almost identical pitchers on a mantelpiece, a glass case filled with butterflies and other exotic species (Atget, *Intérieurs parisiens*).

of collections and the propriety of breaking them up. "A collection made by one man for and by him rarely suits, in its entirety, another man. It is the clothing of the spirit, of a soul that has now died; the collection was made to the measure of that spirit and not to that of another."[62]

We might imagine a similar pronouncement about the furnishings acquired gradually across a lifetime by a noncollector; that they suited their owner and no one else. But the individuality of a collection was thought to be different from that of an ordinary interior, however beautiful. Objects in a collection were thought to be denatured and transformed into something new. Their economic and aesthetic value was thereby also transformed. Whereas the collection represented the individual who possessed it, objects used as part of interior decoration were representative of the family, not of the individual. When the husband died, the wife kept the furniture and vice versa; when both members of the elder generation died, the furniture was divided among the family. It was to live on, but to live on as emblems of the family, of the immortality of the family, not as a means to immortality of the individual creator of the collection. An understanding of the collection as the mirror of the soul was not, of course incompatible with its preservation after death. Although Pinchon argued that his friend's collection should be dispersed as he was now dead and his soul as embodied in the collection should be liberated with his body, others believed equally passionately that the collections *were* their owners and should be kept unified after the death of their creator.

The definition of collecting was permeated with paradox that mirrored and reproduced those of bourgeois masculinity. Bourgeois men were to assure their immortality through reproduction of the family name, living through their sons into the future. But they were also to acquire immortality through their work, through a business, a book, even a painting with their name. Even their political voice required the presence of dependents. Collections could both reinforce and seriously disrupt this bourgeois relation to time, reproduction, and property:

> The true collector is he who would seek to satisfy a complicated need, both cerebral and sensual. He experiences physical joys that are among the most noble that we may ask of our organism. Furthermore, the beau-

62. Catalogue . . . riche mobilier XVIIIe siècle, for private sale, 18–30 mai 1885 (Bibliothèque Forney).

tiful objects that surround us distract us from the idea of death and give to the spirit the idea of eternity, through the past.[63]

In this text Edmond de Gramont characterized the collector as seeking escape from mortality in the past, rather than the future, and as experiencing a mysterious physical joy in acquiring objects rather than in producing children. Indeed, arguably the most famous collectors of the nineteenth century, the Goncourt brothers, were also dandies; not only did they never marry, but Edmond de Goncourt was explicit about the incompatibility of love and collecting:

> For our generation, art collecting is only the index of how women no longer possess the male imagination. I must admit here that when by chance my heart has been given, I have had no interest in the *objet d'art*. . . . This passion . . . gives immediate gratification from all the objects that tempt, charm, seduce: they provide a momentary abandon in aesthetic debauchery. . . . These are some of the causes that invest an almost human tenderness in objects; they have made me in particular the most passionate of collectors.

Edmond created a bedroom for himself that was "an authentic room of a château, where I become a sleeping beauty from the era of Louis XV."[64] Needless to say, since the bed had been made for the princesse de Lamballe he did not quite become the sleeping beauty he had in mind. But the boundary between the collector and the dandy was highly permeable.

The gendering of buying was permeated by the erotic overtones, metaphors, and associations of desire. There was the fear that the desire generated for goods would overflow into sexual desire, causing women to lose control of all other desires. Consumption for the self, understood to be a kind of autoeroticism, was to be reserved for men. Bourgeois women were supposed to desire objects—department stores were explicitly designed to create desire—yet they were not to desire too much. The labeling of women who stole as mad (victims of the new disease of kleptomania), overcome by the excesses of desire, illustrates how terrified contemporaries could be of women's desire.[65]

63. E. de Gramont, *Mémoires: les marronniers en fleurs*, 25th ed. (Paris, 1929), 185.

64. Edmond de Goncourt, *La maison d'un artiste* (1881), quoted in Silverman, *Art Nouveau in Fin-de-Siècle France*, 36.

65. Pierre Giffard, *Paris sous la Troisième République: les grands bazars* (Paris, 1882), 6; Patricia O'Brien, "The Kleptomania Diagnosis," *Journal of Social*

By contrast, normative collecting allowed domestic consumption, normally encoded as feminine, to be recoded as masculine and manly. One could be a manly consumer if in consuming one was really hunting (as in Balzac), liberating captive princesses (and putting them in one's own cave); creating an immortal chef d'oeuvre; creating oneself; competing with other men for the love of women. One could care about beauty, if one controlled it, or used it to control others. It was not, as is sometimes claimed, that men were not conceptualized as consumers. Men were to desire, and consume to acquire the objects of their desire: wealth, women, knowledge, and mastery. Men were not to consume, or desire to consume, as women did; that is, to make *themselves* into the objects of desire. Bourgeois men and women were both consumers, but bourgeois men consumed to produce themselves, bourgeois men must do so "responsibly," as heads of households, entitled to govern because they had dependents. The qualities of the collector were like the qualities of the active male citizen. Masculine consumption contributed to the family's patrimony.

It was not only the family's patrimony that was to be established through collecting in this period, but also the state's. From the founding of the Louvre as a national museum under the Directory through the founding of the Musée des arts décoratifs in the late nineteenth century, the state became increasingly preoccupied with producing organized, classified displays of the national heritage. The intent was both pedagogic and preservationist. Museums, like schools, and the army became a site, outside the home, of the making of the nation. It is not surprising, perhaps, that the form of private consumption most closely resembling state consumption should have been the one defined as "appropriately" masculine. But this appropriateness bore within it the possibilities for its own transgression; collecting could be appropriated by women, as it more and more often was toward the end of the century. Ideally, however, while men and women presumably engaged in all kinds of consumption, with all kinds of goals, the characterization of masculine and feminine consumption was both produced by and reinforced the gendering of the individual in such a way as to render women incapable of political action and men capable of it. Consequently, even if women did indeed create themselves through consumption, that was not how they were allowed to understand their actions.

History 17, no. 1 (fall 1983): 65–77; Elaine Abelson, *When Ladies Go A-Thieving: Middle-Class Shoplifters in the Victorian Department Store* (New York, 1989).

PASTICHE, PARADOX, AND POWER

In French bourgeois society, from the last quarter of the nineteenth century onward, the deployment of purchased goods became not only a critical means of representation—sometimes of class, sometimes of the family, sometimes of the self—but a contradictory one. At other times those goods served to imprison women within the family, sometimes to create group solidarities, sometimes to express individuality. Thus, the making of interiors in the second half of the nineteenth century was simultaneously an individual, familial, class, regional, and national project, but one that also constructed the present, past, and future. The bourgeois home in late nineteenth-century Paris was neither a refuge nor a place of certainty; rather it was a location filled with conflicting desires, needs, and expectations.

Furniture reflected and produced the social standing of the family but also served as a space in which individuals tried to make themselves at ease. Interiors were to help create the unity of the family, and yet the space within them was infinitely divided by usage and by gender. They were to provide a material basis for the history of the family, and yet the furniture was dispersed with every generation. Consumers were simultaneously urged to buy new, innovative furniture and told the right way to use nineteenth-century pastiches. Women were told that the home was to represent their personality, and yet homes also served to constitute families, groups, and the nation. For example, women were best represented by Louis XVI style—unless they were blond, over forty, or under twenty-one. The world was supposed to be divided into binary oppositions, still there were hermaphroditic styles and androgynous spaces. The home was not simply a private, feminized space; it was also a masculine, public space. Thus the home was always simultaneously inside and outside, part of a private narrative and part of a public one as well. Its publicness was social rather than political. As a mixed feminine-masculine, private-public space, it had its own temporality and relation to history. And, not least, this space ostensibly outside of capital was constructed with capital and used to reproduce it.

Bourgeois apartments were characterized by a preoccupation with the creation of a specialized, complete, and apparently enclosed, self-contained world. Yet in its fragmentation and specialization, the haven emulated the world it ostensibly tried to exclude. This world was further inhabited by furnishings named after and resembling those of France's past, but which were in fact new. Through the complexities of elaborate combinations and contradictory codings, interior decoration served to create boundaries against interlopers from within and from the classes beneath, and to forge links with the past while insisting on the importance of the present. Each object was intended to go with every other object, but unlike eighteenth-century aesthetics where the ideal was contemporaneousness, rationality, and symmetry, the aesthetic basis of nineteenth-century interiors was complex pastiche. In these interiors the old world and the new were to meet, the generations were to be brought together and reconciled, hidden rationality and overt sentimentality were to merge. The price of every object in these apartments was known, recorded, and calculated, yet invisible; on the surface all was cozy and protected yet seething with contradictions.

Bourgeois men's forms of transgendered consumerism, in contrast, were to engage in extensive self-adornment through clothing or jewels; to create for themselves alone beautiful, expensive, and carefully chosen interiors; and to consume without producing tangible result. In dressing with great care the dandy embodied the inappropriately narcissistic man or, perhaps more accurately, the model of a man who commodified himself as an object of other people's—either women's or men's—consumption. In creating an elegant home for himself (and his friends), the dandy disrupted the logic of the home as the sacred site of the production and reproduction of the family. Dandies, in their clothing and interiors, seemed to parody bourgeois feminine roles.

But all nineteenth-century consumers, transgressive or not, made choices in their acts of consumption—acting not quite as sovereign subjects nor as mere pawns of clever advertisers and taste professionals. All this should caution us against drawing too simplistic conclusions, sorting various acts of consumption into categories of resistance or accommodation. As in other areas of human experience, the boundaries are not nearly so clear. Some forms of accommodation can become the basis for future resistance; some forms of resistance become safety valves siphoning off potential pressures against the status quo.

It is not surprising then that many bourgeois commentators on taste should have accepted and even embraced and used the middling classes' commitment to ancien régime styles at the same time as they unanimously condemned the same taste in the working class and regretted the bourgeoisie's reluctance to support new styles. The elaboration of systems of internal differentiation through style was deemed appropriate for the bourgeoisie, while the working class was defined as an undifferentiated mass with no individual or collective history.

In all these ways the deployment of style and taste sustained social power. Both the mode of deployment and the context of that power differed profoundly from the ancien régime, however, or even from the early and middle years of the nineteenth century. But the power to make classes, families, and genders ultimately involved the power to make nations, citizens, and politics. We cannot elaborate those constructions without first understanding the crucial roles of markets and other social institutions.

8

Style in the New Commercial World

The furniture industry suffers, above all, from narrow prejudice and stubborn obstruction. How can art possibly develop when the consumers trap the producers in the following dilemma: "Copy, make Renaissance, Louis XIV, Louis XVI; or else make junk furniture." Either one of these kinds of products is the antithesis of all progress. And the public condemns us to making one or the other. If one of us tries to escape from this impasse, if he wants to give himself the luxury of demonstrating that he too is capable of making a beautiful piece of his own design, without worrying about known styles, like in the Renaissance or under Louis XVI, he will pay a high price for his excess of pride. . . . In sum, with the public—and I am not only talking about those who seek the inexpensive above all—having taste just for old styles and forcing the manufacturer to live off imitation, it is clear that the art of *ébénisterie* will soon succumb under this regime.[1]

Railing against consumers' taste, as the preeminent furniture manufacturer Henri Fourdinois was doing in 1897, could not change the fact that by the Third Republic the furniture that sold best was historicist pastiche. Some artisans and manufacturers attempted to counter the current, either taking up their pens to persuade consumers to buy something else or participating in the movements of *style moderne* and later *art nouveau*. Other artisans and manufacturers, the majority in fact, appear to have responded to such market exigencies by inventing new forms of the old. Eugène Rinck, for example, an *ébéniste* active from 1901 to 1935, who was frequently asked to produce reproductions of Louis XIV's famous desk (made originally by Cressent) chose different woods, "improved" the bronzes, and generally altered the details (much to his son's horror).[2]

1. Fourdinois, "Quelques réflexions," 164–65.
2. Fabienne Desaix, "L'art d'être ébéniste en cinq générations," *L'estampille*, 16.

These new versions were often very distinctive, sometimes playful, and sometimes ironic. As was shown in the last chapter, if we compare Henri II, Louis XV, and Louis XVI pieces—some made while the monarch was on the throne and others over the course of the nineteenth century—we realize that the labels Henri II, Louis XV, or Louis XVI could be applied to a wide variety of forms in both the eighteenth and the nineteenth centuries. Some producers were explicit about what they were doing. "French manufacturers have often been reproached for not having created a modern style. One can respond that none of the furniture we make resembles antique furniture; that if in fact we use ornaments from all styles, we create from all these pieces forms appropriate to *our tastes;* and furthermore that a style cannot be invented, because a style emerges from the customs and the social system of an epoch. . . . While we have been inspired by the documents of the period of Louis XV, we have modernized the general form."[3]

This chapter explains how the organization of production and of distribution in the late nineteenth century adapted to meet the exigencies of producing and distributing historicist pastiche styles and how the forms of distribution and production sustained these styles, against a background of increasing fragmentation of labor and growing distance between production and consumption.

Developments only nascent in the 1830s and 1840s, such as mechanization, the division of labor, outwork, piece rates, and provincial production came to maturity in the 1880s and 1890s. The proportion of exclusively custom shops declined as the number of furniture factories increased. New machines (and economic relations with the colonies) made the wood and the veneers necessary to Louis XIV–, Louis XV–, and Louis XVI–style furniture much cheaper. Steam-powered lathes and molding machines made some of the elements of Henri II and Louis XIII style less expensive. The new styles that were tried in this period—*style moderne* and *art nouveau*—were not particularly well suited to these developments, since their production could not be commercialized.[4]

It was also a period in which the fields of sales and advertising were just coming into maturity; forms that could be labeled with Old Regime names

3. BHVP 120, ameub. N–R, Pérol frères, 1906.
4. A close study of over 200 advertisements (BHVP 120, ameub.) from furniture stores in this period reveals that few sold *style moderne* or *art nouveau.* Those that did (Dumas, Gallery, Soubrier, Meubles, Rigaut, Diot, and Nebout) were all high-end stores, with largely luxury furniture, and *style moderne* was among their most expensive.

were easier to sell. Awareness of the possible uncertainties created by the multiplication of retail outlets and the new distance between producer and consumer encouraged the distributors to consolidate their efforts. They sold what they knew had sold before. Furthermore, contemporary advertising theory held that advertisements were quite literally to represent the goods, to prompt people to imagine the goods that they could not see; known styles were easier to visualize. But distributors were also limited by what the organization of production—which they did not absolutely control—could offer. Consumers could now equally easily buy new and old furniture, acquire a custom- or readymade object, and buy at an auction, an open-air market, a specialized furnishings store, a small producer or retailer, or a department store. Thus the period was marked by intense competition among these vendors, each offering a different kind of expertise or convenience, and a different relation between the customer and her furniture.

Despite these changes, we cannot simply categorize the period from 1880 to 1930 as one of mass production and distribution in furniture. Rather the organization of both was highly diversified, favoring the production and sale of historicist pastiche rather than the hegemony of any one style—leading to multiplicity or, in certain critics' eyes, chaos.

CONDITIONS OF LABOR AND THE MAKING
OF STYLE AT THE END OF THE CENTURY

As in the Old Regime, the organization and social relations of production at the end of the century strongly constrained and shaped the possibilities for stylistic innovation and the forms successful styles would assume. The salient features of the organization of production were a significant increase in the number of furniture makers; the augmentation in the number of machine tools in the industry and their sophistication; growing numbers of out- and home workers; the substitution of piece rates for hourly wages; decreasing real wages; persistence of high and low seasons; high worker mobility among shops; more and more finely divided labor; multiplication of large factories; movement of production to the provinces; and, competition from Germany.

The most obvious change, perhaps, was the dramatic expansion of the production side of the trades. As is always the case, head counts in the furniture industry are unreliable, but from a survey of a number of sources, some usable approximate figures emerge. Figures from various censuses between 1860 and 1892 count roughly twenty to forty-six thousand Parisians directly engaged in the industry, with up to one hundred thousand dependent on it.[5] The city as a whole was of course expanding in this period, but the sheer numbers of artisans in the furniture trades meant that the "community" of furniture makers was necessarily differently defined and experienced than in earlier years. Since the industry was still concentrated in the traditional neighborhoods of the faubourg St-Antoine and the rue de Cléry, workshops were increasingly cramped. From the increase in the numbers of producers we can assume a corresponding increase in the number of consumers and in the range of furniture produced.

More significant than this expansion in the workforce were the changes—some dramatic, some subtle—in how the work got done. Workshops based on a "traditional" division of labor and using only human power continued to exist well into the twentieth century but became more and more scarce and needed to expand in order to survive. Thus the maison Gueret, founded in 1851, specializing in sculpted furniture, chairs, and tapestries, operated on a very large scale, even though it still had no machines and used no outworkers, even as late as 1877. It employed on average eighty men, fifteen women, and twenty children (apprentices, sculptors, *ébénistes, menuisiers,* and upholsterers) and had annual sales figures of between 700,000 and 800,000 francs.[6] These shops provided continuity in the trades and the continued possibility of innovation, but their scale meant that often the drawing and building operations had been separated, even if work processes were still relatively undivided. In these large unmechanized shops, the traditional division of labor often involved a team of artisans turning out a given piece or ensemble, working from pattern books and stored drawings to produce variations on the theme of a Louis XV or XVI object. A contemporary commentator, Thomas Funck-Brentano, noted that with this division of labor, including purchased patterns and employers who no longer worked with their hands, stylistic innovation became increasingly difficult. Besides the expansion of unmechanized shops, the pattern of considerable outwork, whose origins may be found in the Old Regime, appears to have greatly increased. Auguste

5. For details on these sources see Auslander, "Social Life of Furniture."
6. V. Brants, "L'état de la petite industrie en France d'après les statistiques récentes," part 1, *Bulletin de l'Académie royale de Belgique* 6 (1900): 513–34. Exceptions include the small-scale sculpture shop of Hyacinthe Guillot, which did separate production and distribution; or M. Lapierre's sculpture shop, which did copies and pastiches of Old Regime styles and employed 20–25 workers and several apprentices; or the maison Edouard Guillaume, with 80 men in the shop, 5 men and women outside, but no machines (AN F^{12}3365, exposition universelle de Paris, 1878; classe 17—meubles).

Chevié, for example, employed 6 to 8 men in the shop, another 6 as full-time *façonniers* and another 8 to 10 as part-time *façonniers*.[7] In many cases the scale again became far larger. The firm of Gallais et Simon employed 125 men and 10 women in the shop and 100 men in outwork. Hertenstein fils expanded the shop his father had founded in 1829 and when he took it over in 1871 added "fabrication du meuble, ébénisterie, sièges, tentures concernant l'industrie de l'ameublement" to his specialties, employing 30 men in the shop and 20 men and 8 women as *façonniers*—a pattern of mixed in- and outwork so common by the 1870s that it usually passed uncommented.

Some manufacturers felt compelled to either defend or apologize for their use of outworkers. Jayer, for example, who specialized in *tables à jeu*, in his application to display work at the 1878 universal exposition divided his production into that done in the shop and that done by *façonniers*, implying that he did not think the work of the same quality. But Emile Lalande, an exhibitor whose shop produced relatively inexpensive Old Regime–style furniture, launched into an elaborate essay on the virtues of home work. He argued that the quality of the work improved when workers labored at home with a plan and raw materials given them by the shop. Workers could then watch their children grow and begin to teach their sons their trade. He insisted that the best workers were those who had been taught by their fathers rather than those who had completed their apprenticeship in a shop.[8] He, correspondingly, employed only thirty artisans in his workshop, but fully one hundred as home workers.

A corollary of the move to home work was a somewhat increased employment of women. Some employers argued that home work was good for women because "these women can take care of their household tasks and work by the piece." In 1866 women were said to make up approximately 4 percent of those employed in the "industries de bois et d'ameublement," 10 percent in 1906, and 11 percent in 1921.[9] Despite the upward trend, it appears that the taboo against women working wood was strong enough to protect male workers against replacement by women in the central trades.

Women in the furnishings trades, of course, earned less than men. The

7. Funck-Brentano, "La ville du meuble," 274; AN F^{12}3365. An example is A. Chambry, who employed 10 in the workshop and 10 outside.

8. Ibid.

9. Ibid., St-Allais-en-Magny-en-Vexin (Seine et Oise) (a chair manufacturer); Henri Nolleau, "Les femmes dans la population active de 1856 à 1954," *Economie et politique* 74 (October 1960): 13.

statistical survey done by the Chamber of Commerce in 1860 claimed that the men employed as *ébénistes* and *menuisiers en meuble* earned between 3 and 6 francs a day, the women 2 francs. Male upholsterers earned between 4 and 6 francs a day, while the women were earning between 2 and 2.50 and the apprentices 4.50. Workers making armchairs and straight chairs, including turners, caners, and "empailleurs de chaises," earned between 4 and 6 francs a day; most men were earning 3 to 6 francs a day with a few as much as 10; the women between 1.25 and 1.75; boys between 1 and 1.75; and girls, 1.25.[10]

Although some male artisans protested that women were invading the masculine parts of the trades, this does not appear to have been the case. Women were consistently employed in caning, finishing, varnishing, making straw seats, and in some branches of upholstery. For example, the 1860 survey listed 7,316 male *ébénistes* and *menuisiers* and only 46 female. In contrast, nearly half of the 3,591 upholsterers were women.[11]

But if the increase in the overall percentage of women in the trades cannot be accounted for by their encroachment into new areas, it must mean that more work was being given to varnishers, chair caners, upholsterers, rush-seat makers, finishers, and gilders. Varnishing, gilding, caning, and upholstering were vital to Louis XIV–, Louis XV–, and Louis XVI–style furniture. Rush seats were used on the least expensive of chairs. Furthermore, the finishing processes in which inexpensive women's labor was concentrated could make cheap furniture look elegant. *Style moderne* used little gilding and no caning. Thus, the expansion of women's labor in these industries simultaneously supported the dominant styles and grew from and encouraged the move to home work.

A necessary side effect of outwork was a wage system based on piece rather than hourly rates for both men and women. The 1851 statistical survey claimed that in 1847 nearly 75 percent of both male and female workers were paid by the hour rather than the piece. In 1860 the majority of *menuisiers* and *ébénistes* were still paid by the day, but most of the upholsterers were paid by the piece: 11.9 percent of the 1,805 men were paid by the day and 4 percent of the 1,589 women were paid by the day.[12] By the 1880s, this trend had developed further and the norm for the majority of the furniture trades was a piecework wage rather than an

10. Chambre de commerce de Paris, *Statistique de l'industrie à Paris, édité pour l'année 1860* (Paris, 1862), 170, 175.

11. Ibid., 15, 211.

12. Out of 508 women, 377 were paid by the day; out of 12,564 men, 9,245 (Van Doren, *Ebénisterie à Paris et à Bruxelles*, 87, 213).

hourly rate. The exceptions to this were the most highly skilled of the *ébénistes* and *menuisiers.*

To some extent, the domination of piecework was determined by the organization of production. All the workers whose trades were defined by the object produced rather than by the tasks they performed—the workers in bedside tables, *ouvriers en commodes, ouvriers en chaises anglaises,* to cite a few—had worked by piece rate since their jobs were created, sometime in the early nineteenth century. These workers often did outwork or worked on speculation, so it was inevitable that they be paid by the piece. Even when the work moved into a shop, however, as sometimes happened, the tradition of piece work continued. This category of worker expanded considerably in the 1870s and 1880s, in part to meet the needs of the new department stores, and perhaps as a side effect of the depression.[13] Consequently, the percentage of workers on piece rate increased.

The continuation of piece rate was determined not only by tradition but also by the low value attributed to the work. Other artisans were also often paid on a piece rate in the 1880s and 1890s, artisans whom it would have been more obvious to pay by the hour: varnishers, finishers, upholsterers, and gilders. In the case of these artisans, specialized by task rather than by object, the employers' choice of piece rate had to do with the employers' goal—to extract maximum labor for minimum wages. The elite of the trades, the artisans whose skill and knowledge were valued as much as their labor, were paid by the hour.

The distinction between daily or hourly rates and piece rates was a crucial one. Although as William Reddy and Michael Sonenscher show, piece rates do not necessarily imply a deterioration in the conditions of labor, or speedup, that was their effect in the Parisian furniture industry at this time. Under this piece-rate system, what was valued was artisans' ability to produce the maximum quantity in the minimum amount of time, making them terribly vulnerable to speedup.

Under a piece-rate system any innovation was clearly a liability to the artisans. Workers were best off when the work remained maximally routine. Thus the turners objected to changing the patterns of the work they produced, even though such changes might have reduced the monotony, because it cost them time and therefore money: "We also need to note an abuse brought about by competition—that is details or additions to the work. It often happens that several manufacturers work for the same client. So, in order to get an edge, one has to change an already finished model.

13. On this process see Funck-Brentano, "La ville du meuble," 290–91.

The worker has to labor, without additional pay, on the piece again. Thus the worker sees his wages diminished by the increase in the work."[14] Some of the limited variations on a common theme that characterized so much of historicist pastiche may have been an effect of this process.

Arguing for piece rates, the manufacturers Rousenel et Goumain prided themselves on both the quality and low cost of their production and stated that "the precise description of each piece including complete details given to each worker facilitates his labor. He is able to work a good day at very much reduced rates and consequently we are able to sell our products for a low price." The artisan—because he did not have to think—could earn more money on a piece rate. But under a daily or hourly rate, artisans were remunerated for the quality as well as the quantity of what they produced. Implied in a pay rate based on the time spent in the shop rather than on the objects produced was a willingness to pay for—the tangible results of its valorization—time spent transmitting knowledge, finely finishing a piece, and making detailed drawings. This is supported both by artisans' demands for hourly wages and by employers' statements. For example, Sauvrezy, a self-described "fabricant de meubles d'art," declared "As I seek perfection in all of the furniture made in my shop, all of my workers are paid by the hour."[15]

Another variation, and one used by one of the largest and most respected shops of the faubourg, was to subcontract out most of the work to a *façonnier* who hired others. The classic difficulty with outwork, from an employer's point of view—and one long noted by historians—is that the employer had less control over the quality and form of the object produced. It is hardly surprising, therefore, that an organization of production emphasizing outwork should have as its dominant style a series of themes with variations. Outworkers were presumably often given the raw materials, and impressionistic sketches and asked to produce a Louis XV chair, or Louis XVI dresser; entrusting them with novel forms would be a far riskier act. Thus the economics of furniture production by the late nineteenth century—from the perspective of both employers and employees—discouraged radical innovation.

Mechanization and Provincial Production

The process of mechanization, which until the 1860s had remained largely a conceptual rather than a pragmatic issue, became much more important

14. Descamps and Beaujean, "Tourneurs en chaises," 3:6–7.
15. AN F^{12}3365.

toward the end of the century. The major heavy machines invented toward the end of the eighteenth century, built in the first two decades of the nineteenth, and perfected from mid- to late century, became widely used by the last quarter of the century.[16]

In Paris, as late as 1860, there were—in workshops doing *menuiserie* and *ébénisterie*—only five steam engines, with two of them in the chair industry. Each steam engine drove a system of belts and pulleys that in turn ran individual machines. Even late in the century machines were largely used for the initial preparation of wood. By the 1889 universal exposition, for example, it was declared that most exhibitors owned a jointer, while only one or two had as late as 1878.[17] Since jointers were used in the initial milling process and reduced production time, they—and other machines— came to influence the dominant styles produced. By 1867 the *ébéniste* worker delegates were already attributing the increase in mechanization to consumers' tastes for veneered furniture and the need to compete with production from abroad. This meant, they claimed, "that French manufacturers must research the best means to make inexpensive furniture, because hand-cut veneers could not be produced in adequate quantities and were very expensive."[18]

Louis XIV, Louis XV, and Louis XVI were all styles in which veneer had an essential role. To cut veneer by hand was not only a time-consuming process, but the veneer could not be cut nearly as thin. By 1860 a new machine to cut veneers achieved considerable reduction in milling time and waste, and savings in wages, thus aiding the popularity of the styles dependent on it.[19]

By the last third of the century renting time on centrally located machines as well as shop ownership of machines were becoming common. Even some very small shops employing three people, like that of Victor Bareau, now had access to considerable machine-tool power—in this case a band saw, table saw, shaper and drills, even though they were all bor-

16. Tresca and Lecoeuvre, "Machines-outils servant spécialement au travail des bois," in *Exposition universelle de 1867, à Paris: rapports du jury international,* ed. Chevalier (Paris, 1868), 9:157–58.

17. *Statistique de l'industrie à Paris, 1860,* 213, 176; Mangeant, "Façon et empilage du bois," 94; Paul Poiré, *La France industrielle, ou description des industries françaises,* 2d ed. (Paris, 1875), 209–10; M. Alheilig, *Recette, conservation, et travail des bois* (Paris, [1894–95?]), 136; Garenc, *L'industrie du meuble en France,* 88; Picard, ed., *Exposition universelle internationale de 1889, à Paris,* 9:437.

18. Baude and Loizel, "Ebénistes," 1:16.

19. Van Doren, *Ebénisterie à Bruxelles et à Paris,* 42.

rowed. Likewise the pool-table maker F. Gerderes, who employed twelve workers and had an annual production worth only 100,000 francs a year, had one band saw. Moreover, mechanization was by no means limited to cheap or mass production. The celebrated furniture maker Henri Fourdinois, whose shop had been founded by his father in 1828 and had been organized according to a traditional division of labor and without machines, rented a 6-horsepower motor by 1877 to drive his milling and molding machines, band saw, and shaper. He employed a total of seventy artisans including operatives who ran the machines, sculptors, *ébénistes*, *menuisiers*, upholsterers, and gilders, together with fifteen women upholsterers and eight apprentices; he subcontracted out the bronze work.[20]

While veneer cutters were essential to the diffusion of ancien régime styles, advocates of *style moderne* also mechanized their shops—but with different machines. Given the emphasis of *style moderne* on solid wood furniture and marquetry rather than veneer, heavy milling machines were used in these shops to rough out the wood that would later be worked by sculptors (see Figure 53). The important manufacturer of *style moderne*, for example, Majorelle, combined machines totaling 50 horsepower with a self-consciously "traditional" organization of production (but employed between eighty and five or six hundred people depending on business).[21]

Regardless of claims to maintain a traditional division of labor, the fact was that the skills needed in large and mechanized shops changed: instead of mastery in the making and use of a chisel, workers needed an understanding of machines, their maintenance and repair. "The art of making tools used to belong to the workers who used them. Everyone knows that in *menuiserie* and *ébénisterie* workers themselves made the tools they used. The introduction of machine tools in the industry necessarily produced a complete revolution in workers' habits."[22] An *ébéniste* or a *menuisier*, until the last decades of the nineteenth century, would have made twenty different planes and jointers, as well as saws of various shapes, chisels, gouges, screwdrivers, measuring instruments and hammers, as well as jigs to guide the saw in cutting certain standard joints. Machines could replace only some of these tools, and certainly not quickly. But not only did machines now replace some tasks for which artisans had previously used hand tools, machines started making the tools. While the report of the *outilleurs en bois*, which dates from 1867, exaggerates the thoroughness

20. Du Maroussem, *La question ouvrière*, 62; AN F^{12}3365.
21. AN F^{12}3365.
22. "Outilleurs en bois," 1:1.

Figure 53. *Armoire à trois corps*, Paris, 1900. Guimard. Pearwood. Musée des arts décoratifs. Photo: L. Sully-Jaulmes.

of this "revolution," it is certain that by the last third of the century woodworkers were making fewer of their tools themselves. Indeed, the toolmakers' use of the term "industry" rather than "métier" is one indication of the shift from a relatively unified craft to the specialized, mechanized industry about which the toolmakers complained.

Consequently, necessity forced many woodworkers to turn their toolmaking skill into skill in machine setups and maintenance. In that transformation they lost a kind of knowledge and replaced it with a kind of skill, because artisans made tools in response to design needs generated in the shop. If a *menuisier* visualized a new kind of joint, he would try to make it with his existing tools; if they failed, he would try to design the necessary tool. Out of such processes new forms were born. In an age of mechanized tool production, if the imagined innovation could not be produced with existing tools, odds were that it would not be made. Thus the gradual loss of the art of toolmaking carried inevitably with it the gradual loss of small, but important, variation and innovation.[23]

Some artisans were conscious of that loss and many continued to make their own hand tools (refusing to use the machinemade ones) well into the twentieth century, even if they had to do so on their own time. Perhaps in part because of an awareness of this loss, many large manufacturers, such as Au Vieux Chêne, MM Dieudonné and Dorenlot, insisted on publicizing the fact they had designed their machine tools themselves.[24]

Machines also forced and enabled the practice of subcontracting within one industrial workspace. For example, essentially all turning (critical for the styles Henri II, Louis XIII, and for many chairs in other styles) was done on steam-driven lathes by this period. Some turners who could neither rent nor buy a lathe to use in their own workshop or home were employed in mechanized factories and obliged to pay rent on the machines they used.[25] Moreover, the rents on such lathes could be high enough to discourage much variation in their designs.

Although it is clear that mechanization was increasing in importance by the last decades of the nineteenth century, it is important not to exaggerate its impact. Most of those applying to exhibit work at the expositions had access to machines, most of the larger shops owned or used machines, but there were multiple factors working against the widespread use of machines in *all* phases of the furniture industry. The typical scale of production was relatively small, making the costs of machines prohibitive. Demand was highly seasonal; if a shop invested in machines, they could sit idle, or almost idle, for six months of the year. The industry had worked out nicely adjustable mechanisms of labor mobility to compensate for market fluctuations. Machines were often too expensive, in relation to the cost of labor and to the savings in raw materials. Even through the twentieth century the Parisian industry combined highly mechanized and essentially unmechanized shops, depending on the kind of work they did, their scale, and their capital. Nonetheless, without the veneer saw, or without the con-

---

23. For examples of the extraordinary array of hand tools made and used by woodworkers, see the collections in the Musée du compagnonnage, Tours; the Maison de l'outil et de la pensée ouvrière, Troyes; and the ATP.

24. Vanloo, 17 rue de Sedaine in Paris made the same claim (AN F^{12}3365).

25. Stoerckel and Prévost, "Tourneurs sur bois," 3:17–18. Stoerckel and Prévost cite the "usine Vaucanson," which employed between 100 and 150 workers renting time on lathes.

sumer demand that encouraged the invention and distribution of the veneer saw, Louis XIV, Louis XV and Louis XVI styles could not have been popular. Without the steam-powered lathe, Henri II dining room sets would have been accessible only to a very few.

Two other equally dramatic transformations in the organization of production were the creation of large factories and the displacement of production to the country. Au Vieux Chêne went from a small shop when it opened in 1820 to selling fifty thousand pieces of furniture per year in 1877. That massive output was produced by two hundred workers and sixty machines driven by two motors totalling 80 horsepower. François Jacob, whose main workshop was on the rue de Charenton in the faubourg St-Antoine in Paris, found it cheaper to both mechanize and locate part of his production in the provinces. Thus he employed a total of twenty-nine people in Paris and nine outside. Some shops originally located in the provinces kept their production there and opened a retailing branch in Paris. François Leglos Maurice had a steam-driven factory in Nantes and a distribution outlet in Paris, employing from three hundred fifty to four hundred men, twenty-five to thirty women, and twenty to twenty-five children. A mechanized chair manufacturer in Seine et Oise was able to produce chairs at remarkably low prices, from 36 to 70 francs.[26]

Large factories and provincial production alike had implications for furniture design: most dramatically, they were relatively rigid production formats, making rapid changes in design difficult. The jigs used in early mechanized furniture production were laborious to produce, and manufacturers would therefore not want to change them frequently in response to new patterns. Furthermore, factories and provincial production made communication between the buyer and the maker impossible; they even attenuated communication between the maker and the seller. Manufacturers often became aware of the failure of a certain style only after producing large quantities of it that did not sell. Both implications tended to make factory production a conservatizing force on design innovation.

The Crisis of the 1880s and 1890s

After a period of considerable expansion in the 1870s, the 1880s were marked in this industry, as in others, by crises. Many of the stores producing luxury goods in the faubourg were able to employ only half their personnel, and those who were kept on were subject to intermittent or seasonal employment. Generally the producers of cheaper furniture fared

26. AN F^{12}3365.

somewhat better.[27] This was also, as has been noted above, a period of intense strike activity and of employers' responses to competition from Germany (a result especially of a new gilding process) and the provinces (cheaper labor for some less delicate operations).

Throughout the nineteenth century, in fact, the furniture market was very seasonal. There was very little work in January and February, the situation improved a bit in March, boomed in April and May, fell off in June, and continued to be slow in July and August. The levels of June were achieved again in September, while October and November mirrored April and May, with a slight drop at the end of the year. Another solution sometimes used to accommodate drops in demand was shortening the workday.[28]

The very long days when there was work and the brutal calm when there was not strongly influenced the structures of work. One result was a very high degree of artisanal mobility from workshop to workshop, which, although the evidence is fragmentary, seems to have been common, and even the norm, from at least the 1830s until the early years of the twentieth century. The few surviving *livrets d'ouvrier*, records from the maison Rinck, and literary and anecdotal evidence indicate that some workers changed workshops as often as every few weeks, although there was often a core of stable workers. As one commentator reported on the well known casting and furniture shop, the maison Barbedienne, its strength was attributable to not relying on "floating personnel" but to keeping stable foremen and a steady elite workforce "protected as much as possible from the vagaries of unemployment that the science of the economists is impotent to conquer."[29] Sometimes departure was the result of a fight with the shop boss or master, sometimes it was a search for better pay,

27. Monthly reports from the Inspecteurs des garnies, préfecture de police, for 1887 and 1888 on the state of Parisian industry (AN F^{12}6172–73).

28. Van Doren, *Ebénisterie à Bruxelles et à Paris*, 53; AN F^{12}6172–73.

29. On Barbedienne see Charles Cauchois-Morel, "Notes d'un ciseleur," May 1892 (AN 368 AP2 dossier 2, 26–27). According to three extant *livrets d'ouvrier* at the ATP (ATP ms 64.6 B 146, livret d'un ouvrier ébéniste, Auguste Braconnier, 1849; ATP-arch ms B 11 59–470, livret de travail délivré au scieur Jean Fouruel, scieur de long, Paris, 22 January 1818; ATP ms 68.40 B 184, livret d'ouvrier de Maurice Marchand, ébéniste, 1858–62), workers sometimes changed jobs as often as eleven times in five years. Government inquiries and the maison Rinck's employment records for workers laid off and rehired at frequent intervals confirm the pattern and suggest an incentive, in wage increases, when workers moved from one job to the next (Ministère du travail, *Apprentissage industriel*, xix). Monthly reports on the state of industries of Paris (AN F^{12}6172–73) document fluctuations in both workforce and profits of a selection of Parisian furniture shops.

sometimes it was a result of layoffs; and sometimes it came because somebody had had enough of a particular workshop or a particular boss.

This extraordinary mobility limited the degree of engagement any artisan could have with any particular piece of work. It did not destroy all sense of craft or solidarity; artisans migrated among a relatively small number of shops all located in the same neighborhood. Everybody knew who had big orders, who small, who was a difficult employer but paid well, and who was nice but always broke. Not only did the workers move around voluntarily, but the foremen and employers seem not to have hesitated to lay off during slow weeks and hire on during the busy. Leaving a shop in a great huff did not at all mean that the artisan would not be back; the odds were that he would be, and within a few months. But *ébénistes* and *menuisiers* belonged to the trades, and to the faubourg; they did not, in general, belong to any particular shop. This lack of allegiance to particular shops meant, however, that the creative work belonged to the owners and the designers. Even if a given shop did not strictly divide the work, artisans might work on one small piece of an object and then move on.

Even as worker mobility among shops decreased the trades' capacity for innovation, it probably contributed to their ability to weather longer-term economic instability. The mechanisms of seasonal, even weekly or monthly adjustments of the labor force meant that small shops and their labor forces could accommodate upturns and downturns without being driven out of business or driven to larger-scale organization with greater capital accumulation for a cushion against hard times. It was this pattern of intershop mobility, combined with the expandable web of isolated, "self-employed" workers, which allowed the industry to grow to meet the increased demand at the end of the century without changing the scale of manufacturing. Employers who suddenly acquired more work than their workers could handle hired on "surplus" workers from another shop, thus saving the other shops from collapse. Labor costs were never fixed, nor were laborers punished by drastic wage cuts or industrywide layoffs or made to bear the whole brunt of a downturn (except in periods of depression).[30]

An equally salient factor in the organization of design and production was the expanded production and use of pattern books in the last third of the nineteenth century. Providing sketches of furniture in various styles, these books were sometimes used by custom shops to give the customer an idea of what they would be buying, but more relevant here is their use

30. See a similar argument in Philip Scranton, *Proprietary Capitalism* (Cambridge, 1983).

as the basis of Old Regime–style furniture (see Figures 47 and 48). By the 1880s the fifty or so of these books in circulation provided impressionistic renderings of a wide variety of objects in Old Regime styles. One book advertised that it offered the manufacturer "twenty rooms, presented in their entirety. This way all error becomes impossible."[31] Another provided illustrations of modernized versions of historical styles specifically to guide the makers. The fact that one author proclaimed his ownership of the models presented in his book and threatened to sue those who stole them raises interesting questions about ownership of design in an age of pastiche. Models were eventually protected by the copyright law of 1902, but the fact that the whole industry was based on reproductions and pastiches of preexisting objects made protecting one person's version of these patterns difficult, if not impossible.[32]

In sum, the structuring of production in the Parisian furniture industry during the Third Republic was more conducive to the wide-scale production of pastiche Old Regime–style furniture than that of *style moderne* or *art nouveau*. Extensive outwork, a combination of limited and cumbersome mechanization, the existence of cheap veneer, and the seasonal and annual instability of demand were all conducive to limiting risk by making a commodity that was known to sell and that was well adapted to existing (and new) production techniques. Historicist pastiche allowed artisans to make small changes in woods used, marquetry designs, and degrees of curvature. These were isolated changes with some small degree of satisfaction for the artisan that did not bring about a major stylistic transformation. Artisans reproduced certain identifiable characteristics and played within them. Figure 54, of an *étagère à deux corps* from a pattern book in the shop library of the maison Schmit, demonstrates the point. Drawn in pencil on top of plate 4 was an alternate design, in the same style, for the piece. The artisan was playing with the idea of enclosing the bottom shelves behind doors with a motif that echoed the carving at the top of the *étagère*. The resulting piece would have been a pastiche of a pastiche. The print in *Le carnet du vieux bois* was already an "imaginative rendering" of a Louis XIII piece; the variation proposed would have taken it one step further away from the original, but it would still have been perfectly recognizable as a Louis XIII *étagère*—a reliable acquisition for one's dining room. Once production shifted more completely into factories, such variations on

31. Bajot, *Du choix et de la disposition des ameublements de style,* n.p.

32. E. Foussier, *L'appartement français à la fin du XIXe siècle* (Paris, ca. 1890) n.p; BHVP 120, ameub. G, Gallery.

Figure 54. "Etagère à deux corps," *Le carnet du vieux bois,* pl. 4. From the library of maison Schmit. Louis XIII style. An alternative possibility—for a closed, carved cupboard— is sketched over the bottom half of the piece.

themes became more difficult to accomplish. Furthermore, by the late nineteenth century the expansion of outwork, the increased difficulty of communication among artisans and between artisans and their clients meant that the incremental innovations based either on artisans' discoveries or on clients' requests no longer organically built up into stylistic change.

DISPLAY AND STYLE: THE EXPANSION OF RETAILING

[This article offers] retail shops [the model for] . . . a luxurious *mise en scène* fully in accord with current ideas. The need to impress buyers has given birth to artistically arranged displays. . . . One could also say that in principle the store should be for the objects found there what a case is for a jewel, a rich binding for a book.[33]

The transformation of production in the last third of the nineteenth century meshed with equally dramatic shifts in how the goods reached the customer. First, the sites of production were separated from those of consumption and an entirely new class of workers was interposed between producers and consumers, armed with novel means of reaching and influencing the latter. Among the first changes in these relations was that workshops exclusively producing custom goods for individual consumers became rarer and rarer in this period. In their stead came a complex array of combined producer-retailers and a few stores that sold but did not make furniture. Many fine furniture workshops now had display rooms in which they sold furniture they and others had made, sold their own products to other retailers, and continued to design custom goods for individuals. These shops diversified their practices of acquisition and sale of finished products and took advantage of the diverse forms of production converging in this period by combining in-house work, outwork, mechanization, hand work, specialized and general labor, and hourly rates and piece rates. This diversity notwithstanding, the industry as a whole moved toward the increasing division of production and distribution, as distributors put greater emphasis on display and custom shops blended with specialized stores.

In the domains of both production and consumption this period saw more than a simple intensification of processes started earlier in the century. With the commercialization of relations of production and consumption, the place of objects, and the meaning of their acquisition and use, also changed. The increasing sophistication of merchandising made available to the upper strata of society a repertoire of ancien régime pastiche (discussed in chapter 7) that suited the retailers as well as the consumers. Stocking a wide range of familiar, but subtly different, goods minimized the risks for merchandisers as they ventured into the still novel world of the ready-made.

The practice of physically separating production and distribution had become widespread by the 1880s. Merchandising was consolidating into a few specialized shopping neighborhoods. Thus, although the vast majority of furniture was still produced in the old woodworking neighborhoods— the faubourg St-Antoine and around the rue de Cléry—many shops opened retail branches in the area around the *grands boulevards* near the place de

33. "Planche 9: menuiserie moderne—boutiques et aménagement des magasins," *Journal de menuiserie* 1 (1863): 33.

l'Opéra, or in the case of some of the very fancy ones, in the rue St-Honoré. The elegant furniture producer, the maison Rinck, opened a shop on the rue du faubourg St-Honoré explicitly to attract customers who would have been put off by the faubourg St-Antoine.[34] Offsetting the inconvenience of having to transport goods across Paris and the cost of a second rent in an expensive district was the additional business the shop attracted. Paris was becoming increasingly divided and segregated by function into residential, industrial, and commercial quarters. As consumption became a distinct activity, connected to leisure and entertainment rather than production, the sites of consumption moved out of the old artisanal neighborhoods and merged into theater and café districts. Now what defined neighborhoods was not the type of goods produced there—furniture, clothing, leather, jewelry—it was their focus as sites of production or of consumption.

The contrasts drawn by contemporary commentators between the retail stores on the *grands boulevards*, "temples built to luxurious tastes," and the "small, dark, and smoke-filled" shops of the faubourg St-Antoine reinforced the spatial separation of production and distribution with social segregation.[35] Artisans no longer engaged in negotiations with the customers concerning the appearance, function, and use of the objects they produced. The separation of production and distribution brought with it the elaboration of the sales professions. A guide to choosing a profession published in the 1890s claimed that sales was the best occupation in the furniture industries. Salespeople were not only paid better than artisans, it claimed; they could hope to share in the profits rather than simple wages and even take over the business. They owed such opportunities to the fact that they controlled the most precious resource—relations with the customers. This was not a universally shared opinion, however; M. Charton in a similar book argued that salesclerks did not earn much more than

34. Most of the custom furniture shops were split between the faubourg St-Antoine and the rue de Cléry. For precise locations see the *Annuaire de l'ameublement et de l'ébénisterie*, 1887–88. For the earlier period see Henri Dulac, *Almanach des 25,000 adresses des principaux habitants de Paris*, 10 vols. (Paris, 1823–48); and for the later one see also J. de La Tynna, *Almanach du commerce de Paris, des départements de la France et des principales villes du monde, par J. de La Tynna, continué et mis dans un meilleur ordre par S. Bottin*, 48 vols. (Paris, 1840). Of 217 specialized stores and custom shops, 190 were on the right bank and only 27 on the left (BHVP 120, ameub.). Information on the maison Rinck came from a private communication to the author by the shop's current manager, Gérard Rinck.

35. Alexis Martin, *Les étapes d'un touriste en France* (Paris, 1890), 167, 247.

artisans and, furthermore, "these salesclerks are obliged to have a certain decorum and are sentenced to black suits and calling cards."[36] But it was precisely the *right* as well as the obligation to wear a suit and have visiting cards that made sales a desirable profession. By the 1880s those who made furniture could often no longer set foot in the store in which it was sold, while those who were selling it knew little, except how to talk about it. The connection between wearing suits and taking over a business had begun.

Of course, not all producer-distributors could afford to have a retail outlet in an elegant part of town. Nonetheless, those who did continue to sell their goods in the faubourg St-Antoine also often detached production from distribution, with the retail store installed on one of the larger, more commercial streets. Thus, the chair manufacturer Redond had his workshop in the obscure passage Raoul, and his showroom on the more centrally located and well known rue de la Roquette. One last new strategy of distancing production from distribution was to open many retail branches all supplied by the same production shop, as did the Compagnie générale de l'ameublement with its fourteen branches.[37]

The elaboration of retailing sites and the changes in consumer relations brought an increased emphasis on display, expertise, and the sales environment. There was, in fact, a four-cornered battle going on among stores that did custom work, stores that sold readymades but only a limited range of furniture, stores that sold a full range of furniture, and department stores.

Among the distribution sites, it was the last ones—the department stores—that proved to be the wave of the future and that attracted the most attention from contemporaries. The sociologists Pierre du Maroussem and Le Play as well as a host of others were quick to condemn department stores as being the cause of the downfall of Parisian artisanal industry. Without an exhaustive (and perhaps impossible) comprehensive study of sales figures in the furniture industry, we cannot be sure that the department stores had such a large proportion of sales. I think that in fact the dominance of department stores in the late nineteenth-century furniture industry has been considerably exaggerated. A great number of contemporary sources heaped blame on the department stores, but this attribution reflects the

36. Paul Jacquemart, *Professions et métiers* (Paris, 1892), 2:39–40; Charton, ed., *Dictionnaire des professions*, 65.
37. AN F^{12}3365; BHVP 120, ameub. C, Compagnie générale de l'ameublement, [n.d.].

revolution in retailing that they implied for the future rather than their real economic impact at the time. The vending of furniture was very different from that of clothing, for example; readymade clothing, sold largely by the department stores, quickly transformed the market. Because furniture was purchased much less frequently than clothing, the convenience offered by department stores—the centralization of consumer goods in one location—was less relevant to furnishings than to fashions. The stereotype of the department store as the dominant mode of bourgeois distribution in late nineteenth-century Paris is, therefore, somewhat too simple. In fact there was intense competition among different forms of retailing.

Indeed, it was the specialized furnishings stores, rather than the department store, that pioneered many of the changes in retailing and remained the dominant distributors during this period of transition. Specialized furniture stores reduced the extent of negotiation or haggling over prices; they removed the possibility of the consumer having a say in the appearance of the object being purchased. Yet they continued to offer expert advice, packaged in the form of decorators, sample rooms, photographs and catalogues. Choice centered not on the form, function, and price of individual pieces after discussion with one of the people who made it but on the selection of the goods before purchase and arrangement of the goods after purchase. As the advertisement for the specialized store C. Balny in Figure 55 demonstrates, these stores emphasized that even if production was out of sight, the goods were still being produced on the premises and that they sold *only* furniture. Unlike department stores, specialized stores still relied on the notion of expertise tied to the practice of a particular trade.

Department stores, in contrast, used diversification to avoid all relations between producer and consumer and between the knowledge needed to make a piece and the knowledge needed to sell it. The overview image of the Grands Magasins Dufayel (Figure 56) emphasized its scale, the busyness of the streets around it. The interior cut of the Dufayel (Figure 57) focused exclusively on the finished goods. Deepening the gulf between production and consumption, department stores were slow to produce their own goods, or even to commission their own goods. Department stores chose to buy their low-quality furniture from the *trôleurs* and high-quality furniture from custom shops like the elegant specialized store, the maison Rinck, partially for economic reasons. To do so was presumably cheaper than to set up their own workshops.

But the most significant contrast, perhaps, between specialized stores and custom shops, on the one hand, and department stores, on the other, is how much the former managed to blend continuities of traditional selling

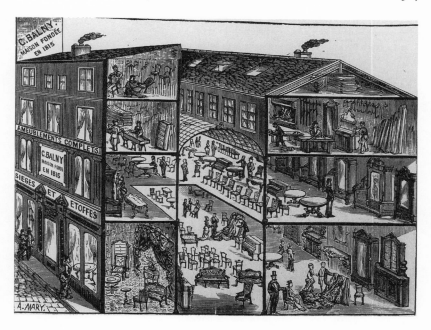

Figure 55.   Advertisement for the specialized store C. Balny. BHVP 120, ameub., Balny.

practices with radical departures. It may well be that this fact actually smoothed the way for the later ever more radical changes made by department stores. Many advertisements for specialized stores played on the idea of rationality and modernity; they created rational displays and used rational sales practices. Stores justified their specific choice of merchandise and·explained why it was better to sell only one kind of object—or in the other extreme, to sell everything under the sun.

The stores emphasizing the virtues of specialization would seem, at first glance, to represent a last stand of traditional distributors against the development of department and household furnishing stores. Yet the specialization offered in the following advertisement was not the same as preindustrial specialization. "The principle of specialization having been recognized today by all buyers because it offers an absolute guarantee and a mark of confidence, I have the honor of inviting you to visit my store specializing in comfortable armchairs of all genres."[38] Stores selling

38. BHVP 120, ameub. C, Carnevali, [n.d.], grande spécialité de fauteuils confortables, 99 boulevard Beaumarchais, 3d arr.

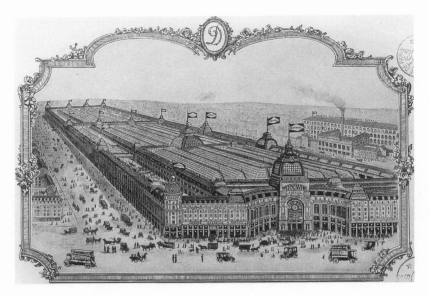

Figure 56.   Advertisement for the department store Dufayel. BHVP 120, ameub., Dufayel.

nothing but comfortable armchairs were a novelty of the late nineteenth century. Earlier there had been stores specializing in *ébénisterie* as opposed to rustic furniture, or in chairs. But a chair specialist would sell all kinds of chairs. And the "principle of specialization" was far from recognized as a virtue by all consumers, if the growing success of department stores for goods other than furniture, founded on precisely the opposite principle, is anything to go by.

Furniture was sold in an extraordinary range of prices, often within the same store, although the fanciest stores did not sell the cheapest furniture and the cheapest did not sell the fanciest. Most styles were available at most prices, although at the absolute bottom end the furniture was often style-less, that is, without any clearly identifiable label (as in Figure 58).[39]

Certain styles cost more to produce and certain woods more than others. Whether the wood was solid or veneer also strongly affected the price. If the wood was veneer, the kind of veneer did not greatly influence the cost. By the end of the century veneers were so thin that the difference in scarcity and import costs had to be very great before the price of furniture varied

---

39. For detailed information on the primary advertising sources, see the bibliography and Auslander, "Social Life of Furniture."

Figure 57. Advertisement for the department store Dufayel. BHVP 120, ameub., Dufayel.

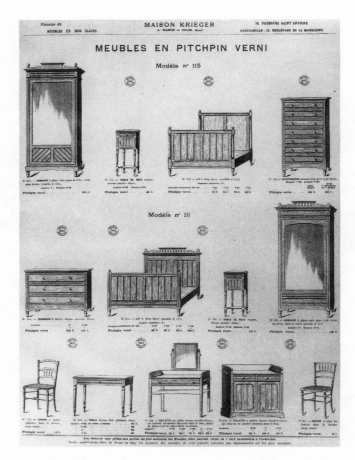

Figure 58.   Bedroom furniture in varnished pine from maison
Krieger. It was given only model numbers, not identified by
style. Cheaper models came to 241 francs for an armoire, bed,
chair, and bedside table.

much. Bronzes, sculpture, and gilding, in contrast, appeared only in the
most expensive sets. Other issues of quality are more difficult to assess; the
advertising materials clearly do not reveal the number of years the wood
was aged, the skill of the artisans who built it, or the keenness of eye of
the designer.

But beyond these issues of richness of materials and quality, it was,
ironically, generally the case that the more one paid the less one got.
Furnishings sold in the lower price range were more likely to come in
complete sets, the most extreme being the very cheap *chambres complètes*,

usually consisting of a bed, a table, a bedside table, two chairs, a small rug, mattress, box spring, linen, and armoire—clearly intended for the poorest of couples setting up housekeeping in one room. The most expensive furniture was rarely sold in sets (although it was often displayed that way). Wealthier consumers appear to have wanted to believe that they were making choices and assembling their rooms themselves, while the poor were not given that option.

In the area of expertise and specialization, specialized stores offering readymade goods were on the defensive, for it was still possible to have one's furniture designed to order. The custom-made shops could argue that they were the keepers of the flame, the maintainers of real quality.[40] In the extant custom shops, goods were sometimes still made to order after careful negotiation between the buyer and seller, prices were negotiated rather than determined beforehand, and buyers had to put their trust in the manufacturers that the finished object would please them and be of the quality they desired. And, as in the Old Regime, the clients of these manufacturer-distributors included both individual consumers and other merchants. Despite this continuity of form, however, much had in fact changed even in this most traditional form of distribution. In order to survive, custom makers needed to be capable of flexibility and diversification. (This is not to say that *no* shops continued to do only custom work for individuals, simply that that became a harder and harder route to follow.) In the records of two custom furniture stores, the maisons Schmit and Rinck, we can see the complex diversification of these stores at the intersection of production and distribution, of retail and wholesale, of custom and readymade.

The maison Schmit was founded in 1818 and opened a large shop at 22 rue de Charonne in the faubourg St-Antoine in 1828. Under the Second Empire and Third Republic, the shop expanded considerably and came to specialize in both pastiche and reproduction of eighteenth-century models. The shop in those years employed a large team of decorators, *ébénistes*, sculptors, upholsterers, *menuisiers en sièges*, and bronze makers. It was one of the largest furniture producers in Paris and a very successful exhibitor at the world's fairs. From the years 1919 to 1939 the shop expanded its range to include producing the interiors of luxury yachts and ocean liners (among them the famous *Normandie*) and selling paintings and antiques. The flexibility and creativity of the maison Schmit is further attested to by its shifts to a focus on the wooden parts of airplanes in the 1940s; the

40. See for example, BHVP 120, ameub. S, Schmit, [n.d.], 18, 20, 22, 24 rue de Charonne, 11th arr.

decoration of banks, Orly airport, shopping malls, and considerable work in Tunisia and Saudi Arabia from the 1950s through the 1960s; and the decoration of the interiors of offshore drilling rigs in the 1970s.

The extant business records of the maison Schmit during the Third Republic illustrate the complex transformations of one of the dominant custom shops of the period. The Schmit address book, started in 1900 and continuing for a number of years, listed some 430 customers and suppliers. Among the customers were not only private individuals but also other producers and retailers to whom Schmit sold furniture.[41] Suppliers referred not only to sources of raw materials but also to other furniture shops from which Schmit bought pieces to complete its sets. Thus, as Schmit did not specialize in selling antiques, the list included antique dealers as well as specialists in Renaissance style, upholsterers, and others. The maison Schmit expanded both its retail and production activities, buying and selling to other retailers as well as to private customers.

The inventories of the maison Schmit for the years 1889–1910 further demonstrate the diversification of the shop. From 1889 to 1910 Schmit decreased from somewhat less than one-half to somewhat less than one-third the proportion of the *ébénisterie* it sold that it had made (see Table 1). The increasing emphasis on retail as opposed to custom production can also be read from the high figures given for goods in stock. While those figures could indicate that there was a long lag time between when custom-made goods were finished and when they were delivered, a more plausible hypothesis is that much of Schmit's production was now of readymades. The exception to this was in the bedding department, where the shop consistently kept large quantities of raw materials on hand. Those raw materials were almost certainly used for making mattresses, which were generally made to order.

The history of the maison Rinck demonstrates another, in some senses more conservative, route to survival of a custom shop.[42] The maison Rinck

41. The archives of the Maison Schmit were unfortunately dispersed in fall 1985. Some are now in my possession. This book held customer and supplier information; notation next to a number of addresses is that the customer did not live there anymore, or that the supplier was not willing to sell to them. The book lists what customers had last bought (and when) and whether they had been persuaded to buy more. The kind of greeting received by the salesperson was also noted.

42. Private archives of the maison Rinck; see the bibliography for the sources to which I had access. I also culled information from interviews with Gérard Rinck, as well as the chapter pertaining to the company in René Minguet, *Géographie industrielle de Paris* (Paris, 1957); and Desaix, "L'art d'être ébéniste," 14–19.

Table 1. Three-year inventories of assets (in francs), Maison Schmit, 1889–1907

	1889	1892	1895	1898	1901	1904	1907
Ebénisterie du dehors	318,367	376,688	488,045	454,972	494,414	561,812	676,937
Ebénisterie des ateliers	241,545	274,080	323,130	333,456	377,489	363,411	357,817
In stock[1]	165,075	174,917	215,125	228,647	245,969	273,129	171,790
In progress[2]	15,869	20,844	18,001	10,263	10,767	5,924	23,260
Work site[3]	59,867	77,699	49,000	93,630	118,810	132,724	161,547
Raw materials	734	620	984	920	1,944	1,834	1,221
Upholstery—chairs	55,982	66,531	90,047	101,109	117,614	121,851	148,452
In stock[1]	35,556	55,496	74,801	91,124	101,632	103,957	133,032
In progress[2]	10,559	8,545	10,329	7,995	13,396	14,598	12,006
Leather	—	—	960	—	—	—	—
Cane/gilding	—	—	2,600	—	—	—	—
Raw materials	9,867	2,490	1,398	1,990	2,585	3,296	3,414
Upholstery—fabrics	25,756	23,800	48,089	47,762	53,591	52,278	20,646
In stock[1]	11,775	10,599	14,917	14,094	18,351	9,271	6,077
Antique fabrics	—	—	23,170	—	—	—	—
Mag. d'étoffes	—	—	800	—	—	—	—
Mag. Hall	—	—	350	—	—	—	—
In progress[2]	8,903	7,311	2,947	6,621	7,462	8,968	4,323
Raw materials	5,078	5,930	5,074	5,938	3,590	2,722	2,642
Carpets	—	—	831	1,744	7,083	1,027	1,276
Upholstery	—	—	—	19,050	20,965	29,365	1,970
Dyes	—	—	—	715	1,140	925	1,359
Bedding	5,375	4,592	5,421	5,315	3,264	2,947	5,499
In stock[1]	1,812	590	1,361	1,645	1,793	445	669
In progress[2]	—	4,002	130	—	—	—	—
Iron beds	—	—	144	423	416	290	1,205
Raw materials	3,562	—	3,786	2,247	1,555	2,211	3,625
Other	858,595	900,367	839,578	850,551	799,219	654,714	849,546
Total	1,505,620	1,646,058	1,794,310	1,793,165	1,845,591	1,757,013	2,058,897

SOURCE: Maison Schmit's private archives, a portion of which came into my possession in 1986.

Note: The categories are taken from Schmit's inventory books, except for the "Other" category, which groups together items that have no relevance to the discussion here. The exact meaning of Schmit's categories is not clear. While I am sure that the figures given for materials purchased from other suppliers are an accurate representation of the prices charged Schmit for those goods, I do not know whether the figures for goods produced by Schmit and still in stock are before or after retail mark-up. I expect after.

[1] Goods on hand, ready to be sold.
[2] Unfinished articles still in the workshop.
[3] Projects being worked on in customers' homes.

was founded in 1841 and has remained within the family, in the same location in the passage de la bonne Graine in the faubourg St-Antoine, from 1871 until the present. From its founding the maison Rinck has always specialized in furniture and woodwork and combined modern design with reproduction and pastiche of the old. The shop never expanded into interior decoration nor moved away from furniture destined for apartments and houses. The diversity of its clientele, however, has grown systematically since its origins to include, in the 1970s, an elaborate set of paneling in the style of Louis XIV intended for the shah of Iran (the shah having been deposed before delivery, the paneling came to grace the lunchroom at the workshop). Most strikingly, the shop reproduced some of the most famous of the royal furniture of the Old Regime, occasionally for new heads of state, but more often not. Louis XIV's desk was remade a number of times by Eugène Rinck and then six more times by his son Maurice, and a chest made by Riesener for the crown was also reproduced four times.[43]

There are no records from the early twentieth century of equally illustrious clients; rather the maison Rinck had a steady customer in the Bon Marché department store. Rinck was also a major supplier of the specialized furniture store, Mercier frères, across the street, on the rue du faubourg St-Antoine. Mercier sold only good quality furniture and did not produce any of it. Mercier clearly provided an outlet for many of the "custom shops" in the neighborhood.[44]

Deciphering the chronology of the development of these transitional stores is difficult. Rinck's founding in 1871 was contemporary with the expansion of department stores and thus the shop could have acquired department stores as clients very early on, but its records go back only to 1900. For older workshop-retailers such as Schmit, the diversification does seem to have increased as the century wore on. By the turn of the twentieth century, they were doing exclusively custom work for some clients and others were buying readymades—either made by Schmit, or by another manufacturer and retailed by Schmit—they were selling to other transitional workshop-retailers, and to stores that were exclusively retailers. Custom shops in the late nineteenth century, therefore, were both like and

43. Desaix, "L'art d'être ébéniste," 16; Minguet, *Géographie industrielle de Paris*, 15.

44. The account books from Rinck noted relatively frequent (a few times a year) deliveries of sets of furniture to the Bon Marché. Rinck supplied nearly all of Mercier's *ébénisterie* while another shop, specializing in chairs, supplied their *menuiserie*.

unlike their eighteenth-century and early nineteenth-century predecessors. In all periods the custom shops exported some of their finest products. The process of negotiation between individual customer and shop changed a little, under the influence of photography and the profusion of printed materials.

The overlap between custom artisan, department store, and specialized furniture store was reinforced by the specializations of the trades. Even though all woodworking shops capable of making beautiful sideboards and tables were theoretically also capable of making chairs, chair making was a separate speciality. For very fancy sets, a custom maker would subcontract to a chair specialist.

Custom furniture shops by definition built goods to order. Completely new designs were not, however, invented for each consumer; rather models, photographs, or prints indicated the possibilities. The models included pieces previously made by the company—displayed in a floor model, a print or a photograph—a model imagined and sketched in-house but never yet built, and commercially produced pattern books.[45] Figure 59 shows a photograph of a complete bedroom in Louis XVI style done by the maison Schmit. Photographs like this enabled the shop to reduce its display space while still offering customers a precise image of what they could acquire. Other photographs (such as Figure 60) were done so as to allow the customer the sense that she already possessed the room. The interior here is complete with the customer (her face carefully obscured). To present a room and its owner rather than a model emphasized the legitimacy of the taste being sold.

But custom shops did not, and could not, rely entirely on printed and photographic materials. After the customers had decided more or less what they wanted, the next step was to make drawings, showing the various possibilities. By the late nineteenth century such drawings, used for informational and persuasive purposes, came in a variety of forms and were very different from the working drawings used by artisans. Some depicted entire rooms in a given style, giving only an impressionistic sense of what

45. Both the maisons Rinck and Schmit had enormously elaborate photographic documentation of all their work, with bound volumes of finished pieces coded to match their inventories and drawings. These photograph albums were presented to potential customers when they came to the store (private archives of the maisons Rinck and Schmit). Besides the photographic documentation, many stores circulated catalogues of line drawings, and sometimes more elaborate drawings of their wares; see the collections at Rinck and Schmit and the iconography collection at the Bibliothèque Forney.

Figure 59.   Sample bedroom, late nineteenth or early twentieth century. Louis XVI–style. Maison Schmit.

the furniture would look like; others were much more detailed studies of individual pieces of furniture, sometimes giving measurements (Figure 61). Yet others demonstrated the variations that could be played on a basic design.

The goal of the drawings then was not to show what the pieces would really look like. The consumers were largely buying an image. Once a customer decided on a piece, the precise working drawings were made. It is clear that custom furniture makers in the late nineteenth century did not think that customers were interested in the details. But the drawings also gave the customers the possibility of intervening in the construction process. They could approve the style of hardware, the shape of the leg or other elements.

The need for drawings arose from the fact that if a store was selling only custom-made objects, then clearly the goods to be sold could not be on display before their purchase. The distributor or maker could make up extra pieces in order to have them on display, but this does not appear to have been a frequent practice. Their absence may in part reflect a lack of capital as well as a notion that each object was to be unique and the result of

Figure 60. Salon showing Louis XV– and Louis XVI–
style furniture. Documentation or advertising photograph
from maison Schmit. The client's face is carefully
effaced.

negotiation between client and producer. Presumably a potential consumer
could also observe the goods and decide whether the style and quality
suited.

These trends—both of continuity and of adaptation to new relations of
production and consumption—persisted until the First World War. Very
few furniture distributors were not also producers, and very few sold only
the things that they themselves had made. There was an increase in the
separation of production from distribution and of mechanization from

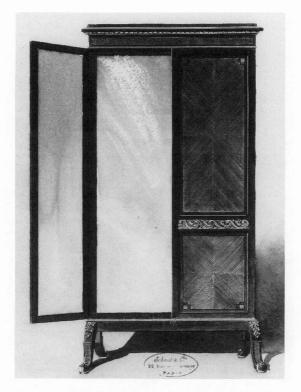

Figure 61. Display drawing of an armoire, late nineteenth or early twentieth century. Maison Schmit.

home work, and an increase in the number of stores.[46] Some were making the furniture in the same building as the shop front, others had workshops in the faubourg St-Antoine, the suburbs or in the provinces. A few stores that specialized in English or Austrian furniture imported all or most of their goods. (Some of these stores eventually set up small factories in France to make their furniture.)

The last third of the nineteenth century also saw the development of a new kind of shopping district, one characterized by an organization for distribution, rather than by type of merchandise being sold. Just as many different kinds of products were grouped under one roof in a department

46. The BHVP 120 series supports this claim.

store, so many department stores were grouped in one neighborhood. Except the Bon Marché, all the department stores were on the right bank, most—the Galeries Lafayette, Au Printemps, Aux Trois Quartiers, and La Belle Jardinière—in the Haussmannian neighborhood of the *grands boulevards* and the Opéra. Others were not far away; the Grands Magasins du Louvre was in the first arrondissement, near the museum, the Bazar de l'Hôtel de Ville was in the fourth, across the street from the city hall and from the Samaritaine.

Department stores were slow to sell furniture and even slower to engage in the actual design and building of it. The Bon Marché was the first to do so. In the 1850s it started selling both wooden and metal beds, adding tables and chairs in the 1870s, and finally, in the 1880s, completed the section with matching room sets in an assortment of styles, deluxe cabinetwork, and country furniture. Many stores avoided furniture altogether; they included the Galeries Lafayette and La Belle Jardinière.[47]

Department stores acquired their furniture from four sources: from custom producers; through a system of outwork to *façonniers;* from the *trôleurs;* and their own workshops. Good quality readymade furniture was acquired from workshops like Krieger, Schmit, and Roll, which employed the full range of woodworkers and designers. These *ateliers* also had their own showrooms and also sold directly to individual clients. The second group of producers were *façonniers* who worked directly for a department store. The stores' agents supplied materials directly to the *façonniers,* which they worked in their own shops.[48] In order to reduce costs, many large department stores managed to transform the *façonniers* who worked directly for them into *trôleurs.* The agents would contract with them to work exclusively for one particular store, advance credit or materials to them, and then refuse to take delivery until they had a large stock on hand. Once the *façonnier* had accumulated enough stock, the agent might refuse to buy. Since the woodworker had, by that point, been working exclusively for one store, he no longer had any other clientele. The producer would then go bankrupt and the department store could buy the goods for below

47. M. Miller, *The Bon Marché,* 50; ADS D12 Z1; François Faraut, *Histoire de la Belle Jardinière* (Paris, 1986).

48. Du Maroussem, *La question ouvrière,* 92–96. See also André Saint-Martin, *Les grands magasins* (Paris, 1900) and the same argument in Emile Levasseur, *Questions ouvrières et industrielles en France sous la Troisième République* (Paris, 1907). Until the late 1860s and 1870s Bon Marché contracted for furniture from small producers—and even after it started an in-house cabinet shop it still had much of the work done outside.

cost. If woodworkers wanted to remain in the business, they then had little choice but to become *trôleurs*.⁴⁹

Eventually most of the department stores heavily committed to the sale of furniture established their own workshops, some bragging about it in their advertisements. "All the industries that cooperate in their manufacturing can be found centralized there. The model organization of our workshops allows us to realize carefully and economically and deliver quickly the most important furnishings." It is possible that in their early years, in the 1870s and 1880s, department stores relied heavily on *façonniers* and *trôleurs*, and as time went on came more and more to have their own shops. Other department stores, like Printemps, did not make the furniture in-house but in the 1920s finally did start to employ designers. The Primavera workshop, the first of the *ateliers d'art* created by a department store, was founded by Printemps in 1912 in order to create models of decorative art applied to industry.⁵⁰

All the early department stores, the Bon Marché (1852), Au Printemps (1865), the Grands Magasins du Louvre (1855), Aux Trois Quartiers, the Bazar de l'Hôtel de Ville (1860), were largely interested in a bourgeois market. They did not offer their goods on credit, and little of the furniture they sold was cheap. The Grands Magasins Dufayel was the largest credit department store in Paris, although Aux Classes Laborieuses also sold furniture on credit. The Samaritaine, founded later than the others, in 1871, also used a credit system.⁵¹ By 1869 Crespin, the store which was to become Dufayel, was selling on the *abonnement* system, where a representative of the store would appear at the customer's door at specified intervals to receive payment for goods purchased.

One department store, the Grands Magasins du Louvre, emphasized that it had no off-season: clients could find the furniture on display and therefore buy it, at any moment of the year.⁵² Presumably, the store was

49. Du Maroussem, *La question ouvrière*, 137; M. Miller, *The Bon Marché*, 206.

50. AN 65 AQ T 116, Grands Magasins du Louvre, catalogue 1908; du Maroussem, *La question ouvrière*, 46–49. They employed twelve men and twelve women in the shop (undated leaflet [probably 1920s], ADS D39Z carton 3).

51. Marjorie Beale, "Mort à Crédit: The Credit Department Store and the Parisian Lower Classes, 1856–1920" (B.A. thesis, Harvard College, 1982), 12.

52. Grands Magasins du Louvre, catalogue 1908 (AN 65 AQ T 116). See also BHVP 120, ameub. F, Meubles Fix, 1911, ameublements de tous styles, 70 and 72 rue du faubourg St-Antoine and 10 and 12 rue de Charonne, 12th arr.; BHVP 120, ameub. C, Compagnie générale de l'ameublement, Siège social, 54, 56, 58, and 60

contrasting itself to specialized furniture stores and custom makers who were still, in the early years of the twentieth century, subject to peak and off-season. The irony of this contrast is that the notion of the seasonality of purchasing probably came from the consumers rather than the producers, who would have been pleased to be rid of the pattern of seasonal overwork and underemployment. But a more even selling pattern across the year, and a large inventory of very high quality furniture, represented a capital investment possible only for the largest distributors. By emphasizing the convenience of the furniture always in stock, the Grands Magasins du Louvre played down the implicit inconvenience for customers of buying a readymade piece with readymade dimensions and upholstery. Without explicitly attacking the traditional organization of distribution—no advertisers did—the store tacitly emphasized its modernity along with the traditionalism of its furniture and its quality. It sold not avant-garde furniture, but rather antiques, copies of antiques, collectors' pieces, and luxury furniture. Its advertisements suggested to potential consumers that they could get the best of both worlds—the security of the tastefulness and status of the object and the "convenience" of being able to take it right home, without negotiation or haggling.

Department stores did, however, sell furniture in a wide range of prices and styles, a range similar to that of the specialty shops. Logically, the generally less expensive department stores sold cheaper furniture than the more elegant ones. Department stores specializing in household goods, like the Bazar de l'Hôtel de Ville and the Colosse de Rhodes, sold a greater variety. The variety of goods available at department stores was generally smaller than at specialty stores and bargaining and negotiating even less of a possibility. Department stores often offered the services of a decorator and had an array of fully decorated rooms to look at to make decision making easier. Clients were never to be left without advice. Even the department stores, which would generally not sell custom furniture, advertised that they would send a qualified salesperson to one's home to work out the best interior.[53] Now the arrangement of readymade objects replaced customization and negotiation in the making and pricing of a piece. It was no longer an artisan's expertise that sold goods, but a salesperson's art.

---

rue de Château d'Eau and 67 rue du faubourg St-Martin, 10th arr.—which had ten other stores in Paris (BHVP 120, ameub. N–R, Palais du Meuble, [n.d.]).
   53. Grands Magasins du Louvre, catalogue 1908 (AN 65 AQ T 116).

Department stores were the most ambitious practitioners of display art. Such displays—often quite elaborate—were one of the novelties of late nineteenth-century merchandising, necessarily post- rather than predating the production of readymades. Department stores worked to create a complete world in the interior of their stores, where the customer could come and pass an entire day, dining, watching a play or a concert, and of course, shopping. The advertisements announcing the entertainments served to attract the public, but then the entertainments themselves had to live up to expectation to get customers to come back repeatedly, which was, of course, the goal (see Figure 62). Besides the active entertainments, the way in which the goods were displayed, as well as the nature and quality of what I have called the shopping experience—the system of pricing, negotiation, and sales strategies—influenced whether customers enjoyed shopping and would come back. Stores often tried to overawe by sheer scale; showing row after row after row of identical or nearly identical beds, or sofas, or sideboards, trying to demonstrate through profusion the extraordinary convenience of buying from them, where all goods were instantly available (see Figure 57). Department stores also sometimes had theme displays—the Far or Middle East, rustic life, English gentility—with a whole floor or department done over in one homogeneous style. These displays also overwhelmed by their power and scale; the goods may not have been very attractive or to one's taste, but there were a lot of them and they came from far away. Thus, department store displays could give the customer the illusion of being linked to a global network of commodities.

Department stores did not enjoy a monopoly on this sales technique. In 1906, for example, Mallet frères put on a "Grande Soirée de gala, suivie d'une tombola gratuite, lot unique: un magnifique salon."[54] The program included a scene from Macbeth (in Italian); a comedy by Rozier, a couple of operatic arias, some popular songs, monologues, and folk songs. Admission prices ranged from 50 centimes to 5 francs and the event was held in the Palais du Trocadéro (Figure 62). This example suggests competition among different kinds of distributors, the common trajectory of changes in retailing notwithstanding.

One of the changes most visible in all forms of distribution was the manner of setting prices and the meaning that that change held for relations

54. BHVP 120, ameub. M, Mallet frères, 1906, 221, 223 rue Lafayette, 9th arr.

Figure 62. Advertisement for Mallet frères, "Grande Soirée de gala, suivie d'une tombola gratuite, lot unique: un magnifique salon." BHVP, Palais du Trocadéro 101, Mallet frères.

between consumers and vendors. As the following sales pitch suggests, the appeal was not simply to the consumers' aesthetic concerns. "Madam, Le Bûcheron, which you have known for a long time, has reserved a surprise for you. It has created 'the furniture department store.' At the moment of moving, or buying a piece of furniture, you hesitate. You are afraid of both the unscrupulousness of stores that advertise profligately and the uncertainty of unmarked items, of specialized stores where the doorman pulls you in and prices are necessarily very high for a decor at the height of fashion. But at the same time you would like to give your home the personalized note that your taste suggests. If only you knew a large, easily accessible store, offering you in its departments a complete range of serious models at moderate prices."[55]

55. BHVP 120, ameub. BE–BU, Au Bûcheron, [n.d.], 10 rue de Rivoli, 4th arr. See also BHVP 120, ameub. K, maison Krieger, advertisement in the *Figaro* of 6 October 1894, A. Damon et Colin Succrs., 74 rue du faubourg St-Antoine, 12th arr.;

The emphasis put on intelligible and visible prices for goods indicates at the same time the prevalence of bargaining and, perhaps, a growing dislike for that style of selling. But to have fixed prices one would need fixed goods—goods bought on sight, not custom goods. To remove bargaining would also take away some of the personalized aspect of buying and selling. To bargain over something implied entering into a debate, a dialogue with the seller. But fixed prices also connoted fairness, equality, and rationality—that there was, if not a "fair price," at least a single price for everybody regardless of personal relations, class, or power of argumentation.

Many, although not all the specialized furniture stores offered possibilities for payment on credit. Some operated with set, marked prices with no negotiation possible; others continued the older tradition of bargaining. Most of the cheaper stores made clear the various provisions, especially furniture rental and credit, for making their furniture even less expensive. Some even used the fact that they were selling on credit to emphasize the quality of their goods since poorly made furniture would fall apart before all the payments were made: "We can't deliver junk because we sell on credit." Others emphasized the discretion with which they made their investigations. "No more vexing inquiries for installment buying (absolute discretion). . . . Nothing in common with *maisons d'abonnement.*"[56] But credit, like price and mechanization, could cut two ways. Some specialized stores made the fact that they did not offer credit a selling point. They claimed that since they did not offer credit they were able to sell more cheaply.

The diffusion of the notion of a fixed price, except for food items—bread being the most obvious—was a late nineteenth-century phenomenon. Prices that were immediately intelligible to the consumer assumed and reinforced a greater social distance between seller and buyer and an underlying rationalization in distribution perhaps parallel to that in production.[57] The discretion of a sales staff that would not importune the cus-

---

BHVP 120, ameub. C, E. Crété, [ca. 1890s], 99 rue du faubourg St-Antoine and 4, 6, 8, 9, 11, 13, 15 passage du Bras d'Or, 11th and 12th arrs.

56. Advertisement addressed to women from the Comptoir français du meuble (1925), specializing in credit sales and guaranteeing furniture for three years (ADS D18 Z9); BHVP 120, ameub. BE–BU, Bellot, founded 1860; ameub. C, Au confortable moderne, 1902, 57 bis avenue de la Motte-Picquet, 15th arr. The older distribution systems based on bargaining gave way to more anonymous transactions as credit mechanisms were systematized.

57. BHVP 120, ameub. BE–BU, Etablissements Béal, 1910, 119 boulevard Voltaire, 11th arr.—entrée libre, prix marqués en chiffres connus; BHVP 120,

tomers assured that distance, as did the fact that one could enter stores without an invitation or any obligation to buy. Such advertisements all reassured potential customers that they were not entering into any kind of social contract when they walked into a store. Stores were no longer within the private sphere; one incurred no guestlike obligations, one needed no invitation. But stores were not defined in the advertisements as completely public either; they offered protection, atmosphere, and guidance.

Another task that all institutions of distribution—custom furniture makers, specialized stores, and department stores—had in common was to convince prospective customers to buy, and to buy from them rather than from one of their numerous competitors. Advertising and display were the two most important means of doing that convincing as well as simply informing potential consumers of their existence, location, and conditions of sale. Advertising had three tasks, to inform, to create need and desire, and to convince consumers that the advertiser could best meet those needs and desires.

Part of the strategy of producers and distributors in the late nineteenth-century capitalist economy, as earlier, was to develop new markets by creating needs. Some new needs could be extracted from definitions of femininity and of what women had to have and do in order to be womanly women. Two examples should make the point. The first example is a table marketed in the late nineteenth century, called "Le Précieux" (Figure 63). This table was to function as a *chiffonnnier, bureau, bibliothèque, coiffeuse,* and *table à ouvrage*—all at the same time. Benefiting from years of research, read one ad, their customers could obtain a table that would be practical, elegant, and adapted to modern life.[58] According to the advertising material, not only would this elaborate table solve all one's decorating problems, but with it came a free offer of ten exciting novels.

More startling, perhaps, than the five-purpose table were the chairs that could convert instantly into bidets and back again. In an advertising leaflet dating from 1902, which seems to have been widely published, the advertiser spent seven paragraphs discussing the epic beauty of Diane de Poitiers and Ninon de Lenclos, both of whom were not only very beautiful but maintained that beauty through extreme old age. And what enabled them to maintain this beauty but douches! Douches, performed

---

ameub. D, Bernard Dorfner, [ca. 1890–1900], 199 rue du faubourg St-Antoine, 11th arr.; BHVP 120, ameub. C, Au Chêne Géant, [n.d.], 7 and 9 boulevard du Temple, 3d arr.

58. BHVP 120, ameub. P, Précieux.

Figure 63.   Advertisement for "Le Précieux." This table was to function as a chiffonier, bureau, bibliothèque, coiffeuse, and table à ouvrage—all at the same time. BHVP 120, ameub., Précieux.

properly, had been confirmed to provide women with long life and beauty but, according to sage medical advice, had to be taken lying down. "All injection taken in another position has no effect on the organ that is the basis of a woman's health, but this prescription is difficult to adhere to without having recourse to one's bed" (Figure 64).[59] Therefore, all women urgently needed a chair that could convert instantly into a bidet without anyone being the wiser. Not only did this advertisement link beauty and longevity, it situated the moral and physical well being of women firmly in the vagina.

Such strategies in advertisements for selling furniture at the end of the nineteenth and beginning of the twentieth centuries are a clear reflection of the wide range of products available, of the continued existence of mixed modes of production and distribution, and of changed media. Pamphlets and catalogues grew elaborate as more stores carried a wider range of goods and

59. BHVP 120, ameub. C, Cerf, [n.d.]; BHVP 120, ameub. literie, M, [no name], 1902, exposition et vente, 10, rue Lacrée, 12th arr.—soixante ans de lis et roses.

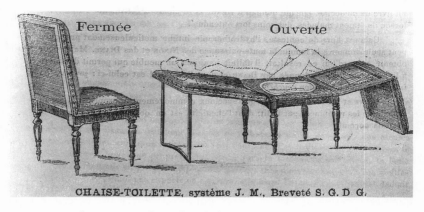

Figure 64.   Advertisement for a chair-bidet, 1902. BHVP 120, ameub., literie.

as color printing became cheaper, and they were heavily supplemented by posters. To inform, inspire, and persuade consumers, advertisers could use the visual form and the pictorial and verbal content of the advertisements. Most furniture retailers used one or more of seven formats for their printed publicity materials: posters, flyers, newspaper advertisements, wallet-size calling cards, postcards, pamphlets, and catalogues.[60] Posters and flyers usually on colored tissue paper or newsprint listed only basic information, were generally the least elaborate forms and were used by the less expensive stores. They gave the name and address of the store, whether it offered credit, a small blurb emphasizing the quality of the products, and a long list of prices, occasionally accompanied by a few line drawings of the wares. Some more elaborate, colored, posters were made, but they were not dominant. Advertisements appearing in newspapers were in a similar, minimalist, format. The postcards and calling cards were often quite elaborate, including ornate scroll work. Occasionally the calling cards would be made out of the material of the trade; in wood for a furniture shop, or leather for a specialist in leather upholstery. Posters, flyers, newspaper ads, and calling cards were all old sales techniques dating from at least the 1830s, but pamphlets and catalogues were linked to new

60. The choice of format depended heavily on the kind of store and where the advertisements were being distributed, many using a variety of formats, adapted for specific distribution. No format was novel; though the quantity of the ads increased greatly over the century, its quality did not match the increasing sophistication of in-store marketing techniques.

larger units of distribution, higher rates of literacy, cheaper printing techniques, and seasonal purchases.[61]

Having convinced people to hold onto their flyer, pamphlet or catalogue long enough to read it, the advertisers then used five general categories of argument (into which the dichotomous pairs outlined above fit). The distributors tried, in different registers according to the kind of store they were advertising, to claim (1) that the "shopping experience" would be enjoyable; (2) that the goods purchased were guaranteed to be tasteful; (3) that the furniture represented good value; (4) that the mode of production used by their suppliers was best; and (5) that their position on credit—either offering or refusing it—was ideal. Different advertisers put these qualities together in different ways, but those were clearly perceived as the issues of central concern to consumers. Late nineteenth-century consumers were inexperienced in the ways of modern consumption; thus, a major part of the task of these advertisements was to provide reassurance.

Once the printed advertising materials, or the manufacturer's or distributor's exhibits at the universal exposition attracted potential customers to the store, the next step was to entice them to buy. Techniques in increasing use as the nineteenth century wore on were elaborate displays and entertainments like those discussed above. Both techniques relied on the appearance of an object that one was selling, rather than the depths of knowledge, skill, and craft sense that went into its production. Distributors were selling the alienated objects of an artisan's alienated labor. Unlike negotiating for a custom-made object—discussing the use, aesthetics, durability, and price of the potential object; making a leap of imagination from a working drawing to the three-dimensional object through belief in the competence of the maker—consumers buying a readymade object were given the illusion of increased knowledge. They could, after all, look at, sit on, or pull out the drawers of a piece of furniture before purchasing it. But the quality of furniture was largely invisible, unless one was an expert. How the springs were tied in a sofa, how the joints were made, what kind of glue was used, how well the wood was seasoned, what was used as stuffing material—all those essentials and many more were invisible to the consumer. Two pieces of furniture might look identical but could be of very unequal quality and durability. Displays acted on customers through mesmeric quantities, by the appearance of luxury, by the art of persuading

61. Many of these can be found in the ADS, since posters, flyers, and newspaper ads were less expensive than glossy catalogues. Elaborate storytelling pamphlets appear to be one of the few innovations of the late nineteenth century.

consumers that they were ignorant of their own needs (and unable to negotiate with an individual maker) and must rely on the knowledge and authority of the distributor.

Entertainments represented a different kind of effort to persuade and, as noted above, were more generally the domain of the department stores. In addition to the entertaining or edifying events they sponsored—such as plays, concerts, lectures, and poetry readings—department stores also often had restaurants, babysitters, lounges, and other amenities to make it possible to spend an entire day shopping. These entertainments were an effort to turn shopping from a chore into a pleasurable, satisfying, and legitimate activity.

Displays and entertainment wove a web of enchantment around their audience. Department stores and specialty stores each sold a particular set of qualities—the department stores their scale, convenience, and capacity to amuse and the speciality stores their expertise and quality. Both sets of attributes differed from what custom furniture makers offered—uniqueness, traditional knowledge, and a say in what one's furniture would look like.

Advertisers used a range of strategies to convince consumers that they needed, wanted and could afford the goods the distributors were selling. They also provided information about the goods available. Distributors made certain assumptions concerning their public: most were women, socially insecure, who did not want to haggle but wanted to be entertained as they shopped. Even more important than these generalizations were the sets of oppositions: mechanization versus hand labor; specialization versus diversification; economy versus luxury—the pairs could go on. To some extent these dichotomies were the inevitable result of a stratified market. It would be foolish to try to sell goods to wealthy and poor customers in the same terms. But the dichotomous discourse also reflects a diversified domain of distribution, where there was not yet any hegemonic model of what an ideal institution of distribution was. All was not chaos; the advertisers consistently laid claim to a rationality of sorts. Even those who sold largely eighteenth-century goods claimed to be selling them in the context best suited to the goods. All was to be orderly, controlled, civilized. There was to be no dickering, no negotiation, no disorder. Such security and rationality were most available in styles that were traditional and established, styles that were familiar.

The late nineteenth century was marked, therefore, by both continuity and radical transformation in the organization of production and distribution, but both favored the making and perpetuation of historicist pastiche rather than the diffusion of a new style. In the Old Regime styles had arisen organically within the trades through incremental innovations and patronage. The older patterns of intense communication among artisans in the trades included mutual borrowing of new techniques and gave some artisans a mastery of all levels of their trade. The work's pace allowed reflection, care, and experimentation. And direct communication with the consumers allowed for responses to their reactions.

By the late nineteenth century, however, there were far fewer artisans who combined skill and knowledge, pattern books were widely diffused, mechanization made many of the techniques needed for Old Regime–style furniture more widely available while colonialism made the wood itself cheaper. The new, more extensive, separation of production and distribution meant that consumers were more uncertain about good form and more inclined to buy what was familiar—it was not clear how much trust they yet put in salespeople to know what they were talking about. In production, extensive outwork enabled artisans to effect small changes on designs—kinds of wood for veneer, shape of leg, detail in the turning—but not major ones. The new styles introduced, *style moderne* and *art nouveau,* were designer-based rather than craft-based styles. They were, therefore, styles that, while aesthetically precedent setting, could not gain widespread commercial success at the time. And, as we will see below, there could, in any case, be no *one* dominant style during the Third Republic because the needs of nation building and of bourgeois consolidation demanded, instead, a plurality of styles. Rather than access to state style, appropriate taste was now the marker of social rather than political power. And yet the economy and the nation were complexly articulated with the social, which was reflected in turn in the world of everyday objects.

9
After the Culture of Production
The Paradox of Labor and Citizenship

 Mid-nineteenth-century efforts to replace the culture of production—by creating a field of industrial art to turn out innovative French furniture and generate class peace—failed. In the eyes of contemporaries, late 1870s laborers and bosses were still at odds and no successful French style had been born. Many contemporaries judged the most innovative work, either *style moderne,* or the style produced by Henri Fourdinois, to be tasteless, or inappropriate to the times. Suggestions for a novel French style arose in response to the failures of the previous generation and in response to a changed world: the industrialization and commercialization of France had dramatically increased in scale and intensity. The class conflict already apparent in the middle years of the century had, in the face of boom and bust economic cycles, intensified. France now had a republican government based on universal manhood suffrage. Socialists now had a legitimate political voice, and male workers had become full citizens as well as laborers. The combination of these factors reframed the debate over the role of the state in social life, the resolution of class inequities, and the making of style.

In the 1830s and 1840s, and even continuing into the 1860s, the knowledge necessary for innovative design appeared at once dangerous and difficult to instill. Reformers were in a double bind: they feared that an industry in crisis would create disgruntled artisans who might rebel, but they also feared that artisans with too much knowledge might become "uppity," recognize their relative deprivation, and take to the streets. To separate knowledge from skills training seemed the answer, thereby producing a new class of industrial artists who could invent forms and direct the labor of a new "moralized" working class. Institutions like the Collège des beaux-arts appliqués à l'industrie (discussed in chapter 5) and the Conservatoire national des arts et métiers would train the petit-bourgeois and bourgeois designers, and evening courses would give the working class enough skill to make the objects imagined by the industrial artists. These new institutions, along with the libraries and universal expositions, were to replace the culture of production, be sites of the invention and production of a new style, and create in the process a specifically working-class repertoire of competencies that differentiated producers according to the technical skills they possessed—thereby ensuring class peace.

Taste professionals of the 1880s inherited these institutions and conceptualizations, and some among them agreed with their premises, but all had to acknowledge the need to find new solutions. Some suggested continuing along the road marked out in the 1860s, but with increasing state involvement. Others agreed with the continued fragmentation of knowledge, skill, and craft sense but argued that the private sector should take the initiative. Yet others argued that the restriction of the education offered to working-class men to that needed for manual labor was both catastrophic for the production of a new national style and was no longer possible in a republic. Most agreed that the contemporary separation of art and industry and the division between public and private responsibility for the decorative arts were problematic aesthetically, economically, and politically. Critics argued that French furniture was unoriginal and could not compete on the international market. Also, both underemployed and over- and undereducated working-class men were considered politically volatile.

Parallel to these debates over artisanal education and a crisis in taste, therefore, were debates over the education of citizens. The Revolution of 1848 had reintroduced universal manhood suffrage in France, and it was a plebiscite that legitimized Napoleon III's ascent to power. In this period the possibility of simultaneously forming the worker and the citizen in the context of a capitalist liberal state based on putative political equality and overt economic inequality had its first clear articulation. Many Third Republic politicians still believed that educating working-class voters and training them in their chosen occupations—equally urgent tasks—were incompatible. Citizens needed abstract knowledge; workers needed concrete skills. Abstract knowledge could lead to expectations of social mobility and, if unfulfilled, to revolution, and abstraction itself could trigger political thought.

Thus to the tasks of producing a successful French style for export, to generating social peace, to determining the appropriate possibilities and limits on state intervention was added that of educating a mass citizenry. Were the tasks contradictory? The transformation of the economy seemed to justify a continuation of the early solutions; industries in which labor was increasingly divided had little use for well-educated workers but considerable need for educated managers and designers. Industries following that course were not producing a new style, however, and were understood to be seriously handicapped. Furthermore, ill-educated labor now voted. Not coincidentally, in this period of nation building, the discussion was further complicated by debate on the racial or genetic nature of taste. Some taste professionals argued that there was really no crisis; intrinsic French tastefulness would produce a new style in due course. Gustave Geoffroy confidently asserted that France's "natural taste" would express itself through producers "who spread decorative objects representative of French work, French taste, and French thought throughout the world." A. Beurdeley expressed even more optimism concerning French artisans' prowess: "Ever since Boulle . . . the strong race of artist workers has never expired in France and has fathered an uninterrupted series of masterpieces that will continue to grow as long as French taste does not expire, that is to say, forever." Individuals who argued passionately for the aesthetic superiority of the French race were not necessarily opposed to institutional transformation, but they were insistent on the genetic heritage that underlay aesthetic achievements. The care with which those passionately engaged in institutional change moved around the issue of innate taste is an indication of the sensitivity of the issue: "French artistic superiority is not simply the result of a gift of nature," wrote Victor Champier: "it is not only a question of territory and of climate; it is a question of study and tradition. Taste is acquired by work. Good workers are obtained by the teaching of drawing . . . the faculties of invention that our race possesses, the taste that one thinks innate . . . will collapse into a dwindling immobility, if it is not stimulated."[1] To simply say outright that taste was something learned might sound like disloyalty to the nation.

BUILDING ON THE HERITAGE:
EDUCATING THE DESIGNER AND THE WORKER

The extent of the perceived crisis in taste and style can be seen in the rapid multiplication of institutions, journals, and books directed toward improving the taste of French producers. The taste professionals continued to flourish and expand their range of activity in both the private and the public sectors from the 1880s well into the twentieth century. Behind most of these efforts, confessed one contemporary, was "the patriotic fear

1. Geoffroy, "Causerie sur le style," 179; A. Beurdeley, fils, "Les meubles d'art," *Revue des arts décoratifs* 3 (1882–83): 2; Champier, "Le pavillon," 70, 77.

generated by seeing the drop in the aesthetic level of our industrial arts workshops."[2] The primary goal of these organizations was to defend the patrimony and improve France's chances of competition in the world market; their secondary goal was to maintain the social order. They tended to worry about social peace but not necessarily about social justice. So far, this sounds very much like the organizations of the 1830s through the 1860s, but there was a striking difference and complication. Earlier discourses had advocated the bridging of art and industry, but institutionally—because of their fear of an educated working class—had encouraged their separation. That institutional separation was reinforced by the growing proletarianization of labor and commercialization of distribution (discussed in chapter 8). The taste professionals of the 1880s, therefore, inherited a world with a real division between art and industry, increasing fragmentation of labor, continued class tensions, and the absence of a new style. This confused heritage produced a very complicated and paradoxical set of responses.

For example, the Patronage industriel des enfants de l'ébénisterie created a school to train artisans in the furniture trades, attempting to reconstruct the complete training of apprenticeship and journeymanship of the culture of production. It tried, in some sense, to turn back the clock. Paralleling its efforts were those of the Comité de patronage of the *tapissiers*, which argued in a letter to the minister of public instruction that "to have good workers in our industry, that is educated intelligent men, it is no longer sufficient to give them notions of manual labor, one has also to develop their taste in giving them teachers of drawing and geometry."[3] Likewise one of the most important technical treatises of the period, *L'art et la science du meuble,* insisted on the importance of renewing the teaching of drawing.[4] One of the initiators of *style moderne,* Emile Gallé, was explicit about the damage done: "We were wrong to dissociate the two curricula, to give to the conservatories the teaching of production, and elsewhere, in the institutes, the means and the virtuosities—drawing, painting, *la plastique,* composition—without reuniting them anywhere."[5]

Others, in contrast, were very explicit that the "age of the artisan" had passed. Emile Molinier argued that the conditions of production were so different in the nineteenth century than in the eighteenth that only the

2. Preface to *Revue des arts décoratifs* 3 (1882–83): 1.
3. AN F^{17}12530, 4 April 1878.
4. Louis Bertin, *L'art et la science du meuble* (Dourdan, [1900]), 2:1.
5. Gallé, "Le mobilier contemporain," 334.

architect now had the means to "truly create a style."[6] And the new category, "Application usuelle des arts du dessin et de la plastique," in which only "models and forms of artistic works destined to be reproduced by industry" were admitted at the 1878 Parisian universal exposition expressed the idea that innovation was now to come only from architects and designers. The organizers argued that this new display category was necessary and important because "architects, painters, decorators, sculptors, *ornemanistes*, engravers, and lithographers are in fact the initiators and the true representatives of the modern school."[7] Creativity and innovation were no longer in the hands of artisans, but rather in the hands of artists.

Lying somewhere in the middle were most of the articles in the new magazines: *L'art décoratif: revue internationale d'art industriel et de décoration* (1898–1914); *Art et décoration: revue mensuelle d'art moderne* (1897–); the *Revue des arts décoratifs* (1880–1902); *L'art et l'industrie: organe du progrès dans toutes les branches de l'industrie artistique* (1877–89); the *Album de l'ameublement: journal de la décoration intérieure* (1882–92); and *L'art ornemental* (1883–86). This last magazine started publication in 1883, with the explicit goal of educating the artisan: "We have dreamed of being the battery that will galvanize the sleeping intellects of artist-workers. . . . We want to give them back to themselves, not with the help of lectures and written discourses, but by the simple sight of masterpieces that were made by their masters." *L'art décoratif* claimed to have similar goals and published a monthly series of masterpieces to benefit artisans' taste under the title *les maîtres du dessin*, but its price and format indicated that it was intended as much for architects and consumers as for artisans. As an organ of progress in all branches of artistic industry, *L'art et l'industrie* followed in the tradition of the *Journal de menuiserie*, offering very technical information for people in the trades that they were not getting in the shop.[8] Except for *L'art et l'industrie*, these magazines were largely directed by architects and painters, including a few decorative artists and manufacturers. They were distant from the production processes and more knowledgeable about, and more interested in, the

6. Molinier, "La décoration dans l'ameublement," 48.
7. AN F^{12}3352, exposition universelle de 1878.
8. Editorial in *L'art ornemental*, 3 February 1883, 1–3; "Les maîtres du dessin," *L'art décoratif* 9 (June 1899): 138; see, for example, "Procédé pour l'entretien des bahuts et des bois anciens," *L'art et l'industrie* 1 (1877): n.p., before pl. 80; or "Dorure sur bois" 2 (1878).

linkages between the fine and the decorative arts. Thus, declared *L'art décoratif* in 1899, it was "real" artists, not artisans, and not even designers who come up with new styles.[9]

Also occupying a complex middle position between the abandonment of artisans to mindless manual labor and the union (or reunion) of art and industry was the Union centrale des arts décoratifs founded in 1882; it grew out of the fusion of the Union centrale des beaux-arts appliqués à l'industrie and of the Société du musée des arts décoratifs and adopted a different stance. In its effort to sustain French production the organization used a quadruple strategy: it created a series of free public lectures; it continued to support the school and library created by the Union centrale des beaux-arts appliqués à l'industrie (discussed in chapter 5); it published the *Revue des arts décoratifs*; and it supported exhibits and ultimately sponsored a permanent museum for the display of French decorative art.

The Union centrale's series of free public lectures for adults were on such topics as "Study of the artistic genius of foreign nations"; "Chronicle of the applied fine arts"; and, "Studies of shadows and of the effects of light on defined surfaces." Through the lectures it hoped to provide those working in the decorative arts industry with the kind of knowledge needed to innovate. The lectures tended to be rather abstract or historical, rather than technical or practical, and attracted audiences of 48 to 140.[10] The magazine created by the organization in 1880, the *Revue des arts décoratifs*, had related articles, including long discussions of eighteenth-century furniture makers, new design happenings elsewhere in Europe, reports on exhibitions, and discussions of the crisis in style. It did not reprint technical manuals or discuss practical problems involved in furniture construction but did sponsor contests and claimed to accept submissions of drawings of new forms of furniture to be published in the magazine (although they very rarely appeared).[11] The magazine was quite expensive, however, and therefore difficult to get. Whatever their intentions, it appears that the lectures and journal sponsored by the Union centrale, like the collège founded in

9. J., "M. Félix Aubert," *L'art décoratif* 4 (January 1899): 158. The editorial committee of *Art et décoration*, for instance, had Puvis de Chavannes (painter), Joseph-Auguste-Emile Vaudremer (architect), Grasset, Jean-Paul Laurens (painter), Cazin, L.-O. Merson, Fremiet, Roty, and Lucien Magne; its director was Thiébault-Soisson.

10. The Union centrale cited the lectures in its request for recognition as a non-profit organization (AN F^{12}2334).

11. Champier, "La maison modèle," 20–21.

the 1860s, almost certainly had a largely leisured public. The same might be true of the museum and library they began, later taken over by the state.

Whereas these lectures and magazines remained under private auspices, from the 1880s onward there was far more blurring of municipal, state, and private initiatives. Through the 1860s, the only institution of state initiative and under state control was the universal exhibition, but by the second decade of the Third Republic the state and the city of Paris were both assuming full responsibility for institutions of private initiative and starting their own. Examples of the former were the museum and library founded by the Union centrale; examples of the latter included the Ecole Boulle and the Bibliothèque Forney.

Besides schools, public lectures, journals, and exhibitions, the taste professionals' intervention into the private domain included museums devoted to the industrial or decorative arts. In 1877 a group of concerned men—the duc d'Audiffret Pasquier, Sir Richard Wallace (the famous English collector), Paul Christofle (a jewelry manufacturer), Henri Bouilhet, and Ernest Lefebure—founded the Société du musée des arts décoratifs. This group, anticipating the *art nouveau* and arts and crafts movements of the end of the century, hoped to create a museum that would breach the division between fine arts and decorative arts.[12] A notion of museums as a means of improving the taste of the nation, and thus aiding in competition with Britain and other industrialized countries, was added to the more traditional idea of museums as a place to preserve the patrimony of the country. In fact, when the Musée des arts décoratifs finally opened twenty-three years later, it was as a branch of the Louvre, on the rue de Rivoli. The museum contained examples of what were judged to be masterpieces of the decorative arts, from glassware to porcelain to fabrics and furniture. The majority of the national collections of furniture remained in the Louvre, with only a small selection of especially fine and typical works going to the new museum. The museum was open only the standard daytime hours (plus Sunday); that schedule, combined with its location, discouraged very heavy artisanal usage though doubtless some artisans did make their way there to look at, study, and sketch the works on display.

The library created by the Union centrale, the Bibliothèque des arts décoratifs, after its founding in 1866 on the place des Vosges, moved around

12. See the excellent discussion of this movement in Silverman, *Art Nouveau in Fin-de-Siècle France;* and on museums, Dominique Poulot, "L'invention de la bonne volonté culturelle: l'image du musée au XIXe siècle," *Le mouvement social* 131 (1985): 35–64.

1886 to its current home in the Louvre and became a publicly (nationally rather than municipally) owned library. The move caused a change in readership as well as ownership, as noted rather sarcastically by the library historian and activist Eugène Morel. "[When the library was located] in the place des Vosges, people came mostly in the evening, [now that it's in] the Louvre, people come in the afternoon. The public has changed. There were more bronze workers, chiselers, *ébénistes*. Now there are many more young ladies doing embossed leather work and pyrography [using a hot tool to decorate leather]. The different neighborhood, the hours, and the building account for the change. It's almost too beautiful, not the reading room, but the vestibule. Workers don't dare to come in."[13]

In 1906 the library was heavily frequented and charged no admission. But most patrons came during the working day rather than in the evening and were not people who worked with their hands. One-third gave no profession and were understood by the library to be "young society ladies, connoisseurs, dilettantes, and unknown." Of those who gave their occupation, there were over 5,000 painters, 3,000 architects, 2,000 sculptors, 1,000 decorators, nearly 400 jewelers, 350 teachers, 178 engravers, and only 44 *ébénistes*.[14] The library became a resource for fine artists, taste professionals, and middle-class women to educate themselves in matters of taste, decoration and craft. Thus, the Union centrale, although it crowed about its success in transforming the taste of artisans, had perhaps a smaller impact than it had hoped.[15]

In both instances, because the focus of the organization had always been on international competition and French honor, once the state was committed to direct engagement in the decorative arts, it took over these institutions, as elements of the French patrimony, and as weapons in the international economic war. As will be seen in chapter 10, by the 1880s, the training of the consumer in national loyalty and patriotism was coming to be as important as that of the producer. The institutions that the state inherited or took over from private initiative were those well suited to that aspect of the state project.

The 1870s saw the further elaboration of schools and the development of libraries, as well as extensive museum planning. A municipal appren-

13. Morel, *Bibliothèque*, 1:92.

14. AN F^{12}2334, no. 11 des pièces d'appui de la demande de l'Union centrale d'être reconnue société d'utilité publique (Morel, *Bibliothèque*, 1:89–90).

15. Champier, "Le pavillon," 69.

ticeship school opened January 1873 in Paris and a national law entitled Ecoles manuelles d'apprentissage passed on 11 December 1880.[16] This law led to the major growth of both day and night courses intended for artisans in the 1880s. The law was the result of efforts of deputies Tolain and Martin Nadaud (an ex-mason, with a career similar to that of Agricol Perdiguier) and had a double goal: "(1) to train workers completely initiated into the work of their trades in these special apprenticeship schools and then to 'pour' them into industry, (2) to give those young men who plan to enter secondary special apprenticeship schools the necessary dexterity of hand and necessary technical know-how."[17]

In the wording of this law the objects of this proposed education were indeed objects. They were to be trained and then poured into the trades. The sole possibility of action for these potential students was to plan and to execute technical skills with their hands. It is indicative of the degree of deterioration of the culture of production, and of the political atmosphere in the National Assembly, that Nadaud, himself the product of that culture, should have sponsored a bill worded in such a way. But this bill fit the generally hierarchical structuring of the public education system in this period. The ideology behind the system was meritocratic, not egalitarian.

The apprenticeship law was thus part of a system of universal free primary education in France, shortly followed by a series of other educational reforms, including the creation of a network of public trade schools. The schools at the top of the hierarchy were the national engineering schools—the Conservatoire national des arts et métiers and the very prestigious Ecole polytechnique. On the next rung down the ladder (although it was a very big step) were the Ecoles nationales professionnelles at Armentières, Vierzon, and Voiron. These schools largely trained the sons of artisans and of the petite bourgeoisie, often placing them in the new occupations of millwright, machinist, and draftsman. Below these were the municipal trade schools, including the Ecole municipale Bernard Palissy and the Ecole Boulle, both of which trained the children of artisans for artisanal jobs in the decorative arts. These schools were highly controversial for both the Right and the Left, as can be seen in the debate around the Ecole Boulle. The Ecole professionnelle d'ameublement, or the

16. Charton, ed., *Dictionnaire des professions*, 34.
17. Leaflet from the Ministère de l'instruction publique et des beaux-arts, on the 11 December 1880 law (AN F[17]11700, p. 11).

Ecole Boulle, founded by the city of Paris in 1886, became the most important school for training workers in the furniture trades.[18] It was located on the rue de Reuilly in the faubourg St-Antoine and was conceived explicitly to "save" the workers and the trade in that neighborhood. While some trades were defined as hopelessly corrupted by industrialization, the luxury trades were viewed as capable of resuscitation through the education of the young. The Ecole Boulle was to "train elite workers, of whom a few will become real artists and will preserve in our products the cachet of elegance and of good taste that have assured them success."[19] Implicit in the design of the school was the formalization and consolidation of a hierarchy of knowledge and skill in the furniture trades. There was to be a small class of school-trained, creative "artists," who would be sandwiched between the foremen and managers produced at the national trade or engineering schools and the mass of undereducated workers. The class of artisans was to disappear, being replaced by a new hierarchy of managers, artists, and workers.

Students were admitted to the Ecole Boulle between the ages of thirteen and sixteen, after they passed an examination consisting of drawing an ornament from a plaster cast and writing a French composition on a simple subject. The course lasted four years, with students choosing their specialty in their second year. Besides formal courses, the students also visited museums, palaces, monuments, as well as factories, forests, and other sites of production of raw materials. The school was serious about accessibility; instruction was free, students were boarded, and at graduation they were given their tools in addition to their certificate.[20]

Teaching was divided into "technical" and "theoretical and artistic" sections. The technical education was essentially manual training; the students worked in the shop under the tutelage of an experienced cabinetmaker. The theoretical and artistic education attempted to fill gaps in their primary education and to teach them to organize their work efficiently. Most significantly, the students were to learn, through drawing, the art of the construction and decoration of furniture and to "more easily absorb the principles of labor instilled in the workshop that have as a goal developing dexterity and taste. Together the knowledge thus acquired

18. This discussion draws on good archival material on the Ecole Boulle (AN F[17]14364) and others (AN F[17]14348); and Gaston Cougny, *L'enseignement professionnel des beaux-arts dans les écoles de la ville de Paris* (Paris, 1888), 192–232.

19. Anonymous article in *Le Temps*, 9 April 1895 (Ecole Boulle dossier, AN F[17]14364).

20. Leaflet advertising competition for the Ecole Boulle, 7 July 1895 (ibid.).

should lessen the bad effects of specialization and should include all that a capable artisan needs to know to create and make works of art."[21]

The logic behind the school was, therefore, not a return to a preindustrial mode of production, nor a recreation of the Old Regime apprenticeship system. It was a response to the new conditions of industrial labor. The dream was a resolutely modern one in which the students were to be completely trained, given a rudimentary liberal education, as well as a firm grasp of the manual aspects of the craft, the theoretical knowledge of geometry and structures needed for design, the ability to graphically represent their ideas, a knowledge of the nature of the materials used—their sources, possibilities, and limitations—an acquaintanceship with the national heritage and with French traditions in interior design. They were to learn good taste and to work quickly and efficiently, turning out finely crafted, beautifully designed objets d'art. To contemporaries, the demands of efficient and scientific artistic production held no contradiction. The logic of the school, unlike that of apprenticeship and journeymanship, was stratified. The school was to train an elite who would direct the work of untrained labor. Those who went would receive a fine training, and those who were not able to go probably had little access to knowledge and skill.

The numbers of students trained in the Ecole Boulle remained small, and those trained in the school rarely remained furniture makers. Full-time students went into the school as potential artisans, part-time students as workers in the furniture industry. By the early years of the twentieth century, all emerged as members of a transitional group who were neither artisans nor members of the working class, nor bourgeois designers. Few continued to work with their hands; most went to work as draftsmen or designers for some of the larger furniture shops of the faubourg. Consequently, by the First World War, there was a multi-tiered system of training in the industrial arts.[22] The last three tiers—the ones most feasible for most working-class adolescents—were the Ecole Boulle, the neighborhood trade schools, and informal training through unskilled or semiskilled work in the shop.

Schools were only one branch of the state's and municipality's efforts to train workers and citizens—libraries were understood to be another important site. Among these, the Bibliothèque Forney was the library equivalent of the Ecole Boulle. It was founded in 1886 as a technical

21. Parisian authorities' announcement of the school (AN F^{17}14346).
22. This division into technical and fine arts training was contested by Bonnaffé among others, but to little avail (*Etudes sur l'art*, 216ff.).

library for the industrial arts, with money from the legacy, ten years earlier, of the industrialist Charles Forney. The library was originally located at 12 rue Titon in the eleventh arrondissement in the middle of the faubourg St-Antoine. It was a significant innovation because at the time of its founding the only public source of iconographic material was the Bibliothèque nationale, whose hours made it almost inaccessible to artisans.[23]

One especially eloquent journalist, Ludovic Simon, lauded the library for providing "the male Parisian worker" with "the tools he needed." He lambasted those who "lived on the ancient prejudice born of the egocentricity of capital and dominating spirit of the clergy, who claimed that the people did not need education." He argued that it was "to the glory of this republic to have started the emancipation of the spirit, by the diffusion of popular education." The library would make "available to the poor man and to the worker the means that are necessary for him to be given a more scientific and elevated character to his knowledge."[24]

The library's purpose was somewhat more limited than Ludovic Simon implied. It did not serve, any more than did the trade schools, to liberate all artisans from routine labor and give them access to unlimited knowledge. The anticlerical, republican discourse obscured a general tendency to give artisans only the information and tools required for manual labor. The founders of the library themselves phrased their intentions differently: "to complete the technical training of artisans, to form, to purify the taste of industrial artists, to prepare the collaboration of *industriels*, retailers, and artists through the appropriate teaching and documentation."[25]

The goals of the founders of this library, therefore, were analogous to those of the founders of the various public schools related to the decorative arts and created a similar hierarchy. According to the municipal council, the artisans were to complete their technical education; the industrial artists— generally low-level designers of artisanal origins who no longer worked with their hands—were to have their taste trained and purified; and industrialists, distributors, and artists were to learn to collaborate and cooperate. The assumption was that those who worked with their hands—the artisans—were exclusively in need of limited training in their craft and that they formed a group distinct from those who worked with their heads, the

23. Among the twenty or so clippings in Bibliothèque Forney is an article by J. G., "Instruction professionnelle," *L'Evenement*, 9 July 1884 (ADS VR216).

24. Simon, "Une grande oeuvre" (ADS VR216).

25. Quoted in Henri Comte, *Les bibliothèques publiques en France* (Lyons, 1977), 298.

artistes industriels, who would benefit from aesthetic education. But these industrial artists, because of their origin, did not, unlike pure artists, possess innate good taste. The owners of capital (and those outside of capital—the real artists) needed only assistance in learning how to work with others. Thus, these late nineteenth-century hybrids, the industrial arts and industrial artists, were embedded in a very complex way in a hierarchy of knowledge and taste and in a particular relation with capital.

The library's holdings reflected this division of labor; they contained subscriptions to thirty-three periodicals, including some British and German, some 10,000 volumes and 80,000 prints (to serve as models or inspiration for readers). In addition, the collection was enlarged at the end of the century by the gift of the drawings and documentary photographs of the production of the famous furniture manufacturer the maison Fourdinois.[26] The holdings were on an open stack system. The prints were in color-coded boxes encircling the room; library users could consult, and even trace, and then reshelve, any images of interest to them. They could also take prints home for further study.

The classification system used by the new library was based largely on the raw materials used, i.e. stone, wood, iron, bronze. Under Stone were grouped architecture, sculpture, marble working, funeral monuments. Carpentry, *menuiserie, ébénisterie,* ivory, and ebonies were discussed together under the rubric Wood. The only exceptions were the first category, General artistic information, and the last two: Science and its applications and Moral and physical sciences (which included geography, statistics, and legislation).[27] This system meant that trades that had little to do with one another were grouped, while others much more interdependent were isolated. Carpentry, for example, had more to do with architecture than with ivory, and *ébénisterie* shared more with *tapisserie* than *tapisserie* did with costumes. The classification scheme was based on natural history, rather than on the history of labor, or the craft traditions behind the industrial arts. (This system of categorization, incidentally, bears a striking resemblance to Le Play's organization of the 1867 Paris universal exposition.) The only liberal arts included were ones that applied very directly to the industrial arts.

Thus the Bibliothèque Forney embodied a construction of knowledge for artisans that implied a focus on limited information necessary to develop

26. Morel, *Bibliothèque,* 1:92; and letters from the prefect to the librarian at Forney, 14 May 1889 (ADS VR216).
27. Morel, *Bibliothèque,* 1:92–93.

technical expertise. While the library of the Union centrale des arts dé-coratifs, as was seen above, chose not to expand its holdings in the direction of artisanal practice and technical treatises, Forney did not venture far into the fine arts. In its efforts to ameliorate the conditions of the industrial arts, the Union centrale mixed fine and decorative arts—theory and product; the Forney, with the same goal, mixed craft and science. This organization provides a marked similarity to the curricula of schools of the period. This library also had far larger holdings on the specific trades than did the private libraries devoted to the decorative arts, which were very little used by artisans.

It is interesting, however, given that the library did not buy only applied texts, to note the abstract books its founders thought appropriate. The paucity of works having to do with the fine arts, most strikingly sculpture and drawing, is especially revealing. It is all the more notable given patterns of usage. The category of books most borrowed was the first and most abstract—*Renseignements généraux: esthétique, peinture, arts décoratifs.* This was true from the library's opening and became more dramatic as time went on. In 1886 there were 2,225 home loans from the first category, with the next most popular being category nine (*science, sciences mathéma-tiques, physiques*) with 1,238 loans. The others trailed far behind. By 1896, 38,268 items were borrowed concerning aesthetics, painting and decorative arts, while 3,804 items were borrowed from category nine, and 3,000 from those concerning wood and textiles.[28] Thus, there clearly was a demand for more abstract texts.

This information concerning the internal usage of the Bibliothèque For-ney should be placed in the context of the library's conditions of access and use. Forney was open from one to three in the afternoon and from seven to ten in the evening. Its hours, the fact that use was free, and its open lending policy made it accessible to working people. Forney was by far the largest industrial arts library in Paris and was clearly heavily used. Also, though no exact records remain, it enjoyed the reputation of serving a large arti-sanal public.[29]

---

28. ADS VR216.

29. Forney's loans rose from 9,413 in 1886 (or 41 percent of all industrial arts libraries of Paris) to 76,135 (or 59 percent) in 1894 (Maurice Pellisson, *Les bibliothèques populaires à l'étranger et en France* [Paris, 1906], 179, 174). See also the librarian's 1898 report: 5,229 library cards since the opening of the library; collection of 66,635 books and prints; in 1898 the Forney had 59,811 loans and 42,954 consultations (ADS VR216).

Forney functioned as a library and, like the Union centrale, sponsored lectures on a variety of subjects perceived to be of interest to artisans working in the decorative arts trades. The topics of the lectures were somewhat more concrete or practical than those given at the Union centrale, ranging from Japanese decorative art or the construction of the Eiffel Tower to the workings of electricity, or jewelry or wallpaper. Some addressed questions of taste and style. In 1899, for example, Robert Thomas, a teacher at the Ecole de la chambre syndicale de menuiserie, gave a talk entitled "Art and customs: Introduction to the study of styles." His proposal indicated that he planned to "document that each style was the result of a series of social phenomena, which profoundly modified the needs and ideas of the world, and consequently the tastes." He would focus especially on the arts of furnishing because "they are the most sensitive to these influences, and because of that carry so powerfully the mark of the moral state of their times."[30]

The lecturers were unpaid and often unsolicited. The talks were advertised widely by enormous posters, published, and distributed. The publicity effort seems to have been successful, garnering a reported audience of from five hundred to eight hundred per lecture.[31] Notably, after the mid-1890s, more and more lectures concerned social problems—such as workers' housing and industrial accidents—than aesthetic and technical subjects.

Any effort to understand the motivations of those who dispensed knowledge through libraries is perhaps doomed from the start, but it is, nonetheless, important to emphasize here the unquestionable complexity of those motivations. The example of Octave Latinne, an importer of exotic woods, who requested the right to give an (unpaid) lecture at Forney serves as a necessary counterbalance to any simplistic image of social control. His father having founded a steam-powered sawmill in 1827, Latinne described himself as "one of the doyens of the wood business," who wished to share his long experience with "the men of the faubourg" and put himself "in contact with the people." He intended to give them some good advice and "alert the male worker to the invasion of department stores by foreign products. If I can be useful to the cause of reviving this industry, I will willingly do so."[32] The condescension of M. Latinne toward the "people,"

30. ADS VR216.
31. Ibid.
32. Letter of 22 April 1898 from Octave Latinne, to the prefect of the Seine (ibid.). Latinne was also one of the editors of *Le Bois: journal spécial des commerces des bois et des industries qui s'y rattachent.*

"the men of the faubourg," is undeniable. Yet his enthusiasm and apparently sincere desire to serve and be useful, and his self-denigration ("lacking talent, I have experience, a taste for hard work, if that can be put to use") is equally palpable. In the eyes of M. Latinne those who made things, the artisans, were the real producers in society, those who truly had talent. In that view, he was not far from Agricol Perdiguier, although theirs was coming to be a minority position. The dominant story is one of artisans' loss of control over the process of acquisition of the necessary knowledge to live and work with some degree of creativity, autonomy and freedom, and its replacement by the more circumscribed mastery of techniques.

Not only were schools and libraries built in an effort by the public sector to train artisans, but public museums were also founded. The first *musée du soir* opened its doors in 1895, ten years before the private Musée des arts décoratifs. It was located temporarily in the Paris Bourse de Travail but moved to the Petit-Palais in 1908. "All of those who are interested in the development of popular education and in the rapid development of thought leading toward a peaceful future, will turn their eyes on the city of Paris. The evening museum can unite scattered good will, can put into contact those who know and those who want to learn—the artist and the artisan."[33] This statement suggests, once again, the perceived links in the late nineteenth century between the right kind of education and social harmony. Artisans were those without knowledge who could learn from artists, who possessed knowledge. The Musée du soir, like the Bibliothèque Forney, sponsored lectures, both to ensure that visitors understood the point of the exhibits and to make the museum more attractive to them. Workers were assumed to be a kind of raw talent, possessing native good taste or "aesthetic instincts," but in need of education to enable them "to be moved by the manifestations of beauty in all its forms." The Musée Galliera was later opened (with evening hours) by the city of Paris in part in the hopes of "bringing to life a new style in furniture and decoration."[34]

The founders of these museums perceived them as institutions alien to the working class, to which a public would come only if cajoled or persuaded. The attendance records from the museums give some credence to those perceptions, even if we do not share the founders' view of a working class generally ignorant and in need of enlightenment. In a commentary

33. Unidentified clipping, 12 April 1895 (ibid).

34. Rapport au nom de la 4e commission sur l'ouverture d'un musée du soir au Petit-Palais, présenté par MM. Henri Turot et Quentin-Bauchart (ibid., p. 6); anonymous article, *Gaulois*, 15 October 1922 (ADS VR247).

on the furniture exhibits in the world's fair of 1878, M. Cousté also based his argument for schools for artisans on the victory of science over misery and immorality. The triumph of the Enlightenment convinced him that schools must "offer to the most modest workers the basic elements of science and industry. That which they don't understand at school will come back to them later. . . . Through simple and precise textbooks, one could bring useful notions that will develop their taste, that will make their work more attractive to them and will increase their happiness and their morality. The future belongs to science."[35] The link Cousté made between taste, enticing work, well-being, and morality typifies the position of the conservative social reformers influenced by Le Play. The focus was on a limited range of knowledge, and on moral values. Petit-bourgeois and bourgeois managers and designers, in contrast, were to be offered a much wider range of material, from the fine arts to free drawing to abstract mathematics, in order to enable them most effectively to direct the labor of others and to imagine new forms.

The development of these institutions, therefore, both marked the final erosion of the culture of production and established crucial cornerstones in the new edifice of the industrial arts. Artisans were now to apply and execute what others had thought out. The schools, libraries, and museums made up critical elements of the new constellation of knowledge in the decorative arts by the end of the nineteenth century. Each, in its own way, provided a context in which aesthetics, production, and consumption were fragmented in new ways and then reunited. They were to provide guidance in unifying the beautiful and the useful, the economical and the tasteful, the rational and the comfortable. They were repositories of knowledge controlled by the taste professionals rather than by the crafts themselves and made that knowledge available to a different public of producers than had been the case before.

In truth, the Ecole Boulle, the Bibliothèque Forney, and the Musée du soir were stuck in a series of double binds. The founders of the Ecole Boulle wanted to provide a theoretical, artistic, and manual education to artisans in order to produce a total artisan for the modern world analogous to what they believed had been the training of furniture makers in the Old Regime. The founders of the Bibliothèque Forney likewise wanted to make available to Parisian furniture makers the books that they needed for complete

35. M. Cousté, "Rapport sur le matériel et les procédés de la confection des objets de mobilier et d'habitation," in *Exposition universelle de 1878* (Paris, 1881), 57–58.

mastery of their craft. Both efforts reflected, in some senses, an anachronistic view of the trade. They were anachronistic in wanting to create
complete artisans for whom there was less and less room in a commer-
cializing and capitalizing economy. Indeed, the Ecole Boulle acted as if the
division of labor between design and manufacture did not exist in the
furniture industries. As a result it produced a small number of very highly
trained men who had difficulty finding employment commensurate with
their training in the 1880s and who by the early years of the century were
becoming the new bosses. The school flourished in its niche—it just wasn't
the niche it had set out to occupy.

The early controversy over the Ecole Boulle raised a further difficulty.
What was the place of specialized, hierarchized state-funded education in
a polity in which all men could vote and all were supposed to be equal before
the law? The controversy mirrored the general debate about the role of the
state in the training of artisans, and the form and the place of technical
training in general.

In a report addressed to the Conseil Municipal de Paris in 1897, MM.
Clairin and Bompard reported that the school, in its first ten years, had
suffered an attrition rate of 45 percent (out of a total student body of 387),
and that those who had finished had not found especially good jobs. Not
only did the school have little success, according to the report, but it was
also costing a fortune. In the eleven years of its existence, the school had
cost a million and a half francs, or 7,150 francs per graduate. Clairin and
Bompard suggested that the school should be transformed, that students
be admitted at a more advanced age (sixteen or eighteen instead of thirteen
or fourteen), the admission test made more difficult, and the teaching less
theoretical. More serious than the expense was the possibility that if
artisans could not find work after graduation, and the state did not—as it
should not—provide it, then the graduates would be "new recruits for the
army of the malcontents and the *déclassés!*"[36]

The ghost of socialism clearly loomed large in a certain set of critiques
of the Ecole Boulle and other trade schools. Rather than become directly
involved in educating artisans, perhaps the state should offer financial

36. Anonymous article in *Le Temps*, 9 April 1895 (AN F^{17}14364). On this
report see other articles: *Le Petit Temps*, 20 May 1897; Edouard Petit, in *Le Voltaire*,
3 June 1897; *Le Radical*, 25 May 1897; *Le Temps*, 30 May 1897. A list of students
leaving in 1893 seems to confirm this negative report—the vast majority of alumni
actually working in the trade earned only around 3.50 francs per day, not a very
good salary for the trade (ibid.).

assistance to employers, who should then train apprentices themselves, "because otherwise they will find themselves . . . dispossessed. And we will have abolished the tyranny of the corporations to fall under the yoke of the Commune or the *état patron*. This servitude is no better or worse than the other, but for liberty to protect its rights, is it not indispensable that it exercises them in a virile manner?"[37]

Furthermore, it was feared that if one educated artisans, they would no longer want to be artisans. Education would make them discontent with their social place, without offering them a real possibility of professional mobility. This argument, deployed here largely against state involvement in trade education, was made by others with different implications. Some argued that the Ecole Boulle and schools like it were providing too much abstract knowledge and thereby not preparing workers for their role in life.

Not only would artisans leave the manual trades after having been to school, but the mere presence of schools would cause them to flee before ever setting foot in a workshop; trades that required schooling or a formal apprenticeship would soon disappear. And, should some children still be interested in learning in a trade, that too would be a poor thing, because they would certainly be rural children and thus schools would cause the depopulation of the countryside.[38]

Others argued in contrast that France needed well educated, highly skilled artisans, in order to ward off the evils of the rationalization and mechanization of labor and to maintain France's position at the head of the international luxury market. The schools were at once to provide protection for national markets and social insurance. The advantage of technical schools was that they could in fact train workers without educating them too much, without elevating them above their station. The overall quality of the workshop would be improved, and intellectual culture and manual skill were to be melded. Trade schools were the necessary accompaniment to the century: "One should make trade education the secondary education of those who will have their tools as a means of earning a living. In our century, starved of freedom, one must admit that the manual laborer is not inferior to the bureaucrat or the salesclerk." The goal of defending the trade against competition from abroad was also explicitly stated in the prospectus of the Ecole Boulle itself. "The goal of this school is to train able and educated workers, capable of maintaining the traditions of taste and the

37. Ibid.
38. Henry Girard, article in *La France*, 9 April 1895 (ibid.).

superiority of French industry."[39] Those fighting against state involvement in workers' education, therefore, were fighting a losing battle. But even when the battle over state responsibility for education had been won, the question remained of what kind of education that would be.

NEW DIRECTIONS: EDUCATING THE CITIZEN

> It's not only the worker who's assaulted in the apprentice, it's the man and the citizen. The habits of orderliness and work, the principles of morality that he brought from school, won't last long. . . . Deplorable school of morals, public as much as private, [apprenticeship] depraves the man in the apprentice, the citizen in the worker, and doesn't even train the worker.[40]

This 1872 comment to the prefect of the Seine from Octave Gréard, the inspector general of public instruction and director of primary education for the département of the Seine, was one of the earliest calls under the Third Republic for the state to replace apprenticeship within the shop by training in schools on the grounds of the need to educate the citizen as well as the worker. He was not alone in his call. The Ecole Boulle and other trade schools provoked so much controversy because much beyond the economic health of one industry was at stake. The question of public education and its content was understood to be central to the republic itself. What that education was to mean—and especially if all French citizens were to receive the same education—was the subject of intense debate. Some, as we have seen, remained unconvinced that the state should be in the education business at all. Others thought that it clearly should and that universal, obligatory, and free primary schooling was essential to the republic and furthermore that all children should receive the same schooling. Others, in contrast, agreed with universal, obligatory, and free schooling but thought it crucial that children of different classes receive different educations.

For example, the political economist Alfred Fouillée, who agreed with state-provided universal and free education argued energetically against *éducation intégrale*—that is, the same education for all—saying, "No socialist system of education can obliterate natural and social inequalities, nor can it make a pyramid stand on its point. Social justice is not a matter of turning society upside down to accomplish the impossible." He claimed

39. Roland, article in *Le Petit Journal,* 30 August 1895; Girard article; 7 July 1895 leaflet advertising Ecole Boulle competition (all in ibid.).

40. Octave Gréard, *Des écoles d'apprentis: mémoire addressé à M. le préfet de la Seine* (Paris, 1872), 5–6 and 17.

that providing all with the same education would create false expectations and disrupt the natural division of labor. "The common basis of education should be . . . basic knowledge of the functions of life in the human body, principles of hygiene, basics of morals and of political economy, the very simplest elements of civil and public law, notions of the constitution and of its workings." Liberal education was to be reserved for an elite, who "not being enslaved to a speciality, should pursue a general culture. . . . The object is to constitute an intellectual, literary, scientific, political, administrative elite, even more necessary to French democracy than to aristocratic monarchies that have their hereditary and artificial props."[41] Thus, in a rather elegant argument, Fouillée asserted that education differentiated by class was, despite appearances, the most appropriate system for a democracy dependent on a meritocratic elite.

The lawyer Alfred Lucet, in contrast, made an economic rather than a political argument. "There has been too much indulgence of inappropriate philosophical and social preoccupations. We have sacrificed the *worker* to the *citizen*." In reference to the public schools, like the Ecole Boulle, he declared that "children go there to learn a manual trade and not to carry off a useless baggage of badly learned bits of knowledge . . . they won't, after all, be literary critics, historians, or geographers; they should be good workers."[42] Lucet thought that young men destined to be factory laborers or artisans were not spending enough time in the shop and were spending too much time reading and thinking. He advocated the further separation of working-class students and bourgeois students into separate schools with separate programs. Working-class students were to learn to be workers, their education as citizens was to be left aside. As will be seen below, implicit in Lucet's argument was the separation of industrial art from fine art. Workers were to learn industrial art, concrete knowledge, pragmatic skill. Abstract knowledge, history, and theory were to be left to the bourgeois citizens. Lucet clearly found that by 1904 working-class students were being given a too civically minded education.

Most socialists did not agree. Gaston Cougny, for example, argued, "One does not educate the people by parsimoniously throwing to their intellect a small provision of canned notions, but by teaching them to . . . teach themselves . . . the citizen has the right to instruction, but that

41. Alfred Fouillée, *La France au point de vue moral*, 2d ed. (Paris, 1900), 205–6, 287, 306.
42. Alfred Lucet, *De l'apprentissage dans l'industrie* (Rennes, 1904), 122, 120; original emphasis.

right's not good for much when he doesn't have the ability [power]!"[43] Socialists Jean Jaurès, Théo Lefèvre, and Jules Renard all likewise made impassioned arguments not just for universal free education, but for uniform and equal education.

The staunch republican Edmond Bonnaffé made a similar argument in direct reference to the arts, but on nationalist grounds:

> If I had the honor to speak to a state that deigned to listen to me, it seems to me that I would say: "We agree on the principle, don't we? Art is one, all artists are of the same blood. Not nobility of the sword or the robe, nor plebeian. . . . [A]ll make up but one family, live in the same home, have the right to eat at the same table." In fact, today, the children are divided into two castes, and you support this division.[44]

Bonnaffé insisted that a split between an education for the fine arts and one for the applied arts was pernicious to both. Thus, in contrast to Lucet, he found that education was already too segregated by class. He noted that working-class students were being taught industrial art, while bourgeois students were taught fine art. The outcome was catastrophic for the students as well as for the decorative arts.

Although Bonnaffé did not explicitly mention education for citizenship, he did talk about the importance of the nation. His thesis was a profoundly nationalistic one—that the French should be unified in their Frenchness, should enjoy equal support from the state, and that unity should not be marred by divisions of class. The division of art into industrial and fine was both symbolic of a class division and created a class division. Bonnaffé went on to suggest the replacement of the schools divided between the fine and the industrial arts into ones in which "a large part will be devoted to the history of art. One will make the old masters known and understood, especially ours, those who practiced French art par excellence and whose work we can therefore best absorb because they were of the same flesh, the same blood, and the same territory as we are." Part of being properly French and taking advantage of France's past was to be imaginative and to learn from the past but not to emulate it. The students in his school were to know that "their first obligation is to make themselves a personality, to avoid at all costs the pastiches that dessicate the imagination and kill all initiative."[45]

43. Cougny, *L'enseignement professionnel*, 317.
44. Bonnaffé, *Etudes sur l'art*, 226.
45. Ibid., 227.

Some, like Charles Fonsegrive, put the case very starkly, stating that "it is the very essence of the Republic to provide an education for the mind, for the soul, of the citizen, that is to say for the voter whoever he may be. This is the only way the Republic can live and guarantee the continuity of national life." The urgency and need for public education was different under a republic than under a monarchy, according to Fonsegrive. "Under a hereditary monarchy in which there are only subjects and a king, only the king is a citizen, he alone needs to receive a spiritual education appropriate to his function . . . it is enough if his subjects are taught obedience . . . docility is their only civic virtue."[46] Although Fonsegrive's Catholicism emerges clearly in the language of souls and spirits, the fact that a Catholic activist should emphasize the importance of civic education in a republic only underscores how widespread such a perception was. In the eyes of many, the republic could not afford to have ill-educated voters. And, as all men could vote, all men needed an adequate education in politics and in civics, not just in manual labor.

Others, occupying a middle position, like Charles Gide, returned to the concept of "the social" to bridge the economic and political discourses, arguing for educations that could provide both a living and freedom for the worker: "the 'professional development' of the worker, [is] not exactly technical education, but that which allows the worker to earn his living and be a useful member of society and a free man." Gide added that people had to be taught to be "social" beings: "The Société pour l'éducation sociale has for its goal . . . the social education . . . of all citizens . . . that is, to create in us the social being." Being a "social being" meant "tak[ing] his share of his obligations and of the joys that civilization demands or gives to people 'of good society,' as one says."[47]

Whatever the particular position taken, this new government involvement was a result of a new definition of the locus of responsibility for social questions such as education and welfare, and of the expansion of industrialization and its transformation of labor. François Ewald identifies an epistemological shift in the late nineteenth century concerning the nature of responsibility in society, especially the responsibility for worker welfare.[48] As responsibility for certain classes of accidents was perceived to be no longer attributable to individuals, it was to be assumed by society at

46. Charles Fonsegrive, *La crise sociale* (Paris, 1901), 409, 410.
47. Charles Gide, "Economie sociale," in *Rapports du jury international: exposition internationale de 1900 à Paris*, ed. Ministère du commerce, de l'industrie, des postes et des télégraphes (Paris, 1903), 5:181, 198.
48. François Ewald, *L'état providence* (Paris, 1986).

large in the form of the state. French society, through its legal and legislative representatives, decided that industrialization brought benefits to society as a whole and its risks should thus be shared by the entire society.

THE FATE OF THE CULTURE OF PRODUCTION
IN A BOURGEOIS AGE

Until the mid-nineteenth century, the formal training of the young in the furniture trades had been largely controlled by the practitioners of those trades. By 1900, however, it appears that it was largely out of the hands of woodworkers, and under the responsibility of the state in the public trade schools or of the taste professionals in the private trade schools. Given the dominant role of private initiatives in the attempts to transform worker education in the mid-nineteenth century, the universal expositions stand out as one of the few, relatively noncontroversial early channels for state intervention in that process. By contrast, the more direct forms of state action—specifically public trade schools—sparked decades of controversy before being accepted as legitimate additional (and even dominant) means of reconfiguring the culture of production. Not only would these later state initiatives be more effective and pervasive, they also changed fundamentally and forever the traditional relation between politics and aesthetics, between the state and the everyday.

The traditional role had, of course, also involved the state in sustaining aesthetic innovations and the creation and reproduction of workers' knowledge, skill, and craft sense. During the Old Regime, the state had taken ultimate responsibility for the training of the young. The crown had controlled the statutes of the guilds—where many apprentices had been trained—and furthermore, the crown had supported an entire extraguild system of training and production (in the workshops of the Louvre and the Gobelins, as well as tacitly by granting exemption from guild regulation to the faubourg St-Antoine). The novelty of the role of the state in apprenticeship and training in the late nineteenth century was that it now became more directly involved through the creation of institutions explicitly intended for that purpose.

By the years just preceding the First World War, the state had a near-monopoly on the training of artisans; either young workers went to school and joined an artisanal elite, or they remained semiskilled workers all their lives. The most important issues raised by this change were, first, the different role of the state in the construction of the beautiful and, second, its role in the identification and separation of those workers in the industrial arts who were to receive knowledge from those who were to remain ignorant. Thus, as the state became more and more actively involved in establishing schools, examining teachers and imposing curricula, it became in some sense one of the panoply of interest groups involved in defining the beautiful and controlling knowledge.

The shift in the locus of control had some visible aesthetic consequences. If we compare the chef d'oeuvre of a compagnon, and the project of certification that gave apprentices their CAP—*certificat d'apprentissage professionnel*—we see that something had profoundly changed. The chefs d'oeuvre for the CAP were at the opposite end of the spectrum from the work of the compagnons. Just as the chefs d'oeuvre of the compagnons were full of humor, fantasy, invention, idiosyncrasy, and beauty, so the examination pieces eighty years later were serious, mundane, technical, and merely skillful. The format of the examination for the CAP was to build a set piece, for which one was given the measurements, materials, and a specific amount of time. There was no opportunity for creativity or fantasy. The only thing the artisan could demonstrate was that he had the skill to follow instructions. The alumni of the finest trade schools could do, and did do, more interesting things, but the corporation clearly no longer functioned in the same way. The trades had ceased to convey skill, knowledge, and craft sense—qualities exemplified in the chefs d'oeuvre—from one generation to the next. Whatever the rhetoric and dreams of the architects of the trade schools and whatever technical skills their students learned, innovation was moving away from the artisanal crafts and into the fine arts. The new designers—the innovators—of the twentieth century were to be artists who no longer worked with their hands.

More than a simple definitional change was at stake in the relocation of responsibility for aesthetic value in the French industrial arts. It was part of a realignment of the social order and signaled the emergence of new class distinctions in the nineteenth century. Furniture workers were increasingly perceived as uneducated and uncultured, incapable because of their class of transmitting aesthetic appreciation or creativity. In the late nineteenth century, the potential for creativity and aesthetic judgment was seen to reside in a small number of people of artisanal parentage who were to be trained in school. So, in addition to commercialization and mass consumerism, the judgment formed that the artisanal class had become atavistic and dysfunctional, leading to its subsequent redefinition as a working class lacking aesthetic capability but susceptible to receiving training in

376 / The Bourgeois Stylistic Regime

technical skill. All these changes helped reduce that culture to its final resting place in the Musée du compagnonnage, the Maison de l'outil et de la pensée ouvrière, and the Musée des arts et traditions populaires.[49]

The contested relation of the state to aesthetic matters also reflected fundamental changes in relations of power and how power might be deployed. The knowledge, skill, and craft sense so essential to the innovative powers of the worker-subject during the Old Regime appeared both necessary and threatening in the hands and minds of worker-citizens under a republican government. As we shall see, this was an antinomy that—in form at least—would appear on the consumption side as well. Lost then was not only the traditional culture of production, but the relations of social order—fragile though they were—that sustained a framework for both creativity and stability for the better part of a century. We need not harbor any nostalgic view of that ancien régime to appreciate the vulnerability of republican, putatively democratic orders, when confronted with similar tasks. Finally, the transformations in training belonged to the new industrialized commercialized world. Even had the artisanal structures of the Old Regime suited the new political world, they would have had great difficulty adapting to the new world of industrial capitalism.

49. These three museums all have as one stated goal the preservation of information concerning traditional work processes. The Maison de l'outil et de la pensée ouvrière, the most specialized and the most idiosyncratic, is funded by the state, the town of Troyes, and the compagnonnage; it consists of a collection of hand tools put together by a Jesuit priest and beautifully displayed in glass cases without explanation: the tools have been completely transformed into works of art. The Musée des arts et traditions populaires, in Paris, with the mission of presenting French folk art, has a large collection of furniture and tools, and a woodworker's shop open to visitors. The Musée du compagnonnage in Tours is largely of compagnons' masterpieces.

10

Style, the Nation, and the Market

The Paradoxes of Representation in a Capitalist Republic

 Living on the same soil, subject to the same climate, hearing the same voices, having the same examples before our eyes, receiving a common education from things and from men . . . we gradually form a common manner of feeling and reacting. Out of all these common things, we constitute an image or idea of the *patrie*.[1]

[S]hould there then be many "beautifuls," one beautiful for the rich, one beautiful for the bourgeois, one beautiful for the wageworker? Exactly. As paradoxical as this may seem, we are not afraid to write it. Or, at least, if there is only one beauty, its forms are infinite.[2]

When I enter a house for the first time and chance has it that I remain alone for a moment in the salon waiting for the mistress of the house, I know in advance her tastes, her mind, her education, and I would willingly say even her face, her figure, and physiognomy, just through inspection of the objects that surround me.[3]

These three statements capture the tensions surrounding the place of objects in the constitution of the French nation and society in the late nineteenth century. In the first, Charles Fonsegrive claimed that the French became a nation by being exposed to the same things. In fact, for Fonsegrive, that homogeneity of objects, of language, and of custom was crucial to assuring the stability and health of the state. In the second, an anonymous author for the magazine *L'art décoratif* argued for different forms of, even definitions of, beauty for each social class. In the third, Marie de Saverny remarked that the individual—her personality, her character, even

1. Fonsegrive, *La crise sociale*, 57.
2. J., "M. Félix Aubert," 158.
3. Marie de Saverny, *La femme chez elle et dans le monde* (Paris, 1876), 41–42.

her body—was reflected in, perhaps even constituted by, the goods she purchased. These three visions of the place of goods in late nineteenth-century France shared one assumption—that objects were critical to the construction of the social world. And they conflicted: was it the nation, the class, or the individual, or all three at once that the objects represented? The multiplicity of these discourses and their contradictions may be explained, at least in part, by the tension between the new republic's needs for symbolic unity and the capitalist economy's needs for maximum consumption. And somewhere between and betwixt those two issues were enduring questions of class and its representation.

The logic of French republicanism added further complexity to the task of finding a means of incarnating the French soul, of creating a new secular and republican patriotism. In French republicanism there was supposed to be only one French soul out of which would emanate one French style and one French taste, yet France consisted of regions and classes, each with its own styles and tastes. If there was to be a national style and taste, therefore, it would have to be produced because it was not being spontaneously generated. Furthermore, the Third Republic had a firm commitment to capitalist development, and capitalism, as a means and product of growth, tends to generate multiplicity and difference, not uniqueness and sameness. Paired with the increasing number and diversity of goods was the structure of display and advertising discussed in chapter 8, designed to persuade people that they wanted and needed these new things. Thus as the task of nation building encouraged the homogenization of style and taste, the market promoted their differentiation. Finally, the Third Republic's support of economic liberalism and the notion of the free market meant that the state could not counter the forces of the market by regulating the appearance of what was made or what was sold. The state could not mandate style. And yet since it was understood that the nation itself was made through its architecture, its art—in sum, its culture—and the unity of that culture was in the public interest, it was therefore a matter of state. For example, Genet-Delacroix traces one way the state attempted to resolve the contradiction between the free market and the national interest: it left contemporary artistic production to market forces while defining all works of art older than fifty years as part of the national patrimony and thus subject to state regulation. In the case of the patrimony, national interest overrode the right to property.[4]

4. Very relevant to these issues are Marie-Claude Genet-Delacroix, "Esthé-tique officielle et art national sous la Troisième République," *Le mouvement social* 131 (1985): 105–20; and Mainardi, *The End of the Salon*, chap. 1.

The task of balancing the need to make homes "French" with respecting the freedom of the market proved more difficult to accomplish. The problem of a national style was so ubiquitous in contemporary discourse because of its salience in a period following a major military defeat, the creation of the first long-lived republic, and the economic problems of the 1880s.

This matter of national taste and style was energetically addressed by the taste professionals whose efforts to influence the education and taste of workers were discussed in the last chapter. The taste professionals employed directly by the state and the authors of etiquette books, decorating magazines, and design books hoped to encourage the public to acquire good French taste and therefore purchase furniture in a soon-to-be-devised national style. There was, naturally, disagreement as to means. Some insisted that private initiative was needed, while others, following in the comte de Laborde's heritage, argued for more intensive and direct state involvement.

In fact, if the taste of bourgeois consumers was to be addressed effectively at all, it had to happen as much through the private sphere as through the public because direct state intervention into what was defined as the private sphere—that is economic relations including production, distribution, and consumption—had long been understood to be of problematic legitimacy. State intervention to improve the conditions of children's (and women's) lives at the workplace contradicted the principles of political economy but based its acts on children's (and women's) status as minorities who could not negotiate as free agents. By the end of the century, moreover, state intervention into the conditions of adult male labor cited the grounds of changing definitions of responsibility for industrial production in a mature capitalist economy. State administration of schools, museums, and libraries, while still controversial, was also usually agreed to be necessary. But after the Revolution of 1789 no regime could claim power to enforce the purchase or the production of certain items or a certain style.

The problem of the inappropriateness of intervention into the home and consumption had been resolved to some extent by the notion of the social and even more powerfully by the attribution to women of responsibility for the home. Since women's fully adult status was by no means established in this period, the heavy hand of advice, when addressed to women, even bourgeois women, would be more acceptable than when addressed to bourgeois men, but it was still necessarily a matter of persuasion and not legislation. Consumers laboring under the weight of advice literature and advertising aimed at gender and class position, not at abstract national interest, had to be convinced that it was in their personal and private interest to acquire certain items. Thus the efforts to persuade consumers tended, insofar as they were nationalistic at all, to be phrased in terms of participation in France's glorious history and tradition of creative production. For example, bourgeois consumers were told that they could be like the kings of the Old Regime if only they would stop buying pastiche of the king's furniture and emulate his support of innovation.[5] The taste professionals worked through museums, universal expositions, libraries, decorating guides, etiquette books, and magazines, and to a lesser extent, schools, in their efforts to improve the taste of the consumers. Although the taste professionals often disagreed with one another and engaged in fierce debate, they systematically, if individually, asserted their legitimacy in the face of new claims to aesthetic authority on the part of the distributors, for they were not the only voices in this discussion of taste and style. The distributors, whose expanded role was discussed in chapter 8, were their powerful interlocutors.

Although not motivated by the same preoccupations, the numerous distributors had an equally strong interest in style and taste in interior decoration. But the distributors' explicit project was to sell as much furniture as possible, both at home and abroad. What that furniture looked like, what it represented, what style it was—these were secondary concerns. The main vehicle of expression for the distributors was advertising, and they would say in those advertisements whatever they thought would help their goods to sell. The satisfaction and challenge in selling came largely from the act itself and from the gain it produced. Changing the taste of consumers to influence the moral order of society was not their dominant preoccupation. They did use the language of taste in their advertisements, however, because that language was the language of authority. In many ways, the taste professionals and distributors embodied the conflicts between the nation and the market that produced so many of the paradoxical relations between taste and power in the bourgeois stylistic regime.

REPUBLICANISM, AND THE GENDERED LABOR OF FORGING THE NATION

Efforts to influence consumers' taste through the middle years of the nineteenth century had focused on its importance as a means of class

---

5. Many of these same commentators were often brutally critical of the new styles born in this period—*style moderne* and *art nouveau*—finding them to be the epitome of bad taste, evil exaggerations of Louis XV style. How truly interested in innovation the taste professionals were remains open to question.

formation, and the impact of consumers' taste on the national economy. In the Third Republic, taste was seen as having yet an additional purpose—internalizing the nation. As early as 1846 Jules Michelet articulated this position in *Le peuple*, arguing first of all for the unity of France: "It is at the moment when France has suppressed all the divergent Frances that lie within her breast that she has given her high and original revelation." This unity was largely produced in the everyday and by means of commodities: "In this great body of a nation . . . [a] certain idea enters through the eyes (fashion, shops, museums, etc.), another through conversation, through the language that is the grand depository of common progress. All receive the thinking of all, perhaps without analyzing it, but they nonetheless receive it."[6] According to Michelet, it was in the small unnoticed moments of life that the nation itself was unconsciously made.

Fifty years later Alfred Fouillée, in one of many texts echoing those sentiments, argued that being French meant sharing certain common attributes, certain styles, certain modes of dress. In making this argument, however, Fouillée worried about the same accusations as César Daly had earlier—that by advocating a single national taste he would produce mediocrity. Fouillée attempted to avoid this by making a distinction between originality of intellect, or genius, and originality of the everyday, or eccentricity. "[A] nation gradually puts its mark on all individuals; those who move too far away from the common type . . . [the] eccentrics . . . risk not succeeding and not founding a family, in which case their posterity will quickly be extinguished. . . . It is not that France rejects real originality—that of merit and intelligence—but that originality must, in some senses, seek forgiveness, by preserving, in exterior manners, in language, in clothing, in conformity in the style of life." This conformity was necessary because it was through "appearances common to everyone that all recognize themselves in others."[7] The nation was thus to be built through a logic of at least superficial sameness and recognition, through commodities and manners. For the nation to hold, all citizens had to identify with other citizens, yet room had to be made for individual genius. In some senses then, Fouillée invoked the legitimacy of individual difference in the sphere of production, but not in the domain of consumption and the everyday. Tellingly, parallel arguments invoked women's engagement in matters of beauty, for it was up to women to train French citizens to have the French

6. Jules Michelet, *Le peuple* (Paris, 1946), 231, 233 n.2.
7. Alfred Fouillée, *Esquisse psychologique des peuples européens*, 3d ed. (Paris, 1903), 470–71.

manners, tastes, and habits that would allow them to recognize each other and would allow them to—beneath that conformity of the everyday—exercise individual genius.

The domestic sphere was, thus, seen as essential to the making of citizens, not only through education as it is usually understood but through the objects by which the child was surrounded, the food the child ate, and the language the child spoke. Given dominant contemporary understandings of women's domestic role, this emphasis on the domestic necessarily gave women a crucial role in the making of the nation. As the Catholic theorist Charles Fonsegrive put it in 1901, "even women, who in our constitution do not enjoy the right to vote should nonetheless be given an education in civics, because they are the presumed mothers of the citizens of the future, educators born of citizens, they should have the souls of citizens." The reason it was so important that women have the souls of citizens was that a republic, unlike a monarchy, needed to instill its values in the very hearts of its citizens. For "a monarchy can be satisfied, if necessary, with material obedience, with the exterior discipline of the movements of the body, for the national organism has one soul, that of the king, and that soul, if necessary, can suffice. But a republic cannot live without a spiritual discipline, a voluntary acceptance, an acquiescence of the spirit that supports the domination of law . . . the spirit of a republican nation must be diffused throughout the social body. There is a republican spirit and it matters to the greatest degree that all the citizens possess it."[8] Fonsegrive understood that it was in the home, through the small gestures and objects by which the child was surrounded, that this "spiritual discipline" and "voluntary acceptance" could best be inculcated. A sense of the nation, of one's belonging in the nation had to be instilled at every moment, even in the most private spaces of the domestic sphere.

This sentiment was not entirely new in the late nineteenth century; rather it represented the maturing of earlier republican themes. Its earliest manifestation had been during the Revolution and First Republic, and it reappeared in republican discourse shortly before the Revolution of 1848, and then again during the Second Republic. For example, Michelet in his 1846 text constructed patriotism as it was to be taught to a child in a dialogue first with his mother, then with his father. The mother said, "You love me, you know only me . . . well, listen, I'm not all. You have another mother . . . we all . . . have a gentle mother, a mother who nourishes us always, invisible and present. Let us love her, dear child, embrace her from

8. Fonsegrive, *La crise sociale*, 440–41.

the heart." This other, mystical, transcendent mother who the child must be taught to recognize and love, was France. Later, when the boy was older, Michelet had his father take him to a city, presumably Paris, on a day of public festival. First they visited the monuments, then they watched a military parade. "See, my child, see: there is France, there is the *patrie*! There are many [soldiers], but they are as one. Same soul, same heart. All would die for one, and each must also live and die for all . . . they go to fight for us. They leave here their father, their old mother, who need them. . . . You will do as much, you will never forget that your mother is France."[9]

Thus, Michelet insisted, children needed to learn that loyalty to the nation came before loyalty to their region, their class, and even their own families. Love for one's mother country did not just come into existence naturally, however, it had to be taught. Michelet distinguished between the different kinds of nationalism taught by mothers and by fathers; France was the fatherland, but it was also mother of all. Fathers brought their sons into the nation by showing them the monuments, the public civic holidays, by telling them about their military obligations; mothers brought their sons into the nation by teaching them about nature, about commonality, about love. Women were essential to the new republic in their role as *producers* of the domestic symbolic nation. But women were also important to the economy as *consumers*, and the tasks—consuming and nation making— were not always easy to combine. Further complicating the story were crosscutting discourses about the role of consumption in fashioning the nation and the class, and its role in representing the self.

Taste professionals and distributors, although they would divide on other matters, united in constructing women as incompetent in these essential, and intimately linked, tasks of society- and family-building. Taste professionals and distributors both, therefore, rushed to provide instruction. Taste professionals and distributors insisted emphatically on the importance of the home in sustaining the moral qualities of the family, and implicitly society itself, for it was at home that the social order was constructed. For example Mme Hennequin in a book published in 1912 asked, "isn't the question of the home one of the many sides of the question of happiness? It's around the home, if one has thought about making it what it should be to fulfill its function, that family ties will form. The influence of the home is immense, and broader than one can say. It is moralizing, or else it is depressing and demoralizing when the home is not

9. Michelet, *Le peuple*, 263–64.

harmonious." Taste professionals and the distributors also agreed that it was up to women to decorate the home. As one advice book put it, "the home . . . occupies such a large place in life . . . that it deserves to always be taken into serious consideration, especially by a woman, for whom it is the prison, or rather the nest, to use a less harsh expression."[10]

Advertising discourses chimed in, sometimes brutally, with characterizations of bourgeois women's place in the household and their need for advice to properly enact their task. As the newly engaged young woman visited the expensive store, Cerf, she was urged (though tired and disoriented) to "think about her living arrangements, an important act, because the happiness of a life depends upon the comfort of the home." The implication of this advertisement, that the happiness of the couple depended largely on the wisdom of the young woman in her choice of decor, was a theme to be found not only in advertisements, but throughout the discussion of women's role. Part of why the home was so important was that it consolidated the family living within it and represented the family to the outside world. As Mme la comtesse Drohojowska put it, "We won't pay much attention to the salon and the dining room, precisely because given the very nature of their usage, and their importance from the point of view of representation, I am sure that they have already attracted all of your attention."[11]

Finally, some distributors and taste professionals emphasized the fetishization of goods by saying that an individual's happiness (and her husband's) depended not only on the good taste and comfort with which she furnished her home, but that it was also destined to be her "most intimate and faithful friend." But in order for furniture to really become a friend, "in order for it to attract and retain [one's affection] as much as the dear people living among it, it is important to know how, with the help of pleasant and likable [*sympathique*] decoration, to create a loving and soft atmosphere."[12] According to this ad, therefore, objects could be animate, loyal, and faithful but only if one had expert assistance in choosing them. If one chose one's furniture friends badly, presumably they could be malevolent and destructive. The consumer needed help.

    10. Mme Hennequin, *L'art et le goût au foyer* (Paris, 1912), 7; Mme de l'Alq, *Le maître et la maîtresse de la maison* (Paris, 1888), 14.
    11. BHVP 120, ameub. C, Cerf, [n.d.]; Antoinette Drohojowska, *Conseils à une jeune fille sur les devoirs à remplir dans le monde comme maîtresse de maison à Paris*, 4th ed. (Paris, [1870?]), 206.
    12. BHVP 120, ameub. Gouffé, [ca. 1910]. See a remarkably similar comment in Maillou, "Causeries sur le mobilier," 139.

The taste professionals and the distributors united to persuade the consumers that objects mattered, that taste mattered, that women were responsible for both, and that women needed help in dealing with both. But they also diverged, both because they were in competition and, more seriously, because aside from a joint interest in matters of furniture and taste their interests were different and they perceived their roles to be different.

FASHION VERSUS TASTE:
BETWEEN THE MARKET AND THE NATION

> We have too many machines and too many newspapers; that is what
> kills art in France and certainly the most useful of arts, that of furnish-
> ing, source of joy, of poetry, of union, treasure of the masses.[13]

Distributors did not, by and large, express disappointment or unhappiness in their consumers' taste. They warned the consumers that they needed advice but assured them that with advice, they could have tasteful homes. Most of the taste professionals, in contrast, perceived a crisis in taste for which the consumers were in part responsible or to which, at any rate, the only possible response was to change the consumers' taste.

The taste professionals saw three great interrelated problems plaguing the Parisian furniture industry in the second half of the nineteenth century: the first was the lack of a properly nineteenth-century style; the second was the poor quality of affordable furniture; the third was the reluctance of wealthy consumers to buy new designs. As we have seen, the taste professionals' efforts to revive and renew the industry were addressed to producers and consumers alike. They understood the interactive nature of the problem. The producers clearly would not make furniture that the consumers refused to buy, and the consumers could not buy furniture that did not exist.

While a very large contingent of the taste professionals (although not all) attacked consumers' taste for Old Regime–style furniture, the distributors were largely silent on that matter. The distributors rarely wrote anything critical about Old Regime style, and although they might suggest that Henri II style was ideal for a dining room, they would never say that a Louis XVI–style dining room was indicative of bad taste. The taste professionals' position on the topic was more complex. Many would in one breath condemn all use of ancien régime style and then spend many pages giving very precise and restricted codifications of which historicist pastiche

13. Noussane, *Le goût dans l'ameublement*, 16.

styles and which woods were appropriate for particular consumers, rooms, locations. On the one hand, the taste professionals were pragmatic—historicist pastiche was what people were buying and the experts would therefore express their opinion concerning how it should best be used. On the other, they called for a new, appropriate, national style, yet most profoundly disliked what innovation they did see. *Style moderne* and *art nouveau* were roundly condemned and deemed to have not solved the taste crisis of the fin de siècle.

Therefore, according to the taste professionals, women were not only to keep their husbands happy, ensure the future, and appropriately represent the social position of their families, they were to support the renaissance of French taste and style as well. In fact, according to the taste professionals, only if they served their nation through the consumption of French taste could they accomplish these other missions. But what was French taste? There were many opinions. Camille Cardelle, for example, asserted with confidence that "Plumet's art is thoroughly French because it is made of clarity and logic . . . the forms [are] . . . of a frankly French character." Some implicitly defined French taste by contrasting it to that of other nations. Thus, the marquis de Rochambeau, after visiting the exhibit of American furniture at the universal exhibition of 1876 in Philadelphia was sure that America would never represent serious competition to the French because "the qualities they lack are in flagrant opposition to their character, it will, consequently, be more difficult for them to acquire them."[14] By making French taste different from American, critics minimized differences among French tastes. But the old dilemma was back: if national taste sprang naturally from the people's breasts, if it was an emanation of national character, then it should not be multiple, for that would mean that there was more than one France.

Furthermore, if taste was the inevitable and natural emanation of national character it need not be (and perhaps could not be) taught or purchased: "You are too good a French woman to think you've fulfilled your duty by simply giving a lot of money and a free hand to a decorator. American women do that willingly—it's so convenient! But you are certainly enough behind the times to prefer your *home* [in English in the text]

14. Camille Cardelle, "Charles Plumet, architecte," *L'art décoratif* 5 (February 1899): 203; le marquis de Rochambeau, "Ameublement et objets d'un usage général dans les constructions et les appartements," *Exposition internationale et universelle de Philadelphia, 1876* (Paris, 1877), 201.

to the most luxurious of furnished hotels."[15] In order to have good French taste, one had to possess it, not rent it or buy it or even be taught it.

Several commentators attempted to circumvent this problem by pointing out that taste had always been taught just as seeds had always been tended to encourage their growth. Providing instruction in taste was analogous to watering a seedling. "Doesn't good taste grow spontaneously on French soil? Yes, it is an indigenous plant, but one which, nevertheless needs cultivation in order to bear its delicate fruit."[16] Thus education in taste could be reconfigured as nurturing an existing quality rather than implanting a new one.

The taste professionals had access to a wide array of resources through which to educate the consumers. Some of those media carried with them the legitimizing cover of the state—the museums, libraries, universal expositions. Others, like etiquette books, enveloped themselves with authority and neutrality through endorsements of unimpeachable (especially religious) figures. Yet others, including the decorating magazines and books, claimed authority through elaborate and scholarly formats.

Despite the problem posed by the belief in innate, national taste, the taste professionals most often acted as if they thought that good taste was learnable, unlike the distributors, who hoped to keep consumers dependent on their expertise, rather than inculcate in them autonomous good taste. As long as consumers doubted their own judgments, it was easier to persuade them to buy more often and more expensively. The taste professionals, because they were teaching morality and even citizenship through taste, hoped—at least in principle—that the consumers would internalize tastefulness. Taste professionals often asserted that certain groups—especially bourgeois women—had more inherent good taste than other groups, but everyone could, to some extent or another, learn good taste. Besides the more passive means of acquiring taste, that is looking at tasteful objects on display in museums and universal expositions, a more active way was through education. No schools to train consumers arose to parallel those for artisans, yet schooling was not absent from the experts' efforts to improve buyers' taste. Learning how to draw would improve one's taste, they thought; drawing courses "would raise the general level of taste, because they produce on the one hand more skillful producers and

15. Landemer, *Le carnet de fiançailles;* see also Noussane, *Le goût dans l'ameublement,* 191.
16. Noussane, *Le goût dans l'ameublement,* 241–42.

on the other more intelligent and delicate consumers."[17] Drawing was to effectively link producers and consumers so that France could become more tasteful.

This concern with the teaching of drawing led gradually to the creation of drawing courses. Some were planned for women, in other cases bourgeois women attended the courses that had been intended for artisans. The popularity of the drawing courses indicates that the taste professionals were not exerting a simply coercive force on women but providing a service that they appreciated, or at least used.

Taste professionals working through the private sector had an ally in the state. Their mission of creating tasteful consumers was in perfect accord with the general cultural model of the time. Primary education became compulsory for both sexes under the Third Republic, but boys and girls were not provided identical educations in the public schools. The basic curriculum was the same, Linda Clark explains, but they were taught in separate classrooms with separate textbooks. Textbooks consistently provided models of married women who were creating tasteful, clean, and attractive interiors. Their clear message was that the primary tasks for women, of whatever social class, were domestic.[18]

The insistence in girls' education on the feminine arts appears to have been duplicated in the private, often Catholic, schools to which bourgeois girls were sent after being tutored at home or going to public primary school. The comtesse Jean de Pange, born in 1888, complained vigorously that her education was too preoccupied with matters of taste and not enough with other issues. In her memoirs Edmée Renaudin cited the way her teachers phrased their frustration with their charges: "Those days we were, she said, girls 'without taste'—that was a serious insult."[19] These efforts to guide girls toward their role as tasteful homemakers through education were not the only public efforts to mold consumers' taste. The universal expositions of the second half of the nineteenth century not only influenced production, functioned as advertising for distributors, and provided a forum for artisans to express their interests but also both entertained and educated consumers. They were immensely popular events, and we can safely imagine that the goods on display there were looked at, even if they were not later purchased. They provided a showcase for both the

17. Brongniart, "De l'enseignement du dessin en 1867," 13:402.
18. Linda L. Clark, *Schooling the Daughters of Marianne* (Albany, N.Y., 1984), chaps. 2 and 3.
19. Pange, *Comment j'ai vu 1900*, 216; Renaudin, *Edmée au bout de la table*, 196.

finest and the most economical of the industrial arts and in many ways mirrored the new techniques of distribution. Their proponents hoped to persuade wealthy consumers to support avant garde, or at least non-pastiche, furniture and lead less wealthy consumers to buy furniture that was durable and appropriate to their position in life.

The taste professionals also created museums of the decorative and fine arts to influence the taste of consumers. The idea of the founders of late nineteenth-century museums was that producers and consumers would visit them and become educated; the producers were not to make reproductions of what they saw, the consumers were not to seek out copies or antiques. Both producers and consumers were to acquire good taste through the mere example of the works behind glass.

Printed texts expanded the consumers' education beyond classrooms, museums, and exhibits at the universal expositions: magazines, books on interior decoration, and etiquette books. The taste professionals writing in books and magazines were often the same as those involved in the schools, universal expositions, and museums—architects, large and successful furniture manufacturers, and interior decorators—and generally had a direct, occupational interest in aesthetics and design. The etiquette-book writers were moralists, popular novelists, or socialites. As a group, therefore, the taste professionals were riven with fractions and factions, each with its own interests. Consequently, consumers and producers were caught in the intersection of a multiplicity of discourses, each making an exclusive claim to legitimacy and authority.

Decorating books and magazines were a form of prescriptive literature produced by a subgroup of taste professionals with particular objectives. Books on decorating addressed a feminine audience, as etiquette books did. Unlike other advice books, most decorating books spoke very explicitly and without shame only to the wealthiest consumers but their readership probably included other groups.[20] For one 1898 classic, Edouard Bajot's *Du choix et de la disposition des ameublements de style*, the intended readership included architects, decorators, *tapissiers*, manufacturers, artists, and *amateurs* (enthusiasts). This book provided two hundred detailed drawings and photographs of twenty complete rooms. Other books were similar in format to the pattern books discussed in chapter 8. A crucial difference, however, is that books intended primarily for consumers never discussed the technical aspects of the furniture; they did not analyze the joints, they did not provide cross sections of the wood frame, they did not

20. Noussane, *Le goût dans l'ameublement*, 185.

break down the construction costs. Consumers were not understood to need such details. The emphasis in the books intended for consumers was on ensembles rather than individual pieces, on arranging rather than building or purchasing. Their domain was taste, which was a matter of convention much more than it was one of art or creativity.

Decorating and fashion magazines were not novelties of the late nineteenth century. The *Journal des dames et des modes,* for example, had been in print since the late eighteenth century. But the number of magazines specializing in decoration did increase as the nineteenth century progressed. The intended public of these magazines varied from *Revue des arts décoratifs,* which was read as much by architects and decorators as by consumers, to other magazines read almost exclusively by the latter group. Magazines included articles not dissimilar to the etiquette books, instructing young women how to decorate their new homes. They were clearly somewhat more fashion-bound because of their ephemeral nature and lighter approach to moral instruction. Decorating magazines took as their task the providing of illustrations of how one's home could look, what the new fashions in decoration were, and what new objects, colors, and furniture had been developed. The development of magazines equivalent to *Better Homes and Gardens* was much later, generally following the First World War.[21]

Etiquette books had also existed since early in the nineteenth century, although they too became more numerous and more specific in their advice as the century wore on.[22] As social mobility became increasingly possible and as consumption became more anonymous, etiquette books self-consciously and explicitly gave their female readers advice on how to accomplish their tasks as wives and mothers and cope with the seemingly chaotic world. Generally, the writers of etiquette books, whether they were advising fashionable young socialites or Catholic housewives intent on a serene household, asserted their neutrality and good will in opposition to the evil intentions of the merchandisers. However seriously their readers took these books, the intentions of their authors were clear.

21. See *Moniteur de l'ameublement,* 1863–68; *Album de l'ameublement,* 1882–92; *Art et décoration,* 1897–; *Revue des arts décoratifs,* 1880–1902; *L'art pour tous,* 1861–1905; *Intérieur,* 1911–12. For more modern magazines see *Maison et jardin,* 1945–; *Maison française,* 1945–; *La demeure française,* 1925–29; *Jardin des arts,* 1945–; *Plaisir de France,* 1934–.
22. The extant etiquette books from the nineteenth century number in the hundreds, of which this is a sampling, and a very interesting source—the only ones in which taste professionals are women. The books are very redundant but, as the discussion indicates, vary to some extent with the social position of the author.

They became guides on how to live and entertain successfully; the authors, and presumably the readers, concentrated first on how to catch and keep a husband. Once the couple was established, the next task was to fit into a particular subgroup of the petite, middling, or haute bourgeoisie. The decoration of the home was defined as central to the task of keeping a husband at home and of being accepted into one's desired social group. Many writers encouraged their readers to look at their decorating tasks as a means of self-expression as well. Most authors had firm opinions concerning what the home ought to look like and the role of the woman in creating that home.

In sum, different groups of taste professionals thus tried to establish their authority and convince consumers of the validity of their perspectives through different uses of this range of institutions and media. The discussions of taste through printed materials all put more stress on combining and arranging and caring for furniture than on assessing the furniture's underlying qualities, but the emphases did vary with the media. In drawing courses, for example, the taste professionals were trying to instill not simply their own notions of good taste but what they defined as the fundamental components of good taste. Through the museums they were trying to teach by example. In the universal exposition exhibits and in the etiquette books, decorating books and magazines, they were simply trying to impose their vision. The strategies chosen depended to some extent on the class of consumer being addressed. Etiquette books, decorating magazines, museums, and drawing courses were generally intended for a bourgeois audience. The universal expositions, which had separate exhibits for wealthy and poor consumers, alone addressed working-class consumers. Whatever their strategy or intent, most of these efforts centered on lengthy discussions of taste; what good taste was, who had it, and how one could acquire it.

There was much else that the experts concerned about taste could not agree on. Taste professionals emphasized that tasteful interiors could be acquired with little money. "In the decoration of a dwelling, it is neither the richness nor the magnificence of the furniture that reveals to the observer the character of the person who lives there—her pure and distinguished taste, her qualities, her virtues; it is rather the disposition and care of the furnishings that are revealing."[23] The distributors, especially the less expensive ones, did sometimes assert that even the less wealthy could have a tasteful interior, but they not surprisingly tended to emphasize the

23. De l'Alq, *Le maître et la maîtresse de la maison,* 122; see also Hennequin, *L'art et le goût au foyer,* 69.

importance of replacing furniture. In contrast, the taste professionals insisted that the woman of the house, if she did not aspire to a station above her own and bought intelligently, could always create a place of beauty. In this age of the mass masculine vote, the tastefulness of all was newly important. Issues of class peace and the social order were still very present but added to them was the issue of a shared Frenchness.

Consequently, as in the case of efforts to influence the training of artisans during the second half of the century, institutional attempts to convert the consumers had a dual trajectory. In one group were the fervent believers in private initiative, in the other were those arguing for state intervention. The strongest group on the side of private initiative was the Union centrale des arts décoratifs, which proclaimed itself to be pursuing "two fundamental ideas, one principle of doctrine—the unity of art; one principle of action—the appeal to private initiative." Its journal was forceful in stating that furnishings touch "most closely the well-being of each person, his life, and his needs," and therefore it would educate the public in good taste. "How many people, confident of their personal taste, imagine that they don't need a guide, while they don't even suspect the barbarisms of which they are innocently guilty! The set of studies that one will find in the *Revue des arts décoratifs* will soon, we are convinced, persuade even the most skeptical on this matter."[24]

Advocates of public action stressed the importance of the universal expositions and of museums. The debate concerning the role of the state in shaping the taste of consumers was, however, less vigorous than that concerning the producers, perhaps because the purchasing life of the bourgeoisie was beyond official control. Although many aspects of private and even intimate life of all classes were regulated by the Napoleonic civil code and subsequent law, and practices of distribution could be legislated by zoning and closing laws, the Third Republic could not legislate what style of furniture citizens were to buy, what clothing they were to wear, or how to prepare their food. Consumption was not a skill like production, to be taught in school—the various school-based programs described above notwithstanding. The taste professionals thus sought to "shake public indifference with respect to the applied arts and to enlighten its taste."[25] Even with a clear idea of their goals, the experts were not at all certain how much influence they had over consumers. Even the typically confident, if not

24. Champier, "Le pavillon," 75; Champier, "La maison modèle," 20.
25. Champier, "La maison modèle," 54.

arrogant, Union centrale des arts décoratifs had doubts on the matter: "Will the Union centrale, which has made such successful efforts to stimulate the zeal of the producers, have enough power to direct the taste of the clientele in a more truly artistic direction? Will the Union be able to exert on the public an analogous action to that which it has already used on the schools and in all questions of teaching—that's what we could not say."[26]

By contrast, late nineteenth-century distributors had access to a new variety of media with which to persuade people to buy, and to buy from them rather than a competitor. Sometimes mischievously or ironically, they found ways to outdo their more respectable rivals in matters of taste. Distributors mimicked the graphic repertoire of the taste professionals' magazines and books; they copied their display techniques; they made overt claims to expertise in taste; and they even borrowed the most sacred names of the taste professionals' institutions, like the Louvre, to christen a department store.

By the 1880s pamphlets and catalogues hawking the wares of the larger or more luxurious stores were usually in color, sometimes on paper of very fine quality, and often very verbose. Pamphlets could and often did go on for pages, defining good taste, good value, women's appropriate role in life, or what a young man's room should look like (see Figures 65 and 66). Nor was the telling of moral tales and parables confined to advertisements for expensive furniture, although it occurred more frequently there.[27] By producing treatises on good taste as advertisements, as the maison Roll did in its ad in Figure 67, the distributors narrowed the gap between themselves and the taste professionals.

Although the advertising of distributors emphasized the importance of good taste in the furnishing of a home, distributors, unlike the taste professionals, only hinted at a definition of good taste. The decoration was supposed to be "sympathique et agréable" and it is clear that comfortableness and good taste were not necessarily synonymous, but there was little real precision. In contrast, the following advertisement expressed a very clear judgment as to the content of good taste, reflecting the distributors' ability to compete with the taste professionals. "The ensembles of modern furniture that I have the honor of suggesting to you were conceived by me, with a sincere and thoughtful attention, following the strictest laws

26. René Ménard, "Rapports des jurys: rapport du jury du premier groupe—le bois," *Revue des arts décoratifs* 3 (1882–83): 80.
27. See for example the advertisements from the Ville d'Aboukir from the 1880s (BHVP 120, ameub. V).

Figure 65.   Advertisement for an *art nouveau*–style
woman's bedroom. Presented in contrast with the
eighteenth-century bedroom in Figure 66. BHVP 120,
ameub., Mercier.

of reason and of good taste . . . GOOD TASTE, by the elegance of the form
of my furniture, elegance that, owing to the simplicity of the lines, com-
plements the sober harmony of my ensembles."[28] Such ads, together with
the long elaborate pamphlets, reinforced the authority and legitimacy of
the distributor as an arbiter of taste and could, at first glance at least, hold
their own when placed next to a learned article in the *Revue des arts
décoratifs*.

Not only did the distributors emulate the taste professionals in their
naming and display practices, but also in the forms of their advertising. For
example, ads from the inexpensive store la Ville d'Aboukir used the strategy of telling a rather unbelievable story with the moral that buying

28. BHVP 120, ameub. literie, M, 1902, exposition et vente, 10 rue Lacrée, 12th
arr.—soixante ans de lis et roses.

Figure 66. Reproduction of an eighteenth-century print used in an advertisement to narrow the gap between taste professionals and distributors. BHVP 120, ameub., Mercier.

furniture appropriate to one's station (and therefore not needing credit), being patient, and gradually working one's way to a more luxurious position in life is the best strategy. "I had the opportunity to sell my furniture at a profit and then furnish my place luxuriously. My boss, paying me a visit, was overwhelmed by my rich installation and found nothing better, to complete the story, than to confide to me the happiness of his daughter and direction of his factory. Despite all of that, I will never forget that I owe my entire fortune and my happiness to the Ville d'Aboukir."[29] Such long tales mimicked the taste professionals' discourses. The moralizing tone and the idea of the importance of buying goods appropriate to one's class was a leaf out of the taste professionals' book, as was the use of long anecdotes to make one's point.

29. BHVP 120, ameub. V, Ville d'Aboukir.

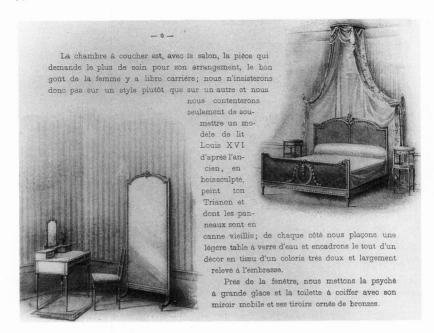

— 6 —

La chambre à coucher est, avec le salon, la pièce qui demande le plus de soin pour son arrangement, le bon goût de la femme y a libre carrière; nous n'insisterons donc pas sur un style plutôt que sur un autre et nous nous contenterons seulement de soumettre un modèle de lit Louis XVI d'après l'ancien, en bois sculpté, peint ton Trianon et dont les panneaux sont en canne vieillie; de chaque côté nous plaçons une légère table à verre d'eau et encadrons le tout d'un décor en tissu d'un coloris très doux et largement relevé à l'embrasse.

Près de la fenêtre, nous mettons la psyché à grande glace et la toilette à coiffer avec son miroir mobile et ses tiroirs ornés de bronzes.

Figure 67.   Part of a pamphlet from maison Roll. BHVP 120, ameub., Roll.

The distributors even learned to emulate the museum techniques pioneered by the taste professionals. "All that concerns Chinese and Japanese art is exhibited, offered, classified, and catalogued in the luxurious stores of M. Rouillier, . . . displayed with an art that only M. Rouillier possesses . . . under the fire of electric light."[30] Here the point was not the yearlong availability of the goods that some of the department stores offered, but the fact that all objects relating to one category—Asian art—were to be found in one location. But not only were they to be found in one place; once there, M. Rouillier exhibited, offered, classified, catalogued, and displayed them (with art) under electric lighting.

In reading this advertisement, consumers saw rise before them, unbidden, the contrasting image of a bazaar or a flea market, where all sorts of exotic treasures were heaped untidily, waiting to be discovered by the assiduous collector. In M. Rouillier's store, the exotic was tamed, murky corners were banished, the whole scene illuminated by the magic (but

30. BHVP 120, ameub. N–R, M. Rouillier, 1895, [newspaper clipping], 8 boulevard des Capucines, 9th arr.; BHVP 120, ameub. D, Dauphin, [n.d.], [magazine clipping], Meubles anciens et objets d'art, 334 rue St-Honoré, 8th arr.

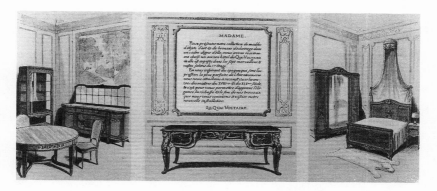

Figure 68. Advertisement for maison Barabas, 1911. BHVP 120, ameub., Barabas.

scientific, rational magic) of electricity. Prospective customers were transported to the simulacrum of a museum, a museum where the goods were for sale, but a museum nonetheless.

Another advertisement addressed to women left aside modernity and electricity to return to prerevolutionary Paris. M. Barabas suggested preindustrial aristocratic luxury in his boutique, housed in a restored eighteenth-century *hôtel*. The furniture and other objects there were to be presented in a context worthy of *them*, not of the consumer (Figure 68). Dauphin made the resemblance explicit in saying that "his stores constitute a veritable museum."[31] Another version of that strategy was to give a store the name of a museum. Thus the Louvre became a department store, one whose very name provoked complaints from some taste professionals. One critic told an anecdote about how his daughters had expressed great enthusiasm about going to the Louvre, an enthusiasm he cheerfully shared until he realized that they were talking about the store rather than the museum.[32] As in the advertisements of Rouillier and Barabas, the prose of the Grands Magasins du Louvre glorified the objects being sold, emphasizing the quality of the pieces being displayed by insisting that they were at the level of collectors' items. Such advertisements were almost challenging the customer to be worthy of the objects she or he was considering purchasing. The furniture itself took on enormous authority and power in these arrangements.

31. BHVP 120, ameub. BA, Etablissements Barabas-Blondeau, 1911, Meubles d'art, 29 quai Voltaire, 7th arr.; BHVP 120, ameub. D, Dauphin.

32. Giffard, *Paris sous la Troisième République*, 12–13.

It is interesting, however, that generally advertisements talked relatively little about the gendering of furniture. They sometimes did identify a room as appropriate for a young girl, or for a young married woman. But unlike the taste professionals, they did not go on into lengthy analyses of what style would be appropriate to what room. The explanation for this silence is not complicated; most furniture stores sold a range of living rooms, dining rooms, studies, and bedrooms. For their advertisements to prescribe a rigid code for each room would be to undermine their efforts to sell a variety of goods, and to convince consumers that they were bored with their Louis XVI and should buy Louis XV or *art nouveau*. If they had created a more rigid coding they might have also had to limit their manufacturing to one style for each kind of room. It was those who were more detached from production and distribution who could express more precise ideas of appropriateness.

One of the clearest examples of distributors' efforts to use the strategies and acquire the legitimacy of the taste professionals was the competition sponsored by Dufayel, the credit store. The contest was organized in the hopes of "provoking the creation of a new style that can synthesize our epoch." To ease the contestants' task, M. Dufayel commissioned a decorator to make twelve models representing the furnishing styles of different periods.[33] Thus Dufayel both attempted to gain prestige within the world of distribution (emulating the practices of the fancier stores) and created competition for the Musée des arts décoratifs and the Louvre—the museum, that is.

The tension between the taste professionals and the distributors was explicit: "*Commerçants* corrupt more and more the crowd's taste. . . . Today, the display of the fake and the imitative have given to modest households ambitions of elegance and vanity of appearances."[34] In the domain of consumption, the taste professionals defined themselves in opposition to the distributors. They labeled the distributors greedy, soulless, and exploitative while they themselves were serving the genuine interests of the consumers and producers. The taste professionals, furthermore, asserted an opposition between taste and fashion as a basis for their claim to authority, arguing that they were the arbiters of taste while the distributors were merely the purveyors of fashion.

To some extent the distinction between taste and fashion was an arbitrary creation of the taste professionals to assert their authority over the

33. BHVP 120, ameub. Dufayel, 1903.
34. Cambry, *Fiançailles et fiançés*.

distributors, but the distinction was far from entirely of their making. The distinction between taste (*le goût*) and fashion (*la mode*) was encoded linguistically. In contrast to good taste (*bon goût*), one could not say that someone had innate good fashion (*bonne mode*); it was a phrase devoid of meaning. The word fashion could barely stand without its preposition, as in *à la mode*, and it could not be used to refer to people. People did not have fashion, rather an item was in or out of fashion. People could, however, grammatically, have good taste (*avoir du bon goût*), or bad. Likewise it was perfectly correct to say that an individual had innate good (or bad) taste. It was nonsense to say that an object was "in taste." An object could be in good or bad taste or could be tasteful.

There was a grammatically built-in temporality to fashion, therefore, that was absent from the concept of taste. Fashionableness was a state through which objects passed, it did not characterize a person. Fashionableness was an indication of the place of a commodity on the market. Tastefulness was an indication of the state of the soul. Taste was deemed eternal, divorced from time and place, and from power.[35]

Indeed, the very legitimacy of the concept of taste was that it was autonomous, in commonsense terms, from power. It was because of the link to the good, the true, and the beautiful—which themselves were constructed as autonomous, transhistorical, and universal qualities—that taste became such a powerful concept. The taste professionals did not invent the opposition between taste and fashion, but they did deploy it.

In addition to the challenge of justifying the education and influence of a taste thought to spring innately from the national breast, the taste professionals also had the problem of reconciling giving advice on good taste (by definition collective) and contemporary notions that each person's taste should be unique, reflecting that particular individual's spirit.

In sharp differentiation from the taste professionals' discourse earlier in the century, both distributors and commentators argued now that women inevitably revealed their personalities, their very selves, through their decor. This exposure could be portrayed as either an opportunity or a burden. For example, Mme Hennequin, the etiquette book writer, explicitly identified the home as one of the few places women had to "express their personalities" without danger of indiscretion (implying, of course, that other forms of self-expression carried that risk). And Noussane, in his guide to decoration, emphasized the fact that tastes were necessarily multiple

---

35. For a fascinating discussion of the parallel phenomenon in America see Karen Halttunen, *Confidence Men and Painted Women* (New Haven, 1982), 64–65.

because personalities were unique. "Tastes cannot, any more than intelligences, be poured in the same mold. It is said that all tastes are in nature. One should cultivate all tastes in order to make them bear abundant fruit, without worrying about variations that will sometimes astonish you."[36] Thus, Noussane was encouraging precisely the pluralism of tastes, of practices of everyday life, that Michelet and Fouillée warned against.

Of course, most taste professionals and distributors did agree that some individual expression was key, but Noussane's easygoing acceptance of wide variation was very rare. More typical was the rather threatening tone in an advertisement from the Trois Quartiers department store. The advertisement first laid out women's responsibility for furnishing the home and then went on to say that "[h]er tastes and her character are so completely reflected in her home that without knowing her . . . [an observer] can represent to himself or herself the mistress of the house as she really is . . . of course, the faults of laziness, absence of taste, and thoughtlessness will also leave their signature."[37]

Not only did the question of the relation between national and individual taste complicate the taste professionals' and distributors' mission, but individuals in both categories also wanted to assert their authority. If all tastes were fine and equal then what role was there for the commentator or salesclerk? Nor was the matter of class now absent from the discussion. Good taste was declared to be the result of both intuition and education, which was "more or less omnipresent in good society, where women work at benefiting from the lessons of history."[38] Good taste did not come naturally; therefore the consumer was always at risk. Since, according to this advertisement, all members of "good society" had the necessary education to decorate their house tastefully and elegantly, not to live up to those standards would be to admit the absence of innate good taste or to risk exclusion from "good society."

Despite this insistence on the expression of self through one's taste, decorating books often detailed what should be put in each room and how much it should cost. Noussane fell into unintentional self-parody when, after a tirade against consumers following the suggestions of journalists like sheep, he went on to give extremely detailed accounts of what really had to be in every woman's house. The same authors who disapproved so energetically of the authority of the *tapissiers* and other distributors could

36. Hennequin, *L'art et le goût au foyer*, 10; Noussane, *Le goût dans l'ameublement*, 245–46.
37. ADS D12 Z1, Trois Quartiers furnishings catalogue, s.d.
38. Ibid.

themselves be specific to the point of pettiness. A well known etiquette-book writer, Mme de l'Alq, insisted, for example, that while *bois noir* was a good and appropriate wood to purchase, neither beech nor oak was truly acceptable.[39]

Both the taste professionals and distributors were caught in a contra-diction. On the one hand they elaborated complex codes of appropriateness and taste; on the other hand, they inhabited a culture that deeply valued individualism. To merely imitate was tasteless, yet to have the wrong things was also tasteless. Women were ideally supposed to manage to find the *juste milieu* between idiosyncrasy and conformity.[40]

Thus, married bourgeois women in the Third Republic were instructed to find the home an adequate site for the expression of their personalities and creativity: expression of those qualities was now in fact part of the job. It had become essential that each bourgeois home look different from every other—but not too different. Women, even respectable married women, were obliged to express their individuality through their consumption practices. Such a notion expressed a considerable shift since the early and middle years of the century and was common enough to become part of contemporary advertising language. Why this change occurred, how it is that bourgeois women's individuation came to be a reality to be expressed through domestic commodities, and the implications of that change are not questions that can be fully addressed here, but some speculation is possible.

I suspect that the change came about, in part, as a result of the increased focus on the domestic market for consumer goods and the need, therefore, to increase demand. As long as consumers were simply representing their husbands and their class there was less need for frequent renewal of goods, and as long as they had etiquette books to tell them exactly what to buy there was also less anxiety. After midcentury, with the multiplication of advice, increased competition among producers and distributors, more so-phisticated advertising, and the idea that one was revealing one's soul in one's things, consumers would be more likely to renew their purchases more often. In a very different domain, the nineteenth century also saw the elaboration of the ideology of individualism and the critique (especially in Britain and the United States) of the exclusion of women from full indi-viduality. The nation now, rather than being embodied in the person of the king as under the Old Regime, was made up of the sum of the citizens, all

39. Noussane, *Le goût dans l'ameublement,* 87; de l'Alq, *Le maître et la maîtresse de la maison,* 62.
40. On this paradox see Forty, *Objects of Desire,* 106–7.

entitled to vote because of their full-fledged personhood or individuality. Women were not allowed to vote precisely because they were not considered full persons, but that position came increasingly under attack—an attack perhaps aided by the steady interpellation of women as full individuals into the world of consumption. But part of the reluctance to grant women the vote may have also derived from their particular role as national consumers. Men were to enact their citizenship through production and war; women were to enact their "citizenship" through reproduction and consumption.

It may be that contemporaries harbored some unease since the varying articulation of citizenship mirrored the nation-market paradox—understood by many as a problem particular to the combination of a republican form of government and industrial capitalism. A report from the universal exposition, for example, mourned the passing of the royal workshops of the Louvre, where under the ancien régime artisans had made things appropriate to their epoch. The article went on to complain that in the current economic and political climate there could not be "a unified direction . . . but there are rather a thousand heads, each obeying and executing the taste of the moment." And Henri Clouzot, the director of the Musée Galliera, faulted the republic for not commissioning work, as the First Empire had done. Another commentator remarked that while in a monarchical system new styles came from above, in a democracy, new styles could only come from below. He did not perceive that that difference made the creation of a new style impossible, just more difficult. Finally, Noussane made the link between royal patronage, national style, and a preindustrial mode of production explicit, complaining first about mechanization and that people were now greedy and bought junk, then saying that "artistic instincts used to flourish in the people when a master worker . . . took three years to make a sideboard. The good people saw this simple man patiently polishing an oak plank, lovingly rubbing a piece of walnut. And the people were proud of this child of their flesh. His work would go in procession to take its place at court. One said with feeling, 'the king complimented François Lheureux whose chest is in the queen's room.' This François Lheureux had put his entire soul, a part of the soul of the people, into his ingenious piece of work."[41] None of these authors were royalists, none were suggesting a

41. Alfred Picard, ed., *Exposition universelle internationale de 1889 à Paris: rapports du jury international*, 19 vols. (Paris, 1891–92), 3:30; Henri Clouzot, *Europe nouvelle*, 2 November 1922 (ADS VR247); Thiébault-Soisson, "A propos d'une décoration intérieure," *Art et décoration* (February 1897): 25–29; Noussane, *Le goût dans l'ameublement*, 15.

return to the regulated economy of the Old Regime, but all were worried about how to make a French style under a capitalist, republican regime.

It is significant, therefore, that many taste professionals perceived as a key difference between themselves and the distributors that they themselves acted in the service and the interests of the nation. The critical importance of objects to the nation was a new theme in the late nineteenth century and a complex and contradictory one. The distributors and the taste professionals were engaged in two different, overlapping, complementary and contradictory projects. Selling furniture, and trying to establish a new French aesthetic in interior decor, were not the same thing. Yet both were in fact deeply enmeshed within capitalist social relations and neither could ignore the issue of the stability of the nation and of the state. Furthermore, although the taste professionals had only bitter things to say about the distributors, the possibility for their existence rested on the existence of distributors. If consumers had still been buying directly from producers, if advertising had not existed, then the taste professionals would not have flourished as they did. Both the taste professionals and the distributors were products of the rationalization of social relations and of the liberal state. Thus the embeddedness of critique within the culture it was critiquing, much discussed recently in the context of the relation of "high" art to "commercial" art, predated modernism and the twentieth century.

One of the paradoxes of bourgeois capitalist society was the need to create areas defined as outside, that is, untainted by, commercial society. Such areas were not only places where the commercialization of social relations were masked (although they were also that), but places where the production of knowledge exceeded and overflowed the reproduction of relations of domination through the power of knowledge. Thus, the cultural institutions and forms through which the taste professionals worked—museums, schools, libraries, and publications—simultaneously served capitalism and undermined it. In their efforts to limit the knowledge acquired by working-class men and women of all classes, in their insistence that commodities were productive of selves, of happiness, and of success, they served capitalism's need for production and consumption. In their argument that tastefulness was something that could be learned, that did not rely on specific goods, they potentially weakened consumer desire. Finally, the taste professionals' self-representation as disinterested, as attempting to provide a counter-weight to the commercialization of society, was not duplicitous; it was at least part of their self-understanding.

Thus the taste professionals tried to establish themselves as disinterested commentators acting only in the interests of the class and the nation, while deriding the distributors as crass middlemen, without culture or scruples, interested only in profit. But distributors, to make or maintain their reputations, had to worry about the quality of the goods they sold. And in order for sales and profits to grow, both social and political stability at home and in foreign markets were needed. Contemporaries thought that the chances of social and political stability were enhanced when each class, each gender, and each generation learned and accepted its place; and that learning of social place could happen through the objects that furnished the domestic world. Just as the distributors had to be concerned with the social order, the taste professionals were, in their preoccupation with social stability and national representation, by no means disinterested nor dissociated from capitalism.

As well as a conflict between groups and between the needs of the nation and the needs of the market, a conundrum lay within the very notion of the nation and the state. The Third Republic had not—any more than any other representative democratic regime ever has—fully worked out how to deal with difference among citizens of the nation. It may well be that this failure made a republican style impossible. Did one have a system of political representation rather than a direct democracy simply because of scale? Because there were too many people to fit into a room to debate? Or, did France have a system of representation because given a citizenry understood to be composed of different people with different interests, each set of interests was to be represented by a representative? In that case the Assembly was acknowledged as a site of conflict and as a site of the very making of the nation.

There could be no republican style in furniture (or in other domains) because the republic was, in fact, a composite of interests (whatever the ideology), and the nation was always in the process of being made. Unlike under absolutism when the state, the nation, the king, and the people were all understood to be one body who could be represented by one style, a representative republic, even without the complication of capitalism, necessarily produced multiple styles. Just as the writing of history became a site of contestation and debate, because history was fundamental to the making of the nation, so style, even in domestic things, became a site of contestation.

But domestic objects did pose yet another layer of complication. The state could impose a curriculum, a vision of history, onto the students in its schools but, given the principle of personal liberty and the free market, could neither impose certain furnishings on its inhabitants nor force producers to make certain goods. Thus, there was an open market in style.

Theoretically, all individuals could make what they wanted to make or (if they had the money) buy what they wanted to buy.

Consequently, the taste professionals preoccupied with the status of the aesthetic and the state of the industrial arts in France from the 1880s to the early years of the twentieth century differed from their elders who had been active at midcentury. The latter years witnessed a growing state bureaucracy concerned with aesthetic matters and increased state funding of the industrial arts. Part of that expansion came in the new flock of pedagogues, from the new fleet of drawing teachers needed to teach drawing courses (made compulsory in 1878) in primary school, through the teachers in the expanded technical schools and colleges, including the professors in the newly created field of art history. Museum and library administration also came to employ more and more people. It was not only the number of taste professionals employed directly by the state whose numbers increased in this period, however. The fin de siècle saw an explosion of decorating magazines, pattern books, and etiquette books, all of private initiative but often deeply preoccupied with the composition and fate of French supremacy in the decorative arts and its relation to the health of the nation and of the state. It is an indication of the degree of preoccupation with the problem of national taste that many taste professionals were not state employees but other members of the bourgeoisie acting privately in the nation's interest.

The battle between the taste professionals and the distributors did not start, therefore, with equal armies. Although the status of merchants had improved since the Old Regime, they still provoked ambivalent reactions, far more ambivalent than those elicited by the occupations exercised by the taste professionals of the Third Republic: university professors, writers, journalists, teachers, and museum administrators. Thus while the taste professionals overtly attacked the distributors in the harshest terms, the distributors attempted to emulate the forms perfected by the taste professionals, as in the example of stores naming themselves after museums and advertisements assuring their readers that the stores were, in fact, museums. It is that order of value that helped differentiate this bourgeois stylistic regime from the mass stylistic regime of the twentieth century. By the mid-twentieth century, the taste professionals' institutions came to imitate the merchandisers rather than the other way around.

The important organs of the taste professionals from midcentury to before the war carried few advertisements, had scholarly pretensions, and reported regularly on what was new and important at the universal expositions. The magazines founded later shifted their emphasis. *La renaissance de l'art français et des industries de luxe* (1918–39), while still published on matte paper, carried large advertisements for luxury goods amidst its serious articles. *Les Echos d'art: revue mensuelle des industries d'art et de luxe, de l'habitation et des arts décoratifs modernes* (1925–) was in large format, glossy paper, and had short heavily illustrated articles that functioned largely as advertisements for some of the major producers. Furthermore the *Echos d'art* had a free designer referral and inquiry service. We are still, in the 1920s and 1930s a distance from the intense commercialization of public cultural institutions, but the commercialization of these private institutions indicates the change in direction and its trajectory.

By the 1980s museums had commodified objects and created desire for them—through display styles, the sale of tickets, and the vast expansion of museum shops—and even more closely resembled department stores.[42] In the late nineteenth century, however, the lack of convergence between taste professionals and distributors meant that there was no one hegemonic discourse that consumers could obediently follow. The cacophony of competing expert discourses meant that there was never only one voice demanding to be heard and claiming authority. The discourses of the taste professionals and the distributors collided and combined in odd and unexpected ways. Consumers in the second half of the nineteenth century were subject to a deluge of advice concerning how they should furnish their homes and the significance of that act of furnishing. The numbers of voices, and the differences in their interests meant that consumers could find no refuge in passivity; they could not simply do as they were told because they were being told many different, mutually contradictory, things at the same time. The frequent dissonance between individual and familial locations meant consumers were faced with contradictory tasks—being true to themselves and to their families. The impossibility of choosing only one fragment of one's social being to represent meant that even being true to oneself was not really possible. And yet consumers made their way through the thicket of advice, admonition, and threat with varying degrees of aplomb.

Grasping the processes of both the acquisition and the use of furnishings, therefore, is essential to understanding the popularity of historicist pastiche in the late nineteenth century. Exploring the discourses around furniture as well as how the objects were used sheds light on the making of distinctions between and within classes, and on the peculiar ways in

42. My argument here has been informed by the work of Neil Harris, *Cultural Excursions: Marketing Appetites and Cultural Tastes in Modern America* (Chicago, 1990).

which the construction of class, gender, nation, and history coalesced in the chairs on which people sat and the tables at which they ate.

STYLE, TASTE, AND POWER: REPRESENTING THE STATE, MAKING THE NATION

The story of the gendered and class meanings attributed to furnishings and spaces in the second half of the nineteenth century, and of the use the Parisian bourgeoisie made of furniture in the construction of personal and national narratives, is now told. Not yet fully articulated, however, is how these questions of everyday life implicated state and nation, how taste and political power were mutually implicated under a bourgeois regime. Their articulation, I suggest, involves explanations and narratives that turn on the crucial role the Revolution plays in French history—a role that illuminates the profound political meanings implicated in the objects of everyday life.

The French Revolution of 1789 divided the eighteenth and nineteenth centuries, inaugurating the latter and inventing the ancien régime. Thus did it cause an epochal rupture stylistically as well as politically, economically and socially, leaving to the future a newly indeterminate past from which to construct intelligible narratives. In destroying the monarchy, the Revolution defined the old order as a historical period of the past—and as a symbolic repertoire available for the representation and production of the present and the past. This ancien régime repertoire served to express the tensions internal to postrevolutionary society, to make a claim to a particular relation to the nation's history, and to mark thicker boundaries among men and women of the bourgeoisie, and between the working, middling, bourgeois, and aristocratic classes. The Revolution inaugurated contests over the form and meaning of representation in the broadest sense, and it is here that we must look to understand how style and taste became so subtly imbricated with the political relations of the modern era. The breaking of historical continuity and the elaboration of class-conflicted industrial society left the French bourgeoisie in the late nineteenth century deeply preoccupied by and ambivalent about the problems of historicity, of boundaries, and of categories.

In the process history became gendered in a new way, the ancient past masculine and heroic, and the more recent past feminized and fragile. And while these distinctions made of the bourgeoisie the visible representation of history and nation, they made of the working class a single category, whose lack of distinctions followed from an inherent incapacity for aesthetic taste. Meanwhile, bourgeois women became targets of intensive media campaigns designed to arouse their consumer desires, but also targets of discursive and even criminal discipline should those desires get out of hand, that is, if they actually sought to represent their personal selves through goods or fell victims to the new disease of kleptomania. Likewise men who strayed beyond the accepted boundaries of "manly" consumption—as collectors or patriarchs—were redefined as somehow "not quite men." Consumption, then, though necessary to the economic health of the country, was understood as potentially and profoundly disruptive of the libidinal economy, capable of either deregulating and destabilizing, or of making, the family and the society.

Consumption was politically significant because it was perceived as capable of producing unfettered individualism incompatible with the survival of the state—composed of individuals whose independence rested on the dependence of others—and the stability of the nation—based on the localization of individuals in families and classes. And yet republican French society rested on the rights of the individual and egalitarianism. The end of the corporate order, the end of a society of estates, and the development of political economy enabled (and perhaps necessitated) the concept of the sovereign, ungendered, autonomous, universal subject. There was, in other words, tension among a concept of society and polity composed of individuals, a society and polity composed of dominant and dependent members of households, and a society composed of classes with differing (and sometimes conflicting) interests. These tensions were expressed and transformed through changing articulations of the nation and the state. The state needed the nation as much as the nation needed the state, and the nation was made as much within the spheres deemed private and social as within the public and political spheres of the state itself.

By the late nineteenth century the understanding that furniture and homes represented their owners had become a commonplace. More novel was the broaching of the particular issue of representation through domestic commodities that coincided with the general questioning of all forms of representation following the establishment of the Third Republic. What political representation meant, the most effective and just means of giving voice to different interests, the relation between identities and interests, and individual entitlement to representation were all hotly debated. Indeed, this particular form of commodity fetishism coincided with the definitive establishment in France of universal manhood suffrage, and with the shift in strategy of suffragists attempting to win the vote for women. Thus, the notion that one's domestic goods could stand in for, almost be oneself, arose at precisely the moment when the problem emerged of creating a unified France, and a unified French culture, out of an assemblage of strongly marked regions with distinctive traditions and languages—at the moment of expansion of French colonialism, of vastly increasing immigration into France.

If one was born on French territory, one was French, and yet birth was not enough; one still needed to be made French, although that process was ideally to be naturalized and hence transparent. The naturalization of the nation coincided with the sustained and exaggerated naturalizing of women in the nineteenth century. The state came to be understood as a constructed object (manmade, quite literally), while the nation was assimilated to the natural, feminized, domestic world. Men were to be members of the state—citizens representing themselves, their families and other men po-litically.[43] Women were to be members of the nation—nationals repre-senting their families socially and instilling patriotism in their children. The definition of the French state was, therefore, relatively clear, because the boundary between inclusion and exclusion was legally explicit. The definition of the French nation was much more problematic, however, because marking its outer (generally physical) boundaries was but a first step in specifying its crucial essence. Those included must exhibit French-ness and it was perceived that many people living within the hexagon were still in need of being made French.

The nation was a cultural entity while the state was a political structure. For the state to function some degree of consensus on the appropriate organization of political process was needed; for the nation to function some degree of consensus on the appropriate organization of the everyday was needed. This division of labor was part of, perhaps a precondition for, the hyphen in the nation-state. That hyphen was not there accidentally; con-

---

43. Joan Scott notes that in French liberal theory the individual (and the citizen) was simultaneously ungendered, abstract, all-inclusive, and constituted in and by the gaze of the Other; see her Berkshire conference paper (1993) and the introduction to her forthcoming book. In the last twenty years a great deal of work has been done on nationalism; the following theoretical discussions grounded in other parts of the world are especially helpful: Lauren Berlant, *The Anatomy of National Fantasy* (Chicago, 1991), 20–22 on the "national symbolic"; Benedict Anderson, *Imagined Communities: Reflections on the Origins and Spread of Nationalism* (London, 1983); Eric Hobsbawm and Terence Ranger, eds., *The Invention of Tradition* (Cambridge, 1983). On France, Eugen Weber's *Peasants into Frenchmen* (Stanford, 1976) remains very useful; the three volumes of Pierre Nora, ed., *Les lieux de mémoire* (Paris, 1986) contain some fascinating articles, although there are equally telling omissions. On the later period see Stanford Elwitt, *The Making of the Third Republic* (Baton Rouge, 1975).

temporaries thought that for the state to be secure, for the votes of its male citizens to be properly cast, nation was also necessary. And these notions were elaborated in a political economy where simultaneous to the development of the liberal bourgeois state—based on the principles of political equality—there was the development of industrial capitalism—based on economic inequality. All these discourses structured the political context within which the meaning and power of everyday objects were reconfigured.

Underlying the notion of nation, moreover, was the problematic fantasy of homogeneity. The French state would be secure if all its citizens became culturally French. Yet what did it mean to be French? What did it mean to be French and not be a voting citizen (as was the case for women)? Or to be French and belong to an economically and socially dominated group, such as the working class or the petite bourgeoisie (or nonwhites or immigrants)? Was the goal to erase all differences—an unlikely hypothesis, since much of the nineteenth century had been spent carefully erecting barriers between classes, between genders, and between races. The dilemma was not so much how to negotiate the reality of difference, but rather how to live with the paradox of the simultaneous desire of dominant groups to maintain difference and the ideal of assimilation that called for incorporating all others into itself. The tensions produced by this paradox were acted out in the expected location of political negotiation and political theorizing, but they were also enacted, in the less obvious everyday worlds of production, distribution, and especially consumption.

In late nineteenth-century France the responsibility for the representation of the nation through consumption was attributed largely to women, and the responsibility for the representation of the state through citizenship was attributed to men. In voting, running for office, and holding government positions, men were to make the state. In shopping, constructing homes, and producing everyday life, women were to make the nation. Women were of course, also to make the state, through their mothering of male children—future citizens.[44] However, women's domestic tasks consisted not only of cultural and biological reproduction but also of representation. Despite the explicit separation of private and public in the postabsolutist nation and the determined defense of the sanctity of domestic privacy, it was understood that the household was an essential building block of both nation and state, and that household was not limited

44. The notion has been well developed in the American case by Linda Kerber, *Women of the Republic: Intellect and Ideology in Revolutionary America* (Chapel Hill, 1982).

to a nuclear family. Furthermore, as the abbé Sièyes indicated in the early nineteenth century, with the end of sumptuary legislation and the development of the free market a new kind of fetishism arose. Goods came to stand in for, represent, people and social relations in a new way. Married women, in their persons and their acquisitions, came to hold a critically important role in the social representation of themselves, their husbands and their families. Women's choice of domestic objects, regulation of sociability, and governance of household affairs were deemed essential to the social and ultimately political legitimacy of the family and the stability of the nation. Thus, contradictory to the ideology of the separation of the social and the political, the political in fact depended on, and helped to construct, the social.

The division of social and political labor, as can be seen by the efforts of contemporaries to naturalize it, and of women to contest it, was far from unproblematic or unchallenged at the time. There was little, if any, theoretical footing within liberalism to exclude women from the polity, and men's consumption was in fact essential to both the health of the economy and the making of the nation. Thus, many of the efforts to naturalize an unnatural situation turned on the making of different forms of individuation and self-realization.[45] Women were defined as consuming in the interests of their families, of their husbands, and then of their children. By creating tasteful interiors they could represent their nation and raise good citizens. Male collectors, in the major form of aesthetic consumption defined as properly masculine, were defined to be participating in a very different kind of creative activity when they consumed. Collectors made themselves through their collections and the collections were, in themselves, understood to be works of art. Through men's acts of consumption they were to reassert and recreate their legitimacy as political actors. But when men refused their task of supporting dependents and reproducing the state, as in the case of dandies, they were demasculinized.

The gendering of consumption, therefore, both reflected and reproduced the complex relationship between the political and the social, on the one hand, and the state and the nation, on the other. And all of these were both shaped by and shaped debates over the place of women in the polity and

45. Although the strength of this task of social representation may also help explain French feminists' relative reluctance to tackle the issue of suffrage, historians usually attribute feminists' social priorities to the fear of destabilizing the republic and fear of other women's piety; but the explanation may have yet another element. Helpful here is Eli Zaretsky's *Capitalism, the Family, and Personal Life,* 2d ed. (New York, 1986).

society and the dual forms of representation that these entities entailed. Again the question of political representation was the most explicit. Feminist demands for political participation started with the Revolution, and feminist voices were never again completely silenced.[46] Suffrage claims were very slow to be met; until 1944 women could neither vote nor run for national office. A consistent argument against women's suffrage was that women were adequately represented by their husbands or fathers; their dependent, nonindividuated status made them incapable of political judgment. An equally important, although unstated, argument was that although men were not legally required to be married or have children in order to vote or run for office, men's independence and capacity for governance was nonetheless signified by their possession of dependents, and by their ability to represent a household.[47] Thus, men's independence depended on women's dependence and was illusory. Autonomy or independence based on the dependence and subordination of another entailed the mutual need of both those occupying the independent and the dependent locations in the dyad. (That mutual dependency did not of course have like consequences for the dominant and dominated.) Indeed, the ferocity of the opposition to women's civil and political emancipation may well be linked to that interdependence. The state was constituted of men but needed women.

The state's need for women was complex and multiple. Women's exclusion from the political was needed to create men's independence (especially once other property qualifications were abandoned), and to give the vote value—in the sense that a privilege from which some were excluded

46. See a fascinating discussion of this process in R. Radhakrishnan, "Nationalism, Gender and the Narrative of Identity," in *Nationalisms and Sexualities*, ed. Andrew Parker et al. (New York, 1992), 77ff. Feminism in France was not limited to or even dominated by demands for suffrage but political emancipation was a consistent issue.

47. This argument has been elaborated in the domain of political theory by Pateman, *The Sexual Contract*; and Anne Phillips, *Engendering Democracy* (University Park, 1991), 30–34; Joan Landes, Gillian Brown, Mary Poovey, Catherine Hall, and Leonore Davidoff make similar arguments, grounded in textual analyses for France, the United States, and Britain, respectively: Landes, *Women and the Public Sphere*, 2; Gillian Brown, *Possessive Individualism* (Berkeley, 1990); Mary Poovey, *Uneven Developments: The Ideological Work of Gender in Mid-Victorian England* (Chicago, 1988), 80. Davidoff and Hall make a rather different argument for the importance of bourgeois men's "independence" in *Family Fortunes*, 199–200. For the implications of this construction in the contemporary world see Nancy Fraser, *Unruly Practices: Power, Discourse and Gender in Contemporary Social Theory* (Minneapolis, 1989), 153.

was more prized. And women were needed to produce the naturalized nation, one whose essential qualities could be taught and yet appear innate, transhistorical, and inevitable. The assimilation of women into nature entailed the naturalization of activities carried out within the home. Indeed, the nation itself was symbolized by the figure of a woman—Marianne— mute and most often portrayed with at least one bare breast.[48]

The exclusion of women from the political sphere and their interpolation as naturally domestic creatures was thus critically important to making the French nation, while masking much of the process of its construction. Frenchness was to appear to grow organically on French soil, even as it was being taught by women. Women became responsible for the cultural as well as biological reproduction of the nation. It was at home that children first learned to be French. Through the creation of French homes, decorated with a French aesthetic, in which French food was eaten with French table manners, and in which good French was spoken, French women created and reproduced the nation—thereby equipping their sons to be good citizens. Thus did domestic and aesthetic matters become matters of state.[49]

But all were not to participate in the same way in this nation. This was a period of bourgeois domination of state and of society, albeit a domination challenged by sections of the working class. This was a bourgeois stylistic regime characterized by a debate within the class concerning how to consolidate possession of the state through control of the nation. On the production side artisans had been largely disenfranchised, and on the consumption side the working classes' possibilities were limited. This bourgeois stylistic regime would terminate in the far-reaching and dramatic changes of politics, society, and economy of the mid-twentieth century. After 1930, and most clearly after 1945, style and taste would be imbricated with nation and state yet again but in fundamentally new ways.

---

48. This story is of course complicated by the fact that women were considered simultaneously closer and further from nature than men (Marina Warner, *Monuments and Maidens* [New York, 1985]; Maurice Agulhon, *Marianne into Battle* [Cambridge, 1981]; Berlant, *The Anatomy of National Fantasy*, chap. 1).

49. For a fascinating analysis of matters of style in nation making see Norman S. Holland, "Fashioning Cuba," in *Nationalisms and Sexualities*, ed. Andrew Parker et al. (New York, 1992), 147–56.

Toward a Mass Stylistic Regime
The Citizen-Consumer

This story ends with the transition to mass society. Following the Second World War, both universal suffrage and mass consumption arrived in France, and with them a changed relation to political and social representation. Furthermore, the definition of Frenchness itself was irrevocably altered with the dissolution of the Empire and the first movement toward a politically and economically unified Europe. Many of the forms nascent in the earlier period developed and expanded in the 1920s and especially in the postwar period, but it was not only a question of expansion of existing structures. The very forms of production, distribution, and consumption were transformed in the ages of Taylorism and then Fordism. Far more people had access to the time, money, and information necessary for full participation in a consumer society. Real mass markets, in other words, developed. More goods became cheaper relative to more people's incomes.

The mass stylistic regime is not merely the outcome of the diffusion of goods through society. It is also characterized by the permeation of society by a commodity logic in which people, groups, interests, and nations are constituted through the acquisition, use, and display of things whose meanings are generated in the domains of distribution and consumption rather than production. The bourgeois stylistic regime was a hybrid system in which production still generated meaning and in which the taste professionals—whose interest in the goods was explicitly more aesthetic and ideological than economic and commercial—outclassed the distributors.

In the decades since the Second World War the world has changed even more drastically. In the domain of production, the division between manual and mental labor analyzed in this book has increased and intensified. With the growing mobility of capital, far more sophisticated and automated machinery, greater standardization, easier and cheaper communication, production sites can and do move around the globe with extraordinary rapidity. Goods move with equal speed in the domains of distribution and consumption. Cash registers in Dijon inform a computer in Paris about what styles are selling well; faxes go out within the hour from Paris to Hong Kong or Sri Lanka relaying that production information based on consumer behavior. Worldwide television uses increasingly sophisticated techniques to market products globally. In the political arena, women were granted the vote in France in 1945, with the resulting individuation of the body of the citizen and of the nation. Furthermore decolonization brought large numbers of nonwhite, non-Christian immigrants to France, some citizens, some not. That immigration along with the dissolution of internal boundaries within Europe since the Second World War transformed the problem of making the nation.

Some of the questions addressed in this book have then either become moot or been dramatically transformed. For example, the decisions of trade unions concerning the balance among creativity, autonomy, money, and time have far less importance in a period when unions are losing (or perhaps have lost) the battle against the mobility of capital and of production. Union strategy was relatively successful from the 1920s through the 1960s (with the exception of the depression years) in that far more people in the United States and western Europe gained access to far more things and had far more leisure time than ever before. By the 1950s there was a genuine mass market. But at what cost? Would unions be less vulnerable today had they been able to fight for the right to creative labor as opposed to shorter work days, higher wages, and better working conditions?

Other dilemmas continue in new social and political contexts. For example, the discussion over the merits and possibilities of an equal and like education for all remains a vivid one. The debate about knowledge and skill was taken up by W. E. B. Du Bois and Booker T. Washington at the turn of the century and has been played out again and again in colonial and postcolonial situations. Of what use is Latin, Molière, or calculus to a child in rural Zaire? Should not that child rather be taught to sow and reap? Is it not imperialist to urge the teaching of abstract, often nonindigenous knowledge to those who will work with their hands? Is it not also presumptuous, arrogant, and self-interested for those who have access to Latin, Molière, and calculus to decide that certain others, on the basis of their class, their nationality, or their race, do not need or want that access?

In the domain of gender women are no longer bound by the legal constraints of the nineteenth century. Women can vote, keep the money they earn, and divorce. It would appear then that the logic of families as the building blocks of society, of women as the keepers of the nation is now over. But when the chaos in American cities is blamed on statistics about women having children too young, about unmarried parents and fatherless children, and about absent "family values," what is being said but that the family is the bedrock of the society and the polity? Without a conventional family, it is said, the social and even political orders will fall apart. The problem, such analyses would lead us to believe, lies not with the global movement of capital, not with social policy, not with racism and sexism, but with the failure of the domestic, with the inability of women to bring up their children to be proper citizens.

A book replete with contradictions and paradoxes, then, concludes with another set. I think that for the descendants of the minority of male artisans who were part of the culture of production, their lives at labor did change over the course of the nineteenth and twentieth centuries. For those who became part of the petit-bourgeois class of designers, their work became less physically strenuous but nonetheless more fragmented—they no longer made what they designed and no longer had the sensuous relation with the wood itself. For those who became "operatives" or "hands," their work remained physically arduous (although the hours were shorter) and grew more tedious and more dangerous. And for a minority of that small number of privileged artisans, little in fact changed—artisans still work in the faubourg St-Antoine to this day. I think, however, that for those who came to work largely with their heads and for those who came to work largely with their hands something indeed was lost. The drastically diminished possibilities for professional reproduction—when the young were trained in school by others instead of in the shop—were a loss. The increasing rarity of the opportunity to meet and talk with the persons who would buy, live with, and use the object one made was a loss. The greater use of machines—with their noise, danger, and boredom—was a loss. The separation of design from production had costs for both sides and for the goods themselves.

Other aspects of artisans' lives improved—male workers could participate in politics, they experienced the benefits of the developing welfare state, and by the early years of the twentieth century their standard of living had improved. Thus working-class men became part of the consumer culture. Not coincidentally, the dominant discourse on the crisis in style also shifted. By the turn of the century the focus of the "art for all" movement was on all being able to *consume* art rather than all being able to *produce* it. Mechanization was now seen as a desirable means whereby the poor could also buy things of style. Many of the taste professionals who, throughout the nineteenth century, continued to think that the conditions of production were relevant abdicated the battle and instead worried more that all should have access as consumers to tasteful goods.

Thus the artisans were gradually transformed into consumers, into people who worked to earn the money to buy the things that made them human rather than becoming fully human through their labor. I have been accused of romanticism in my regret at the passing of creative labor. But how can academics—who themselves choose to earn far less than they could, have less leisure time than they might, face an even more uncertain job market than they must, all in order to have the chance to do labor they find meaningful and creative—say that to regret the passing of that option for those who work with their hands is romanticism?

To return for a moment to my co-workers in Woburn. Their passivity that so frustrated me was in many ways more realistic than my optimism. They had been well trained in school; they knew they had been well trained. They were mistrustful of unions that they felt would cause an already regimented and alienated work-world to become more so. In some sense by choosing to accept boredom, heat, and danger, forty hours a week, they felt they were protecting the other hours in the day, hours they often spent not really at leisure but making things for themselves. They were, in other words, ambivalent about being paid to make beautiful things. They were frustrated and expressed frustration at the ugly stupidity of the instrument boxes and speaker cabinets we labored over. But they were also, in fact, reluctant to be too engaged in the work they were paid for. As one of them put it, this way his head was free to think about his guitars and other projects on the job. From his point of view, if he made guitars forty hours a week he'd have no energy to think about his *own* projects. Thus at some level, once they were selling their labor, they did not care what was done with it. This is a long way from the artisans at the universal expositions of the mid-nineteenth century, who were still defending their right to be paid for making beautiful things. But of course they were working seventy hours a week and not forty—there was no leisure time to defend.

This is thus a mixed story, one full of stubborn ambiguity and paradox. My co-workers in Woburn still did get to make beautiful things. And their ability to make those things—in terms of time, and in terms of knowledge, skill, and craft sense—was in large part a result of union efforts, on the one hand, and the descendants of the taste professionals, in the role of trade-school teachers, on the other. But forty hours a week of tedium is a lot, and indeed they themselves raged against it, resisting in some sense their transformation into consumption machines and by their commitment to their knowledge, skill and craft sense, and by spending many of their leisure hours practicing their trade (much to their wives' frustration). But these were a privileged few. They were employed, first of all, and second, they had a choice about whether to have their lives dominated by production or consumption.

Has the work of researching and writing this book enabled me to understand them any better? My survey of the transformation of the trade, including its metaphorical organization, its system of reproduction, and the ways in which it was embedded within a larger political, social, and economic world has, in fact, made my co-workers in Woburn somewhat more intelligible. I can see that what I perceived as their "macho" attitude was potentially a legacy derived from a trade tradition worked out in relation to the gendering of consumption and production. I can see that their pessimism and what I called in the introduction "passivity in the face of an open market" were not irrational and self-destructive but rather realistic and protective of something they cared deeply about. Finally, I no longer perceive their resistance to unionization as simply reactionary and misguided. I remain very strongly pro-union, yet researching this book, and thinking about the choices unions made concerning which battles to fight and which not, reading other recent labor histories preoccupied with matters of gender and race and noting the often exclusionary behavior of organized labor, I find I cannot judge my co-workers too harshly. But this book has also persuaded me that turning to either leisure-time creative production or consumption as the solution to the alienation of labor is not the answer either.

The change in focus of the world from production to consumption has been mirrored in the academic world, where studies of the meanings of consumption proliferate. As I discussed in the introduction, many books have been written on the creative possibilities of consumption, on self-fulfillment through consumption, on the formation of groups through consumption. Perhaps a return to my grandmothers will help clarify these issues. For my grandmothers, as for the bourgeois consumers discussed in this book, goods provided a means of self-expression that was not in itself of determinate value. They derived considerable enjoyment from shopping, buying, using, and talking about things. Neither their stories nor those of nineteenth-century Parisian bourgeoises were simply stories of alienation or false consciousness. But neither are they simply stories of self-fulfillment, inventiveness, and sociability. In a consumer society, whether of bourgeois or mass orientation, goods become weapons as well as tools, and they are always a means of identification and differentiation. There is always an Other against which the self is constituted, sometimes violently, sometimes peacefully.

Again, as in the case of my co-workers' relation to their work and the objects they made, work on the consumption regimes of the eighteenth and nineteenth centuries have helped me to grasp *why* my grandmothers cared about things so much. And why it was my grand*mothers* who were so invested in their things, especially their interiors. What appeared to me to be rather baffling indirection—what difference did what her dress looked like make?—seems like something rather different when seen as part of a system of self-constitution. This book has described the shifting from a world in which working-class men could articulate a desire to make the beautiful, to a world in which matters of taste were supposed to fall mostly to women and to some elite men. Parts of that system are still in place, others have yielded to historical transformation. In the nineteenth century bourgeois women represented their families, their nations, and eventually themselves through the homes they created. They had few other venues for that task of representation and self-constitution. But that changed with women's suffrage and other forms of emancipation. With the making of a mass-consumption regime, consumption has become a less feminized activity, although making the home is still considered to be largely a woman's task. The woman's task of social representation of the family has not disappeared, but the individualism that was beginning to appear at the turn of the century became more prevalent early in the twentieth century, thus changing the nature of that representation. As consumption has shifted its class location from the bourgeois world to the mass world, therefore, its gendering has shifted as well. Although certain types of consumption are still profoundly gender-coded, the activity as a whole cannot be said to be. With women's accession to the vote, and with the partial shift away from the family to the individual as the constitutive element of society, both women and men have come to constitute themselves in this way.

My grandmothers were, in some sense, right as they unconsciously expressed their mistrust for each other by complaining about each other's taste. The different tastes *did* say something significant about the people they each are, the aspirations they had for their children, the direction in which they hoped the world would go. Their choice of furniture was not inconsequential. But this is not a matter for judgment, for they could not be otherwise. As Jean Baudrillard most eloquently remarks, there is no escape from the semiotic system of consumption. There is no outside, there is no return to neutral goods that communicate nothing. Like the workers in Woburn, then, there was a logic to my grandmothers' behavior. That logic makes the question of resistance or fulfillment or group formation through goods rather beside the point. In a consumer society people necessarily use goods to all of those ends. People's use of things can, as in the case of feminists' use of violet clothing in France in the 1970s, help a political group consolidate and enable members to recognize one another. People's use of things can also be immensely destructive, as in the case of many contemporary American cities where children too often kill each other for the color of their jackets—the means of signification of gang membership—having identified themselves through their commodities as "the enemy." Or when children kill simply to take possession of the goods—jackets, sneakers, or gold chains—that they perceive are necessary for social existence, and that they neither have the money to buy nor the belief that they will one day have that money. Unfortunately perhaps, despite the very different outcomes, the same "logic" runs through each of these examples.

The logic in each instance is the constitution of self, of group, of community through things. Under certain historical circumstances that fetishism can be innocuous—as in the case of my grandmothers—or beneficial—as in the case of feminism or the gay rights movement—or pernicious—as in the case of urban street youth. In a mass society it is likely to be all of those things at once. There is nothing intrinsically liberating or validating about consumption, nothing intrinsically imprisoning or alienating. But as a means of self-making in a world of extraordinary inequality it has real dangers. In the contemporary American version of a consumer society we have apparently conceded that a few are going to have a great deal and many will have very little. But all depend on goods to make themselves nonetheless. If people come to need things in order to exist, in order to have an identity, in order to have "a self," and if they have no possibility of earning the money with which to buy those things, then it is neither as irrational nor disproportionate as it at first glance appears to kill for a jacket. Through the possession of a jacket one comes into oneself and into a place in the community. The gross inequalities of American society are not, however, just an inevitable side effect of capitalist development or a market economy. They are also the result of political choices and decisions. And that leads me back to Michelet.

Michelet suggested that for a republican nation to exist, people had to recognize themselves in one another, through their things, their gestures, and their habits. He insisted that a nation needs a national style and a national taste. In the world of mass consumption, such a thing has become even less imaginable than it was in the nineteenth century. Not only do internal processes of differentiation continuously produce new and different styles and tastes, thus fragmenting the nation, but goods are now designed, produced, and distributed in a global whirlwind. Even more salient is the globalization of the mass media that promote and create desire for those goods. Goods seem to be located in time now rather than space and this in turn seems paradoxically to produce very localized taste and style communities. Very small differences in mass-produced goods, or in a very particular brand or style become the means by which people recognize one another. And such goods become necessary for psychic survival.

And yet the nation lives; national identity continues to emerge in bodies, styles, and gestures. As the debates in France over whether Muslim students should be allowed to wear distinctive dress confirm, the anecdote in the introduction about my experience with handwriting is neither quaint nor anachronistic. The head scarf debate—because it involves issues of equal access to education for boys and girls—is not identical to the handwriting issue, but it is analogous. The analogy lies in the difficulty the French state has in conceiving of citizens whose everyday life practices, including their gestures and their consumption habits, are different from what is defined as the French norm.

My teachers in that French school (and in all the others) were also right—what my handwriting looked like *did* matter; how I walked mattered, and how I wore my hair. They mattered because it is not at all clear what the nation will look like, how the consensus upon which the nation must rest is to be built, if people do not, as Michelet put it, see themselves when they look at others. And in a commodified world, it is in shared things that one sees oneself. In some senses the emphasis on handwriting reflects the optimism of the French national school system. Its ideology holds that if young bodies can be disciplined into becoming French—if children come to look French, sound French, write like the French—then they will indeed be French even if they are not Christian, not white, not of French parentage, and do not possess other French things.

I would like to suggest that there is a linkage between France's long history of association between nationality and items of consumption, whether literal consumption like food, or figurative consumption like furniture, and its difficulty making room for foreigners and French citizens who want to live in France but do not want to adopt the everyday life habits that the French of longer standing define to be properly French. Indeed, that linkage was established in the Revolution and developed during the nineteenth century. Recently the French have almost caricatured themselves in debates about allowing foreign (especially American) culture to implant itself on French soil, and in some of the debates over European unification. But there is legitimacy to their anxiety about the dangers of diversity and capitalist cultural invasion, for there may also be a linkage to be established between French people's ability to see themselves in one another and their relative willingness to pay for a welfare state, just as there may be a similar connection between American tolerance of cultural difference and America's brutal neglect of the poor. Is there some way in which Americans do not see themselves in one another and therefore declare that the survival of the fittest is the only viable political and social system? Finally, there may be a connection between the especially extensive and intensive commodification of American society and the fact that many of those eligible do not vote and the fact that children killing other children for their jackets or sneakers has become a commonplace.

People may understand themselves to be more truly represented by their things than by their elected representatives. And the question goes beyond representation. People exist through their things. In order for political representation to be a viable concept, people have to have some sense of common interest and some sense of collectivity. When people defined themselves as sharing an interest because they lived in the same place, there was a certain fixity to the concept. Within the current democratic regime in the United States, political representatives are fully commodified. They are packaged, distributed, and advertised. Many perceive that they are also bought and sold. It is not implausible to think that those whose access to the world of goods is extremely limited might also think that their access to political representation is equally limited. But again, the economy does not determine all. France is at a comparable moment of capitalism, yet a far greater percentage of the eligible population votes.

Jean Baudrillard notes that consumption has nothing to do with the numbers who can consume, it is not an empirical problem or question. It is a matter of people being defined by and living through the things they own. In a parallel move Pierre Rosanvallon claims, regarding the question of eligibility to vote, that who was in fact able to vote was of lesser importance than the principle of the vote. Both the United States and France established, in the late eighteenth century, the principle of the vote and the principle of political representation. But in France each elector was to elect a representative for the entire nation, and each representative was to understand himself to be representing the nation as a whole. (My use of the male pronoun is intentional.) In the United States, each elector was to elect his own representative, to represent his localities' interests in the national forum. Despite the fact that the distance between the two systems shrinks in the nuances and complexities of enactment, the two principles are quite fundamentally different. In the United States, an elector must feel part of a geographically defined interest group, as well as of the nation as a whole, in order to feel capable of participation in government. In France, an elector must feel part of the French nation.

It is possible that French centralization, even French authoritarianism concerning the style of the everyday, can to some extent protect the polity against the ravages of free market capitalism and commodification. Perhaps the strength of the cultural training of French schools—the instilling of the French hand, for example—makes it easier for electors to feel part of a French nation, even when they cannot buy the things with which to constitute that self. This cultural training also may provide a complicated kind of "protection" for the French nation against the internationalism of the market. People in all places interpret and read global products in local ways, but the French system may have a longer history of such a practice.

I would like to suggest that there may be a powerful paradox underlying the relation between capitalism and democratic states. Democratic states in order to function well may especially need a shared taste and a shared style, in order to create a sense of shared interests and responsibility—of likeness. But democratic states under capitalism have not defined themselves historically as able to impose a style on the nation, for the freedom of the market has been defined as an essential liberty. Part of the reason why the Third Republic emphasized nationalized centralized schooling, language, custom, and handwriting may be precisely because here was a domain it defined as legitimate to control. To control the appearance of goods bought and sold on the market was not legitimate, for that belonged to the domain of free enterprise, to the private (in the sense of economic) sphere. Yet democratic regimes need more urgently than authoritarian ones to instill in people a sense of national loyalty and solidarity, and goods are an obvious site to do that. Yet there is also a need to allow for diversity to differentiate, perhaps because diverse tastes function as a kind of safety valve, a space within which to express difference. Perhaps just as one has a right to choose a representative, one must have a right to choose how one constitutes oneself through goods. Thus we approach the question of the relation between capitalism and democracy from another angle. Is it possible to have the concept of political representation, the delegation *and* constitution of one's interests as part of a group to another person, without having the possibility of constituting one's being through goods? And is it in fact possible for those with different tastes to adhere to the same nation?

These questions must remain open for now. As this book demonstrates, to look at the very small things of life helps us understand the big questions. The study of the everyday is most productive not when it takes on the moral task of restoring the forgotten to history or granting them agency, not when it tries to trace the *longue durée* of climate, soil, and harvest, not when it is on a quest for signs of resistance but when it seeks to grasp how the large-scale transformations of the world are crystallized, reproduced, and changed in the small gestures of the everyday. This is not to suggest that there is a totalizing system that embraces all, within which all can be understood. The institutional, political, economic, and intellectual structures within which we live are thoroughly laced with paradox and contradiction. It is in part because of those paradoxes and contradictions that the need for studying the relation between the small and the large, the concrete and the abstract is a reciprocal one. The study of the manifestations of the state and the economy in institutional and everyday forms gives us a very different and important view on their workings that would be missed if we examined them only more abstractly. Finally, the study of these processes over time allows us to see the contingencies differently. It is of course banal to say that "the state," for example, is a changing entity that embodies and enacts its power differently at different moments, yet despite our knowledge of its historicity, we often write as if it were always the same. Likewise, the place of goods in our lives is easily assumed, and taste, above all, appears the most natural of things. Thinking hard about how taste works can perhaps enable us to also grasp better how nations and economies, as well as our very selves, are made.

Bibliography

PUBLIC ARCHIVES

Archives du département de la Seine (ADS)

DE^1. Papiers de famille: fonds Bucaille, Dubocq, Lestringuez, Marsoulan.
DQ^{10}1667, dossier 351. Prêts aux ébénistes faits par l'état; dépôt des meubles, 1831–32.
VD^{6}21. Fondation de bourses d'apprentissage sous le patronage de la ville, en faveur des meilleurs élèves de l'enseignement primaire, 1847–59.
VR213–16. Bibliothèque Forney.
VR219. Musées du soir, 1895, 1908–9.
VR247. Expositions au musée Galliera.
Séries 6AZ 1814, D12 Z1–3, D17 Z1–4, D18 Z6 and Z9, D39 Z—catalogues des grands magasins, échantillons, factures.
10AZ 24. Livret d'ouvrier.

Archives nationales (AN)

AB XIX, séries 3496–3503. Livres de comptes de familles parisiennes, 1863–1937.
AD XI 2. Bois à bâtir et à ouvrer, 1674–1776.
AD XI 10–11. Communautés d'arts et métiers—réglements et statuts, 1743–88.
AD XI 18. Fondeurs, doreurs, graveurs, ciseleurs, desmasquineurs, 1532–1778.
AD XI 22. Menuisiers, ébénistes, tourneurs, layetiers, 1670–1780.
AD XI 25. Peintres, doreurs, vernisseurs, sculpteurs, marbriers, 1676–1778.
AD XI 27. Tapissiers, miroitiers, marchands de meubles, 1611–1756.
AD XI 45. Manufactures royales des Gobelins, de la Savonnerie, de Beauvais, de Sèvres.
F^{12}1569. Rapport de la Chambre de commerce au ministère de l'intérieur, an V.
F^{12}2332–34. Société d'encouragement, an XI–1843; ouvrages relatifs aux arts et manufactures, an III–1839; fonds accordés, prix, 1810–43; sociétés relatives aux arts et manufactures, 1830–70.
F^{12}2370–74. Organisation ouvrière, salaires, 1849–69.
F^{12}2387. Conservation des bois, an XIII–1841.

F^{12}2410. Ebénisterie, menuiserie, . . . an III–1852.

F^{12}2441. Correspondance relative à la création de musées d'art industriel, 1834–69.

F^{12}2511. Tarifs d'importation; importation et exportation du bois, 1791–1819.

F^{12}2713–14. Notes de statistiques sur le commerce et l'industrie, 1789–1903.

F^{12}3103. Exposition universelle, 1867, commission d'encouragement pour les études des ouvriers—formation des comités.

F^{12}3105–7. Correspondance des organisateurs avec les membres ouvriers de la commission; procès-verbaux d'éléction intéressants sur les rapports d'ouvriers entre eux à l'intérieur des diverses corporations d'ébénistes, de menuisiers.

F^{12}3109. Rapport général de Dewinck et celui de Fourcade.

F^{12}3111–12. Rapports des ouvriers délégués.

F^{12}3115–16. Menuisiers.

F^{12}3121. Tapissiers, tourneurs.

F^{12}3185–97. Exposition universelle de Paris, 1867.

F^{12}3249. Exposition, 1878—délégations ouvrières.

F^{12}3352. Application des arts du dessin et du plastique, 1878.

F^{12}3365–66. Application des arts du dessin et du plastique; classes 17–18—exposition, 1878.

F^{12}4830–33. Apprentissage industriel—loi du 22 février 1851; préparation et exécution, 1841–90.

F^{12}4861–63. Cours du soir, musée et école industrielle—nombre d'élèves, personnel.

F^{12}6171–75B. Statistique industrielle et commerciale, 1869–1900.

F^{12}6359–61. Office du travail; enquête sur l'apprentissage industriel, 1901.

F^{12}7621. Enquête d'apprentissage, 1902.

F^{17}10181. Dossier sur les activités de l'association polytechnique à la période impériale, documents sur les écoles professionnelles de Paris et les oeuvres d'apprentis.

F^{17}11700. Enseignement professionnel, 1865–88.

F^{17}12330. Comité de patronage des apprentis tapissiers.

F^{17}12529. Patronage industriel des enfants de l'ébénisterie, 1882.

F^{17}12530. Ecole polytechnique.

F^{17}14348. Ecoles professionnelles—personnel, décrets, arrêts, et réglements, 1892–96; élèves—nombre, recrutement, placement, 1891–1900.

F^{17}14364. Ecoles municipales, professionnelles de Paris (garçons et filles), 1890–1900.

F^{21}650. Ecole nationale des arts décoratifs.

F^{21}1422. Ecole spéciale de dessin (rue de l'Ecole de médecine), 1832.

F^{22}455. Apprentissage, 1861–1923.

L1051. Abbaye Saint-Antoine.

O^{1}3277. Garde-Meuble royal, administration générale—réglements royaux et intérieurs; mémoires et projets divers, 1657–1792.

Y17291. Lettres patentes de Louis XIV contenant les privilèges en faveur des arts et métiers du faubourg Saint-Antoine, février 1657.

368AP. Papiers Barbedienne, 1810–1955.

371AP2–13. Archives du château de Rosny, comptes et dépenses de Marie-Caroline, duchesse de Berry (1798–1870); factures et mémoires pour achats divers (armes, bijoux, meubles, tableaux . . .), 1816–37.

65AQ. Documentation imprimée concernant les sociétés—séries V, bois, ameublement; T, sociétés commerciales, grands magasins; X, syndicats professionnels, congrès, expositions.

Archives de la préfecture de police (APP)

Ba 168. Grève des ébénistes, menuisiers, ouvriers du sculpté, 1871–89.
Ba 181–82. Grève des ouvriers tourneurs sur bois, 1881–82; grève des ouvriers tapissiers, 1882–83.
Ba 1372. Grève des ouvriers ébénistes de 1891 à 1909.
Ba 1422. Ebénistes en meuble sculpté, 1886–1904; ébénistes en table de nuit, 1893–97; ébénistes, 1884–85; employés du Commerce-meuble, 1895.

Musée des arts et traditions populaires (ATP)

Mss 64.6–68.40B. Livrets d'ouvrier.

Bibliothèque Forney

Advertisements and catalogues in the series CC.
Auction catalogues in the series CV.
Fonds Fourdinois, iconography.

Bibliothèque historique de la ville de Paris (BHVP)

Série 120, ameublement—actualités. Several hundred advertisements from Parisian furniture stores.

Bibliothèque nationale (BN)

Mss français 21679. Anciens statuts des maîtres huchiers de Paris, donnez par le prévost de Paris [December 1290]; Arrest de nos seigneurs de Parlement rendu entre le communauté des tourneurs de la ville et fauxbourgs de Paris et les maitres menuisiers de la dite ville et autre [1 September 1698; Négo, quais des Augustins].
Mss français 21698. Statuts et réglements des maîtres jurez, huchers, menuisiers de Paris et autres patentes portant confirmation d'iceux [April 1580].

PRIVATE ARCHIVES

Maison Rinck

ACCOUNT BOOKS

List of clients and their purchases, 1901–6.
Expenses and sales, 1904–13.
Workers' hours, wages, and addresses, 1907–23.
Inventories, 1916–33.
Cost breakdown, 1917–29.
Workers' wages and work done, 1917–29.
Workers' hours and wages, 1925–28.
Wages, 1928–30.
Classification of models, customers' names, 1928–48.

Summary of cost breakdown, 1928–32.
List of customers, workers, hours, prices, 1929–32.
Classification of models, cost breakdown, 1930.
Cost breakdown, names and addresses of customers, 1930–33.
Cost breakdown, classification of models, 1930–51.
List of customers, of workers, hours, prices, 1932–43.
Cost breakdown, workers' names and salaries without the names of clients, 1943–47.
Classification of models, 1945–46?
Inventories, 1945–48.
Cost breakdown, 1946–50.
Work, wages, prices, 1950–54.

CATALOGUES OF DRAWINGS AND PHOTOGRAPHS
OF WORK PRODUCED

Catalogue, J. Rinck, *Meubles, sièges, tentures* (Paris: Justin Storck, 1889).
Catalogue of models, no date, ca. 1910–20.
Catalogue of models, no date, ca. 1920.
Catalogue of models, no date, 1920s.
Catalogue of models, no date, before 1930.
Catalogue of models, E. Rinck, ca. 1925.
Catalogue of models, no date, ca. 1930.
Catalogue of models, no date, Maurice Rinck, 1935–45.

SKETCHBOOKS

1932–59—one not numbered, 6 bis, 7, 7 bis, 11, 12, 14, 15, 16, 17, 18, 19, 21, 22, 23, 24, 30, 31, 32, 33, 34, 35, 36, 38 bis.

Maison Schmit

The holdings of the Maison Schmit (until 1939 on rue de Charonne; then boulevard de Créteil in Saint-Maur des Fossés) were even greater than those of Rinck. Unfortunately they were in the process of dispersal—some items had been sold, others thrown out—by the time I gained access to the archive and library. I salvaged some illustrations, account books, and other books but had no time to inventory the collection. The holdings were similar to Rinck's and included the financial records of the shop (lists of clients, hours, wages, cost breakdowns); photographic and drawing documentation of the shop's production; technical books; books on the fine arts; and journals and magazines from all over Europe. The documents from this collection mentioned in the text are in my possession.

PERIODICALS

Album de l'ameublement: journal de la décoration intérieure, 1882–92.
Art et décoration, 1897.

L'art décoratif: revue internationale d'art industriel et de décoration, 1899.
L'art et l'industrie: organe du progrès dans toutes les branches de l'industrie artistique, 1877.
L'art ornemental, 1883.
L'art pour tous: encyclopédie de l'art industriel et décoratif, 1861–1905.
Le conseiller des dames [et des demoiselles]: journal d'économie domestique et travaux d'aiguille, 1848–51.
La demeure française, 1925–29.
Intérieur, 1911–12.
Jardin des arts, 1945–55.
Journal de menuiserie, 1863–77.
Journal des dames et des modes, 1811.
Maison et jardin, 1945–.
Maison française, 1945–.
Menuiserie, ébénisterie, emploi du bois dans la menuiserie d'art et de bâtiment, les meubles ordinaires et de style, les mobiliers d'école et d'église, les constructions en bois, etc., 1882–87.
Moniteur de l'ameublement: journal des modes et du confort, 1863–68.
Plaisir de France, 1934–.
Revue des arts décoratifs, 1882–1900.

PRINTED MATERIALS

A. T. [Alfred Toqué]. Review of *Les budgets comparés de cent monographies de famille,* by E. Cheysson and A. Toqué. *Journal de la Société de statistique de Paris* (May 1891): 182.
Abelson, Elaine S. *When Ladies Go A-Thieving: Middle-Class Shoplifters in the Victorian Department Store.* New York: Oxford University Press, 1989.
Accampo, Elinor. *Industrialization, Family Life, and Class Relations: Saint Chamond, 1815–1914.* Berkeley: University of California Press, 1989.
Acker, Joan. "Class, Gender, and the Relations of Distribution." *Signs* 13 (spring 1988): 473–97.
Agnew, Jean-Christophe. *Worlds Apart: The Market and the Theater in Anglo-American Thought, 1550–1750.* Cambridge: Cambridge University Press, 1986.
Aguet, Jean-Pierre. *Les grèves sous la monarchie de juillet: contribution à l'étude du mouvement ouvrier français.* Geneva: E. Droz, 1954.
Agulhon, Maurice. *Marianne into Battle: Republican Imagery and Symbolism in France, 1789–1880.* Cambridge: Cambridge University Press, 1981.
Alheilig, M. *Recette, conservation, et travail des bois: outils et machines-outils employés dans ce travail.* Paris, [1894–95?].
Allwood, John. *The Great Exhibitions.* London: Studio Vista, 1977.
Almanach de Paris contenant la demeure, les noms et qualité des personnes de condition dans la ville et fauxbourgs de Paris. Paris: Lesclaport, 1772–81.
Almanach des corps des marchands et des communautés des arts et métiers de la ville et fauxbourgs de Paris. Paris, 1758, 1769.
Almanach des métiers pour 1852. Paris: G. de Gonnet, 1852.
Almanach du commerce de Paris. Paris, 1797.

Almanach parisien en faveur des étrangers et des personnes curieuses. Paris: la veuve Duchesne, 1765–93.

Alt, John Darrell. "Leisure, Labor, and Consumption: A Critical Sociology of Reification." Ph.D. dissertation, Washington University, 1977.

"Ameublements d'art: Maison Drouard." Special issue, Revue de l'exposition de 1880. *Revue des arts décoratifs* 3 (1882–83): 11–12.

Aminzade, Ronald. *Class, Politics, and Early Industrial Capitalism: A Study of Mid-Nineteenth-Century Toulouse, France.* Albany: State University of New York Press, 1981.

Anceau, Georges. *Organisation industrielle: la fabrication des meubles modernes en grande série.* Paris: Travail du Bois, 1931.

Anderson, Benedict. *Imagined Communities: Reflections on the Origins and Spread of Nationalism.* London: Verso, 1983.

Anderson, Michael. *Approaches to the History of the Western Family, 1500–1914.* London: Macmillan, 1980.

Annuaire de l'ameublement et de l'ébénisterie, 1887–88.

Annuaire des notables commerçants de la ville de Paris, contenant leurs noms et adresses, les spécialités de leur commerce, la date de leurs établissements, les distinctions honorifiques qu'ils ont obtenues. Paris: J. Techener, 1861.

Appadurai, Arjun, ed. *The Social Life of Things: Commodities in Cultural Perspective.* Cambridge: Cambridge University Press, 1986.

Apter, Emily. *Feminizing the Fetish: Psychoanalysis and Narrative Obsession in Turn-of-the-Century France.* Ithaca: Cornell University Press, 1991.

Ariès, Philippe. Introduction to *Passions of the Renaissance,* edited by Roger Chartier, translated by Arthur Goldhammer, 1–11. Vol. 3 of *A History of Private Life,* edited by Philippe Ariès and Georges Duby. Cambridge, Mass.: Harvard University Press, 1989.

Arrest de la cour de Parlement portant Réglement entre les Six Corps des Marchands de la Ville de Paris et les Huissiers-Commissaires-Priseurs au Châtelet de Paris. Au Sujet des Ventes de Fonds de Boutiques, Marchandises et Meubles Neuf [17 June 1777]. Paris: Knappen, 1777.

Atget, Eugène. *Eugène Atget, 1857–1927: Intérieurs parisiens, photographies.* Paris: Musées de la ville de Paris, 1982.

Auclert, Hubertine. *Le vote des femmes.* Paris: V. Biard et E. Brière, 1908.

Audiganne, Armand. *La lutte industrielle des peuples.* Paris: Capelle, 1868.

Auslander, Leora. "The Creation of Value and the Production of Good Taste: The Social Life of Furniture in Paris, 1860–1914." Ph.D. dissertation, Brown University, 1988.

———. "After the Revolution: Recycling Ancien Régime Style in the Nineteenth Century." In *Re-creating Authority in Revolutionary France,* edited by Bryant T. Ragan and Elizabeth Williams, 144–74. New Brunswick, N.J.: Rutgers University Press, 1992.

———. "Feminist Theory and Social History: Explorations in the Politics of Identity." *Radical History Review* 54 (fall 1992): 158–76.

———. "Perceptions of Beauty and the Problem of Consciousness: Parisian Furniture Makers." In *Rethinking Labor History: Essays on Discourse and Class*

Analysis, edited by Lenard R. Berlanstein, 149–81. Urbana: University of Illinois Press, 1993.

———. "'Experience' and Reflectivity: The Politics of Situated Knowledges and Narratives." *Historische Anthropologie* 8 (August 1995).

———. "The Gendering of Consumer Practices in Nineteenth-Century France." In *Force of Things: Essays on Gender and Consumption,* edited by Victoria de Grazia and Ellen Furlough. Berkeley: University of California Press, in press.

"Aux abonnés." *Journal de menuiserie* 1 (1863): 65.

Avril, Paul. *L'ameublement parisien avant, pendant, et après la révolution.* Paris: A. Sinjon, 1929.

Azaryahu, Maoz. "Street Names and Political Identity: The Case of East Berlin." *Journal of Contemporary History* 21 (1986): 581–604.

Azzano, Laurent. *Mes joyeuses années au faubourg: souvenirs du faubourg Saint-Antoine.* Paris: Editions de France-Empire, 1985.

Babeau, Albert. *Les bourgeois d'autrefois.* Paris: Firmin-Didot, 1886.

Bachrach, Susan. *Dames Employées: The Feminization of Postal Work in Nineteenth-Century France.* New York: Haworth Press, 1984.

Bailey, Colin B. "'*Quel dommage qu'une telle dispersion*': Collectors of French Painting and the French Revolution." In *1789: French Art during the Revolution,* edited by Alan Wintermute. 11–26. New York: Colnaghi, 1989.

Bajot, Edouard. *Du choix et de la disposition des ameublements de style: étude des meubles du point au vue de leur destination variée.* Paris: Rouveyre, 1898.

Baker, Keith Michael. "Politics and Public Opinion under the Old Regime: Some Reflections." In *Press and Politics in Pre-Revolutionary France,* edited by Jack R. Censer and Jeremy D. Popkin, 204–46. Berkeley: University of California Press, 1987.

———. *Inventing the French Revolution: Essays on French Political Culture in the Eighteenth Century.* New York: Cambridge University Press, 1990.

Ballot, Marie-Juliette. "Charles Cressent, ébéniste du régent." *Revue d'art ancien et moderne* (1919): 237–53.

Balzac, Honoré de. *Le cousin Pons.* 1846. Paris: Gallimard, 1973.

Bapst, Germain. "Exposition Louis XIV et Louis XV de l'Hôtel Chimay, à Paris." *La Nature* 1 (1888).

Baron, Ava. "Questions of Gender: Deskilling and Demasculinization in the U.S. Printing Industry, 1830–1915." *Gender and History* 1 (summer 1989): 178–99.

———, ed. *Work Engendered: Toward a New History of American Labor.* Ithaca: Cornell University Press, 1991.

Barrielle, Jean-François. *Le style empire.* Paris: Flammarion, 1982.

Barthes, Roland. *Le système de la mode.* Paris: Seuil, 1976.

Bassanville, Anaïs Lebrun. *L'art de bien tenir une maison.* 29th ed. Paris: Victor-Havard, 1892.

Baudeau, Nicolas. *Principes de la science morale et politique sur le luxe et les lois somptuaires.* 1767. Paris: P. Geuthner, 1912.

Baudrillard, Jean. *Le miroir de la production.* Paris: Denoël, 1968.

———. *La société de consommation: ses mythes, ses structures.* Paris: Denoël, 1970.

———. *Le système des objets*. Tournail: Casterman, 1975.

———. *Selected Writings*. Edited by Mark Poster. Stanford: Stanford University Press, 1988.

Baudrillart, Henri. *Histoire du luxe, privé et public depuis l'antiquité jusqu'à nos jours*. Vol. 4. Paris: A. Lahure, 1881.

Baulez, Charles. "Le mobilier et les objets d'art de madame du Barry." In *Madame du Barry: de Versailles à Louveciennes*, edited by Marie-Amynthe Denis, et al., 25–86. Paris: Flammarion, 1992.

Bauman, Zygmunt. "Strangers: Social Construction of Universality and Particularity." *Telos* 78 (winter 1988–89): 7–42.

Bauthian, Charles. *Droit romain: le luxe et les lois somptuaires. Droit français: le luxe et les lois somptuaires. Rôle du luxe au point de vue économique*. Paris: A. Giard, 1891.

Bayard, Emile. *Le style empire: ouvrage orné de 132 gravures*. Paris: Librairie Garnier Frères, [1914?].

Beale, Marjorie. "Mort à Crédit: The Credit Department Store and the Parisian Lower Classes, 1856–1920." B.A. thesis, Harvard College, 1982.

Bechhofer, Frank, and Brian Elliott. "Petty Property: The Survival of a Moral Economy." In *The Petite Bourgeoisie: Comparative Studies of the Uneasy Stratum*, edited by Frank Bechhofer and Brian Elliott, 182–200. New York: St. Martin's, 1981.

Belk, Russell. "Acquiring, Possessing, and Collecting: Fundamental Processes in Consumer Behavior." In *Marketing Theory: Philosophy of Science Perspectives*, edited by Ronald F. Bush and Shelby D. Hunt, 185–90. Chicago: American Marketing Association, 1982.

Benjamin, Walter. "Unpacking My Library." In *Illuminations*, edited by Hannah Arendt, translated by Harry Zohn. New York: Schocken, 1968.

Benker, Gertrud. *Bürgerliches Wohnen: Städtische Wohnkultur in Mitteleuropa von der Gotik bis zum Jugendstil*. Munich: Callwey, 1984.

Bergdoll, Barry George. "Historical Reasoning and Architectural Politics: Léon Vaudoyer and the Development of French Historicist Architecture." Ph.D. dissertation, Columbia University, 1986.

Berger, Georges. *Les expositions universelles internationales: leur passé, leur rôle actuel, leur avenir*. Paris: Arthur Rousseau, 1901.

Bergeron, L. *Manuel du tourneur*. 2 vols. Paris: Chez Hamelin-Bergeron, 1816.

Berlanstein, Lenard R. "Growing Up as Workers in Nineteenth-Century Paris: Case of the Orphans of the Prince Imperial." *French Historical Studies* 11 (1980): 551–76.

———. *The Working People of Paris, 1871–1914*. Baltimore: Johns Hopkins University Press, 1984.

Berlant, Lauren. *The Anatomy of National Fantasy: Hawthorne, Utopia, and Everyday Life*. Chicago: University of Chicago Press, 1991.

Bernard-Bécharies, J. F. *Le choix de consommation: rationalité et réalité du comportement du consommateur*. Paris: Editions Eyrolles, 1970.

Bertaux, Daniel, and Isabelle Bertaux-Wiame. "Artisanal Bakery in France: How It Lives and Why It Survives." In *The Petite Bourgeoisie: Comparative Studies of the Uneasy Stratum*, edited by Frank Bechhofer and Brian Elliott, 155–81. New York: St. Martin's, 1981.

Bertin, Louis. *L'art et la science du meuble: ouvrage d'enseignement professionel moderne.* 2 vols. Dourdan: Lecoux and Bilard, [1900].

Bertrand, Christine. *Le meuble et l'homme: essai sur une philosophie du meuble.* Verviers: C. Vinche, 1946.

Beurdeley, A., fils. "Les meubles d'art." *Revue des arts décoratifs* 3 (1882–83): 2–3.

Bezucha, Robert J. *The Lyon Uprising of 1834: Social and Political Conflict in the Early July Monarchy.* Cambridge, Mass.: Harvard University Press, 1974.

Bhabha, Homi K. "Interrogating Identity: The Postcolonial Prerogative." In *Anatomy of Racism*, edited by David Theo Goldberg, 180–209. Minneapolis: University of Minnesota Press, 1990.

Bimont, J. F. *Principes de l'art du tapissier: ouvrage utile aux gens de la profession et à ceux qui les emploient.* Paris: Lottin, 1770.

Blanc, Charles. "Etude sur les arts décoratifs: les meubles." *Journal de menuiserie* 12 (1875): 22–48.

Blanc, Hippolyte. *Les corporations de métiers: leur histoire, leur esprit, leur avenir.* Paris: Letouzey et Ané, 1898.

Bloch, Jean-Jacques, and Marianne Delort. *Quand Paris alla 'à l'Expo.'* Paris: Fayard, 1980.

Blondel, Jacques-François. *Discours sur la nécessité de l'étude de l'architecture: de l'utilité de joindre à l'étude de l'architecture celles des sciences et des arts qui lui sont relatifs.* 1754. Reprint, Geneva: Minkoff, 1973.

Blondel, Spire. *L'art pendant la révolution, beaux-arts, arts décoratifs.* Paris: Laurens, 1887.

Bluysen, Paul. *Paris en 1889: souvenirs et croquis de l'exposition.* Paris: P. Arnould, 1890.

Boltanski, Luc. *Les cadres: la formation d'un groupe social.* Paris: Editions de Minuit, 1982.

———. "How a Social Group Objectified Itself: 'Cadres' in France, 1936–45." *Social Science Information* 23, no. 3 (1984): 469–91.

Bonnaffé, Edmond. *Inventaire des meubles de Catherine de Médicis en 1589.* Paris: Auguste Aubry, 1874.

———. *Etudes sur l'art et la curiosité.* Paris: Société française d'éditions d'art, 1902.

Bonnardot, Hippolyte. *L'abbaye royale de Saint-Antoine-des-Champs, et de l'ordre de Citeaux: étude topographique et historique.* Paris: Féchoz et Letouzey, 1882.

Bonneville, A. S. *Le faubourg Saint-Antoine, ou considérations sur l'administration politique et municipale du 8ème arrondissement de la ville de Paris.* Paris, 1834.

Borsay, Peter. "The English Urban Renaissance: The Development of Provincial Urban Culture, ca. 1680–1760." *Social History* 5 (1977).

Bossenga, Gail. "Protecting Merchants: Guilds and Commercial Capitalism in Eighteenth-Century France." *French Historical Studies* 15 (fall 1988): 693–703.

Bottin, Sebastien. *Almanach du commerce de Paris, des départements de la France, et des principales villes du monde.* Paris, 1830, 1845.

Boucher, J. *De la vente à tempérament dans des meubles corporels au point de vue économique.* Paris: A. Pédone, 1906.

Bouin, Philippe, and Christian-Philippe Chanut. *Histoire française des foires et des expositions universelles.* Paris: Editions de Nesle, 1980.

Bourdieu, Pierre. "What Makes a Social Class? On the Theoretical and Practical Existence of Groups." *Berkeley Journal of Sociology* 32 (1987): 1–17.

———. *La distinction: critique sociale du jugement.* Paris: Editions de Minuit, 1979.

Boureau, Alain. *Le simple corps du roi: l'impossible sacralité des souverains français XVe–XVIIIe siècle.* Paris: Editions de Paris, 1988.

Bourget, Paul. "Other People's Luxury." In *Domestic Dramas.* Translated by William Marchant. New York: Charles Scribner's Sons, 1900.

Boutemy, André. "L'avènement du style Louis XV." *Connaissance des arts* 70 (December 1957): 132–37.

———. ". . . révèle et définit la personnalité de Pierre II Migeon, ébéniste de qualité, marchand prospère et artiste 'abstrait' de la marqueterie au XVIIIe siècle." *Connaissance des arts* 83 (January 1959): 66–73.

———. *Analyses stylistiques et essais d'attribution de meubles français anonymes du XVIIIe siècle.* Brussels: Université de Bruxelles, 1973.

Bouvier-Ajam, Maurice. *Histoire du travail en France des origines à la Révolution.* Paris: Librairie général de Droit et de Jurisprudence, 1957.

Bowlby, Rachel. *Just Looking: Consumer Culture in Dreiser, Gissing, and Zola.* New York: Methuen, 1985.

Boylesve, René. *Madeleine jeune femme.* Paris: Calmann-Lévy, 1912.

Brants, V. "L'état de la petite industrie en France d'après les statistiques récentes." Part 1. *Bulletin de l'Académie royale de Belgique* 6 (1900): 513–34.

Braudel, Fernand. *The Structures of Everyday Life,* translated by Sian Reynolds. London: Collins, 1981.

Breen, Timothy. "An Empire of Goods: The Anglicization of Colonial America, 1690–1776." *Journal of British Studies* 25 (October 1986): 467–99.

———. "'Baubles of Britain': The American and Consumer Revolutions of the Eighteenth Century." *Past and Present* 119 (May 1988): 73–104.

———. "The Meaning of 'likeness': American Portrait Painting in an Eighteenth-Century Consumer Society." *Word and Image* 6 (October–December 1990): 325–50.

———. "The Meanings of Things: Interpreting the Consumer Economy in the Eighteenth Century." In *Consumption and the World of Goods,* edited by John Brewer and Roy Porter. New York: Routledge, 1993.

Bressani, Martin. "The Spectacle of the City of Paris from 25 bis rue Franklin." *Assemblage* 12 (August 1990): 85–107.

Brewer, John. *Party Ideology and Popular Politics at the Accession of George III.* London: Cambridge University Press, 1976.

———. "Commercialization and Politics." In *The Birth of a Consumer Society: the Commercialization of Eighteenth-Century England,* edited by Neil McKendrick, John Brewer, and J. H. Plumb. London: Europa Publications, 1982.

Briquet, Jean. *Agricol Perdiguier: compagnon du tour de France et représentant du peuple, 1805–1875.* Paris: Librairie M. Rivière, 1955.

Brizon, Pierre. *Histoire du travail et des travailleurs*. Brussels: Editions de l'Eglantine, 1926.

Brongniart, Edouard. "De l'enseignement du dessin en 1867." In *Exposition universelle de 1867, à Paris: rapports du jury international*, edited by Michel Chevalier, 13:402–11. Paris: Imprimerie administrative de Paul Dupont, 1868.

Bronner, Simon J., ed. *Consuming Visions: Accumulation and Display of Goods in America, 1880–1920*. New York: Norton, 1989.

Brown, Gillian. *Domestic Individualism: Imagining Self in Nineteenth-Century America*. Berkeley: University of California Press, 1990.

Brubaker, Rogers. *Citizenship and Nationhood in France and Germany*. Cambridge, Mass.: Harvard University Press, 1992.

Brunhammer, Yvonne, and Monique Ricour. "Les ébénistes parisiens du XVIIIe siècle . . ." *Jardin des arts* 14 (December 1955): 72–80.

Buck-Morss, Susan. *The Dialectics of Seeing: Walter Benjamin and the Arcades Project*. Cambridge, Mass.: MIT Press, 1989.

Bunn, James H. "The Aesthetics of British Mercantilism." *New Literary History* 11, no. 2 (winter 1980): 303–21.

Buonanni, Filippo. *Traité des vernis, où l'on donne la manière d'en composer un qui ressemble parfaitement à celui de la Chine, et plusieurs autres qui concernent la peinture, la dorure, la gravure à l'eau forte, etc.* Paris: Chez L. d'Houry, 1723.

Burawoy, Michael. *The Politics of Production: Factory Regimes under Capitalism and Socialism*. London: Verso, 1985.

Burke, Peter. *The Fabrication of Louis XIV*. New Haven: Yale University Press, 1992.

Butler, Judith. *Gender Trouble: Feminism and the Subversion of Identity*. New York: Routledge, 1990.

Butler, Judith, and Joan Wallach Scott, eds. *Feminists Theorize the Political*. New York: Routledge, 1992.

Cadoux, Gaston. "Contribution à l'étude des salaires réels et du coût de la vie des ouvriers des grandes villes." *Journal de la Société de statistique de Paris* (December 1907): 409–16.

Calagione, John, Doris Francis, and Danien Nugent, eds. *Workers' Expressions: Beyond Accomodation and Resistance*. Albany: State University of New York Press, 1992.

Cambry, Adrienne. *Fiançailles et fiancés*. Paris, 1913.

Capronnier, Janine. *Le prix des meubles d'époque, 1860–1956*. Paris: Armand Colin, 1966.

Caron, ainé. *Manuel de l'ébéniste*. Paris, 1836.

Certeau, Michel de. *The Practice of Everyday Life*. Translated by Steven F. Rendall. Berkeley: University of California Press, 1984.

———. *The Writing of History*. Translated by Tom Conley. New York: Columbia University Press, 1988.

Cerutti, Simona. "Group Strategies and Trade Strategies: The Turin Tailors' Guild in the Late Seventeenth and Early Eighteenth Centuries." In *Domestic Strategies: Work and Family in France and Italy, 1600–1800*, edited by Stuart Woolf, 102–47. Cambridge: Cambridge University Press, 1991.

Chabat, Pierre. "Coloration des bois." *Journal de menuiserie* 14 (1877): 29–31.

Chambre de commerce de Paris. *Statistique de l'industrie à Paris, édité pour les années 1847–48.* Paris: Guillamin et Cie., 1851.

———. *Statistique de l'industrie à Paris, édité pour l'année 1860.* Paris: Guillamin et Cie., 1862.

Champeaux, Alfred de. *Le meuble.* 2 vols. Paris: Société française d'éditions d'art, 1885.

Champier, Victor. "La maison modèle: études et types d'ameublement." *Revue des arts décoratifs* 3 (1882–83): 19–21; 41–58; 180–84; 364–74.

———. "Le Pavillon de la commission française organisé par l'Union centrale à l'exposition d'Amsterdam." *Revue des arts décoratifs* 4 (1883–84): 64–100.

Chartier, Roger. *The Cultural Uses of Print in Early Modern France.* Translated by Lydia G. Cochrane. Princeton: Princeton University Press, 1987.

Charton, Edouard Thomas, ed. *Dictionnaire des professions, ou guide pour le choix d'un état.* . . . 1842. 3d ed. Paris: Hachette, 1880.

Chaveau, Ismael. *De la vente à tempérament des objets mobiliers.* Paris: A. Pédone, 1909.

Chevalier, Louis. *Laboring Classes and Dangerous Classes in Paris during the First Half of the Nineteenth Century.* Translated by Frank Jellinek. New York: H. Fertig, 1973.

Chevalier, Michel, ed. *Exposition universelle de Londres de 1862: rapports des membres de la section française du jury international sur l'ensemble de l'exposition.* 7 vols. Paris: N. Chaix, 1862–64.

———, ed. *Exposition universelle de 1867, à Paris: rapports du jury international.* Vols. 9, 13. Paris: Imprimerie administrative de Paul Dupont, 1868.

Clark, Linda L. *Schooling the Daughters of Marianne: Textbooks and the Socialization of Girls in Modern French Primary Schools.* Albany: State University of New York Press, 1984.

Clark, Peter. *The English Alehouse: A Social History, 1200–1830.* London: Longman, 1983.

Clawson, MaryAnn. "Early Modern Fraternalism and the Patriarchal Family." *Feminist Studies* 6 (summer 1980): 368–91.

Clifford, James. "On Collecting Art and Culture." In *The Predicament of Culture: Twentieth-Century Ethnography, Literature, and Art.* Cambridge, Mass.: Harvard University Press, 1988.

Cochin, M. A. "Classe 91: meubles, vêtements et aliments de toute origine, distingués par les qualités utiles unies au bon marché." In *Exposition universelle de 1867, à Paris: rapports du jury international,* edited by Michel Chevalier, 13:775–86. Paris: Imprimerie administrative de Paul Dupont, 1868.

Cockburn, Cynthia. *Brothers: Male Dominance and Technological Change.* London: Pluto Press, 1983.

Cole, W. A. "Factors in Demand 1700–80." In *The Economic History of Britain since 1700,* edited by Roderick Floud and Donald McCloskey, 1:36–65. Cambridge: Cambridge University Press, 1981.

Colette, Sidonie Gabrielle. *The Vagabond.* Translated by Enid McLeod. New York: Farrar, Straus and Young, 1955.

Comaroff, Jean, and John Comaroff. "Homemade Hegemony." In *Ethnography and the Historical Imagination.* Boulder: Westview Press, 1992.

Comte, Henri. *Les bibliothèques publiques en France.* Lyons: Imprimerie Bosc, 1977.

Coornaert, Emile. *Les corporations en France avant 1789.* Paris: Gallimard, 1941.

Coster. *Projet d'association générale dans toute la France.* Paris, 1851.

Cougny, Gaston. *L'enseignement professionnel des beaux-arts dans les écoles de la ville de Paris.* Paris: Maison Quantin, 1888.

Coulon, G. *Nouveau vignole de menuisier.* Paris, 1835.

Courajod, Louis, ed. *Livre-journal de Lazare Duvaux, marchand-bijoutier ordinaire du roy 1748–1758.* 2 vols. Paris: Société des Bibliophiles françois, 1873.

Coussirat, Lucien. *Manuel du tapissier décorateur.* Paris: Baillière, 1927.

Cousté, J. "Rapport sur le matériel et les procédés de la confection des objets de mobilier et d'habitation." In *Exposition universelle de 1878, groupe VI, classe 59.* Paris: Imprimerie nationale, 1881.

Coward, Rosalind. *Female Desires.* New York: Grove Press, 1985.

Coyner, Sandra. "Class Consciousness and Consumption: The New Middle Class during the Weimar Republic." *Journal of Social History* 10 (spring 1977): 310–31.

Crapanzano, Vincent. *Tuhami: Portrait of a Moroccan.* Chicago: University of Chicago Press, 1980.

Crew, David. "*Alltagsgeschichte:* A New Social History 'From Below'?" *Central European History* 22 (1989): 394–407.

Crow, Thomas. *Painters and Public Life in Eighteenth-Century Paris.* New Haven: Yale University Press, 1985.

Csikszentmihalyi, Mihaly, and Eugene Rochberg-Halton. *The Meaning of Things: Domestic Symbols and the Self.* Cambridge: Cambridge University Press, 1981.

Curtin, Michael. "A Question of Manners: Status and Gender in Etiquette and Courtesy." *Journal of Modern History* 57, no. 3 (September 1985): 395–423.

Daly, César. *Architecture privée de Paris et des environs sous Napoléon III: hôtels privés, maisons à loyer, villas.* 3 vols. Paris: Librairie A. Morel, 1864.

Darcel, Alfred. "Oeben, Riesener, et Maugie aux Gobelins." *Nouvelles archives d'art français,* 3d s., 1 (1885).

Daumard, Adeline. *Les bourgeois de Paris au XIXe siècle.* Paris: Flammarion, 1970.

———. *Les bourgeois et la bourgeoisie en France depuis 1815.* Paris: Aubier, 1987.

Daumard, Adeline, and François Furet. *Structures et relations sociales à Paris au milieu du XVIIIe siècle.* Paris: Armand Colin, 1961.

Daunton, M. J. "Towns and Economic Growth in Eighteenth-Century England." In *Towns in Societies: Essays in Economic History and Historical Sociology,* edited by Philip Abrams and E. A. Wrigley. Cambridge: Cambridge University Press, 1982.

d'Aurevilly, Jules Barbey. *Du dandysme et de George Brummel.* 1845. Paris: Plein Chant, 1989.

Davidoff, Leonore. *The Best Circles: Women and Society in Victorian Britain.* Totowa, N.J.: Rowman and Littlefield, 1973.

Davidoff, Leonore, and Catherine Hall. *Family Fortunes: Men and Women of the English Middle Class, 1780–1850*. Chicago: University of Chicago Press, 1987.

Day, C. R. "The Making of Mechanical Engineers in France: The Ecoles d'Arts et Métiers, 1803–1914." *French Historical Studies* 10 (spring 1978): 439–60.

Delosmois. *Le Vernisseur parfait, ou manuel du vernisseur*. Paris: C. A. Jombert, 1771.

Declaration du Roi portant création, dans la ville de Versailles, d'une communauté de peintres, doreurs, vernisseurs, sculpteurs et marbriers. Paris: 1777.

Defert, Daniel. "The Collection of the World: Accounts of Voyages from the 16th to the 18th centuries." *Dialectical Anthropology* 7, no. 1 (September 1982): 11–20.

Delafosse, Jean-Charles. *Oeuvre*. Vol. 3. Paris, 1772.

de l'Alq, Mme. *Le maître et la maîtresse de la maison*. Paris: Bureaux des causeries familières, 1888.

Delamarre, Théodore-Casimir. *Economie pratique: la vie à bon marché, économie pratique, reformes utiles*. Paris: Levy, 1851.

Delaunay, Jean-Baptiste-Rémy. *L'alphabet du trait appliqué à la menuiserie*. Paris: Roret, 1851.

Delbourg-Delphis, Marylène. *Masculin singulier: le dandysme et son histoire*. Paris: Hachette, 1985.

Deloche, Bernard. *L'art du meuble: introduction à l'esthétique des arts mineurs*. Lyons: Editions l'Hermès, 1980.

Demont. *Nouveau traité d'ébénisterie mis à la portée de tous les ouvriers avec plans, coupes et élévations*. Paris, [1880?].

Denvir, Bernard. *The Late Victorians: Art, Design, and Society, 1852–1910*. London: Longman, 1986.

"Des bois d'oeuvre." *Journal de menuiserie* 1 (1863): 15–16.

Desaix, Fabienne. "L'art d'être ébéniste en cinq générations." *L'estampille:* 14–19.

Deschamps, Madeleine. "Domestic Elegance: The French at Home." In *L'art de vivre: Decorative Arts and Design in France, 1789–1989*, edited by Catherine Armijon, Yvonne Brunhammer, Madeleine Deschamps, et al., 107–41. London: Thames and Hudson, 1989.

Desmaze, Charles Adrian. *Les métiers de Paris d'après les ordonnances du Châtelet avec les sceaux des artisans*. Paris: E. Leroux, 1875.

Desvernay, Arnould, ed. *Rapports des délégations ouvrières contenant l'origine et l'histoire des diverses professions*. Paris: Librairie A. Morel, 1867.

Deville, Jules. *Dictionnaire du tapissier critique et historique de l'ameublement français depuis les temps anciens jusqu'à nos jours*. Paris: C. Claesen, 1878–80.

Deville, Jules, ed. *Recueil de documents et de statuts relatifs à la Corporation des tapissiers de 1258 à 1875: réflexions concernant cette Corporation*. Paris: A. Chaix, 1875.

Devinck, M. F., ed. *Exposition universelle de 1867, à Paris: rapports des délégations ouvrières contenant l'origine et l'histoire des diverses professions, l'appréciation des objets exposés, la comparaison des arts et des industries en France et à l'étranger, l'exposé des voeux et besoins de la classe laborieuse, et l'ensemble des considérations sociales intéressant les ouvriers*. Paris: Librairie A. Morel, 1868.

Dewald, Jonathan. *The Formation of a Provincial Nobility: The Magistrates of the Parlement of Rouen, 1499–1610.* Princeton: Princeton University Press, 1980.

Dictionnaire portatif des arts et métiers. Paris, 1766.

Diderot, Denis, and Jean le Rond d'Alembert. *Encyclopédie, ou dictionnaire raisonné des sciences, des arts et des métiers.* 1751. 30 vols. Reprint, New York: Pergamon Press, 1975.

Dilke, Emilia Frances Strong. *Art in the Modern State.* London: Chapman and Hall, 1888.

Doane, Mary Anne. *The Desire to Desire: The Woman's Film of the 1940s.* Bloomington: Indiana University Press, 1987.

Douglas, Mary, and Baron Isherwood. *The World of Goods.* New York: Basic, 1979.

Doyle, William. "Was There an Aristocratic Reaction in Pre-Revolutionary France?" *Past and Present* 57 (November 1972): 97–122.

———. *Origins of the French Revolution.* Oxford: Oxford University Press, 1980.

Drohojowska, Antoinette. *Conseils à une jeune fille sur les devoirs à remplir dans le monde comme maîtresse de maison à Paris.* 4th ed. Paris: Perisse Frères, [1870?].

Droz, Gustave. *Monsieur, madame et bébé.* Paris: Victor-Havard, 1878.

Du Bois, W. E. B. "Of Our Spiritual Strivings." *Souls of Black Folk.* Chicago: A. C. McClurg, 1903.

Du faubourg Saint-Antoine au bois de Vincennes: promenade historique dans le 12e arrondissement. Paris: Musées de la ville de Paris, 1983.

Duhamel du Monceau, Henri Louis. *Du transport, de la conservation et de la force des bois.* Paris: L. F. Delatour, 1767.

Dulac, Henri. *Almanach des 25,000 adresses des principaux habitants de Paris.* 10 vols. Paris, 1823–48.

Du Maroussem, Pierre. *Les ébénistes du faubourg Saint-Antoine.* Vol. 2 in *La question ouvrière.* Paris: Arthur Rousseau, 1892.

Du Mesnil, Octave. *L'hygiène à Paris: l'habitation du pauvre.* Paris: J. B. Baillière et fils, 1890.

Dumont, Jean-Paul. *The Headman and I: Ambiguity and Ambivalence in the Fieldworking Experience.* Austin: University of Texas Press, 1978.

Duncan, Carol. "Art Museums and the Ritual of Citizenship." In *Exhibiting Cultures: The Poetics and Politics of Museum Display,* edited by Ivan Karp and Steven D. Lavine, 88–103. Washington, D.C.: Smithsonian Institution Press, 1991.

———. "Happy Mothers and Other New Ideas in Eighteenth-Century French Art." In *The Aesthetics of Power: Essays in Critical Art History,* 3–26. Cambridge: Cambridge University Press, 1992.

Duplessis, Georges. "Le département des estampes à la Bibliothèque nationale: indications sommaires sur les documents utiles aux artistes industriels." *Revue des arts décoratifs* 6 (1885–86): 334–41.

Dutheil, F. G. *Aide-mémoire de l'ébéniste tapissier décorateur.* Paris, 1922.

Duveau, Georges. *La vie ouvrière en France sous le Second Empire.* Paris: Gallimard, 1946.

———. *1848: The Making of a Revolution,* translated by Anne Carter. New York: Pantheon Books, 1967.

Eagleton, Terry. *The Ideology of the Aesthetic*. Oxford: Oxford University Press, 1990.

"Ebénisterie et marqueterie; Hunsinger et Wagner." Special issue, Revue de l'exposition de 1880. *Revue des arts décoratifs* 3 (1882–83): 24–26.

Eleb-Vidal, Monique, and Anne Debarre-Blanchard. *Architectures de la vie privée: maisons et mentalités, XVIIe–XIXe siècles*. Brussels: Aux Archives d'Architecture moderne, 1989.

Eley, Geoff. "Labor History, Social History, Alltagsgeschichte: Experience, Culture, and the Politics of the Everyday—A New Direction for German Social History?" *Journal of Modern History* 61, no. 2 (June 1989): 297–343.

Elias, Norbert. *The Court Society*. 1969. Translated by Edmund Jephcott. New York: Pantheon, 1983.

Elwitt, Sanford. *The Making of the Third Republic: Class and Politics in France, 1868–1884*. Baton Rouge: Louisiana State University Press, 1975.

Eriksen, Svend. *Early Neo-Classicism in France: The Creation of the Louis Seize Style in Architectural Decoration, Furniture and Ormolu, Gold and Silver, and Sèvres Porcelain in the Mid-Eighteenth Century*. Translated by Peter Thornton. London: Faber and Faber, 1974.

L'esprit du commerce pour 1754. Paris, 1754.

Etincelle [Henriette Marie Adelaïde Double]. *Carnet d'un mondain . . . gazette parisienne, anecdotique et curieuse*. Paris: Edouard Rouveyre, 1881–82.

Eudel, Paul. *Le truquage: altérations, fraudes et contrefaçons dévoilées*. Paris: Librairie Molière, n.d. [late 19th century].

Everseley, D. E. C. "The Home Market and Economic Growth in England, 1750–1780." In *Land, Labour, and Population in the Industrial Revolution*, edited by E. L. Jones and G. E. Mingay, 206–59. New York: Barnes and Noble, 1967.

Ewald, François. *L'état providence*. Paris: B. Grasset, 1986.

Ewen, Stuart. *All Consuming Images: The Politics of Style in Contemporary Culture*. New York: Basic Books, 1988.

Exposition des produits d'industrie française en 1839: rapport du jury central. 3 vols. Paris: L. Bouchard-Huzard, 1839.

Exposition IVe des produits des membres de l'Académie de l'industrie à l'Orangerie des Tuileries, en 1840: catalogue des produits admis à cette exposition, rédigés sur les notices remises par MM. les industriels. Paris: Guiraudet et Jouaust, 1840.

Exposition universelle (de 1855): galerie de l'économie domestique. Paris: Imprimerie J. Claye, 1855.

Exposition universelle de 1855: rapports du jury mixte international, publiés sous la direction de SAI le prince Napoléon. Paris: Imprimerie impériale, 1856.

Exposition universelle de 1867: enquête ouverte par la réunion des bureaux du 10e groupe . . . Institutions créées par les chefs d'industrie et les ouvriers pour améliorer la condition morale et physique de la population. Paris: Imprimerie impériale, 1867.

Exposition universelle de Vienne, 1873: France—produits industriels. Paris, 1873.

Exposition universelle internationale de 1878: rapports du jury international. 23 vols. Paris: Imprimerie nationale, 1881–85.

"Extrait du rapport des délégués ébénistes à l'exposition universelle de 1867." In *Exposition universelle de 1867: commission ouvrière* . . . , edited by Eugène Tartaret, 1:107–8. Paris: Imprimerie Dugros, 1868–69.

Fairchilds, Cissie. "Women and Family." In *French Women and the Age of Enlightenment,* edited by Samia I. Spencer, 97–110. Bloomington: Indiana University Press, 1984.

———. "Forum: Three Views on the Guilds." *French Historical Studies* 15, no. 4 (fall 1988): 688–92.

Fanon, Frantz. "The Fact of Blackness." *Black Skin, White Masks: The Experiences of a Black Man in a White World.* Translated by Charles Lam Markham. New York: Grove, 1967.

Faraut, François. *Histoire de la Belle Jardinière.* Paris: Belin, 1987.

Farge, Arlette. *La vie fragile: violences, pouvoirs et solidarités à Paris au XVIIIe siècle.* Paris: Hachette, 1986.

———. "The Honor and Secrecy of Families." In *Passions of the Renaissance,* edited by Roger Chartier, translated by Arthur Goldhammer, 571–607. Vol. 3 of *A History of Private Life,* edited by Philippe Ariès and Georges Duby. Cambridge, Mass.: Harvard University Press, 1989.

Farge, Arlette, and Michel Foucault, eds. *Le désordre des familles: lettres de cachet des archives de la Bastille.* Paris: Gallimard, 1982.

Faue, Elizabeth. " 'The Dynamo of Change': Gender and Solidarity in the American Labour Movement of the 1930s." *Gender and History* 1, no. 2 (summer 1989): 138–58.

Favardin, Patrick, and Laurent Bouëxière. *Le dandysme.* Paris: La manufacture, 1988.

Ferry, Luc. *Homo aestheticus: l'invention du goût à l'âge démocratique.* Paris: Grasset et Fasquelle, 1990.

Feuillet, Valérie. *Quelques années de ma vie.* Paris: Calmann-Lévy, 1894.

Fichet, César. *Mémoire sur l'apprentissage et sur l'éducation industrielle.* Faubourg de Paris: Imprimerie de Galban, 1847.

Findlen, Paula. "The Museum: Its Classical Etymology and Renaissance Genealogy." *Journal of the History of Collections* 1, no. 1 (1989): 59–78.

Fishman, Joshua A. *Sociolinguistics: A Brief Introduction.* Rowley, Mass.: Newbury House, 1970.

Fleury, Paul. *Traité pratique de la dorure sur bois: procédé à l'eau, procédé à la mition pour travaux du meuble, du cadre, travaux du bâtiment.* Paris: Garnier, 1908.

Fonsegrive, Charles. *La crise sociale.* Paris: Librairie Victor Lecoffre, 1901.

Fontaine, Arthur. "Musées et expositions." In *Notes sur Paris,* edited by the Société de statistique de Paris. Nancy: Imprimerie Berger-Levrault, 1909.

Fort, Bernadette. "Voice of the Public: The Carnivalization of Salon Art in Prerevolutionary Pamphlets." *Eighteenth-Century Studies* 22 (fall 1989): 368–94.

Forty, Adrian. *Objects of Desire: Design and Society from Wedgwood to IBM.* New York: Pantheon, 1986.

Fouillée, Alfred. *La France au point de vue moral.* 2d ed. Paris: Félix Alcan, 1900.

———. *Esquisse psychologique des peuples européens.* 3d ed. Paris: Félix Alcan, 1903.

Fourdinois, Henri. "Quelques réflexions sur le mobilier à propos de l'Union centrale." *Revue des arts décoratifs* 3 (1882–83): 161–72.

———. "De l'état actuel de l'industrie du mobilier: la maison Fourdinois." *Revue des arts décoratifs* 5 (1884–85): 537–44.

Fournier, Paul. *Traité d'ébénisterie et de marqueterie.* Paris: Garnier, 1905.

Foussier, Ernest. *L'appartement français à la fin du XIXe siècle.* Paris: Thézard Fils, [ca. 1890].

Fraisse, Geneviève. "L'éducation ménagère et le métier de femme au début du XIXe siècle." Special issue, Education des filles, enseignement des femmes. *Pénélope* 2 (1980).

———. *Muse de la raison.* Aix-en-Provence: Alinéa, 1989.

Franklin, Alfred. *Comment on devenait patron.* Vol. 5 of *La vie privée d'autrefois: arts et métiers, modes, moeurs, usages des parisiens, du XIIe au XVIIIe siècle.* Paris: E. Plon, 1889.

Fraser, Nancy. *Unruly Practices: Power, Discourse, and Gender in Contemporary Social Theory.* Minneapolis: University of Minnesota Press, 1989.

"The French Revolution." Special issue, *French Historical Studies* 16 (fall 1989).

Fresson, J. *Enseignement professionnel: conférences sur le meuble.* Paris: Imprimerie de Capiomont, 1887.

Frykman, Jonas, and Orvar Löfgren. *Culture Builders: A Historical Anthropology of Middle-Class Life.* Translated by Alan Crozier. New Brunswick: Rutgers University Press, 1987.

Funck-Brentano, Thomas. "La ville du meuble." *La nouvelle revue* 76 (1892): 271–91.

Furet, François. *In the Workshop of History.* Translated by Jonathan Mandelbaum. Chicago: University of Chicago Press, 1984.

Furlough, Ellen. *Consumer Cooperation in France: The Politics of Consumption, 1834–1930.* Ithaca: Cornell University Press, 1991.

Gailhard-Bancel, Maurice de. *Les anciennes corporations de métiers et la lutte contre la fraude dans le commerce et la petite industrie.* Paris: Bloud et Cie, 1913.

Gaillard, Jeanne. *Paris, la ville, 1852–1870: l'urbanisme parisien à l'heure d'Haussman.* Paris: H. Champion, 1976.

Gaines, Jane, and Charlotte Herzog, eds. *Fabrications: Costume and the Female Body.* New York: Routledge, 1990.

Gallé, Emile. "Le mobilier contemporain orné d'après la nature." *Revue des arts décoratifs* 20 (1900): 333–41.

Gardelle, Camille. "Charles Plumet, architecte." *L'art décoratif* 5 (February 1899): 201–3.

Garenc, Paule. *L'industrie du meuble en France.* Paris: Presses universitaires de France, 1957.

Garmarnikow, Eva, et al. *Gender, Class, and Work.* London: Heinemann, 1983.

Garnier, Athanase. *Nouveau manuel complet du tapissier et marchand de meubles. . . .* Paris: Roret, 1830.

Garrioch, David. *Neighbourhood and Community in Paris, 1740–90.* Cambridge: Cambridge University Press, 1986.

Gascon, Richard. "La France du mouvement: les commerces et les villes." In *L'état et la ville,* 231–479. Vol. 1 of *Histoire économique et sociale de la France,* edited by Fernand Braudel and Ernest Labrousse. Paris: Presses universitaires de France, 1977.

Gates, Henry Louis, Jr., ed. *"Race," Writing, and Difference.* Chicago: University of Chicago Press, 1986.

Gauchat, Nadine. "A Royal Desk by Oeben and Riesener." *International Studio* 98 (February 1931): 47–48.

Gautier, Judith. *Le second rang du collier.* Paris: Librairie Juven, 1909.

Gelber, Steven M. "Free Market Metaphor: The Historical Dynamics of Stamp Collecting." *Comparative Studies in Society and History* 34, no. 4 (October 1992): 742–69.

Genet-Delacroix, Marie-Claude. "Esthétique officielle et art national sous la Troisième République." *Le mouvement social* 131 (1985): 105–20.

Gentry, Jean. *Le petit menuisier.* 4 vols. Paris, 1892–96.

Geoffroy, Gustave. "Causerie sur le style, la tradition et la nature." *Revue des arts décoratifs* 18 (1899).

Gerspach, Edouard. "Chronique de l'enseignement des arts appliqués à l'industrie: les manufactures nationales sous la république de 1848." *Revue des arts décoratifs* 3 (1882–83): 152–55; 219–22.

Gibson, Wendy. *Women in Seventeenth-Century France.* Basingstoke: Macmillan, 1989.

Gide, Charles. "Economie sociale." In *Rapports du jury international: exposition internationale de 1900 à Paris,* edited by Ministère du commerce, de l'industrie, des postes et des télégraphes. Vol. 5. Paris: Imprimerie nationale, 1903.

Giedion, Siegfried. *Mechanization Takes Command: A Contribution to Anonymous History.* New York: W. W. Norton, 1949.

Giesey, Ralph E. *The Royal Funerary Ceremony in Renaissance France.* Geneva: E. Droz, 1960.

———. "Models of Rulership in French Royal Ceremonial." In *Rites of Power: Symbolism, Ritual, and Politics since the Middle Ages,* edited by Sean Wilentz, 41–64. Philadelphia: University of Pennsylvania Press, 1985.

Giffard, Pierre. *Paris sous la Troisième République: les grands bazars.* Paris: Havard, 1882.

Gillispie, Charles Coulston. *Science and Polity in France at the End of the Old Regime.* Princeton: Princeton University Press, 1980.

Gilroy, Paul. *The Black Atlantic: Modernity and Double Consciousness.* Cambridge, Mass.: Harvard University Press, 1993.

Goffman, Erving. *Forms of Talk.* Philadelphia: University of Pennsylvania Press, 1981.

Goldthwaite, Richard. "The Florentine Palace as Domestic Architecture." *American Historical Review* 77 (October 1972): 977–1012.

———. *The Building of Renaissance Florence: An Economic and Social History.* Baltimore: Johns Hopkins University Press, 1980.

Goncourt, Edmond de. *La maison d'un artiste*. 1881. 2 vols. Paris: Charpentier, 1904.

Goncourt, Edmond de, and Jules de Goncourt. *Journal*. 1878. Edited by A. Ricatte. Paris: Flammarion, 1959.

————. *The Woman of the Eighteenth Century: Her Life, from Birth to Death, Her Love, and Her Philosophy in the Worlds of Salon, Shop, and Street.* Translated by Jacques Le Clercq and Ralph Roeder. 1927. Reprint, Westport, Conn.: Hyperion, 1988.

Goodman, Dena. "Enlightenment Salons: The Convergence of Female and Philosophic Ambitions." *Eighteenth-Century Studies* 22 (spring 1989): 329–50.

————. "Filial Rebellion in the Salon: Madame Geoffrin and Her Daughter." *French Historical Studies* 16 (spring 1989): 28–47.

Gordon, Daniel. "'Public Opinion' and the Civilizing Process in France: The Example of Morellet." *Eighteenth-Century Studies* 20 (spring 1989): 302–28.

Gossez, Rémi. *Les ouvriers de Paris*. Paris: Société d'histoire de la Révolution de 1848, 1968.

"Le goût du vieux en art." *Revue des arts décoratifs* 5 (1884–85): 592–94.

Gramont, E. de. *Mémoires: les marronniers en fleurs*. 25th ed. Paris: Grasset, 1929.

Gréard, Octave. *Des écoles d'apprentis: mémoire adressé à M. le préfet de la Seine.* Paris: Charles de Mourgues Frères, 1872.

Greenhalgh, Paul. *Ephemeral Vistas: The Expositions Universelles, Great Exhibitions, and World's Fairs, 1851–1939*. Manchester: Manchester University Press, 1988.

Gribaudi, Maurizio. *Mondo operaio e mito operaio: spazi e percorsi sociali a Torino nel primo novecento*. Turin: Einaudi, 1987.

Grießinger, Andreas. *Das symbolische Kapital der Ehre. Streikbewegungen und kollektives Bewußtsein deutscher Handwerksgesellen im 18. Jahrhundert.* Frankfurt: Ullstein, 1981.

Guiffrey, Jules-Joseph. "Oeben, Riesener: le bureau du roi au Louvre." *Forum artistique* (March 1887): 39–45.

Guilbert, Madeleine. *Travail féminin et travail à domicile: enquête sur le travail à domicile de la confection féminine dans la région parisienne*. Paris: Centre national de la recherche scientifique, 1956.

Gumperz, John. *Discourse Strategies*. Cambridge: Cambridge University Press, 1982.

Günther, Sonja. *Das Deutsche Heim*. Werkbund-Archiv 12. West Berlin: Anabas, 1984.

Guth, Paul. "Le roman d'un estampilleur, L. Boudin." *Connaissance des arts* 54 (August 1956): 26–31.

Habermas, Jürgen. *The Structural Transformation of the Public Sphere: An Inquiry into a Category of Bourgeois Society*. Translated by Thomas Burger and Frederick Lawrence. Cambridge, Mass.: MIT Press, 1989.

Halbwachs, Maurice. *L'évolution des besoins dans les classes ouvrières*. Paris: F. Alcan, 1933.

Hall, Stuart. "The Problem of Ideology—Marxism without Guarantees." In *Marx 100 Years On*, edited by Betty Matthews, 57–85. Atlantic Highlands, N.J.: Humanities Press, 1983.

Hall, Stuart, and Tony Jefferson, eds. *Resistance through Rituals: Youth Subcultures in Post-war Britain.* London: Unwin Hyman, 1976.

Halttunen, Karen. *Confidence Men and Painted Women: A Study of Middle-Class Culture in America, 1830–1870.* New Haven: Yale University Press, 1982.

Hanagan, Michael. *The Logic of Solidarity: Artisans and Industrial Workers in Three French Towns, 1871–1914.* Urbana: University of Illinois Press, 1980.

———. *Nascent Proletarians: Class Formation in Post-Revolutionary France.* Oxford: Basil Blackwell, 1989.

Hanley, Sarah. *The Lit de Justice of the Kings of France: Constitutional Ideology in Legend, Ritual, and Discourse.* Princeton: Princeton University Press, 1983.

———. "Engendering the State: Family Formation and State Building in Early Modern France." *French Historical Studies* 16 (spring 1989): 4–27.

Hansen, Miriam. *Babel and Babylon: Spectatorship in American Silent Film.* Cambridge, Mass.: Harvard University Press, 1991.

Harris, Neil. *Cultural Excursions: Marketing Appetites and Cultural Tastes in Modern America.* Chicago: University of Chicago Press, 1990.

Hart, Keith. "On Commoditization." In *From Craft to Industry: The Ethnography of Proto-Industrial Cloth Production,* edited by Esther N. Goody. Cambridge: Cambridge University Press, 1982.

Haug, Wolfgang Fritz. *Critique of Commodity Aesthetics: Appearance, Sexuality, and Advertising in Capitalist Society.* Translated by Robert Bock. Minneapolis: University of Minnesota Press, 1986.

Hausen, Karin. "Family and Role-Division: The Polarization of Sexual Stereotypes in the Nineteenth Century—an Aspect of the Dissociation of Work and Family Life." In *The German Family: Essays on the Social History of the Family in Nineteenth and Twentieth-Century Germany,* edited by Richard J. Evans and W. R. Lee, 51–83. London: Croom Helm; Totowa, N.J.: Barnes and Noble, 1981.

Hauser, Henri. *Ouvriers du temps passé: XVe–XVIe siècles.* Paris: Alcan, 1899.

Havard, Henry. *Dictionnaire de l'ameublement et de la décoration depuis le XIIIe siècle jusqu'à nos jours.* 4 vols. Paris: Quantin, 1887–90.

———. *Les Boulle.* Paris: L. Allison, 1892.

———. "L'ameublement français: à l'exposition d'Amsterdam." *Revue des arts décoratifs* 4 (1883–84): 39–47.

Hayden, Dolores. *The Grand Domestic Revolution.* Cambridge, Mass.: MIT Press, 1981.

Hebdige, Dick. *Subculture: The Meaning of Style.* London: Methuen, 1979.

Hennequin, Mme. *L'art et le goût au foyer.* Paris: Armand Colin, 1912.

Hertz, Deborah. "Salonnières and Literary Women in Late Eighteenth-Century Berlin." *New German Critique* 14 (spring 1978): 97–108.

Hesse, Carla. "Reading Signatures: Female Authorship and Revolutionary Law in France, 1750–1850." *Eighteenth-Century Studies* 22 (spring 1989): 469–87.

Heywood, Colin. *Childhood in Nineteenth-Century France: Work, Health, and Education among the "Classes Populaires."* Cambridge: Cambridge University Press, 1988.

Hiesinger, Kathryn B., and Joseph Rishel. "Art and Its Critics: A Crisis of Principle." In *The Second Empire, 1852–1870: Art in France under Napoleon III,* edited by George H. Marcus and Janet M. Iandola, 29–34. Philadelphia: Philadelphia Museum of Art, 1978.

Hillairet, Jacques. *Evocation du vieux Paris: les faubourgs.* Paris: Editions de Minuit, 1952–54.

Hirschmann, Albert O. "An Alternative Explanation of Contemporary Harriedness." *The Quarterly Journal of Economics* 87, no. 4 (November 1973): 634–47.

"L'histoire prouvée par les modes." *Journal des dames et des modes* 36 (1 September 1811).

Hobsbawm, Eric, and Terence Ranger, eds. *The Invention of Tradition.* Cambridge: Cambridge University Press, 1983.

Holland, Norman S. "Fashioning Cuba." In *Nationalisms and Sexualities,* edited by Andrew Parker, Mary Russo, Doris Sommer, and Patricia Yaeger, 147–56. New York: Routledge, 1992.

Honour, Hugh. *Chinoiserie.* London: John Murray, 1961.

Huard, Raymond. *Le suffrage universel en France, 1848–1946.* Paris: Aubier, 1991.

Hufton, Olwen. "Women in Revolution, 1789–1796." *Past and Present* 53 (November 1971): 90–108.

Hulot, père. *L'art du tourneur mécanicien.* Paris: Roubo, 1775.

Hunt, Lynn. *Politics, Culture, and Class in the French Revolution.* Berkeley: University of California Press, 1984.

———. "Révolution française et vie privée." In *De la révolution à la grande guerre,* 21–51. Vol. 4 of *Histoire de la vie privée,* edited by Michelle Perrot. Paris: Seuil, 1987.

———. *The Family Romance of the French Revolution.* Berkeley: University of California Press, 1992.

———, ed. *Eroticism and the Body Politic.* Baltimore: Johns Hopkins University Press, 1991.

Hunt, Nancy Rose. "Domesticity and Colonialism in Belgian Africa: Usumbura's *Foyer Social,* 1946–1960." *Signs* 15, no. 3 (1990): 447–74.

Husson, François. *Artisans français: étude historique—les tapissiers.* Paris: Marchard et Billard, 1905.

Huysmans, J.-K. *Les soeurs Vatard.* Vol. 3 of *Oeuvres complètes.* Paris: Cress, 1879.

Hyde, L. *The Gift: Imagination and the Erotic Life of Property.* New York: Random House, 1979.

Hymes, Dell. *Foundations in Sociolinguistics: An Ethnographic Approach.* Philadelphia: University of Pennsylvania Press, 1974.

Impey, Oliver, and Arthur MacGregor, eds. *The Origins of Museums: The Cabinet of Curiosities in Sixteenth- and Seventeenth-Century Europe.* Oxford: Clarendon Press, 1986.

Isaac, Maurice. *Les expositions internationales.* Paris: Larousse, 1936.

Isambert, François-André. *Recueil général des anciennes lois françaises.* Paris: Belin-leprieur, 1829.

J. "M. Félix Aubert." *L'art décoratif* 4 (January 1899): 157–61.

———. "Concours de *l'art décoratif.*" *L'art décoratif* 7 (April 1899).

Jacquemart, Paul. *Professions et métiers: guide pratique à l'usage des familles et de la jeunesse pour le choix d'une carrière.* 2 vols. Paris: Armand Colin, 1892.

Jacques, G. M. "Utopie?" *L'art décoratif* 11 (August 1899): 185–89.

Jameson, Fredric. "Postmodernism and Consumer Society." In *The Anti-Aesthetic: Essays on Postmodern Culture,* edited by Hal Foster, 111–25. Port Townsend: Bay Press, 1983.

Janneau, Guillaume. *Les styles du meuble français.* Paris: Presses universitaires de France, 1972.

———. *Les ateliers parisiens d'ébénistes et de menuisiers aux XVIIe et XVIIIe siècles.* Paris: Editions S.E.R.G., 1975.

Jarausch, Konrad. "Towards a Social History of Experience: Postmodern Predicaments in Theory and Interdisciplinarity." *Central European History* 22 (1989): 427–43.

Jarry, Paul. *Les magasins de nouveautés: histoire retrospective et anecdotique.* Paris: André Barry, 1948.

Jenkins, Brian. *Nationalism in France: Class and Nation since 1789.* Savage, Md.: Barnes and Noble, 1990.

Joanne, Adolphe. *Paris illustré en 1870: guide de l'étranger et du parisien.* 3d ed. Paris: Hachette, 1871.

Johnson, Christopher H. *Utopian Communism in France: Cabet and the Icarians, 1839–1851.* Ithaca: Cornell University Press, 1974.

Judson, Pieter. "Inventing Germans: Class, Nationality, and Colonial Fantasy at the Margins of the Hapsburg Monarchy." *Social Analysis* 33 (1993): 47–67.

Jullian, M. *L'art en France sous la révolution et l'empire.* Paris: Centre de Documentation universitaire, n.d.

Kaplan, Alice, and Kristin Ross. Introduction to *Everyday Life.* Special issue, *Yale French Studies* 73 (1988): 1–4.

Kaplan, Marion A. *The Making of the Jewish Middle Class: Women, Family, and Identity in Imperial Germany.* New York: Oxford University Press, 1991.

Kaplan, Steven L. *Bread, Politics, and Political Economy in the Reign of Louis XV.* 2 vols. The Hague: Martinus Nijhoff, 1976.

———. "The Luxury Guilds in Paris in the Eighteenth Century." *Francia: Forschungen zur westeuropäischen Geschichte* 9 (1981): 257–98.

———. "Les corporations, les 'faux ouvriers' et le faubourg Saint-Antoine au XVIIIe siècle." *Annales: Economies, sociétés, civilisations* 43 (1988): 353–78.

Kaplow, Jeffry. "Parisian Workers at the Universal Exhibitions of 1862 and 1867." Paper presented at the conference on Work and Representations, Cornell University, 1984.

Kerber, Linda. *Women of the Republic: Intellect and Ideology in Revolutionary America.* Chapel Hill: University of North Carolina Press, 1982.

———. "The Paradox of Women's Citizenship in the Early Republic." *American Historical Review* 97 (April 1992): 349–76.

King, Lyndel Saunders. *The Industrialization of Taste: Victorian England and the Art Union of London.* Ann Arbor: UMI Research, 1985.

Kjellberg, Pierre. "Leleu, le plus grand ébéniste français sous Louis XVI." *Connaissance des arts* 123 (May 1962): 58–65.

Kleinman, Ruth. "Social Dynamics at the French Court: The Household of Anne of Austria." *French Historical Studies* 16 (spring 1990): 517–35.

Klejman, Laurence, and Florence Rochefort. *L'égalité en marche: le féminisme sous la Troisième République*. Paris: des femmes, 1989.

Kron, Joan. *Home-Psych: The Social Psychology of Home and Decoration*. New York: Potler, 1983.

La Tynna, J. de. *Almanach du commerce de Paris, pour an VIII de la république française*. Paris: chez Duverneuil, 1799.

———. *Almanach du commerce de Paris, des départements de la France et des principales villes du monde*. Paris: chez de La Tynna, 1815.

———. *Almanach du commerce de Paris, des départements de la France et des principales villes du monde, par J. de La Tynna, continué et mis dans un meilleur ordre par S. Bottin*. 48 vols. Paris, 1840.

Labov, William. *Sociolinguistic Patterns*. Philadelphia: University of Pennsylvania Press, 1972.

Lacombe, S. *Nouveau manuel complet de sculpture sur bois*. Paris: Roret, 1886.

Lacroix, H. *Nouveau manuel complet du tapissier décorateur*. Paris: L. Mulo, 1901.

Lake, Marilyn. "A Revolution in the Family: The Challenge and Contradictions of Maternal Citizenship in Australia." In *Mothers of a New World: Maternalist Politics and the Origins of Welfare States*, edited by Seth Koven and Sonya Michel, 378–95. New York: Routledge, 1993.

Lancaster, Kelvin. "A New Approach to Consumer Theory." *Journal of Political Economy* 74, no. 2 (April 1966): 132–57.

Lanck. "Mobilier." *Journal de menuiserie* 11 (1874): 21–23; 28–32.

Landemer, Georges de. *Le carnet de fiançailles: livret de famille*. Paris: J. Féderlé, 1890.

Landes, Joan B. *Women and the Public Sphere in the Age of the French Revolution*. Ithaca: Cornell University Press, 1988.

Landon, Charles Paul. *Annales du musée et de l'école moderne des beaux-arts*. Paris, 1800.

Larguier, Léo. *Au vieux saint de bois*. Avignon: Aubanel, 1944.

Laumann, Edward O., and James S. House. "Living Room Styles and Social Attributes: The Patterning of Material Artifacts in a Modern Urban Community." *Sociology and Social Research* 54 (April 1970): 321–42.

Leach, William R. "Transformations in a Culture of Consumption: Women and Department Stores, 1890–1925." *Journal of American History* (September 1984): 319–42.

Leblond, Alexandre Jean-Baptiste. *Desseins de développement d'assemblages de differens ouvrages de menuiserie*. Paris, 1711.

Le Camus de Mézières, Nicholas. *Le génie de l'architecture, ou l'analogue de cet art avec nos sensations*. Paris: Morin, 1780.

———. *Traité de la force des bois*. Paris, 1782.

Lecoq, Anne-Marie. "La symbolique de l'état: les images de la monarchie des premiers Valois à Louis XIV." In *La Nation*, 145–92. Vol. 2 of *Les lieux de mémoire*, edited by Pierre Nora. Paris: Gallimard, 1986.

Le Corbusier [Edouard Jeanneret-Gris]. *The Decorative Art of Today*. Translated by James I. Dunnett. Cambridge, Mass.: MIT Press, 1987.

Ledoux-Lebard, Denise. *Les ébénistes parisiens du XIXe siècle (1795–1870): leurs oeuvres et leurs marques*. Paris: F. de Noble, 1965.

Lees, Lynn, and Charles Tilly. "The People of June 1848." Working paper no. 70, Center for Research on Social Organization, 1972.

Lefebvre, Henri. *Critique de la vie quotidienne.* 1947. Paris: l'Arche Editeur, 1958.

———. *Everyday Life in the Modern World,* translated by Sacha Rabinovitch. New Brunswick: Transaction, 1990.

Leffler, Phyllis K. "French Historians and the Challenge to Louis XIV's Absolutism." *French Historical Studies* 14 (spring 1985): 1–22.

Legrand, Louis. *Le mariage et les moeurs en France.* Paris: Librairie Hachette et Cie., 1879.

Leibenstein, Harvey. "Bandwagon, Snob and Veblen Effects in the Theory of Consumers' Demand." *The Quarterly Journal of Economics* 64, no. 2 (May 1950): 183–207.

Leiss, William. *The Limits to Satisfaction: An Essay on the Problem of Needs and Commodities.* Toronto: University of Toronto Press, 1976.

Lemaire, Michel. *Le dandysme de Baudelaire à Mallarmé.* Montreal: Presses de l'Université de Montréal, 1978.

Lenoir, G.-Félix. *Traité théorique et pratique du tapissier: principes de la décoration.* Paris: C. Juliot, 1885.

Le Play, Frédéric. *Oeuvres complètes de Frédéric Le Play.* 6 vols. 2d ed. Tours: A. Mame et Fils, 1878.

———. *Les ouvriers des deux mondes.* 5 vols. Paris: Société d'économie sociale, 1857–85.

Lequin, Yves. *Les ouvriers de la région lyonnaise (1848–1914).* 2 vols. Lyons: Presses universitaires de Lyon, 1977.

———. "Apprenticeship in Nineteenth-Century France: A Continuing Tradition or a Break with the Past?" In *Work in France: Representations, Meaning, Organization, and Practice,* edited by Steven L. Kaplan and Cynthia J. Koepp, 457–74. Ithaca: Cornell University Press, 1986.

Lespinasse, René de. *Orfèvres, sculptures, mercerie, ouvriers en métaux, bâtiment et ameublement.* Vol. 2 of *Les métiers et les corporations de la ville de Paris.* Paris: Imprimerie nationale, 1879.

Levasseur, Emile. *Histoire des classes ouvrières et de l'industrie en France avant 1789.* 2 vols. Paris: Arthur Rousseau, 1901.

———. *Questions ouvrières et industrielles en France sous la Troisième République.* Paris: Arthur Rousseau, 1907.

Le Vent, ed. *Almanach général des marchands, négocians, armateurs et fabricans de la France et de l'Europe et autres parties du monde contenant l'état des principales villes commerçantes.* Paris, 1778.

Lichtenstein, Jacqueline. "Making Up Representation: The Risks of Femininity." *Representations* 20 (fall 1987): 77–87.

Liedekerke, Arnould de. *Talon Rouge: Barbey d'Aurevilly, le dandy absolu.* Paris: Oliver Orban, 1986.

Liepmann, Kate K. *Apprenticeship: An Enquiry into Its Adequacy under Modern Conditions.* London: Routledge and Kegan Paul, 1960.

Liste générale et roolles de tous les arts et métiers qui s'exercent tant en la ville et fauxbourgs de Paris, qu'en autres villes, fauxbourgs, bourgs et bourgades de ce royaume, distingués en cinq rangs selon la bonté et valleur d'iceux. Paris: chez Pierre Charpentier, 1656.

Le livre des expositions universelles, 1851–1989. Paris: Editions des arts décoratifs, 1983.

Londres 1874: oeuvres d'art et produits industriels. Paris, 1874.

Lostalot, Alfred de. *Les arts du bois (sculpture sur bois—meubles): dessins et modèles.* Paris: Rouam, 1890.

Lougee, Carolyn. *Le Paradis des femmes: Women, Salons, and Social Stratification in Seventeenth-Century France.* Princeton: Princeton University Press, 1976.

Lovell, Terry. *Consuming Fiction.* London: Verso, 1987.

Lucas, Colin. "Nobles, Bourgeois, and the Origins of the French Revolution." *Past and Present* 60 (August 1973): 84–126.

Lucet, Alfred. *De l'apprentissage dans l'industrie: initiative privée—intervention de l'état.* Rennes: Simon, 1904.

Luchet, Auguste. *L'art industriel à l'exposition universelle de 1867: mobilier, vêtements, aliments.* Paris: Librairie internationale, 1868.

Lüdtke, Alf. "The Historiography of Everyday Life: The Personal and the Political." In *Culture, Ideology and Politics,* edited by Raphael Samuel and Gareth Stedman Jones, 38–54. London: Routledge, 1982.

Lurie, Alison. *The Language of Clothes.* New York: Random House, 1981.

Lynch, Katherine A. *Family, Class, and Ideology in Early Industrial France: Social Policy and the Working-Class Family, 1825–1848.* Madison: University of Wisconsin Press, 1988.

Lynes, Russell. *The Tastemakers: The Shaping of American Popular Taste.* New York: Dover, 1949.

Maillou, Rioux de. "Causerie sur le mobilier: le bureau." *Revue des arts décoratifs* 6 (1885–86): 138–42; 234–55.

Mainardi, Patricia. *Art and Politics of the Second Empire: The Universal Expositions of 1855 and 1867.* New Haven: Yale University Press, 1987.

———. *The End of the Salon: Art and the State in the Early Third Republic.* Cambridge: Cambridge University Press, 1993.

"Les maîtres du dessin." *L'art décoratif* 9 (June 1899).

Malon, Benoît. *Des réformes possibles et des moyens pratiques.* Vol. 2 of *Le socialisme intégral.* Paris: F. Alcan, 1890–91.

Mandell, Richard D. *Paris 1900: The Great World's Fair.* Toronto: University of Toronto Press, 1967.

Mangeant, A. "Façon et empilage du bois." *Journal de menuiserie* 2 (1864): 92–96.

———. "Des ouvrages de menuiserie." *Journal de menuiserie* 3 (1865).

Mantz, Paul. "Les meubles du XVIIIe siècle." *Revue des arts décoratifs* 4 (1883–84): 313–25; 356–67; 377–89.

Manuel, Frank. *The New World of Henri Saint-Simon.* Cambridge, Mass.: Harvard University Press, 1956.

———. *The Prophets of Paris.* Cambridge, Mass.: Harvard University Press, 1962.

Marbo, Camille [Marguerite Borel]. *A travers deux siècles, souvenirs, rencontres, 1883–1967.* Paris: Grasset, 1967.

March, Lucien. "Les salaires et la durée du travail dans l'industrie française." Part 1. *Journal de la Société de statistique de Paris* (October 1898): 333–47.

————. "Influence des variations des prix sur le mouvement des dépenses ménagères à Paris." *Journal de la Société de statistique de Paris* (April 1910): 135–65.

Marchal, Gaston-Louis. *Jean Jaurès et les arts plastiques.* Castres, 1984.

Mare, Nicolas de la. *Traité de la police.* 12 vols. Paris: J.-F. Hérissant, 1705–38.

Maréchal, Victor. *Le bréviaire de l'ameublement. Recueil des usages, documents, techniques, tarifs, taxes, impôts, lois, décrets et de tous les renseignements concernant les industries de l'ameublement.* Paris, 1927.

Martin, Alexis. *Les étapes d'un touriste en France: Paris, promenade dans les vingt arrondissements.* Paris: A. Hennuyer, 1890.

Martin, Marc. *Trois siècles de publicité en France.* Paris: Editions Odile Jacob, 1992.

Martin-Fugier, Anne. *La bourgeoise.* Paris: Grasset et Fasquelle, 1983.

————. *La vie élégante, ou la formation du Tout-Paris, 1815–1848.* Paris: Fayard, 1990.

Martin Saint-Léon, Etienne. *Histoire des corporations de métiers depuis les origines jusqu'à leur suppression en 1791.* Paris: Guillaumin, 1897.

May, Lary. *Screening out the Past: The Birth of Mass Culture and the Motion Picture Industry.* New York: Oxford University Press, 1980.

Mayer, Arno. *The Persistence of the Old Regime.* New York: Pantheon, 1981.

Maza, Sarah. "The Diamond Necklace Affair Revisited (1785–1786): The Case of the Missing Queen." In *Eroticism and the Body Politic,* edited by Lynn Hunt, 63–89. Baltimore: Johns Hopkins University Press, 1991.

McClellan, Andrew. *Inventing the Louvre: Art, Politics, and the Origins of the Modern Museum in Eighteenth-Century Paris.* Cambridge: Cambridge University Press, 1994.

McClelland, Keith. "Some Thoughts on Masculinity and the 'Representative Artisan' in Britain, 1850–1880." *Gender and History* 1 (summer 1989): 164–77.

McCracken, Grant. *Culture and Consumption: New Approaches to the Symbolic Charcter of Consumer Goods and Activities.* Bloomington: Indiana University Press, 1988.

McInnes, A. "When Was the English Revolution?" *History* 67, no. 221 (October 1982): 377–92.

McKendrick, Neil. "Home Demand and Economic Growth: A New View of the Role of Women and Children in the Industrial Revolution." In *Historical Perspectives: Studies in English Thought and Society in Honour of J. H. Plumb,* edited by Neil McKendrick, 152–210. London: Europa, 1975.

McKendrick, Neil, John Brewer, and J. H. Plumb. *The Birth of Consumer Society: The Commercialization of Eighteenth-Century England.* Bloomington: University of Indiana Press, 1982.

McRobbie, Angela. *Feminism and Youth Culture: From Jackie to Just Seventeen.* Boston: Unwin Hyman, 1991.

Mellet, François-Noël. *L'art du menuisier en meubles et de l'ébéniste contenant des notices sur les bois indigènes et exotiques, la description des meubles de toute espèce.* Paris: Futic, 1825.

Mémoire présenté au roi par les six corps de la ville de Paris. Paris: Nyon, 1788.

Ménard, René. "Rapports des jurys: rapport du jury du premier groupe—le bois." *Revue des arts décoratifs* 3 (1882–83): 69–80.

Ménétra, Jacques-Louis. *Journal of My Life*. Translated by Arthur Goldhammer. New York: Columbia University Press, 1986.

Mercier, Louis-Sébastien. *Le tableau de Paris*. 12 vols. Amsterdam: 1782–88.

Merlin. *Le portefeuille de l'ébéniste: lits, armoires, buffets, étagères, bibliothèques, bureaux, bahuts, chaises*. Paris: Librairie A. Morel, 1883.

Mermet, Emile. *La publicité en France: guide pratique*. Paris: A. Chaix, 1878.

Merot, Alain. "Décors pour le Louvre de Louis XVI (1653–1660): la mythologie politique à la fin de la Fronde." In *La Monarchie absolutiste et l'histoire en France: théories du pouvoir, propagandes monarchiques, et mythologies nationales*, edited by François Crouzet, Chantal Grelle, François Laplanche, et al., 113–37. Paris: Presses de l'Université de Paris, 1986.

Merrick, Jeffrey. "Patriarchalism and Constitutionalism in Eighteenth-Century Parlementary Discourse." *Studies in Eighteenth-Century Culture* 20 (1990): 317–30.

"Meubles en bois simili-courbe, système Bareau et Croisé." Special issue, Revue de l'exposition de 1880. *Revue des arts décoratifs* 3 (1882–83): 6–8.

Meyer, Jean. *La vie quotidienne en France au temps de la régence*. Paris: Hachette, 1979.

Michel, Christian. "Les enjeux historiographiques de la querelle des Anciens et des Modernes." In *La Monarchie absolutiste et l'histoire en France: théories du pouvoir, propagandes monarchiques, et mythologies nationales*, edited by François Crouzet, Chantal Grelle, François Laplanche, et al., 139–54. Paris: Presses de l'Université de Paris, 1986.

Michelet, Jules. *Le peuple*. 1846. Paris: Libraire Marcel Didier, 1946.

Migeon, Gaston. "Les Migeon: une famille d'ébénistes du XVIIIe siècle." *Bulletin monumental* (1918–19): 6–13.

Miller, Daniel. *Material Culture and Mass Consumption*. Oxford: Basil Blackwell, 1987.

Miller, Michael. *The Bon Marché: Bourgeois Culture and the Department Store*. Princeton: Princeton University Press, 1981.

Miller, Toby. *The Well-Tempered Self: Citizenship, Culture, and the Postmodern Subject*. Baltimore: Johns Hopkins University Press, 1993.

Minguet, René. *Géographie industrielle de Paris*. Paris: Hachette, 1957.

Ministère du travail. *Associations professionnelles ouvrières*. 2 vols. Paris, 1894–1904.

———. *L'apprentissage industriel: rapport sur l'apprentissage dans les industries d'ameublement*. Paris, 1905.

Les misères de ce monde, ou complaintes facétieuses sur les apprentissages de differens arts et métiers de la ville et fauxbourgs de Paris, précédées de l'Histoire du Bonhomme misère. London: Cailleau, 1783.

Modleski, Tania. *Loving with a Vengeance: Mass-Producing Fantasies for Women*. New York: Methuen, 1984.

Moers, Ellen. *The Dandy: Brummell to Beerbohm*. Lincoln: University of Nebraska Press, 1960.

Molinier, Emile. "La décoration dans l'ameublement." *Revue des arts décoratifs* 18 (1898): 6–18; 36–49.

———. *Le mobilier royal français aux XVIIe et XVIIIe siècles.* Paris, 1902.

Monnier, Raymonde. *Le faubourg Saint-Antoine, 1789–1815.* Paris: Société des Etudes robespierristes, 1981.

Morel, Eugène. *Bibliothèque: essai sur le développement des bibliothèques publiques et de la librairie dans les deux mondes.* 2 vols. Paris: Mercure de France, 1909.

Morineau, Michel. "Budgets populaires en France au XVIIIe siècle." *Revue d'histoire économique et sociale* 50, no. 2 (1972): 203–37; no. 4 (1972): 449–81.

Moses, Claire. *French Feminism in the Nineteenth Century.* Albany: State University of New York Press, 1984.

Moss, Bernard. *The Origins of the French Labor Movement, 1830–1914: The Socialism of Skilled Workers.* Berkeley: University of California Press, 1976.

Moulin, Jean-Marie. *The Second Empire, 1852–1870: Art in France under Napoleon III,* edited by George H. Marcus and Janet M. Iandola. Phildelphia: Philadelphia Museum of Art, 1978.

Mousnier, Roland E. *La vénalité des offices sous Henri IV et Louis XIII.* Paris: Presses universitaires de France, 1971.

———. *The Institutions of France under the Absolute Monarchy 1598–1789.* Translated by Brian Pearce. 2 vols. Chicago: University of Chicago Press, 1979–84.

Mukerji, Chandra. *From Graven Images: Patterns of Modern Materialism.* New York: Columbia University Press, 1983.

Murard, Lion, and Patrick Zylberberg. *Disciplines à domicile.* Paris: Recherches, 1977.

———. *L'haleine des faubourgs: ville, habitat, et santé au XIXe siècle.* Fontenay-sous-bois: Recherches, 1978.

Nacla, Vicomtesse [Mme Th. Alcan]. *Le boudoir: conseils d'élégance.* Paris: E. Flammarion, 1896.

Nava, Mica. *Changing Cultures: Feminism, Youth, and Consumerism.* London: Sage, 1992.

Nesbit, Margaret. "Atget's *Intérieurs parisiens,* the point of difference." In *Eugène Atget, 1857–1927: intérieurs parisiens, photographies,* 4–32. Paris: Musées de la ville de Paris, 1982.

Nesbit, Molly. *Atget's Seven Albums.* New Haven: Yale University Press, 1992.

Neufforge, Jean-François de. *Recueil élémentaire d'architecture.* Paris, 1757–68.

Nicolet, Claude. *L'idée républicaine en France: essai d'histoire critique (1789–1924).* Paris: Gallimard, 1982.

Nochlin, Linda. *Realism.* Harmondsworth: Penguin, 1971.

Nolan, Molly. "The Historikerstreit and Social History." *New German Critique* 44 (spring–summer 1988): 51–80.

Nolleau, Henri. "Les femmes dans la population active de 1856 à 1954." *Economie et politique* 75 (October 1960): 2–21.

Nord, Philip G. *Paris Shopkeepers and the Politics of Resentment.* Princeton: Princeton University Press, 1987.

Nosban. *Manuel du menuisier en meubles et en bâtiments suivi de l'art de l'ébénisterie contenant tous les détails utiles sur la nature des bois indigènes et exotiques, la manière de les préparer, de les teindre, les principes du dessin géometrique . . . la description des outils les plus modernes.* 2 vols. Paris: Roret, 1827.

———. *Nouveau manuel complet de l'ébéniste et du tabletier.* Paris: Roret, 1827.

Nosban and Maigne. *Nouveau manuel complet du marqueteur et du tabletier, contenant la description des bois d'ébénisterie indigènes et exotiques, l'outillage de l'ébénisterie, des notions sur l'ivoire . . . les principales opérations de marqueterie et de sculpture sur bois.* Paris: Roret, 1877.

Noussane, Henri de. *Le goût dans l'ameublement.* Paris: Firmin-Didot, 1896.

Nouveau Recueil des Statuts et Règlemens des Maîtres Marchands Tapissiers, Hautelissiers, Sarazinois, Rentrayeurs, Courtepointiers, Couverturiers, Coutiers, Sergiers de la ville, Faubourgs et Banlieue de Paris. Paris, 1756.

O'Brien, Patricia. "The Kleptomania Diagnosis: Bourgeois Women and Theft in Late Nineteenth-Century France." *Journal of Social History* 17, no. 1 (fall 1983): 65–77.

Offen, Karen. "Depopulation, Nationalism, and Feminism in Fin-de-Siècle France." *American Historical Review* 89 (June 1984): 648–76.

Oliphant, F. M. *The Air-Seasoning and Conditioning of Timber.* London: His Majesty's Stationery Office, 1927.

Orvilliers, H. de. *Le tapissier pratique, travaux de garniture . . . travaux d'installation . . . rideaux et portières, tapis et teintures, . . . recettes et tours de main.* Paris: Hachette, 1927.

Ory, Pascal. *Les expositions universelles de Paris: panorama raisonné, avec des aperçus nouveaux et des illustrations par les meilleurs auteurs.* Paris: Ramsay, 1982.

Oslet, Gustave, and Jules Jeannin. *Traité de menuiserie.* Paris: G. Fanchon, 1898.

Outram, Dorinda. *The Body and the French Revolution: Sex, Class and Political Culture.* New Haven: Yale University Press, 1989.

Ozouf, Mona. *La fête révolutionnaire, 1789–1799.* Paris: Gallimard, 1976.

Pallach, Ulrich-Christian. "Fonctions de la mobilité artisanale et ouvrière—compagnons, ouvriers et manufacturiers en France et en Allemagne (17e–19e siècles)." *Francia: Forschungen zur Westeuropäischen Geschichte* 11 (1983): 365–406.

Pange, comtesse Jean de [Pauline Laure Marie de Broglie]. *Comment j'ai vu 1900.* Paris: B. Grasset, 1962.

Pardailhé-Galabrun, Annik. *La naissance de l'intime: 3,000 foyers parisiens XVIIe–XVIIIe siècles.* Paris: Presses universitaires de France, 1988.

Pariset, Mme. *Manuel de la maîtresse de maison, ou lettres sur l'économie domestique.* 3d ed. Paris: Gudot, 1825.

Parker, David. *The Making of French Absolutism.* New York: St. Martin's, 1983.

Pateman, Carole. *The Sexual Contract.* Stanford: Stanford University Press, 1988.

Paulin-Desormeaux, A. O. *Art du menuisier en bâtiment et en meubles, suivi de l'art de l'ébéniste, ouvrage contenant des éléments de géométrie descriptive appliquée à l'art du menuisier.* 2 vols. 3d ed. Paris: Audot, 1829.

Pecqueur, Constantine. *Economie sociale, des intérêts du commerce, de l'industrie, et de l'agriculture, et de la civilisation en général, sous l'influence des applications de la vapeur.* Paris: Dessessart, 1839.

Peiss, Kathy. *Cheap Amusements: Working Women and Leisure in Turn-of-the-Century New York.* Philadelphia: Temple University Press, 1986.

Pellisson, Maurice. *Les bibliothèques populaires à l'étranger et en France.* Paris: Imprimerie nationale, 1906.

Percier, Charles, and Pierre Léonard Fontaine. *Recueil de décorations intérieures comprenant tout ce qui a rapport à l'ameublement.* Paris, 1801, 1812.

Perdiguier, Agricol. *Le livre du compagnonnage.* 2 vols. Paris: Pagnerre, 1841.

Perrot, Marguerite. *La mode de vie des familles bourgeoises.* Paris: Presses de la Fondation nationale des sciences politiques, 1961.

Perrot, Michelle. *Les ouvriers en grève, France 1871–1890.* Paris: Mouton, 1974.

———. "L'éloge de la ménagère dans le discours des ouvriers français au XIXe siècle." *Romantisme* 13–14 (1976): 105–21.

———. "On the Formation of the French Working Class." In *Working-Class Formation: Nineteenth-Century Patterns in Western Europe and the United States,* edited by Ira Katznelson and Aristide R. Zolberg, 71–110. Princeton: Princeton University Press, 1986.

Perrot, Philippe. *Les dessus et les dessous de la bourgeoisie.* Paris: Librairie Arthème Fayard, 1981.

Peukert, Detlev J. K. *Inside Nazi Germany: Conformity, Opposition, and Racism in Everyday Life,* translated by Richard Deveson. New Haven: Yale University Press, 1987.

Phillips, Anne. *Engendering Democracy.* University Park: Pennsylvania State University Press, 1991.

Phizacklea, Annie. *Unpacking the Fashion Industry.* London: Routledge, 1990.

Picard, Alfred, ed. *Exposition universelle internationale de 1889, à Paris: rapports du jury international.* 19 vols. Paris: Imprimerie nationale, 1891–92.

Pinkney, David. "The Crowd in the French Revolution of 1830." *American Historical Review* 70 (October 1964): 1–17.

"Planche 6: portes de placard Louis XIII." *Journal de menuiserie* 1 (1863).

"Planche 6: boudoir Louis XVI." *Journal de menuiserie* 3 (1865): 34–35.

"Planche 7: petit banc du 15e siècle." *Journal de menuiserie* 1 (1863): 28–29.

"Planche 9: menuiserie moderne—boutiques et aménagement des magasins," *Journal de menuiserie* 1 (1863): 33–36.

"Planche 10: panneau de porte Louis XIV." *Journal de menuiserie* 1 (1863).

"Planches 3 et 4: magasin." *Journal de menuiserie* 1 (1865).

"Planche 33: cabinet en marqueterie, bronze doré et plaques de Sèvres (pâte tendre) du palais de Madrid." *L'art et l'industrie* 1 (1877): n.p.—two pages before plate 33.

Plum, Werner. *Les expositions universelles au 19e siècle, spectacles du changement socio-culturel.* Translated by Pierre Gallissaires. Bonn: Friedrich-Ebert-Stiftung, 1977.

Plumb, J. H. *The Origins of Political Stability in England, 1625–1725.* Boston: Houghton Mifflin, 1967.

Plumier, Charles. *L'art de tourner, ou de faire en perfection toutes sortes d'ouvrages.* Lyons: J. Certe, 1701.

Poe, Edgar Allan. "Philosophie de l'ameublement." In *Histoires grotesques et sérieuses,* translated by Charles Baudelaire. Paris, 1864.

Poiré, Paul. *La France industrielle, ou description des industries françaises.* 2d ed. Paris: Hachette, 1875.

Pomian, Krzysztof. *Collectionneurs, amateurs et curieux.* Paris: Gallimard, 1987.

Pommier, Edouard. "Versailles, l'image du souverain." In *La nation,* 451–95. Vol. 2 of *Les lieux de mémoire,* edited by Pierre Nora. Paris: Gallimard, 1986.

Poni, Carlo. "Local Market Rules and Practices: Three Guilds in the Same Line of Production in Early Modern Bologna." In *Domestic Strategies: Work and Family in France and Italy, 1600–1800,* edited by Stuart Woolf, 69–101. Cambridge: Cambridge University Press, 1991.

Poovey, Mary. *Uneven Developments: The Ideological Work of Gender in Mid-Victorian England.* Chicago: University of Chicago Press, 1988.

Poulot, Dominique. "L'invention de la bonne volonté culturelle: l'image du musée au XIXe siècle." *Le mouvement social* 131 (1985): 35–64.

Pour l'objet: revue d'esthétique 3, no. 4 (1979).

Pradel, Abraham du. *Le livre commode.* Paris: Chez la veuve de Denis Nion, 1692.

Pradère, Alexandre. *French Furniture Makers: The Art of the Ebéniste from Louis XIV to the Revolution.* Translated by Perran Wood. London: Sotheby's, 1989.

Prat, Jean H. *Histoire du faubourg Saint-Antoine: vieux chemin de Paris, faubourg artisanal, quartier des grands ébénistes du XVIIIe siècle, nerf des révolutions, capital du meuble.* Paris: ANC, Editions du tigre, 1961.

Prather, Charlotte C. "The View from Germany." In *French Women and the Age of Enlightenment,* edited by Samia I. Spencer, 369–79. Bloomington: Indiana University Press, 1984.

Pred, Allan. *Lost Words and Lost Worlds: Modernity and the Language of Everyday Life in Late Nineteenth-Century Stockholm.* Cambridge: Cambridge University Press, 1990.

Procacci, Giovanna. *Gouverner la misère: la question sociale en France, 1789–1848.* Paris: Seuil, 1993.

Quataert, Jean H. "The Shaping of Women's Work in Manufacturing: Guilds, Households, and the State in Central Europe, 1648–1870." *American Historical Review* 90 (December 1985): 1122–48.

Quef, Pierre. *Histoire de l'apprentissage: aspects de la formation technique et commerciale.* Paris: Librairie générale de droit et de jurisprudence, 1964.

Rabinow, Paul. *Reflections on Fieldwork in Morocco.* Berkeley: University of California Press, 1977.

———. *French Modern: Norms and Forms of the Social Environment.* Cambridge, Mass.: MIT Press, 1989.

Radhakrishnan, R. "Nationalism, Gender, and the Narrative of Identity." In *Nationalisms and Sexualities,* edited by Andrew Parker, Mary Russo, Doris Sommer, and Patricia Yaeger. New York: Routledge, 1992.

Rancière, Jacques. *La nuit des proletaires: archives du rêve ouvrier.* Paris: Fayard, 1981.

Rancière, Jacques, and Patrice Vauday. "En allant à l'expo: l'ouvrier, sa femme, et les machines." *Les révoltes logiques* 1 (1975): 5–22.

Ranum, Orest. *Paris in the Age of Absolutism: An Essay.* New York: John Wiley and Sons, 1968.

———. "Courtesy, Absolutism, and the Rise of the French State, 1630–1660." *Journal of Modern History* 52 (September 1980): 426–51.

Rapports des délégués des ouvriers parisiens à l'exposition de Londres. Paris, 1862.

Rearick, Charles. *Pleasures of the Belle Epoque: Entertainment and Festivity in Turn-of-the-Century France.* New Haven: Yale University Press, 1985.

Rébérioux, Madeleine. "Approches de l'histoire des expositions universelles à Paris du second empire à 1900." *Bulletin du centre d'histoire économique et sociale de la région lyonnaise* 1 (1979).

Recueil de menuiserie pratique. Paris, 1876–91.

Reddy, William M. "Skeins, Scales, Discounts, Steam, and Other Objects of Crowd Justice in Early French Textile Mills." *Comparative Studies in Society and History* 21 (April 1979): 204–13.

———. *The Rise of Market Culture: The Textile Trade and French Society, 1750–1900.* Cambridge: Cambridge University Press, 1984.

———. "The Structure of a Cultural Crisis: Thinking about Cloth in France Before and After the Revolution." In *The Social Life of Things: Commodities in Cultural Perspective,* edited by Arjun Appadurai, 261–84. Cambridge: Cambridge University Press, 1986.

Reitlinger, Gerald. *The Rise and Fall of Objet d'Art Prices since 1750.* Vol. 2 of *The Economics of Taste.* London: Barrie and Rockcliffe, 1963.

Renaudin, Edmée. *Edmée au bout de la table.* Paris: Stock, 1973.

Renoy, Georges. *Grands magasins.* Zartbommel, NL: Bibliothèque europiaciéene, 1978.

Révoltes logiques, ed. *Esthétiques du peuple.* Paris: Editions de la Découverte, 1985.

Rheims, Maurice. *The Strange Life of Objects: Thirty-Five Centuries of Art Collecting and Collectors.* Translated by David Pryce-Jones. New York: Atheneum, 1961.

Rice, Danielle. "Women and the Visual Arts." In *French Women and the Age of Enlightenment,* edited by Samia I. Spencer, 242–55. Bloomington: Indiana University Press, 1984.

Richards, Thomas. *The Commodity Culture of Victorian England: Advertising and Spectacle, 1851–1914.* Stanford: Stanford University Press, 1990.

Richet, Denis. *La France moderne: l'esprit des institutions.* Paris: Flammarion, 1973.

Riesman, Paul. *Freedom in Fulani Social Life: An Introspective Ethnography.* Chicago: University of Chicago Press, 1977.

Rigby, Brian. *Popular Culture in Modern France: A Study of Cultural Discourse.* London: Routledge, 1991.

Riley, Denise. *"Am I That Name?" Feminism and the Category of "Women" in History.* Minneapolis: University of Minnesota, 1988.

Ris-Paquot, O. E. *L'art de bâtir, meubler et entretenir sa maison, ou manière de surveiller et d'être soi-même architecte-entrepreneur-ouvrier.* Paris: Henri Laurens, n.d.

Ritter, Gerhard A. "Workers' Culture in Imperial Germany: Problems and Points of Departure for Research." *Journal of Contemporary History* 13 (April 1978): 165–89.

Robiquet, Jacques. *L'art et le goût sous la Restauration, 1814–1830.* Paris: Payot, 1928.

Rochambeau, le marquis de. "Ameublement et objets d'un usage général dans les constructions et les appartements." *Exposition internationale et universelle de Philadelphia, 1876,* 173–201. Paris: Imprimerie nationale, 1877.

Roche, Daniel. *Le peuple de Paris: essai sur la culture populaire au XVIIIe siècle.* Paris: Aubier Montaigne, 1981.

Rogers, Adrienne. "Women and the Law." In *French Women and the Age of Enlightenment,* edited by Samia I. Spencer, 33–48. Bloomington: Indiana University Press, 1984.

Rogers, Katherine M. "The View from England." In *French Women and the Age of Enlightenment,* edited by Samia I. Spencer, 357–68. Bloomington: Indiana University Press, 1984.

Ronteix, Eugène. *Manuel du fashionable, ou guide de l'élégant.* Paris: Dudot, 1829.

Rosanvallon, Pierre. *Le moment Guizot.* Paris: Gallimard, 1985.

———. *Le sacre du citoyen: histoire du suffrage universel en France.* Paris: Gallimard, 1992.

Rose, Sonya O. "Gender Antagonism and Class Conflict: Exclusionary Strategies of Male Trade Unionists in Nineteenth-Century Britain." *Social History* 13 (May 1988): 191–208.

Rotberg, Robert I., and Theodore K. Rabb, eds., *Art and History: Images and Their Meaning.* Cambridge: Cambridge University Press, 1988.

Roubo, André-Jacob. *L'art du menuisier.* 2 vols. Paris: Saillant et Nyon, 1769–70.

———. *L'art du menuisier-carrossier.* Paris: Saillant et Nyon, 1771.

———. *L'art du menuisier en meubles.* Paris: Saillant et Nyon, 1772.

———. *L'art du menuisier-ébéniste.* Paris: Saillant et Nyon, 1774.

———. *L'art du layetier.* Paris: Moutard, 1782.

Rougerie, Jacques. "Remarques sur l'histoire des salaires à Paris au XIXe siècle." *le mouvement social* 63 (1968).

Rourke, Camille. *Machines-outils pour le travail du bois.* Paris: G. Doin et Cie., 1928.

Rudé, Georges. *La population ouvrière parisienne de 1789 à 1791.* Paris: Archives historiques de la Révolution française, 1967.

Rule, John. "The Property of Skill in the Period of Manufacture." In *The Historical Meanings of Work,* edited by Patrick Joyce, 99–118. Cambridge: Cambridge University Press, 1987.

Runte, Roseann. "Women as Muse." In *French Women and the Age of Enlightenment,* edited by Samia I. Spencer, 143–54. Bloomington: Indiana University Press, 1984.

Rybczynski, Witold. *Home: A Short History of an Idea.* New York: Penguin, 1986.

Saint-Martin, André. *Les grands magasins.* Paris: Arthur Rousseau, 1900.

Saint-Sere. "Deux ébénistes favoris de la favorite." *Plaisir de France* 6 (December 1956): 73–77.

Saint-Yves, M. A., and M. August Vitu. "Produits de toute sorte, fabriqués par des ouvriers chefs de métiers." In *Exposition universelle de 1867, à Paris: rapports du jury international,* edited by Michel Chevalier, 13:955–87. Paris: Imprimerie administrative de Paul Dupont, 1868.

Salverte, François de. *Les ébénistes du XVIIIe siècle, leurs oeuvres et leurs marques.* Paris: G. van Oest et Cie, 1927.

Samoyault, Jean-Paul. "L'appartement de madame du Barry à Fontainebleau." In *Madame du Barry: de Versailles à Louveciennes,* edited by Marie-Amynthe Denis, et al., 87–100. Paris: Flammarion, 1992.

Samoyault-Verlet, Colombe. "Furnishings." In *The Second Empire, 1852–1870: Art in France under Napoleon III,* 74–76, edited by George H. Marcus and Janet M. Iandola. Philadelphia: Philadelphia Museum of Art, 1978.

———. "L'ameublement des châteaux royaux à l'époque de la Restauration." In *Un âge d'or des arts décoratifs 1814–1848,* 42–49. Paris: Editions de la Réunion des musées nationaux, 1991.

———. "Louis-Philippe de 1830 à 1840: l'ameublement des palais royaux sous la monarchie de juillet." In *Un âge d'or des arts décoratifs 1814–1848,* 230–34. Paris: Editions de la Réunion des musées nationaux, 1991.

Sandgruber, Roman. *Die Anfänge der Konsumgesellschaft: Konsumgüterverbrauch, Lebensstandard und Alltagskultur in Osterreich im 18. und 19. Jahrhundert.* Munich: R. Oldenbourg, 1982.

Saulo, J. *Nouveau manuel complet de la dorure sur bois à l'eau et à la mixtion par les procédés anciens et nouveaux . . . suivi de la fabrication des peintures laquées sur meubles et sur sièges.* Paris: Roret, 1886.

Savary des Bruslons, Jacques. *Dictionnaire universel de commerce.* Paris, 1761.

Saverny, Marie de. *La femme chez elle et dans le monde par madame Marie de Saverny.* Paris: au bureaux de journal la revue de la mode, 1876.

Say, Jean-Baptiste. *Traité d'économie politique.* 2 vols. 6th ed. Paris: Guillaumin, 1841.

Schama, Simon. "The Domestication of Majesty: Royal Family Portraiture, 1600–1850." In *Art and History: Images and their Meaning,* edited by Robert I. Rotberg and Theodore K. Rabb, 155–83. Cambridge: Cambridge University Press, 1988.

———. *The Embarrassment of Riches: An Interpretation of Dutch Culture in the Golden Age.* Berkeley: University of California Press, 1988.

Schivelbusch, Wolfgang. "The Policing of Street Lighting." *Yale French Studies* 73 (1988): 61–74.

Schnapper, Antoine. "The King of France as Collector in the Seventeenth Century." In *Art and History: Images and Their Meaning,* edited by Robert I. Rotberg and Theodore K. Rabb, 185–202. Cambridge: Cambridge University Press, 1988.

Scott, Joan Wallach. *The Glassworkers of Carmaux: French Craftsmen and Political Action in a Nineteenth-Century City.* Cambridge, Mass.: Harvard University Press, 1974.

———. *Gender and the Politics of History.* New York: Columbia University Press, 1988.

———. "The Evidence of Experience." *Critical Inquiry* 17 (summer 1991): 773–97.

Scranton, Philip. *Proprietary Capitalism: The Textile Manufacturer at Philadelphia, 1800–1885.* Cambridge: Cambridge University Press, 1983.

Searle, William. *The Tasteful Interlude: American Interiors Through the Camera's Eye, 1860–1917.* Nashville, Tenn.: American Association for State and Local History, 1982.

Secrets concernant les arts et métiers. 2 vols. Paris: Jombert, 1716.

Sée, Henri Eugène. *Histoire économique de la France.* Paris: Armand Colin, 1939–42.

Selle, Gert. *Die Geschichte des Design in Deutschland von 1870 bis heute.* Cologne: DuMont, 1978.

Séné, Charles. "Contrat de mariage de Riesener avec la veuve d'Oeben et documents sur l'ébéniste Oeben, 1760–1772." *Nouvelles archives d'art français* (1878): 319–38.

Serrurier, Cornélia. *Bibliothèques de France: description de leurs fonds et historique de leur formation.* The Hague: M. Nijhoff, 1946.

Service, Alastair. *Edwardian Interiors.* London: Barrie and Jenkins, 1982.

Sewell, William H., Jr. *Work and Revolution in France: The Language of Labor from the Old Regime to 1848.* Cambridge: Cambridge University Press, 1980.

———. *Structure and Mobility: The Men and Women of Marseille, 1820–1970.* Cambridge: Cambridge University Press, 1985.

Shammas, Carole. "The Domestic Environment in Early Modern England and America." *Journal of Social History* 14 (fall 1980): 3–24.

———. *The Pre-industrial Consumer in England and America.* Oxford: Clarendon Press, 1990.

Shapiro, Anne Louise. "Paris." In *Housing the Workers, 1850–1914,* edited by M. J. Daunton, 33–66. London: Leicester University Press, 1990.

Shorter, Edward, and Charles Tilly. *Strikes in France, 1830–1968.* London: Cambridge University Press, 1974.

Sibalis, Michael David. "The Mutual Aid Societies of Paris, 1789–1848." *French History* 3, no. 1 (March 1989): 1–30.

Silverman, Debora L. *Art Nouveau in Fin-de-Siècle France: Politics, Psychology, and Style.* Berkeley: University of California Press, 1989.

Simon, Jules. *L'ouvrière.* Paris: Hachette, 1861.

Smith, Bonnie G. *Ladies of the Leisure Class: The Bourgeoises of Northern France in the Nineteenth Century.* Princeton: Princeton University Press, 1981.

Smith, Charles W. *Auctions: The Social Construction of Value.* New York: Free Press, 1989.

Smith, Dorothy E. *The Everyday World as Problematic: A Feminist Sociology.* Boston: Northeastern University Press, 1987.

———. *Texts, Facts and Femininity: Exploring the Relations of Ruling.* London: Routledge, 1990.

Smith, Thomas Spence. "Aestheticism and Social Structure: Style and Social Network in the Dandy Life." *American Sociological Review* 39 (October 1974): 725–43.

Sonenscher, Michael. *The Hatters of Eighteenth-Century France*. Berkeley: University of California Press, 1987.

———. "Mythical Work: Workshop Production and the *Compagnonnages* of Eighteenth-Century France." In *The Historical Meanings of Work*, edited by Patrick Joyce, 31–63. Cambridge: Cambridge University Press, 1987.

———. *Work and Wages: Natural Law, Politics, and the Eighteenth-Century French Trades*. Cambridge: Cambridge University Press, 1989.

Spufford, Margaret. *The Great Reclothing of Rural England: Petty Chapmen and Their Wares in the Seventeenth Century*. London: Hambledon Press, 1984.

Stallybrass, Peter, and Allon White. *The Politics and Poetics of Transgression*. London: Methuen, 1986.

Statistique de la France: résultats généraux du dénombrement de 1872. Nancy: Imprimerie administrative, 1874.

Statuts et ordonnances de la communauté des maîtres tourneurs de la ville, fauxbourgs et banlieue de Paris. Paris: Imprimerie Grou, 1742.

Statuts, articles, ordonnances et privilèges des principaux jurez, anciens bacheliers, maîtres huchers, menuisiers de la ville, fauxbourgs et banlieue de Paris [24 July 1645]. Paris: Imprimerie de la Veuve Alexandre, 1682.

Statuts, ordonnances et réglements de la communauté des maîtres tourneurs de la ville et fauxbourgs de Paris. Paris: Valade, 1773.

Statuts, Privileges, Ordonnances et Reglemens de la Communauté des Maîtres Menuisiers et Ebénistes de la Ville, Fauxbourgs et Banlieues de Paris. Paris, 1751.

Steele, Henry. *The Working Classes in France: A Social Study*. London: Twentieth Century Press, 1904.

Stein, Margot B. "The Meaning of Skill: The Case of the French Engine-Drivers, 1837–1917." *Politics and Society* 8, no. 3–4 (1978): 399–427.

Stendhal [Henri Beyle]. *De l'amour*. Paris: Calmann Levy, 1876.

Stewart, Susan. *On Longing: Narratives of the Miniature, the Gigantic, the Souvenir, the Collection*. Baltimore: Johns Hopkins University Press, 1984.

Stoler, Ann. "Carnal Knowledge and Imperial Power: The Politics of Race and Sexual Morality in Colonial Asia." In *Gender at the Crossroads: Feminist Anthropology in the Post-Modern Era*, edited by Micaela di Leonardo, 51–101. Berkeley: University of California Press, 1991.

Stone, Lawrence, and Jeanne C. Fawtier Stone. *An Open Elite? England 1540–1880*. Oxford: Oxford University Press, 1984.

Stürmer, Michael. *Herbst des Alten Handwerks: Quellen zur Sozialgeschichte des 18. Jahrhunderts*. Munich: Deutscher Taschenbuch-Verlag, 1979.

———. "An Economy of Delight: Court Artisans of the Eighteenth Century." *Business History Review* 53 (winter 1979): 496–528.

Sullerot, Evelyne. *La presse féminine*. Paris: Armand Colin, 1966.

Tableaux de la communauté des maîtres menuisiers, ébénistes, tourneurs et layetiers de la ville, fauxbourgs et banlieue de Paris. 3 vols. Paris: Imprimerie de Chardon, 1782, 1787, 1789.

Tablettes royales de renommée, ou almanach général d'indications des négociants, artistes, célèbres fabricants des six corps, arts et métiers de Paris. Paris, 1773.

Tartaret, Eugène, ed. *Exposition universelle de 1867: commission ouvrière.* . . . 2 vols. Paris: Imprimerie Dugros, 1868–69.

Taussig, Michael. "*Maleficium:* State Fetishism." In *Fetishism as Cultural Discourse,* edited by Emily Apter and William Pietz, 217–47. Ithaca: Cornell University Press, 1993.

Taylor, Barbara. *Eve and the New Jerusalem: Socialism and Feminism in the Nineteenth Century.* New York: Pantheon, 1983.

———. " 'The Men Are as Bad as Their Masters . . .' Socialism, Feminism, and Sexual Antagonism in the London Tailoring Trade in the Early 1830s." *Feminist Studies* 5 (spring 1979): 7–40.

Taylor, George V. "Non-Capitalist Wealth and the Origins of the French Revolution." *American Historical Review* 72 (January 1967): 469–96.

Terrail, Ponson du. *Rocambole.* 1859. Edited by C. A. Ciccione. Monaco: Du Rocher, 1963–65.

Thamer, Hans-Ulrich. "*L'Art du Menuisier:* Work Practices of French Joiners and Cabinet-Makers in the Eighteenth Century." European University Institute, working paper no. 85/171.

Thiébault-Soisson. "A propros d'une décoration intérieure." *Art et décoration* (February 1897): 25–29.

Thirsk, Joan. *Economic Policy and Projects: The Development of a Consumer Society in Early Modern England.* Oxford: Clarendon Press, 1978.

Thomas, Nicholas. *Entangled Objects: Exchange, Material Culture, and Colonialism in the Pacific.* Cambridge, Mass.: Harvard University Press, 1991.

Thornton, Peter. *Seventeenth-Century Interior Decoration in England, France, and Holland.* New Haven: Yale University Press, 1978.

Tilly, Louise. "The Food Riot as a Form of Political Conflict in France." *Journal of Interdisciplinary History* 2 (summer 1971): 23–58.

Tilly, Louise, and Joan Wallach Scott. *Women, Work, and Family.* New York: Holt, Reinhart and Winston, 1978.

Tombs, Robert, ed. *Nationhood and Nationalism in France from Boulangism to the Great War 1889–1918.* New York: Harper Collins Academic, 1991.

Tomlinson, Alan, ed. *Consumption, Identity, and Style: Marketing, Meanings and the Packaging of Pleasure.* London: Routledge, 1990.

Traer, James. *Marriage and the Family in Eighteenth-Century France.* Ithaca: Cornell University Press, 1980.

"Travail du menuisier." *Journal de menuiserie* 14 (1877): 45–48.

Trempé, Rolande. *Les mineurs de Carmaux, 1848–1914.* 2 vols. Paris: Editions ouvrières, 1971.

Tresca and Lecoeuvre. "Machines-outils servant spécialement au travail des bois." In *Exposition universelle de 1867, à Paris: rapports du jury international,* edited by Michel Chevalier, 9:134–59. Paris: Imprimerie administrative de Paul Dupont, 1868.

Trommler, Frank. "Working-Class Culture and Modern Mass Culture Before World War I." *New German Critique* 29 (spring–summer 1983): 57–70.

Troy, Nancy J. *Modernism and the Decorative Arts in France: Art Nouveau to Le Corbusier.* New Haven: Yale University Press, 1991.

Truant, Cynthia M. "*Compagnonnage:* Symbolic Action and the Defense of Workers' Rights in France, 1700–1848." Ph.D. dissertation, University of Chicago, 1978.

———. "Solidarity and Symbolism among Journeymen Artisans: The Case of the *Compagnonnage.*" *Comparative Studies in Society and History* 21 (April 1979): 214–26.

Valabrègue, Antony. "Les arts de la femme." *Revue des arts décoratifs* 18 (1898): 172–78.

Valran, Gaston. *Préjugés d'autrefois et carrières d'aujourd'hui, avec une préface de M. Eugène Etienne.* Toulouse: Privat, 1908.

Van Doren, Auguste. *L'ébénisterie à Bruxelles et à Paris.* Brussels: E. M. Devroye, 1860.

Van Zanten, David. *Designing Paris: The Architecture of Duban, Labrouste, Duc, and Vaudoyer.* Cambridge, Mass.: MIT Press, 1987.

Veblen, Thorstein. *The Theory of the Leisure Class.* 1899. Harmondsworth: Penguin, 1979.

Verchère, J.-T. *Nouveau Traité théorique et pratique de l'ébénisterie d'après Roubo, avec la collaboration d'ébénistes, chefs d'atelier, dessinateurs et sculpteurs des principales maisons d'ameublement.* 2 vols. Dourdan: C. Juliot and P. Coquet, 1900.

Verdellet, Jules. *L'art pratique du tapissier.* Paris: C. Claesen, 1882–83.

Vergesack, Alexander von. *L'industrie Thonet: de la création artisanale à la production en série—le mobilier en bois courbé.* Paris: Editions de la Réunion des musées nationaux, 1986.

Verlet, Pierre. *Les meubles français du XVIIIe siècle.* 2 vols. Paris: Presses universitaires de France, 1956.

———. "Le commerce des objets d'art et les marchands merciers." *Annales: Economies, sociétés, civilisations* 13 (1958): 10–29.

———. *L'art du meuble à Paris au XVIIIe siècle.* Paris: Presses universitaires de France, 1958.

———. *French Furniture in the Eighteenth Century.* Translated by Penelope Hunter-Stiebel. Charlottesville: University Press of Virginia, 1991.

Verlet, Pierre, and Claude Frégnac, eds. *Les ébénistes du XVIIIe siècle français.* Paris: Hachette, collection Connaissance des Arts "Grands Artisans d'Autrefois," 1963.

Viaux, Jacqueline. *Le meuble en France au XVIIIe siècle.* Paris: Presses universitaires de France, 1962.

Vidal, Pierre, and Léon Duru. *Histoire de la corporation des marchands merciers, grossiers, jouailliers: le troisième des six corps des marchands de la ville de Paris, publié sous les auspices de la Chambre syndicale de la mercerie en détail.* Paris: Champion, 1911.

Villermé, Louis. *Tableau de l'état physique et moral des ouvriers employés dans les manufactures de coton, de laine et de soie.* Paris: Jules Renouard et Cie, 1840.

Viollet-le-Duc, Eugène. *Dictionnaire raisonné du mobilier français de l'époque carlovingienne à la renaissance.* 2d ed. Paris: Librairie A. Morel, 1868.

———. *The Story of a House*. Translated by George M. Towle. Boston: James Osgood, 1874.

Vovelle, Michel. *The Fall of the French Monarchy, 1787–1792*, translated by Susan Burke. Cambridge: Cambridge University Press, 1984.

Vovelle, Michel, and Daniel Roche. "Bourgeois, Rentiers, and Property Owners: Elements for Defining a Social Category at the End of the Eighteenth Century." In *New Perspectives on the French Revolution: Readings in Historical Sociology*, edited by Jeffry Kaplow, 25–46. New York: John Wiley and Sons, 1965.

Wallendorf, Melanie, and Michael D. Reilly. "Ethnic Migration, Assimilation, and Consumption." *Journal of Consumer Research* 10 (December 1983): 292–302.

Walton, Guy. *Louis XIV's Versailles*. Chicago: University of Chicago Press, 1986.

Walton, Whitney. *France at the Crystal Palace: Bourgeois Taste and Artisan Manufacture in the Nineteenth Century*. Berkeley: University of California Press, 1992.

Warner, Marina. *Monuments and Maidens: The Allegory of Female Form*. New York: Atheneum, 1985.

Warnod, André. *La brocante et les petits marchés de Paris*. Paris: E. Figuière, 1914.

Watin, Jean-Félix. *L'art de faire ou d'employer le vernis, ou l'art du vernisseur auquel on a joint ceux du peintre et du doreur*. Paris: Quillau, 1772.

Watson, Francis J. B. *Le meuble Louis XVI*. Translated by Robert de Micheaux. Paris: Les Beaux-Arts, 1963.

Weatherill, Lorna. *Consumer Behavior and Material Culture in Britain, 1660–1760*. New York: Routledge, 1988.

Weber, Eugen. *Peasants into Frenchmen: The Modernization of Rural France, 1870–1914*. Stanford: Stanford University Press, 1976.

Weissbach, Lee Shai. "Artisanal Responses to Artistic Decline: The Cabinetmakers of Paris in the Era of Industrialization." *Journal of Social History* 16 (winter 1982): 67–81.

———. "Entrepreneurial Traditionalism in Nineteenth-Century France: A Study of the *Patronage industriel des enfants de l'ébénisterie*." *Business History Review* 57 (winter 1983): 548–65.

———. *Child Labor Reform in Nineteenth-Century France: Assuring the Future Harvest*. Baton Rouge: Louisiana State University Press, 1989.

Wiesner, Merry E. "Guilds, Male Bonding, and Women's Work in Early Modern Germany." *Gender and History* 1 (summer 1989): 125–38.

Wightman, Richard Fox, and T. J. Jackson Lears, eds. *The Culture of Consumption: Critical Essays in American History, 1880–1980*. New York: Pantheon Books, 1983.

Wilberger, Carolyn Hope. "The View from Russia." In *French Women and the Age of Enlightenment*, edited by Samia I. Spencer, 380–94. Bloomington: Indiana University Press, 1984.

Wilhelm, Jacques. *La vie quotidienne au Marais au XVIIe siècle*. Paris: Hachette, 1966.

———. *La vie quotidienne des parisiens au temps du Roi-Soleil, 1660–1715*. Paris: Hachette, 1977.

Williams, Patricia J. *The Alchemy of Race and Rights*. Cambridge, Mass.: Harvard University Press, 1991.

Williams, Rosalind H. *Dream Worlds: Mass Consumption in Late Nineteenth-Century France*. Berkeley: University of California Press, 1982.

Williamson, Judith. *Consuming Passions: The Dynamics of Popular Culture*. London: Marion Boyars, 1986.

Willis, Susan. *A Primer for Daily Life*. New York: Routledge, 1991.

Wilson, Elizabeth. *Adorned in Dreams: Fashion and Modernity*. Berkeley: University of California Press, 1987.

Wood, James B. *The Nobility of the Election of Bayeux, 1463–1666: Continuity through Change*. Princeton: Princeton University Press, 1980.

Woolf, Stuart, ed. *Domestic Strategies: Work and Family in France and Italy, 1600–1800*. Cambridge: Cambridge University Press, 1991.

Zaretsky, Eli. *Capitalism, the Family, and Personal Life*. 2d ed. New York: Harper and Row, 1986.

Zola, Emile. *Son excellence Eugène Rougon*. Paris: Charpentier, 1876.

———. *L'assommoir*. Paris: Charpentier, 1877.

Zylberberg-Hocquard, Marie-Hélène. *Femmes et féminisme dans le mouvement ouvrier français*. Paris: Editions ouvrières, 1981.

General Index

Italic page numbers refer to illustrations.

Inventories, 276; department store, 341; furniture store, 332, 333
Invisibility. *See* Labor

Japanese lacquerwork, 103, 104
Job satisfaction of workers, 7
Jointers. *See* Tools, furniture
Journal de menuiserie, 200
Journal des dames et des modes, 151, 224, 390
Journeymen's organizations. *See* Compagnonnage
July Monarchy of Louis-Philippe, 165–72, 230
"Just price," 100–101, 103

King-as-father metaphor, 31, 98, 137, 144, 189
Kings. *See* Absolutism; *specific kings*
Kinship: biological, 126; fictive, 32, 123–24, 152. *See also* Families
Knowledge: abstract, 111–12, 116, 151, 201, 235, 352, 354, 362–64, 369, 416; artisan opinions on their, 110–11, 234–35; classifications of, 354, 363, 364; as class-specific, 144, 145, 195, 200–201, 352, 363–64; craft repertoire of, 120, 120n, 133, 230; craft sense, 118–21; and culture of production, 110–38; danger of working-class, 191, 199; illusion of consumer, 348; and moral values, 367; and skill of craftsmen, 110–18, 169–72, 234, 249, 250–51, 254, 313–17, 348; transformation in nature of, 107, 230, 415

Labor: and aesthetic objects production, 119, 238–40, 374–75, 418; alienation of aesthetic, 5–6, 237–38, 247–54, 306, 320, 418–19; conditions, 172, 308–22; crisis of 1880s and 1890s, 318–22; home-based, 93, 94, 171–72, 233, 310, 313, 326, 339–40; invisibility of, 255, 348, 415; legitimacy of, 218; as masculine, 8, 31–32, 127–28, 131–32; mechanization,

238–39, 307, 313–17, 417–18; outwork, 153, 170–71, 185, 307, 309–10, 311–13, 339–40; as paternal, 31–32, 122–28, 138, 187; proletarianization of, 172, 354; provincial, 307, 318; right to creative, 237–38, 246, 418–19; strikes, 172, 240, 243–44, 319; subcontracting, 170, 317. *See also* Alienation of labor
Labor, division of: by object or by task, 87–88, 169–71, 312; faubourg St-Antoine, 93–94; furniture-making guilds, 76–89; manual and mental, 415; in mechanized shops, 315–16; provincial production, 307, 318; and specialization of production, 77–80, 86–89, 93, 108, 169–71, 236–37, 309–12, 315–16. *See also* Women in the trades
Labor associations and unions, 416, 418, 419; discourse of, 145, 240–41, 246, 253–54; furniture production, 242–47; gendered construction of, 247–48, 251; male furniture makers in, 145, 226, 247–54; organization without craft, 242–47, 250–51; recruitment, 244; trade unions (*chambres syndicales*), 235, 243–44. *See also* Guilds
Labor at home. *See* Home-based artisans
Labor historians, 7–8
Lacquer work, 56–57, 103, 104, 175, 177
Language: the craft repertoire as, 120, 120n, 234, 316, 407; of the expositions, 251–52; limitations on labor union, 246, 251–52; of taste, 380. *See also* Discourse
Lathes. *See* Tools, furniture
Laws, 159; child labor legislation, 187–88; education system, 359; sumptuary, 47, 47n, 52, 145
Lectures, public, 356, 365–66
Liberal historians, 167
Liberalism, economic, 159
Liberty, 181–83

333n; noble life-style, 47–48, 58–59, 164; wood, 47, 84, 328; working-class furniture, 213, 215–16, 217, 219. *See also* Distribution cost
Primavera workshop, 340
Printemps (store), 168n, 339, 340
Printing media. *See* Media
Private archives, 427–29
Private sphere. *See* Domestic interiors; Space
Prizes, exposition, 208
Producer cooperatives, 243
Production: author's experience in, 5–7, 5n, 6n, 9, 418–19; in crisis times, 147–48, 171–72, 318–22; the culture of pre-Revolutionary, 48, 110–38; custom furniture stores and, 313–17, 331–37, 344; design and, 88–89, 94; design separation from, 230, 372, 375, 417; distribution separation from, 323–24, 337; diversity and convergence of, 323; exclusion of women from, 131, 220–21, 234, 289n, 310; expansion of, 308–09; gendering of, 247–48, 251, 277; linguistic model of, 120, 120n; mass market, 415–16; mechanization of, 172, 185, 201, 238–39, 307, 313–17, 417–18; organization and complexity of, 75–76, 153–54; provincial, 307, 318; quality of, 96–97, 172, 237–38, 312–13, 328, 330, 344, 348; seasonality of, 319–20, 341; sequence of sideboard, 88–89, 94; specialization of, 77–80, 86–89, 93, 108, 236–37, 309–12; technology and, 307. *See also* Manufacturing
Production systems: faubourg St-Antoine, 92–98, 107; guild, 75, 86–89, 108; royal artisans, 89–92, 107; tripartite organization of, 75–76, 86–109, 170, 184
Prostitution and style, 294
Protection legislation, child labor, 187–88
Protests, militant, 172
Provincial production, 307, 318

Prud'hommes (arbitrators), 241
Pseudokinship, 32, 123–24, 152
Public archives, 425–27
Publications. *See* Books and magazines
Public lectures, 356, 365–66
Public schools. *See* Schools
Public space. *See* Rooms; Space
Puissance paternelle, 189

Quality. *See* Beautiful objects; Production
Questions for examination, 8, 23; choice of France for, 24–25; choice of furniture for, 25–27, 26n; innovation, 19, 103n, 137; periodization of, 20
Questions of taste. *See* Taste

Rationalism: and historicism, 179–80; and modernity of stores, 327, 344–45, 349
Raw materials for furniture, 30, 87–89, 110–11; new combinations of, 45, 46, 57, 120–21; nonwood, 41, 47, 57, 84–85, 162. *See also* Wood
Readymade furniture, 100, 323, 325, 331, 332, 341, 344
Record-keeping: business, 332, 333, 335n, 427–29; home, 275–76, 276n
Regency style, 51–52, 54–55
Regional identity. *See* National identity
Renaissance furniture, 41–42
Renaissance style, 262, 263, 287, 288
Representation: of nation by the monarch, 35, 37, 47, 49, 51, 54, 141; political and civil, 2, 61, 407–13, 423; the problem of, 142. *See also* Self-representation
Reproductions, furniture, 120, 165–67, 262–63, 306, 334
Republicanism: iconography of, 149–50; and male furniture makers, 226, 231; and salon culture, 64–66
Republican regime, democratic: gender roles internalizing the, 380–85; relations of state, nation, and capitalism under, 258

State interventions, *(continued)*
184, 257–58; into private matters,
159, 199; into the workplace, 187–
89, 379; in technical education, 121–
22, 351–52, 359–60, 368–70, 374–
76. *See also* Laws; Social
intervention

State-sponsored expositions. *See* Universal expositions

Statistics: 1867 exposition, 232, 232n;
bourgeoisie, 165; custom furniture
shops, 309–10, 309n, 324n, 333; foreign-born guild members, 97; furniture trades, 92, 157, 158–59, 169,
232, 308–12; library use, 358, 364,
364n; on artisans, 308–12; on
women in the trades, 309–11; trade
school, 368; wood trades (eighteenth
century), 83n

Stores. *See* Department stores; Furniture stores

Strikes, labor, 172, 240, 243–44, 319

Style: changes in, 73, 120–21; definitions of, 1–2, 120, 141; failure of,
179–82; and labor conditions, 308–
22; and monarchy under absolutism,
68–69, 70–71, 76; political meaning
of royal, 38–39; and political order,
138–39, 156, 212, 407–13; relation
between taste and, 2, 174–75, 181–
84, 352, 385–86; and retailing, 210,
322–49; sources of, 30, 120–21,
154–55; taste, and political power,
38–39, 141, 407–13

Style moderne, 261, 306, 307, 311, 315,
316

Style pastiche. *See* Pastiche styles

Styles: absence of new, 60–61, 64–66,
179–82, 306–07, 349–50, 352, 354,
385–86; anachronistic, 183–84; architect-created, 154–55; bourgeois,
220–24; Classical influences on, 39,
44, 62, 68, 112–13, 150–51, 167;
coding of, 284–87; consulate and
empire, 154–59, *155*; dates of reigns
and dates of, 38, 68–69, 307;

designer-based versus craft-based,
350; Directory, 150–51; feminization
of royal, 66–67; gendering of Old
Regime, 277–89; Gothic, 166, 167,
180; hermaphroditic, 281; July
Monarchy of Louis-Philippe, 165–
72; labels of, 38, 68–69, 307; lack of
nineteenth-century, 349–50, 352,
385–86; mass consumption, 19, 256,
415–25; names of royal, 38, 68–69;
noncourtly, 64–66; Old Regime pastiche, 38, 154–59, 407; plurality of,
142–43, 183, 350; post-Revolution
state, 143, 183–85; pre-Revolutionary noncourtly, 60–61; Renaissance,
41–42, 262, 263, 287, *288*; restoration monarchies, 159–72; Revolutionary furniture, 147–54; Second
Empire, 175–83; Second Republic,
172–75; working-class, 144, 145–46,
212–20, 276, 276n. *See also* Pastiche
styles; Royal styles

Styles of furniture. *See* Furniture
forms

Subcontracting, 170, 317

Subjectivity, 2; problem of, 18

Suffrage, 423–24; universal manhood,
352, 408–09; women's, 412, 416,
420

Sumptuary laws, 47, 47n, 52, 145

Suppliers. *See* Merchants

Tables, *57–58*, 157, 284, 397; five-
purpose, 345, *346*; pool, 315; writing, *55–56*, 73, *81*, 266. *See also*
Furniture forms

Tapissiers trade, 85, 87, 88n, 96, 104,
164, 191–92, 333, 354; women, 311

Taste: among multiplicity of styles,
142, 350; author's grandmothers',
10–14, 419–20; as class-specific, 142,
195; contradictory aspects of, 1, 306,
386–402; crisis in, 352, 385–86;
fashion versus, 385–407; as feminine, 249–50; political power and
style and, 407–13; as public and pri-

between, 319–20, 319n; department store, 339–40; Garde-Meuble, 69, 89–90, 158, 159; the masculine family of, 31–32, 127–28, 131, 226; subcontracting by, 170, 317; unmecha-

nized and mechanized, 313–18. *See also* Royal workshops (manufactories)

World's fairs. *See* Universal expositions

Index of Names

Italic page numbers refer to illustrations.

Compositor:	Braun-Brumfield, Inc.
Text:	10/13 Aldus
Display:	Aldus
Printer and Binder:	Braun-Brumfield, Inc.